Civil Protection and Domestic Security in Contemporary Hybrid Warfare

Civil Protection and Domestic Security in Contemporary Hybrid Warfare presents a comprehensive approach to civil protection and domestic security in contemporary hybrid armed conflict.

Hybrid warfare encompasses a number of dimensions such as military, political, psychological, cognitive, space, social, economic, informational, or technological. Current conflicts show that hybrid warfare, despite regional differences, is based on a common operational framework that combines conventional and unconventional tactics targeting not only military structures, but also largely targeting civilians (societies). All this makes threats more diffuse, subtle, and difficult to predict. They also often take the form of networked actions and have cascading effects in which they can produce complex secondary effects affecting a range of spheres of society and key infrastructure. In response to this spectrum of threats, individual states need to adapt their security and civil protection systems to the type of threat involved. However, most existing solutions are fragmented, resulting in a reduced ability to coordinate and adequately prepare civilians for hybrid threat conditions. Given these challenges, this book establishes a common language that helps shape coherent risk management and protective mechanisms in dealing with hybrid attacks. It also points in a new direction in ensuring the reliability of information provided to civilians, which is crucial in a hybrid war environment where disinformation is used as one of the main tools of destabilization. Drawing on theoretical knowledge and practical experiences from around the world, this book provides tools to effectively respond to existing and future conflicts and hybrid wars. Above and beyond this, bridging the gap between concrete knowledge of hybrid warfare and operational needs, this book explores how public administrations, public services, NGOs, local communities, and other actors play a key role in protecting the population during such non-traditional armed conflicts.

Civil Protection and Domestic Security in Contemporary Hybrid Warfare is a vital resource to government and civilian specialists responsible for population security and protection, helping them and their civilian populations to strategize and, oftentimes, to individually mitigate the risk of loss of life or health – as has been demonstrated in the Russia-Ukraine conflict.

Civil Protection and Domestic Security in Contemporary Hybrid Warfare

Wojciech Wróblewski, Michał Wiśniewski, and Jędrzej Bieniasz

NEW YORK AND LONDON

Designed cover image: Getty Images

First published 2025
by Routledge
605 Third Avenue, New York, NY 10158

and by Routledge
4 Park Square, Milton Park, Abingdon, Oxon, OX14 4RN

Routledge is an imprint of the Taylor & Francis Group, an informa business

© 2025 Wojciech Wróblewski, Michał Wiśniewski, and Jędrzej Bieniasz

The right of Wojciech Wróblewski, Michał Wiśniewski, and Jędrzej Bieniasz to be identified as author[/s] of this work has been asserted in accordance with sections 77 and 78 of the Copyright, Designs and Patents Act 1988.

All rights reserved. No part of this book may be reprinted or reproduced or utilised in any form or by any electronic, mechanical, or other means, now known or hereafter invented, including photocopying and recording, or in any information storage or retrieval system, without permission in writing from the publishers.

Trademark notice: Product or corporate names may be trademarks or registered trademarks, and are used only for identification and explanation without intent to infringe.

ISBN: 9781032822853 (hbk)
ISBN: 9781032822846 (pbk)
ISBN: 9781003503859 (ebk)

DOI: 10.4324/9781003503859

Typeset in Sabon
by codeMantra

Contents

	About the authors	vii
	Introduction	1
Chapter 1	Characteristics of hybrid warfare	5
Chapter 2	Operations and actors of hybrid warfare	86
Chapter 3	Management of critical infrastructure safety in the context of threats of hybrid warfare	166
Chapter 4	Identification and analysis of threats to the civilian population in hybrid warfare	228
Chapter 5	Population protection in hybrid warfare	291
Chapter 6	Utilizing new technologies for population protection in hybrid warfare	373
Chapter 7	The role of communities in hybrid warfare	420
	Conclusion	457
	Appendix 1: Characteristics of the research methods used	463
	Appendix 2: Results of analysis of media reports characterizing the war in Ukraine	471
	Appendix 3: Glossary	548
	Appendix 4: Interview questionnaire	556
	Index	571

About the authors

Wojciech Wróblewski is Assistant Professor at the Institute of Internal Security of the Fire University, where he also serves as the head of the Postgraduate Studies – Managing Cyber Security in the Public Sector. In 2016, he obtained a PhD in Social Sciences in the discipline of Defence Science. He is an expert in public security, civil protection, humanitarian aid, and contemporary threats such as hybrid warfare, cybersecurity, terrorist threats, and counter-terrorism systems. He has a particular focus on the use of artificial intelligence in civil protection and crisis management. He has authored numerous scientific publications focusing on the analysis of homeland security threats and challenges and security engineering.

Michał Wiśniewski is Assistant Professor at the Faculty of Management at Warsaw University of Technology. In 2018 he defended his doctoral thesis in Situational Security Management of Critical Infrastructure. From 2011 to 2012, he worked on a project funded by the MSHE Optimization Model of the Police Management Organization in the Area of Costs, Transport and Real Estate Management. From 2013 to 2018 he worked on a project funded by the NCRD Risk Assessment Methodology for the Needs of the Crisis Management System of the RP and a Highly Specialized Platform Supporting Civilian and Rescue Planning in the Public Administration of the RP and in the Organizational Units of the NFRS. He is also author or co-author of more than 70 scientific papers in the field of management science on process management, cloud computing, critical infrastructure security management.

Jędrzej Bieniasz is Director of the Cybersecurity Center of Warsaw University of Technology (WUT), Poland, and Assistant Professor at the Cybersecurity Team at the Institute of Telecommunications, WUT. He also holds a PhD Eng in Computer Science from WUT. He has been involved in cybersecurity for the last eight years, and in broad IT for more than ten years. He is the author or a co-author of 30 publications around cybersecurity and IT, and has extensive experience in academic, R&D, and industrial projects. His main areas of interest are building resilient organizations, secure systems, and applications, as well as the operational area of cybersecurity (threat detection, incident management, digital forensics).

Introduction

Hybrid warfare is a term that, on the one hand, is controversial in (mainly academic) debates and, on the other hand, has become a common term for the evolution of modern forms of war. As a consequence, the meaning of the term is today unclear or is interchangeably used, for example, with terms such as hybrid conflict, hybrid threats, asymmetric warfare, or irregular warfare.

Carl von Clausewitz, in his classic theory of war, defined war as an act of violence aimed at forcing the enemy to do our will (von Clausewitz, 2006, p. 15). He also believed that war is like a "chameleon" – it changes its nature depending on the context, but in general it combines three basic elements: violence, hatred, and hostility. Clausewitz used the metaphor of a house on fire to illustrate that in war, decisions and events can spread in unexpected ways, affecting different aspects of the conflict. In order to understand modern hybrid wars, it is particularly important to see war as a process in which it is not possible to look only at single events, but a whole spectrum of seemingly unrelated actions that together shape the nature and dynamics of the conflict (von Clausewitz, 2006, pp. 15, 31, 11–12).

In its nature, hybrid warfare remains the same – it is still an act of violence aimed at subjugating an opponent. However, the scale, intensity, and range of actions and tools are changing, and societies are increasingly being targeted. Hybrid warfare in a very general sense refers to the integrated use of military and non-military actions by state and non-state actors. Frank Hoffman is usually considered to be the progenitor of the term, but the literature does not agree on this. Although the combination of such activities is not new in the history of conflicts, they now complement each other in a particular way, creating networks of flexible linkages that can lead to cascading effects with consequences that are difficult to predict. According to the authors' research, the ratio of non-military to military actions in the war in Ukraine is 3.69:1, which may confirm General Valery Gerasimov's concept of a 4:1 action ratio. This means that non-military actions in the war in Ukraine play an important role in achieving strategic objectives, complementing traditional military operations.

DOI: 10.4324/9781003503859-1

There are currently more than 30 active armed conflicts and wars, but two in particular – the war in Ukraine and the war in Gaza – are so widespread and multidimensional that they have gained the common status of hybrid wars. Although different in objectives, tactics, and scale, both conflicts demonstrate the complexity and diversity of actions characteristic of hybrid warfare. The effects of these actions particularly affect civilian populations. Among the most serious of these are death, starvation, thirst, disease, injury, or the effects of extreme weather conditions and the inability to protect against them. Hybrid warfare, however, is not only about physical effects, but also about the battle for the minds of societies. Information and cognitive operations play an important role in shaping societal attitudes and destabilization. Disinformation, media manipulation, and propaganda are an important part of the operations and can lead to chaos and reduced trust of citizens in each other and in state institutions. This is only a very limited picture of hybrid warfare, but there is no doubt whatsoever that the effects on civilians generated by hybrid operations are more complex today and require security systems to undergo a paradigm shift in civilian protection. This is due to a number of reasons, among which are the pre-emptive nature of hybridity, networking, non-obviousness, or flexibility.

The current approach to civil protection does not directly address hybrid war. Systemic solutions in this area mainly concern peacetime and in a war situation are transformed, as for example in the Polish system, into civil defence, which is largely a response to the classic type of wars. This state of affairs may cause gaps in civil protection in hybrid war. The solution to this problem may lie in the understanding that in such a complex environment compounded by the use of artificial intelligence, it becomes important not to centralize the response to hybrid threats solely in systemic solutions, but to notice the social potential including local communities.

Importantly, given the anticipatory nature of hybrid operations and their complexity, flexibility, and subtlety, community preparedness cannot be based on a mere schematic approach. It is necessary to build maturity in threat assessment and adaptive decision-making. Communities should have the knowledge and tools to not only identify potential hazards, but also anticipate them and respond accordingly. Flexibility in responding to complex and multidimensional hazards should be fostered by developing critical thinking competencies, collaborative skills, and local accountability.

Thus, it becomes important to move away from traditional, top-down managed models of civil protection to a more decentralized, multi-level approach in which societies are active participants in the protection process. Such an approach also requires changes in emergency management strategies, which should take into account the role of local social structures and their ability to respond autonomously to hybrid threats.

This monograph, the methodological layer of which is described in Appendix 1, concentrates on the protection of civilians in the face of the complexities of hybrid warfare. It provides a literature review, empirical analyses, and proposed solutions to enhance the effectiveness of civilian protection. The book consists of six thematically linked chapters with an introduction and conclusion.

The first chapter introduces the topic of hybrid conflict and hybrid war, seen as the most destructive phenomenon that can affect civilians. It then analyses the evolution of the concept of hybrid warfare; its controversies in academic, military, and political discourse; and the difficulties in defining it clearly. An important element is the discussion of the concept of hybrid war as understood by countries such as Russia and the CCP, as well as an analysis of the mechanisms of action used in this type of warfare. This chapter provides an introduction to the key issues that will be discussed in more detail in the following sections of the thesis.

Chapter 2 looks at the role of critical infrastructure that becomes a target in hybrid warfare. Attacks on this infrastructure can lead to catastrophic consequences such as energy supply disruptions, communication disruptions, public health threats, and social destabilization. The chapter discusses the challenges posed by new forms of threats and the need to implement appropriate measures to protect and strengthen the resilience of critical infrastructure. It also considers strategies for detecting, monitoring, and responding to attacks, as well as cross-sectoral and international cooperation as key elements of infrastructure security management in an era of hybrid warfare.

Chapter 3 focuses on the identification and analysis of the threats that affect civilians in hybrid conflicts. In the past, the threats arising from wars were less complex, whereas modern hybrid warfare represents a new and more complex form. The chapter examines the various domains of hybrid warfare, in which military and non-military actions combine to form flexible networks of interconnection, with the aim of, among other things, destabilizing societies. The different types of actors involved in hybrid action – both state and non-state – are discussed.

Chapter 4 addresses the topic of civilian protection in hybrid warfare, emphasizing the need for greater involvement of governments and societies. Attempts to date to curb hybrid activity in the conflict and war phases have not resulted in effective protection mechanisms, as seen in the conflicts in Ukraine and the Middle East. The chapter examines the systemic and individual actions taken by civilians in the face of threats such as famine, disease, extreme weather, or trauma. It also identifies the need for a change in approach to operational strategies in civil protection.

Chapter 5 discusses the impact of new technologies on societies, both as tools for protection and as potential sources of threats. These technologies, such as secure communication systems, cybersecurity, or cloud computing, can play a key role in building resilience to hybrid threats. The chapter presents three main technological dimensions: security-focused conceptual and prescriptive developments, technologies that offer security-relevant functionality, and technology developments to combat vulnerabilities in other technologies. Examples of how these technologies have been used in practice, particularly in the context of the war in Ukraine, are presented.

The final chapter analyses the role of societies and local communities in hybrid conflicts, highlighting their importance in building resilience. These actors can perform a range of functions as well as create solidarity networks and participate in the process of strengthening societal resilience. The role of communities in countering propaganda and disinformation, as well as in providing humanitarian aid and support to war-affected people, is also pointed out.

Each chapter proposes recommendations that are an integral part of the analysis and follow directly from the issues discussed. This approach allows practical solutions and conclusions to be presented on an ongoing basis that can be immediately linked to specific problems, enabling better understanding and application of the content analysed.

The book concludes with a summary that integrates the conclusions of the individual chapters.

BIBLIOGRAPHY

von Clausewitz, C. (2006), *O wojnie*. Kraków: Mireki, ISBN: 978-83-89533-65-4.

CHAPTER 1

Characteristics of hybrid warfare

DEFINITION OF HYBRID WARFARE AND ITS KEY CHARACTERISTICS

According to the Global Conflict Tracker report, there are currently 30 armed conflicts and wars taking place around the world (Council on Foreign Relations, 2024). Many of these conflicts employ traditional methods, but some go beyond the conventional understanding of such threats. Since 2022, the year of Russia's full-scale invasion of Ukraine, a widespread discussion has emerged about the model of modern warfare. This debate intensified in 2023 as a result of the war in the Middle East, commonly referred to as the Israeli-Palestinian war. Both wars are labelled hybrid warfare, although the literature on the subject also sees hybridity in other contemporary and historical conflicts in wars.

This chapter adopts the research hypothesis that hybrid warfare is a phase of a broader, flexible, and integrated hybrid strategy. This strategy, in its first phase, takes the form of a hybrid conflict that, in feedback, may use elements (features) of hybrid warfare.

The use of the term "hybrid warfare" to describe modern war in academic, military, political, social, and media discourse sparks considerable debate, sometimes quite a radical one, among both theorists and practitioners. For some, it represents an unnecessary semantic complication of actions already known from other conflicts and wars, while for others, it reflects an evolving tactical model with characteristics and boundaries that are difficult to clearly define. In truth, there is merit to both perspectives. As Sun Zu wrote,

> War is based on deception. If you can, feign incapacity, if you signal an intent to act, refrain from doing so. When you are near, appear distant, when your enemy is greedy for small gains, entice him. If you notice confusion in his ranks, strike, if his position is stable, strengthen your own. When he is strong, avoid him, when he is quick-tempered,

DOI: 10.4324/9781003503859-2

provoke him, when he is cautious, inflate his ego. If his troops are concentrated, scatter them. Attack when he is unprepared, and appear where he least expects. These are the ways to achieve victory, though they cannot be simply taught.

(Sun Wu et al., 2008, pp. 18–19)

However, it is important to acknowledge the arguments of proponents of the hybrid warfare definition. Modern warfare employs tactics and tools previously well known, but it also expands into domains that were either not utilized at all or were used selectively. What is more, a defining characteristic of contemporary warfare is the intensity, complexity, and interconnectedness of domains, tactics, and tools. All of this makes it increasingly difficult to capture a unified picture of this threat. Carl von Clausewitz, a war theorist who lived in the late 18th and early 19th centuries, stated that war is an act of violence aimed at forcing the opponent to do our bidding, it is like a chameleon adapting to a changing environment (Clausewitz, 2010, p. 15). It appears that the modern environment is far more complex than in previous centuries. The dispersion of the battlefield in contemporary warfare, the multiple attempts to define it through a variety of synonyms, and the lack of consensus on whether the term "hybrid warfare" is legitimate or not contribute to a situation where, much like with the term "terrorism," the pursuit of a clear, universal definition is not prioritized. Instead, there is a tendency towards further complicating the concept (Lindell, 2009, pp. 1–5).

A common example of this is the interchangeable use of the terms "hybrid war" and "hybrid conflict." In the assessment of the authors, these terms should be treated as distinct, as they may represent different stages within a broader strategy. A hybrid conflict can encompass elements of hybrid warfare, but often focuses on less intense and less visible forms of aggression, such as cyber operations, disinformation, psychological or cognitive warfare, or the use of irregular forces. In contrast, hybrid warfare implies full-scale engagement, which can escalate into overt military actions and has long-lasting consequences for domestic and international security, particularly affecting the civilian population. Hybrid conflicts, therefore, may or may not escalate into full-scale hybrid wars, while hybrid wars continue to utilize elements of hybrid conflicts, thus forming part of a broader hybrid strategy.

A representative example is the war in Ukraine, which has experienced two phases of escalation. From 2014, the conflict involved actions without the formal use of military force, which can be classified as the phase of hybrid conflict. However, in 2022, the Russian Federation crossed the threshold into open war through the formal use of military force in what it termed a "special military operation," while continuing to employ tactics from the earlier hybrid conflict phase. The term "war" in the context of the actions in Ukraine was formally used for the first time by the Russian side in a statement by the Russian President's spokesman, Dmitry Peskov, on 22 March 2024 (Otfinowska, 2024). (This conflict will be discussed in greater detail in the subsequent chapters of the book.)

However, the war in Ukraine is not the only contemporary example of hybrid warfare. As Sascha-Dominik (Dov) Bachmann assesses, such actions are increasingly attributed to the conflict in the Middle East as well, specifically the Israeli-Palestinian conflict, which escalated into open war in 2023 (Bachmann, 2023).

Given the complex cognitive and conceptual nature of this issue, this section synthesizes and clarifies the terms that are identified or used interchangeably in the context of hybrid warfare. The aim is to facilitate a better understanding of the concepts used in contemporary discourses on forms of armed conflict. Methodologically, the criterion of representativeness has been adopted, encompassing scientific, institutional, and national perspectives. The concepts of hybrid warfare, as understood by the Communist Party of China (CPC) and the Russian Federation, are discussed in greater detail, highlighting the significant differences in their conceptualization of hybrid warfare compared to Western approaches.

DISTINCTION BETWEEN HYBRID CONFLICT AND HYBRID WAR – CONCEPTUAL ANALYSIS

As noted by Yuriy Danyk and Chad M. Briggs, in the 21st century there is no debate about the existence of hybrid conflicts and wars – only disagreement over their definition and how national security institutions should respond to them. Hybrid conflicts and wars have become a form of adaptation to societal and technological changes, allowing for the control or even the "colonization" of entire states without the need for occupation or open military force. An increasing number of conflicts and wars fit into the category of hybrid warfare, and according to many scholars and practitioners, this may become the dominant form of conflict in the current century (Danyk, Briggs, 2023, pp. 35–50). In this context, Frank Hoffman, Matt Neumeyer, and Benjamin Jensen, in their commentary published on 8 July 2024, by the Centre for Strategic and International Studies (CSIS), highlight the evolutionary nature of conflicts and wars, increasingly oriented towards hybridity. This requires moving away from the rigid division between conventional and irregular warfare. Today, armed conflict should be viewed as a continuum encompassing a wide range of combat techniques, from conventional military operations to asymmetric actions. Russia, by avoiding direct military confrontations, is expanding its hybrid activities across Europe (Hoffman et al., 2024). Vice Admiral Nils Andreas Stensønes, head of Norwegian intelligence, warns of an increase in sabotage activities targeting key European infrastructure, including energy sectors, as a direct response from Moscow to Western support for Ukraine. These operations involve sabotage, arson, and cyberattacks aimed at destabilizing Europe's energy and political security (Politico, 2024; Eye on the Arctic, 2024; SOFX, 2024). Wojcieszek, however, points out that since the beginning of the war Russia, has actively employed sabotage and reconnaissance groups (SRG) that have infiltrated Ukrainian territory on a large scale. Their members are tasked with identifying checkpoints, as well as locating and tracking units of the Armed Forces of Ukraine, and with planning and conducting sabotage operations in operational areas.

The Ukrainian service distinguishes seven forms of sabotage:

- mass attacks on the population that result in death, serious bodily injury, or other harm to health,
- the destruction or damage of facilities crucial to the economy or national defense,
- radioactive contamination,
- mass poisoning,
- actions aimed at the spread of epidemics,
- actions aimed at the spread of epiphytotics (plant epidemics),
- actions aimed at the spread of epizootics (animal epidemics).

These criteria for classifying forms of sabotage help define potential targets, which may include:

- buildings, structures, and other facilities significant for the economy or defense,
- agricultural land, including fields, crops, bodies of water, forests, and similar areas,
- livestock herds, stocked ponds, apiaries, and other such resources.

In practice, the tasks of modern Russian sabotage and reconnaissance groups also include:

- destroying critical and military infrastructure,
- conducting reconnaissance,
- eliminating high-ranking public officials and military commanders,
- carrying out terrorist acts (Wojcieszek, 2024, pp. 261–273).

On the other hand, Poland is a target of Russian disinformation efforts and operations aimed at internal destabilization. The creation and infiltration of radical groups, along with the intensification of propaganda campaigns, are part of a broader strategy to undermine trust in defence and social institutions. According to published documents, Russia is executing a project called "Kylo," which aims to manipulate public opinion through disinformation and incite panic, particularly via social media platforms (Zygiel, 2024). What is more, despite the depletion of military reserves, Russia has significantly increased its military production, as confirmed by a report from the Kiel Institute for the World Economy (Białczyk, 2024). According to the American Enterprise Institute (AEI), supported by China, Russia is capable of continuing the production of key weapons systems, which presents a significant challenge to Western deterrence systems (Critical Threats, 2024).

Both the statements of Hoffman and others, as well as the cited information, clearly indicate that hybrid warfare is undergoing constant evolution while remaining a concept difficult to define precisely. In the context of conceptualizing and defining this phenomenon, Frederik H. Meulman and Pasquale Preziosa, in their work *Hybrid Conflict, Hybrid Warfare, and Resilience*, highlight significant issues with conceptual clarity in previous studies on the topic. They specifically emphasize that the terms "hybrid warfare" and "hybrid conflict" are often treated as synonyms, leading to theoretical confusion (Meulman, Preziosa, 2017). Similar conclusions have been reached by Bianca Torossian and her colleagues (Torossian et al., 2020). The authors emphasize the need for a clear distinction between these terms in the context of the use of armed forces. In hybrid conflict, the use of military forces is covert, whereas hybrid warfare involves the open engagement of military forces (Meulman, Preziosa, 2017; Torossian et al., 2020). Torossian clarifies that hybrid conflict refers to a situation in which parties refrain from overt military confrontation, instead relying on a combination of military intimidation (without direct and open attacks), the use of economic and political tools, as well as diplomatic or technological means to achieve their strategic objectives. In contrast, hybrid warfare is characterized by a state's open use of its armed forces against another state or non-state actor, while simultaneously employing the same economic, political, and diplomatic measures used in hybrid conflict (Torossian et al., 2020).

Additionally, in the literature on hybrid warfare, other terms such as "armed conflict," "war" (in the classical sense), and "hybrid threats" also appear, and are sometimes used interchangeably. However, it is important to note that while these terms may share common characteristics, their meanings differ in relation to the specific features unique to each type of conflict. Therefore, in the following section, an attempt is made to systematize these terms, followed by a discussion of other synonyms used in the context of hybrid warfare, with the aim of clearly defining and distinguishing them both theoretically and operationally (see Appendix 3).

According to the *Encyclopaedia of National Security*, conflict is generally understood as a disagreement of interests and objectives. Its defining feature is the involvement of at least two parties and a subject matter at the centre of the dispute (Urbanek et al., 2024, pp. 283–284). Stephen P. Robbins defines conflict as a process in which Party A makes a conscious effort to thwart the goals of Party B (Robbins, 1998). The source of conflict lies in a situation of contradiction, where each side attempts to impose its intentions. There are various types of conflicts (e.g. social, ethnic, internal, etc.), including armed conflict, which particularly poses a significant threat to security (Urbanek et al., 2024, pp. 283–284). An armed conflict is a type of conflict in which the parties involved use military force, and it occurs when states, coalitions, or organized non-state groups (e.g. Private Military Companies (PMCs)) employ coercion through armed forces to achieve their goals or defend their interests. The objectives of armed conflicts vary and may be related to economic conditions, ethnic differences, historical, religious, or ideological reasons. Many of these causes can coexist (e.g. the conflict in Kosovo). Armed conflicts can be categorized based on various criteria, including geographical scope, the nature and number of participants, the types of combat methods used, the manner in which operations are conducted, and their intensity. In terms of the form and methods of violence used in armed conflicts, the main types include: demonstrations of force (as a form of intimidation), armed blockades, military incidents, armed interventions, military operations below the threshold of war, and the extreme form of conflict, which is war. It is important to note that while every war is an armed conflict, not every armed conflict qualifies as a war, as there is a certain threshold that distinguishes war from other forms of conflict. This threshold includes factors such as the intensity, the level of force and resources involved, the duration of the conflict, and the losses incurred (Balcerowicz, 2013, p. 290). The International Criminal Tribunal for the Former Yugoslavia recognized that an armed conflict exists whenever there is a resort to armed forces between states or protracted armed violence between governmental authorities and organized armed groups, or between such groups within the territory of a single state (Prosecutor v. Dusko Tadic, 1995, p. 70; Falkowski, Marcinko, 2014, pp. 33–34). War is understood and defined in many ways. Today, Balcerowicz considers its fundamental basis to be the definition by Carl von Clausewitz (the most classic of the classic definitions), which states that war is an act of violence aimed at bending the enemy's will to our own (Clausewitz, 2010, p. 24). The most frequently quoted sentence from Clausewitz is the one that says, "War is not merely a political act, but a true instrument of politics, a continuation of political relations, conducted by other means" (what distinguishes war from politics is the finality of its consequences). This interpretation underscores that war is intrinsically linked to political objectives, but unlike politics, its outcomes are often decisive and irreversible (Pawłowski, 2002, p. 155; Clausewitz, 2010, p. 46). The main elements of Clausewitz's definition emphasize the close relationship between politics, the state, and war; the primacy of politics over war; and the treatment of armed violence (war) as a tool of politics. Balcerowicz further highlights the pro-Hegelian trinitarian concept within this definition, where war is seen as a chaotic interplay between force, power, and the people (Balcerowicz, 2024, p. 718). Regardless of its supporters or critics, Clausewitz's theory undoubtedly influenced a paradigm shift in the understanding of war and, consequently, its definition. In the context of international law war is formulated as a state of relations between countries in which an intense conflict, arising from existing political tensions, is resolved through the use of part or all of the political, military, and economic resources at the disposal of these states (Białocerkiewicz, 2005, p. 440 cited in Kołodziejczak, 2018, p. 52). In encyclopaedic and dictionary sources, war is understood as a conflict between political groups involving military actions of significant duration and scale (Encyclopedia Britannica, 202). The *Oxford English Dictionary* defines war as hostile contention by means of armed forces, carried on between nations, states, or rulers, or between parties in the same nation or state, the employment of armed forces against a foreign power, or against an opposing party in the state (Oxford English Dictionary, 2024).

In the context of conceptualizing war, it is worth noting that in some cases, even though war is the subject of analysis, it has not been explicitly defined. For example, in International Humanitarian Law of Armed Conflicts (where the lack of a precise definition also extends to armed conflicts) and in strategic documents and terminology glossaries of NATO, there is no clear and universally accepted definition.

The next step in systematizing terms that are often ambiguously used interchangeably with the term "hybrid war" includes "hybrid conflict" and "hybrid threats." According to the Atlantic Council hybrid conflict (also referred to as hybrid warfare) is a subset of statecraft that uses the diplomatic, informational, military, and economic (DIME[1]) levers of national power across the competition continuum, including cooperation, competition (including grey zone OAA[2]), deterrence, and armed conflict for the purposes of achieving national security objective(s) against a state or non-state actor(s) (Atlantic Council, 2024). On the other hand, hybrid threats, as highlighted by the HybridCoE, are harmful activities that are planned and carried out with malign intent. They aim to undermine a target, such as a state or an institution, through a variety of means, often combined. Such means include information manipulation, cyberattacks, economic influence or coercion, covert political manoeuvring, coercive diplomacy, or threats of military force.

Hybrid threats describe a wide array of harmful activities with different goals, ranging from influence operations and interference all the way to hybrid warfare (Hybrid Co E, 2024).

The European Commission defines hybrid threats as follows: refer to instances when, state or non-state, actors seek to exploit the vulnerabilities of the EU to their own advantage by using in a coordinated way a mixture of measures (i.e. diplomatic, military, economic, technological) while remaining below the threshold of formal warfare. Examples are the hindering of democratic decision-making processes by massive disinformation campaigns, using social media to control the political narrative or to radicalize, recruit and direct proxy actors (European Commission, 2024). On the other hand, NATO defines them as follows: Hybrid threats combine military and non-military as well as covert and overt means, including disinformation, cyberattacks, economic pressure, deployment of irregular armed groups, and use of regular forces. Hybrid methods are used to blur the lines between war and peace, and attempt to sow doubt in the minds of target populations. They aim to destabilize and undermine societies (NATO, 2024).

The concepts discussed above are often used interchangeably with hybrid warfare; however, to maintain consistency in the analysis, it is important to define what hybrid warfare itself is. In a dictionary sense, the term implies the use of a range of different methods to attack an enemy, for example, the spreading of false information, or attacking important computer systems, as well as, or instead of, traditional military action. A detailed discussion of this phenomenon will be provided in the subsequent sections of this chapter.

The presented terms and definitions (Appendix 3) may share some common characteristics with hybrid warfare, but they should not be treated as synonymous. There are many reasons for the ambiguity in defining hybrid warfare, but one of the main causes, as pointed out by Julie C. Bergaust and Stig R. Sellevag, is the lack of clear and precise boundaries between these concepts (Bergaust, Sellevåg, 2023, pp. 169–195). Similar difficulties are confirmed by defence and security experts who were interviewed in partially structured interviews.[3] One of the key issues they highlight is the lack of a clearly defined threshold at which a hybrid conflict escalates into hybrid warfare. This unclear distinction leads to gaps in existing defence and protection strategies, which can be exploited by adversaries.

Given these challenges and the limitations of this study, the authors have decided to conduct a more in-depth analysis of the dichotomy between hybrid conflict and hybrid warfare, which are often used interchangeably. The rationale for this choice is the widespread use of these terms, and as highlighted by the Atlantic Council, precise definition and differentiation of these concepts are crucial for effectively responding to modern hybrid threats and fully leveraging emerging opportunities (Atlantic Council, 2024). In light of the above, it is essential to understand the nature of both hybrid conflict and hybrid warfare. The aim of the analysis in this section is to develop a typology of hybrid conflict and hybrid warfare, which will help eliminate terminological inconsistencies. This approach not only deepens the understanding of the differences between these concepts but also enables the creation of more effective tools for responding to these phenomena. To explore the differences and similarities, a systematic literature analysis was conducted using the VOSviewer program. The results of this study provide valuable insights into the similarities and distinctions between the terms in question and allow for a better understanding of hybrid strategy and its evolution in the context of international security. A detailed description of the research method and inclusion criteria is provided in Appendix 1.

As a result of the data analysis from the SCOPUS database queries, 4,648 studies related to the term "hybrid conflict" and 18,458 studies related to "hybrid warfare" were obtained. These results indicate that the concept of hybrid warfare is addressed much more frequently in academic discussions. Furthermore, the growth dynamics of publications in both areas show the dominant position of hybrid warfare in scholarly research.

The next stage of the study involved developing a keyword co-occurrence map from the literature under analysis. Both the keywords provided by the authors and those indexed by the SCOPUS database were examined. These two sets of keywords were analysed collectively. The reference number of keywords was adopted in accordance with recommendations tested in previous studies (Ciano et al., 2019). The entry criterion was set at five occurrences of a keyword, meaning that a keyword had to appear in at least five different publications to be included on the co-occurrence map. If a higher threshold had been selected, the number of identified keywords would have decreased, potentially leading to the omission of important issues that have not yet been sufficiently researched or adequately highlighted in the literature. Conversely, setting the threshold lower than three occurrences would have returned too many keywords, making the analysis of the co-occurrence map unmanageable. Following this approach, co-occurrence maps were created for the studies on hybrid warfare (Figure 1.1) and hybrid conflict (Figure 1.2).

For the set of studies discussing the issue of hybrid warfare, the total number of keywords is 14,969. Using the VOSviewer program and applying the entry criterion, a network (Figure 1.1) consisting of 1,034 nodes was obtained (a node is a keyword that met the inclusion condition), corresponding to five clusters. Each cluster is distinguished by a different colour. Keyword occurrences were used as weights.

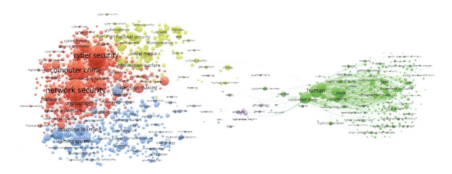

FIGURE 1.1   The keyword co-occurrence map of studies discussing the issue of hybrid warfare

Source: Own study

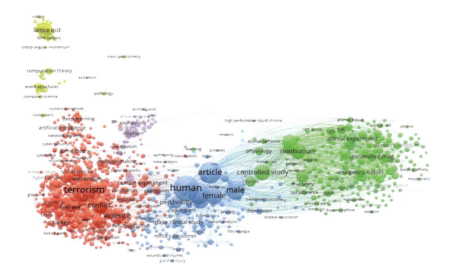

FIGURE 1.2   Keyword link map of studies discussing the issue of hybrid conflict

Source: Own study

The size and prominence of a node correspond to the frequency of its appearance in the analysed dataset. The proximity of individual elements indicates more frequent co-occurrence in specific sets compared to more distant elements. The obtained clusters, for the studies describing the issue of hybrid warfare, are presented in Table 1.1. The cluster

Characteristics of hybrid warfare

TABLE 1.1 Thematic clusters for studies describing the issue of hybrid warfare

Cluster	Keywords	Colour	Cluster Name (Author's Proposal)
Cluster 1	Computer crime, network security, cybersecurity, cyberattacks, critical infrastructure, security of data, decision-making, internet of things, embedded systems, malware, industrial control systems risk assessment, risk management, social network cyber threats	Red	Cybersecurity and Critical Infrastructure Protection
Cluster 2	Human, article, female, male, adult, clinical article, major clinical study, treatment outcome, risk factor, clinical outcome, blood clot lysis, blood vessel graft, cancer surgery, carotid artery diseases, case report, computed tomography, angiography, diffusion-weighted imaging, dizziness	Green	Medical and clinical studies related to hybrid warfare
Cluster 3	5g mobile communication, systems, artificial intelligence, attack detection, machine learning, deep learning, learning systems, intrusion detection, future extraction, neural networks, electric power transmission, simulation	Blue	Advanced technologies and AI in hybrid warfare
Cluster 4	Social media, information warfare, social networking, cyber warfare, cyberspace, computers, national security, terrorism, twitter, internet, fake news, Russia, Syria, Ukraine, United States, South Africa	Yellow	Information warfare and social media dynamics
Cluster 5	Age, analysis, animal experiment, animal model, bottle-nosed dolphin, brain, concentration (composition), data analysis, diagnosis, genetics, mammals, metabolism, nonhuman, physiology, prediction, *Tursiops truncatus*, unclassified drug, water pollutant	Violet	Environmental and biological studies in hybrid warfare context

Source: Own work

name represents the authors' attempt to define a common thematic area addressed in the studies within the cluster.

The identified studies on hybrid warfare are concentrated around the clusters: Cybersecurity and Critical Infrastructure Protection, Medical and clinical studies related to hybrid warfare, Advanced technologies and AI in hybrid warfare, Information warfare and social media dynamics, and Environmental and biological studies in hybrid warfare context. Despite the large number of studies, it is evident that the discussion takes place in five well-defined areas. All clusters have distinct boundaries and are located in a specific area of the map. Cluster 1 (red) includes topics related to Cybersecurity and Critical Infrastructure Protection. Cluster 2 (green) focuses on Medical and clinical studies related to hybrid warfare. Cluster 3 (blue) refers to Advanced technologies and AI in hybrid warfare. Cluster 4 (yellow) pertains to Information warfare and social media dynamics. Cluster 5 (violet) focuses on Environmental and biological studies in the context of hybrid warfare.

Cluster 5 (violet) is the central cluster on the map, serving as the axis of scientific discussion related to hybrid warfare. An interesting observation is that, despite having the fewest publications, this cluster plays a key role as a connector between different research areas. It directly borders Cluster 2 (green), Cluster 3 (blue), and Cluster 4 (yellow). This relationship can be explained as follows: Cluster 5 (violet), although focused on biological and environmental topics, also encompasses issues such as data analysis and genetics, which are relevant to studies on the impact of conflicts on public health (Cluster 2), applications of modern technologies (Cluster 3), and information warfare strategies (Cluster 4). In this way, Cluster 5 serves as a bridge connecting various aspects of hybrid warfare, integrating knowledge from different fields and supporting an interdisciplinary approach to research on this topic. It acts as an essential link between the other clusters, suggesting that an interdisciplinary approach to studying hybrid warfare is crucial for fully understanding its nature and consequences.

The red, blue, and yellow clusters together form a critical triangle for understanding contemporary threats related to hybrid warfare. The connection between these three clusters reflects the complexity and interconnections between various aspects of hybrid warfare in the context of defence. The red cluster (Cybersecurity and Critical Infrastructure Protection) focuses on technological security and the protection of critical infrastructure from cyberattacks, which forms the foundation of national security in the face of hybrid operations. The blue cluster (Advanced technologies and AI in hybrid warfare) introduces elements of modern technologies, such as artificial intelligence (AI) and machine learning, which are essential for detecting and responding to threats in real time. The yellow cluster (Information warfare and social media dynamics) addresses information warfare and manipulation, which are key components of hybrid strategies aimed at destabilizing the adversary through disinformation, influencing public opinion, and shaping social decisions. The combination of these three clusters reflects the complexity and interconnections between various aspects of hybrid warfare. Cybersecurity and Critical Infrastructure Protection (red cluster) form the foundation of defence against both physical and virtual threats. Modern technologies and AI (blue cluster) are essential for detecting and responding to these threats in real time, while Information warfare and social media dynamics (yellow cluster) influence public perception and societal decisions, which can either strengthen or weaken the effectiveness of defensive actions. The integration of these clusters highlights the necessity of a holistic approach to research and defence strategies, taking into account both the technical and social aspects of contemporary hybrid conflicts.

For the set of studies discussing the issue of hybrid conflict, the total number of keywords amounted to 65,939. By applying the same inclusion criteria as used for studies on hybrid warfare, 6,248 nodes corresponding to 9 clusters were obtained. The clusters identified for studies describing the issue of hybrid conflict are presented in Table 1.2. The cluster names represent the authors' attempt to define the common thematic areas addressed in the studies grouped within these clusters.

The identified papers on hybrid conflict are concentrated around Terrorism, radicalization, and social media dynamics, Animal studies and drug effects, Psychological and clinical studies in hybrid conflict, Theoretical and computational physics in conflict studies, Human-wildlife conflict and environmental studies, and Neuroscience and social interaction. Despite the significant number of studies, it is apparent that the scientific discussion is taking place in six clearly defined areas. The clusters have clear boundaries and are located in one defined area of the map. Cluster 1 (red) covers topics related to Terrorism, radicalization, and social media dynamics. Cluster 2 (green) focuses on Animal studies and drug effects. Cluster 3 (blue) relates to Psychological and clinical studies in hybrid conflict. Cluster 4 (yellow) concerns theoretical and computational physics in conflict research. Cluster 5 (purple) focuses on human-wildlife conflict and environmental studies. Cluster 6 (light blue) concerns Neuroscience and social interaction.

Cluster 3 (blue) is the central cluster on the map, forming the axis of the academic discussion related to hybrid conflicts. This cluster directly borders Cluster 2 (green), Cluster 1 (red), and Cluster 5 (purple). This relationship can be explained as follows. Cluster 3 (blue), focusing on psychology and clinical research, is central to understanding the human aspect of hybrid conflict, including the impact on mental and physical health, especially of military personnel. Research includes stress, depression, PTSD (posttraumatic stress disorder), and the effects of medications

TABLE 1.2 Thematic clusters for studies describing the issue of hybrid conflict

Cluster	Keywords	Colour	Cluster Name (Author's Proposal)
Cluster 1	Terrorism, violence, conflict, social media, extremism, radicalization, propaganda, asymmetric conflict, insurgents, counterinsurgency, human right, human experiment, decision-making, Turkey, is real, Palestine, migration, northern Ireland, Mexico, internet, China, Africa, game theory, artificial intelligence, blockchain, chemical warfare agents, war, conflict resolution, education, social behaviour	Red	Terrorism, radicalization, and social media dynamics
Cluster 2	Animal, nonhuman, controlled study, review, physiology, animal behaviour, priority journal, pain, rest, rat, mice, animal tissues, metabolism, drug effect, narcotic analgesic, opioid, unclassified drug, chemistry, kappa opiate receptor, animal cell	Green	Animal studies and drug effects
Cluster 3	Human, psychology, risk factor, major clinical study, adult, female, male, article, procedures, safety, retrospect study, trauma, military personnel, epidemiology, depression, young adult, aged, posttraumatic stress disorder, soldier, cognition, outcome assessment	Blue	Psychological and clinical studies in hybrid conflict
Cluster 4	Hadrons, lattice QCD, elementary particles, form factors, computation theory, pathology, event structures, Petri net, chiral perturbation theory, concurrent systems, matrix elements, nucleon structure, model independent, orbital angular momentum, quantum theory, reversibility, uncertainty analysis, sea quarks, semantics	Yellow	Theoretical and computational physics in conflict studies

(*Continued*)

Characteristics of hybrid warfare   19

TABLE 1.2 (*Continued*) Thematic clusters for studies describing the issue of hybrid conflict

Cluster	Keywords	Colour	Cluster Name (Author's Proposal)
Cluster 5	African elephant, agricultural worker, animalia, Asia, attitude, coexistence, behavioural response, community, conservation management, crop, ecosystem, elephant, environmental protection, foraging behaviour, human–wildlife conflict, India, Kenya, *Loxodonta*, mitigation, participatory approach, primates, punishment, Tanzania, wildlife	Violet	Human–wildlife conflict and environmental studies
Cluster 6	Nerve cell, neurons, photostimulation, social interaction, social status, violent radicalization, vision	Light blue	Neuroscience and social interaction

Source: Own work

used to treat these conditions. Direct links to Cluster 2 (green) may arise from research on the impact of stress and the effects of medication, which is relevant in the context of traumatic conflict experiences. Links to Cluster 1 (red) may be related to the analysis of psychological aspects of radicalization, terrorism, and violence. Cluster 5 (purple) links directly to Cluster 3 (blue) and Cluster 1 (red) and indirectly to Cluster 4 (yellow) through research on the effects of conflict on the environment and human-wildlife interactions, which may have implications for public health and disaster management.

Cluster 4 (yellow) is indirectly connected to the central cluster (blue) through Cluster 1 (red). This connection can be explained by the application of advanced physical and computational theories to the modelling and analysis of hybrid conflicts, including asymmetric attacks and new war technologies. Cluster 6 (light blue), the only cluster with blurred boundaries, suggests that topics related to nerve cell biology and social interactions are not yet sufficiently defined, or that research in these areas is still evolving. This may also indicate their interdisciplinary nature and connections to various other research areas, including studies on radicalization and violence. The conclusions from the analysis show that hybrid conflicts are studied in the context of a wide range of topics, from psychology and public health to technologies and theoretical models, as well as the impact on the natural environment. The interdisciplinarity of these studies is crucial for understanding the full scope of the effects of hybrid conflicts and for developing effective strategies to manage and counter these threats.

An analysis of the keywords showed it is evident that popular topics associated with the concept of hybrid warfare are scattered across all clusters. These include: machine learning, deep learning, cybersecurity, fake news, disinformation, Ukraine, Russia, Internet of Things, malware, cyberattacks, uncertainty, brain arteriovenous malformation, and brain angiography. These keywords suggest that hybrid warfare involves the intensive use of advanced technologies (e.g. AI, machine learning) and informational operations (e.g. fake news, disinformation). Elements such as cybersecurity and cyberattacks indicate a significant cyber component in hybrid conflict.

An analysis of the keyword words related to the issue of hybrid conflict showed that the most popular keywords in the red cluster are: extremism, social medial, AI, peacekeeping, machine learning, Ukraine, Russia, hybrid threat, polarization, fake news. It can be concluded that in the violet cluster, the keywords from this area have been of interest to researchers over the past three years.

In Cluster 1, the dominant theme is the use of advanced information technologies and digital tools for conducting propaganda, disinformation, and destabilization activities. In Cluster 5, research focuses on the impact of conflicts on the environment and ecosystems. This observation highlights that hybrid conflict is characterized by the widespread use of digital technologies and information operations aimed at destabilizing societies and influencing various aspects of life, including the natural environment.

The results of the systematic literature review, using the VOSviewer tool, confirmed the existence of two distinct phases in hybrid strategy: hybrid conflict and hybrid warfare. The analysis of the co-occurrence network of popular topics and keywords demonstrated a dichotomous division of these concepts, primarily based on the scale and intensity of the use of the military component (Ciano et al., 2019, pp. 5284–5317). At the various stages of these hybrid activities, it is possible to identify key areas that differ in terms of the level of involvement and the hybrid threats they generate.

Actions carried out during the hybrid conflict phase include a variety of operations such as information operations, cyberattacks, and asymmetric actions. In this phase, they are characterized by a smaller scale and lower intensity compared to the later phase of hybrid warfare. Examples include spreading disinformation on social media, conducting propaganda campaigns, cyberattacks on critical infrastructure, and supporting paramilitary groups and separatists.

In the hybrid warfare phase, there is an escalation of actions, including conventional military operations that combine regular armed forces with irregular units. Cyberattacks on key infrastructure systems, such as energy, transportation, and financial systems, also intensify. Additionally, integrated operations include both conventional and unconventional actions, supported by precision attacks and sabotage carried out by special forces.

The conclusions from the analysis may confirm previous findings and, as mentioned, highlight the need for clearly defining the boundaries of concepts related to hybrid warfare.

The authors of this study suggest that the existence of a hybrid strategy, which combines two stages: hybrid conflict and hybrid warfare, could be considered. To facilitate analysis, the proposed name for this approach could be the two-phase hybrid strategy model, which accounts for the dynamics of the transition from hybrid conflict to full-scale hybrid warfare. To assess the dynamics of the first phase of the strategy, the theory of hybrid interference, introduced by Mikael Wigell, could be employed. This theory refers to non-military practices primarily aimed at covert manipulation of the strategic interests of other states, often involving a variety of actions simultaneously, as the term "hybrid" pertains to the combination of these activities (Bergaust, Sellevåg, 2023). Interference in this context refers to actions below the threshold of war and can be considered as a precursor or coexisting element with hybrid conflict. In practice, this means that hybrid interference represents a phase of conflict where there is no open use of armed forces, but the objective remains to destabilize the opponent. This is a crucial stage that prepares the ground for more overt military actions, which emerge in cases of escalation to hybrid warfare. However, for this purpose, it is essential to develop indicators to monitor the escalation of actions within this phase of hybrid strategy. Such an indicator could include both qualitative and quantitative elements that reflect the gradual increase in the intensity of hybrid activities below the threshold of hybrid warfare. Bergaust and Sellevag, in their study, employed six parameters inspired by Johansen's morphological analysis for scenario planning in the defence sector: threat actor, target, attack objective, method, tools, and concealment (secrecy of the operation) (Bergaust, Sellevåg, 2023).

The conclusions reached by Bergaust and Sellevåg indicate that the adopted parameters can serve as a starting point for developing organizational, operational, and legal frameworks and indicators that allow for the effective assessment of the dynamics of hybrid actions in the hybrid conflict phase. A key indicator distinguishing hybrid conflict from hybrid warfare could be the scale, intensity, and duration of military involvement – both overt and covert. While this distinction may seem intuitive, it helps avoid situations where responses to increasingly complex hybrid actions result in overly complicated solutions. Particularly in the context of the rapid advancement of technologies, including AI, there is a risk that decision-makers may struggle to keep pace with increasingly coordinated and networked threats (for example, the application of autonomous weapons – the testing of the Russian tank named "Shturm," which utilizes AI, took place during the ongoing war in Ukraine) (Defence News Army, 2024).

Below is a theoretical model of hybrid strategy, which includes the phase of hybrid conflict escalating into the phase of hybrid warfare. It is worth noting that the actions undertaken during the conflict phase can be continued, intensified, and adapted throughout the course of hybrid warfare, allowing for their flexible use in changing operational conditions. Hybrid measures employed during the conflict phase can therefore serve to further destabilize the adversary and enhance the effects of conventional actions during the warfare phase, which will be discussed in more detail in the subsequent sections of this chapter.

Clausewitz wrote that war is inherently divided into two main categories – preparation for war and war itself. The preparation phase is evident in hybrid warfare, but in this case the boundary between preparation and military action is more fluid, as hybrid means are used both before and during the official start of a conflict. These activities, which include disinformation, cyberattacks, or intelligence operations, can therefore intersect with strictly military operations, complicating Clausewitz's classic division between preparation and war itself (Clausewitz, 2010, p. 78).

Figure 1.3 shows the theoretical model of the hybrid strategy.

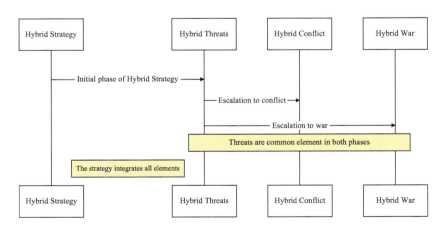

FIGURE 1.3 Theoretical model of the hybrid strategy

Source: Own study

The example of the Russian Federation's actions in Ukraine from 2014, and later in 2022, serves as confirmation of this model. Russia's actions between 2014 and 2021 can be classified as a hybrid conflict (covert military involvement, cyberattacks, cognitive operations, and intense disinformation campaigns). However, after 2022, there was an escalation of these activities with the overt use of armed forces, which can now be referred to as hybrid warfare. Oleg Manko and Yurii Mikhieiev highlight several key aspects of these phases.

Stage (phase) of hybrid conflict (Manko, Mikhieiev, 2018, pp. 11–20):

- Little Green Men – Russia employed soldiers without identifying insignia, known as "little green men." They were prepared to provoke uprisings and engage in street fighting. The lack of official recognition of these forces made it difficult for the international community to respond, and the soldiers were not subject to international law. This contingent represented a hybrid between soldiers and terrorists, with concealed faces, no identification documents, secret leadership, and modern weaponry.
- Ambiguous Command Structure – The ambiguity surrounding the command of these forces made it difficult for both Ukraine and the international community to respond effectively, as it was unclear with whom to negotiate. The local population was forced to submit to the aggressor, leading to the imposition of military emergency regimes, curfews, and the principle of "if you're not with us, you're against us."
- Activities in the Autonomous Republic of Crimea had a strong information component. Cyberattacks and Russian disinformation destabilized Ukraine by propagating false information about the persecution of the Russian-speaking population. The disinformation, confusion, and fear created by the information war made it difficult to respond quickly to Russia's actions.
- Use of Russian financial markets. Russian financial markets were used to justify Russia's actions and prevent international sanctions. The abundance of Russian energy resources enabled business relationships based on mutual financial gain, which became another powerful and covert weapon.
- Intense information warfare. Russia waged an intense information war against Ukraine and the international community. Ukraine sought to minimize losses and gain support, which shifted the emphasis of the war towards avoiding direct military contact. Russia conducted information operations, cyber operations, asymmetric operations, terrorist operations, urban guerrilla warfare, humanitarian warfare, trade warfare, and "emergent warfare," creating controlled chaos affecting the politics of a country subjected to aggression.

Manko and Mikhieiev further signal that the controlled chaos that emerged in Ukraine during the hybrid conflict phase had the following characteristics (Manko, Mikhieiev, 2018):

- involvement of illegal military formations, mercenaries, crime figures, sabotage and reconnaissance forces, units (specialists) and military grade weapons, and power-wielding agencies to the confrontation,
- drawing civilians into a conflict via compulsory mobilization in the introduced war-time regime, voluntary or hired human shields,
- the threat of deployment of Russia's armed forces along the state border in case Ukraine decides to use military force in what was framed by Russia as against its own civilian population,
- blocking attempts of the international community to deal with the conflict under the norms of international law,
- strong information-psychological impact, directed at destabilizing the situation inside the country, decrease people's reliance on the current government system, providing support to insurgents' actions, creation of negative image of the public authorities both in the state and on the world scene,
- greatest possible reinforcement of resistance in economic, diplomatic, information, and other domains.

The activities indicated above have been strengthened and expanded in 2022 to include additional domains, tactics, and actors, using a military component. This will be explored in detail in subsequent stages of this book.

The war in Ukraine, although taken as a reference, especially in Europe, is not the only war to which the label of hybrid is attributed. Irfan Fahmi et al. argue that if one were to ascribe to the framework of the three main characteristics and tendencies of hybrid war presented by Johann Schmidt (focus on non-military centres of gravity, grey area operations, and flexible integration of forms and operations) (Schmidt, 2019, pp. 5–15) they may also be recognized in the context of the present war in the Middle East (the so-called Israeli-Palestinian conflict) (Fahmi et al., 2023, pp. 359–368). Fahmi et al. highlighted that, firstly, a focus on non-military centres of gravity can be observed (both Israel's military operations and Hamas' terrorist tactics are designed to achieve each side's strategic objectives through such operations). Secondly, Hamas often uses asymmetric tactics and covert operations, which leads to blurring the boundaries between the categories of war and peace, operating in a grey area and complicating Israel's response. The State of Israel also uses similar operations against Palestinian civilians, for example.

Thirdly, different civilian and military categories, forms, and means are used in a flexible and integrated manner in the conflict between Hamas and Israel. Israel's use of conventional military force is challenged by asymmetric tactics and Hamas terrorist attacks, leading to new hybrid forms of conflict. This complex situation makes it difficult to identify patterns, underpinnings, and logics of hybrid actions, which supports the element of surprise and complicates the strategic response (Fahmi et al., 2023). Moreover, both sides, Hamas and Israel, engage in cyber-attacks to pursue their strategic objectives. Israel, as a state with an advanced cybersecurity system, focuses on protecting its digital infra-structure, while Hamas conducts cyberattacks against Israeli targets. The Palestinian side often uses militant groups in Gaza to launch attacks against Israel (proxy actions). The Israeli state, in turn, responds with both direct military operations and actions by its regional allies. In unde-tectable operations, Hamas often carries out terrorist attacks that are difficult to attribute directly, and thus allows Hamas to deny respon-sibility for these actions and maintain a level of uncertainty with the opponent. Israel also engages in operations that are difficult to attribute directly. As part of the information war, both sides make heavy use of social media, propaganda, and other forms of communication to influ-ence public opinion both locally and internationally (Fahmi et al., 2023).

Following the 7 October 2023 attack, the Israeli government launched a social media campaign to garner support from Western countries. The propaganda included numerous paid advertisements on platforms such as YouTube, which depicted violent and emotional images of violence. In one week, Israel's Ministry of Foreign Affairs ran 30 advertisements that had more than 4 million views on the X platform. These materials targeted adults in cities such as Brussels, Paris, Munich, and The Hague (Fahmi et al., 2023; Business & Human Rights Resource Centre, 2023). Hamas conducted an intense information war through its Telegram channel, Gaza Now, which had 1.4 million subscribers. This channel was used to post images of children allegedly killed or severely injured by Israeli attacks. Official Hamas channels appealed to their supporters in Arabic, calling for "immediate actions to express anger... without waiting for tomorrow." The Palestinian side sought to portray its fight-ers as freedom fighters with legitimate reasons for killing Israeli civilians. Hamas actively disseminated messages via Telegram to strengthen the resolve of its followers, incite anti-Israeli anger in neighbouring coun-tries, justify the violent actions of its fighters, and garner sympathy for those suffering in Gaza (WUSF Public Media, 2023; Fahmi et al., 2023).

In light of the aforementioned analysis, we can conclude that hybrid warfare serves as a framework for understanding the dynamics of the conflict between Hamas and Israel. The use of diverse elements, both military and non-military, is a fundamental aspect of the strategies employed by both sides, which endeavour to optimally utilize different tools in order to achieve their strategic objectives (Fahmi et al., 2024, pp. 359–365).

Hybrid conflict and hybrid warfare, while central, are not the only concepts requiring clarification. There are several other synonyms used in the context of the analysed area, which are described in detail in Appendix 1. To summarize this section, we conclude that the analysis of terms used in discussions of hybrid conflict and hybrid warfare demonstrates that some of these terms possess characteristics or attributes that can be associated with hybrid warfare but do not encompass its full spectrum. Such an approach may obscure the unique features of each term and the context in which they are most appropriate. The interchangeable use or misapplication of these terms to hybrid warfare may, in turn, obscure the actual characteristics of this type of action and create difficulties, as already mentioned, in designing frameworks for combating it. Therefore, the next section of this chapter will focus on the attempt to define the characteristics of hybrid warfare.

METATHEORETICAL APPROACH TO HYBRID WARFARE

Hybrid warfare in an academic perspective

The word hybrid comes from Latin and was used in the Roman Empire to describe a child born to parents of different social status. Later on, the term evolved to mean phenomena, entities, or activities of a combined nature that are organically integrated, coherent, and coordinated (Bilal, 2024). The first use of the term hybrid war referred to non-state action. William Nemeth researched the first Chechen war and identified how the combination of modern political theory, technology, and traditional customs and ideologies in a decentralized society allowed for a unique form of warfare, which he called hybrid warfare (Nemeth, 2002, pp. 5–28). One of the first definitions was created by Frank G. Hoffman, who called this term a strategic combination of conventional and asymmetric operations. His definition is based on an analysis of low-intensity operations and the prospect of military action outside the traditional framework of warfare (Weissmann, 2019, pp. 17–26; Berdal, 2011, pp. 109–110). In his work *Conflict in the 21st Century: The Rise of Hybrid Wars* from 2007, Hoffman stated that hybrid warfare is a combination of diverse methods of warfare aimed at achieving synergy across different dimensions of conflict and includes military operations, cyberattacks, irregular tactics, terrorism, and information operations. The key here is to use the entire spectrum of available tools to gain strategic advantage. Hoffman emphasized the importance of synergy, which increases the effectiveness of operations. Hybrid warfare, therefore, combines operational elements on different levels – from conventional armed combat to cyber operations, information activities, to influencing public awareness. These activities can take place both in a state of open conflict and in conditions that are not formally recognized as war, making them difficult to classify unambiguously and making hybrid war extremely difficult to predict and counteract (Hoffman, 2007, pp. 11–35). In 2009, Hoffman added that future adversaries will combine traditional, irregular, or catastrophic formations, employing unique combinations or hybrid threats and using all forms of war and tactics simultaneously. Future conflicts will therefore be multimodal or multi-variant.

Hoffman noted that hybrid wars differ from earlier conflicts by blurring the boundaries between regular and irregular operations even at lower operational and tactical levels. In the past, these elements were combined at the strategic level, whereas in hybrid warfare they are integrated into a single battle area (Hoffman, 2009, pp. 35–39). In the assessment of L. Sanchez, despite early criticisms, the concept of hybrid warfare popularized by Hoffman has become somewhat of a new orthodoxy in military thought, as may be confirmed by the use of the term during testimony before Congress in 2008–2010, where, military officials referred to as hybrid warfare the actions undertaken by the enemy in Iraq and Afghanistan, which were to be characterized' by various forms of warfare from conventional to unconventional to irregular (Sanchez, 2010, pp. 88–95).

In turn, in the publication *Hybrid Warfare as a New Type of War. The Evolution of Its Conceptual Construct*, Khayal Iskandarov and Piotr Gawliczek conclude that Hoffman refined the concept of hybrid warfare by analysing a number of earlier theories, mainly "fourth generation war," "complex war," and "unrestricted war," and predicted that future wars would be a convergence of distinct methods and strategies into multimodal wars that would combine the lethality of state conflict with the fanatical fervour of irregular warfare, both in terms of organization and means. They point out, however, that Hoffman's concept focuses only on operational and tactical levels. Hoffman himself acknowledged that his theory does not include non-violent actions, such as economic, financial, subversive, information activities. Iskandarov and Gawliczek believe that a holistic viable concept of hybrid warfare was put forward by the Murata Kaliskana (Figure 1.4) (Caliskan, 2019, pp. 40–58; Iskandarov, Gawliczek, 2023, pp. 96–107).

In the opinion of E. Magda the concept of hybrid war does not have a well-established theoretical basis. According to the author's opinion, in hybrid warfare one can rather speak of hybrid aggression according to a specific algorithm, defined as a finite sequence of precisely defined actions necessary for the implementation of specific tasks.

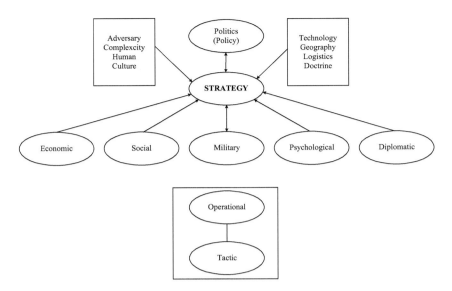

FIGURE 1.4 Concept of hybrid warfare in broader context – grand strategy

Source: Iskandarov, Gawliczek (2023)

The characteristic feature here is the predominance of non-military over military means. For this reason, it is not possible to consider hybrid war as war in the classical sense of the word. Therefore, the author uses the term "hybrid aggression," which more precisely defines the specifics of this type of conflict. The main descriptors of hybrid aggression include actions of an informational-propaganda, intelligence-diversion, political-diplomatic, and economic nature, often with elements of lobbying and corruption. In addition, this type of conflict envisages the possibility of military action using regular armies, guerrilla forces, and the limited use of tactical nuclear weapons (Магда, 2015, pp. 29–30).

In line with the clustering methodology discussed at the beginning of this chapter, a compilation of authors and key characteristics of hybrid warfare was made (Table 1.3).

A common element of these perspectives is the consideration of such aspects of hybrid warfare as the multidimensionality of conflicts, the asymmetry of actions, the integration of various means, and the significant impact on society. At the same time, this comparison highlights the discrepancies in defining and interpreting hybrid warfare, drawing attention to the individual components of each presented concept.

In the authors' opinion, analysing the concept of hybrid warfare solely within an academic context is insufficient for a broader understanding

Characteristics of hybrid warfare

TABLE 1.3 Key characteristics of hybrid warfare by academic perspective

Author/ Organization	Cluster	Features of Hybrid Warfare
Frank G. Hoffman	Multidimensionality, integration	Use of conventional and asymmetric measures, integrated use of the full spectrum of tools to achieve synergistic effects.
Robert G. Walker	New technologies	The use of innovative technologies in low-intensity operations, outside the traditional framework of war, to increase the effectiveness of operations.
Thomas R. Mockaitis	Multidimensionality	The concept of hybrid warfare as an evolutionary process, integrating multiple methods of warfare and adapting to changing conflict conditions.
Peter Mansoor	Integration	Combining conventional military forces with irregular tactics, including special and guerrilla operations, to achieve common political objectives.
Lawrence Freedman	Information and perceptual manipulation	The use of diverse combat tactics, including terrorism and insurgency, to control the narrative and perception of the enemy.
Stephen Blank	New technologies	Making full use of the spectrum of power tools, including cyber warfare and information operations, as an alternative to traditional armed forces.
Borislav Bankov	Asymmetry	Combining traditional combat methods with non-standard forms of action to exploit the enemy's weaknesses and integrated conflict strategy.
Håkanm Gunneriusson	Tactical and operational flexibility	Ability to quickly adapt tactics, exploit cyber space, and manipulate the perception of the opponent while denying involvement.

(Continued)

30 Civil Protection and Domestic Security in Hybrid Warfare

TABLE 1.3 (*Continued*) Key characteristics of hybrid warfare by academic perspective

Author/ Organization	Cluster	Features of Hybrid Warfare
Rakesh Sharma	Actions below the threshold of war	Integration of conventional methods with special operations to achieve results without triggering a full-scale conflict, characterized by non-linearity.
Andrew Mumford and Pascal Carlucci	Impact on society	Combining conventional elements with non-military methods, including propaganda and social manipulation, to achieve strategic political objectives.
Jean-Christophe Boucher	Multidimensionality	Integration of military, paramilitary, and civilian activities to achieve integrated strategic outcomes.
E. Magda	Information and perceptual manipulation	The prevalence of non-military means, such as information propaganda and political-diplomatic activities, to shape perceptions and narratives.
John J. McCuen	Integration of measures, impact on society	Full-spectrum operations covering the physical and conceptual dimensions of war to rebuild security and key elements of the economy.
Margaret S. Bond	Multidimensionality, integration	A continuum of activities from stabilization and security to armed conflict, with an emphasis on adaptive management of resources and methods.
Robert Leonhard	Asymmetry, information and perceptual manipulation, integration	Undeclared activities combining conventional and irregular military operations with non-military operations, information as a key role, blurring the boundaries between strategy and tactics.
Curtis L. Fox	New technologies, impact on society	Defining force in the information age, constructing interrelationships between the use of force and domains, levels and elements of force, operations in one domain initiating actions in another.

Source: Own study

of the phenomenon. A more precise interpretation of the complexity of hybrid wars is possible by examining definitions and concepts beyond academic frameworks.

Hybrid warfare in the view of selected think tanks

Research institutions such as think tanks specializing in armed conflict and war play an important role in understanding hybrid war. Through systematic research and publications, they are shaping international discussions on hybrid warfare, pointing to its evolution and increasing importance for global security. Analyses of think tank publications show that hybrid warfare is clearly defined by its complexity and adaptability, making it one of the most elusive and influential types of contemporary conflict. The key features of the concept in the think tanks' analyses are the crossing of traditional boundaries between a state of war and peace, the combination of conventional and asymmetric methods, and the exploitation of the digital and information space, which requires the development of new approaches in security policy. As highlighted by think tank researchers, understanding and adequately responding to conflict and hybrid war is becoming not only a challenge for states and international organizations, but also an imperative in ensuring global stability and security.

Table 1.4 presents the salient features of hybrid warfare that have been identified through the clustering of think tanks' definition of the issue.

TABLE 1.4   Features of hybrid warfare by think tanks definition

Author/ Organization	Cluster	Futures of Hybrid War
Multinational Capability Development Campaign (MCDC), IISS	Conflict multidi- mensionality	Using variety of instruments of force tailored to the specific weaknesses of the opponent, covering all aspects of social functions, to achieve synergistic effects of action.
(The International Institute for Strategic Science)	Usage of new technologies	Intensive use of technology to extend the reach and increase the effectiveness of hybrid operations, including cyberattacks and advanced intelligence techniques.
RAND Corporation (Andrew Radin)	Asymmetry of actions	A combination of conventional and irregular tactics aimed at influencing the internal politics of target states through actions that do not require direct armed conflict.

(Continued)

32   Civil Protection and Domestic Security in Hybrid Warfare

TABLE 1.4 (*Continued*)   Features of hybrid warfare by think tanks definition

Author/ Organization	Cluster	Futures of Hybrid War
	Actions below the war threshold	Performing covert or deniable actions that are supported by conventional or nuclear forces in a way that makes it difficult to assign responsibility.
Forward Defence	Information and perceptual manipulation	"Grey area" operations aimed at undermining national security and promoting countries' own interests without provoking open conflict.
	Actions below the war threshold	"Grey area" activity, involving activities on the borderline between cooperation and armed conflict, using disinformation and operations to influence public perception.
RUSI (The Royal United Services Institute)	Tactical and operational flexibility	A strategy that combines different forms of warfare, blurring the boundaries between a state of war and a state of peace, enabling tactics to be quickly adapted to changing operational conditions.
	Information and perceptual manipulation	Blurring the boundaries between war and peace through information manipulation to control the narrative and influence the perception of the opponent.
Multinational Capability Development Campaign (MCDC)	Integration of means	Synchronizing military, political, economic, civilian, and information activities in ways that go beyond the traditional military framework to achieve complex strategic objectives.
	Impact on civil society	Consideration and manipulation of the impact of actions on civil society in defence strategies and analysis of potential threats in a social context.

Source: Own study

Operationalization of hybrid warfare in NATO, EU, and U.S. strategies

In the discourse on defining hybrid warfare, international institutions and defence/security organizations play a particularly important role. The understanding of hybrid warfare by NATO, the U.S. Department of Defence, and the European Union is a key element in shaping global strategies to counter this threat.

Definition of NATO. NATO adopted a strategy to counter hybrid warfare in 2015, responding to the growing threats associated with unconventional methods of conflict. This strategy, resulting from decisions made at the 2014 Wales Summit and continued at the 2016 Warsaw Summit, involves the integration of various military and non-military actions. The Alliance enhanced its capabilities to respond to hybrid threats, which led to the creation of specialized analytical units at NATO headquarters in Brussels (Caliskan, 2019, pp. 40–58). Hybrid warfare, as understood by NATO, is an armed conflict that combines the simultaneous use of conventional and irregular methods of warfare, involving both state and non-state actors, applied adaptively in the pursuit of objectives. It is not limited to the physical battlefield or territory. Each attack features its own combinations and mutations of these forms, aimed at undermining the enemy's state and society to achieve its goals. Hybrid warfare can be employed in conflicts not only by states and armed forces but also by various actors operating outside of state authority (Bachmann, 2011, pp. 24–25; Jacobs, Lasconrajias, 2015, pp. 4–5).

EU definition. In J.J. Torreados's assessment, the European Union, due to the difficulties in reaching a unified definition of hybrid warfare, defines this area from the perspective of hybrid threats and hybrid conflict (Terrados, 2019, pp. 43–50). Nevertheless, in general terms, hybrid warfare, as understood by the European Union, refers to the coordinated use of diplomatic, military, economic, and technological means by state or non-state actors. A key feature of hybrid warfare is the ability of such actions to remain below the threshold of formal war, with large-scale disinformation campaigns and manipulation of social media used to disrupt democratic processes. The European Union has developed a joint response plan to hybrid threats, which includes both military and non-military actions, such as combating disinformation (European Commission, 2024).

Definition of the U.S. Department of Defence. The U.S. Department of Defence, in an assessment by General Karen H. Gibson, emphasizes the attempt to achieve strategic objectives without the use of significant military force in defining hybrid warfare. The amorphous nature of hybrid warfare strategy includes information operations, troop movements, disinformation campaigns, cyberattacks, or a combination of all of these. Hybrid warfare may also involve the actual use of force, as is the case with Russia's actions in Ukraine (Garamone, 2019).

A comparison of these three approaches to defining hybrid war shows that each of the aforementioned institutions adapts the concept of hybrid war to its individual needs and strategic experience. NATO focuses mainly on combining military and non-military actions. The European Union does not define hybrid war directly, but refers to the context of hybrid threats, mainly focusing on non-military aspects such as the impact on decision-making and social processes in member states. The U.S. Department of Defence, on the other hand, emphasizes the adaptive and variable nature of hybrid warfare, taking into account a variety of threats. All of these definitions

Civil Protection and Domestic Security in Hybrid Warfare

point to the increasing complexity of modern warfare, where traditional military methods are supplemented by actions aimed at achieving strategic advantage without the need for direct military conflict.

Table 1.5 includes the features of hybrid warfare that emerged during the clustering process, taking into account the approaches used by NATO, the EU, and the U.S. Department of Defence.

TABLE 1.5 Features of hybrid warfare by NATO, the EU, and the United States

Organization/ Person	Cluster	Features of Hybrid Warfare
NATO	Information and cognitive manipulation	Use of subversion, propaganda, disinformation operations, and offensive cyber operations to control the narrative, penetration of intelligence services, acquisition of government officials, funding of political parties, and interference in democratic elections.
	Impact on society	Cyberattacks aimed at destabilizing national economies and media, especially social media platforms, undermining the unity and cohesion of the alliance and eroding the foundations of collective security.
U.S. Department of Defence	Conflict multidimensionality	Integration of information operations, troop movements, disinformation campaigns, cyberattacks and the use of actual force, the use of various forms of hybrid operations by Chinese and Russian initiatives.
	Flexibility	Using a low-risk, low-cost strategy to mask activities and introduce uncertainty about the authorship of activities in the so-called grey area.
European Commission	Asymmetry	Exploitation of the weaknesses of the European Union and its member states by state or non-state actors, using a coordinated mix of measures (diplomatic, military, economic, technological), while remaining below the threshold of formal war.
	Actions below the threshold of war	Disrupting democratic decision-making processes through mass disinformation campaigns, the use of social media to control the political narrative, and the use of non-military forces.

Source: Own study

As mentioned in the introduction to this chapter, the term hybrid warfare is used in the context of several historical and contemporary conflicts and wars. However, the literature highlights two leading states that extensively employ hybrid strategies, which will be discussed in more detail below. According to NATO, one example is the Russian Federation, whose sophisticated hybrid actions include political interference, malicious cyber activities, economic pressure, coercion, subversion, aggression, annexation, and rhetoric. These elements are part of Russia's hybrid strategies aimed at achieving its political objectives and undermining the international order based on democratic principles. Furthermore, large-scale hybrid and cyber operations are also employed by the People's Republic of China (PRC), whose actions, along with confrontational rhetoric and disinformation, pose a threat to international security. The PRC aims to control key technological and industrial sectors, critical infrastructure, as well as strategic materials and supply chains. It uses economic leverage to create strategic dependencies and expand its sphere of influence. Below, we present an expanded analysis of the approaches of both powers, which stem from significant differences in their understanding of hybrid warfare compared to Western theories. In the following sections of this work, we will focus in particular on the specific methods and tactics used by these two states, highlighting their unique approach to hybrid strategies.

The hybrid war in the perspective of the Chinese Communist Party

Since the end of the last century, the PRC has been conducting research on methods of "unrestricted warfare." Techniques associated with this concept include hacking computer systems, creating and spreading computer viruses, destabilizing banking systems, market and currency manipulation, urban terrorism, and media disinformation. The extent to which unrestricted warfare has become an official doctrine in Chinese political strategy remains largely unknown to Western civilization. However, it can be presumed that its influence is present in China's "Three Warfares (3W)" policy, especially concerning territorial claims in the East and South China Seas. To achieve its territorial objectives, China avoids direct military confrontations, instead employing psychological operations, media manipulation, and legal actions (Wither, 2019).

Elements of Chinese hybrid warfare

According to the Chinese military, hybrid warfare is based on integrated and coordinated warfare at the strategic level, while using political (influencing public opinion, diplomacy, law), economic (commercial or energy warfare), military (information warfare, electronic warfare, special operations, and others) means. What emerges here is a marked difference from U.S. concepts, which focus on tactical operations used immediately before a conflict. In China, the role of coordination between different fields of action and cooperation between governmental organizations is emphasized (Peterson, 2023, pp. 1–5).

The assumptions of modern Chinese information warfare were formulated as early as 1929 by Mao Zedong, who emphasized the political role of the Chinese People's Liberation Army (PLA) as a tool of the Chinese Communist Party (CCP). This influenced a threat perception and methods of neutralization that differed from Western and Soviet paradigms (Mattis, 2018). The history of Chinese information, psychological and influence operations suggests their long-standing roots in Chinese military strategy. They were a response to the relative weakness of the Chinese People's Liberation Army (PLA) compared to potential adversaries. To address this, methods now referred to as "hybrid" were used and played a key role in CCP-led conflicts. However, their effectiveness has been judged differently (Damiri, 2013).

Observation of U.S. military activities inspired the PRC to make intensive use of modern technology and methods. The turning point came in 1989 with the events in Tiananmen Square, which meant that the authorities had to confront the problem of military loyalty and adapt the army to the new international realities. In 1999, the publication Unlimited Warfare was published, which, together with the development of the strategy of "local high-tech warfare," set the stage for the development of an extended concept of warfare, elements of which included economic, psychological, and cyber operations (Mattis, 2018; Sugiura, 2021).

Officially, in 2003, the concept of the 3W was introduced: public opinion warfare, psychological warfare, and legal warfare. This followed a review of the political work guidelines of the PLA, the Central Committee of the CPC, and the Central Military Commission (CMC). The interconnectedness, complementarity, and inseparability are key elements of the 3W concept. Actions in the sphere of public opinion create favourable conditions for conducting psychological and legal warfare. Legal warfare, in turn, provides a legal basis for conducting psychological warfare and public opinion warfare. Psychological warfare facilitates the conduct of legal warfare and public opinion warfare (Damiri, 2013). The goal of the aforementioned 3W is to weaken the opponent in such a way that resolving the conflict in favour of China becomes possible without the need to use conventional means. This is facilitated by: exploiting the opponent's weaknesses and leveraging China's own strengths, concealing political objectives, and ultimately creating conditions that enable military victory (Behrendt, 2022).

The 3W strategy gained importance when it became clear that the development of the army and its technology was not sufficient to ensure national security. In 2010, this strategy was expanded and detailed in new guidelines. It then became a key operational strategy, emphasizing the need to train personnel in the 3W (Behrendt, 2022; Charon, Vilmer, 2021).

Public opinion warfare, also referred to as "media warfare," is one of the primary strategic tools used by Chinese authorities to manipulate public opinion, both domestically and internationally. A positive image of Beijing's actions is promoted, morale within the domestic society and armed forces is strengthened, while simultaneously weakening the resolve and will of adversaries to fight. These goals are achieved through large-scale informational activities using radio, television, press, book publications, and the internet, particularly social media. Public opinion warfare is built on three main pillars: shaping the cognitive orientation of the masses, stimulating emotions, and steering behaviours. This is accomplished through official social media accounts, bots, and collaboration with influencers and commentators sympathetic to the PRC. Chinese diplomatic missions invest in content published in local media, reinforcing the desired message. These efforts are based on long-term planning and continuity, which aim to subtly and effectively influence public perception and opinion. To this end, key figures in the enemy camp are targeted, using specific situations to exploit their vulnerabilities. The military weakness of the adversary is highlighted to gain moral superiority and influence the international perception of the situation. Disinformation campaigns not only spread messages favourable to China but also suppress criticism both domestically and abroad.

The key elements of China's media warfare strategy (war on public opinion) are:

- adherence to top-down guidelines – contractors of media operations are obliged to follow the instructions of their top superiors, the CCP and PRC leadership – regarding both the content and timing of news coverage,
- pre-emptive action – the first to publish information, especially on social media, gains an advantage by being able to dominate the message, frame the debate, and influence the subsequent course of the debate,
- flexibility and adaptation to changing conditions – the CHALW requires a flexible response and adaptation to changing political and military conditions,
- use of "all available" resources – the tasks assigned are carried out by all means available to the military and civilian actors.

According to Paul Behrendt, Mattis has identified four phases of Beijing's crisis operations (Mattis, 2013):

- Presenting its own version of events – Beijing issues Chinese position statements on new developments,
- Delineating the principles of conflict resolution – Chinese officials indicate the terms of negotiation at the outset and attempt to shape the discussion, the terms are presented as an acceptable minimum, meeting Beijing's obligations to Chinese public opinion, all dedicated to foreign and domestic audiences,
- Shutting down all unofficial, widely used information channels – the PRC leadership seeks to establish tight control over the flow of information and thereby gain an advantage, while confusing the opponent and exerting psychological pressure,
- Highlighting China's involvement with the United States – Beijing tends to express its full commitment to the bilateral relationship, while suggesting that Washington does not take the relationship as seriously as China does.

Another key dimension of the 3W military strategy is psychological warfare, whose primary objectives are to intimidate and demoralize the enemy, thereby weakening or completely breaking their will to fight. Operations in this area (Psychological Operations – PSYOPS) are directed against individuals, societies, government structures, and the enemy's command. The media, particularly the internet, play a crucial role in disrupting the enemy's operational effectiveness. However, the instruments used in psychological warfare also include military manoeuvres, displays of equipment and weaponry, as well as various provocations that verge on conventional warfare activities (Damiri, 2013).

The PLA divides psychological warfare into four types (Charon, Vilmer, 2021, pp. 47–48):

- Coercion – Forcing the opponent to adopt certain behaviours.
- Deception – Misleading the opponent about the actual situation, thereby influencing their perception and decisions.
- Division – Creating discord and division among opponents by disrupting social bonds and undermining trust.
- Defence – Neutralizing the opponent's psychological warfare efforts and strengthening morale within one's own forces and society. Political officers play a key role in this aspect.

According to Abhijit Singh, psychological warfare is the most destructive element of the 3W strategy, as it undermines the opponent's confidence and determination to defend themselves (Jash, 2019, pp. 96–106). Techniques deployed in psychological warfare during peacetime subtly influence the unconscious beliefs of the opponent, making them more susceptible to external influences. By fostering doubt and distrust towards leadership, the decision-making process of the enemy is disrupted, leading to a weakening of their will to act. As mentioned earlier, in the 3W concept, strategic preparation during peacetime is crucial for achieving victory later. Technology and intelligent systems are playing an increasingly important role in this, creating the need for the development and refinement of appropriate tools (Sugiura, 2021, p. 84; Yamaguchi et al., 2023; Behrendt, 2022).

The concept of legal warfare introduced by the PRC in the context of modern conflicts significantly differs from the traditional (democratic) approach to international law, which in Western culture is often a tool used to prevent wars or regulate their conduct. In China, since the 1990s, law has been one of the main tools in military strategies for conducting offensive, defensive, deterrent, coercive, or punitive actions (Charon, Vilmer, 2021, pp. 47–48). Legal warfare creates the appearance of legality for actions undertaken by China, even when they involve the use of force, while simultaneously portraying the opponent's actions as illegal. Both passive and active measures are employed, with the latter focusing on shaping international law and norms to be favourable to the CCP. This is often achieved through active engagement within international organizations and the training of lawyers specializing in international law (Behrendt, 2022). The goal is to delay and complicate the opponent's actions, shape the desired post-war reality by influencing public opinion, and harass the opposing side. The strategy of legal warfare illustrates the complexity of modern conflicts, where international law becomes a battleground for states seeking to achieve their strategic objectives.

A complementary area of the 3W concept is outer space. Although this domain may seem distant and less obvious, as Paweł Behrend points out, the strategy of the CCP lists it among the techniques of integrated hybrid warfare. The CCP seeks to present itself in the media space as a rising space power, a narrative supported by actual achievements. China emphasizes its commitment to promoting the welfare and progress of humanity, as well as the peaceful use of outer space. Projects highlighted in this narrative include the International Lunar Research Station (ILRS) co-developed with Russia, the Chinese Space Station (CSS/Tiangong), and Mars exploration missions. In the context of media warfare, China's interests are relativized or portrayed as responses to U.S. initiatives. In the realm of psychological warfare, the CCP aims to present China as a future leader in space exploration, thereby undermining the position and confidence of the United States, which has traditionally been the leader in this field. Cooperation with Russia builds a narrative of the potential to jointly break American dominance, including the possibility of coordinated military use. China's collaboration with Russia in legal warfare aims to curb U.S. efforts to maintain its advantage in outer space and promote legal regulations more aligned with Chinese and Russian interests. At the same time, the United States is accused of actions primarily serving its own benefit, such as its leadership in the Artemis Accords, which pertain to the use of outer space in the context of renewed lunar missions. China highlights the lack of African countries' participation and insufficient representation of the Middle East and Asia in these initiatives, while not offering any specific counterproposal. It is important to note that China's activities in the space sector are part of a broader hybrid strategy that combines media, psychological, and legal actions to strengthen China's position on the international stage while simultaneously challenging the dominant role and policies of the United States (Behrendt, 2022).

The concept of 3W is not the only war strategy of the PRC. Kevin Bilms from the Modern War Institute also mentions a less commonly known but significant work – *The Science of Military Strategy*, which is considered by experts to be a foundational text for the development of the operational doctrine of the PLA.

In one of the chapters of this work, the concept of *Non-War Military Activities* (NWMA) is highlighted and explained. NWMA includes guidelines for operations during peacetime, across all domains, aimed at achieving the political objectives of the CCP. NWMA differs from the concept of the 3W, which are practically omitted in this publication. According to Bilms, NWMA is a key element of the PLA's military competition, focused on gaining effective control well before the outbreak of conflict (Bilms, 2022). The authors of *The Science of Military Strategy* describe NWMA as one of the three fundamental elements of the PLA's military power, alongside armed combat and deterrence. They emphasize that NWMA is part of the PLA's modernization efforts and is crucial due to China's increasing responsibilities in relation to its dynamic economic development and global expansion. Within NWMA, four main categories of activities are distinguished:

- confrontational actions – also translated as adversarial,
- enforcement actions,
- relief and rescue operations,
- cooperation actions.

Each category includes additional missions carried out by the PLA.

Confrontational actions and law enforcement involve taking risks through military activities to achieve political or economic gains outside of a declared conflict. An example of this is the PLA's operations in the South China Sea, patrols along the Mekong River, and anti-piracy patrols off the coast of the Somali Peninsula. Through decisive engagement in these regions, which lies at the border between NWMA and active defence – considered the core of the CCP's military-strategic thought – the PLA pursues its defensive objectives. Such limited offensive operations, aimed at securing political goals without leading to strategic escalation, carry the risk of miscalculations or unintended consequences under international scrutiny.

The category of relief and rescue activities is more in line with the concepts of civil defence by military authorities, military diplomacy, and defence cooperation. China's NWMA shows how the PLA sees the use of soft power as a tool to strengthen bilateral relations and control potential crises in important peripheral regions. This interpretation directs the PLA to undertake military exercises, unilateral or in partnership, aimed at achieving strategic dominance in peacetime.

Bilms, analysing the 2013 edition of *The Science of Military Strategy*, notes that by utilizing a wide range of NWMA with varying levels of intensity, the PLA can adjust the use of force to achieve the greatest effect. Taking specific actions before a war yields strategic outcomes in and of itself and allows for greater subtlety in the asymmetric use of the military in low-intensity conflicts or competition below the threshold of war. This approach enables the full force of the PLA to be deployed only when absolutely necessary (Bilms, 2022). This approach is a novelty compared to traditional Western concepts of military planning and doctrines concerning the role of the military in internal affairs and the use of force outside of declared war.

China, by conducting various missions within the framework of NWMA, such as counterterrorism, riot control, armed law enforcement against drug cartels, internal military patrols, and epidemic response, exemplifies both the use of military force and its restraint – both within its own territory and abroad. It should be emphasized that PLA deployments under NWMA may serve hidden objectives, such as strengthening Beijing's influence on the international stage. Meanwhile, China's participation in UN peacekeeping missions provides a platform for gaining operational experience and practising combat concepts. According to *The Science of Military Strategy*, NWMA "reflect the essence of China's traditional concepts of military security."

A distinctive feature of NWMA is the blurring of boundaries between these military activities and the actors carrying them out, especially in the maritime domain. For example, in 2018, the Chinese coast guard was subordinated to the CMC in Beijing, but not as part of the armed forces of the PRC. Consequently, in 2021, it enforced China's interpretation of jurisdictional waters. Analysing NWMA allows for the connection between Beijing's maritime security operations and coastal patrols with China's use of legal warfare. This illustrates a coordinated effort to legitimize the CCP's political claims as facts.

In his assessment, however, Bilms states that not all PLA Non-Military Activities should raise suspicion. For example, embassy protection and security missions abroad to protect Chinese diplomatic missions and interests are types of operations that any military can conduct in cooperation with host states, in accordance with international law. It should be noted, however, that the study and analysis of the NWMA should make Western military planners aware of the secondary implications of the PLA's subtle actions and their strategic impact on achieving objectives without the use of traditional military action (Bilms, 2022).

Table 1.6 presents features of hybrid warfare that emerged during the clustering process, taking into account the approaches used by the CCP.

TABLE 1.6   Features of hybrid warfare by CCP

Perspective	Cluster	Features of Hybrid Warfare
CCP – PLA	Multidimensionality	Using all aspects of state power, including the influence of civil society, to implement indirect confrontation with adversaries, taking into account political, economic, military, and informational aspects.
	Integration of means	Integrated action at the strategic level, combining political, economic, and military means, with an emphasis on coordination between different spheres and governmental organizations to achieve operational synergies.
	Information manipulation	Long-term use of information and psychological operations to shape both national and international perceptions through disinformation, propaganda, and control of the media narrative.
	Asymmetry	The use of asymmetric tactics such as coercion, mystification, division, and demoralization, aimed at undermining an opponent's will to fight and disrupting their ability to respond effectively.
	Flexibility (at tactical and operational level)	Adapting strategies and tactics to changing international conditions, with an emphasis on rapid response and the use of modern technology and innovative methods of warfare.

(*Continued*)

Characteristics of hybrid warfare

TABLE 1.6 (*Continued*)   Features of hybrid warfare by CCP

Perspective	Cluster	Features of Hybrid Warfare
	Legal manipulation	Using international law as a tool for offensive and defensive actions, shaping legal norms that favour the CCP's goals and portraying the actions of opponents as illegal.
	Impacting the society	Promoting a positive image of Beijing as a leader in space exploration, manipulating public perception to build an image of technological power and boosting internal and external morale.
	Economic leverage	Using economic resources to create strategic dependencies and increase influence through investment, loans, and control of key sectors.
	Technological domination	Investing in cutting-edge military and civilian technologies, including cybersecurity, space technology, and artificial intelligence, to gain strategic advantage.
	Actions below the threshold of war	Using measures below the threshold of open conflict, such as promoting space regulation that favours the interests of China and Russia, limiting U.S. dominance in space and avoiding direct military confrontation.

Source: Own study

Hybrid warfare in the Russian perspective

In Russia, hybrid warfare is understood as the systematic and integrated use of military, political, economic, civilian, and information tools, often in grey areas, below the threshold of conventional warfare (NATO, 2024). Arsalan Bilal, in *NATO Review*, assesses that the military instrument in these areas is used unconventionally, in a way that avoids identifying the perpetrators, and sometimes even their detection, which allows for evading responsibility (Bilal, 2024).

An example of this is Russia's actions in Crimea in 2014, when the Russian Federation used unmarked armed forces, the so-called "little green men," to carry out the invasion, while denying its involvement in these events. The broad range of tools in Russia's hybrid warfare arsenal also includes the use of non-state actors, political assassinations, espionage, cyberattacks, election interference, and disinformation.

It is difficult to detect, attribute, and confirm the use of these tools, making it challenging to respond effectively. The use of these methods allows Russia to operate below the threshold of war, maximizing impact while minimizing the risk of strategic escalation. Russia's hybrid warfare strategy also relies on the synchronization of kinetic and non-military actions. This enables the achievement of political and strategic goals without the need to engage in open conflict. A clear example is the intervention in Syria, where military operations were supported by informational, diplomatic, and economic activities aimed at strengthening control over President Bashar al-Assad's regime and weakening Western influence in the region, another similar example is the war in Ukraine (which is analysed in detail later in this study) (Bilal, 2024).

The term "gibridnaya voyna" (hybrid warfare) was introduced into Russian military discussions from the Western debate on hybrid warfare in the late 2000s. However, it gained significant prominence relatively recently, following the publication of articles and books on the subject after the onset of the war in Ukraine in 2014. Similar to the West, in Russian military discourse, the term is used eclectically to describe a war that combines various forms of force, both conventional and non-military. In Russia, this term partially overlaps with the concepts of information warfare and so-called "colour revolutions."

According to Ofer Fridman, the Russian understanding of the term hybrid warfare has little in common with its Western interpretation. Unlike Hoffman, who presents hybrid warfare as tactical-operational methods combining multi-domain resources, Russian scholars define hybrid warfare as a strategic attack on "the spirit of the enemy nation through the gradual erosion of its culture, values, and sense of self-worth." The Russian concept of gibridnaya voyna is a type of war in which the primary objective is to avoid traditional battlefields and destroy the enemy through a mixture of ideological, informational, financial, political, and economic methods that dismantle the fabric of society, leading to its internal collapse (Göransson, 2024, pp. 449–471). In Russia, the term hybrid warfare is used interchangeably with concepts such as "new generation warfare," "nonlinear warfare," "network-centric warfare," "reflexive control," and "active measures." According to the analysis by O.W. Walecki and W.M. Niejelov, in Russian academic literature, hybrid warfare initially described U.S. actions but was later applied to the Russo-Ukrainian conflict. The Russian adaptation of the term focuses on the complexity and multidimensionality of modern conflicts, combining conventional and non-military methods (Валецкий, Неелов, 2015, p. 25).

As Richard Weitz emphasizes, in recent years, Russia has adopted a multidimensional approach to warfare, which includes elements such as cyber aggression, media manipulation, psychological warfare, economic intimidation, proxy actions, sophisticated propaganda, and the exploitation of social divisions. These tactics, when used individually, may seem harmless, but when employed collectively and in a coordinated manner, they have the potential to destabilize target states and pave the way for more aggressive actions (Weitz, 2014).

Since Russia's actions in Ukraine did not fully reflect the previous understanding of the term hybrid warfare, it became necessary to reassess what hybrid warfare truly entails. Russia achieved its political objectives through a combination of unconventional tools, such as cyberattacks, propaganda, disinformation, economic coercion, and diplomatic pressure, alongside military methods – conducting covert operations and involving mercenaries. At the same time, the Russian Federation denied its involvement on Ukrainian territory, thus expanding hybrid warfare to include not only covert military actions but also the use of denial and concealment of the truth. This created ambiguity and the possibility of plausible deniability. As a result, the "hybrid war model" became widely associated with the so-called "Gerasimov Doctrine," which is characterized by blurring the lines between war and peace (Solmaz, 2022).

General Valery Gerasimov, Chief of the General Staff of the Russian Federation, in his address to the Russian Academy of Military Sciences in 2013, presented new advanced methods for planning and conducting military operations by Russia's armed forces. Gerasimov emphasized the necessity of adapting to new forms of conflict, in which the boundaries between war and peace blur, and the role of non-military means in achieving strategic objectives increases. His analysis highlighted the evolving nature of modern conflicts and demonstrated the dominance of non-military actions over the traditional use of armed forces in terms of effectiveness. In his view, this shift in the conduct of warfare is crucial.

> In the 21st century, we have observed a tendency to blur the lines between states of war and peace. Wars are no longer declared, and once begun, they unfold in previously unknown patterns. The experience of military conflicts [...] confirms that a fully thriving state can, within months or even days, be transformed into an area of intense armed conflict, become a victim of external intervention, and sink into chaos, humanitarian disaster, and civil war [...]. The very "rules of war" have changed. The role of non-military means in achieving political and strategic objectives has increased and, in many cases, has surpassed the power of weapons in its effectiveness.
>
> *(Gerasimov, 2013a, 2013b)*

A thorough analysis of General Gerasimov's (2013a, 2013b) speech and his February 2014 article published in the "Voyenno-Promyshlennyy Kurier" provides a clearer understanding of his intentions and approach to modern warfare. Gerasimov does not propose a radically new war strategy, but rather presents reflections on and the evolution of existing methods, emphasizing Russia's readiness to adapt its strategies to complex forms of international competition while maintaining the use of traditional forms of conflict (Galeotti, 2016, pp. 282–301; Pomerantsev, 2017; Terrados, 2019). In his reflections, Gerasimov addressed the topic of modern technologies and the changing conditions on the international stage, as well as their impact on contemporary methods of warfare. He considered conventional methods insufficient and inadequate in the face of modern challenges, which are far more complex and require more integrated responses. Gerasimov specifically mentioned the role of non-military actions, such as informational, cyber, and economic operations, which may prove as effective as, if not more so than, traditional armed actions. According to the Russian general, an effective 21st-century war strategy must combine various means of influence to achieve the desired strategic effect. The use of a full range of tools can help secure a strategic advantage without engaging in open armed conflict.

In his 2014 article, Gerasimov identified the weaknesses of traditional strategies and presented a more flexible and dynamic approach to warfare, one that responds to modern forms of competition. He emphasized the need for continuous adaptation of military strategy, which is crucial for maintaining effectiveness in the ever-changing international environment (Terrados, 2019, pp. 43–50).

In his 2016 speech, Gerasimov emphasized the importance of informational and psychological operations, support for internal opposition, and the use of guerrilla and sabotage tactics as key elements of Russia's modern war strategy. This statement clearly signals an authentic adaptation to the changing nature of contemporary warfare and the complementing of traditional military operations with a wide range of non-military actions. As Gerasimov points out, these actions are designed to minimize direct armed engagement, reducing costs and helping to avoid potential negative repercussions from the international community towards the Russian Federation. Unconventional actions are intended to exert influence on both the domestic and international arenas of the opponent, using techniques that shape perception and political decisions. This strategy, therefore, involves intensive informational operations that manipulate public opinion and media narratives within the target state to cause internal disorganization and conflict. Supporting opposition movements is aimed at undermining the legitimacy of ruling authorities, while guerrilla and sabotage tactics are meant to disrupt infrastructure and reduce the defensive capabilities of the adversary.

The approach outlined by Gerasimov highlights the significant shift in the paradigm of warfare, where symmetrical armed confrontations give way to more diverse and coordinated actions, which can be concealed and, as a result, are harder to attribute to a specific state.

This changes not only the methods of conducting warfare but also requires a new approach from the international community in understanding these tactics and responding to the threats they pose (Pynnöniemi, Jokela, 2020, pp. 828–845; Gerasimov, 2016, pp. 19–23).

In his 2018 speech, General Gerasimov emphasized the growing role of new technologies: precision weaponry, laser technologies, and the strategic use of outer space and cyberspace. By highlighting the importance of dominance in the informational domain and outer space, Gerasimov outlined the direction for the evolution of Russia's military doctrine.

Figure 1.5 illustrates the correlation in Gerasimov's presented tactics between military and non-military means in hybrid conflict, as well as the phases of development of such a conflict. The diagram shows the dominance of non-military actions over both conventional and unconventional military actions. The comparison reveals that for every military action, there are nearly four unconventional actions. Based on conducted research and media report analysis, the authors confirm that in the war in Ukraine, the ratio of non-military to military actions

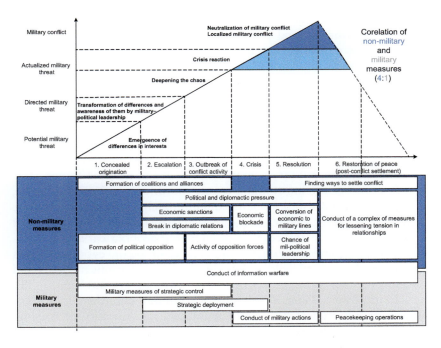

FIGURE 1.5 The ratio of the use of non-military and military measures/actions based on own research and Gerasimov's concept

Source: Own study on the basis of Gerasimov (2018)

(both conventional and unconventional) is 3.69:1, meaning that for every one military action (conventional + unconventional), there are nearly four non-military actions (conventional military actions: seven instances, unconventional military actions: 360 instances, non-military actions: 1,356). Furthermore, the ratio of non-military to conventional military actions is 193.7:1, indicating that non-military actions are almost 194 times more frequent than conventional military actions.

Juan Jose Terrados demonstrated significant parallels between Gerasimov's arguments and the approach adopted by Mattis and Hoffman in 2005, regarding the reorientation of the Russian Federation's military transformation policy. However, there was a notable absence of a clear definition of the new type of conflict or how Russia would conduct warfare in the future (Terrados, 2019). In contrast, Sergey Bogdanov and Sergey Chekinov, high-ranking officers associated with the Center for Military-Strategic Studies of the General Staff of the Armed Forces of the Russian Federation, in their 2013 work *The Nature and Content of a New Generation War*, list pre-war strategies that include establishing no-fly zones, utilizing PMCs, and arming opposition forces to subtly provoke conflict (Chekinov, Bogdanov, 2013, pp. 12–23). Both Bogdanov and Chekinov emphasize the importance of dominance in the realm of information and psychological warfare, aimed at demoralizing enemy forces and society by using disinformation and propaganda against vulnerable segments of the population. An analysis of Bogdanov and Chekinov's works reveals a close connection between contemporary Russian war concepts and the military doctrines of the Russian Empire and the USSR. Their observations, consistent with Gerasimov's presentation, highlight the distinctive features of the so-called "new generation warfare": prolonged asymmetric operations, disorientation of enemy command, intimidation and manipulation, widespread propaganda, control of airspace, military operations preceded by reconnaissance, integrated actions in the information space, coordination of diverse forces, seizing control of resistance points, and ultimately the pacification of the opponent's territory. "New generation warfare" reflects the evolution of strategic thinking in the context of changing geopolitical and technological realities, underscoring the importance of unconventional actions beyond the direct battlefield and the integration of various methods and tools to gain an advantage over the enemy (Wojnowski, 2015, pp. 7–38).

The analysis by General Andrei V. Kartapolov, published in *Military Review* in July-August 2017, also highlights the necessity of employing non-standard strategies. In the author's view, these strategies are intended to offset the technological disparities between Russia and its potential adversaries. Kartapolov notes that the use of propaganda and psychological operations – asymmetric warfare tactics – will characterize armed conflicts in the future (Thomas, 2017, pp. 35–41).

As we can see, the Russian model of hybrid warfare is a synthesis of strategic thought that goes beyond the individual contributions of General Gerasimov. It combines contemporary approaches with the influence of Russian military theorists and strategists from the early 20th century. For example, Soviet strategists Aleksandr Svechin and Georgii Isserson recognized the significant importance of political and informational actions, the rapid and secret deployment of troops, and the avoidance of formal declarations of war in military strategy. This is reflected in the modern Russian war doctrines of Gerasimov and other Russian theorists.

Frank G. Hoffman comments that, in the case of Russia, the combination of various methods of warfare is the realization of practices and experiences tested throughout history over time. He also notes that "the Cold War and recent experiences with Russia suggest that a blend of political, economic, and subversive activity is a constant feature of Russian operational art." The Soviet Union regularly employed so-called active measures in the informational sphere: fabrication, propaganda, and false stories – what we now call fake news – were invented by the Soviet KGB, which used "active measures" and "assistance programmes" or "aid operations" to influence events in a specific country or region by shifting its policies in favour of the Soviet Union's position. These programmes were based on 95% truthful information, to which false content was added, altered, or manipulated in its nuances (Hoffman, 2018).

Some of Russia's tools for disorienting the enemy even have Tsarist origins. *Maskirovka*, which has been the subject of military-academic studies in Russia since 1904, was a set of measures aimed at misleading the enemy regarding "the presence and disposition of forces, their condition, readiness, actions, and plans." During the Cold War, a unique programme of "illegals" was developed – well-prepared intelligence officers sent to foreign countries. Their mission was to integrate into the enemy's society, patiently building networks and gaining positions that would provide the Soviet Union access to the most valuable information. Since espionage did not end with the Cold War, analogies to events from that period are being sought today. Gordon Corera, as cited by James Sherr, even states that it is tempting to speak of a "new Cold War," and although that conflict has long passed, a new war is currently underway, conducted using both old and new techniques (Ramadhan, 2021, pp. 161–184).

Let us examine the differences between the Cold War era and the present. James Sherr points out five significant differences that highlight the shifts in global geopolitics and Russian strategy. The first difference relates to the approach towards borders and the balance of power in Europe. In 1975, by signing the Helsinki Final Act of the Conference on Security and Cooperation in Europe (CSCE), the Soviet Union accepted the principles established therein. Today, however, Russia expresses dissatisfaction with these principles and seeks to change them, aiming to expand its sphere of influence. This suggests that smaller states within its borders might see their sovereignty limited, which would violate the post-World War II principles. The second difference concerns nuclear weapons. Soviet leaders were aware of the dangers posed by the use of such weapons, leading to negotiations and agreements with the West on arms control. In contrast, contemporary Russia undermines previous agreements, exemplified by the violation of the Intermediate-Range Nuclear Forces (INF) Treaty and the rejection of the Treaty on Conventional Armed Forces in Europe (CFE). Another difference between Soviet and Russian Federation policy stems from a differing perception of the opponent's capabilities and intentions. Currently, Russia's assessments are full of contradictions and uncertainties, which increase the risk of misjudgements and misunderstandings of the opponent's actions. The fourth difference relates to the nature of modern Russian warfare, now described as "nonlinear," "network-centric," "new generation warfare," or "hybrid warfare." Its principles revolve around blurring the lines between internal and interstate conflict, as well as between peace and war, necessitating a change in the approach to defence and international response. The fifth difference, highlighted by James Sherr, concerns the shift in the geographic demarcation line. During the Cold War, this line was far from the Soviet Union's borders. Now, there is no longer a buffer zone, and the demarcation line runs along or near the borders of the Russian Federation. This increases the risk of misunderstandings, unintended escalation, and loss of control.

These differences demonstrate how drastically the global security context has changed, and therefore suggest the need for the international community to adapt to Russia's new strategies (Suvari, 2021, pp. 18–20).

Another analysis of hybrid warfare as defined by the Armed Forces of the Russian Federation, authored by Mason Clark of the Institute for the Study of War, identifies well-known characteristics: multidimensionality and the combination of traditional military operations with non-military actions, such as cyberattacks or information warfare. According to Clark's analysis, the primary objective of hybrid warfare is the fragmentation of states and the alteration of their governments and policies. Hybrid wars, based on prolonged actions, aim to weaken the adversary through "crushing and starving." A conflict takes on the nature of hybrid warfare when the aggressor seeks to change the strategic orientation of the target state, employing both kinetic and non-kinetic means integrated into campaigns aimed at achieving desired political and informational objectives. Clark observes that, in the Russian context, the aggressor's clear intent to reshape the strategic orientation and "worldview" of the target state is a key condition for qualifying the conflict as hybrid warfare. While kinetic actions include conventional use of land, air, and naval forces, as well as insurgency and terrorism, non-kinetic actions may involve diplomacy, political activities, information warfare, and the disruption of critical infrastructure. The wide range of actions employed enables complex and multifaceted operations that are difficult to clearly assign and classify. This is one of the key aspects of hybrid warfare. In summary, as presented by Clark, hybrid warfare is a complex conflict in which political and informational goals are achieved through a variety of integrated campaigns, utilizing both kinetic and non-kinetic means, applied in a dispersed or concentrated manner, depending on the current strategic needs (Clark, 2020; Popov, 2019).

Another Russian concept, "gibridnaya voyna," described by V. A. Kiselyova and I. N. Vorobyova, refers to a war whose "primary goal is to avoid the traditional battlefield and destroy the enemy through a mixture of ideological, informational, financial, political, and economic methods that dismantle the fabric of society, leading to its internal collapse" (Kiselyov, Vorobyov, 2015, pp. 92–93). It stems from Igor Panarin's definition of information warfare, based on Aleksandr Dugin's concept of "network-centric warfare" and especially Evgeny Messner's idea of "deceptive warfare." Panarin describes information warfare as encompassing a broad spectrum of actions aimed at manipulating the opponent's decision-making process. He views information warfare as a form of combat that includes political, economic, diplomatic, and military methods of infiltrating the opponent's informational environment. This definition is quite broad and refers to any attempt to use information to gain an advantage over the adversary. Panarin concludes that information warfare has been ongoing since the Cold War, during which the United States effectively destabilized the Soviet elite using informational measures. Today, information warfare remains a key tool of global politics, the dominant method of gaining political and economic advantage in the 21st century (Göransson, 2022, pp. 526–542).

Let's take a closer look at the theory of Aleksandr Dugin, often referred to as Putin's ideologue, for whom network-centric warfare represents a new form of the age-old conflict between the "civilizations of the sea and the civilizations of the land." According to Dugin, the West, representing the civilization of the sea, seeks global domination by imposing its values and political systems on other countries. Network-centric warfare is therefore a tool in this global struggle for influence. Key elements of Dugin's network warfare theory include:

- Primary networks – These consist of criminal groups, ethnic and religious minorities, sects, and loosely organized religious associations that do not have a clear legal status. They effectively mask their destructive activities.

- Secondary networks – These include non-governmental organizations, foundations, think tanks, human rights organizations, scientific and research associations, and youth movements. These networks complement the primary ones and operate within legal boundaries, making it more difficult to detect their subversive activities.
- Networks of influence without direct recruitment – These are often composed of active minorities mobilized through media attention, invitations to academic conferences, or the recognition of their ideas.

According to Dugin, the key is to maximize the synchronization of actions, methods, and means across four domains:

- Physical – Operating on land, sea, air, and in space.
- Informational – Where information is generated, processed, and distributed, particularly regarding infrastructure and mathematical models.
- Cognitive – Encompassing individual and group consciousness, decision-making processes, and motivations.
- Socio-cultural – Focused on human interactions based on historical, cultural, and religious values.

Dugin proposes two solutions to counter the Western network-centric warfare:

- Establishing a Eurasian network to counter Atlanticist countries – This network would unite and apply postmodernist and network-centric methods of Russian strategists. To achieve this, it is necessary to modernize Russia's armed forces, special services, state institutions, and information systems.
- Promotion of a geopolitical ideology – This ideology would disseminate and implement a universal Russian worldview as an alternative to the liberal ideology of the West, uniting societies around a common set of values and opposing Western domination.

According to Dugin, network-centric warfare, by utilizing various "networks," aims to disrupt the social and political fabric of target states in order to take control of their informational and psychological spheres. This is part of a broader effort to adapt modern warfare methods to Russian geopolitical goals, focused on achieving dominance in both the physical and virtual realms (Wojnowski, 2017).

The prototype for modern hybrid warfare concepts is often attributed to the theory of insurgent warfare developed by Colonel Yevgeny

Messner, a Soviet military officer and head of the propaganda department. Messner introduced the idea of blurring the lines between war and peace, as well as between regular and irregular operations. According to him, the primary form of conflict in so-called insurgent wars involves irregular actions such as sabotage, terrorism, guerrilla warfare, and uprisings. Messner emphasized that regardless of legal norms, every citizen has the right to participate in open and underground combat, challenging the traditional distinction between legal and illegal methods of waging war. As a result, regular armies lose their exclusive right to conduct warfare, and new forms of combat can emerge, often disregarding existing laws and the ethics of warfare. Messner also used the term "semi-war," which he understood as actions that conceal open involvement in the conflict (Месснер, 2005, pp. 70–90). Therefore, saboteurs cannot wear identifying insignia, which means that, under international law, they cannot be considered members of the armed forces. This allows the state to officially distance itself from such actions when events spiral out of control. This leads to the phenomenon of the "non-state" nature of armed groups, and the conflict itself, from the outside, resembles a civil war and internal chaos (Banasik, 2015, pp. 22–24). Messner additionally highlights the role of aggressive diplomacy, referring to it as "white-glove politics." This is a less intense form of warfare that, despite its seemingly mild nature, employs tactics of intimidation, imposing will, or achieving agreements on matters of importance to Russia (Месснер, 2005, p. 110). This concept aligns with the principles of hybrid warfare, where the objective can be achieved without open armed conflict. Moreover, Messner places significant emphasis on psychological operations in the context of irregular formations, such as guerrilla, terrorist, and underground party groups. These groups are often less resistant to psychological influence, making them particularly susceptible to informational operations. Additionally, their morale is frequently low, requiring constant motivational support. This is crucial for understanding the mechanisms of psychological operations used in hybrid warfare to destabilize and demoralize the enemy. According to Messner, informational activities in insurgent warfare are an effective weapon for driving social groups into a state of dissatisfaction, creating divisions among political elites, lowering the reputation of a state, causing political isolation, and even influencing hostile international opinion. Similar to the tactics employed in modern hybrid warfare, these strategies are used to weaken the opponent by manipulating perceptions and opinions, rather than through direct military intervention (Месснер, 2005, pp. 232–246).

According to Leszek Sykulski, the response to such a complex strategy should be the competent use of intelligence services and the effective conduct of informational warfare. Long-term psychological and informational operations, which propagate specific narratives, lead to deep changes in the way societies think and perceive reality, often conflicting with local traditions and values (Sykulski, 2015, pp. 103–110) Banasik, 2015, pp. 22–24). The battlefield thus primarily becomes the mental space (noosphere) and cyberspace.

Another intriguing interpretation of the concept of hybrid warfare by Russian military theorists is its geopolitical context, which includes analyses by military strategists, geopolitical experts, and officials from Russian intelligence services. In this regard, the concept of so-called "limitrophic wars" has emerged. In Russian geopolitics, the term "limitroph" refers to unstable peripheral areas that separate large empires or civilizations. The concept of limitrophic wars was introduced into Russian academic discourse by Vadim Tsymbursky, a contemporary Russian geopolitician and author of the metaphor "Russia-Island." Tsymbursky argues for the existence of five major geocivilizations in the Eurasian region: Romano-Germanic, Arab-Iranian, Russian, Chinese, and Indian. After the collapse of the Soviet Union, sovereign states were established in areas surrounding Russia, including Central and Eastern Europe, Transnistria, the South Caucasus, Central Asia, and regions inhabited by Altaic and Turkic-Mongol peoples, stretching to the Russian-Chinese border. Tsymbursky referred to this peripheral zone, which is on the edges of all civilizations, as the "Great Limitroph." According to him, the western part of the Great Limitroph can be used by Western centres to isolate and destabilize Russia, emphasizing the strategic importance of maintaining Russian influence from Kaliningrad to the Crimean Peninsula. Ensuring Russia's security and maintaining its influence in this key geopolitical area requires control over the Great Limitroph. A variety of actions can be used to achieve this: from propaganda and disinformation to supporting separatist movements, and even employing armed forces in the form of "little green men," as was seen during the annexation of Crimea. As demonstrated numerous times, such actions are part of the larger concept of hybrid warfare and align with Russia's strategic objectives, which aim to maximize its influence within its former buffer zone without triggering full-scale armed conflicts with Western powers (Tsymbursky, 1999, pp. 3, 16–32; Sykulski, 2015, pp. 103–110; Fedan et al., 2014, pp. 355–363; Potulski, 2010, pp. 231–232).

The concept of "limitroph" was further developed by Natalia Komleva, who linked it to the issue of hybrid wars. According to her, the term "limitroph," referring to a group of small buffer states, encompasses not only geographical space (land, sea, air, space) but also economic, informational-cybernetic, and informational-ideological spaces. These spaces involve active participants such as transnational organizations, corporations, churches, and religious unions, among others. Komleva asserts that the creation of limitrophs allows a power centre to maintain its independence while enhancing its own security by strengthening its economic, political, and military capabilities. The trophic function of the limitroph, derived from the semantic meanings of the words (from the Latin limes – border and the Greek τροφή – supply, sustenance), means that buffer states can be used as tools in the struggle against a geopolitical opponent across the entire geopolitical space of the limitroph. At the same time, they serve as a kind of "shield" against similar actions from the opposing side. Furthermore, control over the limitroph allows for the expansion of the sphere of influence into previously inaccessible territories (Комлева, 2013, pp. 1–7, 2010, pp. 37–45, 2014, pp. 90–101). Komleva observes that the peripheral areas of the limitroph often become unstable, serving as battlegrounds for wars or as arenas for protracted regional conflicts. Limitrophic wars can encompass various spheres: the geographical, serving as the stage for conventional warfare, the informational-ideological, where psychological and informational battles take place, the economic, involving actions aimed at weakening the opponent's economic potential, and the informational-cybernetic sphere, which includes cyberattacks and other informational-technical actions. According to Komleva's theory, hybrid warfare is a conflict occurring simultaneously in all of these spaces, with an additional dimension – the geopolitical civilization of the adversary. In this light, the Ukrainian crisis can be interpreted as a "limitrophic war," a form of hybrid warfare aimed at weakening the "Russian geocivilization." This perspective significantly explains the geopolitical causes and consequences of hybrid conflicts, which are often overshadowed by other, more visible and apparent international interactions (Комлева, 2015a, pp. 32–42, 2015b, pp. 1–26; Воробьев, Киселев, 2008, pp. 62–70; Wojnowski, 2017).

A further Russian concept related to hybrid warfare, which had been developed by Andrey Mikhailovich Ilnitsky, introduces the notion of "mental warfare," understood as a tool for influencing the opponent's will by targeting their elite and media. Such a type of warfare operates on three levels: tactical, operational, and strategic, encompassing informational campaigns, informational-psychological operations, and battles for societal identity. This approach incorporates the dimension of hybrid warfare where the long-term goals focus on reshaping the social and cultural structure of adversary states. In mental warfare, alongside military methods, new forms of aggression are employed, such as supporting illegal migration and separatism. Ilnitsky's concept of hybrid warfare also includes the use of advanced technologies, like AI, which can provide military, economic, and informational advantages. The propagation of specific narratives, as well as a deeper change in the mindset and perception of reality within entire societies – often in ways that oppose local traditions and values – are examples of actions that blur the lines between war and peace. These strategies serve as tools for gaining geopolitical advantage without the need for open armed conflict (Министерство Обороны Российской Федерации, 2018).

In the analysis of Andrei Alexandrovich Bartosz, hybrid warfare is a complex and concealed conflict, carried out as integrated military-political, financial-economic, informational, and cultural-ideological actions, without a commonly defined status. The redistribution of roles among political actors is primarily achieved through non-military means, without the occupation of the defeated country, destruction of its infrastructure, or mass civilian casualties. Information and communication technologies enable control over a country with minimal military violence. The goal of hybrid warfare is comprehensive competition for leadership and expanding access to resources. The victor is the state or coalition that successfully imposes its worldview, values, and interests on the adversary. Hybrid warfare can also be conducted through the use of regular armies and/or irregular armed and military formations capable of continuous and systematic combat operations, as well as through economic, diplomatic, scientific-technical, informational, ideological, and psychological means (Министерство Обороны Российской Федерации, 2018). In another work, Bartosz expands the definition of hybrid warfare, highlighting the use of both traditional and innovative methods such as digital operations, informational campaigns, low-intensity asymmetric conflicts, and inciting social unrest by supporting illegal migration, ethnic and religious tensions, extremism, and separatism. Hybrid warfare, according to A.A. Bartosz, also employs international organized crime and other destabilizing actions. The resources used in hybrid warfare include not only material assets but also human, technical, financial, and informational resources. Bartosz mentions the concept of the "accelerator" (catalyst) of hybrid warfare, referring to the ability to shape military-political situations by adapting to the changing conditions of a given environment, which enables the rapid intensification of chaos and destabilization in the opponent's state. Particularly significant in this context is the implementation of AI advancements in both the theory and practice of warfare, providing military, economic, informational, and technological advantages. The global trend of increasing the role of new technologies in military strategies is confirmed by the establishment of the Joint Artificial Intelligence Center within the U.S. Department of Defence, which works to accelerate the development of AI-based military solutions.

A form of controlled chaos in hybrid warfare also involves actions aimed at the physical elimination of key political or military figures, organizing mass riots, or utilizing "colour revolutions." As Leon Trotsky pointed out in relation to the use of chaos as a political tool, such actions destabilize state structures.

Also worthy of mentioning is the concept of *balanced warfare* developed by General Alexei Kim, which focuses on minimizing one's own losses by avoiding large, costly battles in favour of asymmetric actions, systematically weakening the enemy by destroying military infrastructure, supply lines, and morale, and maintaining combat capabilities for as long as possible, even with limited resources. Russia applies the principles of balanced warfare in the conflict in Ukraine, which can be observed in such aspects as (Osiecki, Żółciak, 2024):

- rotational attacks on strategic sites, such as Avdeevka, Tveriv Yar, to keep the enemy in constant suspense,
- destruction of infrastructure – systematic destruction of Ukrainian military and logistical infrastructure, including air defence radars and ammunition depots,
- tying up the opponent's forces by forcing them to defend themselves and consume resources for counter-attacks.

This way of waging war by Russia has serious consequences for Ukraine:

- depletion of resources resulting from their continued commitment to defence,
- degradation of military and civilian infrastructure, which makes it difficult for Ukraine to conduct effective defence operations,
- destruction of the morale of the armed forces and the civilian population through the psychological impact of constant threat and pressure.

The strategy of sustainable warfare adopted by Russia also has significant implications for NATO and the global security system through:

- escalating tensions between Russia and NATO countries increasing the risk of direct confrontations,
- the need to change NATO's defence strategies, including an increased military presence in regions bordering Russia,
- long-term instability in the region, affecting the global balance of power.

For Russia, long-term implications related to conducting *balanced warfare* comprise:

- The need for military rebuilding in the event of significant losses, which may take many years.
- The possibility of having to transform existing alliances and the emergence of new geopolitical arrangements.
- The necessity for Russia to acquire and maintain technological know-how in the global arms race.

As noted by Markus Balázs Göransson, it is important to mention that a certain dualism can be observed in Russia's approach to the concept of hybrid warfare. When Russian scholars refer to states other than Russia or the Soviet Union, they use the term "hybrid warfare" in a sense similar to the operational-tactical concept developed by Hoffman, Nathan Freier, Russell W. Glenn, and others. In this context, hybrid warfare signifies a combination of forces across multiple domains. However, when Russian scholars (sometimes the same ones) discuss Western hybrid warfare against Russia or the Soviet Union, the term shifts to describe a strategy of internal destabilization. For instance, Marina Kuchinskaia, a researcher at the Russian Institute for Strategic Studies, employs two distinct meanings of the term. In one article, she describes Western intervention in Libya as a case of operational-tactical hybrid warfare. In another text, she refers to a hybrid campaign against Russia, focusing primarily on non-military-strategic measures: traditional diplomacy, special forces, financial institutions, economic sanctions, non-governmental organizations (NGOs), and global mass media. In this latter article, there is no focus on the operational-tactical level or the combined use of military and non-military tools. Instead, hybrid warfare is used to describe a broad range of alleged harmful actions carried out by various non-military actors in conjunction with special forces. The spectrum of these actions is even broader than in the case of informational warfare and "colour revolutions." Beyond informational influence and protest movements, it can also include financial sanctions and traditional diplomacy, which are elevated in this discourse to potential acts of (hybrid) war. As noted by Markus Balázs Göransson, Aleksandr Neklessa, quoted in the works of Aleksandr Vladimirov, describes hybrid warfare as: the sum of aggressive actions that expand the possibilities of conventional politics, as well as the use of various instruments to subjugate or destroy the opponent, deconstruct unwanted circumstances, and reorganize the existing order or establish a new one (Göransson, 2022, pp. 526–542). Neklessa's definition is so broad that it becomes difficult to determine what harmful actions could not be classified within its scope. Russian military intellectuals Viktor Popov and Musa Khamzatov, not without irony, observe that the result is that [in Russia], the term "hybrid warfare" has come to be understood as anything that doesn't fit the concept of traditional armed combat. This makes the concept a universal term, which could potentially encompass a very wide range of phenomena (Göransson, 2022) as a danger to Russia (Göransson, 2022, pp. 526–542, 2024, pp. 449–471). In reality, hybrid warfare against Russia, in the Russian concept, integrates both non-military and military threats to Russia and its sphere of influence.

The hybrid strategy of Russia, as described by Christopher S. Chivvis, is characterized by at least three main features that distinguish it from traditional forms of conflict and adapt it to contemporary geopolitics. These are as follows.

Economic use of force

The Russian Federation is aware that in a direct prolonged conventional conflict with NATO, its chances of winning would be slim. Therefore, it aims to achieve its interests, whenever possible, without overt use of military force. While it may still utilize its conventional and even nuclear capabilities as part of its hybrid strategy, it prefers to minimize the actual use of traditional military power. The use of cyber tools is an example of a tactic where Russia economizes on force while maintaining the effectiveness of its actions.

Long duration and variable intensity

The reality of hybrid warfare involves an ever-changing intensity of conflict. Hybrid warfare strategies are always in flux, although at certain points they may become more fierce and intense or transition into conventional combat operations. Such variability and flexibility enable Russia to keep its adversaries in a state of uncertainty and constant threat.

Population-based orientation

Russian military experts, observing the actions of the United States and its allies in the Balkans and the Middle East, recognized the importance of influencing the populations of target countries through information operations, proxy groups, and other influence operations. By employing a wide range of tools – from propaganda to psychological operations – Russia shapes the perceptions and behaviours of people to align with its interests. The information operations Russia employs today have evolved from those used during the Cold War, they now have a much broader scope and objectives due to the use of the internet, cable television, social media, and cyber tools. Additionally, Russia uses increasingly extensive economic leverage to influence foreign governments. Being far more integrated with the rest of the world than the Soviet Union was during the Cold War, Russia finds it easier to interfere in Western societies. It is important to note that Russia's current use of these tactics seems less ideologically driven than during the Cold War, making Moscow's actions more flexible and adaptive, no longer constrained by rigid Marxist ideology, but focused on pragmatic strategic goals (Chivvis, 2017, pp. 2, 7–8).

In the *Russian Hybrid Warfare* report, prepared by the Institute for the Study of War, it is noted that Russian armed forces are adapting their capabilities to conduct hybrid warfare. The Russian military does not even hide its intentions to conduct offensive hybrid wars. Russian military theorists openly write about general hybrid strategies and doctrines and discuss the development of their methods. The mentioned report indicates that the Kremlin is currently working on enhancing these capabilities by focusing on integrating both conventional and non-conventional methods to ensure strategic advantage in hybrid conflicts (Clark, 2020):

- Centralization of all Russian decision-making bodies – civil, military, media, and economic – to streamline government actions,
- Adapting traditional military theories and doctrines to hybrid warfare as the primary mission of the Russian armed forces,
- Conducting information campaigns targeting the entire society to improve "patriotic awareness," which the Kremlin considers essential for effective hybrid warfare. This includes enhancing the adaptability and strength of Russian information campaigns to ensure their long-term influence,
- Improving the conventional expeditionary capabilities of Russian armed forces to prepare for supporting hybrid warfare operations abroad,
- Enhancing the use of PMCs and other allegedly deniable proxy forces,
- Subordinating kinetic operations to information operations, which the Kremlin views as the primary change in the nature of warfare, influencing the planning and execution of military actions.

According to Yevhen Vdovytskyi and Stepan Yakymiak, the concept of hybrid warfare most accurately defines the nature of the actions of the Russian Federation, both in theoretical and practical terms, encompassing military, quasi-military, diplomatic, informational, economic, and other means. The specificity of Russian aggression against Ukraine, as well as in other countries where Russia has been and continues to be involved, is also manifested in the unprecedented violation of international legal agreements, the large-scale damage inflicted, and the prolonged duration of the conflict (Vdovytskyi, 2023, pp. 60–72). As Arsalan Bilal emphasizes, hybrid warfare is not only an attractive option for Moscow but also a strategic necessity due to the asymmetry of power in relation to the West. The Russian military budget, technological level, and the scale of its economy cannot be compared to the capabilities of Western powers. The use of hybrid strategies allows Russia to mitigate this imbalance and effectively confront its rivals. However, it remains unclear to what extent this will enable Moscow to achieve its long-term goals (Bilal, 2024).

In Table 1.7, the characteristics of hybrid warfare identified during the clustering process are outlined, considering the approach in Russian studies.

TABLE 1.7   Features of hybrid warfare by Russia

Author/Document	Cluster	Features of Hybrid Warfare
Valery Gerasimov	Information and perception manipulation, influence on civil society	The use of non-military means to achieve political and strategic goals, including informational operations and cyberattacks, with minimal deployment of armed forces.
O.W. Walecki and W.M. Niejełow	Conflict multidimensionality	Description of military action in Iraq and Afghanistan as examples of hybrid warfare, combining guerrilla and non-standard methods.
Suvari, Anders	Tactical and operational flexibility and operational flexibility, integration of measures	Adapting to evolving forms of conflict, emphasizing the importance of innovation and developing capabilities for non-standard and asymmetric warfare.
Sergei Bogdanov, Sergei Chekinov	Use of new technologies, action below the threshold of war	Demoralization of adversary forces and societies through informational and psychological dominance, using information dominance to direct operations.
Mason Clark	Multidimensionality of conflict, impact on civil society	Definition of hybrid warfare as a multidimensional conflict combining military operations with non-military activities such as cyberattacks or information activities.
Natalya Komleva	Multidimensionality of conflict, impact on civil society, integration of measures (limitroph)	Analysis of the "limitroph" as a buffer area for hybrid warfare, use of all spaces (geographic, economic, information-cybernetic) for conflict.
Russia's war doctrine (2014), Russia's security strategy (2021)	Asymmetry of actions, multidimensionality of conflict	Pointing to threats such as strengthening NATO capabilities, terrorism, colour revolutions, highlighting the need to secure maritime transport, port infrastructure, and pipelines.

(Continued)

TABLE 1.7 (*Continued*)   Features of hybrid warfare by Russia

Author/Document	Cluster	Features of Hybrid Warfare
Andrey Mikhailovich Ilnitsky	Information and perception manipulation, influencing civil society (mental warfare)	Mental warfare as a tool to influence the will of the opponent, psychological operations targeting the elite and the media.
Andrei Alexandrovich Bartosz	Multidimensionality of conflict, integration of measures, asymmetry of actions	Hybrid warfare as a process of redistribution of roles in the political process, carried out primarily by non-military means, with key use of information and communication technologies.
Yevgeny Messner	Multidimensionality of conflict, impact on civil society	Description of rebel wars as blurring the lines between war and peace and regular and irregular activities, use of irregular activities such as sabotage and terrorism.
Mark Galeotti	Tactical and operational flexibility, integration of measures	Highlighting Russia's adaptation to complex forms of international competition without departing from traditional forms of conflict.
Vladimir Putin	Multidimensionality of conflict, information and perceptual manipulation	Discuss the methods of destabilization used against Russia, including Secret Service operations and information technology, as elements of hybrid warfare.
Andrei V. Kartapolov	Use of new technologies, action below the threshold of war	Importance of non-standard strategies in the face of technological disparities, use of propaganda and psychological operations.

Source: Own study

An analysis of the perceptions of hybrid warfare by the CPC and the Russian Federation reveals differences and similarities in the strategies of the two global powers. Both countries emphasize the complex and multidimensional nature of modern conflicts, but their viewpoints differ in terms of methods used, strategic objectives, and scope of operations. The Chinese approach to hybrid warfare is based on integration and cooperation across political, economic, military, and other areas, seeking to subtly pursue strategic objectives without escalating to direct conflict.

This strategy differs from U.S. approaches, which focus on direct, tactical pre-conflict action, with less emphasis on long-term coordination between different governmental bodies. Russia, on the other hand, combines military with non-military actions such as cyberattacks, media manipulation, and psychological warfare. The aim is to weaken target states and achieve strategic objectives without the need to use significant military force to influence an adversary's political and social decisions. NATO notes that Russia employs complex hybrid strategies including political interference, malicious cyberattacks, economic pressure, and diversion and annexation. Its actions are part of an overall plan to destabilize the international rule-based order and influence the global balance of power. On the other hand, China also conducts hybrid and cyber operations that threaten international security. The CCP, for example, seeks to control key technology sectors, critical infrastructure, and access to critical materials and supply chains. These actions are part of China's economic strategy, which focuses on building strategic relationships and increasing China's influence on the international stage. In summary, both the CCP and Russia employ conflict and hybrid warfare blurring the traditional distinction between a state of war and peace, allowing them to pursue their strategic objectives without crossing the threshold of armed conflict. Both states are adapting new technologies such as cyberspace and social media for these purposes, which allows them to effectively manipulate information and exert psychological influence. Hybrid warfare is becoming a key tool for these states to achieve geopolitical advantage, requiring the international community to attempt to understand these phenomena and respond to the threats they entail (NATO, 2024).

Hybrid warfare as perceived by experts

In order to deepen the knowledge in the area under analysis, semi-structured expert interviews were conducted with two experts in the fields of defence, security, and humanitarian aid. Their assessment of the concept of "hybrid warfare" was presented anonymously, marking the statement of the first expert with Expert 1 and that of the second with Expert 2.[4] The order of the statements placed follows the dates of the interviews given.

Expert 1

Hybrid warfare is a way of doing things that can be placed somewhere on the spectrum between war and peace. It is an action of a nature outside the patterns of traditional military action. Hybrid warfare is used by: states, quasi-sovereign organizations, legitimate international organizations, terrorist or criminal organizations or interest groups – with a common political, social, or moral interest, occurring online or physically – to create internal or external policy, in other states or regions of the world.

The aforementioned entities may aim to cause social or political destabilization by inciting unrest and social conflicts, with the goal of altering the attitudes of social groups towards specific issues. Such shifts in the perception of reality may be triggered to generate or amplify social anxieties, which can impact the political landscape and may even lead to regime change or a coup.

In simplest terms, the objective of hybrid warfare is to gather information that can be used to achieve pre-determined goals. However, this abstract understanding creates challenges in thoroughly explaining the topic to those interested in it. The difficulty in precisely defining hybrid warfare partially stems from its nature and the fact that it is a phenomenon that is exceedingly hard to pinpoint clearly to define.

Expert 2

Hybrid warfare is a term to describe conflicts fought by an array of different means – from military (invasion) to economic (using a key dependency such as gas or water to force political decisions detrimental to a state's interest – Moldova), political (influence over election), criminal (for example, strategic corruption – Russia in Ukraine), as well as cyber (attacks on infrastructure – in the Baltic states). They are often networked and incorporate a significant element of disinformation. To be clear, I do not consider them to be a new form of warfare – using a variety of means has always been a key element of state strategy.

The key difficulty I see in defining hybrid conflicts is the threshold beyond which they become wars – there is no defined threshold. Hybrid actions are also by design difficult to attribute with reasonable certainty, making it more difficult to ascertain who the adversary is.

Theoretical framework for conceptualizing hybrid warfare

The previously discussed concepts of hybrid warfare in this chapter have been summarized to identify the key characteristics of the phenomenon. The summaries have been subjected to clustering and are included in Tables 1.3–1.7. The authors' approach assumes that within the analysed set, it is possible to distinguish overarching groups (clusters), which contain other lower-level groups (clusters). These methods are deterministic, meaning they guarantee repeatability of results for the same input data. Based on the method of grouping, they are divided into agglomerative (inductive) and divisive (deductive). In agglomerative methods, the starting point is a set of single-element clusters, where the number of elements equals the number of objects. At each subsequent step, the objects are combined into higher-order clusters based on a chosen distance metric between the groups. The final outcome is a single group containing all the elements of the set. Divisive methods proceed in the opposite manner: the starting state is a single group containing all objects, which is subsequently divided into increasingly smaller elements until a set of single-element clusters is obtained. Unlike other grouping methods (e.g. k-means), hierarchical clustering methods do not require the pre-determination of the number of clusters. This means that after carrying out the procedure and visualizing the results, for instance, using a dendrogram, the researcher can decide post hoc which number of clusters is optimal. Typically, the division is made at the points corresponding to the longest branches of the dendrogram (Bobadilla et al., 2013, pp. 109–132).

Table 1.8 was created through clustering to comprehensively present the multidimensionality of hybrid warfare, highlighting how experts from various scientific fields identify and describe its components. Such a synthetic review allows for a better understanding of the dynamics of current conflicts, as well as recognizing common patterns and differences in approaches.

Table 1.8, derived from an interdisciplinary analysis of literary sources, offers a consolidated understanding and definition of hybrid warfare, showcasing this phenomenon in its multifaceted and complex context. In response to these challenges, it is essential to identify the key characteristics that define hybrid warfare. This process is crucial because these features enable the precise description and understanding of the phenomenon under study. By identifying and describing key characteristics, it becomes possible to create a definition that captures the essence and scope of the concept, setting and describing the boundaries within which the object or phenomenon is considered. The conducted analysis of source materials has led to the identification of 11 key characteristics of hybrid warfare:

- multidimensionality,
- synergy,
- complexity,
- asymmetry,
- integration of measures,
- use of new technologies,
- information manipulation,
- flexibility,

TABLE 1.8 Features of hybrid warfare summary of the study

Feature (Cluster)	Description	Authors/Concepts	Key Elements	Domains
Multidimensionality, complexity, synergy	Activities involving various aspects of conflict, both military and non-military, combining traditional forms of warfare with irregular, cyberattacks and information operations.	Hoffman, Mockaitis, Boucher, McCuen, Bond, Mansoor, O.V. Walecki, V.M. Neyelov, Mason Clark, Natalya Komleva, CCP, Russia – War Doctrine (2014), Russian Security Strategy (2021), A.A. Bartosh MCDC, IISS, U.S. Department of Defence, Valery Gerasimov, Suvari, Anders, European Commission, Yevgeny Messner, Mark Galeotti, Vladimir Putin	Integration of regular and irregular forces, cyberattacks, information operations, subversion, political and economic pressure.	Military, Cybernetic, Information, Social, Economic
Asymmetry	Using a variety of asymmetrical means to gain an advantage and surprise the opponent, avoiding direct confrontation.	Bankov, E. Marija, Leonhard, CCP – Psychological warfare, Russia – Gerasimov, A.M. Ilnitsky Rand Corporation, European Commission, A.A. Bartosz	Irregular tactics, avoiding direct confrontation, camouflaging operations, exploiting local conditions.	Military, Cybernetic, Information
Integration of measures (holistic), synergy	Coordinating different methods and means of action to achieve operational and strategic synergies.	Hoffman, Blank, Boucher, McCuen, Bond, Suvari, Anders, CCP, Russia – Suvari, Anders, A.A. Bartosz, Multinational Capacity Development Campaign, V.M. Naylov	Integrated military, political, economic, and information operations, synergy of operations, advanced training.	Military, Cybernetic, Information, Political, Economic
Technological innovations	Use of advanced technologies and innovations (e.g. AI, drones, cyber) to enhance the effectiveness of hybrid operations.	Blank, Walker, Gunneriusson, Sergei Bogdanov, Sergei Chekinov, CCP – Legal warfare, MCDC, IISS, Fox, European Commission, Andrei V. Kartapolov	Military and information technologies, cyberattacks, advanced intelligence techniques.	Technological, Cybernetic

(Continued)

TABLE 1.8 (*Continued*)   Features of hybrid warfare summary of the study

Feature (Cluster)	Description	Authors/Concepts	Key Elements	Domains
Information manipulations	Activities aimed at influencing public perception of reality, decision-makers, and international public opinion through propaganda, disinformation, and psychological operations.	Freedman, Magda, Leonhard, Fox, CCP – Information warfare, Russia – Gerasimov, Forward Defence, NATO, U.S. Department of Defence, Ilnitsky, Gerasimov	Propaganda, disinformation, psychological operations, influencing public narrative and perception.	Information, Social
Flexibility (adaptability)	Adaptation and variability of strategies and tactics to enable rapid adaptation to changing environments and challenges.	Gunneriusson, Leonhard, CCP, Russia – Suvari, Anders, RUSI, U.S. Department of Defence, Suvari, Anders, Mark Galeotti	Rapid adaptation to new conditions, flexibility of operations, use of modern technology and innovative methods.	Military, Cybernetic, Information, Political, Technological
Subliminality	Activities on the borderline between a state of war and a state of peace, aiming to achieve strategic objectives without open armed conflict.	Sharma, Mumford, Carlucci, Fox, CCP, Russia – Sergei Bogdanov, Sergei Chekinov, Rand Corporation, Forward Defence, Andrei V. Kartapolov	Grey area operations, covert operations, strategy to avoid direct armed confrontation.	Cyber, Information, Political
Destabilization	Actions aimed at influencing an opponent's society and one's own society in order to build support or create discontent and division.	Mumford, Carlucci, Boucher, McCuen, Bond, CCP, NATO, Valery Gerasimov, Propaganda, information operations, creating discontent and social divisions, building support, Yevgeny Messner, A.M. Ilnitsky	Propaganda, information operations, creating discontent and social divisions, building support.	Social, Information

Source: Own study

- subliminality,
- destabilization,
- ambiguity.

The last feature – ambiguity – stems directly from the above analysis; however, it can integrate other features of hybrid warfare and reinforce their effectiveness, creating a coherent and flexible system of operations that are difficult to predict and combat (in the view of Andrew Mumford and Pascal Carlucci, this is a defining feature in hybrid warfare, without which it would not exist. However, this position is not supported by the analyses carried out in this study).

Since the image of hybrid war is shaped by information, an examination of media reports of the Ukrainian war was carried out according to the description of the research method in Annex 1 and then the features of hybrid war established on the basis of the literature analysis were compared with media reports. The columns of Table A1.1 present the quantitative results of the codes indicating the features of hybrid war. The results obtained confirm the list of hybrid warfare characteristics established from the literature review. Table A1.1 shows that the dominant area among the features of hybrid war is destabilizing actions. This is followed by media reports indicating flexibility, asymmetry, influencing political decisions. The study also shows the presence of hybrid warfare characteristics such as complexity, spectrum of tools, grey area, new technologies, subliminality, impact on society, and ambiguity. However, in these cases, the indications of individual characteristics were below ten indications.

Table 1.9 presents the interconnections of hybrid warfare features with each other. The percentages at the intersection of codes characterizing hybrid warfare features indicate how often a hybrid warfare feature occurred in conjunction with another feature.

Results presented in Table 1.9 document the associations of hybrid warfare features with each other. The percentages at the intersection of the codes indicate how often a hybrid war feature occurred in association with another feature.

- Ambiguity has only one occurrence (1), which may mean that it is rarely mentioned in the analysis as a separate feature of hybrid warfare.
- Flexibility is a frequent feature, with 40 occurrences. This abundance may suggest that flexibility is a trait used in hybrid warfare.
- Influencing political decisions was mentioned 11 times. Although there are no direct percentage correlations with other traits, this number may indicate its importance as a stand-alone trait.

TABLE 1.9 Overview of hybrid warfare feature links

Code Tree		Ambiguity	Flexibility	Complexity	Integration of Means	Destabilizing Actions	Asymmetry	New Technologies	Subliminality
Code frequency		1	40	9	1	113	12	5	7
Ambiguity	1								
Flexibility	40								
Impacting political decisions	11								
Complexity	9								
Spectrum of tools	1						8.33%		
Grey zone	2								
Destabilizing actions	113								
Asymmetry	12				100%				
New technologies	5								
Below war threshold	7								
Impact on the society	1								

Source: Own study

- Complexity appears nine times, which may also suggest its independence.
- Integration of measures does not occur frequently (one occurrence) and has the only association with destabilizing activities at 8.33%, which may suggest that these features may sometimes co-occur.
- Destabilizing actions are very frequent, with 113 occurrences. The high count indicates the central role of destabilizing actions in hybrid warfare. It is also the only feature having a percentage association with asymmetry at 100%, meaning that every mention of asymmetry was associated with destabilizing actions.
- Asymmetry occurs 12 times and, as mentioned, is always associated with destabilizing actions.
- New technologies appear five times, which may suggest that new technological developments such as AI are also part of hybrid warfare.
- Subliminality has seven occurrences, showing that actions below the threshold of war are an element of hybrid warfare.
- Impact on society although obvious is mentioned only once, which may suggest that this is a less discussed aspect of hybrid war in the context of this study.

In summarizing the connections between the characteristics of hybrid warfare, we can conclude that flexibility and destabilizing actions are the most frequently mentioned features, highlighting their key role in such activities. Asymmetry consistently appears in the context of destabilizing actions, emphasizing that asymmetric methods are often employed to destabilize the opponent. The integration of measures and its connection to destabilizing actions, at a level of 8.33%, may suggest that although less frequently mentioned, this characteristic could play a significant role in specific contexts.

Low occurrence numbers for certain characteristics, such as ambiguity, societal impact, or new technologies, may suggest their more specialized or context-specific use. The study did not show the presence of terms directly indicating hybrid warfare characteristics such as multidimensionality, integration of means, or information manipulation. However, it is important to note that these features can be indirectly confirmed by observing the results of the study in subsequent stages of the book. For example, the multidimensionality of hybrid warfare can be observed by analysing the range of military (conventional and unconventional) and non-military actions. The integration of means can be demonstrated through an analysis of the connections between military and non-military actions and the actors involved in hybrid warfare. Meanwhile, information manipulation can be demonstrated by the occurrence of terms such as disinformation (177 mentions) or propaganda (977 mentions), which will be discussed in more detail in subsequent sections of this work.

The features of hybrid warfare are therefore diverse and may occur in specific contexts. The high specialization of some features may mean that they are not always used together and their co-occurrence is limited to specific situations. For example, destabilizing actions may be more specific to asymmetric strategies, which explains why the two features are closely related.

The number of codes for most features in Table 1.9 is low (often only one or a few occurrences), which naturally limits the number of possible associations. When the number of occurrences is low, the statistical probability of two features co-occurring is also low. In data analysis, the higher the number of observations, the higher the probability of detecting significant associations. In this case, despite the very high number of observations, low code counts limit the possibility of identifying more links. This may be due to the fact that hybrid warfare features are mainly used in scientific publications and reports or the attribution of issues raised in source portals. In contrast, in the context of media reporting, this may mean that specific terms for features are not used in common communication, but as mentioned, subsequent analyses will confirm the existence of most of these features. At the same time, it is important to bear in mind that hybrid warfare is a complex phenomenon in which different features may occur in specific operational contexts. However, understanding these correlations can help to prepare systemic and individual strategies for hybrid warfare. For example, due to their high incidence, destabilizing activities should be a priority in counterinsurgency strategies, and any asymmetric operations should be monitored in detail in the context of their potential destabilizing effects.

As regards the co-occurrence of features, it is worth recalling that, in principle, hybrid warfare is a strategy using military (conventional and unconventional) and non-military actions. The features assigned on the basis of the literature analysis and the analysis of their co-occurrence with other activities in Table A1.1 allow us to understand to what extent hybrid warfare is a new threat and whether it goes beyond the existing definitions. First of all, it should be emphasized that all characteristics (except those in Outcome 1) are linked to conventional (army) actions, which may confirm that hybrid war transcends the traditional understanding of war, let alone armed conflict.

An analysis of the co-occurrence of hybrid warfare characteristics with other activities points to several key findings. The co-occurrence of flexibility, complexity, and destabilizing activities with different domains suggests that hybrid warfare is more complex and versatile than traditional forms of conflict and war. The integration of many different methods and tactics into a single strategy indicates a new level of complexity. The existence of new technologies and asymmetries in destabilizing operations suggests that hybrid warfare uses new tools and irregular methods that were not previously central to traditional conflict and war. This may indicate a new form of threat that is not fully described by existing definitions of war. Ambiguity, in turn, may indicate the difficulty of identifying actors and actions in hybrid warfare, while subliminality may indicate actions that deliberately avoid crossing the threshold of conventional war. Hybrid warfare is characterized by a high degree of flexibility, allowing for rapid adaptation to changing conditions and the use of different methods depending on the situation, which may indicate the dynamic and adaptive nature of this type of conflict.

As in the section on the analysis of concepts and concepts of hybrid warfare, semi-structured expert interviews were conducted with two defence, security, and humanitarian experts to deepen the conducted analyses.

Experts have concluded that one of the main labelling features is the introduction of change by an external actor without the use of direct military tactics and the exclusion of direct involvement of military resources. Another aspect of the characteristics of hybrid warfare is the multiplicity and dispersion of actors actively engaged in it. This causes a problem in the way in which unwanted actions carried out by external actors can be countered. In some ways, hybrid warfare is an extension of tactics from proxy wars (fought through intermediaries), where parties not directly involved in the conflict support one of the parties militarily, financially, or with their knowledge. Part of the effort is aimed at destabilizing the social situation (social aspect), as in the case of directly or indirectly influencing election results, for example. Moreover, there is also the possibility of indirectly affecting the financial situation of the civilian population (financial aspect), e.g. by influencing stock market prices or disrupting the stock market, which may further translate into unemployment rates, investment opportunities, or raising capital on international markets. Experts also stressed that a key variable is uncertainty and lack of clarity: actions below the threshold of war create uncertainty as to whether we are at peace or war. This can be more destabilizing and exacerbate the sense of uncertainty than an objectively worse but clear situation, such as a declared war, during which it is easier to identify countermeasures. The study that was carried out by means of an expert interview points directly and indirectly to the features analysed, among which destabilization also seems to be the main feature. However, to consider it as a specific feature would be a methodological error, as every war aims at destabilization, but considering the catalogue of features in combination with the concurrent slogans, may confirm that hybrid war in Ukraine goes beyond the framework of the traditional understanding of war.

CONCLUSIONS

This chapter, due to the complexity of the topic, attempts to characterize hybrid warfare. An analysis of the literature indicates that there is a lack of consensus among researchers and decision-makers on its definition, although the concept seems to be more widely accepted in decision-making circles. On the one hand, a diversity of interpretations is natural for new phenomena that were previously unknown more widely. On the other hand, hybrid warfare may be one of those conceptual categories that are difficult to define unambiguously, like warfare or terrorism. However, conceptualization is crucial as it enables a clear definition of the object of study, allowing researchers to achieve a coherent understanding and analysis of the phenomenon. A precise definition helps avoid ambiguity and ensures a common understanding of the issues at stake.

The challenge remains to precisely define hybrid warfare, which is a complex, dynamic, and flexible phenomenon. Many authors point out that current definitions, their redefinitions, or attempts to clarify existing concepts often lead to more ambiguity than clarity. Consequently, the authors suggest that for a phenomenon that is so difficult to grasp, it is worth using a simpler definition that captures its essence. Recognizing the limitations of this approach, the authors suggest defining hybrid warfare as a phase of hybrid strategy involving networked military (both conventional and unconventional) and non-military actions conducted by state and non-state actors to achieve strategic advantage, often by producing destabilizing cascading effects. This definition can be a starting point for further and more detailed research and analysis for which the features of hybrid warfare abstracted in this study can be a framework. In the literature, attempts are often made to create a universal definition of hybrid warfare. It should be noted, however, that while certain elements of hybrid warfare are common to different conflicts, there are also significant differences in their dynamics and actions – for example, between the situation in Ukraine and the reality in Gaza. This can be corroborated by Samdesk's analysis of the data, which points to the differentiated nature of the actions, but at the same time demonstrates that both wars operate within a framework of complex, adaptive strategies that skilfully combine elements of conventional military and non-military actions (see Samdesk Analytics, 2024). Therefore, a simple definition allows for regional specificity. Translating operationalization to the regional level allows flexibility to tailor protective measures to the unique tactics employed in a given region, while maintaining the overarching framework of hybrid warfare.

The research hypothesis in this chapter is that hybrid warfare is a phase of a broader, flexible, and integrated hybrid strategy. This strategy, in its first phase, takes the form of a hybrid conflict that, in feedback, may use elements (features) of hybrid warfare. The challenge remains to define the threshold between these phases. The authors propose that the scale, intensity, and continuity of military involvement (overt or covert) should be the key elements determining the classification of an event as a hybrid conflict or hybrid war. While this is a simple division, it provides a clear and practical framework for quickly assessing the operational situation, allowing the focus to be on the most visible elements of the escalation of operations.

The clustering and coding method allowed the identification of 11 key features of hybrid warfare: Multidimensionality, Asymmetry, Synergy, Complexity, Integration of means, Flexibility, Ambiguity, New technologies (use of new technologies), Destabilization, Information manipulation, and Subliminality. A trait is a general property of a phenomenon, giving it a unique character, and therefore these characteristics can be considered to define the theoretical framework of hybrid warfare. All of the above features characterized both the hybrid conflict and hybrid warfare phases, both in Ukraine and in the Middle East. Based on the above characteristics, the authors propose the acronym MASCI-FANDIS which can be used in scientific, strategic, and operational analysis.

The analysis of media reports, carried out according to the procedure described in Appendix 1, confirmed the presence of the indicated characteristics in the selected segments of the study. At the same time, it showed that the characteristics of hybrid warfare are highly variable and contextual. These characteristics do not always occur simultaneously; some are highly specialized and activated depending on the operational specificities of a given conflict environment. Their co-occurrence may be limited to specific moments of escalation, suggesting that hybrid warfare is a distinctly adaptive element of strategy. The complex interaction of these characteristics in specific contexts underlines that hybrid warfare is not a homogeneous phenomenon, but a network of dynamically changing actions that are adapted according to the situation. An extended analysis of the co-occurrence of features within operational activities indicates the emergence of a new multidimensional model of conflict, in which the integration of different domains becomes the standard rather than the exception, making hybrid war uniquely effective (this area is described in more detail in Chapter 2).

As a result of the hypothesis verification, it was shown that hybrid warfare is not a separate, isolated activity, but is part of a broader, flexible, and integrated hybrid strategy that develops in two phases, with a clear feedback mechanism: the hybrid conflict phase and the hybrid war phase. The two phases can seamlessly interpenetrate each other, with features and attributes specific to one phase being applicable to the other, allowing for high adaptability and operational effectiveness.

The above findings systematize the conceptual framework of hybrid warfare, while highlighting the need to standardize key terms.

The standardization of definitions is an important step towards improving communication between states, international organizations, and military institutions, which in turn will translate into more effective development of defence and protection strategies, especially with regard to civilians. Analyses have shown the lack of a single, universally accepted definition of hybrid warfare, indicating the need for further work in this area. While existing disagreements over the concept are likely to persist, developing a common, clear definition of both hybrid conflict and hybrid war is crucial. This is because differences in approach to these concepts can lead to less effective defence and protection strategies.

NOTES

1 Diplomatic, Informational, Military, Economic (DIME) represents the four primary instruments of national power used to achieve strategic objectives.
2 Other Active Measures (OAA) refers to actions taken below the threshold of war or within the so-called "grey zone." The goal of these actions is to achieve strategic advantage without resorting to full-scale and open armed conflict. These are most often covert actions such as disinformation, sabotage, cyberattacks, or activities in the economic and diplomatic spheres.
3 For the full responses of the experts, see Appendix 4.
4 For the full responses of the experts, see Appendix 4.

BIBLIOGRAPHY

Army Recognition (2024), Exclusive: Russia develops AI-powered unmanned T-72 Shturm tanks for deployment in Ukraine, Army Recognition, 18 December. Available at: https://armyrecognition.com/news/army-news/army-news-2024/exclusive-russia-develops-ai-powered-unmanned-t-72-shturm-tanks-for-deployment-in-ukraine. Accessed: 19 December 2024.

Bachmann, S.-D., (2011), Hybrid Threats, Cyber Warfare and NATO's Comprehensive Approach for Countering 21st Century Threats: Mapping the New Frontier of Global Risk and Security Management. *Amicus Curiae*. Available at: https://www.researchgate.net/publication/228214544_Hybrid_Threats_Cyber_Warfare_and_NATO's_Comprehensive_Approach_for_Countering_21st_Century_Threats_-_Mapping_the_New_Frontier_of_Global_Risk_and_Security_Management. Accessed: 28 June 2024.

Bachmann, S.-D., (2023), Hamas attack on Israel: A Lesson in Contemporary Hybrid Warfare. *Australian Institute of International*

Affairs, 12 October. Available at: https://www.internationalaffairs.org.au/australianoutlook/hamas-attack-on-israel-a-lesson-in-contemporary-hybrid-warfare/. Accessed: 04 June 2024.

Balcerowicz, B., (2013), On Peace and War: Between an Essay and a Treaty. Rambler.

Banasik, M., (2015), How to Understand the Hybrid War. *Securitologia*, 1. Akademia Obrony Narodowej, Warsaw. Available at: https://cejsh.icm.edu.pl/cejsh/element/bwmeta1.element.desklight-054d2eee-8c4e-4a27-bf00-4284cb39a504, Accessed: 29 May 2024.

Banasik, M., (2023), Współczesny wymiar strategicznej rywalizacji militarnej. *Facta Simonidis*. Available at: https://akademiazamojska.edu.pl (PDF). Accessed: 9 May 2024.

Baugh, L.S., (2024), Proxy War, *Encyclopedia Britannica*, 5 September. Available at: https://www.britannica.com/topic/proxy-war. Accessed: 23 June 2024.

Behrendt, P., (2022), San zhong zhanfa czyli Trzy Wojny. *Działania hybrydowe po chińsku, Instytut Boyma*, 19 February. Available at: https://instytutboyma.org/pl/san-zhong-zhanfa-czyli-trzy-wojny-dzialania-hybrydowe-po-chinsku/. Accessed: 14 October 2024.

Berdal, M., (2011), The "New Wars" Thesis Revisited. In: H. Strachan and S. Scheipers (eds.), *The Changing Character of War*, Oxford: Oxford University Press.

Bergaust, J.C., and Sellevåg, S.R., (2023), Improved Conceptualising of Hybrid Interference below the Threshold of Armed Conflict. *European Security*, 33(2). https://doi.org/10.1080/09662839.2023.2267478.

Białczyk, P., (2023), Russia is Arming on a Massive Scale. The War Mode Worries Experts, Interia Wydarzenia, 11 September. Available at: https://wydarzenia.interia.pl/raport-ukraina-rosja/news-rosja-zbroi-sie-na-potege-tryb-wojenny-niepokoi-ekspertow,nId. Accessed: 14 October2024.

Białocerkiewicz, J., (2005), *Prawo międzynarodowe publiczne. Zarys wykładu*. Olsztyn: Wydawnictwo UWM.

Bilal, A., (2024), Hybrydowa wojna Rosji z Zachodem. Przegląd NATO, Available at: https://www.nato.int/docu/review/pl/articles/2024/04/26/hybrydowa-wojna-rosji-z-zachodem/index.html,26April. Accessed: 5 May 2024.

Bilms, K., (2022), Beyond War and Peace: The PLA's – Non-War Military Activities Concept. Modern War Institute, 26 January. Available at: https://mwi.westpoint.edu/beyond-war-and-peace-the-plas-non-war-military-activities-concept/. Accessed: 05 May 2024.

Bobadilla, J., Ortega, F., Hernando, A., and Gutiérrez, A., (2013), Recommender Systems Survey. *Knowledge-Based Systems*, 46, 109–132. https://doi.org/10.1016/j.knosys.2013.03.012.

Business & Human Rights Resource Centre, (2023), Graphic Pro-Israel Ads Raise Concern as They Appear in Children's Video Games in Europe. Available at: https://www.business-humanrights.org/en/latest-news/graphic-pro-israel-ads-raise-concern-as-they-appear-in-childrens-video-games-in-europe/. Accessed: 12 September 2024.

Caliskan, M., (2019), Hybrid Warfare Through the Lens of Strategic Theory. *Defense and Security Analysis*, 35. https://doi.org/10.1080/14751798.2019.1565364. Available at: https://www.researchgate.net/publication/331074937_Hybrid_Warfare_through_the_Lens_of_Strategic_Theory#fullTextFileContent. Accessed: 27 June 2024.

Charon, P., and Vilmer, J.-B., (2021), *Les Opérations D'Influence Chinoises: Un moment machiavélien*. Paris: Institut de Recherche Stratégique de l'École militaire (IRSEM). Available at: https://www.academia.edu/88072127/Les_Op%C3%A9rations_D_Influence_Chinoises_Un_moment_machiav%C3%A9lien_Paul_Charon_and_Jean_Babtiste_Jeang%C3%A9ne_Vilmer_Paris_Institut_de_Recherche_Strat%C3%A9gique_de_l_%C3%89cole_militaire_IRSEM_2021. Accessed: 01 May 2024.

Chekinov, S. G., and Bogdanov, S. A., (2013), The Nature and Content of a New Generation War. *Military Thought* (4). Available at: https://www.semanticscholar.org/paper/The-Nature-and-Content-of-a-New-Generation-War-Chekinov-Bogdanov/c8874593b1860de12fa40dadcae8e96861de8ebd, Accessed: 16 May 2024.

Chen, J., and Xu, Y., (2015), Information Manipulation and Reform in Authoritarian Regimes. *Political Science Research and Methods*, 5(1), 1-16. https://doi.org/10.1017/psrm.2015.21. Accessed: 9 June 2024.

Chivvis, C.S., (2017), Understanding Russian "Hybrid Warfare" and What Can Be Done about It. Testimony before the Committee on Armed Services. United States House of Representatives, 22 March. The RAND Corporation. Available at: https://www.rand.org/content/dam/rand/pubs/testimonies/CT400/CT468/RAND_CT468.pdf (PDF). Accessed: 1 May 2024.

Ciano, M.P., Pozzi, R., Rossi, T., and Strozzi, F., (2019), How IJPR Has Addressed Lean: A Literature Review using Bibliometric Tools. *International Journal of Production Research*, 57. https://doi.org/10.1080/00207543.2019.1566667.

Clark, M., (2020), Russian Hybrid Warfare. *Institute for the Study of War*, September. Available at: https://www.understandingwar.org/sites/default/files/Russian%20Hybrid%20Warfare%20ISW%20Report%202020.pdf (PDF). Accessed: 23 May 2024.

Clausewitz, C., O wojnie, Warszawa: Wydawnictwo Ministerstwa Obrony Narodowej, s. 15; cyt. za: Słownik terminów z zakresu bezpieczeństwa narodowego, red. J. Pawłowski, (2002), Warszawa: Wydawnictwo Akademii Obrony Narodowej 2002, s. 155.

Clausewitz, C. v. (2010), On War, A. Rudnicka (ed.), Miraki.

Council on Foreign Relations (CFR), (2024), Global Conflict Tracker. Available at: https://www.cfr.org/global-conflict-tracker. Accessed: 01 June 2024.

Critical Threats, (2024), Russian Offensive Campaign Assessment, *Critical Threats*, 10 September. Available at: https://www.criticalthreats.org/analysis/russian-offensive-campaign-assessment-september-10-2024. Accessed: 12 June 2024.

Damiri, M.H., (2013), China's Three Warfares. Analysis Paper Conducted under the Comprehensive Defence and Security Research Centre (CDSRC), Malaysian Institute of Defence and Security (MiDAS). Available at: https://www.academia.edu/6826107/ANALYSIS_PAPER_Chinas_Three_Warfares. Accessed: 30 June 2024.

Danyk, Y., and Briggs, C.M., (2023), Modern Cognitive Operations and Hybrid Warfare. *Journal of Strategic Security*, 16(1), Article 3. Available at: https://digitalcommons.usf.edu/cgi/viewcontent.cgi?article=2032&context=jss, Accessed: 05 June 2024.

Encyclopedia Britannica, (2023), War. Available at: https://www.britannica.com. Accessed: 11 September 2024.

European Commission, (2024), Hybrid Threats, Defence Industry and Space. Available at: https://defence-industry-space.ec.europa.eu/eu-defence-industry/hybrid-threats_en. Accessed: 14 June 2024.

Eye on the Arctic, (2024), Norway's Spy Chief Sees Russia More Likely to Attempt Sabotage [online]. Available at: https://www.rcinet.ca/eye-on-the-arctic/2024/09/11/norways-spy-chief-sees-russia-more-likely-to-attempt-sabotage/. Accessed: 08 June 2024.

Fahmi, I., Sutanto, R., and Faiq, M., (2024), Analysis of Hybrid Warfare Elements in the 2023 Asymmetric War between Hamas and Israel. *Indonesian Journal of Interdisciplinary Research in Science and Technology*, 2, 359–368. https://doi.org/10.55927/marcopolo.v2i4.8718. Available at: https://www.researchgate.net/publication/380549507_Analysis_of_Hybrid_Warfare_Elements_in_the_2023_Asymmetric_War_between_Hamas_and_Israel/citation/download. Accessed: 18 June 2024.

Falkowski, Z. Marcinko, M. (eds.) (2014), *International Humanitarian Law of Armed Conflicts, 2nd expanded edition*, Military Center for Civic Education, Warsaw. ISBN: 978-83-63755-37-9.

Galeotti, M., (2016), Hybrid, Ambiguous, and Non-Linear? How New Is Russia's 'New Way of War?'. *Small Wars & Insurgencies*, 27(2). https://doi.org/10.1080/09592318.2015.1129170. Available at: https://www.tandfonline.com/doi/full/10.1080/09592318.2015.1129170. Accessed: 11 May 2024.

Garamone, J., (2019), Military Must Be Ready to Confront Hybrid Threats, Intel Official Says. *The Department of Defense*. Available at: https://www.defense.gov/News/News-Stories/Article/Article/1952023/military-must-be-ready-to-confront-hybrid-threats-intel-official-says/. Accessed: 30 June 2024.

Gerasimov, V., (2013a), The Value of Science in Foresight: New Challenges Require Rethinking the Forms and Methods of Warfare, 26 February. Available at: https://moodle.znu.edu.ua/mod/assign/view.php?id=269845. Accessed: 10 May 2024.

Gerasimov, V., (2013b), Ценность науки в предвидении. Новые вызовы требуют переосмыслить формы и способы ведения боевых действий. *Voenno-Promyshlennyi Kurier*, 8(476). Available at: https://vpk.name/news/85159_cennost_nauki_v_predvidenii.html. Accessed: 15 May 2024.

Gerasimov, V., (2016), Организация обороны Российской Федерации в условиях применения противником "традиционных" и "гибридных" методов ведения войны. *Vestnik Akademii Voennykh Nauk*, 2(55). Available at: https://www.avnrf.ru/attachments/article/862/AVN-2%2855%29_001-184_sverka_14-06.pdf?utm_source=chatgpt.com. Accessed: 14 May 2024.

Göransson, M.B., (2022), Russian Scholarly Discussions of Nonmilitary Warfare as Securitizing Acts. *Comparative Strategy*, 41(6). https://doi.org/10.1080/01495933.2022.2130675. Accessed: 26 May 2024.

Göransson, M.B., (2024), Russia's Thinking on New Wars and Its Full-Scale Invasion of Ukraine. *Defence Studies*, 24(3). Available at: https://www.tandfonline.com/doi/epdf/10.1080/01495933.2022.2130675?needAccess=true (PDF). Accessed: 06 May 2024.

Hoffman, F., Neumeyer, M., and Jensen, B., (2024), The Future of Hybrid Warfare. *CSIS*. Available at: https://www.csis.org/analysis/future-hybrid-warfare. Accessed: 06 June 2024.

Hoffman, F.G., (2007), *Conflict in the 21st Century: The Rise of Hybrid Wars*. Arlington: Potomac Institute for Policy Studies. Available at: https://www.potomacinstitute.org/images/stories/publications/potomac_hybridwar_0108.pdf. Accessed: 21 June 2024.

Hoffman, F.G., (2009), Hybrid Warfare and Challenges. *JFQ* (52), 1st Quarter. Available at: https://smallwarsjournal.com/documents/jfqhoffman.pdf. Accessed: 22 June 2024.

Hoffman, F.G., (2018), Examining Complex Forms of Conflict: Gray Zone and Hybrid Challenges. *PRISM*, 7(4). Available at: https://ndupress.ndu.edu/Media/News/News-Article-View/Article/1983462/ (PDF). Accessed: 19 May 2024.

Hybrid CoE, (2024), Hybrid Threats as a Phenomenon. *The European Centre of Excellence for Countering Hybrid Threats*. Available at: https://www.hybridcoe.fi/hybrid-threats-as-a-phenomenon/. Accessed: 14 June 2024.

Iskandarov, K., and Gawliczek, P., (2023), Hybrid Warfare as a New Type of War. The Evolution of Its Conceptual Construct. In The Russian Federation and International Security. Difin Publishing House. Available at: https://www.researchgate.net/publication/373118996_HYBRID_WARFARE_AS_A_NEW_TYPE_OF_WAR_THE_EVOLUTION_OF_ITS_CONCEPTUAL_CONSTRUCT#fullTextFileContent(PDF). Accessed: 27 June 2024.

Jacobs, A., and Lasconrajias, G., (2015), NATO's Hybrid Flanks, Handling Unconventional Warfare in the South and the East. NATO Defence College. Available at: https://www.files.ethz.ch/isn/190786/rp_112.pdf. Accessed: 29 June 2024.

Jash, A., (2019), Fight and Win Without Waging a War: How China Fights Hybrid Warfare. *CLAWS Journal*, Winter. Available at: https://www.claws.in/static/Amrita-Jash.pdf (PDF). Accessed: 02 May 2024.

Kiselyov, V.A., and Vorobyov, I.N., (2015), Hybrid Operations: A New Type of Warfare. *Military Thought*, 2(2015) Available at: https://www.eastviewpress.com/mth-toc-2-2015/?utm_source=chatgpt.com. Accessed: 25 May 2024.

Kołodziejczak, M.E., (2018), Definicyjno-prawne regulacje wojny oraz terminów pochodnych. *Roczniki Nauk Prawnych*, XXVIII(4). https://doi.org/10.18290/rnp.2018.28.4-4. Accessed: 17 June 2024.

Lindell, J., (2009), Clausewitz: War, Peace and Politics. *E-Interna-tional Relations*, 26 November. Available at: https://www.e-ir.info/2009/11/26/clausewitz-war-peace-and-politics/. Accessed: 02 June 2024.

Manko, O., and Mikhieiev, Y., (2018), Defining the Concept of Hybrid Warfare Based on the Analysis of Russia's Aggression against Ukraine. *Information & Security: An International Journal*, 41. https://doi.org/10.11610/isij.4107.

Mattis, P., (2013), Out with the New, In with the Old: Interpreting China's 'New Type of International Relations'. *China Brief*, 13(9). Available at: https://jamestown.org/program/out-with-the-new-in-with-the-old-interpreting-chinas-new-type-of-international-relations/. Accessed: 30 June 2024.

Mattis, P., (2018), China's 'Three Warfares' in Perspective. *War on the Rocks*, 30 January. Available at: https://warontherocks.com/2018/01/chinas-three-warfares-perspective/. Accessed: 30 June 2024.

Meulman, F. H., Preziosa, P. (2017), Hybrid Conflict, Hybrid Warfare and Resilience, in Joint Air Power Following the 2016 Warsaw Summit. Available at: https://www.japcc.org/chapters/hybrid-conflict-hybrid-warfare-and-resilience/. Accessed: 14 October 2024.

Military Advantage. Available at: https://www.atlanticcouncil.org/programs/scowcroft-center-for-strategy-and-security/forward-defense/. Accessed: 14 June 2024.

Ministry of Defence of the Russian Federation, (n.d.), 'Гибридные методы ведения войны', Военная мысль. Accessed: 14 October 2024.

Ministry of Defence of the Russian Federation, (2024), Деятельность вооружённых сил Российской Федерации по борьбе с терроризмом'. Военная мысль. Available at: Accessed: 14 October 2024.

NATO, (2024), Countering Hybrid Threats. Available at: https://www.nato.int/cps/en/natohq/topics_156338.htm, Accessed: 7 May 2024.

Nemeth, W.J., (2002), *Future War and Chechnya: A Case for Hybrid Warfare.* Monterey: Naval Postgraduate School. Available at: https://core.ac.uk/download/pdf/36699567.pdf. Accessed: 20 June 2024.

Osiecki, G., and Żółciak, T., (2024), Rewolucja na Kremlu nie była przypadkiem. Ekonomista ministrem obrony? Rosja wysyła sygnał. Money.pl, 1 June. Available at: https://www.money.pl/gospodarka/rewolucja-na-kremlu-nie-byla-przypadkiem-ekonomista-ministrem-obrony-rosja-wysyla-sygnal-7033425862638336a.html?DCQ=t3-3DxFAAFJHHVcRThEAEVJWRVIAFlZXEgcBTVUFTQUCFwEL EQIHFwZSTAMFTQkGRQsKRgEJRQUHRgMLRgYKRQlFRxE fVkdaGVZAAFJeBBEJRQQCQwEAQAoDCQ. Accessed: 31 May 2024.

Otfinowska, S., (2024), Rosja przyznaje, że jest w stanie wojny z Ukrainą. *EURACTIV.pl*, 22 marca. Available at: https://www.euractiv.pl/section/bezpieczenstwo-i-obrona/news/rosja-przyznaje-ze-jest-w-stanie-wojny-z-ukraina/. Accessed: 03 June 2024.

Oxford English Dictionary, (2024), War. Available at: https://www.oed.com. Accessed: 11 September 2024.

Peterson, N., (2023), The Chinese Communist Party's Theory of Hybrid Warfare. Institute for the Study of War. Available at: https://www.understandingwar.org/sites/default/files/The%20Chinese%20Communist%20Party%27s%20Theory%20of%20Hybrid%20Warfare_0.pdf. Accessed: 30 June 2024.

Politico, (2024), Russian Espionage, Sabotage in Europe Now 'More Likely,' Norwegian Intel Chief Warns. [online] Available at: https://www.politico.eu/article/russian-kremlin-espionage-sabotage-europe-head-of-norwegian-intelligence-service-nils-andreas-stensones/. Accessed: 07 June 2024.

Pomerantsev, P., (2017), Moscow's Shadow: The Gerasimov Doctrine and Russian Non-Linear War. Available at: https://cs.brown.edu/people/jsavage/VotingProject/2017_03_09_MoscowsShadow_GerasimovDoctrineAndRussianNon-LinearWar.pdf. Accessed: 12 May 2024.

Popov, V., (2019), Robust Civil-Military Relations—One of the Most Powerful Tools to Counteract Russian Hybrid Warfare: The Case of Ukraine. March. Available at: https://apps.dtic.mil/sti/pdfs/AD1073658.pdf (PDF). Accessed: 24 May 2024.

Potulski, J., (2010), Współczesne kierunki rosyjskiej myśli geopolitycznej. Między nauką, ideologicznym dyskursem a praktyką. Wydawnictwo Uniwersytetu Gdańskiego, Gdańsk. ISBN: 978-83-7326-681-0.

Prosecutor v. Dusko Tadic, Case No. IT-94-1-AR-72, Decision on the Defence Motion for Interlocutory Appeal on Jurisdiction, International Criminal Tribunal for the Former Yugoslavia (ICTY), 2 October 1995, par. 70, Available at: https://www.icty.org/x/cases/tadic/acdec/en/51002.htm?utm_source=chatgpt.com, Accessed: 15 June 2024.

Pynnöniemi, K., Jokela, M., (2020), Perceptions of hybrid war in Russia: Means, targets and objectives identified in the Russian debate. *Cambridge Review of International Affairs*, 33(6), https://doi.org/10.1080/09557571.2020.1787949.

Ramadhan, I., (2021), The Implication of Cyberspace towards State Geopolitics. *Politicon: Jurnal Ilmu Politik*, 3(2). https://doi.org/10.15575/politicon.v3i2.12660. Available at: https://www.research-gate.net/publication/356798244_The_Implication_of_Cyberspace_Towards_State_Geopolitics (PDF). Accessed: 21 May 2024.

Robbins, S. P., (1998), Behavior in Organizations, translated by A. Ehrlich, Polish Economic Publishing House, Warsaw. Original title: Essentials of Organizational Behavior (1996).

Sanchez, L., (2010), *Hybrid Warfare*. Washington: Government Accountability Office, Available at: https://www.gao.gov/assets/gao-10-1036r.pdf, Accessed: 23 June 2024.

Schmidt, J., (2019), Hybrid Warfare on the Ukrainian Battlefield: Developing Theory Based on Empirical Evidence. *Journal on Baltic Security*, 5(1). Available at: https://www.researchgate.net/publication/334969563_Hybrid_warfare_on_the_Ukrainian_battlefield_developing_theory_based_on_empirical_evidence, Accessed: 09 June 2024.

SOFX, (2024), Norway's Intelligence Chief Warns of Growing Russian Sabotage Threat in Europe. [online] Available at: https://www.sofx.com/norways-intelligence-chief-warns-of-growing-russian-sabotage-threat-in-europe/. Accessed: 09 June 2024.

Solmaz, T., (2022), 'Hybrid Warfare': One Term, Many Meanings. *Conservative News Daily*, 28 February. Available at: https://www.conservativenewsdaily.net/breaking-news/hybrid-warfare-is-one-term-with-many-meanings/. Accessed: 09 May 2024.

Sugiura, Y., (2021), China Security Report 2022: The PLA's Pursuit of Enhanced Joint Operations Capabilities. *NIDS*. Available at: https://www.nids.mod.go.jp/english/publication/chinareport/index.html. Accessed: 03 May 2024.

Sun, T., Sun, P., and Sawyer, R.D. (trans.), (2024), Sztuka wojny. Wydanie IV. Onepress. ISBN: 978-83-289-1113-0 (Print), 978-83-289-1787-3 (Ebook). Accessed: 24 May 2024.

Suvari, A., (2021), The Russian Federation's Use of Non-State Actors in Hybrid Operations in Europe. Available at: https://apps.dtic.mil/sti/trecms/pdf/AD1150814.pdf (PDF). Accessed: 22 May 2024.

Sykulski, L., (2015), Rosyjska koncepcja wojen buntowniczych Jewgienija Messnera. *Przegląd Geopolityczny*, 11, Available at: https://przeglad.org/wp-content/uploads/2014/12/Sykulski_Leszek_PG_tom_11.pdf. Accessed: 30 May 2024.

Terrados, J.J., (2019), Hybrid Warfare. *The Three Swords Magazine*, 35. Accessed: 30 June 2024.

Torossian, B., Fagliano, L., and Görder, T., (2020), Hybrid Conflict: Neither War, Nor Peace. *Clingendael*. Available at: https://www.clingendael.org/pub/2019/strategic-monitor-2019-2020/hybrid-conflict/. Accessed: 14 June 2024.

Tsymbursky, V.L., (1999), Борьба за евразийскую Атлантиду: геоэкономика и геостратегия. *Pro et Contra*, No. 4.

Urbanek, J. et al. (2024), Encyclopedia of National Security, edited by J. Itrich-Drabarek, A. Misiuk, S. Mitkowski, P. Bryczek-Wróbel, WAT.

Vdovytskyi, Y., (2023), An Improvement of the Method for Assessing the Efficiency of the Methods of Performing Tasks by the Naval Forces in the Conditions of Hybrid Operations. *Eastern-European Journal of Enterprise Technologies*, 4(3). https://doi.org/10.15587/1729-4061.2023.285745. Accessed: 2 May 2024.

Weissmann, M., (2019), Hybrid Warfare and Hybrid Threats Today and Tomorrow: Towards an Analytical Framework. *Journal on Baltic Security*, 5(1). Available at: https://www.diva-portal.org/smash/get/diva2:1340789/FULLTEXT03.pdf. Accessed: 14 October 2024.

Weissmann, M., Nilsson, N., Palmertz, B., and Thunholm, P., (2021), Conceptualizing and Countering Hybrid Threats and Hybrid Warfare: The Role of the Military in the Grey Zone. In Hybrid Warfare: Security and Asymmetric Conflict in International Relations. London: I.B. Tauris, pp. 61–82. Available at: https://www.diva-portal.org/smash/get/diva2:1547074/FULLTEXT01.pdf (PDF). Accessed: 18 May 2024.

Weitz, R., (2014), Countering Russia's Hybrid Threats. *ICDS Diplomaatia Magazine*, 21 November. Available at: https://icds.ee/en/countering-russias-hybrid-threats/. Accessed: 08 May 2024.

Wither, J.K., (2019), Defining Hybrid Warfare. *per Concordiam*, 11 December. Available at: https://perconcordiam.com/defining-hybrid-warfare/. Accessed: 30 June 2024.

Wojcieszak, L. (2024). Identyfikatory demaskujące jako narzędzie walki Służby Bezpieczeństwa Ukrainy z aktywnością sabota-żoworozpoznawczą służb specjalnych Federacji Rosyjskiej.Przegląd Bezpieczeństwa Wewnętrznego, (31), Agencja Bezpiecze-ństwa Wewnętrznego, Available at: https://www.abw.gov.pl/ftp/foto/Wydawnictwo/PBW/pbw31/19_-_varia_-_L__Wojcieszak.pdf, Accessed: 09 February 2025.

Wojnowski, M., (2015), Mit "wojny hybrydowej": konflikt na terenie państwa ukraińskiego w świetle rosyjskiej myśli wojskowej XIX-XXI wieku. Przegląd Bezpieczeństwa Wewnętrznego. Available as a digital reproduction from Biblioteka Narodowa (PDF). Accessed: 17 May 2024.

WUSF Public Media, (2023), The Telegram App Has Been a Key Platform for Hamas. *Now It's Being Restricted There*. Available at: https://www.wusf.org/2023-10-31/the-telegram-app-has-been-a-key-platform-for-hamas-now-its-being-restricted-there. Accessed: 12 September 2024.

Yamaguchi, S., Yatsuzuka, M., and Momma, R., (2023), NIDS China Security Report 2023: China's Quest for Control of the Cognitive Domain and Gray Zone Situations. NIDS. Available at: https://www.nids.mod.go.jp/publication/chinareport/pdf/china_report_EN_web_2023_A01.pdf (PDF). Accessed: 04 May 2024.

Zygiel, A., (2024), Strach, panika. Polskie wojsko ostrzega przed rosyjską operacją. Available at: https://wiadomosci.wp.pl/strach-panika-polskie-wojsko-ostrzega-przed-rosyjska-operacja-70692095082 64672a.Accessed: 10 June 2024.

Бартош А.А. Конфликты XXI века, (2019), Гибридная война и цветная революция. М.: Горячая линия-Телеком, 2018; Он же. Туман гибридной войны. Неопределенности и риски конфликтов XXI века. М.: Горячая линия-Телеком.

Бартош, А.А,. (2021), Сдерживание в военных конфликтах XXI века. М.: Горячая линия—Телеком, С. 28.

Бартош, А.А. (2018), Москва по-прежнему цель номер один. США, НАТО и ЕС рассматривают гибридную войну против России как объединительный геополитический проект Запада // Независимое военное обозрение. № 48 (1026). URL: https://nvo.ng.ru/realty/2018-12-14/8_1026_aim.html.

Бартош, А. А. (2018), Стратегия и контрстратегия гибридной войны, (Геополитика и безопасность), Военная мысль, № 10, с. 5–20. ISSN 0236-2058.

Бартош, А.А., (2018), Трение и износ гибридной войны // Военная Мысль. 2018. № 1. С. Он же. Конфликты XXI века. Гибридная война и цветная революция. М.: Горячая линия—Телеком.

БАРТОШ, А.А., (2019), Модель гибридной войны, Военная мысль, Available at: https://www.elibrary.az/docs/JURNAL/jrn2019_180.pdf, Accessed: 14 April 2024.

Бартош, А.А., (2019), Туман гибридной войны. Неопределенности и риски конфликтов современности М.: Горячая линия-Телеком.

Валецкий О.В., Неелов В.М. Особенности партизанских и противопартизанских действий в ходе Иракской войны (2003–2011). — М.: Издатель Воробьев А. В., 2015. — 120 с.: с ил. ISBN 978-5-93883-256-5

Воробьев, И.Н., and Киселев, В.А., (2008), Стратегические категории время и пространство в современных войнах. Военная мысль, no. 8. Accessed: 31 May 2024.

Ильницкий, А.М., (2008), Стратегия гегемона—стратегия войны, Военная мысль, no. 8, Available at: https://cyberleninka.ru/article/n/strategicheskie-kategorii-vremya-i-prostranstvo-v-sovremennyh-voynah/viewer, Accessed: 14 May 2024.

Комлева, Н.А. (2010), Лимитроф как геополитическая технология, "Известия Уральского федерального университета. Серия 1. Проблемы образования, науки и культуры", № 3.

Комлева, Н.А. (2013), Лимитроф в современном геополитическом процессе, "Пространство и Время", № 3.

Комлева, Н.А. (2014), Несколько замечаний относительно природы и типологии геополитических пространств, "Пространство и Время", № 1.

Комлева, Н.А. (2015а), Войны в лимитрофах: эволюция технологий, "Пространство и Время", № 12.

Комлева, Н.А. (2015), Войны сверхдержав: от «горячих» к гибридным, "Вестник Московского государственного областного университета", № 1.

Магда, Е., (2015), Гибридная война: выжить и победить. Харьков: Available at: https://royallib.com/read/magda_evgeniy/gibridnaya_voyna_vigit_i_pobedit.html#0. Accessed: 26 June 2024.

Магда, Е., (2015), Гибридная война: выжить и победить. Харьков. Available at: https://ru.scribd.com/document/412537008/Gibridnaya-voyna. Accessed: 8 June 2024.

Месснер, Е. А. (2005), Хочешь мира, победи мятежевойну! Творческое наследие Е. А. Месснера, М.: Военный университет; Русский путь, 696 с., ил. — (Российский военный сборник. Вып. 21), ISBN 5-85887-134-8.

Министерство Обороны Российской Федерации, (2018), Стратегия и контрстратегия гибридной войны. Военная мысль, 10 October. Accessed: 31 May 2024.

CHAPTER 2

Operations and actors of hybrid warfare

CHARACTERISTICS OF OPERATIONS IN A HYBRID WARFARE ENVIRONMENT

As highlighted in Chapter 1, a feature is a general property of a phenomenon, giving it a unique character, while an action is the practical application of a feature in the context of hybrid warfare.

Actions are specific operations and campaigns conducted within a domain – an area of operations. In hybrid warfare, they can be both military and non-military, including conventional and unconventional, and aim to create conditions to weaken the opponent. Understanding operations is important in the context of discussing domains and threats in hybrid warfare.

Hybrid operations are a set of coordinated activities aimed at achieving military, ideological, or political objectives. They can be conducted by both state and non-state actors, acting alone or in cooperation. When the use or threat of conventional or irregular forces is combined with, for example, cyberattacks, information operations, or disinformation, the effectiveness of such activities increases significantly. Such coordinated operations can significantly increase the level of destabilization of an adversary, optimizing the impact on their defence capabilities and political and social stability (Bilal, 2024). Therefore, the main objective of these activities is to weaken and make dependent the entity under attack. The main principle shaping these operations is the synergy of methods and means, which optimizes the balance of inputs and outputs. As assessed by Arsalan Bilal, kinetic operations – which are themselves becoming increasingly complex – are now commonly combined with non-military strategies aimed at undermining the security of the adversary. The combination of military and non-military instruments and strategies is not arbitrary – it is synchronized and aimed at increasing their effectiveness. In other words, it is this synchronized fusion that

86   DOI: 10.4324/9781003503859-3

optimizes the results of hybrid operations (Bilal, 2024). This is nowadays referred to as networking. Hybrid strategy operations, especially from the perspective of the hybrid conflict phase but also in the war phase, can be compared to the proverbial chasing the rabbit, in the sense that they are characterized by a constant change of methods and tactics, making the termination or unequivocal resolution of hybrid war extremely difficult. This dynamic and adaptive approach means that the adversary is forced to constantly respond to new threats, often without being able to fully neutralize the threats. This type of continuous escalation and adaptation of actions is aimed at gaining an advantage that is not about ultimate victory, but about continually destabilizing the adversary. The implications of such actions for national security and especially for civilians are significant, as will be discussed in later stages of this book.

This chapter adopts the research hypothesis that hybrid warfare is characterized by the integrated and flexible use of both military (conventional and unconventional) and non-military means by state and non-state actors to achieve strategic advantage and leads to the creation of a complex hybrid system with a network character and in which the actions of one element trigger a reaction in other areas (cascade effect).

Military action in hybrid warfare

Military actions in hybrid warfare can be divided into conventional and unconventional actions.

Conventional military operations refer to the traditional forms of combat conducted by the regular armed forces of states. They include land, sea, and air operations that are carried out using standard military units such as infantry, artillery, tanks, warships, and combat aircraft. Examples of such operations include direct military clashes, land offensives, aerial bombardments, and naval blockades (Mumford, Carlucci, 2023, pp. 192–206; Chivvis, 2017; Pettyjohn, Wasser, 2019).

On the other hand, unconventional military operations may include the use of guerrilla warfare, diversion, sabotage, intelligence activities, special operations, private military companies (PMCs). These methods aim to destabilize the adversary and achieve strategic objectives without engaging in direct, open confrontation (Mumford, Carluci, 2023).

An examination of media reports in terms of identifying combinations of military (conventional and unconventional) and non-military activities confirms their wide range.

Table A2.1 presents codes that characterize military conventional and unconventional measures present in the analysed media news (columns of Table A2.1). The percentages at the intersection of the codes characterizing conventional actions with the associated codes indicate how often the action under consideration occurred in the context of the associated code. In contrast, the main conclusions of the analysis are presented below with the help of graphs and discussed.

The conducted research points to a significant disparity between unconventional and conventional military actions. A total of 360 codes related to unconventional actions were identified, compared to only seven codes related to conventional actions. Below is a graph showing the numerical breakdown of the results of the analysis in the study of media reports and the percentage breakdown of the values at the intersection of the codes characterizing the activities with the highest rates (sabotage and diversion) (Figure 2.1).

Unconventional activities are dominated by diversionary (230 indications) and sabotage (118 indications), which are strongly linked to both conventional actors (such as the army) and terrorist groups. Sabotage and diversionary activities also show significant links with propaganda

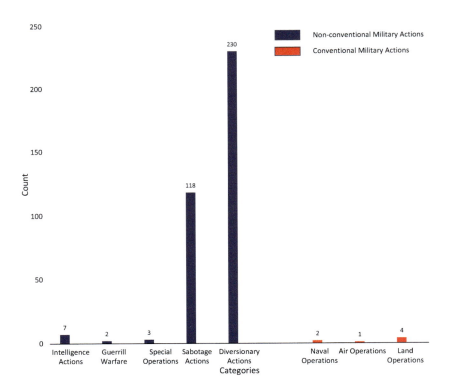

FIGURE 2.1 Numerical breakdown of the results of a review of military action in the study of media reports

Source: Own study

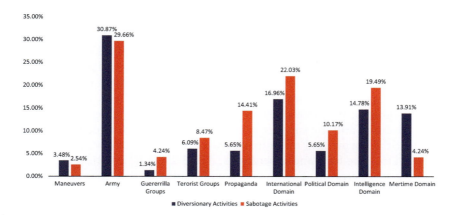

FIGURE 2.2 Percentages at the intersection of codes characterizing sabotage and diversion activities

Source: Own study

operations, with sabotage activities having a higher intensity. Similar trends are observed in the context of activities in the information, intelligence, and political domains. In the maritime domain, on the other hand, sabotage operations are clearly more numerous. Despite the small number of codes, intelligence activities have interesting links with military actors, PMCs, and terrorist groups. These links also include psychological operations (PSYOPs) and disinformation activities, and the information, political, and air domains. Special operations also show significant relationships with military actors and actors involved in irregular and hybrid activities below the threshold of war, as well as the information, intelligence, and air domains (Figure 2.2). This topic will be taken up in more detail in the further part of the book.

Conventional military action in hybrid warfare

The characteristics of conventional military action are based on the use of traditional forms of warfare, such as regular armed forces in land, sea, and air operations (Banasik, 2023; Dobie, 2021, pp. 181–190). The objective of this chapter is not to analyse the military contexts in depth, but to outline a general theoretical background that serves as a basis for further analysis. Definitions of specific areas of action will only be presented in general terms to support the main research objective.

Land operations are activities carried out by ground forces in enemy territory or on the battlefield, in which precise coordination between units of different types plays a key role. In such operations, ground forces carry out complex tactical manoeuvres, such as flanking the enemy, occupying key positions, or breaking through defensive lines, with the support of artillery and tanks. Modern battlefield management systems (BMS) and advanced communication technologies enable the dynamic exchange of information, enhancing the ability to react quickly to changes in the tactical situation. Particular emphasis is placed on the integration of different types of forces, such as engineering troops, special units, and air support systems, allowing more effective combat against the enemy and minimizing own losses (Paździorek, 2021; Joint Allied Doctrine for Land Operations, AJP-3.2 Ed. B, 2022).

Naval operations encompass a wide range of activities conducted on seas and oceans using various types of vessels. Warships, submarines, and naval aviation play a strategic role in these operations, performing diverse tasks of varying complexity. For instance, they can serve as convoy escorts, provide logistical support, participate in naval blockades, and carry out precise attacks on enemy targets at sea. The tactical, flexible, and balanced use of the naval fleet is of great importance for maintaining full control over maritime areas and ensuring maximum security for land-based operations. Naval operations can also involve complex and coordinated actions with other nations, thus forming a broad coalition aimed at jointly protecting and defending maritime interests. Moreover, naval operations demand that military personnel involved possess excellent knowledge of naval tactics, high physical fitness, and the ability to effectively coordinate activities under challenging and ever-changing conditions on the open sea (Kozierawski, Lotarski, 2022, pp. 87–118; Kończal, Kustra, 2021, pp. 109–132).

Air operations involve the effective utilization of combat aviation capabilities to achieve both tactical and strategic objectives. Reliable fighter jets, precision helicopters, and technologically advanced combat drones play an indispensable role in complex and intensive air operations, providing invaluable support to ground forces, destroying enemy targets deep behind the lines, and gaining complete control over airspace. Coordinated and strategically planned air actions have a direct impact on the dynamic course of any armed conflict, significantly influencing its final outcome (Zabrodskyi et al., 2022).

In order to deepen the understanding of conventional military actions in hybrid warfare and their mechanisms, an analysis was conducted in the context of examining media reports to identify conventional actions undertaken in this type of conflict. (The research methodology is described in detail in the Appendix 1.) The analysis of the results revealed the dominant role of manoeuvres, which were recorded 983 times. Codes characterizing the three main domains (land, air, and sea) had significantly lower indicators, below ten mentions, which may suggest that manoeuvres could be a key element in the context analysed. However, it should be clarified that the low indicator for the three primary categories of conventional actions does not imply that these actions are not being conducted in the respective domains, but rather that media reports may not categorize them in this way. Nevertheless, returning to the highest result, the analysis of code correlations related to manoeuvres allowed the identification of several key domains during the preparation phase for hybrid warfare (manoeuvres). The information domain, with 3,516 codes, indicates a strong connection between manoeuvres and informational activities, which include disinformation, propaganda campaigns, and PSYOPs. The high number of codes (actions) in the air domain, amounting to 2,473, may suggest the crucial role of airspace in hybrid warfare strategy. It is complemented by the land domain with 1,427 mentions and activities in the maritime domain with 2,004 mentions. The correlation of these codes (domains) with the term "manoeuvres" may suggest that manoeuvres are a significant indicator of preparation for the transition from the hybrid conflict phase to the hybrid warfare phase.

Figure 2.3 is presented showing the coexistence of manoeuvres with other codes. Detailed data is provided in Table A2.2 in Appendix 2. The rows of the table display the codes associated with the identified codes describing conventional military actions. The percentage values at the intersection of codes characterizing conventional military actions with related codes indicate how often the analysed action occurred in the context of the associated code.

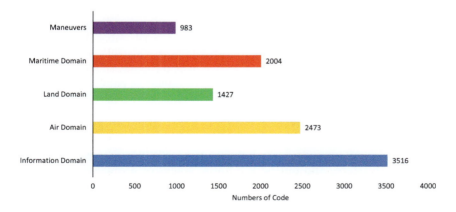

FIGURE 2.3 Diagram of the correlation between the code "manoeuvres" and other terms

Source: Own study

Unconventional military operations in hybrid warfare

Unconventional operations, as suggested by the *Encyclopaedia of National Security* (Polish edition), refer to military actions conducted in enemy-occupied territory, typically involving clandestine groups (guerrilla forces), special services, and government agencies. This type of operation encompasses a wide range of activities, usually long-term, both military and paramilitary, conducted primarily by local forces that are organized, trained, equipped, supported, and commanded externally. Unconventional operations most commonly include guerrilla warfare, covert or overt sabotage actions, diversionary activities, intelligence operations, and actions related to evasion or escape. They may also involve information operations, PSYOPs (although these are more often attributed to non-military activities), and civil-military cooperation (CIMIC).

Unconventional military operations are conducted through interconnected and coordinated phases such as preparation, initial contact, infiltration, organization, build-up, execution, and transformation. The results from the study of media reports concerning unconventional military operations in the hybrid war in Ukraine, conducted by the authors, are presented in Table A2.3. The conclusions and selected results are presented in the following section, where the division is based on the criteria of the most frequently mentioned actions in the scientific literature.

The term guerrilla warfare emerged in modern language during the Napoleonic Wars. It refers to a form of warfare, a technique or method used to achieve objectives, as opposed to a type of war, such as total war or limited war. According to Samuel Huntington's definition, guerrilla warfare is:

> a form of war in which the strategically weaker side takes the tactical offensive in selected forms, times, and places. Guerrilla warfare is the weapon of the weak. It is never chosen as the preferred method of regular warfare, it is used only when the possibility of regular warfare has been ruled out.

Therefore, it is typically employed by small irregular groups of the weaker side, fighting against a superior invading army, aiming to weaken its control over conquered territory, or as an auxiliary measure in conventional warfare, and during the initial stages of a revolutionary war aimed at overthrowing the existing political power. A significant feature of guerrilla warfare is the involvement of citizens from other countries in what were essentially national struggles. This phenomenon reached its peak during the jihad against the Soviet Union in Afghanistan, which led to the formation of global networks of fighters (Kalyanaraman, 2003, pp. 1–20). In contemporary times, guerrilla warfare or its elements serve as a tactic that can be employed in hybrid warfare – more broadly in relation to the war in Ukraine, as described by Manko and Mikhieiev in their study *Defining the concept of "hybrid warfare" based on analysis of Russia's aggression against Ukraine* (the primarily used forms were *urban guerrilla* and *urban guerrilla warfare*). However, as indicated by the frequency of the code (see Table A2.3), the scale of usage of this term in the media reports analysed is low. This may suggest that these actions were not categorized as guerrilla warfare in media reports, or that the use of this component was minimal. Guerrilla warfare was linked to the informational, intelligence, and economic domains (with a 50% strength of association for each of these domains). This may suggest that, despite the low code frequency, such actions could be used, for example, for disinformation, gathering data on enemy movements, and weakening the opponent through economic activities, which will be discussed in more detail later. It has not been determined whether these actions were conducted by the Russian or Ukrainian side.

The central idea underlying the theory of diversionary war suggests that internal unrest is one of the main causes of armed conflict. Faced with domestic challenges to their leadership, political leaders tend to initiate international conflicts to divert public attention from domestic problems to foreign affairs and to maintain their hold on power. At least two rationales can be identified for the choice of diversionary conflict by embattled leaders seeking political survival. The first rationale stems from the rally-around-the-flag effect. Many social psychologists argue that individuals tend to favour members of their own group over members of an out-group, regardless of prior interactions, and that an external threat strengthens this division between in-group and out-group. The second rationale emphasizes the political opportunity to demonstrate leadership competence. Leaders losing domestic support due to political failures or unjust actions need an opportunity to prove their leadership abilities. Winning an international conflict offers such a chance to restore internal support and save their political career (Jung, 2019).

In an encyclopaedic sense, diversion refers to a form of military action conducted in enemy-occupied territory, aimed at disrupting the functioning of its defence system. Diversion is offensive in nature, covert, surprising, and violent in execution. A key feature of diversionary actions is the participation of soldiers (guerrillas), which inherently classifies these actions as armed combat (Kramer, Speranza, 2017). The primary goal of diversion is to reduce the opposing side's ability to respond to crisis and wartime threats, both by institutions and the state's society. Diversionary activities aim to disrupt the political, administrative, and economic life of the opponent's state and weaken its military potential. They are directed at creating uncertainty, weakening and disorganizing the opponent's armed forces, while simultaneously diminishing their combat capabilities and instilling a constant sense of threat within the population. Diversionary actions are carried out to achieve indirect political, economic, and wartime objectives. In modern times, the scope of diversionary tactics has expanded to include ideological activity, an element of psychological warfare. This aspect involves, among other things, exaggerating the effects of diversionary actions, discrediting the governing apparatus, spreading sentiments of uncertainty and panic (disinformation), and encouraging capitulation. Diversionary actions are characterized by secrecy, unconventionality, flexibility, mobility, independence, adaptability, and simplicity. Such actions are often classified as part of so-called special (irregular) operations, which go beyond the traditional frameworks of armed combat. In hybrid warfare, diversion takes on an expanded role, stemming from the fundamental principle of war, which is a key element of its definition by J.F.C. Fuller: *War is the art of identifying, controlling, and exploiting the opportunities it presents* (Fuller, 1926; Weissmann et al., 2021, pp. 62–77; Mumford, Carlucci, 2023, pp. 192–206). In the conducted study of media reports in the context of the war in Ukraine, diversionary actions represent the highest code frequency, which may indicate that they are the most commonly used among the catalogue of unconventional military actions in hybrid warfare. These actions were linked to the army as well as the informational, intelligence, and maritime domains, suggesting that this is an important tactic used alongside conventional military operations.

On the other hand, the objective of sabotage is hindering the enemy's ability to carry out its plans. Typically, sabotage involves destroying or damaging various objects, disrupting economic or political processes, and obstructing significant initiatives of the government or socio-political organizations. These actions are often part of diversionary operations and special operations, and can target strategic sectors of the economy, such as critical systems and infrastructure, particularly military-related facilities like energy and transport. Sabotage is also frequently a form of civilian resistance during occupation, directed against the occupying force. It often takes an unorganized form, making it difficult to identify the perpetrators. Specialized tools are not necessary to carry out such attacks. A thorough understanding of the target facilities or organizations, often coupled with free access and good knowledge of the surroundings, enables precise planning of actions that take into account the specifics and technical security of the targets, thereby increasing the likelihood of success. Sabotage actions can be conducted by individuals or small groups, and in pursuit of a common goal, they can be coordinated into parallel sabotage operations. Given the ever-expanding scope of social, political, and economic life in cyberspace, cyber sabotage has become a significant challenge. This type of sabotage involves disrupting the operation of computer systems or telecommunications networks by destroying, damaging, deleting, or altering information crucial for defence, security in communication, or the functioning of state organs and institutions, as well as other structures critical to the state's operations and economy. It can also involve disrupting or preventing the automatic processing, storage, or transmission of such data (cyberattacks) (Encyklopedia Bezpieczeństwa Narodowego, 2024).

Media reports on the use of sabotage in hybrid warfare are primarily focused on Unit 29155 of the Russian Main Intelligence Directorate (GRU). This unit is attributed with acts of sabotage aimed at destabilizing Europe (Belsat, 2024). As has been mentioned earlier on, and as assessed by a representative of the Polish Institute of International Affairs (PISM), acts of sabotage and other elements of hybrid warfare conducted by Russia can be expected in Poland and across Europe. Sabotage operations, both below the threshold of war and during wartime, are a consistent practice for Russia (Wyrzykowski, 2022). In the conducted study of media reports in the context of the war in Ukraine, acts of sabotage represent the second-highest code frequency, which may suggest that, alongside diversion, it is an equally significant tactic of unconventional military operations. Sabotage actions, similar to diversion, were linked to conventional military operations (the army), as well as propaganda, and to the informational and intelligence domains.

According to its dictionary definition, destabilization refers to a state of imbalance in which something ceases or has ceased to function correctly due to a disruption of its existing equilibrium. In the context of a state's functioning, destabilization affects the political, economic, and social systems. Destabilizing actions aim to cause the loss of power or control by a government or political group, making the political and/or economic situation less stable or secure through intentional changes and the exploitation of the entity's internal weaknesses, which hinder the state's ability to fulfil its fundamental functions. These actions seek to create chaos, undermine the system, and lead to the collapse of power or control by the government or political groups, resulting in political instability and social unrest. Destabilization impacts the security of a state and aims to weaken and possibly exploit the entity's internal weaknesses. Destabilizing actions may include terrorism, war, interstate conflict, economic and political instability, crises triggered by natural disasters, socio-ethnic and/or religious crises, civil war, disruption of community functioning, destabilizing sanctions, psychological warfare, and disinformation (Merom, 1990, pp. 75–95).

In the relevant literature and open sources, a range of activities can be found that fall under the category of destabilizing actions in hybrid warfare. According to the definition of such actions, both in the war in Ukraine and in the war in the Gaza Strip, acts of terrorism, economic, and political instability have occurred and continue to occur. A variety of tools are used for these actions. Destabilizing activities represent the third largest category (after sabotage and diversion) in terms of code frequency in the study of media reports concerning the war in Ukraine. In terms of code correlations, these actions, like diversion and sabotage, are associated with conventional military operations as well as the informational and political domains, with the latter showing stronger associations. This result may suggest that, similar to diversion and sabotage, destabilization is a significant tactic in hybrid warfare, where destabilizing activities are conducted alongside conventional military operations, with a particular emphasis on informational and political actions. This highlights the strong influence of manipulation and disinformation, as well as the weakening of political structures.

Intelligence activities constitute a complex process of gathering, processing, and analysing information that is critical to national security and the achievement of a state's political, military, economic, and technological objectives. These activities encompass various forms of data collection, both open and covert, as well as operations conducted on foreign territory. Intelligence activities can be divided into several categories:

- Military Intelligence – Focuses on gathering and analysing information related to foreign armed forces, including their structures, training, activities, and weaponry. Its objective is to obtain data regarding the defensive and offensive capabilities of other nations.
- Political Intelligence – Concentrates on acquiring information about the political situation in selected countries, the activities of political parties, organizations, factions, and social movements that may influence both domestic and foreign policies.
- Internal Intelligence – Carries out tasks related to identifying domestic entities that may pose a threat to the nation's security.
- Technical Intelligence – Aims to obtain information about technologies employed by other countries, which can be used to enhance one's own technological capabilities.
- Economic Intelligence – Involves acquiring information about economic sectors, business entities, and natural resource reserves, followed by analysis and forecasting.
- Intelligence activities also differ based on the methods used to gather information:
- Operational Intelligence – Responsible for gathering data that facilitates the preparation of operational activities, primarily through surveillance, espionage, and illegal techniques such as coercion or blackmail.

- Agent Intelligence – Relies on a network of agents who, due to their professional positions, obtain and pass on information to their handlers.
- Electronic Intelligence – Increasingly important due to the evolving methods of communication. It employs techniques such as radio signal interception, satellite observation, and hacking methods.

There is also a general classification of intelligence activities (Ogrodowczyk, 2013, pp. 177–199):

- White Intelligence – Based on the analysis of publicly available sources, from which most relevant data can be acquired.
- Grey Intelligence – Involves obtaining information related to the operation of businesses, revealing personal and financial connections, and uncovering real business policies.
- Black Intelligence – Reserved for special services, utilizing advanced techniques like hacking into computer systems and violating communication confidentiality.
- Intelligence activities are a crucial element of state governance, ensuring national security and supporting the implementation of state policy on the international stage.

In the article *Hybrid Intelligence as a Response to Hybrid Warfare*, Jeff Giesea proposes complementing traditional intelligence activities, which are an important element of hybrid warfare, with so-called "civilian intelligence operations," which Giesea refers to as "Hybrid Intelligence." According to the author, it is cheaper, better, faster, and more effective than traditional intelligence methods. It combines many sources of information efficiently, using the latest technologies to surpass traditional methods, which primarily rely on signals, intelligence (i.e., interception), and proprietary technology. Hybrid intelligence integrates human intelligence (HUMINT), aerial intelligence, open-source intelligence (OSINT), and other forms of technology-assisted intelligence (e.g. AI, UAVs, Big Data).

To see how hybrid intelligence could work in practice, one can look at the monitoring of opium production in the Golden Triangle region (Laos, Thailand, Myanmar). The use of satellite technology, drones with cameras, facial recognition systems, and OSINT data enables the identification of poppy fields, processing and distribution locations, and individuals involved in this activity. Constant monitoring made possible by modern technologies allows for real-time collection and verification of information, significantly reducing costs and increasing the efficiency of intelligence operations (Giesea, 2023).

In the conducted study of media reports, intelligence activities, as somewhat expected, represent a small code frequency. Nevertheless, the network of connections for these activities reveals interesting relationships. According to the analysed data, intelligence activities are primarily linked, similar to other actions, with conventional military operations (the army), showing the strongest correlation. However, they are also connected to irregular and sub-threshold activities, as well as to PMCs and terrorist groups. Additionally, intelligence activities were associated with PSYOPs, disinformation, and various domains: the informational domain (which, like conventional operations, has the highest indicator), the political domain, and the air domain. These results suggest that, despite intelligence activities not being the most frequently reported (due to their covert nature), they play a crucial role in hybrid warfare. The findings from the analysis may thus support Giesea's thesis that a modern approach to intelligence – combining traditional methods with new technologies and civilian sources of information – can be more effective. The theory of hybrid intelligence may address these challenges through a highly integrated approach to intelligence gathering and analysis.

Special operations are another category utilized in unconventional military activities. Special operations, also referred to as special missions, are military and non-military actions conducted outside the zone of direct combat by specially organized, trained, and equipped forces that employ unconventional techniques and procedures to achieve political, military, psychological, and economic objectives. These operations are carried out by special forces in situations where the use of other branches of the armed forces (conventional forces) is not possible or advisable due to political or military reasons. Special operations can be conducted during peacetime, crises, and war. They are executed within the framework of special operations and can include a range of specific special missions. These operations are conducted independently or in cooperation with conventional forces. This type of operation requires the use of covert procedures and consideration of both the physical and political risks involved. The objectives of special operations include: supporting the main objectives of conventional forces, reducing the political, military, and economic potential of the enemy, negatively impacting their morale and fighting spirit, gathering and relaying intelligence on the enemy, objects, and terrain, neutralizing key enemy targets, providing assistance and support to damaged military components, allies, and other combat participants (parties to the conflict), as well as to civilian institutions and government and non-governmental organizations (Meredith, 2019).

Within the scope of special operations, tasks such as special reconnaissance, direct actions, and military support can be carried out. Special reconnaissance involves a comprehensive set of activities aimed at acquiring, gathering, analysing, and processing information regarding the enemy's environment, methods, intentions, as well as terrain, weather, and climatic conditions present and expected in the military engagement area. This information is collected using the capabilities and resources of a joint intelligence process, including surveillance (observation, tracking) and patrol activities. Special reconnaissance can provide real-time information when the use of conventional reconnaissance methods is not feasible. It can be conducted independently, as a supporting element, or in a supported role. Special reconnaissance includes: environmental reconnaissance and threat, target, and strike assessment. The choice of methods and techniques for conducting special reconnaissance depends on the nature of the target, its security system, accessibility, location, range, available reconnaissance assets, transport capabilities, terrain and weather conditions, and the ability to ensure the secrecy of the operation.

Direct actions are carefully planned and precisely executed offensive strikes, conducted within a limited time frame and operational scope. Their objective is to destroy, capture, recover, or damage high-value or high-priority targets. Direct actions are characterized by a particularly high level of political and military risk, precision in planning and execution, reliance on the timeliness and accuracy of available intelligence, the ability to leverage local resources, and the use of appropriate methods and techniques. These actions can take the form of raids, ambushes, precision targeting and elimination, destruction, recovery operations, or boarding operations.

Military support involves providing comprehensive assistance to allied forces, coalition forces, authorities, organizations, or armed formations in the form of advice, training, mentoring, and partnerships. Its goal is to effectively utilize local security forces, including civilian forces, as well as local and international organizations. Additionally, military support may include CIMIC and information operations aimed at gaining and shaping social order for the conducted activities, civilian authorities, and security structures. It may also involve assisting international tribunals and courts in prosecuting war criminals. Military support can extend to aiding rebels, insurgents, armed organizations, as well as one's own forces fighting within or behind enemy lines, especially when they are cut off from the main forces (Encyklopedia Bezpieczeństwa Narodowego, 2024). Examples of such actions and their use in achieving strategic objectives include the Russo-Georgian War of August 2008, Russia's actions in Ukraine that began with the annexation of Crimea, and Iran's use of Hezbollah to further its own strategic goals (Królikowski, 2016).

The results for the code special operations/special activities in the study of media reports show a low code frequency, which may indicate that this is a supplementary tactic, as also suggested by the code correlation results. The label assigned to these activities was linked with equal strength to the following codes: conventional operations (army), unconventional operations (guerrilla groups), and the informational, intelligence, and air domains. This may suggest that special operations support conventional activities and that there is cooperation between the army and guerrilla groups in these operations. The domain indicators show that these actions influence or leverage the informational domain, which, while having equal strength with the other two domains, is closely tied to both intelligence operations and the air domain. It is important to note that the air domain also includes technologies enabling the monitoring and collection of intelligence data, for example, through the use of Unmanned Aerial Vehicles (UAVs).

An analysis of the literature points to another significant tactic within the component of unconventional military operations: the use of PMCs in both the hybrid conflict phase and the hybrid warfare phase. PMCs are corporate entities paid to provide military services. These services can vary widely and include specialized tasks such as strategic planning, intelligence, land, sea, or air reconnaissance, air operations (manned or unmanned), satellite surveillance and intelligence, knowledge transfer related to military applications, and logistical or technical support for conventional armed forces (Council of the European Union, 2023). Stefan Pifer and Norman de Castro emphasize that PMCs are becoming a key element in modern conflicts, especially within the framework of hybrid warfare strategies. PMCs offer a wide range of services, from logistical support to combat and intelligence operations (as confirmed by the analyses mentioned above). They are an attractive tool for states because they allow for the conduct of military operations without the need for directly engaging regular armed forces. PMCs provide states with the ability to pursue military objectives while maintaining plausible deniability, thereby reducing political risk and enabling the circumvention of legislative oversight (De Castro, 2021; Pifer, 2014). PMCs operate on behalf of governments and private entities, and their development is part of the process of privatizing security, they are described as a new form of mercenary force. Their growth occurred after the Cold War, in many Western countries, the privatization of military services allowed for an expansion of the range of services provided by PMCs, including: the protection of arms and military equipment transports, the training of armed forces, embargo enforcement in foreign territories, and the protection of military service providers (MSPs). Doug Brooks divides the market of MSPs into the following three sectors:

- Non-lethal Service Providers – intelligence, logistics, demining, etc.
- Private Security Companies (PSCs) – companies that provide passive protection of property and individuals, not only domestically but also in conflict zones.

- Passive and Active PMCs – the former carry out tasks not directly related to combat (e.g. training), while the latter take direct part in combat operations.

Many contemporary researchers of the private security and military firm market refer to current employees of such companies, who provide services in external markets, as "new mercenaries." Interestingly, some of the companies selling these services employ only administrative staff, who handle the recruitment (hiring) of contractors, who are then delegated to tasks with maximum profit potential. The activities of PMCs in international markets are not fully regulated by law, particularly in conflict zones, where mercenaries are not granted combatant rights on the battlefield (Jabłońska-Bonca, 2017; Encyklopedia Bezpieczeństwa Narodowego, 2024).

Most PMCs are established in wealthy Western countries, such as the United States, the United Kingdom, and Germany, but not exclusively. For some time now, they have also been operating in Russia, where they have recently become official. In 2012, President Vladimir Putin, in a speech to the State Duma, argued that PMCs are needed for several reasons – to conduct training in former Soviet states, to protect key sectors of the economy (primarily the extraction industry), and to safeguard gas installations and oil pipelines (Encyklopedia Bezpieczeństwa Narodowego, 2024).

In the study The Business of War – Growing Risks from Private Military Companies, the Council of the European Union highlights that, despite apparent similarities, not all PMCs are the same. South Africa, the United States, and Russia provide examples of three fundamental models.

The South African model is based on the modus operandi of the historical company Executive Outcomes (EOs), resembling the employment of traditional mercenaries. These are private armies conducting autonomous military campaigns and financing their operations from the resources of the country in which they operate. For example, in 1996, EOs support for government forces in Sierra Leone was partially paid for through diamond concessions.

The Blackwater USA model has been described as "military entrepreneurship," integrated with and strengthening traditional state armed forces. Between 1989 and 1993, the U.S. government made significant cuts to the military budget in response to federal budget pressures. More expensive equipment programmes were cancelled, and the total number of soldiers was reduced from 2.2 million to 1.6 million. As part of this process, the Department of Defence began outsourcing a range of administrative tasks, particularly in logistics, to civilian companies contracted by the military, allowing the armed forces to focus on combat operations. Since the end of the Cold War, the company's growth has been part of a broader trend towards the privatization of U.S. military forces. Blackwater became a key tool in the U.S. strategy during the war on terror.

Quite a different approach is represented by the Russian Wagner Group (PMC Wagner) which is much more versatile in its operations. While it can be seen as drawing on elements of American models, it does so with impunity, disregarding human rights and international humanitarian law (IHL). This is a model that emerging powers might be inclined to emulate. It is noteworthy that the extent to which PMC Wagner, as a private group, was able to replace the regular Russian army on the battlefield in Ukraine is extraordinary. However, there was clear tension between Wagner and the military establishment. This culminated in an open rebellion in June 2023, when Wagner forces clashed with the Russian military and began a march towards Moscow after taking control of the city of Rostov, the headquarters of Russia's Southern Military District (The Business of War, 2023). The Wagner Group's rebellion highlighted the limitations and potential risks associated with the use of PMCs.

The first major test for PMC Wagner was its intervention in Ukraine in 2014, where the group supported Russian military operations in Crimea and Donbas by providing direct combat support as well as conducting special operations and intelligence missions. Wagner's actions allowed Russia to deny responsibility, as there was no official deployment of regular Russian armed forces in these regions. This enabled Russia to avoid direct international consequences, despite effectively controlling the operation. PMC Wagner operated without overt legitimacy from Russia until the Kremlin formally acknowledged its connection to the group.

The Wagner Group also operated in Syria, where it supported Bashar al-Assad's government from 2015 onwards. Wagner forces participated in key operations, such as the battles for Palmyra and Aleppo, and secured strategic sites like oil fields, which had direct economic significance for financing their operations. The group's activities in Syria brought financial benefits in the form of contracts for the exploitation of natural resources.

PMC Wagner was also involved in operations in other regions of the world, such as Libya, the Central African Republic (CAR), Sudan, and Venezuela. In each of these cases, the group pursued Russia's strategic objectives, helping to maintain or expand Moscow's influence in these regions. For example, in Libya, the Wagner Group supported the forces of General Khalifa Haftar, aiming to secure Russian interests in a region rich in energy resources (De Castro, 2021, pp. 35–40).

In Ukraine, it became particularly evident that the Wagner Group is a combination of a special forces unit and a mafia-style organized crime group. Wagner operatives functioned there as a paramilitary, para-state criminal organization, carrying out both military and illicit activities to further their objectives, blending traditional combat operations with criminal enterprise (The Business of War, 2023), and wherever they appeared, the Wagner Group was suspected of committing acts of torture, rape, and extrajudicial executions.

The combat role is only part of PMC Wagner's destabilizing activities, which, since 2019, have been closely linked to Patriot Media Group, founded by Yevgeny V. Prigozhin. Through this collaboration, they conducted a massive disinformation campaign to support their own interests as well as those of the Russian government, utilizing over 350 different media outlets. Their activities included the use of troll farms to influence election outcomes in both the United States and Europe. After the failed Wagner Group rebellion in Russia, Patriot Media was shut down (The Business of War, 2023). This practice was confirmed in the authors' research on media reports in Ukraine.

It should be noted that the clients of PMCs are not limited to states. Rolf Uesseler divided them into six categories, based on the size of contracts. These are: strong states with well-established legal systems, private enterprises – both global players and medium-sized companies, weak and failed states, which are unable to ensure adequate levels of security or protection against external threats, civil war parties – terrorist networks, liberation movements, international organizations and institutions, and private associations and individuals (Encyklopedia Bezpieczeństwa Narodowego, 2024).

The largest clients of PMCs are undoubtedly strong and developed states, which rely on their services for security both domestically and internationally. In some cases, PMCs account for up to 50% of the personnel in armed forces participating in conflicts abroad. States turn to PMCs for various reasons, but this trend is part of a broader process of dismantling and reconfiguring certain traditional tools of state sovereignty in response to a rapidly evolving security environment (border/territory control, infrastructure protection, hybrid threats, propaganda, etc.). In the West, this trend is often driven by budget pressures, the public's demand to reduce direct state investments in the military (for example, fatigue from the Cold War in the 1990s), and the increasing complexity of certain overseas operations. Modern weaponry is so complex to operate that armed forces, wanting to avoid lengthy and costly soldier training, purchase weapons along with civilian maintenance services. The rise of PMCs is also linked to the overall weakness of state structures, particularly the military, amidst an expanding zone of conflicts. As a result, governments turn to the private sector to achieve better outcomes for the same cost (The Business of War, 2023).

Newly established military enterprises work in parallel for large international corporations as their security companies and are also directed by them to other tasks. The financing of PMCs by corporations is not very transparent. Some large industrial conglomerates have established and financed companies that not only work for them but are often hired out to other clients. For years, particularly in the United States, there has been a close connection between industrial lobbies, security corporations, and politicians. The broad scope of PMC operations means they represent a military tool with potentially far-reaching consequences, which, in the case of hybrid warfare, becomes another critical element in a hybrid strategy (The Business of War, 2023).

The relevant literature and analyses conducted in the study of media reports confirmed the use of unconventional military actions in the war in Ukraine. The main types were diversionary actions (230 mentions), sabotage (118 mentions), and destabilization activities (112 mentions). It is important to note that the high frequency of these labels may suggest that diversion and sabotage are significantly employed in destabilization efforts. Furthermore, the analysis confirmed the presence of other unconventional actions such as guerrilla warfare, intelligence activities, special operations, and the use of PMCs. However, information regarding these types of actions was not as prevalent as the aforementioned ones. This does not imply that these actions were not used on a large scale, but rather that they may not be as prominently discussed in the media or were employed at a different stage of the hybrid strategy or to a lesser extent, complementing conventional operations.

In this section of the analysis of media report findings, it is important to focus not only on the frequency of individual actions but also on their co-occurrence (interrelationships), which allows for identifying involvement in activities related to the war in Ukraine (see Table A2.3). It is also worth noting that, in many cases, the studies encountered situations where a particular code/term exhibited lower strength in its connections but was highly concentrated in the network of these connections. This indicates that these are highly dispersed activities across many areas. Such is the case with sabotage and diversionary actions, which, like other activities (except guerrilla warfare), were most strongly linked to conventional military operations (the army). This suggests that these actions coexist, confirming the hybrid nature of the conflict. In the case of sabotage, stronger connections were observed with non-military activities, such as propaganda, as well as with actions in the informational, intelligence, and political domains. Similarly, diversionary actions demonstrated stronger connections with the informational and intelligence domains, as well as with the maritime domain. Destabilizing actions, which rank third in code frequency, demonstrated stronger connections with activities in the informational and political domains, as well as with the military.

Interestingly, despite the lower frequency of this code, significant connections were identified in intelligence activities and special operations. In the case of intelligence activities, there is involvement from PMCs and terrorist groups. Actions in this area are linked to PSYOPs, disinformation, and activities within the informational, political, and air domains. Special operations, on the other hand, showed equal percentages of connections with guerrilla groups and activities in the informational, intelligence, and airspace domains. It is important to note that actions with a low code frequency should not necessarily be regarded as methodologically referential. However, in the case of hybrid warfare, which essentially follows no set rules, a low code frequency or co-occurrence may provide insights into the evolving direction of this type of warfare.

The results of media coverage analysis can lead to several key conclusions. The primary unconventional military actions involve diversion and sabotage, which may suggest that these actions serve as catalysts for broader or more complex destabilization campaigns. The analysis also shows that these categories of actions are significantly linked with other activities mentioned above or are dispersed, indicating the complexity of hybrid warfare. Lower frequencies may suggest new directions of evolution in such conflicts. Furthermore, as previously mentioned, the overall results of this study confirm that unconventional actions coexist with conventional military operations, supporting the theory of hybrid warfare in Ukraine. Figure 2.4 shows the connections between main codes and co-occurring terms in area unconventional actions.

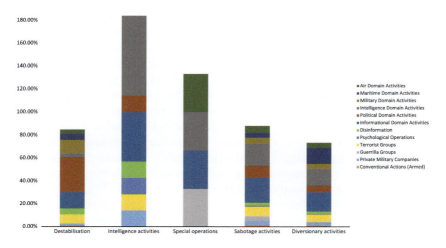

FIGURE 2.4 Connections between main codes and co-occurring terms in area unconventional actions

Source: Own study

Detailed data is provided in Table A2.3 in Appendix 2. The rows of the table display the codes associated with the identified codes describing unconventional actions. The percentage values at the intersection of codes characterizing unconventional actions with related codes indicate how often the analysed action occurred in the context of the associated code.

Non-military actions in hybrid warfare

Non-military actions play a crucial role in hybrid warfare, enabling political objectives to be achieved without the overt use of force. These actions are employed both during the hybrid conflict phase and in hybrid warfare involving military components. The use of these actions varies in scope, scale, and intensity across different phases of a hybrid strategy. The range of non-military actions remains open-ended, due to their opaque nature and the difficulty of clear assessment – likely influenced by the use of AI in such operations. Non-military actions most commonly mentioned in the literature include disinformation, cyber warfare, economic destabilization, and PSYOPs, which often intersect and/or complement each other, creating a web of threats whose impacts on civilians and internal security are difficult to predict. The blurring of boundaries between war and peace, along with the extensive use of non-military means coordinated with societal capabilities, aims to destabilize the opponent without involving significant military resources. As Veronika Stoilova states in her work *The Art of Achieving Political Goals Without Use of Force: War by Non-military Means*, non-military actions in hybrid warfare rely on the principle of synergy, where different forms of pressure are applied simultaneously to achieve the maximum destabilizing effect. This is confirmed by research, which shows that destabilization was a key feature of hybrid warfare with the highest index. These actions are planned and coordinated in such a way that the opponent cannot clearly identify their source or nature, making them difficult to neutralize and increasing their effectiveness. As Stoilova emphasizes, non-military actions are effective tools that can significantly impact the stability of states and societies. Understanding their mechanisms and developing counter-strategies is essential for ensuring security (Stoilova, 2018, pp. 136–142).

So far, no comprehensive catalogue of non-military actions has been developed, primarily due to their concealed nature (the so-called "fog"). Therefore, for the analyses in this section, actions described in scientific and open sources were used, along with the results of media report studies, which are detailed in Table A2.4 in Appendix 2.

Information warfare (disinformation) is one of the greatest threats both in the hybrid conflict phase and during war. This is primarily because it shapes public perception and, in times of war, can impact the physical safety of civilians.

From the NATO viewpoint, information warfare is an operation conducted in order to gain an information advantage over the opponent. It consists in controlling one's own information space, protecting access to one's own information, while acquiring and using the opponent's information, destroying their information systems and disrupting the information flow. Information warfare is not a new phenomenon, yet it contains innovative elements as the effect of technological development, which results in information being disseminated faster and on a larger scale (Media – (Dis)Information – Security, 2020). On the other hand, according to the European Commission, disinformation as a false or misleading content is spread with an intention to deceive or secure economic or political gain, and which may cause public harm. Whereas misinformation is false or misleading content shared without harmful intent though the effects can be still harmful. The spread of both disinformation and misinformation can have a range of harmful consequences, such as threatening our democracies, polarizing debates, and putting the health, security, and environment of EU citizens at risk (Tackling Online Disinformation, 2024).

In the context of information warfare, the acronym FIMI (False, Inaccurate, Misleading Information) is increasingly encountered. In a 2022 report, the Council of the European Union emphasized that FIMI is often used as part of broader hybrid campaigns aimed at misleading, deceiving, and destabilizing societies, as well as creating and exploiting cultural and social tensions. These campaigns also negatively impact both external and internal security. The report highlights that the strategic and coordinated use of information manipulation and interference by Russia, which preceded and accompanied its unprovoked and unjustified military aggression against Ukraine, illustrates this multifaceted threat. It has specific effects on various areas of internal and external policy, particularly on the achievement of CFSP (Common Foreign and Security Policy) and CSDP (Common Security and Defence Policy) objectives (Council conclusions on Foreign Information Manipulation and Interference; FIMI, 2022).

An element of information warfare is information operations (influence operations), which, as indicated by RAND Corporation, involve gathering tactical intelligence about the opponent as well as disseminating propaganda to gain a competitive advantage over the adversary (RAND Corporation – Information Operations, 2024). As part of information operations, actions such as propaganda and disinformation are utilized. (It is important to highlight that the latter term is not precisely defined and may be misused.) According to the EU vs Disinfo platform, 237 disinformation cases relating to Ukraine have been tracked since

February 2022, and over 5,500 total disinformation cases about Ukraine have been tracked since the establishment of the platform, in 2015 (Treyger et al., 2022; Hoyle, Šlerka, 2024, pp. 11–20). The European Union Agency for Cybersecurity (ENISA) Threat Landscape Report 2022 – Disinformation and Misinformation also demonstrated that disinformation was used in Ukraine as a tool of information warfare even before the physical conflict. Russia conducted mass disinformation campaigns to prepare for its invasion of Ukraine, with baseless claims such as "Ukraine planning an attack on Donbas" being used to justify military actions. Maria Avdeeva, a Ukrainian founder and research director of the European Expert Association, explains that the adopted approach aimed to overwhelm people with the sheer volume of false information, producing an effect similar to DDoS attacks (ENISA Threat Landscape 2024, 2023).

All parties involved in the conflict, including Russia, Ukraine, and other countries, have used disinformation campaigns to promote their agendas. Russian disinformation focused on justifying the invasion and portraying Ukraine as the aggressor, while Ukrainian disinformation concentrated on motivating its troops and highlighting Russian military losses. AI-assisted disinformation, such as deepfakes, also played a significant role – spreading fake videos of leaders like Vladimir Putin and Volodymyr Zelensky expressing views contrary to their own (Wypior, 2023).

The latest ENISA Threat Landscape 2023 report indicates that disinformation campaigns also targeted other countries, often in the context of strategic geopolitical objectives. Examples include strengthening Russian influence in Africa and media cooperation between China and Russia, focusing on anti-Western narratives. The report identified 386 disinformation websites related to Russia and Ukraine, operating in various languages such as English, French, German, and Italian. To reflect a broader set of potential threats, the report uses the more general term "information manipulation," emphasizing behaviour rather than the truthfulness of content, highlighting the intent to conduct malicious activities with negative impacts (ENISA Threat Landscape, 2023–2024). According to the report by Hybrid CO, Cause for Concern: The Continuing Success and Impact of Kremlin Disinformation Campaigns, information manipulation is an integral part of Russia's hybrid strategy, particularly in the context of the war with Ukraine. Trend analysis indicates an increase in such activities, aligning with the findings of the ENISA report (Hoyle, Šlerka, 2024) of Microsoft from 2022. The report identifies three phases of hybrid warfare in Ukraine. The first phase involved cyber and influence operations leading up to the invasion. The second phase focused on neutralizing both foreign and domestic support for Kyiv. The third phase consisted of intensifying cyber and influence operations to reinforce Russia's political and military actions (Defending Ukraine: Early Lessons from the Cyber War – report 2022; Hoyle, Šlerka, 2024).

According to data from the *EU vs DiSiNFO* report, during Russia's annexation of Crimea, propaganda and disinformation included false reports about alleged threats to the Russian-speaking population of Crimea and the legality of the referendum. For example, it was claimed that the referendum on Crimea's annexation to Russia was in accordance with international law, whereas the international community deemed it illegal. After the downing of Malaysia Airlines Flight MH17 over eastern Ukraine, Russia propagated various conspiracy theories aimed at shifting the blame to Ukraine or other Western countries. False accusations were spread, such as claims that a Ukrainian fighter jet shot down the plane or that it was a false flag operation organized by the West. Following the invasion of Ukraine in February 2022, Russia intensified its disinformation operations. For instance, claims were spread about the existence of secret American biological laboratories in Ukraine, allegedly developing biological weapons. After the discovery of mass graves and evidence of war crimes in Bucha, Russian propaganda sought to deny Russian responsibility. Russia claimed that the massacre was fabricated by Ukraine or that the victims were the result of Ukrainian attacks. The Russian media have also disseminated disinformation about Western-imposed sanctions, claiming they were ineffective and harmed the countries imposing them more than Russia itself, suggesting that the sanctions caused hunger and humanitarian disasters in Europe (EUvsDisinfo, 2024).

A similar use of disinformation occurred during Operation Cast Lead, the Israeli offensive in the Gaza Strip, where both sides engaged in intense disinformation campaigns. Israel, emphasizing its right to self-defence, portrayed its actions as precise military operations targeting terrorists, despite evidence of widespread civilian casualties. Meanwhile, Hamas disseminated genuine images of civilian victims and destruction caused by Israel, as well as publishing photos of supposed victims of Israeli attacks, which were often from other conflicts or manipulated. During Operation Protective Edge, both sides used social media to spread their versions of events. Israel accused Hamas of using civilians as human shields, while Hamas shared images of civilian casualties.

During the 2018 Gaza protests, known as the Great March of Return, both sides engaged in intense information campaigns. Israel claimed that Hamas organized the protests to launch attacks on Israeli soldiers, sharing videos of Palestinian demonstrators throwing stones and Molotov cocktails. On the other hand, Hamas portrayed the protesters as peaceful demonstrators.

Following the *7 October 2023 Hamas attack*, in which approximately 1,200 people were killed, Israel launched an intensive information campaign, sharing images from the attack to justify its retaliatory actions. The Israeli government used paid advertisements on social media and other platforms to emphasize the brutality of the attack, seeking to gain support for its actions and control the narrative around the conflict. Images from the massacre were distributed across Western social media and even through video games targeting families. Israel also used influencer networks and pro-Israeli organizations to promote its message and discredit pro-Palestinian statements by reducing their visibility and promoting pro-Israeli content. After the 2023 conflict escalation, both Hamas and Israel employed disinformation. Pro-Israeli groups accused Palestinian journalists of collaborating with Hamas during the October 7 attack, allegations that were later debunked. Meanwhile, pro-Palestinian groups spread conspiracy theories about Israel's actions (Accorsi, 2024).

The analysis of media reports confirmed the use of this form of action in the war in Ukraine (both the labels *information warfare* and *disinformation*). The networks of connections (co-occurrences) showed that information warfare has strong links with the diplomatic, political, military, and economic domains. Meanwhile, disinformation is connected to conventional military actions (the army), the informational domain, the political domain, and, slightly below the 10% threshold, the intelligence domain. These findings suggest that both information warfare and disinformation are key components of the hybrid strategy in the war in Ukraine. Information warfare is more strongly associated with broad diplomatic and political activities, while disinformation is heavily utilized in military operations and informational manipulations. This may indicate that this aspect of the hybrid strategy in Ukraine relies on the synergy of these two actions to maximize destabilization.

Directly linked to information warfare and disinformation are propaganda activities. In general terms, propaganda is a process involving the deliberate and planned use of any form of public or mass-produced informational messages, designed to influence the minds and emotions of a target audience for a specific purpose. Most definitions associate propaganda with methods of socio-technical influence, such as manipulation, persuasion, and suggestion, often involving a more or less systematic effort to manipulate the beliefs, attitudes, or actions of others. Propaganda campaigns follow a pattern composed of five elements: source, time, audience, subject, and mission (goal) – these elements are collectively referred to as STASM (Source, Time, Audience, Subject, Mission). Propaganda can be used by states, political parties, social organizations, informal groups, and individuals. In the relevant literature, various typologies of propaganda are distinguished, considering multiple classification criteria. A brief overview of these typologies is provided below (Encyklopedia Bezpieczeństwa Narodowego, 2024; Jowett, O'Donnell, 2006).

Based on the techniques and methods of influence used, propaganda is classified as:

- White propaganda – where the sources and the intentions of the sender are openly disclosed.
- Grey propaganda – where the sources of information and the intentions of the sender are not revealed.
- Black propaganda – which involves attributing one's own propaganda activities to the opponent.
- Another classification criterion divides propaganda into:
- Offensive propaganda – aimed at gaining new supporters,
- Defensive propaganda – focused on retaining existing supporters.

Based on the range of influence, propaganda can be classified as:

- Mass propaganda – directed at broad segments of society,
- Group propaganda – targeting specific social, professional, or ethnic groups,
- Individual propaganda – aimed at single individuals.

Finally, based on the form of communication, propaganda can be:

- Verbal propaganda – any actions using spoken or written words, such as speeches, articles, leaflets, etc.,
- Non-verbal propaganda – using images, sounds, gestures, symbols, etc. Examples include posters, films, music, theatrical performances, and more.
- Given the objective of the propaganda, the following types can be distinguished:
- Conversion propaganda – aimed at changing an individual's awareness, views, and loyalty towards a given social group,
- Divisive propaganda – focused on fragmenting or dividing a community,
- Unifying propaganda – aimed at eliminating divisions and uniting society around a particular cause,
- Counter-propaganda – aimed at weakening or preventing the achievement of the opponent's propaganda goals.

A particular type of propaganda is war propaganda, which involves actions aimed at conveying information that creates a positive image of one's own armed forces and/or a negative image of the enemy, thereby lowering the opponent's morale, causing panic, and encouraging desertion. War propaganda is often regarded as an essential element of warfare. It is believed to have the power to effectively transform the perception of initially unpopular military actions into accepted or even desired ones. It has the capacity to dramatically alter attitudes, value systems, ethical norms, and social legitimacy, introducing new orders and hierarchies within the targeted society. Such actions are widely recognized as destructive and play a significant role during times of war (Kołodziejczak, 2018; Marlin, 2013). For example, during World War II, war propaganda contributed to the creation of a false image of reality aimed at mobilizing both civilians and the military to support war efforts. As numerous studies have shown, these actions, though often based on lies and disinformation, could effectively mobilize people into action. It is fitting here to recall the words of Hiram Johnson: "The first casualty of war is truth." As Adam Kołodziejczyk notes, war propaganda is more complex than what is presented in common knowledge and popular metaphors. Rather than being an all-powerful force capable of easily influencing millions of people and changing their perceptions of reality, these actions mostly serve as a mechanism of self-justification for people. In other words, instead of having the ability to dramatically transform public opinion, most propaganda serves as a cognitive, moral, and legitimizing message that appeals to the values held by the society it targets (Kołodziejczak, 2024). Urszula Jarecka, in Propaganda wojny. Media wizualne XX wieku wobec przyjaźni i solidarności, points out that during wartime, propaganda, the informational sphere (disinformation), and even education become similar and essentially represent persuasion using any method that optimally influences the target group. She identifies three levels of manipulation: the first targets one's own nation, army, and home front, the second focuses on the enemy, its army, and civilian population, and the third is directed at international public opinion (Jarecka, 2008).

Keir Giles notes that the Russian media campaign, both within Russia and in Western countries, has proven to be highly effective. This is the result of long-term efforts, backed by significant investments and skillful use of television and social media. Giles believes that Russia has a sophisticated arsenal of propaganda warfare, which NATO and the EU currently cannot compete with. Russia's practice of information warfare against Ukraine utilizes tried-and-tested influence tools combined with modern technology and new capabilities. When examining the goals and principles of these actions, one can see similarities to the subversive campaigns of the Cold War era. Despite these similarities, it took the West a long time to recognize them. This delay occurred for two reasons. First, there is currently a lack of collective institutional memory in the societies targeted by Russian propaganda, much of these populations consist of people born after the political transformations or those who no longer remember Soviet subversion. Secondly, the substantial resources invested by Russia in internet-based technologies have contributed to the development of media outlets targeting both internal and external audiences (e.g. "Russia Today") and the use of social media and language functions to communicate with target audiences in their own languages. Russia recognized the need for advancement in this area during the Chechen War in 1999, when it became apparent that its opponent was much more adept at using the internet for propaganda purposes. Since then, the Russian Federation has tightened control over public internet access and focused on developing methods to use the internet for attacks as part of information warfare. During the conflict with Georgia in 2008, despite achieving a conventional military victory, significant shortcomings in Russia's warfare and media capabilities were noted. There was a clear disparity between the Georgian president addressing Western audiences in foreign languages and Russia's delayed and ineffective media responses. Although the outcome led to recommendations for creating Russian information warfare forces to manage information campaigns, the focus shifted towards development in other sectors. The protest movements associated with the Arab Spring and the election protests in Russia in 2011–2012 led to further refinement of Russia's information warfare strategy. Attempts to use automated systems proved insufficient, which influenced the decision to create the Kremlin's Troll Army, recruiting foreign-language speakers and journalists. This initiative achieved significant successes – effective media control was established in Russia, and Kremlin-aligned narratives began reaching Western media outlets (an example being the aforementioned media messaging following the downing of Malaysia Airlines Flight MH17).

Before the 2022 invasion of Ukraine, the primary goal of Russian propaganda was to weaken NATO and EU unity and instil fear within societies. During the migrant crisis on the borders of Poland and Lithuania with Belarus, Russian propaganda accused Polish and Lithuanian border guards of human rights violations, publishing false reports and manipulated videos. Keir Giles' report includes data on over 100,000 posts about the migrant crisis published within just a few months. (See more in *Keir Giles, Moscow's Media Campaign on the War in Ukraine*; Giles, 2023).

Aleksander Olech from CyberDefence24 notes that propaganda (especially digital) is pervasive in the context of the Israeli-Palestinian conflict. The published content emphasizes the crimes committed by both sides, and many of the images, opinions, and news used for this purpose are false, leading to strong polarization and even inciting aggression online and in the streets. On social media platforms (Facebook, Instagram, Discord, Twitter), there are anti-Semitic statements calling for boycotts of Israeli products and companies. On the same platforms, Israel conducts its own informational activities against supporters of Palestine. In addition to online actions, there are also dozens of anonymous calls to non-governmental organizations supporting the parties in the conflict (Olech, 2024).

A review of media reports showed that propaganda is a particularly intensively used action in the war in Ukraine (956 mentions). Propaganda demonstrates strong connections with conventional military actions (the army) and the informational and political domains. This result may suggest that propaganda is actively employed in media and other informational channels, aimed at controlling the narrative, shaping public opinion, and manipulating information to influence both societal perception and the opponent. It is also used for political destabilization, strengthening one's own position, and weakening the opponent. This can include, for example, disinformation campaigns targeting political leaders and institutions, aiming to undermine their authority and credibility. Furthermore, the analysis confirmed that the understanding of propaganda aligns with its general definitions, describing it as the deliberate and planned use of informational messages to influence the minds and emotions of recipients. The analysis also confirmed alignment with the STASM elements and the three levels of manipulation mentioned by Jarecka. The results indicated that propaganda is a particularly intensively utilized action with a wide scope, showing strong connections to the key areas of hybrid warfare. It is important to note its evolving and integrated methods, allowing for increasingly precise and effective manipulation. What distinguishes the analysis results is the connection of propaganda with the informational domain. This supports what Jahan Farkas and Christina Neumayer emphasize: that in modern conflicts and hybrid wars, conducted in a highly developed digital era, propaganda has adapted to new platforms and technologies. Social media has become a key tool for disseminating propaganda, with bots and troll farms playing significant roles in spreading disinformation. The use of digital media in hybrid warfare underscores the evolving nature of propaganda and its ongoing relevance in modern conflicts (Farkas, Neumayer, 2020).

Another non-military action is offensive operations in cyberspace. These often involve cyberattacks by intelligence agencies or affiliated hackers. The aim is to paralyse the targeted state, its administration, and its critical infrastructure (Galeotti, 2016). Gazmed Huskaj defines these actions as a sequence of planned activities carried out by an organized group of individuals using hardware and software, intended to compromise the confidentiality, integrity, or availability of the opponent's systems (Huskaj, 2023, pp. 476–479). According to Burt, the most common methods of cyberattacks include wiper malware, ransomware, and phishing.

Strategic documents of Russia, such as the National Security Strategy of Russia from 2021, identify cyberspace as a tool for destabilizing opponents. Cyber operations during the conflict with Ukraine were used by Russia primarily for disinformation and intelligence. Such actions against Estonia, Georgia, and Ukraine were also supported by information campaigns and did not aim to directly support military operations (Dziwisz, Sajduk, 2023). The cyberattack on Estonia in 2007 disrupted the functioning of government websites, the financial sector, and emergency services. Conversely, the cyberattacks on Georgia in 2008 supported both information and military operations, disrupting the communication and strategic actions of the Georgian government. During the annexation of Crimea and subsequent military actions from 2013 to 2022, including the NotPetya attack, Russian cyberattacks had global consequences (Štrucl, 2022, pp. 103–123). For example, there were disruptions in the logistics, pharmaceutical, energy, and transport sectors, as well as financial losses amounting to hundreds of millions of dollars and operational downtimes due to interrupted supply chains. Another example of a Russian cyberattack was the monitoring of email correspondence in major U.S. federal agencies in 2020, which facilitated the hacking of SolarWinds (Hovhannisyan, 2024).

According to Tom Burt, there has been close coordination between cyber operations and land military operations since the onset of Russia's invasion of Ukraine. A day before the invasion on 24 February 2022, strategic Russian cyberattacks targeted Ukrainian objectives. Russia attacked the satellite internet infrastructure of the Ukrainian provider Viasat a few hours before the invasion began, aiming to weaken the operational capabilities of the targeted country by destroying data and disrupting the functionality of government systems. Ukraine successfully countered these threats and mitigated the effects of the attack by using cloud technology to transmit government data across various systems, both within and outside the country, rendering attacks on individual data centres ineffective.

After the withdrawal of Russian forces from previously occupied areas of Ukraine, there was an increase in Russian missile attacks on critical infrastructure, such as energy, water supply, and transportation systems. These attacks deprived 80% of Kyiv of access to running water and left over 10 million Ukrainians without electricity. At the same time, coordinated destructive cyberattacks carried out by the Seashell Blizzard group targeted the same sectors. Although it is not possible to definitively establish the connections between the Russian military and cyber operations, the shared objectives and synchronization of actions provide compelling evidence that war efforts were organized and conducted simultaneously across multiple domains.

Although the cyber tools and tactics used by Russia in the invasion of Ukraine, such as destructive software, espionage attacks, and information operations, are not new or unique, the scale and coordination of their use as strategic elements of a large-scale military campaign are unprecedented.

Similar to other areas, cyber warfare is not confined solely to the conflict in Ukraine. As noted by Check Point Software Technologies Ltd., the first weeks of the war between Israel and Hamas saw an increase in the number of cyberattacks on targets in Israel. Most of these attacks targeted the government and security sector, with a 52% increase in the number of incidents. These operations included various techniques, such as DDoS attacks, the use of wiper malware, and exploiting security vulnerabilities to spread disinformation about missile attacks (The Iron Swords War, 2023).

A Cloudflare report indicates that several such attacks were carried out against Israeli websites on 7 October, leading to millions of demands per second. Newspaper, technology company, bank and government websites have fallen victim to these attacks. One of the most successful DDoS attacks paralysed the Jerusalem Post website for two days. Hackers also used wiper malware, designed to erase data from files by overwriting them or creating random strings. An example of such software is BiBi, named to provoke the Israeli government and Prime Minister Benjamin "Bibi" Netanyahu. The malware in question was detected on both Linux and Windows systems. Although most operations were unsuccessful, the attacks showed potential destruction and were attributed to the Hamas-linked groupArid (Cyber attacks in the Israel-Hamas war, 2023).

Despite the limited resources of Israeli cybersecurity systems, both governmental and private, to protect against hostile cyber operations, Israel manages well against various attack vectors targeting many public and private websites. However, documented cases of successful "hack and leak" practices have emerged, such as the leak of personal data of students from Ono Academic College, which led to the temporary closure of the college's website. Another successful attack targeted the "Red Alert" app, used by Israelis to receive notifications about incoming rocket attacks. The hacktivist group AnonGhost exploited a vulnerability in the app and sent false notifications about an alleged upcoming nuclear attack, aiming to spread disinformation and fear among the population.

On 27 October 2023, internet connectivity in the Gaza Strip was severed for approximately 34 hours due to a telecommunications blackout caused by Israel. This blackout was condemned by several international organizations, such as the World Health Organization (WHO) and the Palestinian Red Crescent, which stated that it prevented ambulances from reaching the injured. The use of telecommunications blackouts by Israel raises significant legal issues, particularly in the context of IHL. While Israel argued that the blackout was necessary for the protection of its forces, critics contend that it hindered humanitarian assistance and disrupted medical communication (Israel–Hamas 2023 Symposium, 2023).

As regards Israeli cyber operations, the main unit is Unit 8200, which is quite frequently compared to the NSA in the United States or GCHQ in the United Kingdom. Unit 8200 has been involved in significant cyber operations, including the Stuxnet attack on Iranian uranium enrichment facilities in Natanz between 2005 and 2010. This operation significantly delayed the Iranian nuclear programme and is considered the first true cyber weapon due to its complexity and impact. In addition to Stuxnet, Unit 8200 developed advanced malware such as Duqu and Flame, which were used in various cyberattacks, particularly against Iran. An example is the cyberattack on the Shahid Rajaee port in Iran in 2020. The Israeli private sector has also played a crucial role, producing well-known spyware programmes like Pegasus and Predator, which are highly regarded for their advanced monitoring capabilities.

Hamas, while lacking cyber capabilities comparable to Israel, has also carried out several significant attacks. In 2019, the Israeli Air Force targeted and destroyed a Hamas unit responsible for cyber operations. Despite these setbacks, Hamas continued attempts to infiltrate Israeli systems through phishing campaigns and malware attacks, albeit with limited success. Notably, there was a lack of increased cyber activity from Hamas prior to the events of 7 October 2023. Google analysts suggest that Hamas assessed the risks associated with cyber operations before the attack outweighed the potential benefits. After the October 7 attack, various regional actors, especially Iran and Hezbollah, intensified their cyber activities against Israel. Iran was responsible for about 80% of phishing attacks on Israel in the six months following the attack, targeting government organizations, think tanks, universities, media outlets, politicians, journalists, and experts. Hezbollah also spread malware through fake websites impersonating institutions like Sheba Medical Center. These efforts aimed to destabilize Israeli society and weaken public trust in state institutions. Israel's response included both defensive measures and offensive cyber operations.

The use of cyber capabilities in conflicts, such as the war between Israel and Palestine and the Russian invasion of Ukraine, demonstrates that cyber operations often accompany kinetic actions, but do not necessarily precede them (Kozłowski, 2024). In the future, we can expect that offensive capabilities in cyberspace will continue to evolve and become even more dangerous. Governments and the international community should therefore urgently work on enhancing security, increasing preparedness, and clearly stating that illegal offensive actions in cyberspace will not be tolerated (Burt, 2023).

The analysis of media report findings did not identify this label as particularly significant in terms of the number of topics addressed in this area, but it confirmed important connections with conventional actions (the army), irregular actions and cybercriminal groups, as well as the informational, political, intelligence, legal, and air domains, alongside cybersecurity. The analysis may suggest that, despite the code's low representation, its connections with other codes allow for the conclusion that these actions support the effectiveness of military operations and activities across key domains of hybrid warfare on multiple levels.

Psychological operations

The highest perfection is to break the enemy's resistance without fighting. This phrase by Sun Tzu perfectly sums up the essence of psychological warfare (Sun Tzu Sun Bin, 2012, p. 6) (PSYOPs). According to the Cambridge dictionary definition "psychological operations" are military activities that involve trying to influence the enemy's beliefs and state of mind (Cambridge Dictionary, 2024). RAND, on the other hand, defines PSYOPs (psychological warfare) as the planned use of propaganda and other PSYOPs to influence the opinions, emotions, attitudes, and behaviour of opposing groups (Psychological Warfare, 2024; Beauchamp-Mustafaga, 2023). On the other hand, according to the report Essential Security against Evolving Threats (ESET) PSYOP is a psychological operation with the goal of conveying selected information and indicators to certain audiences to influence their motives, objective reasoning, and behaviours. This can be aimed at countries, organizations, and groups of power (Kovalová, 2024).

PSYOPs are a significant element of modern hybrid conflicts, combining traditional military actions with advanced techniques of cyber warfare and disinformation. According to Danilo delle Fave and Marco Verrocchio from the International Team for the Study of Security Verona (ITSS) (Fave, Verrocchio, 2022), they encompass all psychological techniques aimed at influencing the behaviour, emotions, and motivations of targets (governments, armies, companies, etc.), intended to support other operations by minimizing efforts and maximizing gains.

Three types of PSYOPs are identified:

- Tactical – employed during a conflict,
- Operational – used before and after a military operation to support the commander's plans,
- Strategic – encompassing actions that a government can take to influence attitudes, perceptions, and behaviours abroad.

Currently, as the authors emphasize, the boundaries between tactical, operational, and strategic PSYOPs are becoming blurred due to the global nature of information dissemination. Furthermore, tactical PSYOPs in contemporary high-intensity warfare are considered more dangerous than strategic and operational ones due to the use of more precise guided weaponry. In tactical PSYOPs, technology plays a crucial role – leaflets are being replaced by SMS and audio messages, and in Ukraine, Orlan-10 drones are used to disseminate information directly to the mobile phones of Ukrainian soldiers. According to Eva Kristinova, psychological warfare operations are difficult to predict, plan, implement, and counteract because they involve mental and emotional processes of which the intended targets may not be aware. Modern strategies and tactics integrate psychological warfare operations, utilizing all forms of traditional and social media platforms. With the spread of information technologies and the multidimensional perspectives of new technologies, such as AI tools, the scope and reach of PSYOPs may soon encompass unprecedented domains and applications (Kristinova, 2024).

Psychological warfare operations have a long history, dating back to ancient times, although such a clear definition likely did not exist then. However, their use significantly increased during the two world wars, where targeting the morale of enemy soldiers via radio stations played a key role. The effects were twofold: first, the intended effect was to demoralize the enemy and break their will to fight; second, the often unintended consequence was increased distrust, confusion, and uncertainty among enemy ranks. After 1945, PSYOPs became more widely utilized. In Korea, the United States established a special unit tasked with persuading enemy soldiers to surrender and preventing support for the enemy from South Koreans. PSYOPs were also closely linked to the actions of Marines during the first Gulf War, achieving significant successes. For example, the 9th PSYOPs Battalion facilitated the surrender of 1,405 encircled Iraqi soldiers on an island by deploying helicopters with loudspeakers. Since the end of the Cold War, psychological warfare has undergone a dramatic transformation. According to NATO's Joint Psychological Operations Doctrine, developed during the "war on terrorism," key elements of PSYOPs include planning, the use of modern communication methods, and collaboration with allies.

Currently, in the context of psychological warfare, precise terms such as "information manipulation" or broader terms like "influence operations" are used. Often, it is overlooked that these definitions typically omit the crucial human aspect susceptible to attacks – emotions. Unlike information manipulation, which targets cognitive processes and perceptions, PSYOPs aim to attack deeper levels and influence fundamental human emotions (anger, fear, hatred). Contemporary PSYOPs encompass a range of tactics and actors, including media propaganda, leaflet distribution, false flag operations, and information warfare. The tactics of PSYOPs are increasingly being incorporated into internal defence planning. In other words, states are interested not only in developing offensive capabilities to strike and demoralize the enemy psychologically but also in ensuring that the same enemy does not succeed in using such tactics against them internally. Many modern examples demonstrate the international and domestic security implications carried by psychological warfare operations (Kovalová, 2024).

Since the beginning of the war in Ukraine, Russia has been using disinformation, propaganda, and false flag operations to target the psychological state of Ukrainian armed forces and the political and military leadership. From the mobilization of troops at and around the Ukrainian border for nearly a month, Russia's goal was not only to prepare for the invasion – an equally important objective was to intimidate Ukraine and break its will to resist even before the fighting began. Similarly, there were widespread and coordinated propaganda narratives aimed at domestic and international audiences, covering topics such as the fascist nature of Ukrainian leadership, genocide in the Donbas and other human rights violations, the development of biological weapons, President Zelensky's capitulation, and anti-refugee sentiments.

Among the campaigns identified by ESET is Texonto, which aimed to weaken the morale of Ukrainian society around the second anniversary of Russia's invasion of Ukraine at the end of 2023. This operation primarily involved sending spam emails intended to sow doubt and fear in the minds of Ukrainians. The first wave of attacks, detected in November 2023, included hundreds of emails with attached PDF files suggesting, among other things, interruptions in heating supplies and shortages of medicines. The second, less complex wave contained darker messages, including appeals from supposed Ukrainian citizens for self-harm to avoid military service. As ESET notes, the emergence of PSYOPs on the digital battlefield adds a new layer to the already complex hybrid war between Russia and Ukraine, and examples like the Texonto operation highlight the shift of the battlefield from the physical to the psychological, aimed at demoralizing and destabilizing communities through disinformation campaigns (Kovalová, 2024), as has already been discussed in other parts of this study.

In the context of utilizing PSYOPs, it is worth noting that both the Russian Federation and the United States have developed their doctrines for PSYOPs. In the U.S. doctrine, PSYOPs leverage information-related capabilities in conjunction with other operational lines and can support military intelligence, cyber operations, electronic warfare, military deception, civil–military operations, and even public affairs. The U.S. doctrine states that PSYOPs aim to influence foreign target groups through the development of messages and actions designed to change the attitudes and behaviours of those groups. A key aspect of the U.S. doctrine is the dissemination of messages based on true information, as false information is considered a double-edged sword that could jeopardize the long-term credibility and effectiveness of future PSYOPs.

The Russian doctrine, on the other hand, acknowledges the use of false information. Russians have developed a military doctrine that envisions the implementation of PSYOPs even in peacetime. The Russian doctrine has expanded the concept of "new generation warfare" and centres around the idea that contemporary threats to the Russian Federation stem from the "informational sphere." Like in Soviet times, information warfare employs reflective control – manipulating the decision-making process by altering key factors in the opponent's perception of the world, leading them to choose actions most beneficial to Russian objectives. Another tool is active measures, which aim to undermine, disrupt, and discredit target countries. One of the most paradigmatic ways to employ PSYOPs is through trolling, utilizing social media algorithms, and targeting key demographics susceptible to their propaganda.

The doctrines of the United States and Russia differ in their approaches to the use of false information, reflecting variations in strategy and tactics for conducting PSYOPs. In a rapidly changing world, where the boundaries between types of PSYOPs are blurring, understanding and adapting to these methods is crucial for effectively conducting modern warfare operations (Kovalová, 2024).

The analysis of media report findings showed that PSYOPs is a poorly represented area in the media coverage. This may stem from both a lack of interest among journalists in this field and difficulties in separating PSYOPs from other activities undertaken within the framework of hybrid warfare. Nevertheless, it is worth noting the network of connections between labels that coexist with conventional military operations, irregular actions, propaganda, and disinformation. This arrangement of dependencies may suggest that psychological manipulation could be an important tool of influence. However, further research in this area is necessary to better understand its role and effectiveness in the context of modern conflicts.

Cognitive operations are linked to PSYOPs, the objective of which is disrupting thought and cognitive processes using advanced tools, primarily conducted in the informational and cyber domains. In a general sense, these actions are used to control the actions of adversaries and allies. Cognitive warfare, in its basic definition, encompasses activities aimed at controlling the mental states and behaviours of individuals. This concept is not new, it has gained significance with the rapid advancement of information and communication technologies. Examples of Russia's interference in the U.S. presidential elections and the Brexit referendum in the United Kingdom demonstrate how these actions can impact democratic processes. Similarly, China has intervened in the politics of Australia and New Zealand and undermined the management of the COVID-19 pandemic in Taiwan. Cognitive warfare poses a particular threat to democracy, where freedom of speech is exploited and undermined by disinformation. According to Tzu-Chieh Hung and Tzu-Wei Hung in *How China's Cognitive Warfare Works: A Frontline Perspective of Taiwan's Anti-Disinformation Wars*, despite the growing importance of cognitive warfare, there is still no consensus on its definition. It is often confused with concepts such as information warfare or cyber warfare. Siman-Tov emphasizes that many political methods, such as propaganda, public relations, and public diplomacy, can be used to influence cognition (Siman-Tov, 2019, pp. 1–39). Rogers argues that confusing operational information warfare with cognitive warfare is a categorical error that needs to be addressed (Rogers, 2021, pp. 81–106). Bernal et al. distinguish cognitive warfare from information warfare, emphasizing that the latter focuses on controlling the flow of information, while cognitive warfare aims to control the responses of individuals and groups to that information (Bernal et al., 2020). In other words, there is still no consensus on the definition of cognitive warfare. Hung and Hung propose to understand cognitive warfare as actions taken to manipulate environmental stimuli aimed at controlling the mental states and behaviours of both adversaries and supporters in the context of both hot and cold wars (Hung, Hung, 2022).

The most effective actions in these areas occur in the cognitive sphere, changing the nature of available information and the perception of target audiences. Contemporary cognitive warfare is a battle for the human mind and the ability to transform the worldview in society within a specific area. While information operations are not new, modern technologies allow for asymmetrical and rapid large-scale actions, meaning the spread of information in cognitive warfare may be beyond the control of states and could lead to the expansion of dominance and the transformation of an independent country into a neocolonial relationship with another entity. Tools of perception and information manipulation can be used to achieve various political, economic, military, and other goals, which in some interpretations constitutes a form of preventive defence (reducing risks and threats associated with conventional wars). If an adversary can be weakened or convinced that only certain alternatives are available, conventional conflict can be completely avoided.

At the same time, cognitive operations can serve as tools for expansion or even specific colonization by transforming the views, values, and interests of target groups. In hybrid conflict and hybrid warfare, where cognitive tools are employed, everyone is a target, even if, theoretically, the country is at peace. Yuriy Yuriy Danyk and Chad M. Briggs define hybrid-cognitive control or expansion as a process of targeted and controlled influence on the value system, views, knowledge, mental space, and personal and social awareness. Such control can provide new opportunities for the colonization of states in the digital age. Hybrid-cognitive influences may emerge during communication at various levels and of different natures. Cognitive operations can encompass specific socio-cultural and linguistic parameters. Efforts for influence or expansion do not occur in a vacuum, they are deliberate and clearly directed processes, not spontaneous and self-regulating. Operations are conducted through in-depth knowledge of the mental space of specific target groups and societies, as well as an understanding of their socio-mental gaps (Danyk, Briggs, 2022, pp. 35–47). Each element of such an operation has a client, a developer, and an organizer.

There is even talk of digital colonization, which is one of the innovative and most effective mechanisms in the digital age due to its impact on people and society, using modern information technologies and artificial intelligence tools, carried out in and through cyberspace. Unlike the seizure and colonization of a state's territory or economy, cognitive operations manage the worldview, interests, and values of individuals. Digital colonization can also refer to data collection and influence efforts, such as situations where *technology companies acquire, analyse, and own user data for profit and market influence with nominal benefits for the data source* (Coleman, 2019).

Danyk and Briggs distinguish four categories in which cognitive operations occur (Danyk, Briggs, 2022, pp. 35–47):

- Physical influence zones (infrastructure and information systems),
- Information and cyber space, where information is created, processed, stored, and disseminated,
- Cognitive processes, meaning the transformation of worldview, awareness, beliefs, interests, and values,
- Critical consequences of cognitive operations.

While many information campaigns in past wars focused on key aspects such as morale, the scope and intentions of contemporary hybrid-cognitive operations have both expanded and changed. Destructive actions can combine various disinformation campaigns with cyberattacks on information resources, infrastructure, economic processes, and democratic institutions. Cognitive operations not only introduce information into cyberspace but are often coordinated with undermining the credibility and trust in critical systems and institutions, such as state governance, national security, social spheres, banks, hospitals, educational and scientific institutions, and official sources of information. The dual aim is to divert people from traditional sources of information and to undermine trust in official state institutions and the community's ability to respond adequately to changing external conditions, attacks, or disasters (Pocheptsov, 2018, pp. 37–43). In the case of the first objective, by undermining trust in traditional sources of information, the recipient can be redirected to alternative information sources that can be micro-targeted to specific populations using, for example, social media.

For example, if a specific population frequently reacts to the topic of hybrid warfare, messages or disinformation can be directed at them as a way to confirm their concerns. Several available analyses discuss this in detail, such as a RAND report on virtual social warfare, understood as efforts to manipulate or disrupt the informational foundations of effective functioning of social and economic systems (virtual social warfare focuses on cognitive rationalization and information availability) (Mazarr et al., 2019). However, as previously noted by Danyk and Briggs, the risk of cognitive distortions increases. This risk can be classified into four categories: information overload, complexity of understanding, the need for rapid response, and the ratio of remembered content to forgotten content (Danyk, Briggs, 2022, pp. 35–47). Equally important, but perhaps more ephemeral, is the impact on the second objective of cognitive operations, which is to undermine trust in institutions and the resilience of communities. Such actions can have a more emotive nature, not based on rationalizations but on more basic fears associated with the brain's limbic system. Everyone has personal experience rationalizing why someone should be trustworthy, yet still feeling distrust based on emotions or intuition (and vice versa). Effective cognitive operations can leverage people's emotions, drawing from their fears, aspirations, loyalties, and perceptions of others to create psychological groups and limit perceived alternatives for action, such as: "we can't call the police, we keep hearing how corrupt they are" or "people of different nationalities, views, orientations are foreign to us." Such information is easier to accept when combined with effective cyber operations, such as initiating discussions on these topics in social networks, various forums, and blogs, alongside cyber actions that increase public dissatisfaction and distrust of authorities, like cutting off electronic access to information resources or shutting down power systems (Danyk, Briggs, 2022, pp. 35–47).

The goal of undermining social resilience is to weaken the ability to respond to changing conditions. It can take various forms – ranging from the destruction of infrastructure to increasing political polarization and corruption. In this sense, resilience can also be defined in psychological terms as the capacity to withstand external pressures, in contrast to more biological concepts of "bouncing back." Undermining the psychological resilience of communities can be an effective tactic when it encourages paralysis of action, polarizes communities, and presents certain actions as hopeless. Appropriately prepared and disseminated information can be used to provoke panic and/or negative reactions (for example, "famine is inevitable"), change attitudes towards state authority (for example, "they do not protect us and are not doing what they should"), and many other consequences. With the use of cyberspace, the rapid dissemination of this information with the right interpretation is possible. The result will ultimately be altered perceptions and attitudes towards what is happening, which will undoubtedly influence decisions made by people, such as during elections.

The most effective campaigns conceal their origin, allowing people to believe that the information comes from someone other than the actual source peers, neighbours, or someone perceived as an authority which strengthens trust in the authenticity of the information or blames these individuals for something that originates far away. This is the foundation of the doctrines of "reflexive control," which shape alternatives and possibilities for thinking in a way that appears organic and based on one's own way of thinking.

In the case of Russian actions against Ukraine, such operations aim to present Ukraine or NATO as the actual aggressor, reinforcing the risk of nuclear escalation and portraying mediated ceasefires (with the Russian Federation retaining control over occupied territories) as the only rational choice for Western countries. This shaping is not only directed at foreign policy decision-makers but also aims to influence social groups and their choices at a time when energy and food prices (linked to the conflict) threaten the welfare of families (Danyk, Briggs, 2022).

Cognitive hybrid expansion always has a specific goal set by beneficiaries, clients, and organizers. Its execution requires significant resources, capabilities, and time.

Cognitive operations can also be linked to another non-military action in hybrid warfare related to finance and the economy (e.g., through information manipulation and financial markets, economic pressure, influencing consumer decisions, or destabilizing currency and banking systems). In a globally connected world, both finance and the economy are inextricably linked to national and international security, impacting the broader geopolitical areas of each country. Economic coercion is one of the most directly applied forms of hybrid warfare as an alternative to the use of force. The main threat to the economic security of any country is economic dependency. A state's economic security is, in turn, a key guarantor of independence, sustainable development, and success, as shown by Mihail Dudin et al. (2018, pp. 459–467).

The strategy of economic coercion as an element of hybrid warfare involves actions aimed at exploiting one's economic advantage and the dependency of the victim. Four types of economic coercion have been identified: foreign aid, monetary power, financial power, and trade (Nordby, 2019). Each of these "tools" is applied according to the level of dependency of the country being targeted. In the context of hybrid threats, it is emphasized that the financial system should be analysed not only in terms of financial stability and security but also by considering the building of economic leverage, interference in internal markets, cyber threats, and information-influencing actions.

In the assessment of Julia Bluszcz and Marica Valente, within the context of the European Union, several key aspects of hybrid warfare related to finance and the economy emerge. The first of these is the centrality of the financial system, which acts as a conduit for capital flow between the private and public sectors, as well as households. Its importance as a link connecting various sectors makes it a potential tool for hybrid threats. Another aspect is the fragmentation of the EU, characterized by strong economic and financial integration, while politics and security largely remain in the hands of individual member states. This asymmetry increases the vulnerability of the financial system to exploitation by external actors and compromises its resilience. The authors further identify the threat posed by foreign loans. China's "going global" strategy has made it the world's largest official creditor. The nature of Chinese loans, often "hidden," presents significant challenges for debt management, oversight, and financial risk assessment in indebted countries, while also heightening the potential for money laundering and illicit financial flows. These are the most glaring examples of the financial system being used as a tool for criminal activity. Money laundering is not only a crime but can also be weaponized against a country's financial system, indicating a close link between money laundering and national security (Aho et al., 2020).

Economic warfare is not a new concept, one could say it has existed as long as the phenomenon of war itself. Today, it manifests in the form of sanctions, embargoes, and other macroeconomic policy measures aimed at resolving conflicts of interest without the use of military force. However, in war, and particularly in hybrid warfare, economic instruments are employed at various levels. Miroslav Mitrović, in *Economic and Energy Aspects of Hybrid Threats to National Security*, points out that economic measures in hybrid warfare aim to create threats to the supply system, the effectiveness of trade mechanisms, and the strategic dimension of markets. Economic pressures, or economic struggles, involve the engagement of the economy, economic resources, and science in bolstering defence and security capabilities. These measures are intended to undermine a state's overall ability to respond to external or internal threats to national security. Their objective is to achieve internal effects and changes in domestic policy, weaken the overall or even defensive strength of the state, and trigger consequences in foreign policy. One could argue that the forces initiating sanctions aim to affect the areas of a nation's economy where it is most vulnerable, applying pressure on state institutions and resulting in repercussions for the defence and security system. However, in addition to the sanctions regime, one of the hybrid methods of influencing a state's overall defence capability – directly stemming from globalization and "open market" policies – is the acquisition of key national resources by an external economic entity. This leads to a loss of sovereignty and, consequently, security (Mitrović, 2017, pp. 304–315; Stefanek, 2024; PAM, 2023).

The financial and economic tools of hybrid warfare employed by Russia include the systematic waging of trade wars aimed at suppressing Ukraine's foreign trade potential and obstructing the diversification of its international trade relations (such as blocking ports, restricting international transit of Ukrainian goods, and imposing discriminatory trade conditions). Significant damage to Ukraine's national interests has been inflicted through the infiltration of Ukraine's economy, aimed at weakening it and establishing either overt or covert control over strategic enterprises. These actions have resulted in the execution of economic terrorism acts. For example, Russia has orchestrated a wide range of economic activities targeting Ukrainian enterprises, leading to the suspension of their financial and operational activities, pushing them towards bankruptcy, and causing a significant rise in social tensions due to employee layoffs, while also gaining access to confidential information about shareholders. Additionally, Russia's financial and economic tools of hybrid warfare have included the infiltration of government management bodies through agents with the aim of influencing the regulation of Ukraine's economy and its international economic relations. Russian aggression in Ukraine, executed across all areas of societal functioning and leading to a decline in the state's security, particularly in its financial component, inevitably impacts international security and the ability to protect the financial interests of all participants in the global community (Yastrubetska, 2024, pp. 158–160).

Due to the war in Ukraine, by the time the conflict erupted in 2022, Ukraine's GDP per capita had fallen by an average of 15.1% between 2013 and 2017. In the absence of war, the GDP would have followed a stable, gradually increasing trend. Prior to the Ukrainian revolution in 2014, the Donbas region accounted for approximately 25% of the country's exports and over 15% of capital investments. In August 2014, industrial production in Donetsk declined by 60% and by 85% in Luhansk (Bluszcz, Valente, 2020).

Experts from the Kyiv School of Economics Institute (KSE Institute) are working to summarize Ukraine's losses resulting from Russian aggression. Compared to June 2023, the amount of direct losses Ukraine has incurred has increased by over $700 million. The largest portion of total direct losses comes from housing assets, amounting to $55.9 billion. In total, approximately 167,200 housing units have been destroyed or damaged due to the war, of which 147,800 are private homes, 19,100 are multi-family residential buildings, and another 350 are dormitories, among others. The Donetsk, Kyiv, Luhansk, Kharkiv, Mykolaiv, Chernihiv, Kherson, and Zaporizhzhia regions are among the areas most affected by the destruction of housing. The second and third largest categories of losses are in infrastructure and industry, as well as business losses, amounting to $36.6 billion and $11.4 billion, respectively. Since the beginning of the war in Ukraine, 18 airports, including civilian ones, have been damaged, along with at least 344 bridges and overpasses, more than 25,000 kilometres of state highways, regional roads, and municipal streets. Industrial and business losses include at least 426 large and medium-sized private and state-owned enterprises, whose assets were damaged or destroyed due to the war.

According to experts, the education sector is also among those most affected by the war. As of early September 2023, the sector has suffered losses totalling $10.1 billion due to the war. Compared to June 2023, this figure has increased by over $400 million. The total number of damaged or destroyed educational institutions now exceeds 3,500, including over 1,700 secondary schools, more than 1,000 kindergartens, and 586 higher education institutions.

Losses in the healthcare sector are also rising, with estimates as of 1 September 2023 reaching $2.9 billion. In total, 1,223 medical facilities have been destroyed or damaged due to the war, including 384 hospitals and 352 outpatient clinics (Kyiv School of Economics, 2023; Trusewicz, 2024).

According to Iikka Korhonen of the Bank of Finland Institute for Emerging Economies, as air defence systems in cities stabilized and improved, economic activity began to recover. This was particularly noticeable in the western parts of the country, bolstered by the influx of displaced people (which, of course, meant that the workforce in the eastern and southern regions was significantly diminished). Ukraine's economy returned to positive growth by the end of 2022, and the recovery continued last year. GDP growth in 2023 is currently estimated at around 5% (potentially slightly higher). The stabilization of the conflict in the east and south also fuelled domestic demand, as many who fled the country at the onset of the war were able to return. Additionally, industrial production supporting the war effort increased significantly, and access to international financing became more readily available.

Ukraine has successfully pushed the Russian navy away from its territorial waters, allowing an increase in grain shipments through the Black Sea, approaching pre-invasion levels. In addition to this critical Black Sea shipping, Ukraine has also developed alternative grain export routes to global markets, such as the Danube River. Well-functioning land borders with the European Union are now considered essential for Ukraine's economy. As highlighted by Korhonen, Ukraine's growth is expected to continue. In January 2024, the research firm Consensus Economics reported that its average of key forecasts for 2024 projects a GDP growth of 4.3% for Ukraine this year and 5.4% the following year. While these forecasts are naturally dependent on developments in the ongoing war, last year's positive trends suggest cautious optimism. The economy could recover quite robustly once the fighting ceases. However, as long as the majority of Ukraine's infrastructure and production capacity remain damaged, destroyed, or under Russian control, only partial recovery is possible. A recent joint study conducted by the World Bank, the UN, the European Commission, and Ukraine estimated the cost of repairing the current war damages at $486 billion – nearly three times Ukraine's GDP in 2023 (Korhonen, 2024).

The conflict in the Gaza Strip also illustrates the use of finance and the economy as tools in hybrid warfare. According to a report from the United Nations Conference on Trade and Development (UNCTAD) and data presented by Abdallah Al Dardari, Director of the UNDP's Regional Bureau for Arab States, Gaza's GDP contracted by 24% in 2023 (Shortell, 2023; Preliminary Assessment of the Economic Impact of the Destruction in Gaza, 2024).

The International Labour Organization (ILO) estimated that unemployment in Palestinian territories rose to 57% in the first quarter of 2024, resulting in the loss of 507,000 jobs. Gaza was particularly affected, with unemployment reaching 85%, leading to the loss of 200,000 jobs. This severe increase in unemployment has caused a significant slowdown in economic activity, reducing operations to just 16% of full capacity. This situation underscores the devastating impact of conflict on employment and the broader economy, particularly in regions already facing substantial challenges (Siddiqui, Motamedi, 2024). A total of 37,379 structures have been damaged or destroyed, accounting for 18% of the buildings in Gaza (Preliminary Assessment of the Economic Impact of the Destruction in Gaza, 2024). Before the war, 61% of Gaza's population lived below the poverty line. As a result of the conflict, this percentage increased by approximately 20% within the first month of fighting, followed by an additional 34% increase in the second month (Siddiqui, Motamedi, 2024).

According to Bloomberg's assessment, since the start of the war in October, 148,000 people from the West Bank have lost their jobs due to losing access to employment opportunities in Israel. Additionally, 144,000 jobs in the West Bank were lost as a result of the escalation of violence and disruptions in supply chains (Agencies, TOI Staff, 2023).

The United Nations Development Programme (UNDP) predicts that the ongoing conflict will set back social development in Gaza and the West Bank by 11–16 years. By the end of December 2023, the Palestinian Central Bureau of Statistics estimated economic losses at

$1.5 billion. In February 2024, the World Bank reported that Gaza's economy had contracted by 80% in the fourth quarter of 2023, and by May 2024, investments worth $50 billion had been destroyed, with 1.8 million people falling into poverty (Dietrich, 2024; Al Jazeera and News Agencies, 2023).

The World Bank has issued a warning regarding the Israel-Gaza conflict, highlighting its potential to trigger a significant global economic shock. One of the possible consequences could be a sharp increase in oil prices, which would have serious implications for the global economy, leading to higher food prices and potentially causing hunger among millions of people (Dietrich, 2024).

The analysis of media reports on economic activities in the context of the war in Ukraine did not demonstrate that such actions are widely used or described. The impact of these activities was found to be minimal. However, network analysis revealed that these actions are interconnected with the political and intelligence domains. It is important to note, however, that due to the small sample size, this area requires further research to draw more definitive conclusions.

Another non-military action in hybrid warfare is the blockade of food supplies. Ukraine is a major producer and exporter of several key food products, particularly wheat, corn, and oilseeds. As a result of Russia's war on Ukraine, global food supply chains have experienced significant disruptions. Prior to the war, the EU also imported a substantial amount of food and fertilizers from Ukraine. Therefore, it can be stated that the Russian invasion has caused severe disruptions to global food security, leading to sharp increases in food prices and other essential commodities.

At the beginning of the war, the Russian blockade of Ukrainian ports in the Black Sea severely hindered exports. Russia also deliberately targeted silos and warehouses storing agricultural products. From July 2022 to July 2023, the situation was alleviated by a multilateral agreement between the United Nations, Russia, and Turkey – the Black Sea Grain Initiative. However, in July 2023, Russia announced that it no longer supported the initiative, leading to a spike in grain prices. World leaders have called on Russia to rejoin the programme, but this has not occurred. Currently, Ukraine exports grain and other agricultural products through the territorial waters of Romania and Bulgaria, as well as via "solidarity corridors" (inland waterways, roads, and railways). EU leaders have consistently supported the solidarity corridors in their meeting conclusions. In addition to these logistical challenges, the war has devastated farms, soils, and crops in Ukraine, often referred to as the breadbasket of Europe. According to Ukraine's Ministry of Agriculture, around 20% of the land used for crops in 2021 is now inaccessible. Some fields have been mined, and efforts are underway to clear them and restore them for agricultural use. The destruction of the Kakhovka Dam has further damaged the surrounding agricultural areas, causing contamination and irrigation problems (Welsh, Glauber, 2024).

The war has also affected farmers in the EU, notably through high energy and fertilizer prices. European food producers' organizations recently expressed concerns that imports from Ukraine could disrupt the EU's single market by lowering prices and threatening local production of goods such as sugar, eggs, and poultry. The difficult overall conditions faced by farmers, combined with the negative effects of the war, have led to farmer protests in 2024.

Russia is using food as a weapon of hybrid warfare, aiming to destabilize societies and exert pressure on governments. In response to the crisis, many countries have implemented export controls on agricultural goods, further disrupting global markets. Currently, export restrictions cover 17% of globally traded calories, a level comparable to the food crisis of 2007–2008. Countries such as India, Argentina, Egypt, and Turkey have introduced bans on the export of certain agricultural products (Welsh, Glauber, 2024).

The war in Ukraine has affected global food supplies through three main factors (Guénette et al., 2022):

- Significant reduction in the export and production of key commodities: Ukraine, being a major exporter of grains and other essential agricultural products, has seen a sharp decline in output due to the conflict.
- Global increase in food prices and the cost of agricultural inputs (such as fertilizers and energy): The war has led to higher prices, straining both global food markets and the agricultural sector.
- International responses to these factors: These can either exacerbate the crisis (primarily through uncoordinated protectionist or speculative measures) or mitigate it by applying lessons learned from the 2007–2008 food crisis.

The use of food blockades as a tactic in hybrid warfare also occurs on a regional scale. For example, during the siege of Mariupol in 2022, civilians experienced severe shortages of food and water. The city was besieged by Russian forces, which made the delivery of supplies impossible. As a result of these actions, thousands of residents found themselves in a critical situation, without access to basic means of survival. In eastern Ukraine, in regions such as Donetsk and Luhansk, there were multiple instances where humanitarian aid convoys were blocked or shelled. Russian armed forces and pro-Russian separatists deliberately hindered the delivery of food and other resources to besieged cities and villages. Russian attacks on infrastructure, such as food warehouses, farms, and food processing facilities, significantly disrupted food distribution in Ukraine. The destruction of these key facilities affected Ukraine's ability to provide food for its citizens (Guénette et al., 2022).

The blockade of food is also occurring in the Gaza Strip. Human Rights Watch (HRW) has accused Israel of using hunger as a tool of war by blocking the delivery of essential resources such as water, food, and fuel, and hindering humanitarian aid. HRW points out that such actions are a violation of IHL (World Report 2024: Our Annual Review of Human Rights Around the Globe, 2024). The United Nations (UN), in reports cited by Oxfam International, states that the situation in the Gaza Strip is catastrophic, and the use of hunger as a weapon of war is evident. Although a limited number of aid trucks are allowed to pass through the Rafah border crossing, this number is insufficient to meet the immense needs of the civilian population. Many Palestinian families lack access to adequate drinking water, and the shortage of energy and destruction of infrastructure prevent the proper storage and preparation of food (Starvation as weapon of war being used against Gaza civilians, 2023).

The analysis of subject literature, available reports, and open sources clearly indicates that the violation of food security is a component of hybrid warfare strategy. This action, which has a direct and severe impact on the civilian population, manifests primarily through the creation of food shortages, leading to hunger. Media reports suggest that, in the context of food security in hybrid warfare, it is crucial to identify links with various operational domains. The strongest connections were observed with conventional actions conducted by armed forces. However, the analysis also revealed a broad network of links involving irregular actions, including operations carried out by terrorist groups. In the examined category of activities, in addition to military aspects, diplomatic, political, water, and land domains were also significant. These interconnected links suggest that such actions aim at multidimensional destabilization, where food security is used as a tool of pressure and blackmail, coordinated with other forms of hybrid aggression.

Another non-military action in hybrid warfare is the use of energy instruments. Galeotti points to energy blackmail through threats of cutting off supplies of strategic resources, sabotage of the energy grid, and terrorist acts targeting gas transportation systems (Galeotti, 2018). In Miroslav Mitrovic's assessment, current trends indicate an escalation in the struggle for energy, replacing the former arms race with a race to ensure energy security. Energy security has become a key element of national strategies, with a direct impact on geopolitics, the economy, and political power of states.

Energy security is a relatively new concept. Abdelrahman Azzuni and Christian Brayer define energy security as the *uninterrupted availability of energy sources at an affordable price* (Mitrović, 2017, pp. 304–315). Energy security can be interpreted from the perspective of producers, consumers, and transit countries. In this context, three categories can be distinguished:

- Energy-exporting countries – dependent on the continuity of demand in the global market to ensure stable revenue from energy exports.
- Developing countries – reliant on energy prices, which directly impact the development of technology and production capacities.
- Energy-importing countries – for whom energy security means ensuring a reliable supply of energy from sources outside their own territory.

Energy security is closely tied to national security. In situations where the energy system is threatened and political, economic, and diplomatic measures fail, military strength becomes a key factor in response. Stable energy resources enable the development of effective defence capabilities and the protection of energy infrastructure (Mitrović, 2017). Actions during both the hybrid conflict stage and outright war demonstrate that disrupting energy supplies or increasing their costs is a key element of hybrid strategy. These tactics are used to weaken adversaries by creating economic strain and destabilizing essential infrastructure.

In their study Global Energy Security Index and Its Application on National Level, Azzuni and Brayer provide the example of Russia as a state employing various hybrid threats against the energy policies, assets, and supplies of not only NATO allies but also other nations. The challenges posed by hybrid warfare to the energy sector can weaken the defence and development of nation-states in both peacetime and conflict. The ongoing dependence on fossil fuels or their substitutes creates vulnerabilities in which major energy exporters can leverage their position to exert political, economic, and military influence over countries that are energy-dependent on them (Azzuni, Breyer, 2020).

Arslan Sheikh asserts that the current war in Ukraine serves as an excellent example of how energy security is utilized as a strategic element in hybrid warfare (Sheikh, 2020). Arnold C. Dupuy and co-authors, in a publication for NATO Review, also emphasize that Russia employs various hybrid threats against energy resources and supplies, combining political and economic pressure with disinformation campaigns, as seen in Bulgaria, Romania, and Ukraine.

Russia also leverages its economic and political influence to pursue energy projects, such as the expansion of the Paks nuclear power plant in Hungary and the construction of the Nord Stream II pipeline in Germany. Russian cyberattacks on the energy sector have been reported in Germany, Poland, Turkey, the United Kingdom, and the United States. These attacks often accompanied other forms of hybrid aggression, such as limiting natural gas supplies. Over the past decade, Russia has intensified its campaigns aimed at destabilizing NATO's energy security.

Before the outbreak of war in 2022, Ukraine was particularly affected by Russia's hybrid campaigns, which included supply disruptions, cyberattacks, and disinformation efforts. One example is the gas supply interruption in 2009, as well as the 2015 cyberattack on a power plant, which cut off electricity to a large part of the country. Another attack in 2016 targeted the power grid in Kyiv, using advanced malware known as CrashOverride (Dupuy et al., 2021; Biznes Newseria, 2022).

In the conducted study of media reports, there were no codes related to energy security breaches; however, these actions are mentioned in reports by international security organizations, as well as in publications and media reports about attacks on power plants or the deliberate blocking of energy supplies to civilians. Such actions are used in both the war in Ukraine and the conflict in the Gaza Strip (this aspect is discussed in more detail in the chapter on civilian protection).

Another tactic used in hybrid warfare is triggering refugee flows (known as migration profiling) and humanitarian crises to create large movements of refugees, placing additional economic and social burdens on neighbouring countries. Examples include the refugee crisis in Syria, the conflict in Venezuela, the conflict in Yemen, and the migration crisis in Europe. In the context of ongoing wars, migration profiling pertains to actions carried out by both Russia and those in the Gaza Strip.

In the first case, the ongoing migration profiling on the Polish-Belarusian border since 2021 can be identified as a hybrid action. According to the Polish government website gov.pl, Russia, with the support of Belarus through the use of artificially created illegal migration routes, is carrying out an action to destabilize the countries of NATO's eastern flank. This tactic, used against Poland, has a dual objective: testing Poland's border protection procedures and seeking to undermine the integrity of its national border, which is also the external border of NATO and the EU. A successful breach of the border would not only challenge Poland's sovereignty but could also be leveraged for future aggressive actions. Additionally, the strategy against Poland involves the infiltration of a large number of individuals of unknown and unverifiable origin. Their influx poses significant internal risks, including the potential entry of individuals linked to criminal activity, foreign intelligence services, or terrorist organizations. The presence of such individuals would strain the institutions responsible for national security, affecting their capacity to maintain internal stability (Serwis Rzeczypospolitej Polskiej – gov.pl, 2024).

The hybrid operation against Poland can also be seen as an attempt to test the crisis response procedures of both Poland and the broader NATO and EU frameworks. These actions may serve to assess the effectiveness of security protocols under pressure, identify differences in approaches to crisis management among policymakers, influencers, and the public, and evaluate the effectiveness of engaging various structures in national defence during a crisis. Additionally, Russian and Belarusian intelligence services likely had the opportunity to collect similar data regarding international-level responses and actions.

The actions of Belarusian and Russian entities were complemented by an intense information warfare campaign directed against Western countries. These information warfare tactics were an integral part of the broader hybrid warfare strategy, amplifying the impact of physical incidents and testing response procedures. In Poland, this included attempts to influence and destabilize public debate. Russian and Belarusian propaganda infiltrated certain segments of Polish society and opinion leaders. The main objectives of these information operations included (Serwis Rzeczypospolitej Polskiej – gov.pl, 2024):

- Exerting pressure on Poland to accept the illegal migration route organized by Belarus and Russia.
- Promoting narratives aimed at isolating Poland within NATO and the EU.
- Discrediting the Polish government by portraying its policies as dangerous for Europe, in violation of international law, and irrational in its relations with Russia.

The crisis on the Polish-Belarusian border also has a very clear military aspect. The actions at Poland's border began one month before the active phase of the Zapad 2021 exercises, the largest Russian-Belarusian military manoeuvres directed towards the West. The scenario of these exercises assumed that the onset of military operations by three states referred to as "western" – "Neris," "Polar Republic," and "Pomoria" (in fact, Poland, Lithuania, and Latvia) – against the "Republic of Polesia" (Belarus) and the "Central Federation" (Russia) would be preceded by a border crisis (Kristinova, Alvarez-Aragones, 2024; Dyner, 2022). The significance of these manoeuvres as part of a hybrid strategy was confirmed by the analysis of media reports, where the exercises were characterized by a very high frequency of codes, indicating that they could be one of the direct indicators preceding a military invasion.

According to Caitlin Procter, based on Israel's actions aimed at destabilizing the region by triggering mass migration, influencing refugee flows is also relevant to the war in the Gaza Strip, where residents are forced to emigrate in various ways. In addition to military attacks and the constant threat of violence, as previously mentioned, Israel also employs economic blockades and restricts access to resources, leading to an economic crisis, high unemployment, and the lack of basic services such as healthcare, education, and food supplies. Furthermore, information warfare is utilized, including propaganda and disinformation campaigns aimed at creating fear and uncertainty, which drives people to leave the region. An example of this can be seen in intense media campaigns portraying life in Gaza as unbearable and migration as the only viable option for survival (Procter, 2024, pp. 2359–2383).

The result of migration profiling, both in times of peace and war, is the creation of humanitarian crises. According to a UNICEF report, as a result of the war in Ukraine, 3.7 million people remained internally displaced in 2023, and approximately 6 million were spread across Europe. In the Gaza Strip, 1.8 million people were internally displaced in 2023, while 3.1 million required humanitarian assistance.

In the conducted analysis of media reports, the frequency of the term "humanitarian crisis" was not high, but the network of connections is noteworthy, with the highest frequency associated with conventional actions (military), suggesting that this is another phenomenon coexisting with hybrid warfare. The analysis also highlights that these actions are linked to the informational, diplomatic, and maritime domains, which may indicate a coordinated and multidimensional approach to regional destabilization.

The final issue in the section on non-military actions is intimidation. There is limited research on this topic in the literature, with most studies focusing on the use of such tactics by Russia and China (Novossiolova, Georgiev, 2023) in the context of security of NATO and the EU. However, there is also a context that remains unnoticed in publications, which pertains to intimidation as a form of action against the civilian population during the conflict phase and the phase of hybrid warfare. The conclusions drawn from the analysis of media reports indicated that this form of action is linked to conventional operations (the military), as well as the informational and diplomatic domains. This may suggest that in hybrid warfare, such actions are directed both at the civilian population and the administration.

The non-military actions in hybrid warfare described above, as mentioned in the introduction to this section, do not constitute a closed catalogue and likely never will, due to the nature of hybrid warfare. Nevertheless, there are certain indicators that may suggest, even before a full-scale invasion, that non-military threats are evolving towards the war phase. However, very often the various agencies responsible for internal security, including civilian protection, do not approach this issue holistically but rather in a fragmented manner. Moreover, the communication to the civilian population about non-military threats remains quite limited. It is rather unrealistic to expect that societies will follow all publicly available reports in real time. The lack of verified and reliable information provided to the public can lead to an expanded perception of reality, ultimately devaluing the actual threat, which may directly impact preparedness for the dangers emerging from hybrid strategy phases.

The results of the analysis of media reports on the war in Ukraine have shown that non-military actions coexist with other types of actions (conventional and unconventional military) and play a significant role in hybrid strategy. Given the complexity of these findings, the most important conclusions for this section are graphically presented and described below. The complete catalogue of results is provided in Table A2.4.

Figure 2.5 presents the frequency of codes in non-military actions. Each category is represented by a different colour, and the frequency values are displayed at the ends of the bars.

The most frequently occurring codes in non-military actions are: propaganda (956 mentions), disinformation (177 mentions), and intimidation (71 mentions). Other actions, such as cyberattacks, influencing food security, causing humanitarian crises, terrorist activity, diplomatic actions, offensive actions in cyberspace, and information warfare, appear less than 50 times. Codes such as political pressure, international isolation, special services activities, economic actions, and instigating internal conflicts are characterized by only single occurrences. Among non-military actions, no reports were identified that indicated food blockades, migration manipulation, creation of an alternative power

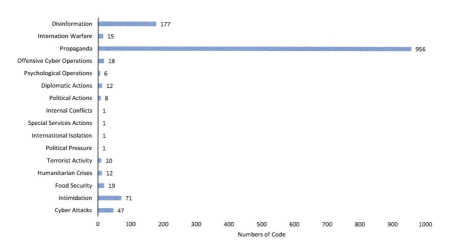

FIGURE 2.5 Frequency of codes in various categories of non-military actions

Source: Own study

138 Civil Protection and Domestic Security in Hybrid Warfare

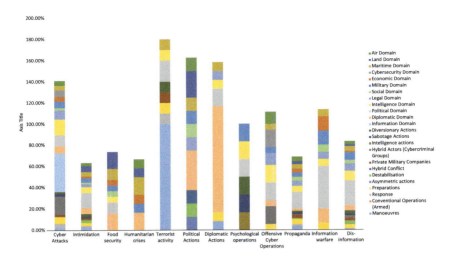

FIGURE 2.6 Layered graph representing the main co-occurrence of codes in various categories of non-military actions

Source: Own study

centre, reflexive control, ideological subversion (this term has been explained earlier), energy-related actions, ideological actions, or social actions. As in the other analyses, non-military actions also showed interesting co-occurrences. Figure 2.6 is presented, showing the primary co-occurrences of codes across different categories. Each bar represents a category, and the different colours depict the percentage share of each code's co-occurrence. This allows for a clear view of how various co-occurrences are distributed within each category.

The conclusions from the analysis of the study revealed diverse patterns of code co-occurrences across different categories of non-military actions. In the case of cyberattacks, the dominant co-occurring themes were conventional actions (military), hybrid actions (cybercriminal groups), the political domain, and the intelligence domain. For the intimidation category, key co-occurring themes included conventional actions (military), the political domain, the maritime domain, and the land domain. When analysing food security, the most significant co-occurring themes were conventional actions (military), hybrid actions (terrorist groups), the diplomatic domain, the political domain, the maritime domain, and the land domain. In the context of terrorist activity, the highest co-occurrence was observed with manoeuvres, response, preparedness, conventional actions (military), PMCs, diversionary actions, the informational domain, the political domain, the intelligence domain, and the maritime domain. Humanitarian crises most frequently co-occurred with conventional actions, the informational domain, the diplomatic domain, the intelligence domain, and the maritime domain. Political actions co-occurred with asymmetric actions, the informational domain, the diplomatic domain, destabilization, hybrid conflict, the legal domain, the social domain, the military domain, the maritime domain, the land domain, and the air domain. Diplomatic actions most frequently co-occurred with conventional actions (military), the informational domain, and the political domain. PSYOPs were linked with conventional actions (military), intelligence activities, sabotage actions, diversionary actions, the informational domain, the political domain, the intelligence domain, and the military domain. Offensive actions in cyberspace most often co-occurred with conventional actions (military), cybercriminal groups, the informational domain, the political domain, the intelligence domain, the legal domain, cybersecurity, and the air domain. Propaganda most frequently co-occurred with conventional actions, the political domain, and the informational domain. Information warfare showed co-occurrence with the informational domain, the diplomatic domain, the political domain, the economic domain, and the military domain. Disinformation co-occurred with conventional actions (military), the informational domain, and the political domain. An especially interesting finding is the high frequency of propaganda and disinformation (the highest occurrence) in the context of their connections with other themes. In both categories, a few themes dominate in terms of frequency indicators. In both categories, the key co-occurring themes are the military, the informational domain, and the political domain. However, in both cases, many themes show very low indicators. This may suggest that propaganda and disinformation are broadly dispersed across many areas, but they are not as intensively utilized as in the key domains. Table 2.1 shows the assigned dispersed areas for the categories of propaganda and disinformation.

The most frequently co-occurring non-military activities are those in the information domain, political domain, and conventional activities carried out by the military. The high co-occurrence of these categories suggests that they are key areas of focus and action in the context of non-military strategies. In contrast, the low co-occurrence in some categories, such as cyber, intelligence, or sabotage activities, may suggest their widening or narrower application or new directions of evolution in this type of conflict. As mentioned earlier, the findings may point to the coexistence of military and non-military actions as a hybrid strategy. Furthermore, it can be clearly observed that in many cases these activities intermingle and complement each other, thus creating a network of cascading effects, which in the context of the protection of civilians becomes much more challenging than in conflicts and wars known so far.

140 Civil Protection and Domestic Security in Hybrid Warfare

TABLE 2.1 Keywords co-occurring with the category of propaganda and disinformation that had low percentage scores

Propaganda	Disinformation
Manoeuvres	Manoeuvres
Armed conflict	Territorial defence
Psychological factor	Social media
Social media	Tactics
Public opinion	Tools
Tactics	Techniques
Tools	Prevention
Techniques	Preparation
Prevention	Counteracting
Response	Hybrid operations
Preparation	Destabilization
Counteracting	Reconstruction
Destabilization	Impacting political decisions
Restoration	Complexity
Reconstruction	Destabilizing actions
Flexibility	Regular armed forces
Impacting political decisions	Army
Asymmetry	Private military companies
Actions below war threshold	Terrorist groups
Regular armed forces	Cybercrime groups
Army	Intelligence actions
Little green men	Sabotage actions
Private military companies	Diversionary actions
Guerrilla groups	Information domain
Terrorist groups	Diplomatic domain
Cybercrime groups	Political domain
Sabotage actions	Intelligence domain
Diversionary actions	Legal domain
Information domain	Social domain
Diplomatic domain	Cultural domain
Political domain	Military domain
Intelligence domain	Economic domain
Legal domain	Cognitive domain
Social domain	Cyberspace
Cultural domain	Space domain
Military domain	Water domain
Economic domain	Land domain

(*Continued*)

TABLE 2.1 (*Continued*) Keywords co-occurring with the category of propaganda and disinformation that had low percentage scores

Propaganda	Disinformation
Cognitive domain	Air domain
Air domain	
Land domain	
Space domain	
Maritime domain	
Cybersecurity	
Cyberspace	

Source: Own study

The methodology for building dependency networks and analysing cascading effects has been described in detail in Chapter 3, using essential services and critical infrastructure objects as an example. Figure 2.7 is a sample network diagram illustrating the co-occurrence of codes related to non-military actions in hybrid warfare. The nodes represent different categories, and the edges indicate the strength of co-occurrence, which is illustrated by the thickness and colour of the edges.

To summarize the results of the analysis in the section on hybrid warfare actions, it is evident that these actions form an integrated and complex system, often characterized by flexibility. The objective of these actions is to destabilize all levels of state security. In hybrid warfare, military actions complement non-military actions (as mentioned earlier, this ratio is 3.69 non-military actions to 1 military action). Furthermore, the analyses showed strong integration between conventional and unconventional actions. In terms of the highest frequency, conventional military actions were most often associated with manoeuvres, while unconventional actions were dominated by sabotage, diversionary, and destabilizing activities. Both types of actions were supported by information operations. In non-military actions, the key labels were propaganda and disinformation. The high frequency of codes assigned to these categories highlights that they are key elements of information manipulation, which is the most commonly linked domain in non-military actions. Additionally, disinformation plays a particularly significant role in the political and intelligence domains. The cumulative results demonstrate that both military and non-military actions create more or less obvious networked systems, which today pose a challenge to security. Experts who participated in the semi-structured study stated that the most important actions are aimed at creating disruptions (destabilization) – broadly speaking – in the following systems: (1) social, (2) political, (3) financial,

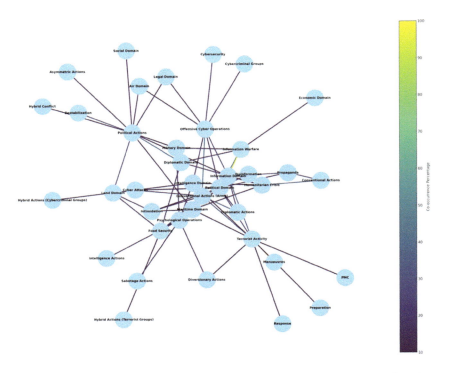

FIGURE 2.7 A network diagram showing the co-occurrence of codes related to non-military action in hybrid warfare

Source: Own study

(4) military, (5) critical infrastructure, more specifically, (6) the healthcare system, (7) the justice system, (8) the banking system, (9) broadly understood transport and logistics, and (10) the IT infrastructure.

Depending on the specific objective of a given action, certain elements of the state or society may prove to be the most effective in achieving that goal. This, in turn, may explain the occurrence of numerous dispersed outcomes across diverse areas. For example, effectively leveraging religious views may facilitate changes in legislation, which could lead to protests and social unrest. As previously mentioned, some actions may be aimed at generating social unrest, increasing societal divisions, undermining trust in particular social groups, or influencing the results of elections or referenda. Additionally, this may involve funding organizations or entities that can impact the aforementioned actions, or hacking and using data for these purposes (through controlled leaks of personal data and information in general, or blackmailing decision-makers). It could also include efforts aimed at reducing military capabilities (e.g. by undermining trust in the decision-makers of states intending to purchase military systems or equipment). Furthermore, a second expert pointed more directly to military actions and the use of key economic dependencies, such as gas or water, to force political decisions unfavourable to the state's interests, as seen in the case of Moldova. In the political context, this includes influencing elections. Criminal actions involve strategic corruption, as in the case of Russia in Ukraine. In cyberspace, these actions include attacks on infrastructure, as seen in the Baltic states. Furthermore, hybrid warfare contains a significant element of disinformation, often organized through networks and difficult to attribute to a specific perpetrator. The actions mentioned by experts have been confirmed and further expanded upon in this analysis.

However, all actions must be organized, coordinated, and executed by someone. Therefore, the next section will discuss the actors identified in hybrid warfare. This section, like the previous ones, will be based on an analysis of literature reviews, reports, open sources, and media reports concerning the war in Ukraine.

CHARACTERISTICS OF ACTORS AND THEIR ROLES IN HYBRID WARFARE

Despite intense debates about what constitutes hybrid warfare, less attention has been given to who is involved in these actions and how these interdependencies influence one another. Hybrid warfare is undoubtedly characterized by the blurring of boundaries between various types of military and non-military actions, as well as the actors involved, leading to exploitable ambiguity (Thornton, 2015, pp. 40–48).

The last decade has brought significant changes in the dynamics of global security. Non-democratic states, as well as those questioning their democratic systems, are facing difficulties in achieving strategic objectives through traditional and transparent means, such as foreign policy, diplomacy, trade agreements, and legal frameworks. The past decade has also been marked by turbulence in the international order, intensifying great power rivalry, and the resurgence of competition over values and narratives (Giannopoulos et al., 2021).

General Patrick Sanders and other experts emphasize the emergence of a new axis formed by Russia, China, and Iran. This axis is considered more dangerous than the alliance of Germany, Italy, and Japan before World War II due to better coordination and greater interdependence. These countries possess significant potential to provoke conflicts and collectively form a new axis of power, distinct from their historical predecessors through deeper alliances and mutual dependencies (Bilal, 2024; Niedziński, 2024).

As the world becomes more complex and interconnected, the concentration of power is shifting from resource-based economic and military might to relational power, which relies on the ability to influence the beliefs, attitudes, preferences, opinions, expectations, emotions, and actions of others. This shift makes influencing international affairs more complex and multidimensional, extending beyond mere material power. The use of hybrid threats has become a tactic for actors who lack the capacity to pursue their strategic interests through traditional methods (Giannopoulos et al., 2021).

Hybrid warfare actors aim to weaken democracies by exploiting vulnerabilities across various domains, creating new weaknesses through interference, exploiting potential vulnerabilities, fostering ambiguity, and undermining citizens' trust in democratic institutions. They can also be characterized by the goals they pursue, such as: undermining the integrity and functioning of democracy, attacking vulnerabilities in various sectors, creating new ones, manipulating established decision-making processes, obscuring situational awareness, exploiting information gaps, intimidating individuals, and instilling fear in target societies. They seek to maximize their impact by generating cascading effects, combining elements from different domains to overwhelm even the best-prepared systems (Jungwirth et al., 2023).

Actors in hybrid wars fall into two main categories: state and non-state actors

State actors which mainly include authoritarian states often support hybrid operations directly or indirectly, using their resources to destabilize target countries. For example, Russia and China use sophisticated cyber operations, propaganda, and covert military action to achieve their goals. Russia, in particular, is known for escalating its actions from preparation and destabilization to actual coercion, as in the case of the annexation of Crimea and the conflict in Ukraine (Danyk, Briggs, 2024).

As noted by the authors of The Landscape of Hybrid Threats, one of the key aspects of authoritarian state actors' activities is their effort to undermine the rule of law, which is a cornerstone of democracy. Over the past decade, authoritarian regimes that systematically suppress political pluralism and freedom of expression have increasingly applied these same principles on the international stage. Authoritarian states such as Russia, China, and Iran are developing internal political strategies that are mirrored in their international actions. The primary goal of these regimes is to maintain power through societal control and manipulation of information, in order to reinforce their own rule and weaken the ability of democratic states to respond effectively (Giannopoulos et al., 2021). Information manipulation is a key tool used by authoritarian states to control perceptions and discourage citizens from collective action against the regime. Authoritarian governments leverage the media to instil trust in their leadership while simultaneously fostering distrust among social actors (Chen, Xu, 2015, pp. 1–16).

Authoritarian states, in contrast to democracies where the rule of law is the foundation of the system, use legal frameworks as tools of repression and social control. These regimes manipulate legal systems to maintain control and project power. In international relations, they favour a Westphalian approach, emphasizing non-interference, while simultaneously exploiting legal systems to gain asymmetric advantages. In authoritarian states, the boundary between the public and private sectors is much more blurred than in democracies. Authoritarian governments can compel companies and individuals to act in the interests of the state. An example of this is China's 2015 National Security Law, which imposes obligations on citizens and corporations to support the government in protecting national security. In democracies, cooperation between the public and private sectors is more regulated and transparent (Kaja et al., 2015).

The concept of hybrid actions largely originates from non-state actors who sought to free themselves from the influence of stronger parties through manipulated tactics (Giannopoulos et al., 2021). Non-state actors in the context of hybrid threats are entities that play a role in international relations and possess sufficient power to interfere, influence, and cause changes without being tied to established state institutions. The role of non-state actors has evolved alongside changes in international politics, driven by globalization and the emergence of new dependencies. These changes have strengthened network-based actions to such an extent that non-state actors can influence nation-states and put pressure on democratic governments. Non-state actors exert influence through interference, sometimes gradually and subtly, as demonstrated by the case study on Salafists in Sweden (Giannopoulos et al., 2021).

Non-state actors are often linked to states that operate through these entities, allowing such states to conduct hostile actions in a way that is difficult to detect and attribute. The use of non-state actors also enables states to deny involvement in the actions being carried out, which is particularly useful in politically sensitive areas. The use of PMCs for risky operations is a fitting example of this strategy (Giannopoulos et al., 2021).

One aspect of hybrid activities is the potential use of non-state entities with specific skills in critical sectors of the target state's infrastructure. An example is the real estate company Airiston Helmi in Finland, which could have potentially served as a tool for preparing operations harmful to the target state. Criminal organizations also represent useful entities in the context of hybrid threats. Iran, for instance, leverages its relationship with Hezbollah to conduct criminal and terrorist activities worldwide (Giannopoulos et al., 2021).

From 2002 to 2014, the concept of hybrid threats was also applied to transnational organized crime, terrorism, and insurgencies. Hybridization from this perspective is characterized by the intersection of various non-state actors, including insurgent networks, criminal groups, and ideological or religious organizations. The use of social media and cyber tools has expanded the ability to influence and manipulate target groups, which has been exploited by state actors in hybrid campaigns. The Islamic State, for example, uses these tools to spread its agenda among Western populations, although their ability to conduct such operations is limited (Giannopoulos et al., 2021).

Vladimir Rauta proposes a division of non-state actors into four categories based on their functions in hybrid wars:

- Proxy forces – Armed groups that are not part of regular military forces but fight on behalf of states seeking to alter the strategic outcome of a conflict while remaining external to it. An example is the separatists in Donbas, supported by Russia, who fought for autonomy, independence, or unification with Russia. In August 2014, Russia deployed around 4,000 regular soldiers to support these groups, highlighting the limitations of the proxy strategy (Savage, 2018, pp. 77–85).
- Auxiliary forces – These are not part of the regular armed forces but are directly integrated into combat structures, operating in cooperation with regular forces. An example would be the pro-Russian self-defence militias in Crimea, such as the Night Wolves and Afghan war veterans, who supported Russian special operations by blocking access to OSCE observers and organizing protests (Galeotti, 2016, pp. 281–301).
- Surrogate forces (surrogates) – Groups used by states to conduct warfare on their behalf when the state is unable to independently control the use of violence. An example would be Ukrainian volunteer battalions, such as the Azov and Donbas battalions, which were formally integrated into the National Guard of Ukraine and fought against separatists in eastern Ukraine (Rauta, 2020, pp. 868–887).
- Affiliated forces – These unofficially form part of regular armed forces and fight on behalf of states seeking to change the strategic outcome of a conflict. An example is the Wagner Group, a Russian PMC that has operated in Ukraine, Syria, and other locations, conducting military operations and supporting rebel groups while maintaining a de facto illegal status (Sukhankin, 2019; Marten, 2019, pp. 181–204).

Understanding the role of non-state actors in hybrid warfare is important for developing effective defence and protection strategies. The relationships between these actors and regular armed forces create complex and often unclear structures that influence the dynamics of the conflict.

This is confirmed by a study of media reports in which the spectrum of actors involved in the conflict was analysed.

The results of the survey of media reports indicate that the most frequent group of actors in hybrid warfare is the regular armed forces, including the army, with a total of 8,703 indications. Terrorist groups also have a high incidence rate (554 indications). Other actors, i.e. special forces, international organizations, green men (little green men), irregular forces, separatist forces, PMCs, and guerrilla groups, appear in media reports much less frequently, with their numbers fluctuating around 100 indications for each label.

The dominant role of regular armed forces demonstrates that they continue to be the main component in hybrid warfare, playing a key role in both military and non-military operations. However, there is significant involvement of this component in unconventional and non-military activities (which has not traditionally been as evident). Besides this, terrorist groups serve as an important indicator, suggesting that they complement the actions of regular forces. Other entities with significantly smaller numbers confirm their participation in the war in Ukraine, but it may also indicate that, despite their involvement, their actions are much less visible in media reports, which is characteristic of hybrid warfare. These data may also suggest a trend in media reporting, where more attention is given to traditional actors. Such an approach may influence public perception of hybrid wars, leading to a limited awareness of the more subtle and concealed elements of these conflicts.

The network of connections between the labels related to actors is diverse. Both the highest indicators and those with lower indexes are interesting (as these may represent evolving issues). Regular armed forces intersect significantly with the informational, air, political, and land domains, creating a catalogue of actions attributed to military actors. Special forces primarily intersect with diversionary and intelligence activities, as well as the air domain, but they also engage in the diplomatic, political, and military domains. In the case of non-military actors, three main groups dominate: terrorist groups, guerrilla groups, and cybercriminals. For terrorist groups, the main vectors of connection involve the informational and political domains, but these groups also engage in areas such as social media, propaganda, diversionary actions, and intelligence activities, as well as a range of other domains with varying degrees of involvement. Guerrilla groups are most strongly connected to the informational, political, and intelligence domains, but they also exhibit activity in sabotage and diversionary actions, as well as legal efforts and operations across three military domains (maritime, air, and land). In the case of cybercriminal groups, their actions are typical for this type of actor, primarily focusing on the informational, intelligence, and political domains, as well as cyberattacks. Interestingly, these groups also engage in propaganda, disinformation, and the maritime domain. PMCs and separatist forces are not as frequently coded as the actors mentioned above, but in the case of PMCs, it is worth noting their broad involvement. With a 100% indicator, they are highly active in the informational and intelligence domains. Their involvement is slightly lower in the legal and political domains, but they also show a strong presence in propaganda activities. PMCs are involved in the military domain and political, sabotage, diversionary, economic, and social actions.

It is also important to note the significant connection with preparation (especially when considering the link with manoeuvres), which suggests that PMCs play a key role in hybrid strategy. PMCs also conduct destabilizing actions and operate below the threshold of war. In the case of separatist groups, the analysis indicates that their involvement in the war in Ukraine primarily focused on the diplomatic domain. To a lesser extent, their activities involved political, intelligence, and legal actions. These groups were also engaged in actions below the threshold of war and participated in the preparation phase.

The extensive involvement of diverse actors in hybrid warfare has been confirmed through the analysis of sources, media reports, and expert opinions gathered during the study. Experts highlighted that one of the primary entities participating in such conflicts are states. Holding the status of a state provides many advantages, such as access to resources and the ability to use them creatively. Through the use of armed forces, intelligence services, and other tools, states are able to influence the economic, social, and political situations in other countries, not necessarily limited to neighbouring ones. Such actions can enhance effectiveness in both the military and political spheres, although they simultaneously reduce the ability to deny involvement in the conflict.

Quasi-state organizations (para-states) represent another group of actors in hybrid wars. They fight for territory or the recognition of their independence on the international stage, seeking the right to self-determination. International organizations also engage in hybrid conflicts, operating in an institutionalized manner and influencing the dynamics of the conflict. Terrorist and criminal organizations play a significant role as well, acting independently by acquiring resources for their operations or being supported by other entities, including states.

Interest groups also participate in hybrid conflicts, operating either in an organized manner or on an ad hoc basis. Their activities can include both online engagement and on-the-ground actions, aiming to influence domestic or international policy. Often, these groups seek to shape narratives that align with their interests, regardless of the consequences for regional stability.

Experts also highlight the involvement of PMCs and theoretically independent structures that are linked to governments, such as Gazprom or the Wagner Group. While these entities have greater operational freedom, they possess fewer resources than regular military forces. Their role is not to capture and hold territory, but rather to sow chaos and destabilization. Thus, hybrid warfare encompasses a wide spectrum of actors whose actions are difficult to predict and even harder to attribute clearly to specific sides in the conflict.

In summary, the analysis revealed that hybrid warfare involves a complex interaction of engaged entities that are connected through a wide range of actions and domains. State actors dominate in conventional operations but also actively participate in unconventional and non-military activities. Non-state actors employ asymmetric tactics and modern technologies to compensate for limited capabilities. The significance of the informational domain and the widespread use of propaganda and disinformation by all actors highlight the strategic importance of controlling information and influencing public perception. This multidimensional activity is characteristic of hybrid warfare, where the boundaries between military and non-military actions blur, and actors use a combination of means to achieve their objectives. However, what is important in the context of this study is not the degree of engagement, which may change depending on operational or tactical needs, but rather the number of entities involved in such conflicts and their networks of connections. For a better understanding of these relationships, a diagram of mutual dependencies and connections is presented based on the results from the analysis of media reports (Figure 2.8). Detailed results are shown in Table A2.5 in Appendix 2.

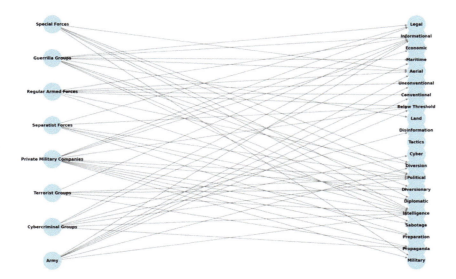

FIGURE 2.8   Connections of actors and actions in hybrid warfare

Source: Own study

CONCLUSIONS

As highlighted in the introduction, a feature is a general property of a phenomenon, giving it a unique character, while an action is the practical application of a feature in the context of hybrid warfare. Actions in this study are categorized as military actions, including both conventional and unconventional actions, and as non-military actions. The analysis of sources confirmed that there is a spectrum of operations (actions) and state and non-state actors in the wars in Ukraine and the Middle East. Statistics from the analysis of media reports prove that unconventional military actions are used to a much greater extent than other types of actions. This is dominated by sabotage and diversionary activities, which are primarily associated with conventional operations and regular armed forces, as well as terrorist groups. The label of destabilization is also an important indicator, which can denote both deliberate action and the effect of integrated actions. In the case of non-military actions, the main labels are propaganda and disinformation activities, which coexist with conventional operations and regular military forces, as well as activities in the information and political sphere. But also noteworthy is the growing importance of cognitive operations, PSYOPs, and intimidation.

In the study *The Landscape of Hybrid Threats*, the authors found that, in line with Frank Hoffman's analysis, hybrid strategies emphasize non-state actors (Giannopoulos et al., 2021). However, an analysis of media coverage of the war in Ukraine shows that although non-state actors, in particular terrorist groups, cyber groups, and PMCs, are an important element of hybrid operations, they do not dominate over regular armed forces (state actors). This may also suggest that hybrid warfare differs at certain levels between regions. Considering the statistics from the analysis of media reports, state actors account for 8,736 compared to 760 non-state actors, a ratio of 11.49:1. Another aspect is also worth noting. The Gerasimov doctrine suggests that non-military actions are four times more significant than military actions. In our analysis, the ratio of non-military actions to all military actions is 3.69:1, and to conventional military actions as high as 193.7:1. These data confirm that non-military actions, such as propaganda and disinformation, play a key role in hybrid conflicts, but are carried out to varying degrees by both state and non-state actors. In conventional military actions, it is also worth noting the increasing number of manoeuvre codes, which may be an indicator suggesting an impending armed conflict.

This chapter adopts the research hypothesis that hybrid warfare is characterized by the integrated and flexible use of both military (conventional and unconventional) and non-military means by both state and non-state actors to achieve strategic advantage and leads to the creation of a comprehensive hybrid system.

This hypothesis has been positively confirmed by research, which has shown that hybrid warfare is indeed characterized by the integrated and flexible use of military and non-military means by state and non-state actors to achieve strategic advantage and leads to the creation of a complex hybrid system with a network character, in which the actions of one element triggered reactions in other areas (cascade effect).

The complex nature of this type of war necessitates changes at both the systemic and individual security level. Systems for the protection of civilians need to be reviewed and adapted to the networked conditions of hybrid warfare. Traditional lines of defence are no longer adequate in such a complex environment, especially when actions primarily target societies. Globalization, which plays a key role in facilitating hybrid operations, is also an additional complication. It increases the availability of technologies and tools that can be used to carry out complex operations. An example of this is the global failure of the Microsoft and CrowdStrike operating systems on 19 July 2024 (Reuters, 2024). This failure highlighted the potential ease of destabilizing the global technology infrastructure. The incident was immediately exploited by the Russian Federation, which presented a narrative of its strategic technological superiority as part of its information and propaganda efforts. Such activities are aimed not only at strengthening the internal legitimacy of power, but also at weakening the geopolitical position of opponents by highlighting its own technological independence capabilities and the lack of such independence among other states.

Ensuring internal security, including the protection of civilians, requires an integrated and flexible approach that not only responds to existing threats but also anticipates future challenges. A key element here is the ability to build resilience at strategic, operational, and societal levels. Social resilience, understood as society's ability to adapt and survive in the face of crises, is as important as other means of defence and protection. Colin S. Gray rightly observed *that humanity is the best evidence of the age-old basis of war.* Technologies may change methods of operation, but it is human decisions, motivations, and responses that are central to war strategies. In the context of hybrid warfare, the human capacity for adaptation and resilience becomes a key factor supporting systemic models of homeland security (Hoffman, 2020).

BIBLIOGRAPHY

Accorsi, A., (2024), How Israel Mastered Information Warfare in Gaza. *Foreign Policy*, 11 March. Available at: https://foreignpolicy.com/2024/03/11/israel-gaza-hamas-netanyahu-warfare-misinformation/. Accessed: 9 May 2024.

Agencies and TOI Staff, (2023), World Bank Warns War Causing 'Unparalleled' Damage to Palestinian Economy. *The Times of Israel*, 12 December. Available at: https://www.timesofisrael.com/world-bank-warns-war-causing-unparalleled-damage-to-palestinian-economy/. Accessed: 21 June 2024.

Aho, A., Midões, C., and Šnore, A., (2020), *Hybrid Threats in the Financial System*. Hybrid CoE Working Paper 8. Available at: https://www.hybridcoe.fi/publications/hybrid-coe-working-paper-8-hybrid-threats-in-the-financial-system/ (PDF). Accessed: 9 June 2024.

Al Jazeera and News Agencies, (2023), Israel-Gaza War 'Devastating' Palestine Economy, UN Warns. *Al Jazeera*, 10 November. Available at: https://www.aljazeera.com/economy/2023/11/10/israel-gaza-war-having-massive-impact-on-palestinian-economy. Accessed: 23 June 2024.

Azzuni, A., and Breyer, C., (2020), Global Energy Security Index and Its Application on National Level. *Energies*, 13(10), 2502. https://doi.org/10.3390/en13102502. Accessed: 27 June 2024.

Banasik, M., (2023), Współczesny Wymiar Strategicznej Rywalizacji Militarnej. Facta Simonidis. Available at: https://akademiazamojska.edu.pl (PDF). Accessed: 9 May 2024.

Beauchamp-Mustafaga, N. (2023), Chinese Next-Generation Psychological Warfare: The Military Applications of Emerging Technologies and Implications for the United States, RAND Corporation, Santa Monica, CA. ISBN: 978-1-9774-1106-8 (PDF).

Belsat, (2024), Rośnie zagrożenie rosyjskim sabotażem i aktami terroru w Europie. *Jak odpowie NATO?* Available at: https://belsat.eu/pl/news/11-05-2024-rosnie-zagrozenie-rosyjskim-sabotazem-i-aktami-terroru-w-europie-jak-odpowie-nato. Accessed: 20 May 2024.

Bernal, A., Carter, C., Singh, I., Cao, K., and Madreperla, O., (2020), Cognitive Warfare: An Attack on Truth and Thought. *NATO, Johns Hopkins University*. Available at: https://innovationhub-act.org/wp-content/uploads/2023/12/Cognitive-Warfare.pdf. Accessed: 3 June 2024.

Bilal, A., (2021), Hybrid Warfare – New Threats, Complexity, and "Trust" as the Antidote. *NATO Review*, 30 November. Available at: https://www.nato.int/docu/review/articles/2021/11/30/hybrid-warfare-new-threats-complexity-and-trust-as-the-antidote/index.html. Accessed: 19 June 2024.

Bilal, A., (2024), Hybrydowa wojna Rosji z Zachodem. *Przegląd NATO*, 26 April. Available at: https://www.nato.int/docu/review/pl/articles/2024/04/26/hybrydowa-wojna-rosji-z-zachodem/index.html. Accessed: 5 May 2024.

Biznes Newseria, (2022), Atak na spółki energetyczne to element wojny hybrydowej. *Executive Magazine*, 11 October. Available at: https://executivemagazine.pl/przemysl-logistyka/atak-na-spolki-energetyczne-to-element-wojny-hybrydowej-ma-oslabic-ich-pozycje-i-bezpieczenstwo-energetyczne-kraju/. Accessed: 30 June 2024.

Bjerregaard, T., (2012), Hybrid Warfare: A Military Revolution or Revolution in Military Affairs? Master's Thesis. US Army Command and General Staff College. Available at: https://apps.dtic.mil/sti/tr/pdf/ADA569384.pdf. Accessed: 3 June 2024.

Blank, S., (1995–2023), Collected Works. Foreign Policy Research Institute. Available at: https://www.fpri.org/contributor/stephen-blank/. Accessed: 10 June 2024.

Bluszcz, J., and Valente, M., (2020), The Economic Costs of Hybrid Wars: The Case of Ukraine. *VoxUkraine*, 30 July. Available at: https://voxukraine.org/en/the-economic-costs-of-hybrid-wars-the-case-of-ukraine. Accessed: 14 June 2024.

Bobadilla, J., Ortega, F., Hernando, A., and Gutiérrez, A., (2013), Recommender Systems Survey. *Knowledge-Based Systems*, 40, 109–132. https://doi.org/10.1016/j.knosys.2013.03.012. Available at: https://www.sciencedirect.com/science/article/abs/pii/S0950705113001044. Accessed: 4 May 2024.

Boucher, J.-C., (2017), Hybrid Warfare and Civil-Military Relations. *Policy Update*, December. Available at: https://d3n8a8pro7vhmx.cloudfront.net/cdfai/pages/3090/attachments/original/1512422821/Hybrid_Warfare_and_Civil-Military_Relations.pdf?1512422821 (PDF). Accessed: 7 June 2024.

Bryjka, F., (2021), *Wojny Zastępcze*. Warsaw: Polski Instytut Spraw Międzynarodowych. Available at: https://www.researchgate.net/publication/349956085_WOJNY_ZASTEPCZE. Accessed: 16 June 2024.

Burt, T., (2023), The Face of Modern Hybrid Warfare. *Digital Front Lines*, 25 May. Available at: https://digitalfrontlines.io/2023/05/25/the-face-of-modern-hybrid-warfare/. Accessed: 23 May 2024.

Cambridge Dictionary, (2024), Meaning of Psych Ops in English. Available at: https://dictionary.cambridge.org/dictionary/english/psych-ops. Accessed: 25 May 2024.

Chen, J., and Xu, Y., (2015), Information Manipulation and Reform in Authoritarian Regimes. *Political Science Research and Methods*, 5(1), DOI: 10.1017/psrm.2015.21. Accessed: 9 June 2024.

Chivvis, C.S., (2017), Understanding Russian Hybrid Warfare and What Can be Done About It. Testimony before the Committee on Armed Services, United States House of Representatives, 22 March. The

RAND Corporation. Available at: https://www.rand.org/content/dam/rand/pubs/testimonies/CT400/CT468/RAND_CT468.pdf (PDF). Accessed: 1 May 2024.

Coleman, D., (2019), Digital Colonialism: The 21st Century Scramble for Africa through the Extraction and Control of User Data and the Limitations of Data Protection Laws. *Michigan Journal of Race & Law*, 24(2). Available at: https://repository.law.umich.edu/mjrl/vol24/iss2/6 (PDF). Accessed: 6 June 2024.

Connell, M.E., and Evans, R., (2015), *Russia's 'Ambiguous Warfare' and Implications for the U.S. Marine Corps.* CNA Occasional Paper, Strategic Studies, CNA Analysis and Solutions. Available at: https://www.cna.org. Accessed: 28 June 2024.

Council of the European Union, (2022), *Council Conclusions on Foreign Information Manipulation and Interference (FIMI)*. Brussels: General Secretariat of the Council. Document 11429/22. Available at: https://data.consilium.europa.eu/doc/document/ST-11429-2022-INIT/en/pdf. Accessed: 10 November 2024.

Council of the European Union, (2023), *The Business of War – Growing Risks from Private Military Companies*. ART – Research Paper, 31 August. Available at: https://www.consilium.europa.eu/media/66700/private-military-companies-final-31-august.pdf. Accessed: 27 May 2024.

Cyber attacks in the Israel-Hamas war, (2023), Cloudflare Blog, 23 October. Available at: https://blog.cloudflare.com/cyber-attacks-in-the-israel-hamas-war/. Accessed: 20 May 2024.

Danyk, Y., and Briggs, C.M., (2022), Modern Cognitive Operations and Hybrid Warfare. *Journal of Strategic Security*, 16(1). Available at: https://digitalcommons.usf.edu/jss/vol16/iss1/3 (PDF). Accessed: 5 June 2024.

De Castro, N., (2021), On Private Military Companies and Hybrid Warfare. *IJOIS*, Spring, Volume VIII (1), Program in Arms Control & Domestic and International Security, Sciences Po, Paris. Available at: https://ugresearchjournals.illinois.edu/index.php/IJOIS/article/view/765 (PDF). Accessed: 28 May 2024.

De Wijk, R., (2012), Hybrid Conflict and the Changing Nature of Actors. In: J. Lindley-French and Y. Boyer (eds.), *The Oxford Handbook of War*. Oxford: Oxford University Press.

Dietrich, M., (2024), Economic Fallout of Israel's Gaza Strip Operation Threatens Growth Prospects. *Military Balance Blog*, 16 February. Available at: https://www.iiss.org/online-analysis/military-balance/2024/02/economic-fallout-of-israels-gaza-strip-operation-threatens-growth-prospects/. Accessed: 22 June 2024.

Dudin, M. N., Fedorova, I. J., Ploticina, L. A., Tokmurzin, T. M., Belyaeva, M. V., and Ilyin, A. B., (2018), International Practices to Improve Economic Security, *European Research Studies Journal*,

XXI(1). Available at: https://www.ersj.eu/dmdocuments/2018_XXI_1_38.pdf. Accessed:15 November 2024.

Dupuy, A.C., Nussbaum, D., Butrimas, V., and Granitsas, A., (2021), Bezpieczeństwo energetyczne w czasach wojny hybrydowej. *NATO Review*, 13 January. Available at: https://www.nato.int/docu/review/pl/ articles/2021/01/13/bezpieczenstwo-energetyczne-w-czasach-wojny-hybrydowej/index.html. Accessed: 29 June 2024.

Dyner, A.M., (2022), The Border Crisis as an Example of Hybrid Warfare. The Polish Institute of International Affairs, 2 February. Available at: https://www.pism.pl/publications/the-border-crisis-as-an-example-of-hybrid-warfare. Accessed: 2 June 2024.

Dziwisz, D., and Sajduk, B., (2023), The Russia-Ukraine Conflict from 2014 to 2023 and the Significance of a Strategic Victory in Cyberspace. *ACIG*, 2(1). https://doi.org/10.60097/ACIG/162842. Available at: https://www.acigjournal.com/pdf-184308-105065?filename=The%20Russia_Ukraine.pdf (PDF). Accessed: 16 May 2024.

Encyclopedia Bezpieczeństwa Narodowego, Itrich-Drabrek J., Misuk A., Mitkov Sz., and Bryczek-Wróblel P., (red.), (2024), Elipsa, Warszawa, Available at: https://encyklopedia.revite.pl. Accessed: 11 May 2024.

ENISA Threat Landscape – reports (2024), Available at: https://www.enisa.europa.eu/publications/enisa-threat-landscape-2024. Accessed: 6 May 2024.

European Commission, (2024), Hybrid Threats. Available at: https://defence-industry-space.ec.europa.eu/eu-defence-industry/hybrid-threats_en. Accessed: 30 June 2024.

European Commission, (2024), Tackling Online Disinformation. Available at: https://digital-strategy.ec.europa.eu/en/policies/online-disinformation. Accessed: 10 November 2024.

EUvsDisinfo, (2024), MH17: dziesięć lat rosyjskich kłamstw i zaprzeczania, 16 July. Available at: https://euvsdisinfo.eu/pl/mh17-dziesiec-lat-rosyjskich-klamstw-i-zaprzeczania/. Accessed: 8 May 2024.

Farkas, J., Neumayer, C. (2020). Disguised Propaganda from Digital to Social Media. In: Hunsinger, J., Allen, M., and Klastrup, L. (eds.), *Second International Handbook of Internet Research*. Dordrecht: Springer. Available at: https://doi.org/10.1007/978-94-024-1555-1_33. Accessed: 14 May 2024.

Fave, D., and Verrocchio, M., (2022), Psychological Warfare in a Changing World. Available at: https://www.itssverona.it/psychological-warfare-in-a-changing-world. Accessed: 28 May 2024.

Fox, A., (2017), Hybrid Warfare: The 21st Century Russian Way of Warfare. https://doi.org/10.13140/RG.2.2.35922.38086. Accessed: 30 June 2024.

Fuller, J.F.C., (1926), *The Foundations of the Science of War*. London: Hutchinson & Co. Available at: https://archive.org/details/foundationsofsci00jfcf. Accessed: 17 May 2024.

Galeotti, M., (2016), Hybrid, Ambiguous, and Non-Linear? How New is Russia's 'New Way of War? *Small Wars & Insurgencies*, 27(2). DOI: 10.1080/09592318.2015.1129170. Available at: https://www.tandfonline.com/doi/full/10.1080/09592318.2015.1129170. Accessed: 11 May 2024.

Galeotti, M. (2018), (Mis)Understanding Russia's Two 'Hybrid Wars', Available at: https://www.eurozine.com/misunderstanding-russias-two-hybrid-wars/?pdf. Accessed: 20 November 2024.

Giannopoulos, G., Smith, H., and Theocharidou, M. (2021), *The Landscape of Hybrid Threats: A Conceptual Model*, European Centre of Excellence for Countering Hybrid Threats (Hybrid CoE) & Joint Research Centre (JRC), European Commission. Available at: https://euhybnet.eu/wp-content/uploads/2021/06/Conceptual-Framework-Hybrid-Threats-HCoE-JRC.pdf. Accessed: 6 June 2024

Giesea, J., (2023), Hybrid Intelligence As A Response to Hybrid Warfare? *Small Wars Journal*, Available at: https://smallwarsjournal.com/jrnl/art/hybrid-intelligence-response-hybrid-warfare. Accessed: 24 May 2024.

Giles, K., (2023), Russian Cyber and Information Warfare in Practice: Lessons Observed from the War on Ukraine. *Russia and Eurasia Programme*, Available at: https://www.chathamhouse.org/sites/default/files/2023-12/2023-12-14-russian-cyber-info-warfare-giles.pdf (PDF). Accessed: 12 May 2024.

Guénette, J.D., Kenworthy, P., and Wheeler, C., (2022), Implications of the War in Ukraine for the Global Economy. *Equitable Growth, Finance, and Institutions Policy Note*. Available at: https://thedocs.worldbank.org/en/doc/5d903e848db1d1b83e0ec8f744e55570-0350012021/related/Implications-of-the-War-in-Ukraine-for-the-Global-Economy.pdf. Accessed: 24 June 2024.

Gunneriusson, H. (2021). Hybrid Warfare: Development, Historical Context, Challenges and Interpretations, *Icono 14*, 19(1), pp.15–37. Available at: doi: 10.7195/ri14.v19i1.1608. Accessed: 4 June 2024.

Hoffman, F. G. (2020), Fifty Shades of Gray: A Tribute to Colin S. Gray (1943–2020), Foreign Policy Research Institute. Available at: https://www.fpri.org/article/2020/03/fifty-shades-of-gray-a-tribute-to-colin-s-gray-1943-2020/. Accessed: 25 November 2024.

Hovhannisyan, G., (2024), Cyber Warfare: Understanding New Frontiers in Global Conflicts. *Dark Reading*, 21 March. Available at: https://www.darkreading.com/cyberattacks-data-breaches/cyber-warfare-understanding-new-frontiers-in-global-conflicts. Accessed: 18 May 2024.

Hoyle, A., and Šlerka, J., (2024a), *Cause for Concern: The Continuing Success and Impact of Kremlin Disinformation Campaigns*. Hybrid CoE Working Paper 29. The European Centre of Excellence for Countering Hybrid Threats. ISBN 978-952-7472-94-1 (web), ISBN 978-952-7472-95-8 (print). Available at: https://www.hybridcoe.fi (PDF). Accessed: 4 May 2024.

Hoyle, A., and Šlerka, J., (2024b), *Cause for Concern: The Continuing Success and Impact of Kremlin Disinformation Campaigns*. Hybrid CoE Working Paper 29. Available at: https://www.hybridcoe.fi/wp-content/uploads/2024/03/20240306-Hybrid-CoE-Working-Paper-29-The-impact-of-Kremlin-disinformation-WEB.pdf (PDF). Accessed: 7 May 2024.

Huber, T. M. (2002), *Compound Warfare: A Conceptual Framework*. In: T. M. Huber (ed.), *Compound Warfare: That Fatal Knot*, Combat Studies Institute Press, Fort Leavenworth, KS, pp. 1–12. Available at: https://www.armyupress.army.mil/Portals/7/combat-studies-institute/csi-books/compound_warfare.pdf. Accessed: 29 June 2024.

Hung, T.-C., and Hung, T.-W., (2022), How China's Cognitive Warfare Works: A Frontline Perspective of Taiwan's Anti-Disinformation Wars. *Journal of Global Security Studies*, 7(4), ogac016, Available at: https://doi.org/10.1093/jogss/ogac016. Accessed: 4 June 2024.

Huovinen, P., (2011), *Hybrid Warfare – Just a Twist of Compound Warfare? Views on Warfare from the United States Armed Forces Perspective*. Department of Military History, Senior Staff Officer Course 63, Finnish Army, National Defence University, Available at: https://www.doria.fi/bitstream/handle/10024/74215/E4081_HuovinenKPO_EUK63.pdf. Accessed: 22 June 2024.

Huskaj, G., (2023), Offensive Cyberspace Operations for Cyber Security. *International Conference on Cyber Warfare and Security*, 18(1), 476–479. https://doi.org/10.34190/iccws.18.1.1054 (PDF). License: CC BY-NC-ND 4.0. Accessed: 15 May 2024.

Interia, (2024), Rosja zbroi się na potęgę. Tryb wojenny niepokoi ekspertów. Available at: https://wydarzenia.interia.pl/raport-ukraina-rosja/news-rosja-zbroi-sie-na-potege-tryb-wojenny-niepokoi-ekspertow, nId,7778402. Accessed: 11 June 2024.

Israel–Hamas 2023 Symposium – Cyberspace – The Hidden Aspect of the Conflict, (2023), by T. Mimran, Lieber Institute West Point, 30 November. Available at: https://lieber.westpoint.edu/cyberspace-hidden-aspect-conflict/. Accessed: 21 May 2024.

Jabłońska-Bonca, J. (2017), *Prywatna ochrona bezpieczeństwa. Koncepcje – podmioty – zadania – normy – konteksty*, Wolters Kluwer Polska, Warszawa. Wydanie 1. Seria: Monografie, ISBN (druk): 978-83-8107-409-4, ISBN (PDF): 978-83-8107-706-4, ISBN (EPUB): 978-83-8107-692-0.

JAPCC, (2024), Hybrid Conflict, Hybrid Warfare and Resilience. Available at: https://www.japcc.org/chapters/hybrid-conflict-hybrid-warfare-and-resilience/. Accessed: 13 June 2024.

Jarecka, U. (2008), Propaganda Wizualna Słusznej Wojny: Media Wizualne XX Wieku Wobec Konfliktów Zbrojnych, Wydawnictwo Instytutu Filozofii I Socjologii PAN, Warszawa. ISBN: 978-83-7388-146-4.

Jordan, J., (2021), 'International Competition Below the Threshold of War: Toward a Theory of Gray Zone Conflict'. *Journal of Strategic Security*, 14(1), pp.1–24, Available at: https://doi.org/10.5038/1944 -0472.14.1.1836, Accessed: 17 June 2024.

Jowett, G.S., and O'Donnell, V., (2006), *Propaganda and Persuasion*. Washington: Sage Publications. ISBN 1412908981. Accessed: 10 May 2024.

Jung, S.C., (2019), *Diversionary Theory of War*. Oxford Bibliographies. https://doi.org/10.1093/OBO/9780199743292-0265. Accessed: 16 May 2024.

Jungwirth, R., Smith, H., Willkomm, E., Savolainen, J., Alonso Villota, M., Lebrun, M., Aho, A., and Giannopoulos, G., (2023), *Hybrid Threats: A Comprehensive Resilience Ecosystem*. Luxembourg: Publications Office of the European Union. Available at: https://publications.jrc.ec.europa.eu/repository/handle/JRC129019. Accessed: 8 June 2024.

Kaja, A., Luo, Y., and Stratford, T.P., (2015), China's New National Security Law. *Global Policy Watch*, 7 July. Available at: https://www.globalpolicywatch.com/2015/07/chinas-new-national-security-law/. Accessed: 10 June 2024.

Kalyanaraman, S., (2003). Conceptualisation of Guerrilla Warfare. *Strategic Analysis: A Monthly Journal of the IDSA*, 27(2), pp. 1–20, Available at: https://ciaotest.cc.columbia.edu/olj/sa/sa_apr03/sa_apr03kas01.html, Accessed: 15 May 2024.

Kołodziejczak, M. E., (2018), Definicyjno-prawne regulacje wojny oraz terminów pochodnych, Roczniki Nauk Prawnych, XXVIII(4). DOI: http://dx.doi.org/10.18290/rnp.2018.28.4-4, Accessed: 17 June 2024.

Kończal, A., and Kustra, W., (2021), Koncepcja bezpieczeństwa morskiego Unii Europejskiej. *Świat Idei i Polityki*, 20(2). https://doi.org/10.34767/SIIP.2021.02.06. Accessed: 13 May 2024.

Korhonen, I., (2024), Ukraine's Economy Grows Amidst the Rising Toll of War. *BOFIT Bulletin*, 23 February. Available at: https://www.bofbulletin.fi/en/blogs/2024/ukraines-economy-grows-amidst-the-rising-toll-of-war/. Accessed: 17 June 2024.

Kovalová, A., (2024), What Is a PSYOP, and How Can It Be Used in Hybrid War? *ESET Blog*, 21 February. Available at: https://www.eset.com/blog/consumer/what-is-a-psyop-and-how-can-it-be-used-in-hybrid-war/. Accessed: 27 May 2024.

Kozierawski, D.S., and Lotarski, P., (2022), Konflikty zbrojne na Bliskim Wschodzie i ich wpływ na zmiany na polu walki. Influence of Middle East armed conflicts into battlefield changes. *Zeszyt*, 159(1). https://doi.org/10.5604/01.3001.0015.8557. Accessed: 12 May 2024.

Kozłowski, A., (2024), Wojna toczy się na cyber-Bliskim Wschodzie. Nawet Hamas rzucił wyzwanie. *Onet*, Available at: https://www.onet.pl/informacje/nowaeuropawschodnia/wojna-toczy-sie-na-cyber-bliskim-wschodzie-nawet-hamas-rzucil-wyzwanie/ch2tfyw, 30bc1058. Accessed: 22 May 2024.

Kramer, F. D., and Lauren M. Speranza. (2017), Meeting the Russian Hybrid Challenge: A Comprehensive Strategic Framework. Atlantic Council, ISBN: 978-1-61977-415-5.

Kristinova, E., (2024), Psychological Warfare and Hybrid Threats – Attacks on Hearts and Minds. Available at: https://londonpolitica.com/conflict-and-security-watch-blog-list/psychological-warfare. Accessed: 29 May 2024.

Kristinova, E., and Alvarez-Aragones, P., (2024), Hybrid Threats 101 – Conceptual and Historical Context. Available at: https://londonpolitica.com/conflict-and-security-watch-blog-list/hybrid-threats. Accessed: 1 June 2024.

Królikowski, H., (2016), Siły operacji specjalnych (Wojska Specjalne) w konfliktach hybrydowych. *Bezpieczeństwo: Teoria i Praktyka*, 34(XVII). Available at: https://cejsh.icm.edu.pl/cejsh/element/bwmeta1.element.desklight-b6e55ad8-a277-4b14-b30c-98fc83 1bd3ff/c/BTiP_2016_3_01_Krolikowski.pdf. Accessed: 26 May 2024.

Kublik, E., (2019), Strategic Meaning of Reflexive Control Methods in the CO. *Kultura Bezpieczeństwa*, 33. https://doi.org/10.5604/01. 3001.0013.1944. Accessed: 19 June 2024.

Kyiv School of Economics, (2023), $147.5 Billion—The Total Amount of Damages Caused to Ukraine's Infrastructure Due to the War, Available at: https://kse.ua/about-the-school/news/147-5-billion-the-total-amount-of-damages-caused-to-ukraine-s-infrastructure-due-to-the-war-as-of-april-2023/. Accessed: 15 June 2024.

Marten, K. (2019), Russia's Use of Semi-State Security Forces: The Case of the Wagner Group, *Post-Soviet Affairs*, 35(3), pp. 181–204 Available at: doi: 10.1080/1060586X.2019.1591142. Accessed: 15 June 2024.

Marlin, R. (2013) Propaganda and the Ethics of Persuasion. 2nd edn. Ontario: Broadview Press.

Mazarr, M.J., Bauer, R.M., Casey, A., Heintz, S.A., and Matthews, L.J., (2019), The Emerging Risk of Virtual Societal Warfare: Social Manipulation in a Changing Information Environment. RAND Corporation. Available at: https://www.rand.org/t/RR2714 (PDF). Accessed: 8 June 2024.

McCuen, J. J. (2008), Hybrid Wars, Military Review, 88(2), pp. 107–113. Available at: https://www.armyupress.army.mil/Portals/7/military-review/Archives/English/MilitaryReview_20080430_art017.pdf. Accessed: 25 June 2024.

MCDC Countering Hybrid Warfare Project, (2019), Countering Hybrid Warfare. Available at: https://assets.publishing.service.gov.uk/media/5c8141e2e5274a2a51ac0b34/concepts_mcdc_countering_hybrid_warfare.pdf. Accessed: 11 June 2024.

Meath Baker, C., (2017), Hybrid Warfare in the Middle East: We Must Do Better. *RUSI*, 7 March. Available at: https://www.rusi.org/explore-our-research/publications/commentary/hybrid-warfare-middle-east-we-must-do-better. Accessed: 12 June 2024.

NATO (2020), Information Warfare, NATO Deep Portal. Available at: https://www.nato.int/nato_static_fl2014/assets/pdf/2020/5/pdf/2005-deepportal4-information-warfare.pdf. Accessed: 2 May 2024.

Nordby, G., (2019), The Four Types of Economic Coercion, Available at: https://medium.com/@gnorby01/the-four-types-of-economic-coercion-810f1fd7f11a#:~:text=The%20four%20types%20are:%20Foreign,,%20Financial%20Power,%20and%20Trade. Accessed: 16 November 2024.

Meredith, S., (2019), Countering Russian Strategic Approaches: Special Operations in Hybrid Warfare. *National Defense University*, June. Available at: https://nsiteam.com/countering-russian-strategic-approaches-special-operations-in-hybrid-warfare/. Accessed: 25 May 2024.

Merom, G., (1990), Democracy, Dependency, and Destabilization: The Shaking of Allende's Regime. *Political Science Quarterly*, 105(1). Published by Oxford University Press. https://doi.org/10.2307/2151226. Accessed: 22 May 2024.

Mitrovic, M., (2017), Economic and Energy Aspects of Hybrid Threats to National Security. *Vojno delo* (6/2017). https://doi.org/10.5937/vojdelo1706304M. Accessed: 10 June 2024.

Mumford, A., and Carlucci, P., (2023), Hybrid Warfare: The Continuation of Ambiguity by Other Means. *European Journal of International Security*, 8. https://doi.org/10.1017/eis.2022.19. Available at: https://www.cambridge.org/core/services/aop-cambridge-core/content/view/1B3336D8109D418F89D732EB98B774E5/S2057563722000190a.pdf (PDF). Accessed: 19 May 2024.

Murray, W., and Mansoor, P.R., (2012), *Hybrid Warfare: Fighting Complex Opponents from the Ancient World to the Present.* Cambridge: Cambridge University Press. https://doi.org/10.1017/CBO9781139199254. Accessed: 9 June 2024.

Niedziński, B., (2024), Rosja, Chiny i Iran. To nowa oś zła zdaniem byłych brytyjskich dowódców. *Bankier.pl*, 9 July. Available at: https://www.bankier.pl/wiadomosc/Rosja-Chiny-i-Iran-To-nowa-os-zla-zdaiem-bylych-brytyjskich-dowodcow-8779826.html. Accessed: 7 June 2024.

Novossiolova, T., and Georgiev, G., (2023), *Countering Hybrid Warfare in the Black Sea Region: Strengthening Institutional Frameworks for Protection and Resilience.* Center for the Study of Democracy, 29 December. Available at: https://csd.eu/publications/publication/countering-hybrid-warfare-in-the-black-sea-region/ (PDF). Accessed: 4 June 2024.

Noyes, A., and Egel, D., (2023), *Winning the Irregular World War.* RAND Corporation, 6 November. Available at: https://www.rand.org/pubs/commentary/2023/11/winning-the-irregular-world-war.html. Accessed: 26 June 2024.

Ogrodowczyk, P., (2013), Special Services in the Modern State System. *SBN*, 4(1). https://doi.org/10.37055/sbn/129802. Available at: https://sbn.wat.edu.pl/pdf-129802-56672?filename=SPECIAL%20SERVICES%20IN%20THE.pdf. Accessed: 23 May 2024.

Olech, A., (2024), Izrael-Palestyna. Rywalizacja w cyberprzestrzeni zaognia się. *Cyber Defence* 24, 8 February. Available at: https://cyberdefence24.pl/cyberbezpieczenstwo/izrael-palestyna-rywalizacja-w-cyberprzestrzeni-zaognia-sie. Accessed: 13 May 2024.

PAM, (2023), Gigantyczna kwota ujawniona. Rosja wydała na wojnę prawdziwą fortunę. *Money.pl*, 17 September. Available at: https://www.money.pl/gospodarka/rachunek-za-wojne-putina-rosja-wydala-ponad-167-mld-dolarow-6942496814578304a.html. Accessed: 12 June 2024.

Paździorek, P., (2021), Operacyjne aspekty koncepcji A2/AD. Operational Aspects of A2/AD Concept. *Wiedza Obronna*, 275(2). https://doi.org/10.34752/2021-c275. Available at: https://wiedzaobronna.edu.pl (PDF). Accessed: 11 May 2024.

Pettyjohn, S.L., and Wasser, B., (2019), *Competing in the Gray Zone: Russian Tactics and Western Responses.* RAND Corporation. Available at: https://www.rand.org/pubs/research_reports/RR2791.html. Accessed: 8 May 2024.

Pifer, S., (2014), Watch Out for Little Green Men. *Der Spiegel*, 7 July. Available at: https://www.spiegel.de/international/europe/nato-needs-strategy-for-possible-meddling-by-putin-in-baltic-states-a-979707.html. Accessed: 29 May 2024.

Pocheptsov, G., (2018), Cognitive Attacks in Russian Hybrid Warfare. *Information & Security*, 41. https://doi.org/10.11610/isij.4103. Accessed: 7 June 2024.

Preliminary Assessment of the Economic Impact of the Destruction in Gaza and Prospects for Economic Recovery (2024), UNCTAD Rapid Assessment, January. Available at: https://unctad.org/publication/preliminary-assessment-economic-impact-destruction-gaza-and-prospects-economic-recovery. Accessed: 19 June 2024.

Procter, C., (2024), Coerced Migration: Mobility Under Siege in Gaza. *Journal of Ethnic and Migration Studies*, 50(10), 2359–2383. https://doi.org/10.1080/1369183X.2024.2312229. Accessed: 3 June 2024.

Psychological Warfare, (2024), RAND Corporation. Available at: https://www.rand.org/topics/psychological-warfare.html. Accessed: 26 May 2024.

Pynnöniemi, K., and Jokela, M., (2020), Perceptions of Hybrid War in Russia: Means, Targets and Objectives Identified in the Russian Debate. *Cambridge Review of International Affairs*, 33(6). Available at: https://doi.org/10.1080/09557571.2020.1787949. Accessed: 13 May 2024.

Radin, A., (2017), *Hybrid Warfare in the Baltics: Threats and Potential Responses*. RAND Corporation. Available at: https://www.rand.org/t/RR1577. Accessed: 13 June 2024.

RAND Corporation – Information Operations, n.d., RAND Corporation. Available at: https://www.rand.org/topics/information-operations.html. Accessed: 3 May 2024.

Rauta, V., (2020), Towards a Typology of Non-State Actors in "Hybrid Warfare": Proxy, Auxiliary, Surrogate and Affiliated Forces. *Cambridge Review of International Affairs*, 33(6). https://doi.org/10.1080/09557571.2019.1656600. Accessed: 13 June 2024.

Reuters, (2024), Microsoft Says about 8.5 Million of its Devices Affected by Crowdstrike-Related Outage, Available at: https://www.reuters.com/technology/microsoft-says-about-85-million-its-devices-affected-by-crowdstrike-related-2024-07-20. Accessed: 20 November 2024.

Rogers, Z., (2021), The Promise of Strategic Gain in the Digital Information Age: What Happened? *The Cyber Defense Review*, 6(1), Available at: https://www.researchgate.net/publication/377398125_The_Promise_of_Strategic_Gain_in_the_Digital_Information_Age_What_HappenedAccessed: 2 June 2024.

Russell, J. A., (2004), Asymmetrical Warfare: Today 's Challenge to U.S. Military Power, *Naval War College Review*, 57(1), Article 19. Available at: https://digital-commons.usnwc.edu/nwc-review/vol57/iss1/19. Accessed: 24 June 2024.

Savage, P.J., (2018), The Conventionality of Russia's Unconventional Warfare. *The US Army War College Quarterly: Parameters*, 48(2). https://doi.org/10.55540/0031-1723.2946. Available at: https://press.armywarcollege.edu/parameters/vol48/iss2/9 (PDF). Accessed: 11 June 2024.

Schnaufer, Tad A. (2017), II. Redefining Hybrid Warfare: Russia's Non-linear War against the West, *Journal of Strategic Security*, 10(1), 17–31. DOI: http://doi.org/10.5038/1944-0472.10.1.1538, Available at: https://digitalcommons.usf.edu/jss/vol10/iss1/3. Accessed: 21 June 2024.

Scowcroft Center for Strategy and Security, (2024), Forward Defense: Promoting an Enduring Military Advantage. Available at: https://www.atlanticcouncil.org/programs/scowcroft-center-for-strategy-and-security/forward-defense/. Accessed: 14 June 2024.

Serwis Rzeczypospolitej Polskiej (2024), Hybrydowy atak na Polskę, Available at: https://www.gov.pl/web/sluzby-specjalne/hybrydowy-atak-na-polske. Accessed: 20 November 2024.

Sharma, R., (2019), Contextual Evolution of Hybrid Warfare and the Complexities. *CLAWS Journal*, 12(2), Winter 2019. Centre for Land Warfare Studies (CLAWS), New Delhi, India. Available at: https://www.claws.in/static/Amrita-Jash.pdf. Accessed: 5 June 2024.

Sheikh, A., (2020), Energy Security and Hybrid Threats – A General Overview. Available at: https://londonpolitica.com/conflict-and-security-watch-blog-list/energy-security. Accessed: 28 June 2024.

Sherr, J., (2017), The Militarization of Russian Policy, Transatlantic Academy Paper Series, No. 10. Transatlantic Academy, Washington, DC. Available at: https://www.gmfus.org/sites/default/files/Militarization%2520edited.pdf. Accessed: 20 May 2024.

Shortell, D., (2023), UN Report Warns War Has Already Set Gaza and West Bank Economy Back More Than a Decade. *CNN*, 9 November. Available at: https://edition.cnn.com/2023/11/09/middleeast/un-report-gaza-economic-impact-poverty/index.html. Accessed: 18 June 2024.

Siddiqui, U., and Motamedi, M., (2024), Israel's War on Gaza Updates: World Condemns Al Jazeera Journalist's Arrest. *Al Jazeera*, 18 March. Available at: https://www.aljazeera.com/news/liveblog/2024/3/18/israels-war-on-gaza-live-ceasefire-push-as-rafah-invasion-looms?update=2780902. Accessed: 20 June 2024.

Siman-Tov, D., (2019), Disinformation Campaigns and Influence on Cognition: Implications for State Policy, Memorandum No. 197, Institute for National Security Studies (INSS), October 2019. Available at: https://www.inss.org.il/publication/disinformation-campaigns-and-influence-on-cognition-implications-for-state-policy/. Accessed: 1 June 2024.

Starvation as weapon of war being used against Gaza civilians (2023), Oxfam, 25 October. Available at: https://www.oxfam.org/en/press-releases/starvation-weapon-war-being-used-against-gaza-civilians-oxfam. Accessed: 26 June 2024.

Stefanek, M., (2024), Niemcy. Horrendalny koszt wojny w Ukrainie. *DW*, 21 February. Available at: https://www.dw.com/pl/niemcy-horrendalny-koszt-wojny-w-ukrainie/a-68322430. Accessed: 11 June 2024.

Stoilova, V., (2018), The Art of Achieving Political Goals Without Use of Force: War by Non-Military Means. *Information & Security: An International Journal*, 39(2). https://doi.org/10.11610/isij.3911. Available at: https://connections-qj.org/ru/system/files/3911_stoilova_war_by_non-military_means.pdf (PDF). Accessed: 1 May 2024.

Štrucl, D., (2022), Russian Aggression on Ukraine: Cyber Operations and the Influence of Cyberspace on Modern Warfare. *Contemporary Military Challenges*, 2022(2), https://doi.org/10.33179/BSV.99.SVI.11.CMC.24.2.6 (PDF). Accessed: 17 May 2024.

Sukhankin, S., (2019), War, Business and Ideology: How Russian Private Military Contractors Pursue Moscow's Interests. *Jamestown Foundation*, 20 March. Available at: https://jamestown.org/program/war-business-and-ideology-how-russian-private-military-contractors-pursue-moscows-interests/. Accessed: 14 June 2024.

Sun-Tzu, Sun Bin., (2012), Sztuka wojny i 36 forteli: Sztuka wojny wg Suna Wu i Sun Bina, tłum. J. Zawadzki, Createspace Independent Publishing, 6 marca 2012. ISBN-10: 1470102323, ISBN-13: 978-1470102326.

The Business of War – Growing risks from Private Military Companies, (2023), Council of the European Union. *ART – Research Paper*, 31 August. Available at: https://www.consilium.europa.eu/media/66700/private-military-companies-final-31-august.pdf. Accessed: 31 May 2024.

The Iron Swords War – Cyber Perspectives from the First 10 Days of the War in Israel, (2023), Check Point Research, 18 October. Available at: https://blog.checkpoint.com/security/the-iron-swords-war-cyber-perspectives-from-the-first-10-days-of-the-war-in-israel/. Accessed: 19 May 2024.

Thornton, R., (2015), The Changing Nature of Modern Warfare. Responding to Russian Information Warfare. *The RUSI Journal*, 160(4). Accessed: 5 June 2024.

Treyger, E., Cheravitch, J., and Cohen, R. S., (2022), Russian Disinformation Efforts on Social Media, RAND Corporation, Santa Monica, CA. ISBN: 978-1-9774-0968-3.

Trusewicz, I., (2024), Ile kosztuje Ukrainę agresja Rosji? Nowe wyliczenia. *Rzeczpospolita*, 25 March. Available at: https://www.rp.pl/gospodarka/art40054041-ile-kosztuje-ukraine-agresja-rosji-nowe-wyliczenia. Accessed: 16 June 2024.

Weisiger, A., (2013), *Logics of War: Explanations for Limited and Unlimited Conflicts*. Ithaca and London: Cornell University Press. Available at: https://library.oapen.org/bitstream/handle/20.500.12657/30789/642713.pdf?sequence=1&isAllowed=y. Accessed: 18 June 2024.

Weissmann, M., Nilsson, N., Palmertz, B., and Thunholm, P., (2021), Conceptualizing and Countering Hybrid Threats and Hybrid Warfare: The Role of the Military in the Grey Zone. In: *Hybrid Warfare: Security and Asymmetric Conflict in International Relations*. London: I.B. Tauris. Available at: https://www.diva-portal.org/smash/get/diva2:1547074/FULLTEXT01.pdf (PDF). Accessed: 18 May 2024.

Welsh, C., Glauber, J., (2024), Food as the "Silent Weapon": Russia's Gains and Ukraine's Losses, Center for Strategic and International Studies (CSIS), Available at: https://www.csis.org/analysis/food-silent-weapon-russias-gains-and-ukraines-losses. Accessed: 20 November 2024.

Wojnowski, M., (2017), Koncepcja wojny sieciowej Aleksandra Dugina jako narzędzie realizacji celów geopolitycznych Federacji Rosyjskiej. *Przegląd Bezpieczeństwa Wewnętrznego*, 9(16). Available at: https://bibliotekanauki.pl/articles/501810 (PDF). Accessed: 27 May 2024.

World Report 2024: Our Annual Review of Human Rights Around the Globe, (2024), *Human Rights Watch*. Available at: https://www.hrw.org/world-report/2024. Accessed: 25 June 2024.

Wschodnia Flanka NATO W Dobie, (2021), Wyzwań A2/AD. Europa Środkowa i Wschodnia. Dekady wolności – czas przemian. Available at: https://www.researchgate.net (PDF). Accessed: 10 May 2024.

Wypior, E., (2023), ENISA's Threat Landscape Report 2022 – Part 9 – Disinformation & Misinformation. Available at: https://seqred.pl/en/enisas-threat-landscape-report-2022-part-9-disinformation-misinformation/. Accessed: 5 May 2024.

Wyrzykowski, K., (2022), PISM Analyst: We Can Expect Acts of Diversion and Other Elements of Hybrid Warfare by Russia in Poland. Available at: https://www.polandatsea.com/pism-analyst-we-can-expect-acts-of-diversion-and-other-elements-of-hybrid-warfare-by-russia-in-poland/. Accessed: 21 May 2024.

Yastrubetska, L., (n.d.), *Financial and Economic Tools of Hybrid Warfare*. Lviv: Ivan Franko National University of Lviv. https://doi.org/10.30525/978-9934-26-356-9-44 (PDF). Accessed: 13 June 2024.

Zabrodskyi, M., Watling, J., Danylyuk, O.V., and Reynolds, N., (2022), *Preliminary Lessons in Conventional Warfighting from Russia's Invasion of Ukraine: February–July 2022*. Royal United Services Institute for Defence and Security Studies. Available at: https://static.rusi.org/359-SR-Ukraine-Preliminary-Lessons-Feb-July-2022-web-final.pdf (PDF). Accessed: 14 May 2024.

CHAPTER 3

Management of critical infrastructure safety in the context of threats of hybrid warfare

GENESIS OF THE METHODOLOGY OF ESSENTIAL SERVICES SECURITY MANAGEMENT

The global security landscape has undergone a significant transformation in recent years, requiring a new way of thinking and acting by security actors and the vulnerable public. The notion of traditional war, based on open armed conflict between states, has been significantly expanded by new strategies and tactics known as "hybrid warfare." Under the new warfare paradigm, hostile states deploy various tools and methods, such as military-political operations, cyberattacks, disinformation, sabotage, terrorism, and many others, to achieve their goals while avoiding open confrontation.

One area that has become particularly vulnerable to the threats posed by hybrid warfare is the essential services (ES) and the critical infrastructure (CI) that enables it. The terms ES and CI are defined differently in legal systems of various countries. The lack of a uniform definition of UK and CI makes it challenging to identify a universal framework for its designation and management. The common feature of ES and CI in each country is that they play a fundamental role in the country's sovereignty, stability, and development in the economic, social, or environmental areas. ES and CI are emerging in critical sectors such as energy, transport, telecommunications, healthcare, access to drinking water, and many others.

The results of a survey of civilians affected by the hybrid war in Ukraine showed that attacks on CI, such as power plants, water supply systems, communication networks, and hospitals, led to:

166   DOI: 10.4324/9781003503859-4

- feeling of hunger in 52.6% of cases,
- feeling of thirst in 77.8% of cases,
- limitations in getting help for injuries in 36.4% of cases,
- limitations in obtaining assistance related to illness in 53.8% of cases,
- feeling too cold in 71.4% of cases.

Moreover, respondents, in assessing their country's readiness to detect, respond to, and counter computer security incidents, indicated that CI operators are moderately prepared for such activities. Respondents made a subjective assessment of CI operators' ability to detect, respond to, and counter computer security incidents on a 5-point scale. A score of 1 indicated a complete lack of preparedness, while 5 indicated the capability of implementing cybersecurity best practices. The resulting score, a weighted average in this area, was 3.1.

In addition to assessing the readiness of state institutions to respond to cyber threats, respondents were asked to rate their country's readiness to detect, respond to, and counter hybrid threats. In this area, the weighted average readiness rating was 4.0.

The results of a survey of media reports on the PAP and Defense.24 news portals, discussed in Chapter 4, indicate that besides sabotage and cyberattacks, CI is being attacked with conventional military tools, such as missile attacks, artillery fire, or drone attacks. In addition, media reports indicate that energy system elements are most often attacked to cut off civilians from electricity.

CI sectors are always dependent on the characteristics of a specific country and are determined by needs of the population affected by ES. In this sense, CI is a resource necessary for the continuity of ES operations. The process approach becomes in this context a methodological framework for characterizing ES, regardless of where it is provided and the legal framework. The decomposition of ES into activities that directly create added value and activities necessary for the added value to be created allows the identification of a complete list of entities on which the uninterrupted operation of the service depends.

Further analysis of the internal processes of the identified entities enables identifying resources, services, or further entities necessary for an effective (at the appropriate level of efficiency) implementation of the process. This analysis results in a verifiable list of resources needed to provide ES. In other words, it is possible to determine the elements of CI based on an analysis of the cause-effect relationships arising from the process dependencies of providing a specific ES. Subsequently, taking advantage of the fact that each resource is susceptible to certain risks, it is possible to determine a list of risks that could interrupt the continuity of operation of individual processes implemented by ES. Lack of continuity of processes carried out by CI (unavailability of a component ES[1]) leads to a loss of continuity of operation of the entire ES. Knowing the risks, operators of ES components can introduce safeguards to mitigate the level of risk.

EVOLUTION OF SECURITY MANAGEMENT – FROM CI TO ES

Ensuring the security of the modern society is a complex and multifaceted process. In view of the ambiguity of this need, it seems equally difficult to assess efficiency and effectiveness in this domain and to define its essence, given the diversity of stakeholders (citizen, business, state). However, the state significantly depends on uninterrupted access to services that condition existence, survival, and development. The ability to identify and protect what is "critical" and to trace the entire value creation chain, in which completely non-obvious entities may be involved, becomes a considerable problem. Maintaining the ability to continuously supply the entities on which state security depends on with essential goods and services has become a fundamental issue for state rulers and researchers (Wiśniewski, 2020).

In terms of practical achievements, one can point to the EU/L333 legislative package, which represents the culmination of an evolution that the approach to CI security management has undergone from an object-oriented approach (protection of specific resources designated as critical by decision-makers) to a service-oriented approach (protection of the value-added created as part of the process of manufacturing and delivering the product/service to the recipient). This package, as of the date of publication of this book, represents the most advanced solution in the field of ES and CI security assurance in the world, indicating the need to protect the value-added capabilities of different audiences.

However, the first stage of evolution towards ensuring the security of entities on which state security depends was an attempt to determine which characteristics should be met by a critical facility. A significant influence on the inclusion of such facilities in state protection mechanisms was a terrorist threat. Starting with the USA Patriot Act, CI was understood to mean systems and physical or virtual resources so essential to the United States that "the failure or destruction of those systems and resources would have a debilitating effect on security, the security of the national economy, national healthcare, or any combination of these matters" (Moteff, Copeland and Fischer). What is more, it was noted that public security could be compromised not only due to CI dysfunction but also due to the interdependencies between different facilities (Rubin, 2001).

To solve this problem in the United States, it was assumed that CI falls within the field of social logistics, understood as the shaping of material flows and accompanying information with a specific social role in order to achieve accessibility to places and to goods that ensure the proper functioning of society and respect for civil and human rights (Szołtysek, 2018). This means that certain services, such as those related to saving endangered lives and providing security (public and in public spaces), are either not for profit or their performance, in addition to making a profit (Szołtysek, 2014), serves a public purpose (Skomra, 2019). In order to identify which material and information flows serve public objectives, one should use the process management theory and note that CI operators, regardless of the nature of the organization (business entity, public administration, or non-profit organization), function as process organizations. This means that the organization's goal is to satisfy customer needs. In contrast, the organization itself is shaped and managed through the viewpoint of the activities carried out in it, i.e. processes. Those processes should adapt closely to the changing environment's dynamics and internal structures (Eusgeld et al., 2011).

A proposal for linking customer needs to the processes implemented by CI operators is provided by the "Six Ways to Die" methodology. It assumes that the primary task of the state is to eliminate factors that can lead to death in six areas (Bennett and Gupta):

- hunger,
- thirst,
- trauma,
- illness,
- excessively high temperature,
- excessively low temperature.

Eliminating sources of danger should take place at three levels of need: the person, groups of citizens, and the state as an organization. For each level of needs, conditions for survival can be described by processes for achieving them. Cybersecurity and Infrastructure Security Agency (CISA) applies the "Six Ways to Die" methodology at the level of central U.S. public administrations. CISA defines critical state functions. Then, by creating a table of critical state functions, it successively defines the processes that serve to achieve them. Critical functions of the state are defined as government and private sector functions of such importance to the United States that their disruption, damage, or destruction would have a detrimental effect on public safety, the security of the national economy, national healthcare, or any combination of these matters. Critical functions are divided into four groups (Table 3.1).

170   Civil Protection and Domestic Security in Hybrid Warfare

TABLE 3.1   National critical function set

Connect	Distribute	Manage	Supply
• Operate Core Network • Provide Cable Access Network Services • Provide Internet-Based Content, Information and Communication Services • Provide Internet Routing, Access and Connection Services • Provide Positioning, Navigation, and Timing Services • Provide Radio Broadcast Access Network Services • Provide Satellite Access Network Services • Provide Wireless Access Network Services • Provide Wireline Access Network Services	• Distribute Electricity • Maintain Supply Chains • Transmit Electricity • Transport Cargo and Passengers by Air • Transport Cargo and Passengers by Rail • Transport Cargo and Passengers by Road • Transport Cargo and Passengers by Vessel • Transport Materials by Pipeline • Transport Passengers by Mass Transit	• Conduct Elections • Develop and Maintain Public Works and Services • Educate and Train • Enforce Law • Maintain Access to Medical Records • Manage Hazardous Materials • Manage Wastewater • Operate Government • Perform Cyber Incident Management Capabilities • Prepare for and Manage Emergencies • Preserve Constitutional Rights • Protect Sensitive Information • Provide and Maintain Infrastructure • Provide Capital Markets and Investment Activities • Provide Consumer and Commercial Banking Services • Provide Funding and Liquidity Services • Provide Identity Management and Associated Trust Support Services • Provide Insurance Services • Provide Medical Care • Provide Payment, Clearing, and Settlement Services • Provide Public Safety • Provide Wholesale Funding • Store Fuel and Maintain Reserves • Support Community Health	• Exploration and Extraction of Fuels • Fuel Refining and Processing Fuels • Generate Electricity • Manufacture Equipment • Produce and Provide Agricultural Products and Services • Produce and Provide Human and Animal Food Products and Services • Produce Chemicals • Provide Metals and Materials • Provide Housing • Provide Information Technology Products and Services • Provide Materiel and Operational Support to Defence • Research and Development • Supply Water

Source: National Critical Functions Set | CISA

Efforts to protect CI were also made in the EU after the attacks on the Tokyo Metro (1995), the WTC (2001), Madrid's railroad infrastructure (2004), and the London Underground (2005), and culminated in the 2008 Directive on the Identification and Designation of European CI and Assessment of Needs to Improve its Protection. This established the criteria for identifying CI, a formal framework for cooperation and exchange of information on threats, and how to protect such facilities in EU member states. Preparing CI protection plans for physical, technical, legal and personal security, ICT security, and business continuity were mandatory. As a result, it became necessary to change the purpose of the protectors' actions and orient themselves to ensure the continuity of service provision, which is considered essential by the state.

In parallel, efforts have been made to strengthen coordination and cooperation in combating the effects of natural disasters and catastrophes within the Union Mechanism for Civil Protection (*Euratom: Council Decision of 23 October 2001 Establishing a Community Mechanism to Facilitate Reinforced Cooperation in Civil Protection Assistance Interventions*, 2001) (UMCP) framework, established in 2001. Through subsequent amendments, the scope of protected assets was expanded. In addition to civil protection, areas such as the environment and property, including cultural heritage, were identified. The catalogue of threats against which the actions described in UMCP must be taken has also been expanded. These threats are all natural and anthropogenic disasters, including the aftermath of terrorist acts, technical, radiological, or environmental disasters and catastrophes, marine pollution, and health emergencies occurring within or outside the EU. In addition, the revised decision emphasizes disaster prevention and building and maintaining emergency capabilities. As a result, it obliges EU member states to, among other things, develop and improve risk management plans.

Due to the volatility of threats and protected facilities, security systems must adapt to current challenges constantly.

The EU institutions have faced this problem, and the effort to enhance CI security is just one of many initiatives for the security of the EU population. These efforts are consistent with the 2010 EU Internal Security Strategy, which identifies five strategic objectives and links CI protection to:

- Objective 2: Combat terrorism and combat radicalization and terrorist recruitment,
- Objective 5: Increase Europe's resilience to crises and disasters.

As a result, it is assumed that an essential determinant of internal security in the EU is CI's resilience to cyberattacks and terrorist attacks. Moreover, in the context of countering these two threats, the European approach to CI protection is evolving, as manifested in two parallel processes.

The first, the European Programme of Critical Infrastructure Protection (EPCIP), culminated in the 2006 EC Communication (*Communication from the Commission on a European Programme for Critical Infrastructure Protection*, 2006) and regulatory framework in the form of Directive 2008/114/EC, which provided the legal basis for recognizing, identifying, and protecting facilities considered European CI. The programme had flaws, but it provided a unified framework for distinguishing and protecting European CI whose disruption may be experienced by two or more EU member states. How the directive was transposed into national law depended on the varying maturity of member states' security management of strategic facilities. The directive took a sectoral approach to selecting CI facilities. When evaluating the results of the programme, it is noticeable that:

- The focus on the two selected sectors was not accidental. The various types of energy networks (electricity, gas, fuel) constitute a very complex and vulnerable structure of supply, which is not constrained by the borders of the member states despite the need for a coherent purchasing policy for energy resources from outside the EU. Efficient transport, in turn, is a prerequisite for the free movement of people and goods, the foundations of the EU starting with the Maastricht Treaty and reaffirmed in the Treaty on the Functioning of the EU (TFEU), among others. However, this freedom may have been curtailed as a result of terrorist attacks, and enhancing resilience to such threats is strongly evident in the genesis and one of the priorities of EPCIP.
- As the directive's creators acknowledge as early as the preamble, it was necessary to extend similar protection mechanisms to the ICT sector.
- The object-oriented approach has limitations, and the strict treatment of CI through the viewpoint of sector membership prevents a correct perception of the functioning of complex systems and networks. As a result, many countries have already taken a systems or services approach at the risk assessment stage.

Therefore, in the document published based on the review signalling a new approach to EPCIP, the sectoral approach has been maintained where it makes sense, sector-specific risk assessment methodologies exist, and a systems approach has been exposed where CI should be treated as a network of interdependencies. Under the programme's financial support framework, projects have been initiated to develop methodologies for assessing the interdependence of ICT systems and energy production and to simulate the effects of ICT infrastructure interdependence. A pilot programme was also launched to demonstrate how to protect transnational facilities using examples of particularly complex systems (EUROCONTROL, GALILEO, Electricity Transmission Grid, and European Gas Transmission Network). As envisioned in the project roadmap, it made sense to identify further types of infrastructure with similar pan-European reach and cover them with consistent protection mechanisms based on the cycle familiar in crisis management: prevention, preparation, response, and recovery.

Independent third parties (EY and RAND Europe) evaluated the programme in 2018 to verify the utility of EPCIP, and the results were published in 2019. The conclusions of the reports indicate that (Directorate-General for Migration and Home Affairs (European Commission), EY, and RAND Europe, 2020):

- EPCIP has had a positive impact on improving awareness of the need to protect CI, but it is not easy to assess the importance of this project's contribution, given the varying state of maturity of countries in protecting CI at the start of the initiative.
- The revised approach had many limitations and insufficiently took into account new risks, especially those associated with new technologies (e.g. AI, UAV).
- Despite the positive impact on awareness and the undertaking of specific legislative changes by member states, it was necessary to revise the approach to the protection of critical facilities, which exposes the complementarity of CI systems more than the previous one and thus exposes the criteria of resilience and continuity of delivery of the effects of the systems as the actual expected outcome of the protection process.

The conclusions of the report developed by EY and RAND Europe indicate that the security problem had to be viewed systemically, and the system's boundaries became defined by the service provision process. A source of good practice in this area could be the NIS Directive, which better considers the phenomenon of interdependence and its impact on the security status of facilities and the security process.

The NIS Directive is the fruit of a second parallel process aimed at strengthening the resilience of CI within the EU, which concerns the ICT space. The problem of protecting the digital space was highlighted, among others, in the Stockholm Programme, whose authors, on the one hand, postulate the need to complement EPCIP with other sectors of strategic importance and postulate the development and implementation of a policy for a high level of network and information security in the EU containing mechanisms for strengthening the resilience of CI, including ICT and service infrastructure. As a result, significant legislative changes were already adopted in 2009, imposing an obligation on EU member states to ensure that digital service operators make due technical and organizational efforts to ensure a level of service security commensurate with the risks involved and to ensure continuity of service provision, taking into account the consequences of the interconnection of networks and information systems (*Directive 2009/140/EC of the European Parliament and of the Council of 25 November 2009 Amending Directives 2002/21/EC on a Common Regulatory Framework for Electronic Communications Networks and Services, 2002/19/EC on Access to, and Interconnection of, Electronic Communications Networks and Associated Facilities, and 2002/20/EC on the Authorisation of Electronic Communications Networks and Services (Text with EEA Relevance), 2009*). These obligations were expanded in the 2018 Electronic Communications Code, an amendment to the above directive (*Directive (EU) 2018/1972 of the European Parliament and of the Council of 11 December 2018 Establishing the European Electronic Communications Code (Recast) Text with EEA Relevance, 2018*), which focuses on four main issues:

- Network and device security:
  - physical security,
  - environmental security,
  - supply security,
  - network access control,
  - network integrity;
- Responding to computer security incidents:
  - creating procedures to deal with computer security incidents,
  - creation of incident detection capabilities,
  - reporting and reporting computer security incidents;
- Monitoring, controlling, and testing:
  - establishing strategies for monitoring and recording incidents,
  - exercising and testing contingency plans,
  - testing networks and services,
  - security assessments,
  - compliance management;
- Business continuity management:
  - establishing service continuity strategies (BCS),
  - creation of contingency plans (BCP),
  - establishing disaster recovery capabilities (IT DR).

One of the principles of EPCIP that was abandoned in the formulation of the NIS directive is the so-called "no-sanctions" approach, based on the principle of voluntary participation and the belief that CI operators are responsible and rational. As has been shown by experience, despite the business and economic rationale, this approach has only worked in some countries. As a result, it was replaced by the so-called regulatory approach (Szwarc, 2018), which includes defined protection requirements and criminal sanctions imposed on the operator in case of evasion of the requirements. In the case of a digital service operator, the requirements under the NIS Directive are consistent with those of the Electronic Communications Code. In contrast, obligations have been imposed on ES operators[2]:

- assessing the risk and protecting the ability to provide the service in proportion to its level,
- ensuring continuity of ES provision covering the full spectrum of operations, i.e. emergency response, resumption of critical processes and sustaining system operation at a minimum acceptable level, restoration of full system performance to the state prior to the security incident,
- reporting computer security incidents in such a way that it is possible to assess the significance of the disruption using the criteria of the number of users, the duration of the disruption, and the geographic scope.

The mode of implementation of the provisions of the NIS Directive is similar to EPCIP – a dedicated law (Cybersecurity Act) and implementing documents or an amendment to the existing law. A peculiar practice is the amendment of sectoral regulations, which, in an extreme case, meant the dispersion of requirements into 12 pieces of legislation (Denmark). All member states have also developed national cyber security strategies. Implementing the NIS Directive by EU member states has contributed to boosting the resilience of service providers in key sectors of economies and the cyber security capabilities of individual countries and establishing a framework for cooperation in this field. On the other hand, however, the varied way the directive has been implemented has made the achieved level of resilience of countries, sectors, and businesses enormously different and, in many cases, unsatisfactory. Despite the attempt to create a system for notifying and transmitting computer security incidents to entities in other countries potentially or realistically affected by the disruption, an effective mechanism for building situational awareness and responding to cyber crises has yet to be created.

A particular test of the effectiveness of this mechanism was during the COVID-19 pandemic, during which much activity moved to the network, and the network became a particular target for attacks. On the one hand, introducing a minimum cybersecurity framework has made it possible for public administrations and many businesses to be prepared to operate in this environment. However, many service providers critical to the functioning of societies have yet to be included in the list of ES operators.

176 Civil Protection and Domestic Security in Hybrid Warfare

As a result of the review of the impact of the implementation of the NIS Directive and the shortcomings identified, its provisions were replaced by a second version of the Directive (NIS2). This led to a substantial increase in the number of operators and a significant expansion of the scope of mandatory protection of networks and information systems by service providers (Table 3.2).

TABLE 3.2 Evolution of security requirements contained in NIS directives

NIS	NIS2
Obligations of key services operators	
Take appropriate and proportionate technical and organizational measures to manage risks	Have expertise in cybersecurity risk management and be aware of the need to acquire capabilities to identify, manage, and develop knowledge of cybersecurity risks
Take preventive and reactive measures to reduce the impact of incidents and ensure continuity of service provision	Implement policies: analysis of the risk and security of information systems assessing the effectiveness of risk management measures in the use of cryptography
Immediate reporting of computer security incidents	Provide measures to handle incidents
Monitoring, controlling, and auditing the state of security	Have mechanisms to ensure business continuity
Compliance management	Ensure supply chain security by, among other things, managing relationships with suppliers
Inform service recipients about cyber threats	Ensure the security of information system components throughout the life cycle and identify and disclose vulnerabilities
	Personal security management
	Access and asset management
	Use of multi-component authentication systems
	Securing data transmission and communications in emergency situations
	Reporting computer security incidents without undue delay
	Informing service recipients about cyber threats
Obligations of states	
Identify, review, and update the list of key service operators	Organize the technical means of reporting
Assess the significance of disturbing effects	Ensure the ability to report vulnerabilities anonymously
Set out national cyber security strategies	Establish a national cyber security strategy and detail policies

(*Continued*)

TABLE 3.2 (*Continued*) Evolution of security requirements contained in NIS directives

NIS	NIS2
Designate national cybersecurity authorities and a national single point of contact, and monitor the application of the Directive at national level	Establish competent entities and single points of contact and provide them with resources Establish authorities responsible for crisis/cybersecurity incident management
Designate the CSIRT	Establish a CSIRT and appoint the one that reveals vulnerabilities
Ensure the handling of reports of cyber incidents	Adopt national cyber incident response plans
Ensure that key service operators/digital service providers protect facilities	Ensure that operators select security measures appropriate to identified supply chain vulnerabilities
Encourage the use of international standards	Promote the use of accepted norms and standards
Transpose the provisions of the Directive into national law	May impose the use of ICT products, services, and processes on certified entities
	Require registration of domain names in a dedicated database
	Ensure that operators who fail to meet safety requirements take corrective action without undue delay
	Create conditions for the exchange of knowledge and good practices on threats, vulnerabilities, and ways to counter them
	Ensure and enforce that the legal provisions laid down pursuant to the Directive are applied
	Control and supervise the application of the safeguards
	Provide regular targeted security audits
	Conduct security scans
	Issue warnings, orders, injunctions, and sanctions for failures in relation to the security systems set up, risk management, and continuity of supply of the critical/important service
	Order the withdrawal of the certificate or apply to the court for a ban on acting as a manager

Source: Own study

178 Civil Protection and Domestic Security in Hybrid Warfare

Due to the inconsistent implementation of the provisions of the NIS Directive, the amendment clarifies the recommendations so that member states have no room for interpretation of the scope of the required protection. Changes introduced by the NIS2 directive are part of a legislative package developed based on lessons from both the COVID-19 pandemic and the war in Ukraine, as well as the identified deficits of the first version of this document. An equally important element of the postulated changes is the CER directive, which formulates tasks for CI operators, EU member states, and the European Commission (Table 3.3).

TABLE 3.3   Critical infrastructure protection requirements under the CER directive

CI Operators	• Carry out a risk assessment and a business impact analysis (BIA) of disruptions to the provision of a key service • Prevent disruptive incidents • Provide physical protection • Ensure continuity of operations of critical facilities • Provide personal protection • They can check the past of employees (identity, non-punishment) • Create plans to ensure the resilience of the facility • Establish bodies responsible for communication • Reporting of incidents
Governments of EU Member States	• Identify Critical Entities • Create a strategy for the resilience of critical entities • Carry out an assessment of the risk of disruption of the critical entity's work • Designate or establish one or more authorities responsible for the correct application and enforcement of the provisions of the Directive and one single point of contact • Support critical entities by ensuring: guidelines, methodologies, organization of exercises, counselling, training, and in specific cases of financial support • Consult with other countries • Lay down rules containing sanctions which should be effective, proportionate, and dissuasive
European Commission	• Organize, at the request of a member state, advisory missions to assess the measures taken by the State that has identified a critical entity of particular European interest • Supports member states and critical entities in fulfilling their obligations under the Directive • Complements member states' activities at the international level (exercises, training, methodologies) • Inform member states of the financial resources available to enhance the resilience of critical entities

Source: Own study

Management of critical infrastructure safety

The NIS2 and CER directives should be considered necessary and complementary components of the exact protection mechanism. Both directives take a sanctioning approach with the assumption that penalties are effective, proportionate, and dissuasive, implying continuity with the NIS Directive and a departure from the preferred principle of non-sanctions contained in EPCIP.

In the evolution of the EU approach to protecting strategic infrastructure, the perceived problem of interdependence should be highlighted (Table 3.4).

An analysis of data in Table 3.4 indicates that in recent years, dependence on the continuity of digital services has been identified as crucial, and the impact on trust sectors such as finance and public administration is considered critical.

TABLE 3.4 References to interdependence in the EU directives under review

Document	References to the Problem of Interdependence
EPCIP	A European CI is one that is located in the EU and affects at least two member states – i.e. located (geographical), subject to a common legal regime (legal), whose ability to operate depends on the ability of others to operate (physical) and whose effects are felt by a similar population (social).
	Cross-cutting criteria refer to physical and social interdependencies.
	They contain mechanisms for recognizing ECIs in the form of bilateral or multilateral consultations.
NIS	A service-oriented model is introduced to identify strategic infrastructure. Physical and information interdependencies are recognized as specific types. Interdependencies of operators of networked critical services through ICT infrastructure are recognized. The cross-border nature of the relationship is indicated, which requires standardization at EU level.
	Criteria used to assess the materiality of the impact of a disruption include the number of affiliated entities, the dependency on other sectors, the geographical extent of the impact of a computer security incident.
	The establishment of a Collaboration Group has been set up, whose tasks include the exchange of good practices in identifying critical service operators, taking into account cross-border dependencies.
NIS2	The identification of key operators is done through the viewpoint of their role in the supply chain. It also points to the need of assessing the operator's independence from business partners and other related companies to avoid placing non-key actors under protection obligations.

(Continued)

TABLE 3.4 (*Continued*)   References to interdependence in the EU directives under review

Document	References to the Problem of Interdependence
	It is cautioned that the effects of a disruption, even if seemingly limited, can have a cascading effect, the consequences of which can be long-lasting and far-reaching. The basis for identifying strategic actors is an assessment of the effects of disruption manifested in: • the uniqueness of their action (non-substitutability), • significant impact on multiple spheres of state functioning (security and public order, public health), • the potential for serious systemic and, in some sectors, cross-border risks. A coordinated EU risk assessment policy for critical supply chains is implemented. A coordinated crisis management mechanism is being set up for cyber incidents requiring coordinated action at supranational (Community) level. Underpinning this capability is the creation of situational awareness through a much more specific reporting system.
CER	The awareness of interdependencies is a basis for the establishment of harmonized rules containing minimum standards for the protection of CI. As in the NIS2 Directive, attention is paid to the risk of cascading effects and systemic risk. CI of particular European interest is singled out if its disruption has the potential to affect six or more MS. National strategies are created which should define strategic objectives and priorities for improving CI resilience, taking into account existing geographical and cross-sectoral dependencies. When conducting risk assessments, MS should take into account risks arising from interdependencies between sectors and CI operators from EU and non-EU MS. A Critical Entity Resilience Group is being set up to, inter alia, share good practice in identifying CI operators, taking into account cross-border dependencies.
DORA	Particular attention is paid to the financial sector's dependence on the continuity of digital services. It is accepted that the financial entity is fully responsible for the risks arising from its relationship with an external ICT service provider, and therefore the impact of disruptions to their operations on the continuity of financial services should be assessed and appropriate business continuity mechanisms undertaken.

(*Continued*)

TABLE 3.4 (*Continued*) References to interdependence in the EU directives under review

Document	References to the Problem of Interdependence
	A lead supervisor responsible for assessing the extent of interdependencies with the ICT service provider is designated. The regulation requires that all information and ICT assets are inventoried and those considered critical are recorded. Financial entities carry out a business impact analysis (BIA), during which they assess the dependence on external entities and the impact of the disruption on these entities. Systemic risks arising from the scale of dependence on the digital service provider are identified and estimated, taking into account the impact on the stability of the financial sector, the number of financial entities dependent on the provider, the type (criticality) of financial entity functions that may be disrupted as a result of a digital service disruption, the substitutability of the provider. Crisis management exercises can be conducted to demonstrate the degree of dependence of the financial sector on the ICT sector and other sectors of the economy.

Source: Own study

December 2022 integrated previous efforts to improve the security of critical facilities, resulting in the following:

- Regulation (EU) 2022/2554 of the European Parliament and of the Council on operational digital resilience of the financial sector;
- Directive on measures for a high common level of cyber security within the Union (NIS2);
- Directive amending a number of other directives with regard to operational digital resilience of the financial sector (DORA);
- Critical Entity Resilience Directive (CER).

In parallel with bureaucratic efforts, possible CI and ES protection methods have been a subject of scientific interest. An analysis of the scientific discussion of ES protection indicates that only some of the articles discuss ES. The number of leading topics in the papers indicates that researchers' attention is broadly dispersed. Analysis review of leading topics of papers shows that researchers' interest in ES topics focuses on their relevance to actors (social groups, businesses, states). Population-related papers discuss the ES from the perspective of smart cities, traffic management and optimization, municipal services, fire services, and municipal buildings. Other articles address the impact of the COVID-19 pandemic on the ES, especially in the context of drug production and the impact on business operations.

There are also articles on sustainability and corporate social responsibility. Available publications touch on government funding for ES conservation and the ES aspect for the agricultural sector. More comprehensive work needs to be done on ES, and the issue of ES business continuity has been addressed in only 27 studies (based on SCOPUS and WoS CC database, as of 20/03/2024).

Moreover, the available literature covers only selected elements of ES and often focuses on the importance of ES for specific entities or the impact of specific events on ES. No work has yet been observed on a holistic approach to ES security that considers physical security, technical security, legal security, personal security, ICT security, and business continuity. Studies on ES and business continuity have also yet to identify a framework that defines the principles of security management understood as maintaining ES business continuity. Work in this area provides research results on several partial forms of ES business continuity management:

- application of standard risk management methods,
- risk mitigation strategies: collaborative management, proactive planning,
- effectiveness of rapid response measures,
- a set of resources at the organizational level that supports resilience and contributes to an empirical evidence base for business continuity planning (BCP):
  - awareness,
  - human resources,
  - information and communication,
  - leadership and culture,
  - operational infrastructure,
  - physical resources,
  - social capital,
- the importance of standardizing procedures and resources,
- business continuity framework for IoT.

The review of available scientific studies on ES protection indicates that government institutions play the dominant role in setting the direction of UK and CI protection at the level of specific countries (United States) or communities (EU). In addition, the need for a comprehensive solution in ES business continuity management has been demonstrated. This solution should include the ability to simulate the spread of adverse events of the so-called "domino effect" using simulation tools. In the analysed literature, isolated papers relating to this topic were observed.

Nowadays, specific safeguards for ES and CI are not defined at the level of normative acts, as emphasized by the provisions of the CER

Management of critical infrastructure safety   183

and NIS2 directives. A common assumption is that the need for action depends on the ES or CI operator's results of a risk assessment. The level of risk justifies the development of a detailed risk response plan and its implementation in the company's operations on a project basis. In this context, a key element is to ensure uniformity in the risk management process for all designated ES and CI operators. The risk assessment process for ES and CI operators is often regulated in national risk assessment methodologies for emergency management or CI protection plans. These studies provide knowledge of the steps in the risk management process and provide a source of workable methods for ES and CI security operators (Table 3.5).

TABLE 3.5   List of action steps of selected risk assessment methodologies for crisis management purposes

Item	Methodology	Stages of Risk Assessment Methodology for Crisis Management	Best Practices
1	Poland (Skomra, 2015)	• Setting the context • Identification of risks • Risk analysis • Risk estimation • Risk assessment	• List of initiating and secondary risks • Inclusion of competency analysis of the risk assessment team • Identification of risk dependencies • Forecasting the spread of risks
2	Australia ('National Emergency Risk Assessment Guidelines', 2020)	• Establishment of context • Risk identification • Risk analysis • Risk evaluation • Risk handling	• A structured approach to identifying control mechanisms and the possibility of applying adequate solutions • Linking the causes of the risk and its effects • Standardized risk tolerance matrices
3	Sweden ('Swedish National Risk Assessment', 2019)	• Starting point (role and area of responsibility, and defining the method and perspective of risk analysis) • Risk assessment (risk identification, risk analysis, and risk evaluation)	• Determination of the impact on society and the studied organization • Multi-criteria analyses • Use of scenario methods

(*Continued*)

TABLE 3.5 (*Continued*)   List of action steps of selected risk assessment methodologies for crisis management purposes

Item	Methodology	Stages of Risk Assessment Methodology for Crisis Management	Best Practices
		• Vulnerability assessment (capability assessment and vulnerability analysis) • Risk treatment (results and conclusions, and continuous work, forces and resources, response plans)	
4	Ireland ('A Framework for Major Emergency Management', 2022)	• Establishment of context • Identification of risks • Risk assessments • Presentation of risks on a risk matrix	• Visualization of results of the risk analysis in the form of an extensive risk matrix that takes into account the areas of: risk prevention and reduction, increase of response forces
5	Canada ('All Hazards Risk Assessment Methodology Guidelines', 2022)	• Establishment of context • Risk identification • Risk analysis • Risk evaluation • Risk handling	• Identification of a set of methods and techniques to support the various stages of the methodology • Medium- and long-term analyses (5–25 years)

Source: Own study

The basis for the risk assessment methodologies analysed is the PN-EN ISO 31000:2018 risk management guidelines, which assumes that the risk assessment process is carried out in three stages: establishing the context, risk assessment (identification, analysis, and evaluation), and the decision to deal with risks.

Table 3.5 shows that almost all risk assessment methodologies begin with establishing the context. At this stage, the resources needed for the activities and the vulnerabilities for which the risk assessment is to be performed are defined. An exception to this rule is the Swedish methodology, which is started by defining areas of responsibility and adopting a risk analysis method.

The Swedish methodology also provides an additional step, not found in PN-EN ISO 31000:2018, involving resource vulnerability assessment. All methodologies provide for implementing the components of the risk assessment process recommended by PN-EN ISO 31000:2018, i.e. risk analysis and estimation.

The concluding stage of the risk assessment analysed methodologies is to decide how to deal with the risks. The decision is made based on the results obtained from the risk assessment stage and concerns the selection of adequate safeguards to eliminate or reduce the risk. As can be seen, the analysed risk assessment methodologies fully align with the approach adopted in the NIS2 and CER directive for establishing safeguards for ES and CI.

An analysis of the evolution of the approach to managing the security of facilities on which state security depends indicates that the current approach involves the identification of a value chain in the form of ES, which determines the resources necessary for its implementation. The resources necessary for the implementation of the ES constitute the CI that must be protected from the materialization of threats or reduce the consequences of their occurrence. Hence, the developed methodology of the ES should ensure that it is possible to determine the characteristics of the CI, assess the risks arising from threats to which the CI is susceptible, and identify safeguards to mitigate the risk to an acceptable state. Given the above, it is proposed that the Methodology of Essential Services Security Management (MESSM) be implemented in the following stages:

- appointment of a team – the stage in which members of an analytical team selected according to an analysis of characteristics of the CI under consideration are identified,
- mapping of CI characteristics – the stage within which current characteristics of the considered CI are established,
- determination of safety thresholds – the stage in which the safety threshold for the functionalities characterizing the considered CI is established,
- generation of adverse event scenarios (AES) – the stage within which AES are generated for identified risks in order to supplement the analytical team's knowledge of the potential consequences of the occurrence of risks,
- formulation of the decision problem – the stage in which the analytical team formulates the decision problem regarding threats and safeguards that can be applied to achieve resilience to the threats or minimize their effects,
- risk estimation – the stage in which the analytical team verifies whether safeguards will allow the CI security threshold to be met,
- implementation of safeguards – the stage where the analytical team decides whether to implement safeguards, updates the CI characteristics, and completes the cycle.

CHARACTERISTICS OF THE MESSM

The purpose of the MESSM is to provide those responsible for the security of the CI with a standard of conduct to allow achieving the assumed security threshold through the selection of security combinations for threats stemming from the characteristics of the CI. It is assumed that providing the required level of security for ES components will translate into the security of the entire ES. The security of the ES is understood as resilience to provide the ES as a result of the materialization of the threat or its restoration within the assumed time.

The starting stage of the MESSM methodology is the establishment of the analysis team. This stage is carried out in two steps:

- Analysis of the stakeholders of the CI under consideration and selection of team members,
- Verification of the analytical team's competency matrix.

The direct beneficiaries of the MESSM are operators of CI and ES; their representatives constitute the main stakeholders who make up the analytical team (internal stakeholders). The list of internal stakeholders in the MESSM is derived from the characteristics of CI and is related to the following:

- CI functionalities,
- resources that implement CI functionalities.

Dependence of the list of internal stakeholders on the list of CI functionalities makes it possible to identify the resources necessary for their implementation. Knowledge of these resources allows identifying people familiar with the specifics of their operation, able to determine what risks they are susceptible to,[3] and identify possible safeguards to mitigate the level of risk.

Facilities considered CI function within communities represented by public administration bodies and services established to assist. Representatives of both groups must be part of the composition of the analytical team (external stakeholders). Their participation allows the team to take a broader view of both the risks and the effects of the materialization of risks on the community within which the CI operates.

The role of the analytical team is to establish the current characteristics of CI, to adopt the values of security thresholds for the CI functionalities being implemented, to estimate the risk of loss of functionality, and, if necessary, to make decisions aimed at determining additional safeguards to achieve the assumed security threshold. Implementing this task requires that the analytical team has the right competencies, which are understood as the totality of knowledge, skills, experience, attitudes, and readiness of the employee to act under the given conditions. Their completeness can be verified by the competency matrix (Table 3.6).

The rows of the matrix show the required competencies of the analytical team established based on the threats to which the CI under consideration is susceptible. The competencies of the team members regarding knowledge of measures to eliminate or reduce the effects of threats in the assumed areas of protection are verified.

Each stakeholder representative is familiar with one or more protection areas related to specific threats and can identify safeguards for them. Before the team starts work, it is essential to check that each threat has a designated person with proven competence in the assumed protection areas. If the team's competence is lacking, expanding the team to include persons with the required competence is necessary. Synthetically, the stage of team establishment is summarized in Table 3.7.

The next stage of the MESSM is to determine the characteristics of CI. The goal of the stage is to map the current situation of CI. Determining CI characteristics allows synthetic collection of CI security data, which can be exchanged between entities responsible for CI security and related entities that jointly provide ES. Establishing the characteristics of CI in the further stages of the MESSM allows:

- estimating the risk of loss of functionality,
- generation of the AES,
- formulation of the decision problem and determination of a set of safeguards to achieve the adopted safety threshold.

The definition of CI characteristics is carried out in six steps (Table 3.8).

In the MESSM, the CI operator's determination of the safety threshold for CI functionality is carried out expertly based on its knowledge regarding its obligations. This step is carried out in three steps (Table 3.9).

The goal of the risk estimation stage is to quantify the risk of loss of functionality, taking into account variables that determine:

- probability of occurrence of threats,
- effects of threat occurrence on CI functionality,
- vulnerability of CI to threats,
- impact of applied safeguards on CI resilience.

Identifying the risk of loss of functionality allows the identification of decision problems, which are solved in the stage of formulating the decision problem. The risk estimation procedure is carried out in four steps (Table 3.10).

TABLE 3.6 Competency matrix of the analytical team

Description		External Stakeholders				Internal Stakeholders		
Threats	Protection areas	A representative of local government	A representative of the fire department	A representative of the police	...	Person 1	...	Person n
Threat 1	Physical security							
	Technical security							
	Personal security							
	ICT security							
	Legal security							
	Business continuity							

Source: Own study

Management of critical infrastructure safety 189

TABLE 3.7 Characteristics of the stage of the MESSM – establishment of the team

Stage Name	Establishment of the Team	
Goal of Stage	**Input Data**	**Output Data**
Identification of the composition of the analytical team responsible for CI security characteristics of CI	Identification of the composition of the analytical team responsible for CI security characteristics of CI	Identification of the composition of the analytical team responsible for CI security characteristics of CI
Procedure	• Analysis of the stakeholders of the CI under consideration and selection of team members • Verification of the competency matrix of the analytical team	

Source: Own study

TABLE 3.8 Characteristics of the stage of the MESSM – mapping of CI characteristics

Stage Name	Mapping of CI Characteristics	
Goal of Stage	**Input Data**	**Output Data**
Mapping of CI characteristics	Data on: • CI functionality • Resources required to implement the functionality • The vulnerability of the resources • Safeguards used	CI characteristics
Procedure	• Definition of a set of CI resources • Definition of a set of functionalities for each CI resource • Determination of the set of threats to which CI resources are susceptible • Determination of the set of dependencies occurring between threats • Determination of the set of applied security features for each CI resource • Determination of the set of dependencies occurring between CI resources	

Source: Own study

TABLE 3.9 Characteristics of the stage of the MESSM methodology – establishment of the safety threshold

Stage Name	Establishment of Safety Threshold	
Goal of Stage	**Input Data**	**Output Data**
Declarative adoption of levels of functionality that guarantee the tasks of the considered CI	List of functionalities of the considered CI	List of functionalities of the CI under consideration with specific security thresholds
Procedure	• Adoption of a list of CI functionalities derived from CI characteristics • Determination of the safety threshold for each CI functionality • Recording the adopted safety threshold in the CI characteristics	

Source: Own study

TABLE 3.10 Characteristics of the stage of the MESSM – risk estimation

Stage Name	Risk Estimation	
Goal of Stage	**Input Data**	**Output Data**
Estimating the risk of loss of CI functionality	Characteristics of CI Set of security features used	Value of the risk of loss of functionality taking into account safeguards
Procedure	• Identifying the value of risk parameters on the basis of CI characteristics • Calculation of the value of the risk of loss of the considered CI functionality • Forecasting the availability of functionality in the next period • Decision-making on the handling of risks	

Source: Own study

The stage of generating the AES is a response to the needs of those responsible for the security of CI and ES, as indicated in EU normative acts.[4] The purpose of this stage is to identify possible scenarios of adverse events resulting from the dependence of ES and CI operators on other entities. This knowledge makes it possible to verify whether the assumptions made about the consequences of the materialization of threats are correctly estimated. Besides, an analysis of the obtained AES allows the verification of whether risks were overlooked during the work of the analytical team, thus limiting the possibility of protecting against

Management of critical infrastructure safety

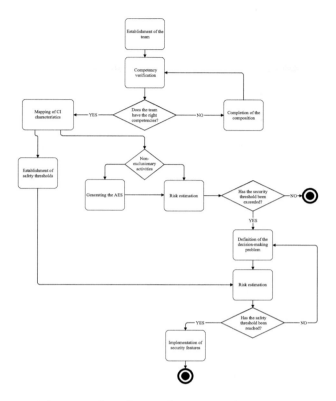

FIGURE 3.1 The procedure for implementing the MESSM

Source: Own study

TABLE 3.11 Characteristics of the stage of the MESSM – generation of the AES

Stage Name	Generation of the AES	
Goal of Stage	**Input Data**	**Output Data**
Recognition of possible AES	CI characteristics	Characteristics of CI links List of AES
Procedure	• Development of the characteristics of CI links • Preparation of the list of AES	

Source: Own study

them. This stage is optional to maintain the continuity of inference within the framework of the MESSM, as illustrated by the methodology implementation procedure (Figure 3.1). The stage of generating the SNF is implemented in two steps (Table 3.11).

The inputs for the decision problem formulation stage are derived from the characteristics of the CI or AES. Decision areas within the decision problem are determined by the threats to which the CI is susceptible. Elementary decisions within decision areas illustrate the possibilities of protection against the threats. The solution to the decision problem provides the analysis team with knowledge of the safeguards that need to be applied to reach the designated security threshold. The procedure for formulating the decision problem is carried out in four steps (Table 3.12).

The final stage of the MESSM involves the implementation of safeguards (Table 3.13). It is assumed that the implementation of safeguards in the structures of the CI under consideration is carried out by the CI operator according to separate methods of proceeding, for example,

TABLE 3.12 Characteristics of the stage of the MESSM – definition of the decision-making problem

Stage Name	Definition of the Decision-Making Problem	
Goal of Stage	Input Data	Output Data
Develop a list of acceptable decisions to ensure that the required safety threshold is achieved for the CI functionalities under consideration	Characteristics of the considered CI List of considered AES	List of permissible decisions that can be applied in response to identified threats
Procedure	• Building a model of the decision-making problem • Generating a set of acceptable decisions • Making a choice and making a decision • Analysing the consequences of the decision	

Source: Own study

TABLE 3.13 Characteristics of the stage of the MESSM – implementation of safeguards

Stage Name	Implementation of Safeguards	
Goal of Stage	Input Data	Output Data
Security recommendation	Characteristics of CI excluding new security features	Characteristics of CI incorporating new security features
Procedure	• Recommendation of safeguards to the CI operator • Updating the characteristics of the considered CI with data on implemented safeguards	

Source: Own study

using project management principles. From the point of view of ES and CI security management, the analysis team needs to update the CI characteristics with the safeguards recommended to the CI operator, ensuring a solution to the decision problem. This provides a starting point for the implementation of the next cycle of the MESSM.

The process of implementing the MESSM is illustrated in Figure 3.1.

The integrity of the MESSM is achieved by maintaining the principle that the output of one stage is the input for the next one. The relationship between stages of the MESSM and the tools necessary for its application is discussed in the next section.

TOOLS OF THE MESSM

In the MESSM, it is assumed that CI is an object whose characteristics comprise the dimension of a resource that performs functionalities, which is vulnerable to threats and which applies safeguards to reduce the value of risks associated with threats. Understanding the characteristics of CI in this way makes it possible to define the CI situation model:

$$<V, \Phi, Z, H, M, G, T> \tag{3.1}$$

where:

V – considered CI,
Φ – set of CI functionalities,
Z – set of threats to which CI is susceptible,
H – set of relationships between risks,
M – set of CI security,
G – set of links of the considered CI with other CIs,
T – time signature for which the CI situation was determined.

The CI security entity determines individual elements of the CI situation model based on available data or expert knowledge. Attributes of the CI situation model are presented in Table 3.14. The collection of these data is a prerequisite for using the MESSM. Those attributes can be freely expanded depending on the needs determined by normative acts in force in the country under consideration.

The primary metric for the MESSM is a risk of the loss of functionality. The expression of risk using a numerical value is a facilitation in the process of ES and CI security management, which allows the decision-maker to adopt a strategy for dealing with risk (examples of possible strategies for dealing with risk: hazard reduction, impact reduction, risk transfer, undertaking) (Zawiła-Niedźwiecki, 2014). Risk in the MESSM is understood as a numerical value expressing a percentage of

TABLE 3.14 Basic attributes of the CI situation model

	Attributes	Symbol	Scale
Resource	Name of the resource V with index α	V_α	–
	Threat Z with index β for a resource with index α	$Z_{\alpha,\beta}$	–
	Functionality Φ with index γ of a resource with index α	$\Phi_{\alpha,\gamma}$	–
	Vulnerability level U of a resource with index α to a threat with index β	$U_{\alpha,\beta}$	<0, 1>
Threat	The link G with index n	G_n	–
	Name of the threat Z with index β affecting the resource with index α	$Z_{\alpha,\beta}$	–
	Type of threat	IN or OUT	–
	Effect $\Delta\Phi$ of the occurrence of a hazard affecting the functionality Φ of a resource with index γ of a resource with index α	$\Delta\Phi_{\alpha,\gamma}$	<0%, 100%>
	Probability P of a threat with index β affecting a resource with index α	$P_{\alpha,\beta}$	<0, 1>
	Safeguarding M with index λ against a threat with index β for resource α	$M_{\alpha,\beta,\lambda}$	–
Dependence of threats	Threat relationship	H_n	–
	Name of the inducing threat	$Z_{\alpha,\beta}$	–
	Name of the threat induced	$Z_{\alpha,\beta}$	–
Functionalities	Functionality Φ with index γ resource with index α	$\Phi_{\alpha,\gamma}$	–
	Value ϕ functionality Φ with index γ resource with index α in the period under consideration	$\phi_{\alpha,\gamma}$	<0%, 100%>
	Safety threshold value ϕ^{PB} functionality Φ with index γ resource with index α in the considered period	$\phi^{PB}_{\alpha,\gamma}$	<0%, 100%>
Safeguards	Safeguarding M of index λ against a threat of index β for resource α	$M_{\alpha,\beta,\lambda}$	–
	The value of increasing the resistance of the considered CI with index α to a threat with index β as a result of the application of the security of index λ	$m_{\alpha,\beta,\lambda}$	<0, 1>

(*Continued*)

Management of critical infrastructure safety 195

TABLE 3.14 (*Continued*)   Basic attributes of the CI situation model

	Attributes	Symbol	Scale
	Objective A of crisis management realized by the collateral	A	–
	Area O of CI protection secured by the considered protection measure	O	–
CI link	Link G with index n	G_n	–
	Name of the incoming resource V	V_α	–
	Name of dependent resource V'	V'_α	–
	Name of threat Z affecting resource V'	$Z_{\alpha,\beta}$	–

Source: Own study

the expected degree of loss of CI functionality that may arise due to the materialization of a hazard. Hence, the variable characterizing the effect of the occurrence of a hazard in the classical risk formula is replaced by variable ($\Delta\Phi$), which symbolizes the change in the availability of CI functionality due to the materialization of the hazard.

The risk formula considers the CI's vulnerability to the threat (U). Vulnerability is the probability of the loss of the considered CI functionality due to the occurrence of a hazard arising from the CI's design features. The vulnerability of CI to a hazard increases the risk associated with the hazard. Hence, in the risk formula, it is necessary to distinguish between the variable responsible for the probability of occurrence of the threat and the variable indicating the probability of consequences.

As a result of introducing a variable identifying the vulnerability of the CI, the logical corollary is to link it to a variable determining the impact of the applied safeguards (M) on the resilience of the CI under consideration, i.e. the ability of the facility to perform functionality under the impact of disturbances.

Taking into account the above considerations, a risk formula 3.2 that fits the CI situation model was proposed:

$$R_{\alpha,\beta} = P_{\alpha,\beta} \times |\Delta\Phi_{\alpha,\gamma}| \times (U_{\alpha,\beta} - M_{\alpha,\beta})$$
$$U_{\alpha,\beta} - M_{\alpha,\beta} = 0 \text{ for } M_{\alpha,\beta} {}^3 U_{\alpha,\beta} \tag{3.2}$$

where:
α – CI index,
β – threat index,
γ – index of functionality of the CI under consideration,
$R_{\alpha,\beta}$ – risk value <0%, 100%>,

$P_{\alpha,\beta}$ – probability of threat β in the scale <0, 1>,
$U_{\alpha,\beta}$ – CI vulnerability β in the scale <0, 1>,
$\Delta\Phi_{\alpha,\gamma}$ – effect of threat materialization β <0%, 100%>,
$M_{\alpha,\beta}$ – sum of the impact of collateral on a CI vulnerability β in the scale <0, 1>.

An extension of formula 3.2 is formula 3.3, which allows establishing the aggregate value of the risk of loss of CI functionality derived from the entire set of considered threats to which the CI is susceptible. The loss of availability of CI functionality is a discrete random variable with specific weights for each threat to which the considered CI is susceptible. These weights are equal to the probability of the threat materializing $P_{\alpha,\beta}$ divided by the sum of the probabilities of the threats affecting the CI. Hence, the formula 3.3 for the sum of CI risks takes the form of:

$$R_{\Phi_{\alpha,\gamma}} = \sum_{\alpha=1}^{n}\sum_{\beta=1}^{j} \frac{P_{\alpha,\beta}}{\sum_{\alpha=1}^{n}\sum_{\beta=1}^{j} P_{\alpha,\beta}} \times \left| \Delta\Phi_{\alpha,\gamma} \right| \times \left(U_{\alpha,\beta} - M_{\alpha,\beta} \right) \qquad (3.3)$$

where:
$R_{\Phi_{\alpha,\gamma}}$ – risk for the CI functionality under consideration,
j – number of threats to which a CI with index α is susceptible,
n – number of CIs under consideration.

Knowledge of the value of the risk of loss of functionality, combined with data from the CI situation model, allows identifying the availability of functionality when a threat materializes and whether it will fall below the assumed safety threshold. The safety threshold is understood in the MESSM as the level of functionality considered by the CI operator to be sufficient to carry out the CI tasks arising from its obligations to society. Formula 3.4 illustrates this relationship:

$$\Phi_{\alpha,\gamma}\left(t_{n+1}\right) = \Phi_{\alpha,\gamma}\left(t_n\right) - R_{\Phi_{\alpha,\gamma}}\left(t_n\right) \qquad (3.4)$$

where:
$\Phi_{\alpha,\gamma}\left(t_{n+1}\right)$ – predictive level of functionality at the time t_{n+1},
$\Phi_{\alpha,\gamma}\left(t_n\right)$ – estimated level of functionality at time t_n, resulting from the model of the situation considered CI,
$R_{\Phi_{\alpha,\gamma}}\left(t_n\right)$ – value of the risk of loss of functionality at the time of t_n.

Another component of the MESSM is the method for generating the AES. For its application, it is necessary to define the Model of Essential Service (MES). The MES is formed based on an analysis of the ES value-added process and is the sum of CI objects necessary for the implementation of the ES. The characteristics of each CI object necessary for implementing the ES are established using the CI situation model. Knowledge about the course of the AES is supplemented by information about the risks to which the considered CI is susceptible.

The adverse event spreads due to the relationships between the CI (characterized by the set G of the CI situation model) and threats (characterized by set H of the CI situation model). The creation of an MES involves the development of a model consisting of:

- nodes, which represent random variables,
- probability of occurrence of threats (symbols of rectangles),
- CI's vulnerability to hazards (ellipse symbols),
- arrows connecting the nodes, interpreted as representing the dependence of threats (dashed arrows) and CIs (continuous arrows).

Relationships in the case of the CI situation model are expressed by:

- CI dependencies (elements of the set G) – communication of vulnerability $U_{\alpha,\beta}$ CI V_α and the probability of occurrence of the threat $P_{\alpha,\beta}$, expressed on a scale of <0, 1>, determining the probability of loss of functionality after taking into account the vulnerability of CI to the considered threat, which can be expressed as $P(P_{\alpha,\beta}|U_{\alpha,\beta})$, where: α – CI index; β – threat index,
- threat link (elements of set H) – communication of the probability of threat $P_{\alpha,\beta}$ under the condition of occurrence of another threat $P'_{\alpha,\beta}$ expressed in a scale <0, 1>, determining the probability of materialization of the considered pair of threats, which can be expressed as $P(P_{\alpha,\beta}|P'_{\alpha,\beta})$ where: α – CI index; β – threat index.

In order to generate the AES and establish the value of risk, it is necessary to synthesize the data characterizing the considered CIs included in the MES, which relate to the vulnerability of CIs to threats and the dependence on threats. Table 3.15 shows an idealized notation mapping the vulnerabilities of the components of the MES to threats.

TABLE 3.15 Idea notation mapping the vulnerabilities of MES components to threats

Description	Resource (V_α)	
Column 1	Column 2	
Threat ($Z_{\alpha,\beta}$)	$P_{\alpha,\beta}$	$U_{\alpha,\beta}$
		$M_{\alpha,\beta,\lambda}$

Source: Own study

TABLE 3.16   Idea notation mapping hazard dependencies in MUK

Description	Threat $(Z'_{\alpha,\beta})$	
Threat $(Z_{\alpha,\beta})$	$P'_{\alpha,\beta}$	$p'_{\alpha,\beta}$
	$P_{\alpha,\beta}$	$p_{\alpha,\beta}$

Source: Own study

Column 1 lists all the threats $(Z_{\alpha,\beta})$ that have been identified for CIs that are components of the MES.

Columns 2 and the following ones contain resources $(V\alpha)$, which are components of MES. In the fields of column 2, the following are entered:

- probability $P_{\alpha,\beta}$ of occurrence of threat $Z_{\alpha,\beta}$,
- vulnerability $U_{\alpha,\beta}$ of the resource $V\alpha$ to the threat $Z_{\alpha,\beta}$,
- impact of $M_{\alpha,\beta,\lambda}$ protection, reducing the vulnerability of the V_{α} resource to the $Z_{\alpha,\beta}$ threat.

Table 3.16 shows an ideological notation mapping the threats' dependencies in the MES. The rows and columns list all the threats to which the components of the MUK under consideration are susceptible. If a hazard marked in row $(Z_{\alpha,\beta})$ creates conditions for the materialization of a threat marked in column $(Z'_{\alpha,\beta})$ at their intersection, the probabilities of occurrence of these threats are entered.

The compiled data allows the application of the chosen technique for generating the AES. In order to speed up the process of generating the AES, it is proposed to use computer simulation, deploying Bayes' theorem, which assumes that it is possible to record any information as a sequence of events, and that will allow determining the probability of occurrence of the considered event under the condition of occurrence of another threat or set of threats (Bolstad, Curram, 2016).

Decision-making is a feature of the management process, which in the MESSM requires the formulation of a decision problem, understood as a set of decision areas to indicate the solutions sought (elementary decisions) to solve it. The set of decision areas result from the risks to which the CI facilities under consideration are susceptible:

- decision areas are denoted by the symbol $Z_{\alpha,\beta}$, and their relevance to the decision problem by the symbol $D_{\alpha,\beta}$,
- elementary decisions are denoted by the symbol $M_{\alpha,\beta,\lambda}$, and their relevance to the decision area by the symbol $d_{\alpha,\beta,\lambda}$.

Importance of the decision area ($D_{\alpha,\beta}$) stems from the share of risk related to the analysed risk in the total of risk values contained in the CI characteristics, which may be expressed by formula 3.5:

$$D_{\alpha,\beta} = \frac{R_{\alpha,\beta}}{\sum_{\beta=1}^{j} R_{\alpha,\beta}} \times 100 \qquad (3.5)$$

where:

α – CI index,

β – threat index,

$D_{\alpha,\beta}$ – relative importance of the decision area related to the threat with index β,

$R_{\alpha,\beta}$ – value of risk associated with the β-index threat to which the CI is susceptible, calculated from formula 3.2,

j – number of threats to which CI is susceptible, as determined by the CI situation model.

Elementary decisions $M_{\alpha,\beta,\lambda}$ for decision areas symbolize safeguards and response measures to the threat. The parameter describing the elementary decision in the MESSM refers to the increase in resistance to the considered threat. Therefore, the relative relevance of the elementary decision is defined as a share of the impact of the considered safeguard in the total impact of the safeguards indicated for the considered decision area $Z_{\alpha,\beta}$, which is represented by the equation:

$$d_{\alpha,\beta,\lambda} = \frac{m_{\alpha,\beta,\lambda}}{\sum_{\lambda=1}^{i} m_{\alpha,\beta,\lambda}} \qquad (3.6)$$

where:

λ – safeguard index,

$d_{\alpha,\beta,\lambda}$ – relative relevance of the elementary decision λ related to the risk with index β, to which a CI with index α is susceptible,

$m_{\alpha,\beta,\lambda}$ – value of raising the resistance of the considered CI with index α to a threat of index β as a result of applying a safeguard of index λ,

i – number of all safeguards available to the CI security entity that can be applied in response to a threat with an index β.

There may be contradictions between the elementary decisions in each decision area due to technical, legal, organizational, or financial obstacles.

The solution to the decision problem is to identify a combination of safeguards, one for each decision area, implementing the adopted objective in one of three options:

- maximum value of cost assessment,
- minimum value of cost assessment,
- value of the cost assessment is within the adopted range.

Because it is the loss of functionality that is responsible for the adverse consequences for the life and health of the population, the environment, and the economic consequences for the CI operator, it is assumed that the goal in the area of CI safety is to maintain the availability of the considered CI functionality above the assumed safety threshold.

The solution to the decision problem requires calculations. For this purpose, the decision problem can be presented as a matrix equation, the solution of which will identify the set of safeguards that achieves the adopted objective. The decision areas should be written in the formula of sets. The decision problem will then take the form (3.7):

$$Z_{\alpha,\beta}\left\{M_{\alpha,\beta,1}, M_{\alpha,\beta,\lambda+1}, \ldots, M_{\alpha,\beta,i}\right\}$$

$$Z_{\alpha,\beta+1}\left\{M_{\alpha,\beta+1,1}, M_{\alpha,\beta+1,\lambda+1}, \ldots, M_{\alpha,\beta+1,i}\right\}$$

$$\ldots\left\{\ldots, \quad \ldots, \quad \ldots, \quad \ldots\right\} \tag{3.7}$$

$$Z_{\alpha,j}\left\{M_{\alpha,j,1}, M_{\alpha,j,\lambda+1}, \ldots, M_{\alpha,j,i}\right\}$$

where:
α – CI index,
β – threat index,
i – number of possible safeguards for the threat under consideration,
j – number of threats to which CI is vulnerable.

Having a record of decision areas in the notation of sets, it is necessary to indicate all the solutions to the decision problem. Then, from the set of the resulting solutions, those that contain pairs of contradictory elements are removed. In this way, acceptable decisions are obtained that solve the decision problem under consideration. The resulting solutions can be written in matrix form where the columns denote successive areas of decisions, and the rows denote acceptable decisions (combinations of security). By substituting the values of the relative importance of elementary decisions $d_{\alpha,\beta,\lambda}$ in place of the collateral symbols $M_{\alpha,\beta,\lambda}$, a matrix of collateral values solving the decision problem is formed. Multiplying this matrix by the matrix of relative relevance of individual decision areas $D_{\alpha,\beta}$, the cost evaluation of individual solutions to the decision problem is obtained (Table 3.17).

Management of critical infrastructure safety 201

TABLE 3.17 An example of calculating the value of the estimate of the cost of solutions to a decision-making problem

	$d_{2,1,\lambda}$	$d_{2,2,\lambda}$	$d_{2,3,\lambda}$	$D_{2,\beta}$			Cost Assessment
Decision 1	$M_{2,1,1}$	$M_{2,2,1}$	$M_{2,3,1}$	$D_{2,1}$			$(M_{2,1,1} * D_{2,1}) + (M_{2,2,1} * D_{2,2}) + (M_{2,3,1} * D_{2,3})$
Decision 2	$M_{2,1,1}$	$M_{2,2,1}$	$M_{2,3,2}$	$D_{2,2}$			$(M_{2,1,1} * D_{2,1}) + (M_{2,2,1} * D_{2,2}) + (M_{2,3,2} * D_{2,3})$
Decision 3	$M_{2,1,1}$	$M_{2,2,2}$	$M_{2,3,1}$	$D_{2,3}$			$(M_{2,1,1} * D_{2,1}) + (M_{2,2,2} * D_{2,2}) + (M_{2,3,1} * D_{2,3})$
Decision 4	$M_{2,1,1}$	$M_{2,2,2}$	$M_{2,3,2}$		*	=	$(M_{2,1,1} * D_{2,1}) + (M_{2,2,2} * D_{2,2}) + (M_{2,3,1} * D_{2,3})$
Decision 5	$M_{2,1,2}$	$M_{2,2,2}$	$M_{2,3,1}$				$(M_{2,1,2} * D_{2,1}) + (M_{2,2,2} * D_{2,2}) + (M_{2,3,2} * D_{2,3})$
Decision 6	$M_{2,1,2}$	$M_{2,2,2}$	$M_{2,3,2}$				$(M_{2,1,2} * D_{2,1}) + (M_{2,2,2} * D_{2,2}) + (M_{2,3,2} * D_{2,3})$
Decision 7	$M_{2,1,3}$	$M_{2,2,1}$	$M_{2,3,2}$				$(M_{2,1,3} * D_{2,1}) + (M_{2,2,1} * D_{2,2}) + (M_{2,3,2} * D_{2,3})$
Decision 8	$M_{2,1,3}$	$M_{2,2,2}$	$M_{2,3,2}$				$(M_{2,1,3} * D_{2,1}) + (M_{2,2,2} * D_{2,2}) + (M_{2,3,2} * D_{2,3})$

Source: Own work

Using the cost evaluation of solutions to a decision problem, it is possible to identify the best solution for the goal directly, assuming maximization or minimization of the assumed effect. The solution is a decision with the highest or lowest cost evaluation. The cost evaluation of the solutions to the decision problem does not allow direct indicating of decisions that achieve the goal, assuming the maintenance of functionality in the assumed range. In this case, the obtained solutions should be substituted sequentially into the risk formula (3.2), its value calculated, and then the availability of functionality after materializing the considered threats estimated (3.4).

EXAMPLE OF APPLICATION OF THE MESSM

This chapter presents a computational experiment to illustrate the application of the MESSM using the example of two geographically related CIs. Let V_1 denote a hospital, V_2 denote an oil refinery, and V_3 denote the surroundings of the CIs under consideration (a city).

CI Hospital V_1 is vulnerable to the threat of:

- fire $(Z_{1,1})$,
- drought $(Z_{1,2})$,

- environmental contamination – heavy smoke ($Z_{1,3}$),
- personnel limitations ($Z_{1,4}$)

The hospital operator has put in place the following safeguards in response to the identified threats:

- fire extinguishing agent system ($M_{1,1,1}$),
- own drinking water intake ($M_{1,2,1}$),
- air filter system ($M_{1,3,1}$),
- the ability to mobilize non-call staff ($M_{1,4,1}$).

Three functionalities characterize the hospital:

- burn treatment unit ($\Phi_{1,1}$),
- an airstrip for LPR ($\Phi_{1,2}$),
- staff availability ($\Phi_{1,3}$).

Refinery CI V_2 is susceptible to the threat of:

- fire ($Z_{2,1}$),
- drought ($Z_{2,2}$),
- technical failure ($Z_{2,3}$).

The refinery operator has implemented the following safeguards in response to identified threats:

- plant fire department ($M_{2,1,1}$),
- fire extinguishing agent system ($M_{2,1,2}$),
- protective suits ($M_{2,1,3}$),
- drinking water supply ($M_{2,2,1}$),
- maintenance department ($M_{2,3,1}$).

Three functionalities characterize the refinery:

- olefins production facility ($\Phi_{2,1}$),
- flue gas cleaning ($\Phi_{2,2}$),
- personnel safety ($\Phi_{2,3}$).

In addition, the surroundings of the hospital and refinery (V_3) are susceptible to the threat of drought ($Z_{3,1}$) with a probability of 0.2 and vulnerability $U_{3,1} = 0.11$. In addition, the threat of $Z_{2,1}$ – fire gives rise to the threat of $Z_{3,2}$ – environmental contamination – heavy smoke, which has a probability of 0.1 and to which the surroundings of V_3 are susceptible ($U_{3,2} = 0.32$).

Synthetically, the characteristics of CI V_1 and V_2 are illustrated in Table 3.18, showing data on resources, functionality, threats, and safeguards. Complementing the V_1 and V_2 characterization models in Table 3.18 is Table 3.19, which illustrates the relationships between CIs.

Figure 3.2 shows the example of the CI situation of a hospital (V_1), a refinery (V_2), and its surroundings (V_3).

Analysing Figure 3.2, it is possible to recognize some of the dependencies of the CIs indicated in Table 3.19. These dependencies stem from internal threats indicating that the considered CI interacts with itself (Figure 3.2, dependencies: G_3, G_6, and G_7). Other dependencies result from information about the threats to which the considered CI is susceptible. An example is threat $Z_{2,1}$ – fire in a refinery, which, in addition to the adverse effects on the functionality of the refinery, induces threat $Z_{1,3}$ – environmental contamination – heavy smoke. The hospital is susceptible to this threat, for which it is an external threat. A fire at the refinery creates conditions conducive to an adverse event ($Z_{1,3}$) affecting the hospital, indicating a relationship (G_5) between the refinery and the hospital.

Relationships between CIs, although they arise from the CI characteristics considered, cannot be generated automatically. An example is the threat $Z_{1,1}$ – fire, to which the hospital (V_1) is susceptible. Materializing this hazard, as in the case of the $Z_{3,1}$ thread – drought, should arouse the $Z_{2,1}$ threat – fire, to which the refinery is susceptible. However, the situation shown in Figure 3.2 does not consider such a link. This dependence was omitted due to the excessive distance between the hospital (V_1) and the refinery (V_2). In such cases, a significant role is played by the experience of the analytical team, which has to interpret the available data and decide whether there is a relationship.

Another example of the lack of impact is the case of threat $Z_{1,3}$ – environmental contamination – heavy smoke, the occurrence of which creates favourable conditions for the materialization of threats $Z_{2,3}$ – technical failure and $Z_{1,4}$ – restriction of personnel. In Figure 3.2, the possibility that the threat $Z_{1,3}$ will induce the threat $Z_{1,4}$ is marked, omitting the threat $Z_{2,3}$. This was done because the characteristics of CI (V_1) do not indicate that it is susceptible to this threat.

The way of recognizing dependencies between CIs points to two rules:

- if the considered threat induces another threat to which the considered CIs are susceptible, then there is a potential link between them, which must be verified and confirmed by the analytical team,
- if the considered threat creates conditions conducive to the occurrence of another threat to which the considered CIs are not susceptible, then there is no link between them.

TABLE 3.18 Synthetic note on the CI situation V_1 in V_2

	Functionalities		Threats						Safeguard			
CI	Symbol	Functionality Value (%)	Symbol	Type	Induced Threat	Probability	Reduction of CI Functionality	Symbol	Degree of Reduction in Vulnerability	Goal of Crisis Management	CI Protection Area	Vulnerability
V_1	$\Phi_{1,1}$	70	$Z_{1,1}$	IN	–	0.3	–30% ($\Phi_{1,1}$) –20% ($\Phi_{1,3}$)	$M_{1,1,1}$	0.05	Taking control	Technical security	0.5
			$Z_{1,2}$	OUT	Technical failure	0.4	–10% ($\Phi_{1,3}$)	$M_{1,2,1}$	0.9	Prevention	Business continuity	0.8
	$\Phi_{1,2}$	100	$Z_{1,3}$	OUT	Technical failure increased number of victims	0.05	–100% ($\Phi_{1,2}$) –15% ($\Phi_{1,3}$)	$M_{1,3,1}$	0.3	Prevention	Technical security	0.7
	$\Phi_{1,3}$	85	$Z_{1,4}$	OUT	–	0.65	–50% ($\Phi_{1,1}$) –5% ($\Phi_{1,3}$) –10% ($\Phi_{1,2}$)	$M_{1,4,1}$	0.04	Taking control	Business continuity	0.65
V_2	$\Phi_{2,1}$	85	$Z_{2,1}$	IN	Environmental contamination; strong smoke increased number of casualties	0.5	–100% ($\Phi_{2,1}$) –50% ($\Phi_{2,2}$) –30% ($\Phi_{2,3}$)	$M_{2,1,1}$	0.4	Prevention	Technical security	0.7
								$M_{2,1,2}$	0.1	Taking control	Technical security	
								$M_{2,1,3}$	0.05	Response in case of occurrence	Physical security	
	$\Phi_{2,2}$	100	$Z_{2,2}$	OUT	Technical failure	0.4	–10% ($\Phi_{2,3}$)	$M_{2,2,1}$	0.1	Response in case of occurrence	Business continuity	0.8
	$\Phi_{2,3}$	90	$Z_{2,3}$	IN	Fire	0.35	–40% ($\Phi_{2,1}$) –35% ($\Phi_{2,2}$) –15% ($\Phi_{2,3}$)	$M_{2,3,1}$	0.35	Prevention Response in case of occurrence	Technical security Business continuity	0.65

Source: Own study

TABLE 3.19 Synthetic note of the dependence of threats and CIs

Resource Symbol:		V_3
Threat symbol:	Dependent resource	Influential threat
G_1	V_1	Drought
G_2	V_2	Drought
Threat symbol:	V_1	
G_3	V_1	Fire
Threat symbol:	V_2	
G_4	V_1	Increased number of victims
G_5	V_1	Environmental contamination – heavy smoke
G_6	V_2	Fire
G_7	V_2	Technical failure
G_8	V_3	Environmental contamination – heavy smoke

Source: Own study

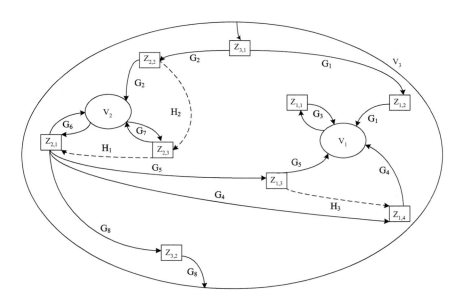

FIGURE 3.2 Illustration of the links considered CI

Source: Own study

TABLE 3.20 Illustration of the impact of threats on the CI in question

Description	V_1		V_2		V_3	
	P	U M	P	U M	P	U M
$Z_{1,1}$	0.30	0.50 0.05				
$Z_{1,2}$	0.40	0.80 0.90				
$Z_{1,3}$	0.05	0.70 0.30				
$Z_{1,4}$	0.65	0.65 0.04				
$Z_{2,1}$			0.50	0.70 $0.4 + 0.1 + 0.05$		
$Z_{2,2}$			0.40	0.8 0.10		
$Z_{2,3}$			0.35	0.65 0.35		
$Z_{3,1}$					0.20	0.11 0
$Z_{3,2}$					0.10	0.32 0

Source: Own study

Table 3.20 presents a synthetic note of the vulnerability of the CIs under consideration (Figure 3.2) to threats (Table 3.18).

Table 3.21 presents a synthetic record of the dependence of threats[5] occurring between the CIs under consideration (Figure 3.2), prepared on the basis of Table 3.18.

The data collected in Tables 3.20 and 3.21 allowed the development of a model of the dependencies of the CIs under consideration. It was implemented in an IT tool that allows simulating business processes by IBM Websphere Business Modeler 7.0 Advance. Based on the simulation of 1,000 conditions conducive to $Z_{3,1}$ threat – drought, 18 AES were obtained, 11 of which ended with negative consequences for the hospital, refinery, or their surroundings. Sample data on the obtained the AES is shown in Table 3.22.

TABLE 3.21 Illustration of the interdependence of the threats to the CIs under consideration

Threat	$Z'_{1,1}$	$Z'_{1,2}$	$Z'_{1,3}$	$Z'_{1,4}$	$Z'_{2,1}$	$Z'_{2,2}$	$Z'_{2,3}$	$Z'_{3,1}$	$Z'_{3,2}$
$Z_{1,1}$									
$Z_{1,2}$									
$Z_{1,3}$				$P'_{1,4}$ 0.65 $P_{1,3}$ 0.05					
$Z_{1,4}$									
$Z_{2,1}$			$P'_{1,3}$ 0.05 $P_{2,1}$ 0.50	$P'_{1,4}$ 0.65 $P_{2,1}$ 0.50					$P'_{3,2}$ 0.10 $P_{2,1}$ 0.50
$Z_{2,2}$							$P'_{2,3}$ 0.35 $P_{2,2}$ 0.40		
$Z_{2,3}$					$P'_{2,1}$ 0.50 $P_{2,3}$ 0.35				
$Z_{3,1}$		$P'_{1,2}$ 0.40 $P_{3,1}$ 0.20				$P'_{2,2}$ 0.40 $P_{3,1}$ 0.20			
$Z_{3,2}$									

Source: Own study

208 Civil Protection and Domestic Security in Hybrid Warfare

TABLE 3.22 Example of AES for threat $Z_{3,1}$ – drought

| Description | Sequence of Events | | | Number of Cases | Distribution (%) |
	Incitation	Materialization	Effect		
Scenario 7	$Z_{2,1}$-D	$Z_{2,1}$-P		1	0.10
	$Z_{2,2}$-D	$Z_{2,2}$-P			
	$Z_{2,3}$-D	$Z_{2,3}$-P	$Z_{2,3}$-R		
	$Z_{1,2}$-D				
	$Z_{1,3}$-D				
	$Z_{1,4}$-D	$Z_{1,4}$-P	$Z_{1,4}$-R		
	$Z_{3,1}$-D	$Z_{3,1}$-P			
	$Z_{3,2}$-D				
	$Z_{2,3}$-D				
	$Z_{1,2}$-D	$Z_{1,2}$-P			
	$Z_{3,1}$-D	$Z_{3,1}$-P			
Scenario 18	$Z_{2,1}$-D			2	0.20
	$Z_{2,2}$-D	$Z_{2,2}$-P			
	$Z_{2,3}$-D	$Z_{2,3}$-P			
	$Z_{1,2}$-D				
	$Z_{3,1}$-D	$Z_{3,1}$-P			

Source: Own study

The data in Table 3.22 should be read as follows:

- a single scenario element marked with the letter "D" means that the $Z_{\alpha,\beta}$ threat has been triggered, i.e. conditions conducive to its occurrence have occurred. If there is no $Z_{\alpha,\beta}$ element marked with the letter "P" in the next column, i.e. despite favourable conditions, the threat has not materialized;
- the sequence of scenario elements $Z_{\alpha,\beta}$-D, $Z_{\alpha,\beta}$-P should be read as the occurrence of favourable conditions and the materialization of the threat $Z_{\alpha,\beta}$. Supposing there is no $Z_{\alpha,\beta}$ element marked with "R" in the next column, i.e. despite the materialization of the threat, the Vα resource has not been affected, i.e. in that case, the functionalities of the Vα resource are available at the level before the materialization of the threat. Such a situation means that the Vα resource has proven to be resistant to the $Z_{\alpha,\beta}$ threat;
- the sequence of scenario elements $Z_{\alpha,\beta}$-D, $Z_{\alpha,\beta}$-P, $Z_{\alpha,\beta}$-R should be read as the materialization of the threat $Z_{\alpha,\beta}$, as a result of which the resource Vα was affected, i.e. the functionality level

of the resource $V\alpha$ is lower than before the materialization of the threat or the functionality of the CI under consideration has been wholly lost.

Data in Table 3.22 is interpreted in Scenario 7 (an example of a scenario with negative impacts) and Scenario 18 (an example of a scenario without negative impacts).

Within scenario 7, which occurred once, eight threats were induced ($Z_{1,2}$; $Z_{1,3}$; $Z_{1,4}$; $Z_{2,1}$; $Z_{2,2}$; $Z_{2,3}$; $Z_{3,1}$; and $Z_{3,2}$). As a result of favourable conditions, five threats materialized ($Z_{1,4}$; $Z_{2,1}$; $Z_{2,2}$; $Z_{2,3}$; and $Z_{3,1}$), as a result of which resource V_1 – the hospital and resource V_2 – the refinery were exposed to adverse effects manifested in reduced functional availability. The materialization of threats triggered adverse events ($Z_{1,4}$ and $Z_{2,3}$)[6] for resource V_1 (threat $Z_{1,4}$ – reduction of personnel caused the adverse effects specified in Table 3.18) and resource V_2 (threat $Z_{2,3}$ – technical failure caused the adverse effects specified in Table 3.18).

Under scenario 18, which occurred twice, five hazards ($Z_{1,2}$; $Z_{2,1}$; $Z_{2,2}$; $Z_{2,3}$; and $Z_{3,1}$) were induced. As a result of favourable conditions, three threats materialized ($Z_{2,2}$, $Z_{2,3}$, and $Z_{3,1}$), resulting in the V_2 resource refinery being exposed to negative impacts. However, the materialization of the threats did not trigger an adverse event, causing a decrease in the availability of the functionality of the CI under consideration. This means that the safeguards in place proved effective according to this scenario.

Calculating the value of the risk associated with the contemplated threat to which the CI is susceptible requires the entity responsible for CI security to determine which functionality is exposed to the adverse effects of threat materialization. The AES can integrate multiple CIs, as shown in scenario 7 (Table 3.22). In such a case, standard functionality for the CIs present in the scenario may not exist. However, this does not prevent the calculation of risks associated with the AES.

When there is no standard functionality for the CIs under consideration, as in scenario 7, the CI security entity decides which functionality, among the set of functionalities of the CIs under consideration, is of interest to it.

Once the functionality is selected, the risk formula (3.3) is applied, considering all CIs included in the AES that affect the functionality under consideration ($\Delta\Phi \neq 0$).

An example illustrating the calculation of risk values for the AES uses data from scenario 7 (Table 3.22). The computational experiment examines the impact of threats in the scenario on the functionality of the olefins production facility ($\Phi_{2,1}$). Scenario 7 assumes that the materialization of threats triggered adverse events ($Z_{1,4}$ and $Z_{2,3}$) for hospital V_1 (threat $Z_{1,4}$ – staff reduction) and refinery V_2 (threat $Z_{2,3}$ – technical failure).

From the point of view of the considered functionality $\Phi_{2,1}$, only threat $Z_{2,3}$ is relevant. Using the CI dependency model (Figure 3.2), it is possible to reconstruct the course of the AES and determine that the occurrence of threat $Z_{2,3}$ was preceded by threats $Z_{2,2}$ and $Z_{3,1}$. This allows calculating the probability of occurrence of threat $Z_{2,3}$ on the condition of materialization of threats $Z_{2,2}$ and $Z_{3,1}$ using Bayes' theorem.

$$P\left(Z_{2,3} | Z_{2,2}; Z_{3,1}\right) = \frac{P_{2,3} \times 0.(3)}{0.(3) \times \left[\left(P_{2,3}\right) + \left(P_{2,2}\right) + \left(P_{3,1}\right)\right]} = 0.316$$

The obtained result of the probability of occurrence of threat $Z_{2,3}$ under the condition of materialization of threats $Z_{2,2}$ and $Z_{3,1}$ substituted into the risk formula (3.3) allows calculating the risk of loss of functionality $\Phi_{2,1}$ that is associated with AES No. 7.

$$R_{2,3} = P_{1,1} \times |\Delta\Phi_{2,1}| \times \left(U_{2,3} - M_{2,3,1}\right)$$
$$= 0.316 \times |-40\%| \times (0.65 - 0.35) = 3.792\%$$

The computational experiment shows that the risk of loss of functionality of $\Phi_{2,1}$ – olefins production facilities resulting from scenario 7 is 3.792%.

This value is the total of all the risks that negatively affected scenario 7 regarding the functionality under consideration. In the case at hand, only threat $Z_{2,3}$ materialized and negatively affected functionality $\Phi_{2,1}$. Hence, the value of the risk for this threat is simultaneously the value of the risk for functionality $\Phi_{2,1}$ resulting from AES No. 7.

The CI V_2 characteristics (Table 3.18) distinguish three threats: $Z_{2,1}$ – fire, $Z_{2,2}$ – drought, and $Z_{2,3}$ – technical failure. The materialization of these threats has a negative impact (defined in Table 3.18) on the functionality of the considered CI olefins production facility ($\Phi_{2,1}$), flue gas treatment ($\Phi_{2,2}$), and personnel availability ($\Phi_{2,3}$).

The decision problem in question concerns the impact of materialization of threats contained in the characteristics of the refinery on the functionality of $\Phi_{2,3}$ – personnel availability.

For the example, it is assumed that the CI operator does not apply any safeguards to the identified threats. Hence, the risk of loss of availability of functionality as a result of the materialization of three threats is 17.113%, which means the possibility of loss of functionality $\Phi_{2,3}$ in this dimension. This value results from the total of risks associated with threats calculated by multiplying the probability of materialization of threats ($P_{\alpha,\beta}$), the effects of their materialization on functionality ($\Delta\Phi_{2,3}$), and the vulnerability of the refinery to the threats ($U_{\alpha,\beta}$) (Table 3.18) according to formula (3.3).

$$\sum_{\beta=1}^{3} R_{\alpha,\beta} = 17.113\%$$

$$R_{2,1} = 0.5 \times 30\% \times 0.7 = 10.5\%$$

$$R_{2,2} = 0.4 \times 10\% \times 0.8 = 3.2\%$$

$$R_{2,3} = 0.35 \times 15\% \times 0.65 = 3.413\%$$

The risk of loss of functionality $\Phi_{2,3}$ associated with threats $Z_{2,1}$, $Z_{2,2}$, and $Z_{2,3}$ of 17.113% suggests a potential availability of functionality due to threat materialization of 72.887% according to formula (3.4).

If we assume that the CI operator's goal is to maintain a functionality level of $\Phi_{2,3}$ in the <80%, 90%> range, this means that with the current level of functionality $\Phi_{2,3}$ equals 90%, the risk of loss of availability of functionality $\Phi_{2,3}$ has to be reduced by a minimum of 7.113%.

The CI operator can apply the following safeguards to the threat to reduce the risk of a loss of $\Phi_{2,3}$ functionality:

- $Z_{2,1}$ – $M_{2,1,1}$ company fire department ($m_{2,1,1} = 0.4$), $M_{2,1,2}$ fire extinguishing agent system ($m_{2,1,2} = 0.1$), $M_{2,1,3}$ protective suits ($m_{2,1,3} = 0.05$),
- $Z_{2,2}$ – $M_{2,2,1}$ potable water supply ($m_{2,2,1} = 0.1$), $M_{2,2,2}$ potable water delivery ($m_{2,2,2} = 0.3$),
- $Z_{2,3}$ – $M_{2,3,1}$ maintenance department ($m_{2,3,1} = 0.35$), $M_{2,3,2}$ production on another machine ($m_{2,3,2} = 0.2$).

The decision problem resulting from the considered refinery characteristics (V_2) is illustrated in Figure 3.3.

The relative importance of decision areas was calculated according to formula (3.5) and rounded to integer values.

$$D_{2,1} = \frac{R_{2,1}}{\sum_{\beta=1}^{3} R_{\alpha,\beta}} \times 100 \approx 61$$

$$D_{2,2} = \frac{R_{2,2}}{\sum_{\beta=1}^{3} R_{\alpha,\beta}} \times 100 \approx 19$$

$$D_{2,3} = \frac{R_{2,3}}{\sum_{\beta=1}^{3} R_{\alpha,\beta}} \times 100 \approx 20$$

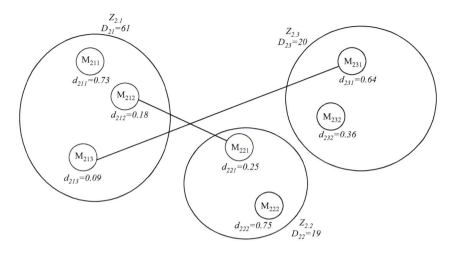

FIGURE 3.3 Decision problem based on CI V_2 characteristics

Source: Own study

The relative significance of elementary decisions was calculated according to formula (3.6) and after rounding to two decimal places was as follows:

$$d_{2,1,1} = \frac{m_{2,1,1}}{\sum_{\lambda=1}^{3} m_{\alpha,\beta,\lambda}} \approx 0.73$$

$$d_{2,1,2} = \frac{m_{2,1,2}}{\sum_{\lambda=1}^{3} m_{\alpha,\beta,\lambda}} \approx 0.18$$

$$d_{2,1,3} = \frac{m_{2,1,3}}{\sum_{\lambda=1}^{3} m_{\alpha,\beta,\lambda}} \approx 0.09$$

$$d_{2,2,1} = \frac{m_{2,2,1}}{\sum_{\lambda=1}^{2} m_{\alpha,\beta,\lambda}} \approx 0.25$$

$$d_{2,2,2} = \frac{m_{2,2,2}}{\sum_{\lambda=1}^{2} m_{\alpha,\beta,\lambda}} \approx 0.75$$

$$d_{2,3,1} = \frac{m_{2,3,1}}{\sum_{\lambda=1}^{2} m_{\alpha,\beta,\lambda}} \approx 0.64$$

$$d_{2,3,2} = \frac{m_{2,3,2}}{\sum_{\lambda=1}^{2} m_{\alpha,\beta,\lambda}} \approx 0.36$$

Considering the contradiction of pairs of elementary decisions, a matrix of acceptable solutions to the decision problem was indicated (Table 3.23).

The cost evaluation of individual decisions was identified by substituting the values of relative importance of individual elementary decisions and multiplying the resulting matrix by the matrix of relative importance of decision areas (Table 3.24).

Based on the significance indexes of elementary decisions $(d_{\alpha,\beta,\lambda})$, safeguards being components of each decision have been determined $(M_{\alpha,\beta,\lambda})$. On this basis it was possible to establish values of collateral influence on CI resilience $(m_{\alpha,\beta,\lambda})$. After substituting values of the impact of safeguards on CI's resilience $(m_{\alpha,\beta,\lambda})$ into the risk formula (3.3), it turned

TABLE 3.23 Matrix of possible solutions to the decision problem

	$M_{2,1,\lambda}$	$M_{2,2,\lambda}$	$M_{2,3,\lambda}$
Decision 1	$M_{2,1,1}$	$M_{2,2,1}$	$M_{2,3,1}$
Decision 2	$M_{2,1,1}$	$M_{2,2,1}$	$M_{2,3,2}$
Decision 3	$M_{2,1,1}$	$M_{2,2,2}$	$M_{2,3,1}$
Decision 4	$M_{2,1,1}$	$M_{2,2,2}$	$M_{2,3,2}$
Decision 5	$M_{2,1,2}$	$M_{2,2,2}$	$M_{2,3,1}$
Decision 6	$M_{2,1,2}$	$M_{2,2,2}$	$M_{2,3,2}$
Decision 7	$M_{2,1,3}$	$M_{2,2,1}$	$M_{2,3,2}$
Decision 8	$M_{2,1,3}$	$M_{2,2,2}$	$M_{2,3,2}$

Source: Own study

TABLE 3.24 Calculation of the values of possible solutions to the decision problem

	$d_{2,1,\lambda}$	$d_{2,2,\lambda}$	$d_{2,3,\lambda}$	$D_{2,\beta}$	Cost Assessment
Decision 1	0.73	0.25	0.64	61	62.37
Decision 2	0.73	0.25	0.36	19	56.77
Decision 3	0.73	0.75	0.64	20	71.81
Decision 4	0.73	0.75	0.36		66.27
Decision 5	0.18	0.75	0.64		38.1
Decision 6	0.18	0.75	0.36		32.5
Decision 7	0.09	0.25	0.36		17.48
Decision 8	0.09	0.75	0.36		26.98

Source: Own study

TABLE 3.25 Summary of the level of risk of loss of functionality and value of functionality for solutions to the decision problem

Decision	Cost Assessment	Value of Risk (%)	Value of Functionality (%)
1	62.37	8.875	81.125
2	56.77	9.663	80.333
3	71.81	8.075	81.925
4	66.27	8.863	81.138
5	38.1	12.575	77.425
6	32.5	13.363	76.638
7	17.48	14.913	75.088
8	26.98	14.113	75.888

Source: Own study

out that the decisions numbering 1, 2, 3, and 4 (Table 3.25) implemented the adopted goal of the CI operator, which was to maintain functionality within the range of <80%, 90%> after taking into account the risk of materialization of threats to which CI V_2 – oil refinery is susceptible.

The most practical combination of safeguards for the considered set of threats is Decision No. 3, which assumes the use of the corporate fire department, potable water supply, and the establishment of a maintenance department to counter the identified threats. The implementation of Decision No. 3 achieves a loss-of-function risk value of $\Delta\Phi_{2,3}$ of 8.075%, potentially reducing the considered functionality to 81.925%.

$$\sum_{\beta=1}^{3} R_{2,\beta} = 8.075\%$$

$$R_{2,1} = 0.5 \times 30\% \times (0.7 - 0.4) = 4.5\%$$

$$R_{2,2} = 0.4 \times 10\% \times (0.8 - 0.3) = 2\%$$

$$R_{2,3} = 0.35 \times 15\% \times (0.65 - 0.35) = 1.575\%$$

The decision problem for the AES was formulated based on scenario No. 7 (Table 3.22), in which:

- threat $Z_{1,4}$ – personnel restrictions negatively affect CI V_1 – hospital,
- threat $Z_{2,3}$ – technical failure negatively affects CI V_2 – refinery.

The goal assumed by the operators of the CIs in question is to reduce to the extent possible the vulnerability of the related CIs (V_1 and V_2) to the threats arising from AES No. 7.

For the computational experiment, the state resulting from the CI situation models V_1 and V_2 is assumed (Table 3.18). This means that the baseline vulnerability:

- CI V_1 Hospital to threat $Z_{1,4}$ is $U_{1,4} = 0.65$,
- CI V_2 Refinery to threat $Z_{2,3}$ is $U_{2,3} = 0.65$.
- CI operator V_1 applies protection against threat $Z_{1,4}$ in the form of $M_{1,4,1}$ – mobilization of personnel not on duty, which reduces the vulnerability of CI V_1 to the $Z_{1,4}$ threat by 0.04 to $U'_{1,4} = 0.61$,
- CI operator V_2 applies protection against threat $Z_{2,3}$ in the form of $M_{2,3,1}$ – maintenance department, which reduces CI V_2 vulnerability to threat $Z_{2,3}$ by 0.35 to a level of $U'_{2,3} = 0.3$.

Making assumptions about the vulnerability of CI V_1 and V_2 to threats $Z_{1,4}$ and $Z_{2,3}$ and the impact of safeguards, the relative importance of decision areas was calculated according to formula (3.5).

$$D_{1,4} = \frac{U'_{1,4}}{U'_{1,4} + U'_{2,3}} \times 100 = \frac{0.61}{0.61 + 0.3} \times 100 \approx 67$$

$$D_{2,3} = \frac{U'_{2,3}}{U'_{1,4} + U'_{2,3}} \times 100 = \frac{0.3}{0.61 + 0.3} \times 100 \approx 33$$

Additional safeguards that can be applied in response to identified threats are as follows:

- for threat $Z_{1,4}$:
  - collateral $M_{1,4,2}$ – transport of victims to other hospitals, which reduces CI V_1 vulnerability to threat $Z_{1,4}$ by $m_{1,4,2} = 0.45$,
  - protection $M_{1,4,3}$ – mobilization of personnel from other hospitals, which reduces CI V_1 vulnerability to threat $Z_{1,4}$ by $m_{1,4,3} = 0.42$,
  - security $M_{1,4,4}$ – mobilization of military medical personnel, which reduces CI V_1 vulnerability to threat $Z_{1,4}$ by $m_{1,4,4} = 0.35$,
- for threat $Z_{2,3}$:
  - protection $M_{2,3,2}$ – production on another device, which reduces CI V_2 vulnerability to threat $Z_{2,3}$ by $m_{2,3,2} = 0.2$,

- protection $M_{2,3,3}$ – outsourcing production to another plant, which reduces CI V_2 susceptibility to threat $Z_{2,3}$ by $m_{2,3,3} = 0.1$.

Making assumptions about safeguards against $Z_{1,4}$ and $Z_{2,3}$, the relative importance of elementary decisions in decision areas was calculated using the formula (3.6).

$$d_{1,4,2} = \frac{m_{1,4,2}}{\sum_{\lambda=2}^{4} m_{1,4,\lambda}} = \frac{0.45}{0.45 + 0.42 + 0.35} \approx 0.37$$

$$d_{1,4,3} = \frac{m_{1,4,3}}{\sum_{\lambda=2}^{4} m_{1,4,\lambda}} = \frac{0.42}{0.45 + 0.42 + 0.35} \approx 0.34$$

$$d_{1,4,4} = \frac{m_{1,4,4}}{\sum_{\lambda=2}^{4} m_{1,4,\lambda}} = \frac{0.35}{0.45 + 0.42 + 0.35} \approx 0.29$$

$$d_{2,3,2} = \frac{m_{2,3,2}}{\sum_{\lambda=2}^{3} m_{2,3,\lambda}} = \frac{0.2}{0.2 + 0.1} \approx 0.67$$

$$d_{2,3,3} = \frac{m_{2,3,3}}{\sum_{\lambda=2}^{3} m_{2,3,\lambda}} = \frac{0,1}{0.2 + 0.1} \approx 0.33$$

For the decision problem at hand, pairs in a contradictory link were assumed as follows:

- $M_{1,4,4} - M_{2,3,2}$
- $M_{1,4,4} - M_{2,3,3}$

Figure 3.4 illustrates the decision problem resulting from AES No. 7 for CI V_1 and V_2.

Considering the contradiction of pairs of elementary decisions, a matrix of possible solutions to the decision problem was indicated (Table 3.26).

The cost evaluation of individual decisions was obtained by substituting the values of relative importance of individual elementary decisions and multiplying the resulting matrix by the matrix of relative importance of decision areas (Table 3.27).

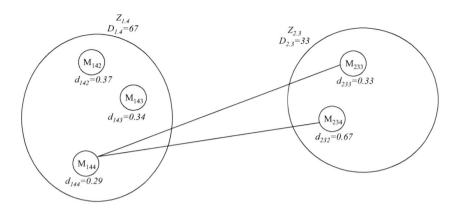

FIGURE 3.4 Illustration of the decision problem resulting from AES No. 7 for CI V_1 and V_2
Source: Own study

TABLE 3.26 Matrix of possible solutions to the decision problem resulting from AES No. 7 for CI V_1 and V_2

	$M_{1,4,\lambda}$	$M_{2,3,\lambda}$
Decision 1	$d_{1,4,2}$	$d_{2,3,2}$
Decision 2	$d_{1,4,2}$	$d_{2,3,3}$
Decision 3	$d_{1,4,3}$	$d_{2,3,2}$
Decision 4	$d_{1,4,3}$	$d_{2,3,3}$

Source: Own study

TABLE 3.27 Calculation of the values of possible solutions to the decision problem resulting from AES No. 7 for CI V_1 and V_2

	$d_{1,4,\lambda}$	$d_{2,3,\lambda}$	$d_{\alpha,\beta}$		Cost Assessment
Decision 1	0.37	0.64	* 67	=	46.9
Decision 2	0.37	0.64	33		35.68
Decision 3	0.34	0.36			44.89
Decision 4	0.34	0.64			33.67

Source: Own study

Data presented in Table 3.27 indicates that securing the transport of victims to other hospitals and production on another device most effectively achieves the stated goal (maximally reduces the related CIs V_1 and

218 Civil Protection and Domestic Security in Hybrid Warfare

TABLE 3.28 Summary of the risk level of loss of functionality and the value of functionality for solutions to the decision problem resulting from AES No. 7 for CIs V_1 and V_2

Decision	Cost Assessment	Vulnerability Value Taking into Account New Safeguards V_1	Vulnerability Value Taking into Account New Safeguards V_2
1	46.9	0.16	0.1
2	35.68	0.16	0.2
3	44.89	0.19	0.1
4	33.67	0.19	0.2

Source: Own study

V_2 to the threats arising from AES No. 7). Vulnerabilities of CIs V_1 and V_2 after implementing the suggested safeguards are shown in Table 3.28.

ENSURE BUSINESS CONTINUITY OF ES

More often than not, the ES is a collection of values provided by independent entities that pursue their own business goals. This fact poses an additional problem in the area of ES security management. A contractual example of ES could be a service that allows withdrawing money from an ATM.[7] In order for a user to satisfy his need to access cash, the component services must be available:

- availability of power supply to the ATM,
- availability of the internet network to provide connectivity to the clearing system,
- availability of the clearing system of the bank from which the money is withdrawn,
- provision of cash at the ATM, which is mainly the responsibility of ATM network operators.

Consequently, the ability to withdraw money from an ATM is, in fact, a set of relationships between the components of the above services, and it can only take place as a result of the simultaneous availability of all component services. Consequently, more than the unavailability of one of the component services is needed to make ES available.

The unavailability of the ES is a decision-making problem. Usually, the business entity providing the service in question would solve this problem by developing BCP for all component services. In the case of the ES, the solution to the decision problem is complicated because independent business entities manage the component services, and they are all responsible for the availability of the entire ES. This observation is the rationale for developing a method to manage ES availability.

In business practice, there are several ways to ensure uninterrupted service access; these are:

- structural redundancy, which involves duplicating elements deemed critical,
- functional excess, which consists of adapting selected elements of the system to perform additional functions,
- parametric redundancy, which consists of standard powering of the system to a degree that exceeds ensuring its usability.

Since the ES does not have a single operator responsible for its availability, no entity can fund additional system components to secure the analysed ES. Moreover, no component service operator doing business will be interested in maintaining an excess level of availability of a service that is a component of the ES. Such action generates additional costs that reduce the entity's profit, which contradicts the primary purpose of the existence of enterprises. Hence, the right way to ensure uninterrupted ES access is to rely on functional excess.

Using the MESSM, the institution that supervises ES and CI operators can, using the UK list, identify entities on which the analysed ES depends. The component services can then be treated as functionalities of CI facilities. In the event of an incident limiting or eliminating the availability of a functionality, it is possible to identify facilities with similar functionality and, within the framework of the BCP, supplement the missing component ES with functionality implemented by another facility. Figure 3.5 shows the components of the considered ES (objects and their functionalities) that will enable the withdrawal of money from an ATM:

- $\Phi_{1,2}$ – power access,
- $\Phi_{2,2}$ – internet access,
- $\Phi_{3,2}$ – availability of the bank's clearing system,
- $\Phi_{4,1}$ – ATM cash access.

As a result of the incident loss was sustained of the functionality $\Phi_{1,2}$ – power access, which was replaced by a V_5 object symbolizing a generator, which for a certain period became an object necessary to maintain ES availability (until the base object regains functionality).

Using the principles of similarity of functionality, it is possible to define a set of backup objects for the resources on which ES access depends and hence automate the creation of the ES BCP. For this purpose, the inference assumptions may be used by analogy, particularly the Case-Based Reasoning (CBR) method. Adopting the assumptions of inference by similarity, the decision-making task (ZP) is defined as:

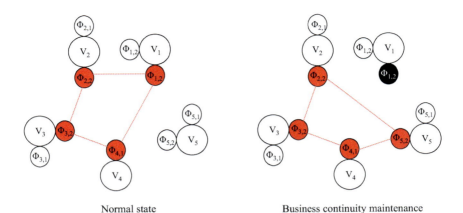

FIGURE 3.5 Illustration of the change in the components of the essential service

Source: Own study

$$ZP \cup \{PD, ZIK, ZR\} \qquad (3.8)$$

where:
pd_n – n-th decision problem ∈ PD,
zik_n – n-th characteristics of the CI facility ∈ ZIK,
zr_n – n-th result ∈ ZR.

The similarity between two decision problems pd_0 (base decision problem) and pdn (the n-th decision problem) is a non-negative real number, which is determined by:

$$s(pd_0, pd_n) = 1 - \frac{\sum_{pd \in PD} \text{distance}(b_{pd_0}, b_{pd_n})}{\sum_{pd \in PD} b_{pd_n}} \qquad (3.9)$$

where:
b – feature in common with the base case,
$s(pd_0, pd_n)$ – similarity of the n-th decision problem to the baseline decision problem,
distance (b_{pd_0}, b_{pd_n}) – for attributes belonging to a qualitative domain assumes values of 0 for identical values of compared elements and 1 in the opposite case.

Comparing the values of their attributes is sufficient to determine the similarity of cases. Describing the case with attributes used in the

MESSM, i.e. resources, threats, functionalities, and safeguards, indicates that there are four essential criteria for assessing the similarity of cases:

- resource similarity – determined by the V resources present in the decision problems being compared,
- functionality similarity – determined based on the functionalities Φ present in the compared decision problems,
- similarity of threats – determined based on threats Z occurring in the compared decision-making problems,
- security similarity – occurs when the same M actions have been taken in response to a threat in the compared decision-making problems.

In order to select a substitute ES component, it is necessary to describe as accurately as possible features of the functionality sought in the base case that would affect the degree of similarity of the cases. Associated with each n, this decision problem is a degree of security utility allowing the determination of the level of satisfaction $k(zr_n)$ of the entity responsible for ES security. The value of case utility informs the decision-maker about how far the considered resource can replace the lost functionality.

Based on the similarity of decision problems and the utility of safeguards, entities responsible for the security of ES components can order the considered problems according to the value of case utility K_{pd_n}:

$$K_{pd_n} = s(pd_0, pd_n) \times k(zr_n) \qquad (3.10)$$

where:

K_{pd_n} – case utility,

$s(pd_0, pd_n)$ – similarity of the n-th decision problem to the baseline decision problem,

$k(zr_n)$ – utility of the result,

zr_n – n-th result $\in$ ZR.

The decision-maker compares possible solutions with the base case and selects the resource offering the functionality sought, which has the highest utility (Table 3.29).

After sorting out the decision problems, the decision-maker compares the set of case security features with the set of features of the sought functionality of the underlying decision problem with the set of features with the highest case utility. In a situation where the elements of both sets are in agreement, the CI security entity has grounds to replace the ES component with the functionality of the object under consideration.

TABLE 3.29   Example of determining the utility of power sharing equipment

PD	Resource Similarity Criterion Mains Power from UPS	Fire	Threat Similarity Criterion Technical Failure	Explosion	Functional Similarity Criterion Power Sharing	Power Storage	Security Similarity Criterion Maintenance	Service	Battery Meter	Similarity	Usefulness of Safeguards	Usefulness of Case
Aggregate	1	0	0	0	0	1	0	0	1	0.67	0.5	0.33
UPS	1	0	0	0	0	0	0	0	0	0.89	0.2	0.18
Solar panel with UPS	1	0	0	0	0	0	0	0	0	0.89	0.4	0.36

Source: Own study

In the case at hand, the availability of ES was lost due to the disappearance of $\Phi_{1,2}$ functionality – power access at the facility where the ATM was located. A possible solution for the recovery of the ES component is to use substitute resources to recover power at the ATM. Available options are Genset, UPS, and solar panels with UPS. Table 3.29 shows an example of determining which available options should be used as a contingency measure to enable the continuity of ES operations. A comparison was made regarding resource similarity, threats, functionality, and security features.

In resource similarity, it was ascertained that all the available emergency options are not the same as the base resource, as it is not an additional power line provided by another operator. As regards threats, it was considered that all options are susceptible to the same threats as the base case. In the context of the implemented functionalities, the base case comprises two features: it makes power available and sustains it with UPS energy storage. In this area, the functionalities of UPS resources and solar panels with UPS were considered identical. In the case of the genset, the lack of power backup was indicated. In the area of applied safeguards, it was pointed out that the three features of the base solution are technical inspection, service, and battery metre. In this area, it was pointed out that the genset does not have a battery consumption metre. Considering all areas and using formula (3.8), a case similarity index was calculated. For the genset, the similarity index was 0.67; for the UPS and the solar panel with the UPS, the similarity index was 0.89. In order to establish the utility of the case that will indicate the preferred solution, an evaluation of the effectiveness of each solution was taken into account. The evaluation was determined expertly based on experience. By substituting the values of variables into formula (3.9), it was found that the variant with the highest utility in terms of similarity to the base case and effectiveness was the solar panel variant with UPS. For this reason, it is this particular solution that should replace the lost base case functionality until its availability is restored.

CONCLUSION

The analysis of the threats resulting from the hybrid war observed in Ukraine indicates a change of approach towards identifying and managing CI security. Identifying critical facilities should be linked to the critical services and resources required to maintain their business continuity. Conversely, CI security management should be based on a CI Situation Model that takes into account:

- implemented functionality that can be interpreted as components of an ES,

- threats to which the resource is vulnerable,
- safeguards that are applied as a response to identified risks,
- the organization of the process that determines the interdependence of resources.

The CI situation model integrates functionalities with resources, which are vulnerable to threats, the materialization of which may damage or destroy the resource and adversely affect the availability of functionalities. Threats, in turn, indicate the need for safeguards to ensure the correct operation of resources and access to functionality. The data collected in the resource situation model forms the input package for further activities:

- Risk value estimation – based on the derived risk value, the availability of functionality is forecast in the event of a specific hazard. If the predicted functionality value does not reach the safety threshold, a decision problem is formulated, considering the hazards from which the considered risk arises.
- Generation of AES – data from the asset situation model allows the development of a network of dependencies. Determining this network enables the identification of AES. AES are determined by the probability of a hazard occurring and the asset's vulnerability to that hazard. For each scenario, it is possible to determine the risk value associated with the hazards included in the scenario. If the risks associated with the scenario do not allow a safety threshold to be reached, a decision problem is formulated for the hazards present in the scenario. Determining the probability of a hazard occurring under the condition that another hazard materializes is done using Bayes' theorem. A detailed example illustrating the mechanics of creating AES for crisis management can be found in the publication.
- Decision problem formulation – the solution to the decision problem is a set of safeguards for each identified threat, allowing the safety threshold to be reached. The decision problem formulation method modifies the Analysis of Interconnected Decision Areas (AIDA) method. The set of safeguards resulting from the solution to the decision problem provides the resource operator with a recommendation for action in response to the risks arising from the threats to which the resource is vulnerable.

In addition, using the CI situation model makes it possible to identify resources that can replace those that have lost the ability to deliver their functionality (the ES components). Using the assumptions of analogy theory in combination with resource assessment criteria derived from the characteristics of resources mapped in the CI situation model, it is possible to quickly identify similar resources and integrate them into the ES delivery process, either temporarily or permanently.

NOTES

1 ES component – CI implements functionalities of the value chain of terrorizing ES, which is managed by the entity pursuing its business goals.
2 In the case of digital service operators, the extent of service disruption and the extent of impact on economic and social activities are examined when determining the materiality of the impact.
3 Vulnerability determinations are based on stakeholders' experiences or historical data on past incidents.
4 Directive (EU) 2022/2555 of the European Parliament and of the Council of 14 December 2022 on measures for a high common level of cyber security within the Union, amending Regulation (EU) No 910/2014 and Directive (EU) 2018/1972 and repealing Directive (EU) 2016/1148 (NIS Directive 2) Directive (EU) 2022/2557 of the European Parliament and of the Council of 14 December 2022 on the resilience of critical entities and repealing Council Directive 2008/114/EC (CER Directive).
5 The data in Table 2.21 should be interpreted as follows, e.g. threat $Z_{1,3}$ induces threat $Z_{1,4}$. The probability of a pair of these threats together is 0.0325 ($P_{1,3} * P_{1,4}$).
6 Whether a threat will cause negative effects on a resource is determined by the vulnerability of the resource $V\alpha$ to the threat $Z_{\alpha,\beta}$.
7 The authors used an example of a service that the reader can easily imagine. Despite its apparent triviality, the service of withdrawing money from an ATM is of considerable importance to many people. Lack of access to cash, primarily provided by ATMs today, can cause difficulties in buying food, medicines, etc. A prolonged lack of this service can lead to the inefficiency of stationary banking facilities and reduce access to cash in real terms. This, in turn, affects citizens' living comfort and health, as was confirmed during the onset of the COVID-19 pandemic.

BIBLIOGRAPHY

'A Framework for Major Emergency Management', (2022). Available at: https://www.gov.ie/en/collection/ca182-a-framework-for-major-emergency-management/. Accessed: 7 March 2024.

'All Hazards Risk Assessment Methodology Guidelines', (2022). Available at: https://www.publicsafety.gc.ca/cnt/rsrcs/pblctns/mrgnc-mngmnt-pnnng/index-en.aspx#ahral-2-5. Accessed: 7 March 2024.

Bennett, M., and Gupta, V., (n.d.), Dealing in Security Understanding Vital Services and How They Keep You Safe. Available at: https://www.scribd.com/document/16355390/Dealing-in-Security-understanding-vital-services-and-how-they-keep-you-safe Accessed: 31 Januar 2025.

Bolstad, W., and Curram, J., (2016), *Introduction to Bayesian statistics.* John Wiley & Sons, Inc., Hoboken, New Jersey.

Communication from the Commission on a European Programme for Critical Infrastructure Protection (2006). Available at: https://eur-lex.europa.eu/legal-content/EN/TXT/?uri=CELEX:52006DC0786. Accessed: 9 September 2024.

Directive 2009/140/EC of the European Parliament and of the Council of 25 November 2009 Amending Directives 2002/21/EC on a Common Regulatory Framework for Electronic Communications Networks and Services, 2002/19/EC on Access to, and Interconnection of, Electronic Communications Networks and Associated Facilities, and 2002/20/EC on the Authorisation of Electronic Communications Networks and Services (Text with EEA Relevance), (2009), OJ L. Available at: https://data.europa.eu/eli/dir/2009/140/oj/eng. Accessed: 9 September 2024.

Directive (EU) 2018/1972 of the European Parliament and of the Council of 11 December 2018 Establishing the European Electronic Communications Code (Recast) Text with EEA Relevance, (2018). Available at: https://eur-lex.europa.eu/eli/dir/2018/1972/oj. Accessed: 9 September 2024.

Directorate-General for Migration and Home Affairs (European Commission), EY, and RAND Europe, (2020), *Evaluation Study of Council Directive 2008/114 on the Identification and Designation of European Critical Infrastructures and the Assessment of the Need to Improve Their Protection: Final Report.* Luxembourg, Publications Office of the European Union. Available at: https://data.europa.eu/doi/10.2837/864404. Accessed: 9 September 2024.

Euratom: Council Decision of 23 October 2001 Establishing a Community Mechanism to Facilitate Reinforced Cooperation in Civil Protection Assistance Interventions, (2001), OJ L 2001/792/EC. Available at: https://data.europa.eu/eli/dec/2001/792/oj/eng. Accessed: 30 July 2024.

Eusgeld, I., Nan, C., and Dietz, S., (2011), "System-of-Systems" Approach for Interdependent Critical Infrastructures. *Reliability Engineering & System Safety*, 96(6), 679–686. Available at: https://doi.org/10.1016/j.ress.2010.12.010.

Moteff, J., Copeland, C., and Fischer, J., (2003), Critical Infrastructures: What Makes an Infrastructure Critical?

National Critical Functions Set | CISA, (n.d.), Available at: https://www.cisa.gov/national-critical-functions-set. Accessed: 9 September 2024.

'National Emergency Risk Assessment Guidelines', (2020), Australian Institute for Disaster Resilience. Available at: https://www.aidr.org.au/media/7600/aidr_handbookcollection_nerag_2020-02-05_v10.pdf. Accessed: 7 March 2024.

Rubin, C., (2001), *The Terrorist Attacks on September 11, 2001: Immediate Impacts and Their Ramifications for Federal Emergency Management.* Center University of Colorado (Natural Hazards research and Applications Information), Boulder, Colorado.

Skomra, W., (2015), *Metodyka oceny ryzyka na potrzeby zarządzania kryzysowego RP.* I. Warszawa: belStudio.

Skomra, W., (2019), Usługi logistyczne jako element infrastruktury krytycznej. *Przemysł Chemiczny*, 1(7), 16–19. Available at: https://doi.org/10.15199/62.2019.7.1.

'Swedish National Risk Assessment', (2019). Available at: https://www.government.se/contentassets/70c9762f411144dbbaf1020b1a5425b3/swedish-national-risk-assessment-2019-english-20191205-.pdf. Accessed: 8 March 2024.

Szołtysek, J., (2014), Przesłanki i założenia koncepcji logistyki społecznej. *Gospodarka Materiałowa i Logistyka* [Preprint] 1(2), 2–7.

Szołtysek, J., (2018), Social Logistics. How the Perception of the Role of a Man Changed the Logistics Decisions. *Logistyka* [Preprint] 1(6), 5–11.

Szwarc, K., (2018), National Key Infrastructure Protection – Sanction-Free or Regulatory Approach? *National Security Studies*, 14(2), 211–230. Available at: https://doi.org/10.37055/sbn/132133.

Wiśniewski, M., (2020), Methodology of Situational Management of Critical Infrastructure Security. *Founding Management*,12, 43–60. https://doi.org/10.2478/fman-2020-0004.

Zawiła-Niedźwiecki, J., (2014), *Operational Risk as a Problematic Triad: Risk, Resource Security, Business Continuity.* Legionowo and Kraków: Edu-Libri.

CHAPTER 4

Identification and analysis of threats to the civilian population in hybrid warfare

HYBRID THREATS AND THEIR IMPACT ON SECURITY

In the evaluation of the NATO-published study Hybrid threats and hybrid warfare, the concepts of hybrid warfare and hybrid threats have gained considerable attention in both academic and practical circles over the past decade. Although, as highlighted in the remaining chapters of this book, the terms are not synonymous, there is an important relationship between them due to their common purpose: to describe complex and changing phenomena in the international security environment. Both concepts, hybrid warfare and hybrid threats, seek to define a wide range of activities that can threaten international stability, often without the explicit use of traditional military means. Hybrid warfare and hybrid threats attempt to capture phenomena that fall in the space between conventional warfare and subtler, sometimes more difficult to discern methods of action. The terminology also encompasses concepts such as grey zone threats, information warfare, cognitive warfare or irregular warfare. Each of these terms refers to actions aimed at undermining the international order mainly by weakening societies, institutions and states, often to achieve specific political or military objectives mainly by external actors. These phenomena are not obvious to clearly classify and cover a wide range of activities. Hybrid threats often use information and communication technologies, manipulating information to create chaos and destabilisation. Although many of these terms are not officially recognised in military doctrine, they are gaining wider recognition in security and defence circles and also in popular messages. As NATO emphasises, understanding and analysing these concepts are crucial to contemporary defence strategies,

228   DOI: 10.4324/9781003503859-5

especially in the context of changing adversary methods (NATO, 2024). According to the authors of Hybrid threats and hybrid warfare, hybrid threats mainly refer to operations below the threshold of formal war, but this does not mean that such threats do not also occur during formal war (NATO, 2024). With this assertion, the authors of this study disagree. In this book, we have attempted to demonstrate that hybrid warfare cannot be an ontological concept that accommodates anything outside the traditional framework of war or is a review of previous concepts in different wars or an undefined area. Such an approach obscures more than it illuminates. Based on the authors' research (as expressed in the previous chapters and will be emphasised in the following ones), hybrid war is a stage of hybrid strategy in which the first phase is hybrid conflict (i.e. actions below the threshold of war resulting in hybrid threats also below the threshold of war). However, it is important to emphasise that hybrid threats are not limited to the effects of actions below the threshold of war; they often gain intensity and play a key role in hybrid war, as discussed in this and the other chapters of this book. Above and beyond this, as the authors of Hybrid Threats and Hybrid Warfare go on to write, hybrid threats refer to potential overt and covert military and non-military actions that states or non-state actors may take to undermine the target society and achieve their political objectives. These actions go beyond normal interactions between states, without necessarily pursuing war aims. Not all hybrid threats can be clearly classified as military problems (NATO, 2024). The analyses carried out within the framework of this study allow for some suggestions towards understanding and defining hybrid threats. Firstly, it should be made clear that hybrid threats are the result/effect of specific actions, which as individual actions are integrated into a web of actions, leading to hybrid threats. Each of these actions taken in isolation will not be entitled to the hybrid label. Therefore, the verb refers should not be used, which remains an imprecise term. Next, the definition uses military and non-military actions, forgetting that in hybrid war we have military actions (conventional and unconventional). Within the framework of this study, it is proposed that hybrid threats should be considered as the result/impact of actions in the different domains of hybrid conflict and hybrid war, which together create complex and multidimensional (networked) threats. One other aspect of the NATO-labelled study is worth noting on this occasion. The authors used the conjunction 'and' in the title. However, as the empirical evidence in this study as in many others shows, hybrid threats and hybrid warfare are inextricably linked, as both phenomena encompass a broad spectrum of activities that aim to destabilise the adversary and achieve strategic objectives. Evidence suggests that these threats are part of a broader warfare strategy, and their separation can lead to a misunderstanding of the nature of contemporary conflicts. In addition to the definition of hybrid threats cited above, there are a number of other definitions in the literature among which one of the most commonly cited is the definition developed by the Hybrid CoE which states that Hybrid threats are harmful activities that are planned and carried out with malign intent. They aim to undermine a target, such as a state or an institution, through a variety of means, often combined. Such means include information manipulation, cyberattacks, economic influence or coercion, covert political manoeuvring, coercive diplomacy, or threats of military force. Hybrid threats describe a wide array of harmful activities with different goals, ranging from influence operations and interference all the way to hybrid warfare (Hybrid Co E, 2024a, 2024b). Also relevant for further analysis is the definition of hybrid threats orpacated by the European Commission and Hybrid Coe, which states that Hybrid threats refer to specific types of interference and influence methods by authoritarian state or non-state actors targeting democratic *systems and those in the process of democratisation. Democratic states use different types of method, while an authoritarian state acting against another authoritarian state uses yet different methods. There are similarities, such as using multiple means, but here, when talking about hybrid threats we refer to authoritarian states and non-state actors targeting specifically systemic vulnerabilities in democracies* (Hybrid Co E, 2023). Given the diversity of definitions, it can be argued that understanding and precisely defining hybrid threats, as in the case of hybrid warfare, remains a complex issue and difficult to reach consensus especially among scholars and practitioners. The aim of this chapter is to attempt to identify and deepen the understanding of hybrid threats and their impact on internal security and civilian protection. In this context, it is hypothesised that the threats in hybrid warfare represent a network of flexible linkages between military and non-military threats that interact with each other, leading to likely cascading effects on the population civilian.

ANALYSIS OF OPERATIONAL DOMAINS IN HYBRID WARFARE

Domain, according to Jeffrey Reilly, refers to a critical macro-level manoeuvring space whose access or control is essential to the freedom of action and advantage required by the mission (Nettis, 2020, cited in Reilly, 2018). Jared Donnelly and Jon Farley, from the Air Command and Staff College (ACSC), point out that the understanding of the domain becomes more important as these intangible spaces begin to have a real impact on operations (Donnelly, Farley, 2018). The literature speaks of five basic domains of hybrid warfare: air, sea, land, space and cyberspace. This division can be supplemented by military, information, economic, political and technological. *The landscape of Hybrid Threats:*

A conceptual model (HybridCo), in the context of hybrid threats, proposes the following catalogue of domains: infrastructure; economy; military/defence; culture; social/sociality; public administration; legal; intelligence; political; diplomacy; information (Giannopoulos et al., 2021).

Recently, the cognitive domain (also referred to as the sixth traditional domain) has become increasingly important as a result of the growth of information operations. General Robert Brown, commander of U.S. Army Pacific, suggests that this is the most important domain that should be treated separately (cited in Nettis, 2020), as the public's broad access to information can undermine traditional control mechanisms, which in turn makes it easier for any actor, state or non-state, to exert influence across domains. Traditional control structures are being overtaken by platforms such as Twitter, Facebook and other social media in terms of speed of information dissemination (Nettis, 2020). David Patrikarakos *in War in 140 Characters,* for example, describes how Twitter has become the main source of relevant real-time information in the Russian-Ukrainian conflict (Patrikarakos, 2017). Patrikarakos highlighted both the advantages and disadvantages associated with the speed of social media reporting, noting the discrepancies in pro-Russian and pro-Ukrainian reporting and the problem of disinformation *being passed on thousands of times.* As a result, he stated that he was observing not just propaganda, but *a rediscovery of reality,* in which social media played a key role. In addition, he noted that mass *recruitment,* involving not only fighters but also civilians, is taking place through these channels, which has a real impact on the war (Patrikarakos, 2017; Galus, Nesteriak, 2019).

All of the mentioned domains are broad fields in which hybrid activities can take place. In addition, these domains can combine to create an even more complex hybrid threat environment. In this section, domains will be discussed, the catalogue of which was established on the basis of a literature analysis and then juxtaposed with a survey of media reports. The survey was performed according to the description of the research method in Appendix 1. The quantitative results of the codes indicating the occurrence of hybrid warfare domains are presented in the commons of Table A4.1. Figure 4.1 shows a list of domains and the number of codes indicating their occurrence.

The results obtained confirm the list of hybrid warfare domains established on the basis of the literature review. At the same time, the hierarchy of the use of domains in the war in Ukraine was established. Figure 4.1 shows that the dominant domains of hybrid warfare are:

- Information domain – 3,516 indications,
- Political domain – 3,069 indications,
- Air domain – 2,473 indications,

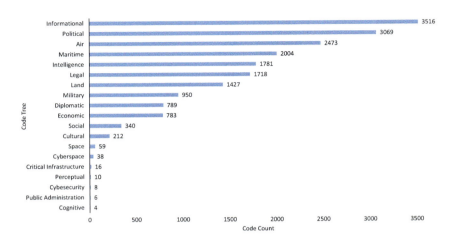

FIGURE 4.1 Number of codes in different domains in descending order

Source: Own study

- Maritime domain – 2,004 indications,
- Intelligence domain – 1,781 indications,
- Political domain – 1,718 indications,
- Land domain – 1,427 indications.

Table A4.2 (Appendix 2) presents the associations of hybrid warfare domains with each other. The percentages at the intersection of the codes characterising hybrid warfare features indicate how often a hybrid warfare feature occurred in conjunction with another feature.

All domains showed significant co-occurrence values with conventional (army) activities. The only exception for the lack of such a link in the tabulation is the cognitive domain, but this should be read together with the cognitive domain which shows a 50% strength of association with the army. The network of links is another piece of evidence that shows the coexistence of military and non-military activities that can be defined as hybrid warfare.

As part of a comprehensive domain analysis in the context of hybrid warfare, it has been assumed that the first step is to study and analyse the critical infrastructure domain. In the scientific literature on critical infrastructure (CI), there is no uniform definition of the term, but all definitions emphasise its critical role for society and the negative consequences that may result from its disruption (Wisniewski et al., 2023). According to the European definition, adopted by the Council of the European Union in 2022, critical infrastructure: *means a component, facility, equipment, network or system, or part of a component, facility, equipment, network or system, necessary for the provision of a critical service* (Directive of the European Parliament and of the Council (EU) 2022/2557, 2022).

Under NIS 2, the focus is on ensuring the continuity of critical services, defined as services that are critical to the maintenance of essential societal functions, essential economic activity, public health and safety or the environment (European Parliament and Council Directive (EU) 2022/2555, 2022, pp. 80–152).

Regardless of the nature of the enemy actor (state or non-state), infrastructures, essential services and supply chains can be attractive targets for intimidation and pressure.

These activities may aim to:

- a reduction in the quality of the goods and services offered (e.g. reduction in availability, reliability),
- destruction of key parts of the infrastructure,
- increased operating costs,
- impact on demand, creating pressure on infrastructure,
- reducing/removing redundancy and causing unilateral dependence on the enemy actor,
- gaining or limiting access to key resources needed for their functionality (raw materials, technology, expertise, etc.), and others.

Any tool that can create or exploit a vulnerability in the infrastructure (internal vs. external vulnerabilities) and achieve one of the above effects can potentially be used as part of a hybrid toolkit. It is important to note that a vulnerability is often sector specific, and can also be temporary (e.g. increased demand for a service due to a natural disaster) or recurring (cyclical) based on specific conditions. The critical infrastructure domain can be considered a mega-domain as it covers several sectors. In a survey of media reports carried out, the critical infrastructure domain achieved a low code count score, which may suggest that these activities do not occur frequently in the media space, but the effects of these attacks are usually very extensive and measurable for security systems and civilians. The IK domain co-occurs mainly with the maritime and air domain, but to a lesser extent is also linked to the information and intelligence domain. In the context of the co-occurrence of CI with other domains, it co-occurs mainly with conventional military activities and cyber-attacks. The pattern of domain and area linkages with CI in hybrid warfare confirms the complexity hypothesis, where domains intersect and attacks on critical infrastructure, despite their rare appearance in the media, are crucial due to their potentially catastrophic consequences for national security and social stability.

Another domain in hybrid warfare is the domain of cyberspace. The literature on the use of this domain is extensive and will be discussed further in Chapter 6. Hybrid Co E and the European Commission highlight the special nature of cyberspace in war, due to the fact that every significant event in the real world also takes place in cyberspace. The new European defence doctrine approved by the European Council in March 2022, the Strategic Compass, recognised cyberspace as an area of warfare (Strategic Compass for Security and Defence, 2022; Duguin, Pavlova, 2023). Cyberspace introduces new mechanisms for executing attacks, increasing their speed, proliferation and power, as well as ensuring undetectability. The low cost of entry, anonymity and asymmetries in vulnerabilities enable a greater ability to exert influence in cyberspace than in traditional domains. The dimension of cyberspace, according to Giannopoulos et al, refers to the information environment, consisting of interdependent networks of information technology infrastructure, including hardware, software, data, protocols and information, such as the Internet, telecommunications networks, computer systems and embedded processors and controllers. Tools are aimed at degrading, disrupting or destroying networks or access to data and information. Intelligence operations and the reduction of detection through access to information may also be targets (Giannopoulos et al., 2020).

As Goncalves, Giannopoulos, Smith, Theocharidou et al. note, the combined nature of cyberspace and artificial intelligence has given rise to hybrid threats reinforced by cyber, where technology is used to achieve its strategic objectives, making cyber operations now a key component of hybrid strategies and tactics, shaping the profile of hybrid threats and wars. According to Goncalves et all, hybrid strategies rely on the use of information and communications technology (ICT) and artificial intelligence (AI) tools to combine conventional and unconventional operations, thus enhancing their impact (Giannopoulos et al., 2020). In the context of contemporary hybrid operations, three main dimensions of hybrid strategic power, understood as the ability to achieve strategic objectives through hybrid operations, can be distinguished. These are network force, AI force and collaborative force. The first type of force is realised through social networks and the ability to use cyberspace for propaganda, disinformation and viral campaigns, a form of information warfare. It also includes launching cyber attacks that can disrupt various sectors and the theft and possible disclosure of critical data. The second type of force involves the use of AI, particularly machine learning (ML) tools, in support of various cyber operations that can support hybrid strategies. The range of AI applications includes network force operations and cyber disruption of critical infrastructure. The third type of force is specific to today's defence and security environment and involves the collaboration of various state and non-state actors. The latter include, for example, organised crime and terrorist groups, which can work together to mutually support and enhance each other's operations (Goncalves, 2019).

Goncalves highlights that the main drivers of hybrid operations are cyber psychological operations (cyops), in which information superiority plays a key role. The new face of conflict involves the use of non-military actions and means using information and communications technology (ICT) to target all public institutions in the target country (Goncalves, 2019). While illustrative of the Russian perspective on war, Treverton, former chairman of the US National Intelligence Council, takes a similar view. Treverton identified typical cyberspace-based tactics of war in a pattern of hybrid operations, using propaganda, fake news, strategic leaks, funding organisations and supporting political parties, organising protest movements using social networks, using cyber tools for espionage, attacks and manipulation, economic leverage, using intermediaries and unacknowledged war, and supporting paramilitary organisations. Although the thinking of strategic studies and military practice is deeply rooted in the past, the above references show that the renewal of the concept of hybrid operations and their relevance in contemporary strategic doctrine is due to the fact that these operations have gained effectiveness through the use of cyberspace. This is the decisive factor changing the profile of defence and security threats arising from hybrid operations. As already mentioned, hybrid operations can be carried out by both state and non-state actors, signifying a shift in strategic power, where individuals and groups that may not be state-sponsored can use cyberspace and AI-based systems to execute hybrid operations that can have a significant impact on internal security and the protection of civilians (Treverton, 2018, pp. 9–35; Hanko, Spily, 2018, pp. 144–159). Three types of hybrid cyber operations can be distinguished: state-sponsored operations (implemented by a specific state, involving the human and technical resources of the country's armed forces); non-state-sponsored operations (carried out by non-state actors and groups that are not financially, politically or logistically supported by any state); and state-sponsored operations carried out by non-state actors (use of hackers and technological mercenaries, political, financial and logistical support to non-state actors and groups, opening the way for joint operations that involve non-state actors and different states – with an additional level of deniable responsibility for states) (Goncalves, 2019; Treverton, 2018, pp. 9–35).

The report *The Role of Cyber in the Russian War Against Ukraine: Its Impact and the Consequences for the Future of Armed Conflict*, states that the kinetic invasion of Ukraine by the armed forces of the Russian Federation in February 2022 was accompanied by massive cyber operations. Such activities as a means of warfare have also been observed previously, including between Russia and Georgia, Israel and Iran, and Russia and Ukraine (where Russia has been conducting cyber attacks against Ukraine since 2014). As the report assesses, the number and scope of cyberattacks in the Ukraine war were characterised by intensity and cross-linking with other domains, although in terms of innovation of technology and methods, these were mostly already familiar activities. In this context, cyber attacks and operations in cyberspace also became a type of military operation, coordinated or synchronised with kinetic operations (Dugin, Pavlova, 2023). As Christian-Marc Liflander, head of the Cyber and Hybrid Policy Section in NATO's Security Challenges Division, points out: (quoted in Duguin, Pavlova, 2023, p. 6)... unlike military buildups or other forms of military mobilisation, which are rare and highly visible, cyber operations are the result of operational cycles that take place covertly and continuously during peace and war. Targeting vulnerable networks during peacetime allows attackers to prepare malware for use in wartime. The methods attackers use to establish an initial beachhead for operations are indistinguishable from those that precede cyber attacks. For cyber units, war does not fundamentally change the way they prepare for or initiate combat (Dugin, Pavlova, 2023, p. 6).

As mentioned above, the war in Ukraine, demonstrates the dynamics regarding cyber threats and new and emerging vectors and vulnerabilities. Cyber attacks and operations have been deployed to destroy data and systems, disrupt critical infrastructure and services, control information space, exfiltrate significant amounts of data, conduct reconnaissance and espionage, and conduct influence operations, including disinformation campaigns to devalue trust in public information and institutions, create confusion and discredit belligerents and their allies (cf. Dugin, Pavlova, 2023; Shamsi, 2024, pp. 1–14; Danyk, 2019, 2023, pp. 35–50).

As well as being used for hybrid cyber operations in Ukraine, this tactic is also being used in the war in the Middle East. As Tal Mimran reports, research conducted by Israeli cyber security firm Check Point indicates that in the first weeks of Israel's war against Hamas, there was a significant increase in the number of cyber attacks against targets in Israel. In particular, a 52% increase in the number of attacks targeting the government and security sector was observed, for obvious strategic reasons. These operations included various techniques such as distributed denial of service (DDoS) attacks, wiper malware and the exploitation of security vulnerabilities to spread misinformation about missile attacks, with the aim of intimidating the population. DDoS operations aimed to disable websites or stop their functionality by 'flooding' them with multiple access requests. These attacks often consisted of overloading the site with fake requests coming from a large number of computers, sometimes without the knowledge of their owners (Mimran, 2023). The Cyber Attacks in the Israel-Hamas report by Cloudflare Blog Cloudflare indicates that several DDoS attacks have targeted Israeli websites, generating up to millions of requests per second. Sites of newspapers and other media outlets, software companies, banks, financial services, insurance companies and government administrations have all been affected by DDoS attacks. One of the most successful DDoS attacks was against the Jerusalem Post website, which was down for two days. Hacking groups 'Team_insane_Pakistan' and 'Anonymous Sudan', known as religious hacking groups linked to pro-Russian groups such as 'Killnet', claimed responsibility for carrying out this attack. The hackers also used more advanced wiper malware. An example of such software was BiBi, named for political reasons to provoke the Israeli government and Prime Minister Benjamin 'Bibi' Netanyahu. This software was detected on both Linux and Windows systems. Although most of these operations failed, they had destructive potential and have been attributed to the Arid Hamas group (Yoachimik, Pacheco, 2023). An example of a direct attack on civilians, was an attack targeting the Israeli Red Alert application, which is used to receive notifications of incoming rocket attacks. The pro-Palestinian hacking group AnonGhost exploited a vulnerability in the app and sent out false notifications, falsely stating that "a nuclear bomb was coming". This attack, was part of a wider disinformation effort that showed similarities to Russian disinformation regarding the war in Ukraine (Mimran, 2023). In his analysis, Mimran notes that even security vulnerabilities were exploited to hack into digital billboards and display the Palestinian flag. Potential actions could have been much more egregious, for example, by using billboards to display drastic videos documenting attacks on civilians (some of these assaults including murders, rapes, severing of limbs and other cruel ways of inflicting pain, were filmed using victims' mobile phones, which were then put back into the victims' pockets for their families to find later) (Mimran, 2023). In addition to these actions, there were also telecommunications blockades in Gaza and when internet access was restored, the connectivity rate was only about 15% of the usual level. This type of action translates into a direct threat to civilians, for example through the lack of connectivity to medical or humanitarian aid, In his analysis, Mimran, highlights another important aspect of hybrid warfare in cyberspace. This is the legal liability of this type of action, which has only been recognised by some countries as stemming from actions in the reality of armed conflict (see more extensively Mimran, 2023).

The literature indicates that the cyberspace domain is actively used in hybrid strategies. An analysis of the results of the media reports showed that a total of 38 text passages relating to the cyberspace domain were identified and coded. However, this is not the total result, as cyberspace should be seen in the context of domains such as the information domain, which has the highest occurrence rate, and the political and intelligence domains, which also have a high code count. The co-occurrence analysis of codes revealed that codes pertaining to this domain most frequently co-occurred with codes pertaining primarily to the information domain and the political, space, maritime and land domains. The results of the association of the codes of the cyberspace domain with other areas (codes), i.e. the code of military conventional actions and actions below the threshold of war (cyber groups), propaganda, disinformation and tools, confirm, the growing role of cyberspace in hybrid warfare. Although operations in this domain are not directly characterised by large numbers, which may be due, for example, to their covert nature, their importance for the ability to coordinate and amplify the effects of operations in other domains is significant and measurable.

Another domain used in hybrid warfare is the Spice domain. As assessed by Jana Robinson et al. in *Europe's Preparedness to Respond to Space Hybrid Operations* hybrid operations in space are not a new phenomenon. Until now, however, issues related to these operations have been largely confined to classified, often isolated environments and open discussions of hybrid threats have focused almost mainly on classical domains. Today, global dynamics in space are driven by rivalries between the US, China and Russia, along with other factors such as the emergence of new space players (including commercial ones) and the advancement and diffusion of space technologies (Robinson et al., 2018, pp. 6–19).

In NATO's assessment, the space domain in hybrid warfare can be the target of malicious attacks aimed, for example, at disrupting or spoofing satellite services used in critical infrastructures and networks. Other activities include cyber or physical operations against space assets and ground infrastructure, foreign direct investment in strategic space companies, the creation and exploitation of infrastructure dependencies or the deliberate production of space debris, which threatens satellites and can lead to loss of access to space (NATO, 2024).

The Prague Security Studies Institute (PSSI) defines hybrid space operations as deliberate, temporary, mostly reversible and often harmful actions/activities in space that are specifically designed to exploit linkages with other domains and conducted just below the threshold of requiring significant military or political responses (PSSI, 2018).

Examples of hybrid space operations (PSSI, 2018):

- Directed energy operations that can result in space debris – low-power laser attenuation or blinding, high-power microwave (HPM) or wideband (UWB) emitters.
- Orbital operations that do not normally produce space junk – tracking and identification of space objects; Rendezvous and Proximity Operations (RPO).
- Electronic operations – jamming (orbital/uplink, terrestrial/downlink); impersonation (spoofing)

- Cyber operations – attack on satellite or ground station antennas; Attack on ground stations connected to terrestrial networks; Attack on user terminals connected to satellites.
- Economic and Financial (E&F) operations – investment in a target country's space infrastructure for impact/control; Lending and construction/shooting of the target country's space systems.

In recent years, space has become a key area within hybrid warfare, thanks to the increasing availability of space technology and the strategic importance of satellites and other space assets. Matthew Mitkov and Ralph Thiele, highlight that the war in Ukraine has proven that space is no longer a distant reality, but a real threat to every domain of conflict and hybrid warfare. Activities such as satellite intelligence, GPS navigation and communication systems, have become essential in the conduct of warfare, but have also affected the security of civilians. An example is Maxar Technologies' satellite imagery, which provided detailed information on Russian troop movements and the extent of infrastructure damage. Thanks to these images, Ukraine was able to better prepare for its defence by observing the concentration of Russian forces near the Ukrainian border even before the war started. Satellite navigation systems, such as GPS, on the other hand, were crucial for precise targeting and coordination of military operations. Signal jamming by Russian forces was designed to hamper the Ukrainian military's operations, which could lead to problems in determining the position and altitude of flights. SpaceX's Starlink system played a key role in maintaining reliable communications. These systems were powered by generators or powerbanks, ensuring their reliability in harsh environments. Radio-electronic attacks on satellites supporting Ukraine, such as the Starlink system, were aimed at blocking communication services (Mitkov, 2023; Thiele, 2019). Another example is the Russian cyber-attack on the Viasat satellite network (KA-SAT), which rendered modems inoperable, causing thousands of disruptions to organisations across Europe. The incident took place just before the invasion began, significantly affecting communication capabilities and situational data exchange (Viasat, 2022; Holmes, 2023).

Similar conclusions are also pointed out by the authors of the report The space domain and the Russo-Ukrainian war: Actors, tools, and impact Hybrid Co E, which states that the space domain has probably never before been used so comprehensively in any other conflict as in the war in Ukraine, where it has been described as the first bilateral space war (Höyhtyä, Uusipaavalniemi, 2023). Within this war, the authors of the report identified the following links between hybrid threats in the space domain and threats in other domains in the Russian-Ukrainian war, as shown in Table 4.1.

240 Civil Protection and Domestic Security in Hybrid Warfare

TABLE 4.1 Links between domains and hybrid threats

Domain	Link/Impact on Hybrid Threats and Tools
Infrastructure	Satellite technologies are key enablers of critical infrastructure such as energy, transport, and communications networks.
Cyber	A cyberattack on satellite networks (such as Viasat) can prevent communications in Ukraine and cause service disruptions in organisations across Europe. Russia is actively jamming GPS signals around Ukraine, and there have been hacking attempts targeting the Starlink system.
Economy	The space industry in Ukraine has been disabled. Launching capacity is restricted since Russia pulled out of the collaboration. Economic sanctions can be bypassed as Russia achieves access to capabilities through allies and the black market.
Military/ Defense	Space-based capabilities are essential for intelligence, environmental monitoring, missile warning, and command and control on the battlefield. Russia has demonstrated the threat of new types of weapons, such as those to destroy satellites.
Social/Societal	Space-based capabilities can support vital functions in society during a crisis, such as Starlink ensuring internet availability and communications in Ukraine. Citizens can provide assets to support operations, like the 'dronations' campaign in Ukraine.
Public Administration	Commercial space capabilities and information are important for Ukrainian ministries. The Ministry of Defence supported the public acquisition of an ICEYE satellite, and the Ministry of the Interior uses satellite images for decision-making and information sharing.
Legal	Russia claims private space assets as legitimate targets in war. Russia states the use of private satellites for military purposes to be provocative and questionable under the Outer Space Treaty. Private actors use legal arguments to prevent their equipment from being used.
Intelligence	Satellites enable intelligence operations in areas that would be very challenging to work in with other means.
Diplomacy	Russia has decided to resign from the International Space Station (ISS) collaboration. There are growing international tensions in space extending from Russia. The loss of ISS as a diplomatic tool impacts diplomatic relations significantly.
Political	Russia has tried to politicise the ISS, which has been a purely scientific collaboration platform. International collaboration between other countries and Russia is expected to remain frozen for an extended period.

(Continued)

TABLE 4.1 (*Continued*)   Links between domains and hybrid threats

Domain	Link/Impact on Hybrid Threats and Tools
Information	Russia has made provocative statements about commercial and civilian satellite assets becoming legitimate targets in wartime operations. Roscosmos has used the ISS for pro-Russian, anti-Ukrainian propaganda.
Culture	Collaborative culture in exploring and developing space is endangered due to Russia's resignation, increasing tensions, and the growing quest for strategic autonomy.

Source: Own compilation based on Höyhtyä and Uusipaavalniemi (2023, pp. 10–15)

Similar to cyber, the literature also indicates an increase in the involvement of hybrid activities and threats in the war in Ukraine in space. The results of the analyses in the survey of media reports showed that the space domain is not a widely covered area (a total of 59 text excerpts concerning the space domain were coded). The result may suggest that activities in this domain are still not evident in the common perception of the risks of such activities. However, the result of the analyses of the space domain in the context of code co-occurrence (interconnection) shows that the activities conducted in this domain were mainly cross-linked with codes relating to the conventional military domain, which may confirm that this is still an area mainly used by the military component in the war in Ukraine.

The next domain that is used in hybrid warfare relates to actions in the economic space (the economic domain), which is becoming increasingly integrated today as a result of globalisation, creating numerous opportunities for manipulation of economic and financial systems. Actions generating hybrid threats in this domain can take various forms, for example: attacking confidence in the system, manipulating currency markets, undermining economic foundations and the efficiency of the economy. Financial systems can also be used as tools to achieve geopolitical objectives (e.g. influencing capital flows or infiltrating financial centres) and/or to create chaos (e.g. initiating financial crises in stock markets). Some countries use trade, aid, investment and threats of sanctions to influence the actions of states in disputed regions. Economic responses to economic and financial coercion can include retaliatory sanctions, blockades and embargoes. It is also worth considering the international technology and social media platforms (e.g. Amazon, Google, Meta and Apple), whose financial turnover exceeds the GDP of many countries. These platforms wield enormous power and influence over politics and trade. At the same time, technologies and social media platforms have allowed individuals and groups to shape both national and international affairs in online spaces (Hybrid Threats and Hybrid Warfare, 2024). Similarly, she sees economic warfare as part of hybrid warfare (Rusnáková, 2017, pp. 343–380). In her view, these are actions that aim to influence the economic, technological and military balance in favour of the country or alliance conducting these actions through the use of instruments such as freezing bank accounts, import and export bans, travel restrictions, measures that cause a decline in production and investment, energy supply disruptions and various forms of economic blackmail and intimidation.

In light of the need to preserve the possibility of denial and avoid provoking open military conflict, the use of the economic (economic) domain rarely has the same objectives as an open military campaign. The purpose of economic domain action is to comprehensively weaken the target state, undermining public confidence in democracy and government. For example, economic measures or policies may be used to add political pressure and economic coercion may seek to change a state's foreign policy stance, weakening the resilience of its economy, society and security.

The ubiquity in international relations of the tools used to act in the economic domain (instruments of international economic policy) makes the economy one of the first possible targets of a hybrid strategy. At the same time, this enables a long primary phase and makes it difficult to determine whether an action is part of hybrid threats or not. These relationships are largely due to the actions of firms, which can be controlled by an actor willing to exploit hybrid threat activity. For example, as Giannopoulos et al. (2021) and Chivvis (2017, pp. 1–10) point out, these can be energy and other infrastructural dependencies, generating economic dependencies and/or creating tools for economic pressure. An example is Russia, which uses its position as a natural gas exporter not only against Ukraine, but also against the European Union. Above this, infrastructure development usually involves capital projects that attract foreign direct investment, whose intentions may be questionable. Another important argument is that economic difficulties and/or inequalities can be used to influence the outcome of elections. Economic difficulties, such as a balance of payments crisis or rising public debt, can also be used as a narrative to undermine the legitimacy of the government, or even to justify actions and/or geopolitical positions.

Iskandarov and Gawliczek, in their study Economic coercion as a means of hybrid warfare: The South Caucasus as a focal point, on the example of the South Caucasus region, point to the application of hybrid methods in the economic domain. The main activities concern areas such as (Iskandarov, Gavlichek, 2022, pp. 45–57):

- Foreign aid – due to the economic backwardness of the countries of the South Caucasus compared to developed countries, external sanctions can seriously damage their economies. These sanctions, threats to sever important trade ties and overt or covert economic pressure are tools to weaken and manipulate target countries.
- Escalatory dominance – this concept relies on the ability of the aggressor to conduct attacks at different levels of escalation. An example is the crisis in Kazakhstan in early 2022, which demonstrated how the economy can be used as a tool to destabilise a state and undermine its national security.
- Economic dependence – economic dependence is one of the most important factors leading to effective economic pressure. In the case of Armenia, Georgia and Azerbaijan, this dependence is particularly pronounced. Armenia is economically dependent on Russia and Iran, which makes it vulnerable to external pressure. Georgia, on the other hand, has experienced various forms of economic pressure from Russia, including embargoes on Georgian products and manipulation of gas prices.
- Natural resource advantage – Azerbaijan, with its abundant natural resources, especially oil and gas, is able to reduce its economic dependence. However, despite this, it remains vulnerable to economic pressure from external actors such as Russia, which is the main source of income for many Azerbaijanis working in Russia.

Sandeep Jain, in *Economic war to energy war: Ukraine war reflects new dimensions of warfare*, highlights, using the example of the war in Ukraine, that actions in the economic domain can be used both offensively and defensively in a hybrid strategy. Sanctions imposed on Russia have transformed the conflict into an energy war in which Russia seeks to cut off its opponents' access to energy and the West minimises Russia's financial gains by capping prices and forcing compliance on other states. Economic sanctions were designed to weaken Russia's economy and reduce its ability to wage war. Russia responded by creating an energy crisis and reducing gas and oil supplies to destabilise Western economies. In contrast, attacks on Ukraine's energy infrastructure are aimed at weakening Ukraine's ability to wage war (Asthana, 2022). Adeela Naureen, in Hybrid war and economy, goes even further and assesses, using the example of Pakistan, that economic action is at the heart of hybrid warfare. According to her analysis, examples from the Middle East, North Africa, Ukraine and Venezuela show that hybrid wars have one main component – economic warfare in an environment of a growing gap between rich and poor. Elites in Libya, Ukraine, Syria, Iraq and

Yemen have failed to understand that depositing billions of dollars in foreign accounts has created serious security risks, exacerbating class disparities and allowing this money to be used to finance domestic destabilisation. In her view, economic warfare is unfolding in an environment filled with elite corruption, mismanagement, nepotism, poverty, money flowing abroad, marginalisation of the youth, unchecked media and a growing gap between rich and poor. In Pakistan's political and economic context, these factors are clearly present. Elites continue to benefit from an exploitative system of patronage and nepotism, and the gap between rich and poor continues to grow. Pakistan's youth are becoming increasingly excluded. The public is bombarded with political rubbish on TV screens, leading to political atomisation and the formation of sub-groups dependent on the political elite. The build-up of debt has crossed the Rubicon of sustainability, upsetting the financial equilibrium to the point where Pakistan needs a new Marshall Plan (Naureen, 2017, cited in The Nation).

As with the previous domains, an intensification of hybrid activities can also be seen in the economic domain. The results of the analysis in the study of media reporting in the war in Ukraine showed 783 text fragments concerning the economic domain. On the other hand, the analysis of co-occurrence of codes revealed that codes pertaining to this domain most often co-occurred with codes pertaining to the political domain and the military (conventional) domain. What was peculiar to this domain was the diffuse network of other links, which may prove extensive networking with other domains in hybrid warfare.

Another domain in the context of hybrid wars and threats is the military domain. According to the *Hybrid Threats and Hybrid Warfare* assessment, in this domain, hybrid war actors typically operate in the grey zone, balancing war and peace, friend and foe, internal and external security, and civilian and military actors, both state and non-state. Military operations may include the use of regular, irregular and proxy military forces; overt and/or covert military operations; and symmetric and asymmetric warfare at different levels of escalation. Demonstration of force, power projection and the threat of military force can be as important as active military action. Combining different methods of warfare and distinguishing between lethal and non-lethal (kinetic and non-kinetic) elements is key (Hybrid Threats and Hybrid Warfare, 2024). Giannopoulos et al., in The Landscape of Hybrid Threats define the military domain as the action of the military to preserve independence and the inviolability and unity of territory, especially in the context of maintaining and defending sovereignty (Giannopoulos et al., 2021).

Activities conducted in the military domain are commonly described in media messages and literature studies. At this stage of analysis, it is not the aim to describe them in detail but only to signal the existence of this category in hybrid warfare and the scale of its involvement. The results of the analysis of the survey of media reports confirm the extensive use of this domain in the war in Ukraine. A total of 950 text fragments relating to the military domain were identified and coded, but in this case basic sub-domains such as naval (2,004 results), land (1,427 result) and air (2,473 results) were also examined, which adds up to 5,904 indications resulting from the combination of sub-domains. The military domain was most frequently networked as co-occurring with codes relating to the political domain and the information domain. In the case of the three sub-domains, each sub-domain also co-occurred predominantly with the information and political domains, which is consistent with the military domain score, but these were in the nature of scattered codes. Above this, each of the sub-domains co-occurred with each other. An important link of the military domain is its association with manoeuvres, which may suggest that this is an important element prior to a military invasion. In the case of the military domain, it is worth mentioning that despite the significant number of codes, it is not the leading domain. In the course of the analyses in this book, it was found that actions in the non-military domain are used much more frequently in the war in Ukraine. Giannopoulos et all., conclude that the military domain is an important element in the analysis of contemporary hybrid wars, directly influencing not only military actions, but also the shaping of strategy in other areas (Giannopoulos et al., 2021). However, in light of the research for this book, it appears that in hybrid warfare it is actions in other domains that influence the military domain and the shaping of strategy in its areas.

Further domains in the analysed area, are the political, cultural/ cultural and social domains, which are used to generate or exploit divisions in the society of the country under attack. Activities in these domains are complex and targeted by deliberate hybrid campaigns. In the targeted countries, various themes are used to foment divisions in society. These themes may include: the manipulation of shared history to create an impression of legitimacy as a pretext for invasion – for example, portraying the annexation or occupation of territory as a protection against 'aggressive states' or the defence of an ethnic group against discrimination; the confrontation of traditional, religious or ideological values with modern ideologies such as liberal democratic principles; and the use of migration as a tool of pressure (e.g. the threat of mass migration) or an aggressive approach to migrants, including those of the second and third generations. Actors can steer public opinion and influence large parts of the population using disinformation and propaganda. Catalysing events can lead to violent confrontations and create social tensions (NATO, Hybrid Threats and Hybrid Warfare, 2024).

In the context of war and hybrid threats, according to Christopher S. Chivvis of RAND, the political domain is closely linked to diplomacy, mainly because of foreign policy's ability to strongly influence domestic policy – the relationship between the two is often described as a two-level game – and to public administration, as the latter exists to implement public policy but can also influence policy-making. (Chivvis, 2017, pp. 1–10). A study of media reports conducted for this book, shows that while politics has some influence on diplomacy (5.28% code linkage count rate) diplomacy is much more significant for policy making (20.53% code linkage count rate). In other words, diplomatic activities have a significant impact on policy, while the impact of policy on diplomacy is less significant. The study also showed that in the relationship between the political domain and public administration, this relationship is at 0.03% in the linkage of these codes. Some political domain tools try to change the public's perception of political choices and/or actors. Therefore, tools from the information domain can be used to support hybrid threat activities that seek to exploit the political domain. In addition, actors, as they seek to avoid open confrontation, will continue to exploit legal loopholes and operate at the boundaries between national and international law. In this sense, it is the legal domain that shapes the environment in which an actor may seek to exploit the political domain. Ultimately, the success of many tools in this domain depends on the nature of the actions involved (Chivvis, 2017, pp. 1–10).

In the analysis conducted in the study of media reports, a total of 3,069 text fragments relating to the political domain were identified and coded. This is the second most abundant domain (after the information domain). The co-occurrences of the codes are mainly a network built with the information, legal and economic domains, but it should be noted that the results are scattered, suggesting that activities from the political domain are used in all domains (the exception being the critical infrastructure domain).

Cultural elements such as ideas, customs and behaviours are used as activities to influence, recruit, divide and manipulate communities, pitting them against each other, national governments and international institutions (Chivvis, 2017, pp. 1–10), which is the domain of the cultural domain. In this domain, the aggressor uses cultural diplomacy to support specific objectives. These actions are part of strategies to destabilise and influence an adversary by violating its cultural sphere. The scope of cultural diplomacy can be internal, external or a combination of both. Internally, cultural diplomacy involves using cultural and civilisational motives to define the fundamental elements of national identity, while as a foreign policy strategy, it seeks to promote culture as a means to project an attractive image abroad. Although similar to the concept of soft power, cultural diplomacy differs fundamentally in its origins.

Identification and analysis of threats to the civilian population 247

While soft power is born out of an autonomous civil society, cultural diplomacy is fundamentally a state endeavour and is linked to national identity, history and religion. Like cultural diplomacy, the cultural domain of hybrid action originates from the state sphere and aims to support these activities (Chivvis, 2017, pp. 1–10).

In the study of media reports, a total of 212 text fragments relating to the cultural domain were identified and coded. The co-occurrence analysis of the codes revealed that codes pertaining to this domain most often co-occurred with codes pertaining to the political domain and the information domain. The results of the cross-linking of culture domain codes with other domains in hybrid warfare, showed mainly co-occurrences with codes for conventional military action and propaganda. Such cross-linking suggests that the cultural domain actively supports other activities in hybrid war by shaping public opinion and reinforcing the aggressor's narrative.

The third domain, the social domain, is typically used to generate, exacerbate or exploit socio-cultural divisions that provoke the social confusion necessary for hybrid threat operations to begin or succeed. The NATO Handbook, (NATO, Hybrid Threats and Hybrid Warfare, 2024), assesses that social polarisation is created to undermine trust or highlight inequalities in areas such as income, access to basic services, social protection and social capital. Controversial issues such as unemployment, poverty and education are always debated in Western societies, making them easy targets. However, issues that can create or sustain a crisis are particularly attractive. Examples include economic crisis, irregular immigration and terrorist attacks (active shooter incidents, cyber-attacks, CBRNE incidents). The ultimate goal of operations in this domain is to influence the way society functions in the target state in order to create a vulnerable environment for hybrid operations (Giannopoulos et al., 2021). In the case of the social domain, a total of 340 codes relating to this domain were identified and coded as a result of the analyses in the study of media reports. The co-occurrence analysis of the codes revealed that codes relating to this domain most often co-occurred with codes relating to the information, political (very strong association), legal and economic domains. The results of the association of codes of the social domain with other domains in hybrid warfare, showed mainly co-occurrence with destabilising actions, hybrid operations below the threshold of conflict, conventional military actions, propaganda and diversionary actions, which supports the hypothesis of the complex use of this domain in hybrid warfare to destabilise societies and its increasing importance.

The three domains listed above demonstrate not only their presence in the hybrid war in Ukraine, but also their potential degree of involvement (based, of course, on information in the common environment).

The next domain analysed is that of Public Administration. According to Giannopoulos et all, public administration is interpreted in the broadest possible sense as the process of transforming public policies into results. The policy-administration dichotomy is highlighted as a fundamental feature of societies. In other words, public administration exists to implement laws and policies. While this is clear in theory, it can be difficult to apply in practice. Firstly, in interpreting the law in order to bring it to life, administrators may inadvertently make value judgements that may be political in nature. Secondly, public administration naturally contributes to policy-making by evaluating existing policies and organising the formulation of new ones (Giannopoulos et al., 2021; Seibel, 2016, pp. 309–332). A detailed discussion of the activities carried out in this domain can be found in a number of reports that analyse both cyber attacks and broader aspects of hybrid warfare in Ukraine. Reports such as Defending Ukraine: Early Lessons from the Cyber War (Microsoft), Cybersecurity and Hybrid Threats in Ukraine (Institut Jacques Delors), Russian Hybrid Warfare in Ukraine (CNA) and Ukraine's Lessons for the Future of Hybrid Warfare (RAND Corporation) detail coordinated efforts to destabilise public administration. In a survey of media reports, the public administration domain was identified and coded a total of 6 times. This is one of the lowest in terms of abundance, which may indicate that it is not an area covered in widespread coverage. The low abundance is also characterised by the co-occurrence of codes with the public administration domain, which was only linked to codes relating to the information and political domain, which may suggest the importance of information flow and political processes in administrative management during hybrid warfare (this is also confirmed by the above reports). Other links of this domain are the co-occurrence with the code of conventional military operations and terrorist groups. The low abundance of this domain suggests the need for further research in this area.

Another domain increasingly used in the context of war and hybrid threats is the legal domain. This domain, refers to the set of legal rules, actions, processes and institutions, including both their normative and physical manifestation, that are or can be used to achieve legal or non-legal outcomes in the context of hybrid threat campaigns. Hybrid actions and threats in this domain can be realised through, for example, the use of legal thresholds, gaps, complexity and uncertainty; the circumvention of legal obligations; the avoidance of accountability; the exploitation of compliance by the targeted state; the exploitation of the lack of legal cooperation between targeted states; the use of their regulatory powers under national law; and the use of law and legal processes to create narratives and counter-narratives. While some of these actions may involve violations of existing principles of national or international law, not all of them do so. As a label for hybrid actions in this domain, the following characteristics can be adopted – first, actors who wish to undermine democratic or democratising states use the law to exploit specific weaknesses in democratic societies. For example, relying on the right to freedom of expression creates space for disinformation campaigns. Second, the law is used as a tool to achieve destabilising, subversive or harmful objectives against the target state, undermining its interests and furthering the goals of the attacker. Third, the law is often abused or used in ways that undermine the rule of law. Fourth, law is often used as a tool to achieve intended effects in other domains, especially in the information space, while actions in other areas are designed or used to produce effects in the legal domain (Giannopoulos et al., 2021). An example is legal warfare which is a key element of China's strategy to use international and domestic law to highlight Chinese positions and gain legitimacy for its policies. These activities include creating new domestic laws, increasing legal expertise and participating in international legal forums. China's legal warfare is evident in disputes such as the South China Sea, where China uses selective legal interpretations to support its claims. China's legal warfare involves four main strategies: legal deterrence, legal attack, legal counterattack and legal protection. Unlike Western strategies that emphasise legal resilience, China's approach is more offensive, focusing on achieving legal superiority and shaping international law in its favour. This methodology includes influencing the interpretation and implementation of international law, particularly in disputed areas such as the South China Sea (Mosquera, Chalanouli, 2020).

Analysis of the results in a study of media reporting in the Ukraine war revealed a total of 1,718 identified and coded text fragments relating to the legal domain. The co-occurrence of this domain with the main domains in terms of numbers concerned the political and information domain and, to a lesser extent, conventional military actions and a number of dispersed links forming a network of the use of legal actions in different domains in the hybrid war. It is worth mentioning that partial results which relate to private military companies (PMCs), terrorist groups and propaganda, among others, may suggest that this domain is being used to create a legal framework that can legitimise actions in these areas.

According to Mark Lowenthal, domain-intelligence operations are the process by which specific types of information relevant to national security are requested, collected, analysed and delivered to decision-makers; the products of this process; the protection of these processes and information by counterintelligence operations; and the execution of operations at the request of legal authorities (Lowenthal, 2012). Intelligence provides decision-makers with situational awareness, which is essential for strategic and security-related decisions. Therefore, intelligence operations must be designed and implemented to meet the needs identified by decision-makers or derived from their policy guidance. Modern intelligence draws from disciplines such as Open-Source Intelligence (OSINT); Signals Intelligence (SIGINT); Geospatial Intelligence (GEOINT); Imagery Intelligence (IMINT); Measurement and Signature Intelligence (MASINT); Cyber Intelligence (CYBINT) and Human Intelligence (HUMINT). According to the literature, intelligence activities can be used to support a wide range of activities, making this domain considered related to many other domains, in particular the information, cyber and space domains (Giannopoulos et al., 2021). Analogous findings have emerged from studies of media reporting in the war in Ukraine. The domain of intelligence has been identified and coded a total of 1781 times. The cross-linking is mainly links to the political and information domain. Further (less numerous) network vectors form links to conventional military operations, private military companies (PMCs), terrorist groups and propaganda. The co-occurrence of the intelligence domain with the above-mentioned areas shows, as in all the previous domains, that these types of activities are distributed and used in hybrid warfare.

One of the more relevant domains in hybrid strategy is that of diplomacy. Diplomacy is a key tool in state governance. Following the Peace of Westphalia in 1648, the foundations of modern international relations were established, based on the balance of power and the recognition of states as formal representatives of their citizens. Although this principle is still valid, new challenges are emerging, such as the growing role of non-state actors, including terrorist organisations and corporations. New elements of diplomacy have been introduced in response to these threats, such as the Budapest Convention on Cybercrime. However, the development of an international consensus in the context of hybrid wars, actions and threats faces numerous difficulties, as many states feel that the introduction of new norms may infringe on their sovereignty (Hybrid Threats and Hybrid Warfare, 2024). Normative theories of international relations argue that war can be justified as a means of defence against provoked aggression, provided that the principles of proportionality and protection of civilians are respected. Hybrid actions, particularly those in the sphere of diplomacy, are designed to provoke divisions at both national and international levels. The aim of these activities is to support information campaigns and to influence decision-making processes. Tools used in this context include diplomatic sanctions, boycotts, embassy actions and the creation of misleading or contradictory narratives (Aho et al., 2023). As stated in *Hybrid Threats a Comprehensive Resilience Ecosystem*, diplomacy in world politics refers to the process of communication between international actors who, through negotiation, seek to resolve conflict without resorting to war, as well as attempts to manage and create order in the global system. Nowadays, in the context of the issue under consideration, the scope of these negotiations includes a wide variety of misunderstandings, as the peace/war dichotomy is not obvious (Aho et al., 2023; Giannopoulos et al., 2021).

The diplomatic domain in the study of media coverage of the war in Ukraine was identified and coded a total of 789 times, which is not a particularly high score compared to many other domains. At the same time, however, this figure may be indicative of the important role of diplomacy in the context of hybrid war, where diplomatic activity, despite its lower visibility in the media, has a function in shaping the international narrative, political support and managing international responses to aggression. Networking this domain is the dominant links to the political, legal intelligence and information domains. Above this, there are also links between this domain and conventional military operations and propaganda.

One of the last domains in the analysed section is the information domain, which is characterised by informational and psychological (cognitive) operations and is a major field of action in hybrid warfare, where narratives, disinformation and propaganda play key roles in shaping perceptions and outcomes (Peter, 2015, pp. 191–198).

As assessed by Abdyraeva, Cholpon and Hensoldt Analytics, information domain operations are a key component of hybrid and non-linear strategies. They are used to undermine a sense of social security by deliberately antagonising political, social and cultural identities. They aim to manipulate identity and loyalty politics, thereby destabilising influential interest groups and breaking up political alliances. As a result, society is plunged into disorientation and chaos, which heightens feelings of insecurity. A key tool in this domain is disinformation, including cyber propaganda, black propaganda and fake news. The latter often take the form of material designed to discredit specific individuals or groups, creating the appearance of authenticity. Fake news, particularly on social media, becomes a powerful propaganda tool, spreading disinformation on a massive scale. The information domain is closely linked to the cultural and social domains, as disinformation and other techniques aim to undermine the social homogeneity and cultural identity of target states. It is also linked to the intelligence domain, as information gained through intelligence operations can be used to influence public opinion and political debates. Ultimately, one of the key objectives of operations in the information domain is to destabilise political processes in target states, which links it to the political domain (Abdyraeva, 2020, pp. 20–28; Hensoldt Analytics, 2021).

Examples of the use of this domain are plentiful, but to illustrate, one can cite the Russian information attack of July 2024, in which hackers published calls to arms by Ukrainians on hundreds of Telegram channels. The post describes the difficulties of the war advocated by the Ukrainian president and once false information regarding his wife: We will have to delete this message and some of us will even be fired from our jobs or imprisoned, but we cannot tolerate this any longer... While his wife (Zelensky – Belsat.eu) drives a new Bugatti, you send your sons to defend what... Fatherland? Wake up! What are you fighting for? This is not your war! The West is using Ukraine for its own ends, with complete disregard for the victims (Belsat, 2024, quoted in Russian Information Attack). Information is the foundation on which states and societies rely. There is a wide and complex debate about the role of information in the hybrid threat environment and hybrid warfare, mainly because information can shape public opinion. Nowadays, people function in the information sphere both through traditional media such as press, radio or television and through social media, including blogs, videos, vlogs, live streaming, etc. Information can be used by state and non-state actors to create false narratives. Information in hybrid warfare has become a central tool for manipulation, disinformation or cognitive operations (Hybrid Threats and Hybrid Warfare, 2024). Adam Ure, in an analysis by the Centre for Information Resilience, points out that in the case of the war in Ukraine, one of the key priorities was the control of information in Ukraine's media space. Russian forces and security services sought to quickly take over the media, seizing television studios, radio towers and telecommunications infrastructure. Numerous incidents of violence against journalists were reported during this period, including detentions and even killings (Ure, 2023). Ure identified five steps that Russia took in an attempt to take over the information space in occupied Ukraine, noting that these steps were not sequential or applied uniformly across the entire temporarily occupied territories and their implementation varied depending on local circumstances and the effectiveness of Ukrainian resistance.

- Infrastructure takeover: Russia took control of major infrastructure and key municipal buildings such as town halls, mayors' offices, schools, hospitals and universities, enabling the takeover of local media infrastructure.
- Media takeover: Russian forces and agents, sometimes supported by Ukrainian collaborators, established control over public and private media, including broadcast towers, TV and radio stations and media offices. The technique of 'TV tower war' was used, which involved building taller broadcast towers and blocking Ukrainian channels.
- Blocking Ukrainian sources: The Russians blocked media from government-controlled Ukraine and pro-Ukrainian local organisations, opening up space for intensive broadcasting of pro-Russian content, often with the support of local collaborators.

Identification and analysis of threats to the civilian population 253

- Silencing Ukrainian voices: Russian agencies identified key pro-Ukrainian journalists, educators, influencers, activists and religious leaders, who were then kidnapped, silenced or coerced. These techniques ranged from financial incentives to threats and torture.
- Importing resources from Russia and other occupied territories: Russian authorities imported media resources from other regions to support the work of local collaborators, while training a new generation of pro-Russian journalists.

In many cases, Russian bodies simply took over existing media assets in the occupied territory, such as newspapers and television stations, forcing the owners to leave and publishing pro-Russian content in their place. An example is the Russian takeover of the local newspaper Melitopol Vedomosti in April 2022, whose familiar logo and branding was used to distribute pro-Russian content without informing residents of the change of ownership (Ure, 2023).

The information domain has the highest score in the study of media reporting in the war in Ukraine. A total of 3,516 text fragments relating to the information domain were identified and coded, confirming those studies that consider this domain as the most important in hybrid war. The cross-linking of this domain in the main vectors concerns the linkage to the political domain, intelligence domain. conventional military operations and propaganda. There are also a number of distributed code linkages to the information domain, indicating the extensive use of this domain in hybrid warfare.

The last domain discussed is the cognitive domain, which Johns Hopkins defines as a key area of warfare where the human mind becomes the central battleground. The aim of cognitive warfare is not only to modify the beliefs and behaviours of individuals and social groups, but also to influence their ways of thinking and decision-making. In extreme cases, this can lead to social disintegration and the weakening of a society's ability to resist collectively against an aggressor. These actions can be both short-term, such as sabotaging military operations, and long-term, aiming to destabilise the political or social system. Cognitive warfare uses cyber, information and psychological tools, with social media becoming a platform for selective attacks targeting specific groups and individuals. These aim to polarise opinion, reinforce radical attitudes and create internal conflicts that lead to destabilisation. Smart technologies and social media play a key role here, which, through the collection of user data, personalise messages and contribute to the creation of closed 'information bubbles'. An effective defence against cognitive warfare requires not only awareness of its existence, but also the ability to monitor and neutralise the campaigns conducting it, using advanced analysis and warning systems (Hopkins, 2021).

Both in the literature and in the conducted study of media reporting in the war in Ukraine, the cognitive domain is not widely described. A total of 14 text fragments relating to this domain were identified and coded. When cross-linking this domain with other codes, these were mainly links to the information, political, intelligence, social, military, cyber and land domains. Although the number of occurrences is low the strength of co-occurrence is the highest of all network domain connections. Although, as mentioned, operations in the cognitive domain require further research, it is undoubtedly one of the most important domains in hybrid warfare.

The analyses carried out have shown both the existence, hierarchy and very broad activities formed in the network of links between the different domains and the domains and activities in hybrid warfare.

In order to more fully illustrate the analysed area, using the results of the media reporting on the war in Ukraine, Figure 4.2 to illustrate

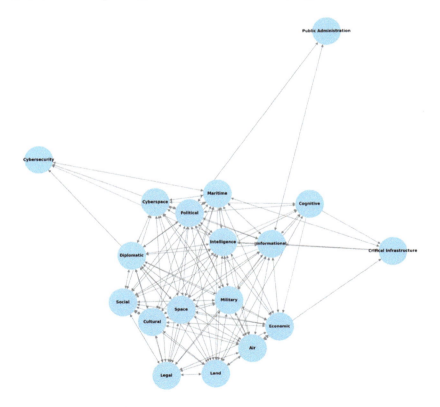

FIGURE 4.2 Interdomain interconnections

Source: Own study

the interrelationships between domains. Each circle represents a distinct domain, and the lines connecting domains indicate the presence and nature of the relationships between them.

IDENTIFICATION AND CHARACTERISATION OF HYBRID THREATS

Herbert R. McMaster, former director of the US Army Capabilities Integration Center (ARCIC), posits that modern threats seek to bypass defensive capabilities, disrupt strategic advantages, mimic successful strategies and penetrate new battlefields, including emerging domains. McMaster supports the concept of hybrid warfare as a real and present threat doctrine (cited in: Fox, 2017, pp. 22–52) Fox, 2017, cit. McMaster, 2016). The reference example is undoubtedly Russia, for which, as assessed by Amos C. Fox, hybrid warfare represents a contemporary take on these theories, focusing on covert operations, neutralising the adversary's superiority, exploiting the adversary's weaknesses through indirect methods in multiple domains that are constantly evolving, and sequencing operations across time, space and target. This perspective indicates that the concept of hybrid warfare is deeply rooted in classical theories of war, while adapting them to contemporary challenges (Fox, 2017, pp. 22–52).

One of the two key concepts of hybrid warfare concept/theory is hybrid threats. In encyclopaedic and classical terms, hybrid threats are defined as any adversary who uses a combination of conventional weapons, irregular tactics, terrorism and criminality at the same time and on the same battlefield to achieve political objectives (this is similar to Frank Hoffman's theory) and/or any adversary who reaches for a variety of methods of warfare, who creatively employs a mix of weapons and tactics and other actions. An adversary that simultaneously and adaptively employs some combination of means (political, military, economic, social, informational) and preferred methods (conventional warfare, irregular warfare, terrorism, diversion, criminality). A hybrid threat may be a state or non-state actor or a combination of both (Balcerowicz, 2024, p. 768).

In the literature and open studies, hybrid threats are defined in varying contexts. For example, the European Commission defines hybrid threats refer to when, state or non-state, actors seek to exploit the vulnerabilities of the EU to their own advantage by using in a coordinated way a mixture of measures (i.e. diplomatic, military, economic, technological) while remaining below the threshold of formal warfare (European Commission, 2024). Hybrid Co E studies (The landscape of Hybrid

Threats: A conceptual model and Hybrid threats: A comprehensive resilience ecosystem) address hybrid threats in a similar context. According to the Hybrid Co E, Hybrid

> threats aim to restrict the political room for manoeuvre by targeted states, including by undermining their citizens' sense of security. They are designed to create fear or anxiety, and sow distrust towards authorities and other people, citizens, or groups. They target and exploit vulnerabilities inherent in democratic systems of government and in the fabric of democratic societies, such as political rights and individual liberties. By using hybrid threat activities, malign actors seek to aggravate wedges in society, to undermine social cohesion and trust among citizens and towards their democratic institutions.
>
> *(Hybrid Co E, 2024a, 2024b)*

The institutional studies cited above define and classify hybrid threats. However, the classifications largely refer to threats in an environment below the threshold of war, which this study understands to qualify as the hybrid conflict phase (i.e. operations without open or formal war). In contrast, the literature does not address this type of threat in hybrid war more broadly. In the context of the topic of this study, this is of fundamental importance. Hybrid threats below the threshold of war and in hybrid warfare differ in both nature and effect. In the former, actions are less networked and do not usually affect civilians in an immediate and direct way. In contrast, actions taken in a war environment evolve into a complex network with a military component and can affect the health and lives of civilians directly. For example, a cyber-attack on power plants below the threshold of war will most often cause a reversible problem (even if the paralysis of service lasts longer it will not make much difference to the functioning of society and state organisations) but if such an attack is coordinated with the shelling of power plants and attacks on civilians, then the effect will be complex and long-term (e.g. no heating in winter). The purpose of this section is to identify the threats in hybrid warfare. The identification of these threats was carried out using the methodology and tools described in Appendix 1.

In order to deepen the analysis, a code correlation analysis was additionally carried out (Tables 4.5 and 4.6). For a better understanding of the code correlation analysis, a description of the approach has been included in a footnote.[1]

Analysis of media reports showed a spectrum of threats in three groups: conventional military threats, unconventional military threats and non-military threats. Codes pointing to conventional military threats were stamped 21,569 times in media reports. The result indicates that this type of threat is dominant in the hybrid war studied. Non-military threats came in second place. Codes indicating this group of threats occurred 3695 times. The least represented threat group is unconventional military action. Codes indicating this group of threats occurred 946 times in media reports.

The above results indicate a significant preference for military over non-military threats. This is a crucial difference in the context of the result of the study of actions and domains in hybrid warfare, where non-military actions were in a ratio of 3.69:1 against military ones. Such an arrangement may imply, on the one hand, a vagueness of the boundaries in distinguishing between these aspects, but it may also indicate that non-military actions generate military threats, confirming hybridity and networkedness. The reason for this relationship in the outcome, may also be an issue of attribution. Attribution in the context of hybrid warfare refers to the process of attributing responsibility for specific actions or attacks to specific actors, usually state or non-state actors. It is a key element of hybrid threat analysis that significantly influences threat perception and responses. In the context of non-military activities, which are more numerous, attribution is particularly challenging due to the covert nature of these activities. Non-military hybrid threats, such as cyber attacks, disinformation campaigns or political manipulation, are difficult to attribute to specific actors due to their complexity and covert nature. In contrast, conventional military threats, such as bombings or the use of tanks, are more direct and visible, making the process of attributing them to responsible actors much easier. An analysis of media reports indicates that the difficulties associated with the attribution of non-military actions can lead to their underestimation in threat assessments, despite their numbers and importance in hybrid strategies. In the media, the attribution of military actions tends to increase threat perception, which can be used as part of hybrid strategies to put pressure on states not directly involved in the conflict. The attribution problem in the context of hybrid warfare highlights the need for continuous improvement in attribution methods, which may be relevant not only from a threat analysis perspective, but also for understanding and countering hybrid threats in war. Tables 4.2–4.4 present the results of the identified threats divided into the conventional military threats, unconventional military threats and non-military threats.

Analysis of the data collected in Table 4.2 shows that the dominant conventional military threats in the conflict analysed are: missiles (18.4%), rockets (14.4%), artillery (13.6%), tanks (11.7%), shelling (8.5%), bombs (6.1%), infantry (4.6%), and manoeuvres (4.6%). Note also the cumulative share of threats such as unmanned aerial systems (3.3%) and drones (3.2%).

TABLE 4.2 Quantitative summary of conventional military threats

Code Tree	Number of Codes	Percentage Share
Rockets	3,969	18.401
Bullets	3,107	14.405
Artillery	2,930	13.584
Tanks	2,521	11.688
Fire	1,828	8.475
Bombshells	1,320	6.120
Infantry	993	4.604
Maneuvers	983	4.557
Unmanned systems	710	3.292
Drones	692	3.208
Occupation	518	2.402
Slavery	511	2.369
Bombing	501	2.323
Patrols	231	1.071
Raid	197	0.913
Scouting	106	0.491
Ambushes	84	0.389
Siege	58	0.269
Special forces	50	0.232
Kinetic	45	0.209
Landmine	39	0.181
Cluster bomb	26	0.121
Explosive charge	23	0.107
Offensive operations	21	0.097
Chemical weapons	14	0.065
Non-kinetic	12	0.056
Weapons of mass destruction	10	0.046
Nuclear attack	10	0.046
Air attacks	9	0.042
Fire support	9	0.042
Fights in the city	6	0.028
Street fighting	5	0.023
Artillery support	4	0.019
Medical evacuation	4	0.019
Land operations	4	0.019
Attacks on energy security	3	0.014
Chemical attack	3	0.014
Armed clashes	3	0.014

(*Continued*)

Identification and analysis of threats to the civilian population   259

TABLE 4.2 (*Continued*)   Quantitative summary of conventional military threats

Code Tree	Number of Codes	Percentage Share
Maritime blockade	2	0.009
Maritime operations	2	0.009
Air operations	1	0.005
Biological weapons	1	0.005
Attacks on critical infrastructure	1	0.005
Torpedo attacks	1	0.005
Biological attack	1	0.005
Special operations	1	0.005

Source: Own elaboration

TABLE 4.3   Quantitative summary of unconventional military threats

Code Tree	Number of Codes	Percentage Share
Private military companies	405	42.812
Diversionary activities	230	24.313
Torture	162	17.125
Sabotage activities	118	12.474
Proxy	9	0.951
Intelligence activities	7	0.740
Irregular activities	4	0.423
Special operations	3	0.317
Signal interference	2	0.211
Guerrilla warfare	2	0.211
Grey area	2	0.211
Jamming	1	0.106
Asymmetric operations	1	0.106

Source: Own elaboration

TABLE 4.4   Quantitative summary of non-military threats

Code Tree	Number of Codes	Percentage Share
Propaganda	956	25.873
Influencing elections	258	6.982
Protests	258	6.982
Rape	196	5.304
Disinformation	177	4.790
Terrorist attacks	147	3.978

(*Continued*)

260 Civil Protection and Domestic Security in Hybrid Warfare

TABLE 4.4 (*Continued*) Quantitative summary of non-military threats

Code Tree	Number of Codes	Percentage Share
Riots	141	3.816
Corruption	139	3.762
Terrorism	139	3.762
Hunger	130	3.518
Destabilising actions	113	3.058
Homicides	100	2.706
Kidnapping	74	2.003
Intimidation	71	1.922
Injuries	54	1.461
Disease	44	1.191
Cyber attack	43	1.164
Theft	38	1.028
Price increases	35	0.947
Beatings	35	0.947
Abduction	35	0.947
Espionage	34	0.920
Manipulation	34	0.920
Desire	32	0.866
Temperatures too low	28	0.758
Collaboration	27	0.731
Fake news	26	0.704
Import ban	26	0.704
Mutilations	24	0.650
Crime	22	0.595
Export ban	21	0.568
Persecution	20	0.541
Polarisation	16	0.433
Information warfare	15	0.406
Fraud	14	0.379
Humanitarian crisis	13	0.352
Surveillance	12	0.325
Diplomatic action	12	0.325
Psyop	12	0.325
Radicalisation	10	0.271
Extremism	9	0.244
Attacks on civilians	8	0.217
Poverty	8	0.217
Nepotism	7	0.189

(*Continued*)

Identification and analysis of threats to the civilian population   261

TABLE 4.4 (*Continued*)   Quantitative summary of non-military threats

Code Tree	Number of Codes	Percentage Share
Power cuts	6	0.162
Psychological operations	6	0.162
Political changes	5	0.135
Activities in cyberspace	5	0.135
Drinking water supply interruptions	4	0.108
Excessively high temperatures	4	0.108
Social divisions	3	0.081
False accusations	3	0.081
Social divisions	3	0.081
Social discontent	3	0.081
Spreading disinformation	3	0.081
Internal voltages	2	0.054
Psychological operation	2	0.054
Increase in unemployment	2	0.054
Increase in commodity prices	2	0.054
Commercial restrictions	2	0.054
Economic sanctions	2	0.054
Extortion	2	0.054
Attack on the hospital	2	0.054
Cyber terrorism	2	0.054
Dissemination of false information	2	0.054
Influence operations	2	0.054
Political persecution	1	0.027
Restrictions on freedom of expression	1	0.027
Increase in violence	1	0.027
Internal conflicts	1	0.027
Social conflicts	1	0.027
Social tensions	1	0.027
Economic inequalities	1	0.027
Threats to National Security	1	0.027
Organised crime	1	0.027
Political pressure	1	0.027
International isolation	1	0.027
Activities of the secret services	1	0.027
Internal conflicts	1	0.027
Policy instruments	1	0.027
Psychological warfare	1	0.027

Source: Own elaboration

Analysis of the data collected in Table 4.3 shows that the dominant unconventional military threats in the conflict analysed, are: private military companies (42.8%), diversionary activities (24.3%), torture (17.1%). The list of unconventional military threats is completed by sabotage activities (12.5%). Taken together, the listed threats account for almost 97% of the identified unconventional military threats.

Analysis of the data collected in Table 4.3 shows that the dominant non-military threats in the conflict analysed, are: propaganda (25.9%), influencing elections (7%), protests (7%), rape (5.3%), disinformation (4.8%), terrorist attacks (4%), riots (3.8%), corruption (3.8%), terrorism (3.8%), famine (3.5%), destabilising actions (3%), assassinations (2.7%), kidnapping (2%), intimidation (1.9%), injuries (1.5%), illness (1.2%). The listed threats together account for 81.1% of the non-military threats in the conflict studied.

In addition to collating and analysing the identified threats, a categorisation of media reports was carried out using a code tree which included categories of military (conventional and unconventional) and non-military threats. Each report was assigned to a corresponding code, which allowed quantitative analysis and identification of the co-occurrence of threats in hybrid warfare. In this way, an attempt was made to understand how military actions are linked to non-military actions. Tables A4.3 and A4.4 (Appendix 2) detail the juxtaposition of the linkages (networking) of the identified military threats (conventional and unconventional) with non-military threats. Analysis of these results identifies the most important general patterns.

The juxtaposition of conventional military and non-military threats revealed many complex, multi-vector linkages, often of a diffuse nature, as detailed in A4.3. The hierarchical arrangement of the identified conventional threats shows that missile attack, the most represented in terms of codes, showed the main co-occurrence with propaganda. In addition to missile attacks, bombs and bombing were the next threats in the catalogue of conventional threats. The threats associated with their use were linked in the case of bombs mainly to propaganda, but bombing showed co-occurrence with famine and rape. Cluster bombs, which are prohibited by international humanitarian law, co-occurred with killings and rape. Tanks and the use of artillery were another identified threat, which showed co-occurrence with propaganda, as did artillery-related shelling and firing. The threat of drone use and unmanned systems also co-occurred with propaganda. Another code indicating a kinetic threat was landmining which co-occurred with maiming, disinformation, disease, starvation and propaganda. In the case of the use of weapons of mass destruction (CBRNE), despite the coding of all threats, there were codes for chemical and mass destruction weapons and nuclear and chemical attack. In the first case, chemical weapons showed co-occurrence with disinformation while weapons of mass destruction showed co-occurrence with propaganda. In the second case, nuclear attack co-occurred with influencing elections, protests and kidnappings, while chemical attack showed a very strong co-occurrence with rape, which may seem an unusual co-occurrence but may suggest a cycle of violence. Another threat identified was that of patrols and special forces with the main co-occurrence being rape, abduction, espionage, rioting and extremism. The threat of siege co-occurred with destabilisation activities, propaganda, disinformation, mutilation, extortion and beatings. In contrast, the next threat-assault-is linked to collaboration, rape and propaganda. The last threats to be identified in this section relate to the large number of occupation and captivity codes. In the former case, co-occurrence was mainly related to propaganda and abductions. In the case of captivity, the co-occurrence was much more numerous and concerned influencing elections, collaboration, riots, protests, rape, abduction, kidnapping and propaganda. To the catalogue of threats, we should also add manoeuvres which showed also in this section a high number with co-occurrence mainly with propaganda, which may suggest, as already mentioned, that these activities are a key element in the hybrid conflict strategy.

The main axis of intersection between the codes identified as conventional military threats and non-military threats was propaganda.

After analysing media reports, a correlation analysis of military and non-military threat codes was developed (Tables 4.5 and 4.6). For this purpose, a correlation mapping table was created, which orders the codes according to the number of times they occur.

A correlation mapping table was created to analyse the correlation of the codes. This table segregates and orders the codes according to the number of code records. The higher the number of code records, the higher they rank. However, the code records were not sorted by correlation coefficient. The correlation coefficient is derived from an analysis of media reports – the more frequently the two codes co-occur, the higher the index. This allowed the more correlated codes to be separated from the less correlated ones, regardless of the number of code records. The column and row 'Correlation strength in axis...' sums up the X-axis and Y-axis correlation coefficients respectively, i.e. the codes in the rows relative to the codes in the columns. In this way, we have obtained a table that shows us not only the number of occurring records and the correlation coefficient, but also a simplified picture of the media content – the strength of correlation in this context allows us to indicate which codes we should pay special attention to. This means that we can infer correlation trends from this method of segregation and measuring correlation strength. We can see that some codes, despite a significant number of records, do not co-occur, i.e. are not correlated, more frequently or more strongly than those that occur in fewer records. Conditional formatting

TABLE 4.5 Correlation of codes of association between conventional military and non-military threats

Code tree	Number of codes	Rockets	Bullets	Artillery	Tanks	Fire	Bombshells	Infantry	Maneuvers	Unmanned systems	Drones	Occupation	Slavery	Bombing	Patrols	…	Strength of correlation in the X axis
Number of codes		3969	3107	2930	2521	1828	1320	993	983	710	692	518	511	501	231	…	
Propaganda	956	1,84%	1,54%	1,33%	1,47%	1,31%	2,42%	0,91%	3,56%	1,83%	1,88%	5,98%	4,70%	1,80%	0,00%	…	66,81%
Influencing elections	258	0,18%	0,23%	0,10%	0,16%	0,55%	0,38%	0,00%	0,81%	0,42%	0,43%	1,74%	0,98%	0,60%	0,43%	…	17,95%
Protests	258	0,18%	0,23%	0,10%	0,16%	0,55%	0,38%	0,00%	0,81%	0,42%	0,43%	1,74%	0,98%	0,60%	0,43%	…	17,95%
Rape	196	0,25%	0,39%	0,31%	0,20%	0,44%	0,98%	0,30%	0,61%	0,28%	0,29%	1,74%	0,78%	1,00%	1,30%	…	60,35%
Disinformation	177	0,25%	0,16%	0,24%	0,36%	0,44%	0,61%	0,10%	0,20%	0,28%	0,29%	0,19%	0,59%	0,20%	0,00%	…	18,06%
Terrorist attacks	147	0,23%	0,19%	0,07%	0,12%	0,66%	0,30%	0,20%	0,31%	0,14%	0,14%	0,97%	0,00%	0,60%	0,43%	…	9,92%
Riots	141	0,18%	0,26%	0,17%	0,20%	0,38%	0,30%	0,10%	0,00%	0,00%	0,00%	1,93%	0,20%	0,40%	1,30%	…	6,44%
Terrorism	139	0,13%	0,13%	0,03%	0,16%	0,55%	0,23%	0,20%	0,20%	0,00%	0,00%	0,97%	0,00%	0,60%	0,43%	…	9,15%
Corruption	139	0,08%	0,00%	0,03%	0,16%	0,11%	0,00%	0,00%	0,20%	0,14%	0,14%	0,00%	0,39%	0,00%	0,00%	…	1,25%
Hunger	130	0,05%	0,39%	0,48%	0,04%	0,38%	0,45%	0,20%	0,00%	0,28%	0,29%	0,77%	0,59%	1,00%	0,43%	…	7,91%
Destabilising actions	113	0,15%	0,00%	0,03%	0,12%	0,22%	0,15%	0,20%	0,31%	0,00%	0,00%	0,39%	0,39%	0,00%	0,43%	…	5,05%
Homicides	100	0,10%	0,03%	0,17%	0,04%	0,38%	0,53%	0,00%	0,20%	0,00%	0,00%	0,39%	0,59%	0,20%	0,00%	…	8,70%
Kidnapping	74	0,03%	0,00%	0,03%	0,08%	0,05%	0,08%	0,00%	0,31%	0,00%	0,00%	1,35%	0,59%	0,20%	0,43%	…	13,15%
Intimidation	71	0,13%	0,13%	0,10%	0,08%	0,27%	0,30%	0,00%	0,20%	0,00%	0,00%	0,00%	0,00%	0,00%	0,43%	…	1,84%
Intimidation	71	0,13%	0,13%	0,10%	0,08%	0,27%	0,30%	0,00%	0,20%	0,00%	0,00%	0,00%	0,20%	0,00%	0,43%	…	1,84%
Injuries	54	0,05%	0,10%	0,07%	0,04%	0,16%	0,15%	0,00%	0,00%	0,00%	0,00%	0,77%	0,20%	0,20%	0,00%	…	1,74%
Disease	44	0,00%	0,00%	0,07%	0,00%	0,05%	0,00%	0,00%	0,00%	0,00%	0,00%	0,19%	0,39%	0,00%	0,43%	…	3,69%
Cyber attack	43	0,03%	0,00%	0,07%	0,08%	0,05%	0,00%	0,00%	0,10%	0,00%	0,00%	0,00%	0,00%	0,00%	0,00%	…	2,33%
Theft	38	0,15%	0,03%	0,00%	0,08%	0,05%	0,00%	0,00%	0,00%	0,14%	0,14%	0,39%	0,20%	0,00%	0,00%	…	1,18%
Abduction	35	0,08%	0,03%	0,03%	0,08%	0,22%	0,08%	0,20%	0,00%	0,00%	0,00%	1,16%	1,17%	0,20%	0,00%	…	6,19%
…		…	…	…	…	…	…	…	…	…	…	…	…	…	…	…	…
Strength of Y-axis correlation		4,91%	4,30%	3,89%	4,19%	7,93%	9,09%	3,21%	9,02%	4,63%	4,74%	24,51%	14,54%	8,80%	7,76%	…	

Source: Own elaboration

TABLE 4.6 Correlation of codes for linking unconventional military and non-military threats

Code tree		Private military companies	Diversionary activities	Torture	Sabotage activities	Proxy	Intelligence activities	Strength of correlation in the X axis
Number of codes		405	230	162	118	9	7	
Propaganda	956	7,90%	5,65%	1,85%	14,41%	0,00%	0,00%	29,81%
Influencing elections	258	0,74%	0,43%	1,23%	0,85%	0,00%	0,00%	3,25%
Protests	258	0,74%	0,43%	1,23%	0,85%	0,00%	0,00%	3,25%
Rape	196	0,74%	0,00%	13,58%	0,00%	0,00%	0,00%	14,32%
Disinformation	177	1,23%	2,17%	0,62%	2,54%	0,00%	14,29%	20,85%
Terrorist attacks	147	0,49%	2,17%	1,85%	2,54%	0,00%	0,00%	7,05%
Riots	141	1,23%	0,87%	0,00%	0,85%	0,00%	0,00%	2,95%
Terrorism	139	0,25%	1,74%	1,85%	2,54%	0,00%	0,00%	6,38%
Corruption	139	0,00%	0,43%	0,00%	0,00%	0,00%	0,00%	0,43%
Hunger	130	0,49%	0,43%	0,00%	0,00%	0,00%	0,00%	0,92%
Destabilising actions	113	0,49%	2,17%	0,00%	0,00%	0,00%	0,00%	2,66%
Homicides	100	0,99%	0,43%	10,49%	1,69%	0,00%	14,29%	27,89%
Kidnapping	74	0,00%	0,43%	4,32%	0,85%	0,00%	0,00%	5,60%
Intimidation	71	0,25%	0,87%	0,62%	0,85%	0,00%	0,00%	2,59%
Intimidation	71	0,25%	0,87%	0,62%	0,85%	0,00%	0,00%	2,59%
Disease	44	0,25%	0,00%	0,00%	0,00%	11,11%	0,00%	11,36%
Cyber attack	43	0,25%	0,43%	0,00%	0,85%	0,00%	0,00%	1,53%
Theft	38	0,25%	0,00%	0,00%	0,00%	0,00%	0,00%	0,25%
Abduction	35	0,00%	0,00%	0,62%	0,00%	0,00%	0,00%	0,62%
Beatings	35	0,25%	0,00%	0,00%	0,00%	0,00%	0,00%	0,25%
Espionage	34	0,49%	1,30%	0,00%	1,69%	0,00%	14,29%	17,77%
Manipulation	34	0,00%	0,00%	0,00%	0,85%	11,11%	0,00%	11,96%
...	...	...	...	...	...	...	...	...
	Strength of Y-axis correlation	11%	18%	39%	21%	33%	57%	

Source: Own elaboration

of the coefficient and strength of correlation with a colour spectrum (on a red-green scale) makes it easy to identify the range of record numbers and correlation trends in a more visually accessible way. Based on this, a diagonal curve or boxes on the mapping can be drawn that roughly separate the more frequent and more frequently correlated records. With this curve, we can separate codes whose number, coefficient and strength of correlation indicate codes and correlations that are favoured in media reports from those that are not. We can plot an example of a diagonal curve starting with the non-military code information war.[2] We can plot it up to the conventional military threat codes on the borderline Kinetic, Terrain mining, Cluster bomb. We can also plot two example boxes: one that, based on the number of records and the correlation coefficient, seems to indicate, as it were, the universality of the codes used and their correlations (a box leaning towards the yellow spectrum), and another box that indicates the non-universality of the codes used and their correlations (a box leaning towards the green spectrum). Point correlations whose coefficients are high in the non-universal field (leaning towards the orange and red spectrums) emerge to us in the mapping as peculiar anomalies.

Based on the delineation of the sample curve, the two fields and with the indication of the anomaly points, and taking into account the correlation strength indices in the X and Y axes, we can conclude that Weapons of Mass Destruction (WMD) have the least coverage in the non-military codes, which means that they define this type of threat very unambiguously and within a narrow range of non-military codes. Other values of the Y-axis correlation strength index also seem to indicate this. Based on what the correlation strengths of conventional military threat codes and non-military threat codes are, with a coefficient almost equal to or higher than 10%, it is possible to infer in which area of codes and, as it were, also the subjects of media reports the conflict takes place in the information sphere: occupation, captivity, reconnaissance, siege, special forces, land mines, nuclear attack, chemical attack, weapons of mass destruction, and propaganda, rape, disinformation, influencing elections, protests, kidnappings, terrorist attacks. In our view, the analysis shows that the mapping of the links indicates a distortion of the image of the conflict in media reporting in a way that is directed at maintaining social control and maintaining an advantage in the information domain.

Data from the results on the links between unconventional military threats and non-military threats were also analysed. Despite 216 labels/phrases, the analysis showed only 6 results with different degrees of abundance. This may suggest that these are the main directions of unconventional military threats described in the media. The highest score indicates a strong involvement of PMCs in military activities. The co-occurrence of PMCs in this threat section is mainly threats related to riots, disinformation and propaganda, but PMCs were used in many other areas that were direct threats or led to them (e.g. effects): influencing elections, assassinations, maiming, espionage, intimidation, protests, economic sanctions, beatings, crime, theft, excessively cold temperatures, disease, famine, intimidation, rape, terrorist attacks, destabilising activities and involvement in cyber attacks. The high numbers of PMCs and their widespread use may suggest that this is an important threat link in hybrid warfare. The next non-military threat is diversionary activities which coexist with other forms of violence, largely propaganda, but the remaining numbers are only slightly smaller and also indicate involvement in generating threats such as destabilisation, terrorism, disinformation, espionage and collaboration as well as influencing elections, assassinations, corruption, intimidation, riots, protests, polarisation, manipulation, famine, kidnappings, PSYOPS operations and cyber attacks. Alongside diversionary activities, we have sabotage activities that co-exist with other forms of violence. The main co-occurrence here is assassination, collaboration, espionage, disinformation, terrorism and a very strong link to propaganda. Above this, the involvement of sabotage activities is influencing elections, intimidation, riots, protests, manipulation, kidnappings, PSYPOS operations and cyber attacks. An equally important non-military threat is torture, which coexists with other forms of violence, mainly assassinations, rapes and kidnappings, but also with influencing elections, maiming, intimidation, protests, persecution, disinformation, abductions, terrorism and propaganda. Further threats include intelligence activities and threats from the involvement of proxy groups. This code is related to PMCs, but points to additional aspects. Both PMCs and proxies affect the threat of famine, but additionally point to manipulation and PSYPOS operations. In the case of intelligence operations, they too coexist with other forms of violence, but there are only four threats: assassination, espionage, disinformation and PSYOPS operations.

Similar to the compilation of code correlations of conventional military and non-military threats, a code correlation analysis was also conducted for unconventional military and non-military threats following an analysis of media reports.

An analysis of the data presented in the linking of unconventional military and non-military threats, indicates that private military companies are primarily political targets. Consequently, they themselves also function as political tools. Given that they are classified as unconventional code, we find these conclusions intriguing. Clearly, intelligence activities and torture are seen as the most problematic, as there is the strongest correlation in the Y-axis and torture, due to the stronger psychological factor, has a higher distribution. Diversionary and sabotage activities are also a big problem because of the high distribution in the X-axis and at the same time quite strong correlation in the Y-axis and quite strong point correlations in the X-axis – here you can clearly see the construction of fear. E.g. torture = murder, rape. To put it another way: the soldier is not afraid of e.g. the Wagner Group, but he is afraid of torture, diversion and sabotage. The public, on the other hand, is afraid of all this and, in addition, in the most extensive but also vague way, of mercenaries. It is thus a vague but personalised threat, which explains such a strong focus on one non-military code: propaganda.

Briefly, in the correlation (Tables 4.5 and 4.6), we observe a complex information landscape that reveals the adversary's objectives and defensive strategies. This analysis allows us to understand which enemy actions are designed to create the greatest fear and which threats are of greatest concern to the defender and its public. The results also suggest that the problem for Russia and Ukraine is occupation and propaganda in Table 4.5, and propaganda, assassination, disinformation, espionage with intelligence, torture and sabotage in Table 4.6. This may suggest that the battle is primarily about the morale and fighting spirit of the soldier, as this society will be quite easy to manipulate once the soldier surrenders.

In addition, summaries of the links between the characteristics of hybrid warfare and the identified military and non-military threats have been prepared (Table A4.5). As a reminder, the catalogue of characteristics established in the previous chapters are: multidimensionality, synergy, complexity, asymmetric, integration of means, use of new technologies, information manipulation, flexibility, subliminality, destabilisation, ambiguity. However, not all characteristics showed results in this summary. In Table 4.7 is a summary of the interrelationships of military and non-military threat codes that were identified in each trait.

To complement the analyses conducted, semi-structured expert interviews were conducted with two defence, security and humanitarian experts. According to the experts, there is a broad catalogue of potential hybrid warfare threats and their potential wide-ranging consequences for internal security and civilians. The experts assessed that the current impacts of hybrid threats are diverse and regionally dependent. For example, mental health problems and weakened social ties are evident in Ukraine, while social and political consequences, as well as weakened social ties, are observed in Moldova. Limited access to health care is also seen in Moldova, while physical threats are more prevalent in Ukraine.[3]

In the context of hybrid warfare, critical impacts on civilians include hunger, thirst, injury, illness, exposure to extreme heat and cold, all of which are particularly relevant in the more militarised stages of conflict. In less militarised situations, although they are not completely excluded, their occurrence is less likely, especially when below the threshold of war and non-military measures are used, except in situations involving attacks on infrastructure. Above and beyond this, one can identify, mental health problems associated with a lack of stability, certainty and predictability,

Identification and analysis of threats to the civilian population 269

TABLE 4.7 Linkages of the military and non-military threat codes that were identified in each feature

Features of Hybrid Warfare	Risks Identified
Destabilisation	Conventional actions: captivity, occupation, manoeuvres unconventional actions: diversionary actions non-military actions: influencing elections, espionage, corruption, riots, protests, polarisation, disinformation, famine, terrorist attacks, terrorism, propaganda
Synergy	Conventional actions: unmanned systems, maneuvers, missiles, artillery, drones, tanks, infantry, raid, kinetic, non-kinetic unconventional actions: private military companies, diversionary actions non-military actions: corruption
Subliminality	Conventional actions: missiles, rockets unconventional actions: diversionary actions, sabotage actions non-military actions: polarisation, terrorist attacks, terrorism, propaganda, cyber attack
Use of new technologies	Conventional actions: missiles non-military actions: terrorist attacks, terrorism
Asymmetry	Conventional actions: manoeuvres, patrols, infantry unconventional actions: private military companies, sabotage actions, diversionary actions non-military actions: economic inequality, polarisation, radicalisation, terrorist attacks, terrorism, propaganda
Multidimensionality	Conventional operations: missiles, tanks unconventional operations: proxies, diversionary operations non-military actions: crime, disinformation, terrorist attacks, terrorism
Complexity	Conventional actions: missiles, tanks unconventional actions: proxies, non-military actions: crime, disinformation, terrorist attacks, terrorism
Ambiguity	Conventional actions: manoeuvres, infantry, shelling unconventional actions: diversionary actions non-military actions: influencing elections, disinformation, protests, propaganda, terrorist attacks
Flexibility	Conventional operations: unmanned systems, manoeuvres, missiles, artillery, drones, tanks, infantry, missiles, shelling unconventional operations: private military companies, sabotage operations, diversionary operations non-military action: propaganda

Source: Own elaboration

social and political consequences, including stunted national economic development and an ineffective political system, weakened social ties and cohesion, health and well-being problems associated with limited access to health care resulting from the country's limited economic development, physical threats. Broadly speaking, the overall effect is a deterioration of the living environment and sense of security and stability, which then translates into poorer social, economic and political outcomes, such as increased polarisation. It can also lead to a deterioration of the international security environment. Above and beyond this, the wide range of impacts is due to the multi-faceted and intricate nature of modern social systems and the way they operate. The more developed economies of the world rely on complex systems and technologically advanced elements that are inextricably linked. Dysfunction in one of these interdependent elements causes disruption, obstruction or inefficiency in other systems. Thus, for example, a disruption or collapse of the banking system can cause an inability to check or use one's own funds (either by withdrawing them directly or using non-cash settlements) or a disruption in communication between banks (e.g. in the SWIFT system) can affect problems with incoming and outgoing transfers. Similarly, disconnection from IT systems can have far-reaching consequences for the functioning of citizens. If there is a collapse in electricity or gas transmission systems as a result of external actors, citizens will feel it immediately. The situation is similar with disruptions to, for example, rail transport. The same could happen if there is a disruption in the availability of systems facilitating the location of objects such as GPS or Galileo, which will affect the ability to move around smoothly. All of the above situations cause inconvenience and a kind of inconvenience in everyday life. However, it is difficult to prioritise the magnitude of these risks.

Undoubtedly, an important area of risk is attacks on CI, which reduce civilians' access to key services, including electricity, heat and healthcare, resulting in both short-term and long-term negative impacts (poorer health outcomes, more limited educational opportunities for children and mental health consequences). In the medium to long term, this can reduce trust in government and undermine social cohesion. Attacks on cultural institutions, for example, can cause public confusion and loss of trust in those institutions that have not taken sufficient measures to protect their resources. Sometimes these types of events can serve as perfect surrogate topics acting as a distraction from other social or political problems. Another example concerns submarine cables. Potentially, gaining access to undersea fibre-optic cables can cause direct and indirect danger to citizens. Other critical infrastructure (its location, role, and access) may be at risk if the transmitted information is accessed. Disruption of such fibre-optic cables may threaten complete or partial inability to transmit and receive information. In addition, depending on the role such cables play (civilian or military), the lives and health of citizens may be at risk if their integrity is compromised and information (e.g. location and geolocation data of critical or military infrastructure) is obtained.

Experts have highlighted information activities that can result in social destabilisation. The personal safety of civilians may be at risk in the case of electronic warfare aimed at disrupting the transmission of information or its acquisition. The same is true for propaganda activity targeting a particular section of society. Various actors may wish to take advantage of some already existing social divisions in this regard and seek only to amplify them. This can be done using a process known in English as scapegoating. This is a phenomenon that accompanies crises and major social change. In this process, a person, individuals or specific social groups are identified as a threat to social integrity. A process of stigmatisation occurs in this respect and these persons or groups are identified as socially undesirable or threatening. Due to the strong amplification of negative emotions directed at these very individuals, their safety is at risk, as they may become the target of direct attacks that threaten their health and lives. Disinformation, especially at the local/tactical level, can have a direct negative impact on security outcomes, especially if it distorts information about available services, safe evacuation routes and military movements and behaviour towards civilians.

The analyses carried out clearly indicate the expansive nature of hybrid threats. The main characteristics of these threats are flexibility, synergism and asymmetry, while the goal is destabilisation. The catalogues of hybrid threats in hybrid warfare are open-ended and difficult to identify due to their covert nature. Nevertheless, one can clearly see their cross-linking and complementarity depending on operational needs.

A METHODICAL APPROACH TO RESPONDING TO HYBRID THREATS

In the search for a methodical response to identified risks in hybrid warfare, it is possible to adapt the concept of risk management commonly used in management science.

Risk management theory indicates that if an action taker is able to identify the risks to which an initiative is susceptible and determine the likelihood of their occurrence and their impact then he or she is dealing with a risk. Failure to be able to identify risks and parameterise them leaves the taker of an action in the realm of uncertainty of achieving the intended outcome. Moving in the sphere of uncertainty has consequences for the management of the action taken, making it impossible to take rational decisions aimed at reducing the level of uncertainty. Risk as a parameterisable phenomenon makes it possible to analyse actions and adopt strategies that increase the probability of achieving the objective.

Linked to the issue of risk is the concept of hazard. Hazard in this case is not synonymous with risk. A hazard has a form and characteristics that can be measured objectively e.g. natural hazards i.e. fires, hurricanes, floods have a source and defined mechanisms of origin. Similarly, any identified military, non-military and hybrid threat.

Threats affect resources through their vulnerabilities causing disruption. The disruption (access restriction or permanent destruction) of a resource affects the process in which the considered resource is used. The occurrence of a disruption generates a measurable effect on the activities undertaken, affecting the expected outcome. This effect will always depend on the organisation of the process and be subjectively perceived by the one taking the action.

In the case under consideration, instead of a resource, we are considering civilians who are impacted by the effects of the identified hazards. These impacts can cause a spectrum of effects, the most significant of which are permanent injury and death.

There are many definitions of risk in the literature. Current knowledge of risk has become a broad and multifaceted theory. On the one hand, it formulates generally accepted and unquestionable basic findings, such as, inter alia, the inextricable link between risk and action (Penc, 2000). On the other hand, it is divided into a number of strands related to, inter alia (Zawiła-Niedźwiecki, 2013, pp. 31–32):

- areas of economic activity (banking, insurance, capital market, industry, trade, etc.),
- the perspective of individual social sciences (especially sociology, psychology, economics, finance, management, security sciences),
- mechanism the emergence and realisation of risk.

A particular conceptual character is attributed to the changing environment of broad economic, sectoral, social as well as universal security. J. Pronko notes that some authors state that it is not possible to define risk unambiguously as through a set of characteristics describing it, which include: the source and object of risk, i.e. the reason that makes the consideration of risk legitimate and the situation (phenomenon) equivalent to the object of risk analysis; the possible consequences of risk, i.e. the potential nature of the effects of decisions taken and the measures of these effects in terms of subjects and objects; the taking of risk, i.e. the decision to take active measures related to the implementation of tasks needed to obtain benefits and minimise losses; risk realisation, i.e. the occurrence of anticipated or unforeseen consequences of events whose source is the subject of risk; and the possibility of risk manipulation, i.e. the susceptibility of the subject of risk to the application of measures and methods aimed at the occurring processes in the desired direction (Jedynak, Szydło, 1997, pp. 14–46).

Another general criterion classifying the perception of risk is the sectoral and holistic approach. Increasingly, studies can be found that exclude the validity of looking at risk in a sectoral way in favour of a holistic, multifaceted and multi-sectoral view of risk. This is an approach with which one has to agree. It is based on the fact that risk arises from people and their activities, and from a range of other risks that are partly the result of those activities and partly independent of them. As a consequence of this, hybrid risks emerge. The term hybrid threat refers to an action taken by states and non-state actors with the aim of destabilising the object of attack or inflicting harm on it through the combined use of overt and covert, military and non-military means (Zwęgliński et al., 2020, pp. 22–23).

In the literature, risk is often defined as the product of the value of the probability of a hazard occurring and the consequences resulting from that hazard, as expressed by formula (Eq. 4.1) (Monkiewicz, 2004, p. 26).

$$R = P \times S \qquad (4.1)$$

where:
R – stands for risk,
P – probability of hazard occurrence,
S – effect of hazard occurrence.

Expressing risk in terms of a numerical value is a facilitation in the risk management process that allows the decision-maker to dimension the various aspects of the risks under consideration into an indicator in order to then adopt a strategy for dealing with the risk.

The basic view of risk as the product of the probability of a hazard occurring and its effect is often inadequate. Today, researchers use two complementary approaches to describe risk (Zwęgliński et al., 2020, p. 53).

The first defines risk as the product of the probability (P) of a hazard materialising (moving from potential to dynamic) and its negative consequences (S). Since the processes of shaping safety are carried out by and for people, where a purely social factor, e.g. the perception of safety and risks, is not without influence on the decisions taken, it must also be taken into account. So the above product needs to be extended to include this aspect. This is realised by including in formula (Eq. 4.2) the aspect of social perception referred to as "social agitation" (SA).

$$R = P \times S + SA \qquad (4.2)$$

A second, equally frequently used approach to risk is to understand it as the probability of the materialisation of a threat that adversely affects the protected good (value, entity, service) as a result of the exposure and vulnerability of the good in question to that threat. This definition can be reduced to equation (Eq. 4.3):

$$R = P[H, V(A), E]$$

$$(4.3)$$

where:

R – risk associated with the impact of multiple factors (economic, social, cultural, political, environmental, scientific and technical);

P – probability of occurrence (in relation to place and time);

H – hazard;

A – the good at risk (a good is by definition a specific tangible or intangible value);

V – vulnerability or resilience of the protected good, e.g. entity or service (vulnerability/resilience);

E – exposure to the threat (exposure).

An extension of the aforementioned approach is to consider the relationship between the resources under consideration and the threats that affect them (Eq. 4.4). This concept is based on a situation model of a resource that, in combination with other resources, creates a space for the propagation of threats in a domino or cascade effect (Wisniewski, 2019, pp. 44–58).

$$R_{\Phi_{\alpha,\gamma}} = \sum_{\alpha=1}^{n} \sum_{\beta=1}^{j} \frac{P_{\alpha,\beta}}{\sum_{\alpha=1}^{n} \sum_{\beta=1}^{j} P_{\alpha,\beta}} \times |\Delta\Phi_{\alpha,\gamma}| \times (U_{\alpha,\beta} - M_{\alpha,\beta})$$

$$(4.4)$$

where:

$R_{\Phi_{\alpha,\gamma}}$ – risk to the resource functionality under consideration,

j – the number of threats to which a resource with index α is susceptible,

n – the number of stocks under consideration,

$R_{\alpha,\beta}$ – risk value <0%, 100%>,

$P_{\alpha,\beta}$ – probability of hazard β on a scale of <0, 1>,

$U_{\alpha,\beta}$ – vulnerability of the resource β on a scale of <0, 1>,

$\Delta\Phi_{\alpha,\gamma}$ – effect of materialisation of threat β <0%, 100%>,

$M_{\alpha,\beta}$ – sum of the impact of safeguards on the vulnerability of a resource β on a scale of <0, 1>.

The approach outlined is part of risk management and is the basis for the development of practical tools to support the risk estimation process, such as the risk matrices disseminated in public emergency management.

The mathematical definition of risk is a general definition and can therefore be applied regardless of the type of hazard. All formulas

Identification and analysis of threats to the civilian population   275

considered are based on the probability and effect components extending them with additional variables. Each parameter should be determined individually by adopting criteria for their determination.

Determining the probability of a hazard occurring refers to the expected frequency of the event under consideration. There are two basic types of scale for assessing probability:

- continuous scale,
- discrete scale.

Each entrepreneur individually tailors the scale to the needs of the organisation and the data it has.

A discrete scale is a scale that does not require a large dataset, but compared to a continuous scale, the results produced are less precise. There are many types of scale that differ in the number of steps. Table 4.8 shows examples of a discrete scale for determining the probability of risk.

A characteristic of the discrete scale is the definition of a limited number of steps described in terms of words or points. Each degree should be accompanied by a description which is a criterion whose fulfilment determines the possibility of assigning the degree in question. This criterion should be measurable so that different users of the scale make comparable estimates, independent of subjective judgements.

A continuous scale requires a large amount of historical data. An example of a continuous scale is presented in Table 4.9.

TABLE 4.8   Example of a five-level scale for determining probability

Keyword Description of the Probability of an Event Occurring	Examples of Detailed Descriptions	Probability Value on a Point Scale
Very high	It is expected that timing is very likely to occur. Regularly, every two weeks.	5
High	The event is very likely to occur. Regularly, at least once a month.	4
Medium	The event is very likely to occur once every six months.	3
Low	There is a low probability of the event occurring. It will occur once per tok.	2
Very low	An event can only occur in exceptional circumstances. Once every five years, and most likely not at all, it has not occurred so far.	1

Source: Jajuga (2019, p. 428)

TABLE 4.9 Example of a continuous scale in determining probability

Keyword Description of the Probability of an Event Occurring	Examples of Detailed Descriptions	Probability Value in Percentage
Very high	Regularly, monthly or more often.	81–100
High	Regularly, at least once a year.	61–80
Medium	The event will occur a maximum of five times in five years.	41–80
Low	There is a low probability of an event occurring. It will occur once every five years.	21–40
Very low	Once every ten years or the event has not yet occurred.	0–20

Source: Jajuga (2019, p. 428)

When estimating the effects of the risk under consideration, similar principles apply as for the probability variable. A certain complication in the case of the effects variable is their differentiated nature, which in management science is divided into financial and non-financial. The differentiated nature of the effects forces a decision on how to calculate the risk indicator.

It is possible to calculate an indicator for each type of effect separately, which, on the one hand, makes the analysis more difficult by having to take into account multiple indicators characterising a single hazard. On the other hand, the segmentation used allows a more precise selection of risk mitigation actions.

Another option is to calculate a single risk indicator for the hazard under consideration, which takes into account all types of impacts that occur. In this case, formula 4.5 is used (Jajuga, 2019, p. 430):

$$S = \sum_{i=1}^{n} S_i \qquad (4.5)$$

where:
S – denotes the effect of the risk,
Si – effect for each criterion,
n – natural count,
i – summation index.

Knowing the values of the probability of a hazard occurring and its effect on the organisation under consideration, it is possible to calculate the value of the risk according to equation 1. Based on the results of the risk assessment, the company can rank the hazards to which it is susceptible using, for example, the criteria in Table 4.10.

Identification and analysis of threats to the civilian population 277

TABLE 4.10 Example of risk materiality classification

Breakdown of the Risk Scale	Slogan Description of Risks	Description of Risks
20–25	Unacceptable risks	The level of risk is unacceptable. Materialisation of the risk will cause large losses to the company. It will prevent the achievement of objectives. A given level requires immediate action.
15–19	High level of risk	If a risk materialises, it is very likely to cause serious damage to the company. If it concerns new tasks, it should not be carried out.
10–14	Average risk level	Risk is a threat to the company, there is the possibility of financial and material loss.
5–9	Low risk	The materialisation of risks will result in a small threat to the achievement of the company's goals and objectives; the level of risk should be monitored and controlled.
1–4	Acceptance	Risks do not affect the core business of the unit; they do not prevent the tasks and objectives of the organisational unit from being achieved, and require monitoring and, where necessary, checking that risks are properly controlled.

Source: Own elaboration

The fundamental difficulty in classifying risks is mainly due to the need to take into account both the causes of risk (causal approach), the manner and process of its fulfilment (vulnerability approach) and the manifestations of its materialisation (effect approach).

Awareness of risk regardless of its classification enables an organisation to start the risk management process.

Risk management is implemented on two levels: risk diagnosis and action strategy. According to ISO 31000:2018, the risk management process consists of six.

1. Communication and consultation – a key recommendation of the ISO standard is to communicate at all stages of processes. Therefore, communication and consultation plans should be established as early in the process as possible. Communication ensures that those responsible for risk management know and understand the entire process, particularly the rules and decisions that are being made. Furthermore, proper communication and consultation ensures that possible risks are correctly

identified. It also enables knowledge from the different experiences of staff to be used.

2. Setting the context – at this stage, the company defines its objectives both externally and internally, as well as setting the scope and recommendations for risks. The context for each of the company's processes may vary, and may include:
   - defining general and specific objectives for risk management activities,
   - defining responsibilities for and within the risk management process,
   - defining the scope as well as the level of detail and scale of risk management activities, including specific inclusions and exclusions,
   - defining an activity, process, function, project, product, service or asset in the context of time and place,
   - defining dependencies between a particular project, process or activity and other projects, processes or activities of the organisation,
   - defining a risk assessment methodology,
   - defining ways to estimate the performance and effectiveness of risk management,
   - identifying and determining the decisions that should be taken,
   - identifying, defining the scope or framework of the research needed, its scale.

3. The risk assessment consists of stages:
   - Risk identification – the main purpose of identification is to create a list of risks that threaten the company. Unidentified risks will not be taken into account during the next steps. It is recommended that all risks are included in a given list, regardless of the origin or likelihood of the risk. The enterprise should use tools and techniques that are best suited to the enterprise's objectives,
   - Risk analysis – The purpose of the risk analysis is to provide information for risk evaluation and to help decide how to proceed with the risk. The analysis stage includes consideration of the causes and sources of the risk, both positive and negative consequences, as well as the likelihood of these consequences occurring. Risk analysis can be carried out at different levels of detail depending on the purpose and the data available. Consequences and their probability can be determined by modelling event outcomes or by extrapolation from experimental studies or available data. A number of tools are applicable in risk analysis, such as brainstorming,

interviews, the Delphi method, checklists, preliminary risk analysis and SCA (sneak analysis & sneak circuit analysis) and Monte Carlo simulations.
- risk evaluation – the main purpose of evaluation is to support decision-making. Evaluation assists in the implementation of corporate behaviour and also indicates what the priorities should be when dealing with risks,
4. Dealing with risks – the stage where strategies for dealing with risks are identified.
5. Monitoring and review – a stage involving regular review and oversight of the risk handling process. In this way, the company can make sure that the decisions taken are having the desired effect. In addition, regular monitoring and review can allow new risks to be detected before they have an adverse effect.
6. Documentation and reporting – represents a set of methods and tools that can be used in future analyses.

In summary, the risk management process is designed to create a situation in which the analyser is aware of the risks and, by analysing the causes and mechanisms of materialisation, has made a risk assessment. Knowledge of the probability and impact of risks enables both the selection of the right strategic course of action (choice of risk management strategy) and the identification of operational measures in the form of specific safeguards and risk response plans.

A risk management strategy is an overall plan of action, in an important area for the organisation, consisting of the formulation of objectives and forms of action related to anticipated changes in factors affecting the level of probability of loss of benefit or loss (Bizon-Górecka, 2001). The literature on organisational management distinguishes the following strategies for dealing with risk (Staniec, Zawiła-Niedźwiecki, 2008):

- strategies for avoiding risk by not getting involved in ventures where the risk appears extremely high,
- reducing the magnitude of risks through analysis and monitoring,
- transferring risks to others mainly by insuring them,
- diversifying risks by reducing the likelihood of losses, engaging in other areas or introducing new activities,
- reducing negative impacts on the company's position by increasing capital, creating reserves and using insurance.

Individual strategies are assigned to areas designated by the criterion of probability and impact of the risk (Figure 4.3). Through this exercise, strategic directions for dealing with risks classified into a specific category are indicated.

Risk responce strategy

High effect	Risk transfer Reducing negative impacts	Avoidance
Low effect	Acceptance of risk	Risk diversification Risk monitoring
	Low probability	**High probability**

FIGURE 4.3 Example of risk strategy assignment for general risk categories

Source: Own study

A complementary activity to the identification of a risk management strategy is the identification of specific safeguards in response to the identified causes of risks and the development of contingency action plans in response to the adverse effects of risks. A method dedicated to this task is the Bow-Tie. Bow-tie is a graphical method to link the causes of an event to its effects. The method is a combination of event tree analysis and fault tree analysis. Within the bow-tie method, in addition to the identification of effects and their causes, it is possible to mark barriers between risks and their causes and risks and their consequences. The data sources for the bow-tie method are (Kosieradzka, Zawiła-Niedźwiecki, 2016, p. 77):

- FTA method,
- the brainstorming method,
- BIA method.

The bow-tie method allows the integration of the risk with the multiple factors that initiate it and the range of consequences to which the materialisation of the risk can lead. This knowledge provides an opportunity to build a team of experts that will be able to propose appropriate barriers affecting the likelihood of risk materialisation as well as plans to mitigate the effects of risk materialisation.

Using the methodological apparatus of risk management, threats in hybrid warfare can be classified in terms of frequency of occurrence and impact on the civilian population. General handling strategies can then be adopted for the four groups of threats thus defined, which

Identification and analysis of threats to the civilian population   281

can be supplemented by, specific to each group, a spectrum of specific safeguards and handling plans. In this way, civilians wishing to reduce the risks associated with hybrid warfare threats will themselves be able to take precautions or prepare to respond to the occurrence of threats. Ultimately, the effects of the threats will be reduced.

SUMMARY

The aim of this chapter was to try to identify and deepen the understanding of hybrid threats and their impact on internal security and civilian protection. In this context, it was hypothesised that threats in hybrid warfare represent a network of flexible linkages between military and non-military threats that interact with each other, leading to likely cascading effects on civilians. The hypothesis was verified positively. The analyses conducted clearly showed that the actions and resulting threats in hybrid warfare are networked and flexibly adapt to the operational environment and the needs of the attacker. The networks of linkages are diverse and have varying scales of use. Nineteen domains have been identified in which activities are conducted and the effects of these activities, i.e. hybrid threats, interact. Hierarchically, the leading domains are: the information domain; the political domain; the air domain; the maritime domain; the intelligence domain; and the land domain. However, this does not mean that the use of domains has to be limited to only those confirmed above. In each of the nineteen domains, there are complex activities, which in different ways and at different scales create a web of interconnectedness. The study also indicates the evolution of activities in the cognitive (cognitive) domain. This is an important indicator because activities in this domain have the potential to manipulate perception and control minds resulting in the ability to control societies on an unprecedented scale. This can be confirmed by the strong link between this domain and the information domain, which has one of the highest rates. However, there is undoubtedly a need for more in-depth research focused on these relationships, especially in the context of artificial intelligence. Hybrid threats are the result of activities in the different domains. The study showed that conventional military threats dominate non-military threats. This is a premise that, in the context of the outcome of non-military and military actions (3;69:1), proves that non-military actions can generate military threats as well as the fact that, media coverage focuses on more visible military threats. Attribution in this case poses a serious problem, as contemporary information shapes threat perception, which in the case of civilians and the context of hybrid warfare can have tangible consequences in preparing for threats. Arguably, this is why disinformation and propaganda activities are so widely used in the war in Ukraine. However, the networking and flexibility of these remains a significant problem. The spectrum and scale of threats traditionally attributed to different actors is being expanded. The numerical scales in the networks of linkages in hybrid warfare show the involvement of state and non-state actors in a feedback loop, meaning that the actions taken are not only interconnected but also interact with each other. The consequence of this is precisely a complex environment of hard-to-predict hybrid threats with cascading effects. In response to the complexity of the hybrid threat environment, states and security organisations are implementing strategies to counter hybrid threats. The solutions implemented are often geared towards a systemic response. However, given the not only networked and flexible, but also anticipatory nature of hybrid threats, it is important to rethink the decentralisation of responsibility for preparing for threats to smaller social communities starting as early as the individual. This is because a civilian mindset that is only focused on security based on systemic solutions can lead to passive social attitudes, especially in the context of intensive information and preparation activities. In view of this, involvement at the micro level is a necessity. Contemporary hybrid threats also require a full rethinking of security paradigms. The institutional system cannot be the only tool in dealing with such a complex nature of threats. The civilian population should be fully aware of the mechanisms of such threats as well as having an adaptive response capability.

ACKNOWLEDGMENT

The authors would like to express their gratitude to Łukasz Przybyszewski for his consultation on one of the sections in this chapter.

NOTES

1 Blank fields in the correlation table were filled with the entry '0%'. The codes were sorted in descending order of the number of times they occurred, and then the column and row correlations were segregated in the same way. A column summing % correlation was added to express the strength of correlation on the X-axis, and a row summing % correlation was added to express the strength of correlation on the Y-axis. Conditional formatting was then introduced in a spectrum of colour shades from red (high correlation score) through yellow (medium correlation score) to green (low correlation score). In this way, the results were grouped into a heat map. The qualitative analysis of the quantitative results and

Identification and analysis of threats to the civilian population 283

the image, i.e. the heat map, was based on the assumption that newspaper articles are written according to a key from the editorial guidelines and/or according to the author's own self-imposed guidelines in relation to political correctness, the most widely held views, etc. This assumption is supplemented by a logical conclusion in the form of a "heat map". This assumption is supplemented by the logical conclusion that such a key will strengthen some codes in terms of numbers and weaken others. Correlations with other codes, on the other hand, will indicate what newspaper article writers and editors avoid and what they combine. The lower the abundance and the lower the correlation, the more a particular code is avoided. As the heat map was analysed, both the correlation strength indicators and the area of the matrix that was covered were important. In this way, the correlation strength indices served as vectors that indicated which way the narrative was going on the matrix. The code or codes that ranked, so to speak, in the middle in each of the tables were considered to be the most significant code, since it or they indicated the tendency, typical in human psychology, to hide the main theme or message in speech or writing in the middle of a speech or article. The same tendency is observed in examiners who, when arranging a multiple-choice test (a) (b) (c) (d), reflexively place the correct answers under (b) or (c) more often. The qualitative analysis and description of the observations continued with the author's experience in analysing open sources, especially press and official messages and government statements from countries which, in the opinion of Western countries, are regarded as subjecting the press and new media to strong censorship and enforcing a high level of self-censorship in social network users and journalists. This experience shows that users and journalists avoid revealing the issue at all costs by hiding in the thicket of other information. At the same time, they keep silent on those topics that are at the heart of the problem. This can be called self-confessed anomie. The qualitative analysis of the tables was supposed to indicate a result that would guide further research questions. This succeeded because proving the conclusions of this analysis, as well as gaining a fuller picture of the media narrative and identifying new codes, requires probing the content of the materials. This means that it will probably be necessary to probe selected samples of articles in terms of the message they convey and therefore the framework within which the codes are contained, as well as the volume of the text, because, for example: usually, accusations of propaganda are supported by anti-propaganda content (or simply their own propaganda), which lengthens news reports or articles.

2 In the report *When words become weapons: the unprecedented risks to civilians from the spread of disinformation in Ukraine*, the mechanism of information warfare is detailed. Russia has intensified its information operations and disinformation activities, using them to achieve its strategic, operational and tactical objectives. Much of the disinformation disseminated by Russian-linked actors was aimed directly at Ukrainian civilians, with the aim of influencing their behaviour, often in ways that threatened their lives. For example, civilians who made decisions to flee frontline areas exposed to mines and bombardment encountered disinformation regarding the timing, location and existence of organised evacuation efforts. It also included false claims that the Ukrainian military was blocking some evacuation routes or attacking civilians attempting to evacuate. The scale of these disinformation activities was significant. Of the approximately 6,300 messages shared by pro-Russian Telegram channels that were analysed by CIVIC as part of this research project, some 5,400 posts contained evacuation-related material – https://civiliansinconflict.org/wp-content/uploads/2023/11/CIVIC_Disinformation_Report.pdf.

3 For the full responses of the experts, see Appendix 4.

BIBLIOGRAPHY

Abdyraeva, C., (2020), Information Warfare Operations in the Cyber Domain, in the Use of Cyberspace in the Context of Hybrid Warfare: Means, Challenges and Trends. *OIIP – Austrian Institute for International Affairs*. Available at: https://www.jstor.org/stable/resrep25102.8. Accessed: 14 August 2024.

Aho, A., Alonso Villota, M., Giannopoulos, G., Jungwirth, R., Lebrun, M., Savolainen, J., Smith, H., and Willkomm, E., (2023), *Hybrid Threats: A Comprehensive Resilience Ecosystem*. Available at: https://www.hybridcoe.fi/wp-content/uploads/2023/04/CORE_comprehensive_resilience_ecosystem.pdf (PDF). Accessed: 22 June 2024.

Asthana, S.B., (2022), Economic War to Energy War: Ukraine War Reflects New Dimensions of Warfare. *WION News*, 27 November. Available at: https://www.wionews.com/opinions-blogs/economic-war-to-energy-war-ukraine-war-reflects-new-dimensions-of-warfare-537830. Accessed: 19 June 2024.

Balcerowicz, B., (2024), Zagrożenie hybrydowe. In: Encyklopedia Bezpieczeństwa Narodowego. Wojskowa Akademia Techniczna. Available at: https://encyklopedia.revite.pl/articles/view/672, Accessed: 20 August 2024.

Belsat, (2024), Russian Information Attack: Hackers Published Calls to Arms by Ukrainians on Hundreds of Telegram Channels, 22 July. Available at: https://belsat.eu/pl/news/22-07-2024-rosyjski-atak-informacyjny-hakerzy-opublikowali-na-setkach-kanalow-telegramu-wezwania-do-zlozenia-broni-przez-ukraincow. Accessed: 23 June 2024.

Ber, J., (2023), Wagner's Group in the Russian-Ukrainian War. From Popasna to Bakhmut. Centre for Eastern Studies. *OSW Commentaries*, 511, 28 April. Available at: https://www.osw.waw.pl/pl/publikacje/komentarze-osw/2023-04-28/od-popasnej-do-bachmutu-grupa-wagnera-w-wojnie-rosyjsko. Accessed: 24 June 2024.

Bizon-Górecka, J., (2001), Strategies for Managing Risk in a Business Organisation. *Organization Review*, 1. Available at: https://przegladorganizacji.pl/artykul/2001/10.33141po.2001.01.01. Accessed: 25 June 2024.

Chivvis, C.S., (2017), *Understanding Russian 'Hybrid Warfare' and What Can Be Done About It.* CT-468, Testimony Presented before the House Armed Services Committee on March 22, 2017. Available at: https://www.rand.org/pubs/testimonies/CT468.html (PDF). Accessed: 19 June 2024.

Danyk, Y., (2019). Methodical and Applied Aspects of Creation and Application of Cyber Ranges. *Theoretical and Applied Cybersecurity*. 1. https://doi.org/10.20535/tacs.2664-29132019.1.169089.

Danyk, Y., (2023). Modern Cognitive Operations and Hybrid Warfare. *Journal of Strategic Security*, 16(1). https://doi.org/10.5038/1944-0472.16.1.2032.

Directive (EU) 2022/2555 of the European Parliament and of the Council of 14 December 2022 on Measures to Promote a High Common Level of Cyber-Security within the Union (NIS Directive 2), PE/32/2022/REV/2, OJ L 333, 27.12.2022. Available at: https://eur-lex.europa.eu/legal-content/PL/TXT/?uri=CELEX%3A32022L2555. Accessed: 15 June 2024.

Directive (EU) 2022/2557 of the European Parliament and of the Council of 14 December 2022 on theRresilience of Critical Entities and Repealing Council Directive 2008/114/EC (Text with EEA relevance), PE/51/2022/REV/1. Available at: https://eur-lex.europa.eu/legal-content/PL/TXT/?uri=CELEX%3A32022L2557. Accessed: 15 June 2024.

Donnelly, J., and Farley, J., (2018), Defining the 'Domain' in Multi-Domain. *Over The Horizon*, 17 September. Available at: https://othjournal.com/2018/09/17/defining-the-domain-in-multi-domain/. Accessed: 14 June 2024.

Duguin, S., and Pavlova, P., (2023), *The Role of Cyber in the Russian War against Ukraine: Its Impact and the Consequences for the Future of Armed Conflict,* Policy Department for External Relations,

Directorate General for External Policies of the Union, European Parliament, PE 702.594. Available at: https://www.europarl.europa.eu/RegData/etudes/BRIE/2023/702594/EXPO_BRI(2023)702594_EN.pdf. Accessed: 15 June 2024.

European Commission (2024), Hybrid Threats. European Commission - Defence Industry & Space, https://defence-industry-space.ec.europa.eu/eu-defence-industry/hybrid-threats_en. Accessed 27 November 2024.

Fox, A.C., (2017), Hybrid Warfare: The 21st Century Russian Way of Warfare. Thesis. Available at: https://www.researchgate.net/publication/344174453_Hybrid_Warfare_The_21st_Century_Russian_Way_of_Warfare (PDF). Accessed: 15 June 2024.

Galus, A., and Nesteriak, Y., (2019), Digital Media in Contemporary Conflict – The Example of Ukraine. *Central European and Balkan Studies*, No. 4. Available at: https://doi.org/10.14746/ssp.2019.4.2. Accessed: 15 June 2024.

Giannopoulos, G., Smith, H., and Theocharidou, M. (eds), (2020), The Landscape of Hybrid Threats: A Conceptual Model. *Public Version*, 26 November 2020. Available at: https://ec.europa.eu/newsroom/cipr/items/713833/en. Accessed: 15 June 2024.

Giannopoulos, G., Smith, H., and Theocharidou, M. (eds), (2021), The Landscape of Hybrid Threats: A Conceptual Model. *Public Version*. Available at: https://www.hybridcoe.fi/publications/the-landscape-of-hybrid-threats-a-conceptual-model/ (PDF). Accessed: 20 June 2024.

Gonçalves, C. P., (2019), Cyberspace and Artificial Intelligence: The New Face of Cyber-Enhanced Hybrid Threats, Available at: 10.5772/intechopen.88648, Accessed: 20 June 2024.

Hanko, M., and Spily, P., (2018), Digital Subversion. *Security Dimensions*, 26(26), https://doi.org/10.5604/01.3001.0012.7247. Accessed: 23 June 2024.

Hensoldt Analytics, (2021), Modern Battlefield Is Multi-Domain: HENSOLDT Analytics Webinar on Hybrid Warfare, 18 May. Available at: https://www.anetakpawlik.eu/wp-content/uploads/2022/06/Modern-Battlefield-is-Multi-Domain-HENSOLDT-Analytics-Webinar-on-Hybrid-Warfare-HENSOLDT-Analytics-v2.pdf. Accessed: 15 June 2024.

Holmes, M., (2023), 10 Defining Moments in Cybersecurity and Satellite in 2022. *Via Satellite*, 25 January. Available at: https://interactive.satellitetoday.com/via/january-february-2023/10-defining-moments-in-cybersecurity-and-satellite-in-2022/. Accessed: 19 June 2024.

Hopkins J., (2021), Countering Cognitive Warfare: Awareness and Resilience. *NATO Review*, 20 May. Available at: https://www.nato.int/docu/review/pl/articles/2021/05/20/przeciwdzialanie-wojnie-kognitywnej-swiadomosc-i-odpornosc/index.html. Accessed: 24 June 2024.

Höyhtyä, M., and Uusipaavalniemi, S., (2023), *The Space Domain and the Russo-Ukrainian War: Actors, Tools, and Impact.* Hybrid CoE Working Paper 21, January. Available at: https://www.hybridcoe. fi/wp-content/uploads/2023/01/20230109-Hybrid-CoE-Working-Paper-21-Space-and-the-Ukraine-war-WEB.pdf. Accessed: 18 June 2024.

Hybrid Co E, (2023), Comprehensive Resilience Ecosystem. Available at: https://www.hybridcoe.fi/publications/hybrid-threats-a-comprehensive-resilience-ecosystem/. Accessed: 15 June 2024.

Hybrid Co E (2024a), Frequently Asked Questions on Hybrid Threats. Available at: https://www.hybridcoe.fi/wp-content/uploads/2024/01/FAQ-on-Hybrid-Threats.pdf (PDF). Accessed: 24 June 2024.

Hybrid Co E, (2024b), Hybrid Threats as a Phenomenon. Available at: https://www.hybridcoe.fi/hybrid-threats-as-a-phenomenon/. Accessed: 15 June 2024.

Iskandarov, K., and Gawliczek, P., (2022), Economic Coercion as a Means of Hybrid Warfare: The South Caucasus as a Focal Point. *Security and Defence Quarterly*, 40(4). https://doi.org/10.35467/sdq/151038 (PDF).

Jajuga, K., (2019), *Risk Management.* Warsaw: Wydawnictwo Naukowe PWN.

Jedynak, P., and Szydło, S., (1997), *Risk Management.* Wrocław: Ossolineum.

Kosieradzka, A., and Zawiła-Niedźwiecki, J. (eds), (2016), *Advanced Risk Assessment Methodology in Public Crisis Management.* Kraków-Legionowo: edu-Libri.

Listner, M., (2023), Law as Force in Hybrid Warfare. *Irregular Warfare Initiative*, 5 October. Available at: https://irregularwarfare.org/articles/law-as-force-in-hybrid-warfare/. Accessed: 22 June 2024.

Lowenthal, M.M., (2012), *Intelligence: From Secrets to Policy.* Los Angeles: SAGE/CQ Press, pp. xxi–417. Available at: https://archive.org/details/intelligencefrom0000lowe_t8r9. Accessed: 22 June 2024.

McMaster, H. R., (2016), Harbingers of Future War, Lecture, Pritzker Military Museum and Library, Chicago.

Mimran, T., (2023), Israel – Hamas 2023 Symposium – Cyberspace – The Hidden Aspect of the Conflict. Available at: https://lieber.westpoint.edu/cyberspace-hidden-aspect-conflict/. Accessed: 15 June 2024.

Mitkov, M., (2023), The Year of Russia's Invasion of Ukraine. *Space Domain in the Age of War*, 24 February. Available at: https://space24.pl/bezpieczenstwo/technologie-wojskowe/rok-inwazji-rosji-na-ukrainie-domena-kosmiczna-w-dobie-wojny-komentarz. Accessed: 17 June 2024.

Monkiewicz, J. (ed.), (2004), *Basics of Insurance.* Warsaw: Poltext.

Munoz Mosquera, A., and Chalanouli, N., (2020), China, an Active Practitioner of Legal Warfare. *Guest Post on Lawfire*, 2 February. Available at: https://sites.duke.edu/lawfire/2020/02/02/guest-post-andres-munoz-mosqueras-and-nikoleta-chalanoulis-essay-china-an-active-practitioner-of-legal-warfare/. Accessed: 22 June 2024.

NATO, (2024), Hybrid Threats and Hybrid Warfare. Available at: https://www.nato.int/nato_static_fl2014/assets/pdf/2024/7/pdf/241007-hybrid-threats-and-hybrid-warfare.pdf. Accessed: 15 June 2024.

Naureen, A., (2017), Hybrid War and Economy. *The Nation*, 17 October. Available at: https://www.nation.com.pk/17-Oct-2017/hybrid-war-and-economy. Accessed: 20 June 2024.

NATO, (2024), *Hybrid threats and hybrid warfare*, Available at: https://www.nato.int/nato_static_fl2014/assets/pdf/2024/7/pdf/241007-hybrid-threats-and-hybrid-warfare.pdf. Accessed 15 June 2024.

Nettis, K., (2020), Multi-Domain Operations: Bridging the Gaps for Dominance. *Wild Blue Yonder*, 16 March, Maxwell AFB, AL. Available at: https://www.airuniversity.af.edu/Wild-Blue-Yonder/Article-Display/Article/2109784/multi-domain-operations-bridging-the-gaps-for-dominance/. Accessed: 15 June 2024.

Patrikarakos, D., (2017), War in 140 Characters: How Social Media Is Reshaping Conflict in the Twenty-First Century. New York, Books, ISBN-139780465096152.

Penc, J., (2000), *Decisions in Management*. Warsaw: Placet.

Peter, P., (2015), Optimizing Armed Forces Capabilities for Hybrid Warfare – New Challenge for Slovak Armed Forces. *Incas Bulletin*, 7(3). Available at: https://doi.org/10.13111/2066-8201.2015.7.3.18 (PDF). Accessed: 23 June 2024.

Preparedness to Respond to Space Hybrid Operations, Prague Security Studies Institute, Prague. Available at: https://www.pssi.cz/download//docs/8252_597-europe-s-preparedness-to-respond-to-space-hybrid-operations.pdf. Accessed 17 June 2024.

Rashi, T., and Schleifer, R., (2023), The Ethics of Psychological Warfare – Lessons from Israel. *Democracy and Security*, 19(2), 199–210. https://doi.org/10.1080/17419166.2023.2210472.

Reilly, J., (2018), OTH Video: Beyond the Theory-A Framework for Multi-Domain Operations, 13 April. Available at: https://othjournal.com/. Accessed: 16 June 2024.

Robinson, J., Šmuclerová, M., Degl'Innocenti, L., Perrichon, L., and Pražák, J., (2018), Europe's Preparedness to Respond to Space Hybrid Operations. *Prague Security Studies Institute, Prague*. Available at: https://www.pssi.cz/download//docs/8252_597-europe-s-preparedness-to-respond-to-space-hybrid-operations.pdf. Accessed: 17 June 2024.

Rusnáková, S., (2017), Russian New Art of Hybrid Warfare in Ukraine. *Slovak Journal of Political Sciences*, 17(3–4). https://doi.org/10.1515/sjps-2017-0014.

Seibel, W., (2016), Hybridity and Responsible Leadership in Public Administration: 26th wissenschaftlicher Kongress der Deutschen Vereinigung für Politische Wissenschaft. https://doi.org/10.5771/9783845266039-309 (PDF).

Shamsi, Z.U.H., (2024), Introducing the Framework Model for the Evaluation of Deterrent Value of States. *NUST Journal of Interna-tional Peace & Stability*, 7(2). Available at: https://www.researchgate.net/publication/385949956_Introducing_the_Framework_Model_for_the_Evaluation_of_Deterrent_Value_of_States, Accessed: 15 June 2024.

Staniec, I., and Zawiła-Niedźwiecki, J., (2008), *Operational Risk Management*. Warsaw: C.H. Beck.

Strategic Compass for Security and Defence, (2022), Council of the European Union. Available at: https://www.consilium.europa.eu/en/policies/strategic-compass/. Accessed: 15 June 2024.

Thiele, R., (2019), #SpaceWatchGL Op'ed: Space and Hybrid Warfare – Part One. *SpaceWatch.Global*, 21 December. Available at: https://spacewatch.global/2019/12/spacewatch-oped-space-in-hybrid-warfare/. Accessed: 18 June 2024.

Treverton, G.F., (2018), *The Intelligence Challenges of Hybrid Threats: Focus on Cyber and Virtual Realm.* Sweden: Center for Asymmetric Threat Studies. ISBN: 978-91-86137-75-5. Available at: https://fhs.diva-portal.org/smash/get/diva2:1250560/FULLTEXT01.pdf. Accessed: 15 June 2024.

Ure, A., (2023), Information Warfare: Five Ways Russia Captured Ukrainian Media. *Info-Res,* 5 July, Updated: 12 July. Available at: https://www.info-res.org/post/information-warfare-five-ways-russia-captured-ukrainian-media. Accessed: 24 June 2024.

Viasat, (2022), KA-SAT Network Cyber Attack Overview. Available at: https://news.viasat.com/blog/corporate/ka-sat-network-cyber-attack-overview. Accessed: 18 June 2024.

Wiśniewski, M., (2019), Zarządzanie Sytuacyjne Bezpieczeństwem Infrastruktury Krytycznej Państwa, Warszawa, OWPW.

Wisniewski, M., Szwarc, K., and Skomra, W., (2023), Continuity of Essential Services as an Emerging Challenge for Societal Resilience. *IEEE Access*, 11, 44614–44635. https://doi.org/10.1109/ACCESS.2023.3271751. Accessed: 15 June 2024.

Yoachimik, O., and Pacheco, M., (2023), Cyber Attacks in the Israel-Hamas War. Cloudflare Blog, Available at: https://blog.cloudflare.com/cyber-attacks-in-the-israel-hamas-war/. Accessed: 27 June 2024.

Zawiła-Niedźwiecki, J., (2013), *Operational Risk Management in Ensuring Business Continuity in Organisations*. Kraków-Warsaw: edu-Libri.

Zwęgliński, T., Smolarkiewicz, M., and Gromek, P., (2020), *Efekt kaskadowy współczesnym wyzwaniem zarządzania kryzysowego*. Warsaw: SGSP.

Zawiła-Niedźwiecki, J. (ed.), (2020), *Introduction to Public Crisis Management*. Warsaw: Oficyna Wydawnicza Politechniki Warszawskiej.

CHAPTER 5

Population protection in hybrid warfare

INTRODUCTION TO CIVIL PROTECTION

The contemporary security situation, as assessed by the European Commission, is characterized by dynamic changes driven by a range of complex factors. Key determinants of this evolving reality include phenomena such as climate change, demographic trends, and political instability in regions beyond the borders of the European Union. Furthermore, the impact of globalization and digital transformation is becoming increasingly significant. While these processes bring benefits and innovation, they also generate new threats. Notably, there has been an increase in threats related to terrorism, organized crime and the illegal trafficking of drugs and human beings.

In the context of digitalization, there is also a significant rise in cybercrime and cyberattacks, which are becoming more sophisticated due to the transnational nature of operations and the close interconnection between the physical and digital worlds. In this regard, modern technologies and artificial intelligence are being increasingly utilized in criminal activities (European Commission, 2020). Additionally, during peacetime, the security of EU member states is further threatened by so-called hybrid threats, which can be exploited as potential tools for conducting hybrid warfare.

As states evolved into sovereign entities with defined territories, populations, legal systems, and enforcement mechanisms, it became essential to ensure protection against both external and internal threats. This led to the distinction between external security, which focuses on protection against military threats to sovereignty, territorial integrity and the inviolability of borders, and internal security, which concerns the prevention of internal threats aimed at the political, legal, and enforcement institutions of the state (Kitler, 2023). According to Waldemar Kitler, however, the boundaries between internal and external security—which is often considered paramount—are becoming increasingly blurred.

DOI: 10.4324/9781003503859-6

Contemporary challenges, such as hybrid threats, demonstrate that actions related to internal security often originate from external factors, involving both state and non-state actors. Internal security pertains to the process of addressing the needs and interests of a nation's society. It is carried out in a complex environment and impacts not only the individuals and social groups directly involved but also other communities, due to the cross-border nature of threats such as terrorism, which do not recognize national boundaries. This concept originates from state theory, which distinguishes between its external and internal functions. Consequently, the term "internal security of the state" is frequently used in legal doctrine. In the field of security studies, it is considered an integral component of national security (Kitler, 2023, pp. 117–133). Kitler, however, proposes defining internal security as a complex set of measures across various domains, including political, economic, social, cultural, ecological, public, general, informational and cyberspace security, and in certain situations, even military security. These measures aim to protect national interests, which are a composite of the interests of the state (public authorities), social groups, and individual citizens within the territory of a given country, against all external and internal challenges and threats that jeopardize these interests. In other words, it is the maintenance and protection of national security (of the state) within the borders inhabited by the state's citizens, against both external and internal threats to national interests (Kitler, 2023, p. 146).

Internal security can therefore be understood in two ways. In a narrower sense, it encompasses the fundamental functions of the state, such as the protection of territory, political order, social stability and the safeguarding of citizens' safety (including the protection of life and health). On the other hand, human security is a multi-sectoral approach to security that identifies and addresses common and cross-cutting challenges related to the survival, well-being and dignity of individuals. This concept was developed by the United Nations (UN), and the North Atlantic Treaty Organization's (NATO) approach to human security is based on this very concept (NATO, 2022). In a broader sense, internal security extends beyond state institutions and takes on a global character, linked to liberalism and international cooperation. In this context, it encompasses all forms of social and cultural activity, including the work of non-governmental organizations, which raises issues related to the privatization of security and social security. Although the subject of internal security has not yet been thoroughly studied, the concept lacks a universal definition and is interpreted differently across various countries. The scope of this concept depends on the nature, type and specific characteristics of the threats faced (Encyclopaedia of Public Administration).

The aim of this chapter is to examine the consequences that the materialization of threats caused by hybrid warfare has on the civilian population. In this context, the hypothesis is put forward that these threats necessitate the implementation of multifaceted systemic and individual actions aimed at effectively minimizing their impact on civilians.

INTERNATIONAL MECHANISMS FOR THE PROTECTION OF THE CIVILIAN POPULATION IN CONFLICTS AND WARS

Internal security and the protection of civilians constitute two key pillars that together form the foundation of a stable and secure functioning state. As previously mentioned, internal security refers to actions taken to maintain public order, ensure political security, and counter threats such as terrorism, organized crime, and cyber threats. On the other hand, the protection of civilians focuses on safeguarding citizens from various threats, including natural disasters, calamities, epidemics, and other emergency situations. These two areas are inextricably linked, both conceptually and operationally, meaning that the protection of civilians is one of the fundamental components of internal security. The effective functioning of the internal security system therefore requires the integration of civilian protection efforts, particularly in the context of crisis management and the prevention of various types of threats. In this context, the protection of civilians serves both as a strategic objective and as a tool that supports the broader implementation of internal security measures. Effective coordination of these efforts is crucial to creating a cohesive and effective security policy (NATO, 2024a, 2024b).

The definition of civilian protection, much like that of security, depends on the temporal context and encompasses both peacetime and wartime periods. Karolina MacLachlan emphasizes that civilian protection is not only a crucial aspect of military operations but also an ethical and strategic imperative in all types of conflicts, including hybrid wars. In such conflicts, the adversary often employs tactics aimed at harming civilians, which further underscores the importance of protecting civilian populations (MacLachlan, 2022). Traditional frameworks of international humanitarian law have established the protection of civilians within the context of conventional forms of warfare. However, with the emergence of hybrid wars, existing definitions and protection mechanisms have proven to be inadequate. The absence of a well-defined concept of civilian protection in the context of hybrid warfare creates a gap in the ability to build systemic and societal resilience.

In Poland, according to the Law on the Protection of the Population and Civil Defence, civilian protection is defined as a system comprising public administration bodies that carry out tasks aimed at ensuring the safety of the population by protecting human life and health, property, essential infrastructure, cultural heritage, and the environment in situations of threat. This system includes both the civilian protection authorities and entities responsible for these tasks, as well as the forces and resources allocated for their implementation. In the event of the introduction of martial law or during times of war, civilian protection transitions into civil defence, which focuses on safeguarding the civilian population from threats arising from military actions and their consequences (Act on Civil Protection and Civil Defence in Poland, 2024).

This understanding of civilian protection aligns with the approach adopted by the member states of the European Union, which in their strategic documents define civilian protection as a set of actions aimed at minimizing the impact of future natural disasters and man-made crises. Additionally, civilian protection encompasses both preventive measures and the direct provision of assistance to those affected after such events. Contemporary approaches to civilian protection therefore emphasize the comprehensiveness of actions, integrating preventive aspects with immediate response efforts in response to crises (EUR-Lex, 2024; Treaty on the Functioning of the European Union [TFEU], 2024).

To accomplish these tasks, the Union Civil Protection Mechanism was established, which coordinates rescue and relief efforts in the event of natural disasters and other emergencies (Decision No 1313/2013/EU of the European Parliament and of the Council of 17 December 2013, pp. 924–947, on a Union Civil Protection Mechanism, 2013). The mechanism, in addition to the European Union (EU) member states, also includes several non-EU countries such as Albania, Bosnia and Herzegovina, Montenegro, Iceland, North Macedonia, Norway, Serbia, Turkey and Ukraine. According to information from the European Council, Moldova and Ukraine joined the mechanism in 2023. It is important to note that this mechanism is not a direct response tool for hybrid warfare. Its primary goal is the organization of humanitarian aid and logistical support, rather than the direct protection of civilians in conflict zones. Nonetheless, in response to the Russian military aggression, the EU initiated an operation under this mechanism. EU member states, along with some cooperating countries, provided Ukraine with assistance in the form of medical supplies, power generators, firefighting equipment, food and water pumps. To strengthen the mechanism, the rescEU capacities were established in 2021. These capacities are used as a reserve of additional European resources dedicated to prevention and can be deployed to provide assistance in extremely challenging situations (Regulation (EU) 2021/836 of the European Parliament and of the Council of 20 May 2021 Amending Decision No 1313/2013/Eu, pp. 1–22, on a Union Civil Protection Mechanism). Through this mechanism, the EU also supported Ukrainian refugees across Europe by providing supplies to various countries and international organizations. According to the European Council, these actions demonstrate the European Union's commitment to broad-based civilian protection, encompassing both prevention and response to international crises (European Council, 2024). However, the EU lacks a direct mechanism to comprehensively support the protection of civilians both below the threshold of hybrid warfare (during the hybrid warfare phase) and in wartime situations. According to Luigi Lonardo, this limitation stems from the nature of these threats, which are difficult to clearly classify and detect. In his view, two legal approaches could potentially harmonize the EU's actions in the future: the application of horizontal emergency provisions or the introduction of constitutional changes (Lonardo, 2021, pp. 1075–1096).

A more direct mechanism for the protection of civilians in hybrid warfare is provided by NATO actions. This issue was specifically addressed in the NATO Policy for the Protection of Civilians, approved during the NATO Summit in Warsaw in July 2016. This policy aims to integrate the protection of civilians into the planning and execution of military operations, which is a fundamental aspect of NATO's strategy in armed conflict. According to the adopted guidelines, the protection of civilians involves all actions aimed at avoiding, minimizing, and mitigating the negative impacts that NATO military operations may have on civilians. When necessary, these actions also involve protecting civilians from physical violence resulting from the conflict and threats posed by other entities by creating a safe and stable environment (NATO, 2016). To ensure the effectiveness and consistency of this approach, NATO developed the Military Concept for the Protection of Civilians, which was approved by member states in June 2018. The primary objective of this concept is to fully integrate the protection of civilians into the planning and execution of NATO military operations. This concept defines the framework and guidelines for the armed forces, enabling them to identify and gain a deeper understanding of the threats that civilians may face during military operations (NATO, 2019). The Military Concept for the Protection of Civilians, as an integral part of NATO's Policy, serves as a foundation for the development of detailed guidelines, such as the Protection of Civilians Handbook developed by Allied Command Operations (ACO). This document not only sets standards but also systematizes NATO's approach to civilian protection, integrating it into the planning and execution of military operations (NATO Allied Command Operations, 2021).

Another mechanism for the protection of civilians in armed conflicts is the United Nations (UN) Policy on the Protection of Civilians in Peacekeeping Operations. The goal of this policy is to provide a conceptual framework, guiding principles, and key considerations for the implementation of civilian protection mandates by UN peacekeeping operations (United Nations Department of Peace Operations, 2023). The UN pursues this objective through a wide range of actions, from the use of force to protect civilians from immediate threats to creating conditions that enable the delivery of humanitarian aid. It also supports security in refugee camps and facilitates the safe return of internally displaced persons and refugees (Global Protection Cluster, 2023). An operational complement to the policy is the *Protection of Civilians in United Nations Peacekeeping: Handbook*, developed by the United Nations Department of Peace Operations (UNDPO) in 2020. This handbook provides detailed guidance and practical tools for implementing the protection of civilians within UN peacekeeping missions (UNDPO, 2020). An additional support mechanism for the UN is the humanitarian cluster system. One of the clusters, the Global Protection Cluster (GPC), developed the Protection Analytical Framework (PAF), which aids in the analysis of protection risks in crisis situations. The PAF is a structured analytical tool that enables a deep understanding of threat dynamics in various humanitarian contexts, thereby facilitating more effective risk management (Figure 5.1). It allows the systematic organization of data and information necessary to conduct a comprehensive assessment of a crisis situation. The use of the PAF can support decision-making within the framework of multi-sectoral and multidisciplinary strategies aimed at reducing protection risks and preventing violations of international legal norms, including humanitarian law and human rights. According to the GPC, its usefulness extends across various humanitarian contexts, including situations involving internally displaced persons, returning refugees and refugees. The flexibility of this tool can facilitate ongoing analysis and adaptation of protection strategies at different stages of a crisis, allowing for dynamic adjustments to protective actions in response to changing conditions (Global Protection Cluster, 2023).

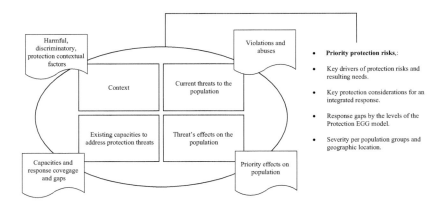

FIGURE 5.1   PAF analytical conclusions

Source: Global Protection Cluster (2023)

The EU Civil Protection Mechanism, NATO's Policy on the Protection of Civilians, and the UN's Policy on the Protection of Civilians, along with all additional solutions that extend these mechanisms, are distinct initiatives implemented by different organizations, even though they operate in parallel. Each of these initiatives aims to protect civilians, especially in crisis situations, but they differ in their scope of actions and priorities. The EU Civil Protection Mechanism primarily focuses on coordinating humanitarian aid and supporting civilians in the case of natural disasters and crises (although it has also been utilized in the context of the war in Ukraine). On the other hand, NATO and UN policies are to a much larger extent focused on the military context, with emphasis on protecting civilians during military or peacekeeping operations. These mechanisms operate within their specific mandates and competencies, meaning that each organization carries out its actions based on defined goals, priorities and resources, targeting different aspects of civilian protection. However, the lack of a comprehensive and holistic approach to civilian protection limits the effectiveness of these mechanisms, leading to gaps in protective actions during crisis situations.

The mechanisms outlined above can serve as important components in the protection of civilians during hybrid wars, yet they cannot replace the fundamental role of international humanitarian law (IHL). The Global Protection Cluster emphasizes that the protection of civilians is an integral part of international law, which, through various declarations, pacts, and conventions, regulates the broad rights of individuals and societies and unequivocally mandates the safeguarding of civilians from all forms of attacks (Global Protection Cluster, 2024). Complementing this legal framework is the international humanitarian law (IHL), which directly addresses the protection of civilians in wars (also referred to as the law of armed conflict or the law of war). International humanitarian law is based on two main sources: treaty law and customary law, similarly to other branches of public international law. The Treaty law, which comprises international agreements, obliges the parties to adhere to specific actions and conditions as stipulated by the agreements. These treaties regulate key aspects related to the protection of persons and objects during armed conflicts and introduce prohibitions on the use of certain types of weapons and methods of warfare. A central element of IHL consists of The Hague Conventions of 1899 and 1907 and the Geneva Conventions of 1949, which were supplemented in 1977 by two additional protocols. The Hague Conventions from the late 19th and early 20th centuries marked a significant step in codifying customary law by regulating the rights and obligations of warring parties and limiting the methods and means of warfare. These agreements primarily focused on the rules governing the conduct of hostilities and are commonly referred to as "Hague Law".

In contrast, the Geneva Conventions of 1949, which address the protection of war victims, concentrate on safeguarding wounded and sick soldiers as well as civilians, forming what is known as "Geneva Law." The two additional protocols adopted in 1977 expanded the protection of war victims and introduced certain modifications to Hague Law, further enhancing the legal framework governing armed conflicts (Ministry of Foreign Affairs in Poland, 2024). In addition to treaty law, customary humanitarian law also serves as a source of rights and obligations for warring parties. It arises from the prolonged practice of states that recognize certain principles as legally binding. A customary legal norm is formed through the repeated practice of states (*usus*) and the belief in its legal obligatory nature (*opinio iuris*). This practice includes actions taken by states in the physical, normative, diplomatic and judicial spheres. Notably, customary IHL has a universal nature and applies to all parties in an armed conflict, including irregular armed groups, regardless of their adherence to treaty law. Although the norms of customary law may be less detailed than those found in treaty law, they often have a foundational character, meaning that many treaty-based principles directly derive from customary norms. The Hague Conventions of 1899 and 1907, as well as the Geneva Conventions of 1949, represent the codification of these customary norms (International Committee of the Red Cross, 2024).

The fundamental principles of international humanitarian law (IHL) form the foundation upon which the entire structure of this legal framework is built, encompassing both treaty and customary norms. These principles are the bedrock of IHL, ensuring that warfare, while inherently destructive, is conducted in a manner that minimizes its impact on the civilian population and adheres to essential standards of humanity (Marcinko et al., 2019, pp. 6–11).

The first and most fundamental principle is the principle of distinction, which imposes an obligation of differentiating between combatants and civilians, as well as between military objectives and civilian objects. Without this principle, humanitarian law would lose its effectiveness, as it would be impossible to ensure the protection of those not involved in hostilities. The primary aim of this principle is to safeguard civilians and civilian property from the consequences of armed conflict, requiring a clear distinction between legitimate military targets and protected objects. An example of an application of this principle is the prohibition against attacking *hors de combat* individuals, such as the wounded, sick, shipwrecked and prisoners of war. While soldiers can be targeted under normal circumstances, this principle mandates that they must not be attacked if they are no longer capable of fighting or have surrendered, which is crucial for ensuring the protection of those who no longer pose a threat (Diakonia, Basic Principles of IHL, 2024).

A further key principle is the principle of humanity, which emphasizes the protection of human life and health and the minimization of human suffering. International humanitarian law prohibits inflicting suffering and destruction that is not necessary to achieve legitimate military objectives. Warring parties must always act in accordance with minimum standards of humanity, which includes the prohibition of unnecessary violence and the obligation to treat those under their control humanely, such as prisoners of war and civilians in occupied territories (Marcinko, 2020). An example of the application of this principle is the prohibition against the use of weapons that cause excessive injury or unnecessary suffering, such as laser weapons that induce blindness (Diakonia, Basic Principles of IHL, 2024).

The principle of proportionality, closely linked to the principle of humanity, aims to balance military interests with the necessity of protecting the civilian population. This means that any military action must be proportionate to the anticipated military advantage and must not cause excessive civilian casualties or damage to civilian property. This principle requires parties to a conflict to refrain from attacking if the consequences of the attack would be disproportionately harmful compared to the expected military gain (Marcinko et al., 2019, pp. 6–10). An example of the application of this principle is a situation where an attack on a military target is legally permissible, but if the harm inflicted on civilians is excessive in relation to the military advantage gained, such an attack would be prohibited (Diakonia, Basic Principles of IHL, 2024).

Finally, the principle of military necessity recognizes that the use of force is permitted only to the extent necessary to achieve military objectives, such as compelling the enemy to surrender. However, this principle also emphasizes that even the necessary use of force must be controlled and limited to avoid causing excessive destruction and suffering beyond what is required for military purposes. An example of this is the use of force in a manner that is necessary to achieve a military objective while simultaneously avoiding unnecessary civilian casualties and the destruction of civilian property (Diakonia, Basic Principles of IHL, 2024).

An important aspect of international humanitarian law is the Martens Clause, which is one of its key principles. The original version of this clause, formulated in 1899, was included in the preamble to the Second Hague Convention thanks to the initiative of Russian lawyer and diplomat Fyodor Martens. It was later reiterated in the preamble to the Fourth Hague Convention of 1907. In its original wording, the Martens Clause emphasized that in situations not covered by treaty provisions, civilians and combatants remain under the protection and authority of the principles of international law, derived from established customs, the principles of humanity, and the dictates of public conscience. In later versions, some of the wording of the Martens Clause was updated to better reflect contemporary realities, but its core essence remained unchanged. This clause establishes the fundamental principle that the absence of specific regulations in International Humanitarian Law does not imply permission for certain actions. In other words, the principle that "everything not explicitly prohibited is allowed" does not apply. In the absence of specific prohibitions, actions must additionally be assessed for their compliance with customary law and the broader principles of humanity and public conscience. The Martens Clause has been included in many key documents, such as the four Geneva Conventions of 1949 (common Article 63/62/142/158), the Additional Protocols I and II of 1977 (Article 1 and preamble), and the 1980 Convention on Certain Conventional Weapons (Article 1). The inclusion of the Martens Clause in these documents, not only in preambles but also in substantive provisions, underscores its status as a binding treaty norm, rather than merely a humanitarian guideline. The significance of the Martens Clause has been affirmed in the jurisprudence of both national and international courts. In the context of assessing the legality of actions taken during World War II, the Martens Clause was invoked in the rulings of courts in Belgium, the Netherlands, Norway, and by the U.S. military tribunal in Nuremberg. In modern times, the constitutional courts in Colombia and Germany have emphasized the fundamental nature of the Martens Clause within International Humanitarian Law. In international jurisprudence, special attention is given to the decisions of the International Criminal Tribunal for the former Yugoslavia and the advisory opinion of the International Court of Justice on nuclear weapons, both of which underscore the universal and undeniable significance of the Martens Clause (Widłak, 2012, pp. 173–186).

International humanitarian law (IHL) is not fully effective as a tool in the context of hybrid warfare. Even in traditional armed conflicts, it is often not adhered to, and in the case of hybrid wars, it faces additional challenges. Not only is it sometimes disregarded, but it also fails to cover certain aspects that are not evident in the classical definition of war. Kashi Komijani emphasizes that IHL faces significant challenges in the event of modern conflicts, such as hybrid wars. Although the Geneva Conventions assert that the type of weapons used and the manner in which hostilities are conducted do not affect the application of IHL provisions, certain actions—such as cyberattacks or the operations of irregular armed groups—may not fit neatly into the traditional definitions of armed conflict. An example of this is a cyberattack that leads to massive destruction or loss of life, which may not necessarily be classified as an armed conflict in the traditional sense. This creates difficulties in categorizing such actions and introduces uncertainty regarding the application of international humanitarian law (Komijani, 2023, pp. 3–15).

Another issue, as noted by Komijani, is the geographical and functional scope of IHL application. Traditionally, IHL is applied within specific territories and in the context of clearly defined armed conflicts. However, hybrid wars, which may involve actions in cyberspace, disinformation campaigns, cognitive operations, economic attacks and activities in the space domain, blur the boundaries within which humanitarian law should be applied. This ambiguity leads to a lack of clear answers and opens the door to potential abuses and uncertainties in the application of the law (Komijani, 2023, pp. 4–14).

In traditional wars, it is relatively easy to identify the parties involved in the conflict. However, in hybrid wars, non-state actors often play a significant role and are informally supported by states. The challenge lies in determining when the actions of such entities can be attributed to a state, which is crucial for the application of IHL. In some cases, it can be difficult to establish whether certain actions, such as attacks carried out by paramilitary groups, are initiated or supported by a state, complicating the classification of the conflict and the application of relevant international law provisions. Moreover, hybrid wars often blur the line between military and civilian targets, further complicating the situation. Attacks on critical infrastructure, such as energy, water or telecommunications systems, can have a direct impact on the civilian population. In this context, adhering to the principle of distinction between civilian and military targets becomes particularly challenging, leading to violations of the fundamental principles of IHL. Ultimately, as Komijani assesses, although IHL presumes accountability for violations of humanitarian law, enforcing these rules in the context of hybrid and cyber warfare faces significant obstacles. The difficulties in tracing perpetrators, the lack of effective international oversight mechanisms, and issues related to state sovereignty make the enforcement of the law in these cases exceptionally complex (Komijani, 2023, pp. 9–15).

Aurel Sari shares a similar view to Komijani, highlighting several key issues related to the functioning of international humanitarian law (IHL) and international law more broadly in the context of hybrid wars. According to Sari, IHL is not effectively equipped to regulate hybrid warfare. For example, there are no clear criteria that define when a cyberattack reaches a level that allows the application of IHL (noting that a cyberattack can manifest and result in tangible harm to civilians). Furthermore, Sari points out that states often manipulate international law to justify their actions, which, in reality, contradict the spirit of humanitarian law. An example of this is Russia's argumentation regarding the annexation of Crimea, where legal justifications were used to legitimize aggressive actions. Such behaviour undermines trust in international law and weakens its authority. States can exploit gaps and ambiguities in international law to pursue their interests while avoiding accountability for actions that violate international norms. This creates a situation where, instead of protecting those affected by conflict, IHL can be instrumentalised to support aggressive policies. Sari notes that an increasing number of states are retreating from multilateralism, favouring unilateral actions, which weakens international institutions responsible for enforcing humanitarian law. These institutions, such as the International Criminal Court, are becoming less effective in holding violators of IHL accountable, leading to a rise in impunity among states that breach these norms (Sari, 2019). An example of this can be found in the latest report by the UN Security Council Secretary-General on the protection of civilians in armed conflicts in 2023. The report indicates that, while there has been some progress in holding perpetrators accountable for international crimes, these efforts are minimal compared to the vast scale of the impact that wars have on civilian populations (ONZ, 2024).

Sari argues that the existing humanitarian law not only requires the adaptation and updating of its provisions but also a shift in the approach to its enforcement. In his view, contemporary forms of conflict, particularly hybrid wars, challenge the effectiveness of current norms, necessitating the introduction of a resilience model that would better align the law with modern warfare realities and enhance its capacity to protect conflict victims. In this context, Sari proposes a resilience-based approach as a tool to strengthen international humanitarian law (IHL). In Sari's framework, the resilience model consists of two key aspects: the systemic resilience of international law and the enhancement of the resilience of societies and states. The first aspect involves the adaptation and evolution of IHL provisions in response to new forms of warfare, such as cyberattacks or disinformation campaigns, and the ability to absorb disruptions. This means that the legal system must be resilient to manipulation and instrumentalisation by states and other actors who may exploit legal loopholes to pursue their interests. In the second aspect, Sari suggests that humanitarian law should be closely integrated with military and operational practices, which requires the training and preparation of armed forces to act in accordance with IHL norms, even in the context of complex and hybrid forms of warfare. This also involves enhancing the capacity for rapid response and societal adaptation, meaning that societies and states must be prepared for swift changes in the nature of conflict, including sudden escalations or the emergence of new threats. To achieve this, it is essential to strengthen cooperation between states and develop early warning and information-sharing mechanisms, ensuring that humanitarian law can be effectively applied in real-time.

In order for the resilience model to work effectively, Sari highlights some practical steps:

- States should update their military doctrines and security policies to incorporate the specific characteristics of hybrid warfare and the role that International Humanitarian Law (IHL) plays in regulating such conflicts. In particular, it is essential to develop strategies that can be applied in the context of cyber warfare, information warfare, and other irregular forms of aggression.

- It is crucial that both policymakers and military personnel receive appropriate training in the application of International Humanitarian Law (IHL) in modern conflicts. Education should cover not only the fundamentals of humanitarian law but also its application in a rapidly evolving combat environment, along with an understanding of the threats posed by hybrid warfare.
- The resilience model of International Humanitarian Law (IHL) requires collaboration between states, international organizations and other global actors. Establishing joint information-sharing platforms, supporting initiatives for the harmonization of regulations, and cooperating within international institutions can strengthen the IHL system, making it more resilient to new challenges.

Sari also suggests the necessity of developing new legal instruments that better align with the contemporary realities of hybrid warfare. These could include, for example, additional protocols to existing conventions that clarify the application of International Humanitarian Law (IHL) in contexts such as cyber warfare or disinformation, as well as mechanisms for rapid legal response to violations (Sari, 2019, pp. 4–6, 15–19).

All of the aforementioned mechanisms for the protection of civilians, despite differences in their approaches, strive toward a common goal: ensuring the safety of civilians at both the operational and formal levels. Unfortunately, as highlighted by international reports from humanitarian organizations and governments in countries affected by armed conflicts and hybrid wars, civilians continue to pay the highest price. According to Karolina MacLachlan, it is estimated that around 100 civilians die each day as a result of warfare, underscoring the insufficiency of current solutions and the urgent need for more effective implementation and enforcement of civilian protection mechanisms (MacLachlan, 2022).

The significant inadequacy of current efforts to protect civilians is highlighted in the aforementioned UN Security Council Secretary-General's Report on the Protection of Civilians in Armed Conflict. The report emphasizes that the situation regarding civilian protection in 2023 was particularly alarming, as hundreds of thousands of civilians were killed or seriously injured due to both deliberate and unintentional attacks, as well as actions deemed legal under international humanitarian law. The United Nations recorded at least 33,443 civilian deaths in 2023, representing a 72% increase as compared to 2022. The proportion of women and children killed has doubled and tripled, respectively, as compared to 2022. In 2023, women accounted for 40% of civilian deaths, while children made up 30%. Seventy percent of all recorded fatalities occurred in the Occupied Palestinian Territories and Israel, making this conflict the deadliest for civilians in 2023. In October 2023, attacks by Hamas and other armed groups on Israel resulted in the deaths of approximately 1,200 people, the majority of whom were civilians. These events followed widespread destruction and casualties caused by Israeli military operations in Gaza, which, according to the Gaza Ministry of Health, led to the deaths of 21,672 Palestinians and injured 56,165 individuals, the majority of which were women and children.

In addition to the Israeli-Palestinian conflict, significant civilian casualties were also reported in the Democratic Republic of the Congo, Mali, Mozambique, Myanmar, Somalia, South Sudan, Sudan, Syria and other locations. In the Democratic Republic of the Congo, over 219,000 conflict-related casualties were reported, while in Mali, 1,300 civilians were killed in security incidents. In Myanmar, the last quarter of 2023 saw an escalation in the ongoing conflict, including airstrikes, shelling and the burning of villages. Violence in north-eastern Nigeria claimed 4,533 civilian lives in 2023, and over 1,400 civilians were killed or injured in attacks in Somalia. In South Sudan, 848 incidents were recorded in 2023, resulting in 1,527 civilian deaths, 1,040 injuries, and 597 abductions. In Sudan, following the outbreak of conflict in April between the Sudanese Armed Forces and the Rapid Support Forces, approximately 12,260 people were killed and 33,000 were injured, primarily due to attacks on residential areas using explosive weapons, executions and sexual violence, particularly against women and girls. In Syria, at least 556 civilians were killed as a result of conflict-related violence. In Ukraine, following the Russian Federation's invasion, 1,958 civilians were killed and 6,572 were injured in 2023.

In 2023, nearly 30,000 civilians were killed or injured due to the use of explosive weapons in six major conflicts: in Gaza, Myanmar, Sudan, Syria, Ukraine and Yemen. Civilians accounted for 90% of the casualties when explosive weapons were used in populated areas. The use of explosive weapons in residential areas was the primary cause of civilian casualties in Sudan and Ukraine, where entire cities and towns were devastated by such attacks. A significant number of civilian casualties also resulted from the use of Improvised Explosive Devices (IEDs) in Afghanistan, Burkina Faso, Cameroon, the Democratic Republic of the Congo, Mali, Niger, Nigeria, the Philippines, Somalia, Syria and other locations.

Armed conflicts in 2023 had a severe impact on critical infrastructure supplying electricity, water and healthcare. In Burkina Faso, the destruction of 48 water infrastructure facilities left over 149,000 people without access to water. In Gaza, warfare rendered 23 hospitals and

56 healthcare centres inoperative, damaged 370 educational facilities, and destroyed 11 bakeries. In Myanmar, bridges, schools, hospitals and power plants were targeted. In Sudan, water, sewage and electrical networks, as well as medical facilities, were destroyed. In Syria, damage to water infrastructure affected access to water for millions of people. In Ukraine, repeated attacks on power plants and transformer stations disrupted electricity and water supplies, and 103 medical facilities and 294 educational institutions were destroyed or damaged. Additionally, massive floods following the destruction of the Kakhovka dam damaged 37,000 homes and disrupted water supplies for 1 million people. Critical infrastructure in Ukraine was also targeted by cyberattacks, highlighting the need to protect civilians from such actions.

Another significant threat to civilians arising from war was landmines and unexploded ordnance. These were the second leading cause of civilian casualties in Afghanistan, killing and maiming over 60 people per month, primarily children. In Colombia, 96 casualties from landmines and unexploded ordnance were recorded in 2023. These hazards threatened approximately 600,000 people in 146 municipalities, severely hampering socio-economic activities. In Myanmar, the number of landmine victims increased by 270% as compared to 2022, with 1,052 people killed or injured, including children who accounted for 20% of the victims. In Ukraine, civilian casualties from landmines and unexploded ordnance increased by 16%, causing 116 deaths and 383 injuries. In Yemen, 183 incidents were reported, leading to 189 casualties, including 132 fatalities.

In 2023, concerns also grew regarding the involvement of private military and security companies (PMCs) in violations of international humanitarian law and human rights. The Montreux Document on Pertinent International Legal Obligations and Good Practices for States related to Operations of Private Military and Security Companies during Armed Conflict (Montreux Document Forum, 2008) and the International Code of Conduct for Private Security Service Providers (The Responsible Security Association, 2010), define best practices, emphasizing the application of existing international law to the activities of private military and security companies (PMCs). Since then, the employment of PMCs in conflicts has significantly increased, and their role has evolved in some cases to conducting military operations alongside or on behalf of states. With this evolution, concerns have grown regarding the potential involvement of PMCs in violations of international humanitarian law.

By mid-2023, 110 million people worldwide had been displaced due to conflicts, persecution, violence or human rights violations. 60% of these were internally displaced persons. The war in Sudan resulted in

6 million new internal displacements and 1.4 million refugees. In the Democratic Republic of the Congo, 2.9 million new displacements were recorded. In Gaza, the conflict forcibly displaced 1.9 million people, representing 85% of the population. Other conflicts, such as those in Colombia, Myanmar, Azerbaijan, Nigeria, the Sahel, Syria and Ukraine, also contributed to an unprecedented level of displacement.

In 2023, over 2,370 incidents of violence against healthcare workers and patients were recorded across 21 conflicts, with the most significant impact in Palestine, Myanmar, Sudan and Ukraine. More than 700 healthcare workers were killed, and hundreds of others were injured, kidnapped or arrested. In Gaza, the war drastically reduced the number of operational hospitals from 36 to 13. In Sudan, less than one-third of medical facilities in conflict areas were functioning by the end of 2023. In Ukraine, 18 medical facilities were destroyed, and 85 were damaged. In Burkina Faso, 402 medical centres were closed, affecting the safety and well-being of 3.6 million people.

War remained a major factor in profound food insecurity, forcing people off land and grazing areas for animals, destroying food stocks and agricultural resources, and disrupting food systems and markets. As a result, food prices have risen, household purchasing power has declined and access to supplies needed for food preparation, including water and fuel, has decreased. In 2023, some 117 million people experienced severe hunger in 19 countries or territories affected by war, often at a catastrophic level Integrated Food Security Phase Classification Phase 5 (IPCinfo, 2024).

The consequences of war include the degradation or permanent destruction of the natural environment, which is of key importance from the perspective of civilian protection. In Gaza, damage to water infrastructure led to sewage leaks into residential areas and the sea, worsening environmental conditions and the quality of soil and groundwater. In Sudan, the use of explosive weapons damaged water, industrial and energy infrastructure, further contributing to environmental contamination. In Ukraine, airstrikes on fuel infrastructure caused air and groundwater pollution, and the destruction of agro-industrial facilities increased the risk of civilian exposure to hazardous substances. The conflict also contributed to the degradation of biodiversity and natural ecosystems. The destruction of the Kakhovka dam resulted in the washing of chemicals and hazardous materials into the Black Sea, affecting river morphology, pollution levels, and the destruction of habitats.

In 2023, over 11,300 children were killed or maimed in armed conflicts, primarily in Afghanistan, the Central Sahel, Sudan, Syria, Ukraine, and the Occupied Palestinian Territory. The number of attacks on schools and hospitals increased, depriving children of access to education and healthcare. Children continued to suffer from recruitment, abductions, rape, and sexual violence, further exacerbating their already dire situation.

In 2023, there was a significant increase in incidents of sexual violence in armed conflicts worldwide, particularly against women and girls, who accounted for 95% of the victims. The number of UN-verified cases of conflict-related sexual violence rose by 50% compared to 2022. In the Central African Republic, over 3,169 cases of gender-based violence were recorded, with women making up 50% of the victims and girls 46%. In the Democratic Republic of the Congo, 733 cases were documented, including rape, gang rape and sexual slavery, affecting 509 women, 205 girls, 18 men and 1 boy. In Sudan, at least 118 cases of conflict-related sexual violence were reported. Sexual violence was also prevalent in other regions, including Myanmar, Somalia, Israel, Syria, Palestine, Ukraine and others. This violence often accompanied displacement, family separations, and shortages of essential goods. Due to insufficient funding for support programs, only 29% of victims had access to necessary medical and psychosocial assistance within the first 72 hours.

In Sudan, at least 118 cases of conflict-related sexual violence were reported. Sexual violence was also present in other regions, such as Myanmar, Somalia, Israel, Syria, Palestine, Ukraine, and elsewhere. This violence often accompanied displacement, family separations, and shortages of essential goods. Due to insufficient funding for support programs, only 29% of victims had access to the necessary medical and psychosocial assistance within the first 72 hours.

In 2023, people with disabilities were particularly affected by armed conflicts worldwide. In Afghanistan, they faced barriers to accessing aid; in Myanmar and Gaza, they often could not evacuate due to destruction or lack of accessible transport, putting them in direct danger. In north-eastern Nigeria, people with disabilities were killed while remaining in conflict areas or under the control of armed groups, and women with intellectual disabilities were victims of killings based on accusations of witchcraft. In Ukraine, the number of people with disabilities increased from 300,000 to approximately 3 million, primarily due to the use of explosive weapons. In many conflict zones, such as Gaza, Sudan and Ukraine, people with disabilities had limited access to medical care and rehabilitation and were also exposed to future risks associated with unexploded ordnance.

In 2023, the International Committee of the Red Cross (ICRC) registered 40,000 new cases of missing persons and was handling over 212,000 cases, the majority of which were related to armed conflicts. This represents the highest annual registration number, largely due to the conflict in Ukraine, where approximately 23,000 people went missing (UNSC, 2024).

The total number of civilians who were affected in some way in 2023 across 25 major armed conflicts, including hybrid wars (such as those killed, injured, displaced, victims of sexual violence, victims of landmines and unexploded ordnance, missing persons, etc.), amounts to approximately 150 million civilians. This staggering figure clearly demonstrates that the protection of civilians in conflicts and wars, including in hybrid warfare, still requires significant effort and improvement.

The analysis of the report reveals certain differences between traditional conflicts and hybrid warfare. In traditional wars, we often see large-scale military operations that can lead to mass civilian casualties, typically resulting from bombings, artillery shelling or urban combat. In contrast, in hybrid wars, the scale of direct military operations may be smaller, but civilian casualties often result from actions deliberately targeting critical infrastructure. These actions lead to long-term consequences, such as the lack of access to essential services, which over time can have equally severe impacts. However, it is important to note that, considering the war in Ukraine and the conflict in the Middle East as examples of hybrid wars, the hybrid nature of these conflicts differs in terms of operational complexity and advancement.

In traditional wars, the primary objective is often territory or the enemy's military forces. In hybrid wars, however, the focus is on destroying civilian infrastructure, with the aim of destabilizing the functioning of society.

Hybrid wars are often characterized by the asymmetric use of force, where one side employs unconventional means to minimize direct military confrontation while maximizing cognitive impact on the civilian population. In traditional conflicts, such as full-scale wars, civilian casualties are easier to estimate due to visible and direct military actions. However, in hybrid wars, the number of casualties and the impact on civilians may be underestimated because not all effects are immediately apparent.

Given the findings so far, it is clear that the hybrid nature of wars introduces new humanitarian challenges that call into question the ability of international humanitarian law to fully protect civilian populations (UNSC, 2024). Alexander Kolb and others point out that one of the main issues with humanitarian law in the context of the war in Ukraine is the inconsistency between national and international regulations, leading to legal gaps and hindering the effective legal protection of conflict victims. An example of this is the difference in terminology, such as between the term "refugee" in international law and "temporarily displaced person" in Ukrainian legislation. These inconsistencies create practical difficulties in enforcing the rights of conflict victims, particularly in the international arena. Another issue is the improper application of international law, as seen in the use of the Ukrainian criminal code by the separatist republics of Luhansk People's Republic (LPR) and Donetsk People's

Republic (DPR), which prosecute Ukrainian soldiers for general criminal offenses without recognizing them as prisoners of war. This practice contradicts international legal norms governing the status of prisoners of war and is an example of the misapplication of law. Additionally, as noted by Kolb and others, Ukraine faces challenges related to the dualism and monism in the relationship between international and domestic law. In practice, Ukraine seems to operate on the border between these two theories, leading to difficulties in fulfilling international obligations. Additionally, the challenge of implementing international norms in the context of hybrid warfare, as seen in Ukraine, highlights the difficulties in adapting international humanitarian law to new forms of armed conflict. In this context, there is a need to redefine certain humanitarian law norms to effectively protect the victims of such conflicts. Kolb and others confirm what the analyses presented in the earlier sections demonstrate that in the face of the challenges posed by hybrid warfare, it is also necessary to rethink and adapt existing international legal norms to the new realities of armed conflict (Kolb et al., 2021, pp. 334–349).

In concluding this section, it may be worthwhile to highlight the concept of "mirror imaging," a cognitive bias where analysts or decision-makers project their own beliefs, experiences, and values onto others. This can lead to errors in assessing the motivations and strategies of an adversary (Witlin, 2008, pp. 89–90). In the context of hybrid warfare, adapting civilian protection systems and international humanitarian law to the realities of modern conflicts requires a focused understanding of the adversary's specific tactics. Mirror imaging, the assumption that the opponent operates under similar principles and values—such as the protection of civilian populations—can lead to significant analytical errors. Such assumptions may result in ineffective protection strategies that fail to account for the unique nature of hybrid warfare, where attacks on infrastructure and cognitive operations may be the adversary's primary objectives, rather than traditional military targets.

ASSESSMENT OF THREAT PERCEPTION AND THE EFFECTIVENESS OF CIVILIAN PROTECTION STRATEGIES IN HYBRID WARFARE: RESULTS OF A SURVEY CONDUCTED AMONG CIVILIANS IN THE WAR ZONE IN UKRAINE

The conducted analyses clearly highlight significant challenges associated with civilian protection in the context of hybrid wars. In response to these challenges, the authors decided to delve deeper into the issue. To this end, a study was conducted based on the methodology described in Appendix 1. The survey, which consisted of 144 questions, allowed an

TABLE 5.1   Age structure of respondents

Age Range	Number of Respondents	Percentage Share
Below 18 years	1	2.5
18–29	4	10
30–39	9	22.5
40–49	16	40
50–59	2	5
60–70	4	10
Above 70	4	10

Source: Own study

in-depth analysis and capture of the complex aspects of the experiences and perceptions of respondents in the context of hybrid warfare. Despite limitations related to the sample size, it is important to emphasize that the study was conducted exclusively with civilians directly affected by the war in Ukraine. The data collected and analysed may serve as a foundation for further research, which could contribute to building both systemic and individual as well as societal resilience to hybrid wars.

The study included 40 respondents from the war zone in Ukraine, of whom 87.5% were women. The predominance of women in the study is expected due to the characteristics of the target group. Table 5.1 presents the age structure of the respondents.

The respondents primarily came from rural areas (33.3%) and cities with populations over 500,000 (30.8%). Additionally, other areas represented included towns with populations up to 50,000 (12.8%), towns with populations between 50,000 and 150,000 (7.7%), and cities with populations over 150,000 but less than 500,000 (12.8%).

The respondents primarily had higher education (63.2%), with others having completed secondary education (18.4%) and vocational or technical education (18.4%).

Among the respondents, 11 individuals reported having various disabilities:

- mobility impairment (one person),
- respiratory and cardiovascular diseases (three people),
- visual impairment and deafness (one person),
- hearing and/or speech impairment (one person),
- genitourinary system diseases (three people),
- cancer (three people),
- obesity (one person),

Population protection in hybrid warfare 311

TABLE 5.2 Summary of respondents' perceptions of life-threatening danger or long-term health damage due to threats

Threat	Perception of Life-Threatening Danger	Belief in Permanent Health Damage
Hunger	12	12
Thirst	11	11
Injuries	12	11
Diseases	14	15
Excessively high temperature	4	7
Excessively low temperature	8	12
Other	13	13

Source: Own study

- neurological diseases, including neurodegenerative conditions (multiple sclerosis [MS], cerebral palsy [CP], stroke, epilepsy, Alzheimer's disease and dementia, Parkinson's disease) (three people).

As a result of the materialization of hybrid warfare threats, 32 respondents reported experiencing negative effects. In 25% of cases, hunger was reported, 18.8% experienced thirst, and 9.4% sustained injuries. The most common effect, reported in 34.4% of cases, was illness. Additionally, 18.8% of respondents suffered from excessive heat, and 9.4% were too cold. The range of effects from hybrid warfare, based on the "Six Ways to Die" methodology, was expanded by respondents to include extreme stress, nervous breakdowns, exhaustion, insomnia, fear for the safety of their children, and the death of loved ones. Table 5.2 presents data indicating whether the respondents who experienced these effects believed that their lives were at risk or that they were exposed to permanent health damage.

Respondents also reported that incidents had occurred in their surroundings where others suffered due to threats posed by hybrid warfare. In 41.9% of cases, the negative effects were related to hunger and injuries, in 29% to thirst, and in 61.6% to illness. Adverse effects associated with excessive heat were noted in 6.5% of cases, while 22.6% were related to the experience of excessive cold. What is more, respondents indicated that people around them experienced psychological disorders and fear. In several cases, respondents mentioned incidents of heart attacks, the death of loved ones, or the loss of property. Table 5.3 summarizes the data showing whether the respondents who observed these effects believed that they posed a threat to the lives of others or exposed them to long-term health damage.

312   Civil Protection and Domestic Security in Hybrid Warfare

TABLE 5.3   Summary of respondents' perceptions of threats to the lives or long-term health of others due to the occurrence of hazards

Threat	Perception of Life-Threatening Danger	Belief in Permanent Health Damage
Hunger	14	16
Thirst	12	11
Injuries	21	19
Diseases	19	20
Excessively high temperature	5	7
Excessively low temperature	10	7
Other	7	5

Source: Own study

Respondents (20 individuals) identified the causes of hunger they experienced as a result of threats arising from hybrid warfare. The threats were categorized into three groups:

- natural threats,
- human-induced threats – military,
- human-induced threats – non-military.

Respondents indicated that the primary causes of hunger were natural events, such as extreme weather conditions (27.9%), and human-induced events, specifically military actions (33.3%). The list of causes of hunger in this category also includes the need for evacuation and missile shelling.

In the category of human-induced military threats, respondents indicated that the causes of hunger were primarily direct ground military operations, such as gunfire, accounting for 70% of cases, and direct aerial military attacks, such as missile strikes, bombings, and other air-based combat actions, accounting for 75% of cases. To a lesser extent, hunger was caused by special operations, such as landmines and other tactics aimed at creating traps and obstacles, in 40% of cases, and the use of chemical, biological, radiological weapons, or toxic substance leaks in 25% of cases.

In the category of human-induced non-military threats, respondents identified that the dominant causes of hunger are attacks on critical infrastructure, such as sabotage or assaults on essential services like power plants, water systems, communication networks, and hospitals, which accounted for 52.6% of cases. Other significant causes included disinformation and propaganda (36.8% of cases) and psychological operations, such as actions aimed at manipulating public perception and attitudes, influencing morale, and behaviour (31.6% of cases). To a lesser

Population protection in hybrid warfare 313

extent, the causes of hunger in this category were attributed to terror-ist attacks (21.1% of cases), social and cultural threats, such as stoking social tensions, reinforcing divisions, and exploiting cultural differences to incite conflict (21.1% of cases), and economic threats, including the use of economic instruments like sanctions, embargoes, and market manipulation to weaken the enemy's economy (15.8% of cases). Only 5.3% of respondents cited cyberattacks as a cause of hunger. Notably, no respondent identified international law as a means of exerting political pressure or achieving strategic advantage.

Respondents identifying the consequences of threats that led to the experience of hunger pointed out several physical consequences. These included the blocking of access to food in 52.9% of cases, loss of food due to deliberate destruction, and forced migration in search of food in 47.1% of cases. Additionally, the consequences involved an increase in malnutrition and hunger-related diseases in 29.4% of cases, as well as physical violence and theft in 5.9% of cases.

In the area of non-physical consequences that led to the experience of hunger, respondents highlighted stress and anxiety related to food availability in 90.5% of cases, weakening of social bonds, such as within families or among neighbours, in 23.8% of cases, and the intensification of local conflicts without the use of violence in 14.3% of cases.

The final area of consequences examined in relation to the material-ization of threats leading to the experience of hunger involved the impli-cations for particularly vulnerable individuals (Table 5.4).

Individuals suffering from hunger most commonly felt this sensation for up to 24 hours (50% of respondents). The remaining respondents reported experiencing hunger for up to 48 hours (22.2%), up to 72 hours (5.6%), and more than 72 hours (22.2%).

Respondents indicated that among the systemic actions taken in response to the events that caused them to suffer from hunger, humani-tarian actions were the most dominant, such as organizing and distribut-ing food packages, ready-to-eat meals, and other forms of food assistance

TABLE 5.4 Experience of hunger among particularly vulnerable groups due to the materialization of hybrid warfare threats

Impact	Number of Respondents	Percentage
Impact of hunger on the elderly	10	55.6
Impact of hunger on sick persons	4	22.2
Impact of hunger on the persons with disabilities	8	44.4
Impact of hunger on pregnant women	5	27.8
Impact of hunger on children	15	83.3

Source: Own study

TABLE 5.5   Assessment of the effectiveness of systemic actions in response to the experience of hunger among the civilian population

Assessment	Number of Indications
Highly ineffective	9
Rather ineffective	2
Partially effective	6
Rather effective	1
Very effective	0
No effective systemic actions have been taken	2

Source: Own study

(50% of responses). Additionally, protective actions were noted, such as directing individuals to shelters (33.3% of responses), rescue operations, such as deploying rescuers, organizing evacuations from areas affected by hunger and firefighting (22.2% of responses), medical actions, such as providing medical care for hunger-related illnesses (16.7% of responses), and informational actions (11.1% of responses). What is more, in a few cases respondents mentioned legal actions, such as ensuring the respect for the rights of civilians in armed conflict, and actions related to psychological support. Furthermore, none of the respondents indicated preventive measures, such as training related to hunger situations during war. Table 5.5 presents the results of the assessment of the effectiveness of systemic actions taken in response to the experience of hunger among the civilian population.

Respondents indicated that the most common method of disseminating information about systemic actions was through digital means, such as social media, websites, and news portals, accounting for 65.2% of responses. To a lesser extent, respondents gained information from traditional media (radio, television) and alarm and warning systems (SMS alert systems), which were mentioned by 30.4% of respondents. Additionally, respondents pointed to printed materials (4.3%), direct communication (13%), and social and religious organizations (17.4%).

Among the individual actions taken in response to the event that caused respondents to experience hunger, the following were mentioned:

- Physical Security Actions – Physical Protection: For example, self-evacuation to a safe shelter with access to food (52.6%),
- Health-Related Actions – Health and Medical Care: For example, access to basic healthcare, medicines, medical supplies, hunger management, first aid training, and medical care during wartime (21.1%),

Population protection in hybrid warfare 315

- Psychological Security Actions – Psychological Support: For example, stress and trauma management, emotional and psychological support during times of hunger (10.5%),
- Economic Security Actions – Financial Stability: For example, maintaining financial stability, access to resources necessary for survival (26.3%),
- Food Security Actions – Access to Food: For example, ensuring access to sufficient food and water (21.1%),
- Housing Security Actions – Housing and Shelter: For example, providing safe shelter (26.3%),
- Digital and Information Security Actions – Cybersecurity and Information: For example, protection against cyber threats, access to reliable information (5.3%),
- Social Security Actions – Community and Cooperation: For example, maintaining social cohesion, community support, protection against isolation (15.8%),
- Mobility Security Actions – Mobility and Organized Evacuation: For example, the ability to move safely, organized evacuation when necessary (10.5%),
- Legal Security Actions – Legal Protection: For example, access to legal protection and respect for human rights (5.3%),
- Actions to Ensure the Security of Particularly Vulnerable Groups: For example, protection and support for elderly, sick, disabled individuals, pregnant women, and children (10.5%).

Table 5.6 shows the results of an evaluation of the effectiveness of individual actions taken in response to the civilian population experiencing hunger.

Respondents indicated that in most cases, they required special resources, such as medication supplies, specialized food and additional

TABLE 5.6   Assessment of the effectiveness of individual actions in response to the experience of hunger among the civilian population

Assessment	Number of Indications
Highly ineffective	4
Rather ineffective	2
Partially effective	10
Rather effective	3
Very effective	0
No effective systemic actions have been taken	0

Source: Own study

316   Civil Protection and Domestic Security in Hybrid Warfare

training, in order to implement individual actions that could prevent the recurrence of the situation that led to hunger. This need was expressed by 81% of the respondents.

Experience of hybrid warfare: experience of thirst

Respondents (ten individuals) identified the causes of experiencing thirst as a result of threats arising from hybrid warfare. The threats were categorized into three groups:

- natural threats,
- human-induced threats – military,
- human-induced threats – non-military.

Respondents identified the main causes of suffering of thirst as primarily natural events, such as extreme weather conditions (30%) and human-induced events, particularly military actions (20%). The list of causes for experiencing thirst in this category also includes fleeing from war and power outages.

In the category of human-induced military threats, respondents indicated that the causes of suffering thirst included direct ground military operations (46.2% of cases) and direct aerial military attacks, such as missile strikes, bombings, and other air-based combat actions (53.8% of cases). To a lesser extent, thirst was caused by special operations (30.8% of cases) and the use of chemical, biological or radiological weapons (15.4% of cases). Additionally, respondents pointed to restrictions on movement and the lack of access to purchasing drinking water.

In the category of human-induced non-military threats, respondents identified the dominant causes of experiencing thirst as attacks on critical infrastructure (77.8% of cases), disinformation and propaganda (44.4% of cases), and social and cultural threats, such as stoking social tensions and reinforcing divisions (33.3% of cases). To a lesser extent, the causes of thirst in this category included terrorist attacks (22.2% of cases). Only 11.1% of respondents cited cyberattacks, economic threats, and political manipulation as causes of thirst. No respondents indicated legal actions or psychological operations as threats leading to thirst during the hybrid war.

Respondents identifying the consequences of threats that led to the experience of thirst pointed out several physical consequences. These included forced migration in search of access to drinking water in 54.5% of cases, and dehydration and related illnesses in 36.4% of cases. None of the respondents indicated physical violence or theft as consequences of experiencing thirst.

TABLE 5.7 Perception of thirst by groups particularly vulnerable due to the materialization of threats caused by hybrid warfare

Impact	Number of Respondents	Percentage Share
Impact of thirst on the elderly	1	10
Impact of thirst on the sick	1	10
Impact of thirst on people with disabilities	1	10
Impact of hunger on pregnant women	1	10
Impact of thirst on children	6	60

Source: Own study

In the area of non-physical consequences that led to the experience of thirst, respondents highlighted stress and anxiety related to water availability in 63.6% of cases, the exacerbation of local non-physical conflicts in 18.2% of cases, and the weakening of social bonds, such as within families or among neighbours, in 23.8% of cases. Additionally, 9.1% of respondents mentioned financial problems that made drinking water too expensive or difficult to access. None of the respondents indicated the intensification of non-violent local conflicts. Moreover, those experiencing thirst expressed fear for themselves, their children, and their parents, and noted that the lack of water made it impossible to prepare meals for infants.

The last examined area of the consequences arising from the materialization of threats that led to the sensation of thirst comprised implications for particularly vulnerable groups (Table 5.7).

In most cases those suffering from thirst had to endure it for up to 24 hours (66.7% of respondents). The remaining respondents reported enduring thirst for up to 48 hours (22.2%), and more than 72 hours (11.1%).

The respondents indicated that among the systemic actions taken in response to the event that caused them to suffer from thirst, humanitarian efforts, such as organizing and distributing food packages, ready-to-eat meals, and other forms of food assistance, held a dominant position (44.4% of responses). Additionally, search operations were noted by 33.3% of respondents, and actions focused on ensuring the safety of particularly vulnerable groups, such as the elderly, sick, disabled, pregnant women, and children, were mentioned in 22.2% of cases. In a few instances, respondents also pointed to medical, informational and protective actions. None of the respondents identified rescue operations, preventive measures or legal actions as examples of systemic tools used to address the issue of thirst experienced by the civilian population. Table 5.8 presents the results of the assessment of the effectiveness

TABLE 5.8   Assessment of the effectiveness of systemic actions in response to the perception of thirst by the civilian population

Assessment	Number of Indications
Highly ineffective	2
Rather ineffective	1
Partially effective	5
Rather effective	3
Very effective	0
No effective systemic actions have been taken	0

Source: Own study

of systemic actions taken in response to the experience of thirst among civilians.

Respondents indicated that digital means, such as social media, websites, and news portals, 54.5% of indications, and direct communication (45.5%) were the most common means of disseminating news about systemic measures. Respondents did not indicate other channels for obtaining information about systemic measures to counter thirst among the civilian population.

Among the individual actions taken in response to an event that caused respondents to feel thirsty were listed:

- Physical Security Actions – Physical Protection: For example, self-evacuation to a safe shelter with access to food (50%),
- Health-Related Actions – Health and Medical Care: For example, access to basic healthcare, medicines, medical supplies, hunger management, first aid training, and medical care during wartime (20%),
- Economic Security Actions – Financial Stability: For example, financial stability, access to resources necessary for survival (30%),
- Food Security Actions – Access to Food: For example, access to sufficient food and water (10%),
- Mobility Security Actions – Mobility and Organized Evacuation: For example, the ability to move safely, organized evacuation when necessary (10%).

Table 5.9 shows the results of evaluating the effectiveness of individual actions in response to the civilian population's feelings of thirst.

Respondents indicated that in most cases, they required special resources, such as medication, supplies, specialized food, and additional training as necessary to implement individual actions that could prevent

TABLE 5.9 Assessment of the effectiveness of individual actions in response to thirst experienced by the civilian population

Assessment	Number of Indications
Highly ineffective	1
Rather ineffective	2
Partially effective	4
Rather effective	3
Very effective	0
No effective systemic actions have been taken	0

Source: Own study

a recurrence of the situation that led to suffering of thirst. This need was expressed by 66.7% of the respondents.

Experience of hybrid warfare: experience of injuries

Respondents (ten individuals) identified the causes of injuries they sustained as a result of threats arising from hybrid warfare. The threats were categorized into three groups:

- natural threats,
- human-induced threats – military,
- human-induced threats – non-military.

Respondents indicated that the primary causes of injuries were natural events, such as extreme weather conditions (20%) and human-induced events, specifically warfare actions (40%). The list of causes of injuries in this category also includes direct actions by Russian soldiers and shrapnel from missiles.

In the category of human-induced military threats, respondents stated that the causes of injuries were primarily direct ground military operations, such as gunfire (75% of cases) and direct aerial military attacks, such as missile strikes, bombings, and other air-based combat actions (75% of cases). To a lesser extent, injuries were caused by special operations (41.7% of cases) and the use of chemical, biological, or radiological weapons, or toxic substance leaks (16.7% of cases).

In the category of human-induced non-military threats, respondents identified terrorist attacks as the dominant cause of injuries (54.5% of cases). To a lesser extent, injuries were caused by attacks on critical infrastructure (36.4% of cases), socio-cultural threats (27.3% of cases), as well as disinformation and propaganda, and economic threats, each accounting for 18.2% of cases. Other causes, such as cyberattacks, political manipulation, and border blockades, were responsible for 9.1% of the injuries sustained by the civilian population.

Respondents identified the consequences of threats that led to injuries, particularly in the area of physical consequences. The most frequently mentioned were injuries caused by explosions (61.5% of cases), bruises and fractures (53.8% of cases) and forced migration (46.2% of cases). To a lesser extent, physical consequences included blocked access to medical care (23.1% of cases), gunshot wounds (15.4% of cases), burns (15.4% of cases), physical violence (7.7% of cases), and psychological disorders (percentage not specified).

As regards non-physical consequences that led to injuries, respondents highlighted stress and anxiety related to food availability in 92.3% of cases, financial problems in 23.1% of cases, and weakening of social bonds in 15.4% of cases. No respondent indicated an increase in local non-violent conflicts. Additionally, respondents mentioned trauma, particularly among children.

The last area examined concerning the consequences of threats that led to injuries was the implications for particularly vulnerable groups (Table 5.10).

Individuals who sustained injuries most commonly felt their effects for more than 72 hours, as reported by 63.6% of respondents. For less severe injuries, the effects were felt for up to 24 hours in 27.3% of cases, and up to 72 hours in 9.1% of cases.

Respondents indicated that among the systemic actions taken in response to the incidents that caused injuries, rescue operations held a dominant position, accounting for 33.3% of cases. Additionally, in this area, the following actions were noted:

- Search Operations: 8.3% of cases,
- Humanitarian Actions: 8.3% of cases,
- Medical Actions: 16.7% of cases,

TABLE 5.10 Incidence of injuries among particularly vulnerable groups due to the materialization of threats caused by hybrid warfare

Impact	Number of Respondents	Percentage
Impact of injuries on the elderly	1	11.1
Impact of injuries on the sick	2	22.2
Impact of injuries on people with disabilities	1	11.1
Impact of injuries on pregnant women	0	0
Impact of injuries on children	5	55.5

Source: Own study

TABLE 5.11   Assessment of the effectiveness of systemic actions in response to the incidence of injuries among the civilian population

Assessment	Number of Indications
Highly ineffective	2
Rather ineffective	2
Partially effective	4
Rather effective	1
Very effective	2
No effective systemic actions have been taken	1

Source: Own study

- Protective Actions (e.g., directing individuals to shelters): 8.3% of cases,
- Informational Actions (e.g., warnings and reports on danger zones): 25% of cases.

Table 5.11 presents results of an assessment of the effectiveness of systemic actions taken in response to injuries sustained by the civilian population.

Respondents indicated that the most common method for disseminating information about systemic actions was through digital means, such as social media, websites and news portals (45.5% of responses), as well as direct communication (36.4%). To a lesser extent, respondents gained knowledge from traditional media, such as radio, television, and alarm and warning systems (e.g., SMS alert systems) (18.2%). Additionally, 9.1% of respondents also mentioned printed materials. None of the respondents identified social or religious organizations as sources of information. In one instance, a respondent reported having no access to information about systemic response methods for dealing with injuries.

Among the individual actions taken in response to the event that caused respondents to sustain injuries, the following were mentioned:

- Physical Security Actions – Physical Protection: For example, self-evacuation to a safe shelter with access to food (50%),
- Health-Related Actions – Health and Medical Care: For example, access to basic healthcare, medications, medical supplies, hunger management, and first aid training and medical care during wartime (33.3%),
- Psychological Security Actions – Psychological Support: For example, stress and trauma management, emotional and psychological support during times of hunger (33.3%),

- Economic Security Actions – Financial Stability: For example, financial stability and access to resources necessary for survival (8.3%),
- Food Security Actions – Access to Food: For example, access to sufficient food and water (16.7%),
- Housing Security Actions – Housing and Shelter: For example, ensuring access to safe shelter (25%),
- Social Security Actions – Community and Cooperation: For example, maintaining social cohesion, community support, and protection against isolation (16.7%),
- Mobility Security Actions – Mobility and Organized Evacuation: For example, the ability to move safely and organized evacuation when necessary (8.3%),
- Legal Security Actions – Legal Protection: For example, access to legal protection and respect for human rights (8.3%),
- Actions Ensuring the Safety of Particularly Vulnerable Groups: For example, ensuring the safety of the elderly, sick, disabled, pregnant women and children (25%).

None of the respondents specified actions related to digital and informational security such as cybersecurity and information protection against cyber threats as measures taken in response to the injuries.

Table 5.12 presents the results of the assessment of the effectiveness of individual actions taken in response to injuries sustained by the civilian population.

Respondents stated that in the majority of cases, they required special resources, such as medication supplies, specialized food, and additional training, to implement individual actions that could prevent a recurrence of the situation that led to their injuries. This need was expressed by 83.3% of the respondents.

TABLE 5.12 Assessment of the effectiveness of individual actions in response to the incidence of injuries among the civilian population

Assessment	Number of Indications
Highly ineffective	1
Rather ineffective	0
Partially effective	4
Rather effective	3
Very effective	2
No effective systemic actions have been taken	1

Source: Own study

Experience of hybrid warfare: experience of illness

Respondents (12 individuals) identified the causes of illness resulting from threats associated with hybrid warfare. These threats were categorized into three groups:

- natural threats,
- human-induced threats – military,
- human-induced threats – non-military.

In the category of natural threats, respondents indicated that the causes of illness comprises warfare activities (33.3% of cases) and extreme weather events (25% of cases). The list of causes of illness in this category also includes stress and other related illnesses.

In the category of human-induced military threats, respondents pointed out that the causes of illness were primarily direct aerial military attacks, accounting for 100% of cases. To a lesser extent, the causes included direct ground operations conducted by military units (25% of cases), special operations (12.5% of cases), and the use of chemical, biological, or radiological weapons, as well as the release of toxic substances (6.3% of cases).

In the category of human-induced non-military threats, respondents identified attacks on critical infrastructure as the dominant cause of illness, cited in 53.8% of cases. Following this, respondents mentioned terrorist attacks (38.5%), psychological operations, such as actions aimed at manipulating public perception and attitudes, influencing morale and behaviour (30.8%), disinformation and propaganda (23.1% of cases), and economic threats (15.4% of cases). The least impact on the experience of illness was attributed to political manipulation, legal conditions, and social and cultural threats, each cited in 7.7% of cases.

When identifying the consequences of threats that led to the experience of illness in the area of physical consequences, respondents pointed to the worsening of pre-existing conditions in 70.6% of cases and limited access to first aid in 58.8% of cases. To a lesser extent, respondents mentioned an increased risk of infectious diseases (17.6% of cases), injuries and skin diseases caused by exposure to high temperatures and flames (17.6% of cases), an increased risk of infection in overcrowded temporary shelters (11.8% of cases), and disability among children (5.9% of cases).

In the area of non-physical consequences that led to the experience of illness, respondents pointed to stress and anxiety in 68.8% of cases, financial problems caused by the illness in 31.3% of cases, and weakening of social bonds in 12.5% of cases.

TABLE 5.13   Implications of illness experience among particularly vulnerable groups due to the materialization of threats caused by hybrid warfare

Impact of Illness	Number of Respondents	Percentage Share
Impact of illness on the elderly	6	40
Impact of illness on the sick	2	13.3
Impact of illness on people with disabilities	5	33.3
Impact of illness on pregnant women	2	13.3
Impact of illness on children	9	60

Source: Own study

The final area examined concerning the consequences of threats that led to the onset of illness involved the implications for particularly vulnerable groups (Table 5.13).

Individuals experiencing illness reported they felt its effects mainly for more than 72 hours (68.8% of cases). Additionally, the effects of the illness were felt by respondents for up to 24 hours in 18.8% of cases, up to 48 hours in 6.3% of cases, and up to 72 hours in 6.3% of cases.

Respondents indicated that among the systemic actions taken in response to the event that caused them to become sick, medical actions held the dominant position, such as providing healthcare when the illness was recognized (41.2% of cases). Following this, respondents mentioned humanitarian actions, such as medical support, psychological assistance, and other forms of humanitarian aid (35.3% of cases); actions related to ensuring the safety of individuals, particularly vulnerable groups such as the elderly, sick, disabled, pregnant women and children (29.4% of cases); rescue operations, such as sending rescue teams, organizing evacuations to safe locations, and extinguishing fires (17.6% of cases); informational actions, such as warnings and notifications about danger zones where access to medical treatment might be challenging (11.8% of cases); and protective actions, such as directing individuals to shelters (11.8% of cases). According to the respondents, preventive actions, such as training for illness related to war (5.9% of cases), and psychological support actions (5.9% of cases) had the least impact. Table 5.14 presents the results of the assessment of the effectiveness of systemic actions taken in response to the experience of illness by the civilian population.

Respondents indicated that the most common methods for disseminating information about systemic actions were digital channels, such as social media, websites, and news portals (40% of responses), as well as direct communication (40% of responses). To a lesser extent, respondents gained knowledge from traditional media (13.3% of responses), printed materials (20% of responses), and alarm and warning systems

Population protection in hybrid warfare

TABLE 5.14   Assessment of the effectiveness of systemic actions in response to the experience of illness among the civilian population

Assessment	Number of Indications
Highly ineffective	4
Rather ineffective	1
Partially effective	9
Rather effective	2
Very effective	1
No effective systemic actions have been taken	0

Source: Own study

(20% of responses). Additionally, some respondents mentioned obtaining information from social and religious organizations (6.7%).

Among the individual actions taken in response to an event that caused respondents to suffer from hunger, the following were indicated:

- Physical Security Actions – Physical Protection: For example, self-evacuation to a safe shelter (60% of cases),
- Health-Related Actions – Healthcare and Medical Care: For example, access to basic healthcare, medications, medical supplies, disease management, first aid, and medical care training during wartime (46.7% of cases),
- Psychological Security Actions – Psychological Support: For example, stress and trauma management, emotional and psychological support (26.7% of cases),
- Economic Security Actions – Financial Stability: For example, financial stability and access to resources necessary for survival (20% of cases),
- Food Security Actions – Access to Food: For example, access to sufficient food and water (20% of cases),
- Housing Security Actions – Shelter and Housing: For example, ensuring access to safe shelter (13.3% of cases),
- Actions related to digital and information security – cybersecurity and information – e.g., protection against cyber threats, access to reliable information (13.3% of cases),
- Social Security Actions – Community and Cooperation: For example, maintaining social cohesion, providing assistance within the community, and protecting against isolation (6.7% of cases).
- Mobility Security Actions – Mobility and Organized Evacuation: For example, the ability to move safely and organized evacuation when necessary (13.3% of cases),

TABLE 5.15 Assessment of the effectiveness of individual actions in response to the experience of illness by the civilian population

Assessment	Number of Indications
Highly ineffective	1
Rather ineffective	3
Partially effective	7
Rather effective	3
Very effective	2
No effective systemic actions have been taken	0

Source: Own study

- Actions to Ensure the Safety of Particularly Vulnerable Individuals: For example, ensuring the safety of the elderly, sick, disabled, pregnant women, and children (20% of cases).

None of the respondents indicated any actions related to legal security such as legal protection, access to legal assistance, and respect for human rights.

Table 5.15 presents the results of the assessment of the effectiveness of individual actions taken in response to the experience of illness by the civilian population.

Respondents indicated that, in most cases, they required special resources such as medical supplies, specialized food, and additional training to implement individual actions that could prevent the recurrence of the situation that led to their illness. This was reported by 85.7% of respondents.

Experience of hybrid warfare: experiencing excessive heat

Four respondents identified the causes of suffering from excessive heat due to threats triggered by hybrid warfare. These threats were categorized into three groups:

- natural causes,
- human-caused military threats,
- human-caused non-military threats.

Respondents indicated that the causes of suffering from excessively high temperatures were primarily natural events, such as extreme weather phenomena (50%), as well as human-caused events, including warfare and floods, each accounting for 25% of cases.

In the category of human-caused military threats, respondents indicated that the causes of experiencing excessive heat were primarily direct airstrikes, accounting for 66.7% of cases, and special operations, accounting for 33.3% of cases.

In the category of human-caused non-military threats, respondents identified disinformation and propaganda, political manipulation, and social and cultural threats, such as inciting social tensions, exacerbating divisions, and exploiting cultural differences to provoke conflict. Each of these factors was mentioned in 33.3% of the cases.

When discussing the consequences of threats that led to experiencing excessive heat, respondents pointed out that heat stroke was reported in all cases as a physical consequence.

As regards non-physical consequences that led to experiencing excessive heat, respondents pointed to the intensification of local non-physical conflicts in 66.7% of cases, and financial problems caused by illness in 33.3% of cases.

The last examined area of the consequences of threat materialization that led to experiencing excessively high temperatures were the implications for particularly vulnerable individuals (Table 5.16).

Individuals experiencing excessive heat most commonly felt this sensation for up to 24 hours, up to 48 hours, and for more than 72 hours, each accounting for 33.3% of cases.

Respondents indicated that among the systemic actions taken in response to the events that caused them to experience excessive heat, they observed humanitarian actions, such as the provision of water, medical

TABLE 5.16 Experience of excessively high temperatures among particularly vulnerable groups due to the materialization of threats caused by hybrid warfare

Impact of Excessively High Temperature	Number of Respondents	Percentage Share
Impact of excessively high temperature on the elderly	0	0
Impact of excessively high temperature on the sick	2	66.7
Impact of excessively high temperature on people with disabilities	1	33.3
Impact of excessively high temperature on pregnant women	0	0
Impact of excessively high temperature on children	0	0

Source: Own study

TABLE 5.17 Assessment of the effectiveness of systemic actions in response to the experience of excessively high temperatures by the civilian population

Assessment	Number of Indications
Highly ineffective	0
Rather ineffective	0
Partially effective	1
Rather effective	2
Very effective	0
No effective systemic actions have been taken	0

Source: Own study

support, psychological support, and other forms of humanitarian aid in 66.7% of cases. Additionally, medical actions, such as providing medical care in cases of fever, were noted in 33.3% of cases. Table 5.17 presents the results of the assessment of the effectiveness of systemic actions in response to experiencing excessive heat by the civilian population.

Respondents indicated that the methods of disseminating information about systemic actions included digital means such as social media, websites, and news portals (25% of responses), traditional media (25% of responses), and alarm systems (SMS alert systems) (50% of responses).

Among the individual actions taken in response to the event that caused respondents to experience excessively high temperatures, the following were mentioned:

- health-related actions – health and medical care – e.g., access to primary healthcare, medications, medical supplies, management of hunger, first aid training, and medical care during wartime (100%),
- actions related to ensuring the safety of particularly vulnerable groups, such as the elderly, the sick, people with disabilities, pregnant women, and children (33.3%).

Table 5.18 presents the results of the assessment of the effectiveness of individual actions taken in response to the experience of excessively high temperatures by the civilian population.

Respondents indicated that in 50% of cases, they needed special resources, such as medication supplies, specialized food and additional training to implement individual actions to prevent a recurrence of the situation that led to exposure to excessively high temperatures.

TABLE 5.18   Assessment of the effectiveness of individual actions in response to the experience of excessively high temperatures by the civilian population

Assessment	Number of Indications
Highly ineffective	0
Rather ineffective	0
Partially effective	3
Rather effective	0
Very effective	1
No effective systemic actions have been taken	0

Source: Own study

Experience of hybrid warfare: experience of excessively low temperature

Respondents (eight individuals) identified the causes of experiencing excessively low temperatures as a result of threats arising from hybrid warfare. The threats were categorized into three groups:

- natural,
- human-caused – military,
- human-caused – non-military.

Respondents indicated that the causes of experiencing excessively low temperatures were mainly natural events such as extreme weather phenomena (12.5%), prolonged stays in bomb shelters (12.5% of cases), the time of year (12.5% of cases), disconnection of heating (12.5% of cases), and the warfare itself (25% of cases).

In the category of human-caused military threats, respondents indicated that the causes of experiencing excessively low temperatures were direct ground military operations (62.5% of cases) and direct airstrikes (75% of cases). To a lesser extent, the causes comprised special operations (37.5%) and migration to escape the war (12.5% of cases).

In the category of human-caused non-military threats, respondents indicated that the dominant cause of experiencing excessively low temperatures was attacks on critical infrastructure (71.4% of cases). To a lesser extent, the causes in this category of threats included economic threats, terrorist attacks, and waiting at the border (four days), each accounting for 14.3% of cases.

When speaking of the consequences of threats that led to experiencing excessively low temperatures in the area of physical consequences, espondents pointed to respiratory illnesses (50% of cases), physical

TABLE 5.19 Experience of excessively low temperatures among particularly vulnerable groups due to the materialization of threats caused by hybrid warfare

Impact of Excessively Low Temperature	Number of Respondents	Percentage Share
Impact of excessively low temperature on the elderly	2	33.3
Impact of excessively low temperature on the sick	0	0
Impact of excessively low temperature on people with disabilities	2	33.3
Impact of excessively low temperature on pregnant women	2	33.3
Impact of excessively low temperature on children	3	50

Source: Own study

exhaustion (37.5% of cases), and hypothermia, circulatory disorders, and cystitis, each accounting for 25% of cases. In one instance, a respondent mentioned the death of a loved one.

In the area of non-physical consequences that led to experiencing excessively low temperatures, respondents pointed to stress and anxiety (66.7% of cases), financial problems (33.3%), and the weakening of social bonds, such as within the family or among neighbours (16.7% of cases).

The last examined area of the consequences arising from the materialization of threats that led to experiencing excessively low temperatures were the implications for particularly vulnerable groups (Table 5.19).

Individuals suffering from excessively low temperatures most often experiences this sensation for more than 72 hours (57.1% of cases). The remaining individuals experienced excessively low temperatures for up to 24 hours (14.3% of cases), up to 48 hours (14.3% of cases), and up to 72 hours (14.3% of cases).

Respondents stated that among systemic actions taken in response to the event that caused them to experience excessively low temperatures, the following were observed: search operations, such as organizing searches (16.7% of cases), humanitarian actions, such as medical support, psychological support, and other forms of humanitarian aid (16.7% of cases), medical actions (16.7% of cases), informational actions (16.7% of cases), and protective actions, such as directing people to shelters (33.3% of cases). In two cases, respondents indicated a lack of systemic actions in this area. Table 5.20 presents the results of the assessment of

Population protection in hybrid warfare 331

TABLE 5.20 Assessment of the effectiveness of systemic actions in response to the experience of excessively low temperatures by the civilian population

Assessment	Number of Indications
Highly ineffective	2
Rather ineffective	0
Partially effective	3
Rather effective	0
Very effective	1
No effective systemic actions have been taken	2

Source: Own study

the effectiveness of systemic actions taken in response to the experience of excessively low temperatures by the civilian population.

Respondents indicated that the methods of disseminating information about systemic actions included direct communication (50%) and printed materials (25%). Among the individual actions taken in response to the event that caused respondents to experience excessively low temperatures, the following were mentioned:

- actions related to physical safety – physical protection – e.g., self-evacuation to a safe shelter (50%),
- actions related to health – health and medical care – e.g., access to primary healthcare, medications, medical supplies, coping with the effects of extreme cold, first aid, and medical care training during wartime (16.7%),
- actions related to housing security – shelter and housing – e.g., providing safe shelter (33.3%),
- actions related to social security – community and cooperation – e.g., maintaining social cohesion, community assistance, protection from isolation (16.7%),
- actions aimed at ensuring the safety of particularly vulnerable individuals, such as the elderly, the sick, people with disabilities, pregnant women, and children (16.7%).

In one case, a respondent indicated a lack of individual actions taken to stop experiencing excessively low temperatures. Table 5.21 presents the results of the assessment of the effectiveness of individual actions taken in response to the experience of excessively low temperatures by the civilian population.

Respondents indicated that in 100% of cases, they needed special resources, such as medication supplies, specialized food, and additional

TABLE 5.21 Assessment of the effectiveness of individual actions in response to the experience of excessively low temperatures by the civilian population

Assessment	Number of Indications
Highly ineffective	0
Rather ineffective	1
Partially effective	3
Rather effective	1
Very effective	0
No effective systemic actions have been taken	0

Source: Own study

training, to implement individual actions that could prevent a recurrence of the situation that led to experiencing excessively low temperatures.

Cyberspace and technology in the world of hybrid warfare

In the last section of the survey, respondents answered questions regarding cyberspace and technology in the world of hybrid warfare. A total of 34 respondents participated in this part of the study. The majority of respondents indicated that they use IT systems daily (91.2% of cases). Among them, 32.4% use IT systems for personal reasons, while 58.8% use IT systems in connection with their professional duties. Additionally, respondents reported using IT systems four to six times per week, very rarely, a few times per quarter, or almost never. In each of these cases, the percentage of respondents was 2.9%.

Respondents indicated that in the past 90 days, they encountered misleading information available on the Internet in the form of texts, emails, or websites. Table 5.22 presents information on the frequency of such occurrences.

The results indicate that a significant majority of respondents (64.8%) were exposed to misleading information disseminated via the Internet. According to the respondents, the misleading information pertained to manipulation (54.2% of cases), half-truths (29.2% of cases), false events (50% of cases), the spread of fake news (33.3% of cases), phishing attempts (8.3%), and the presentation of sponsored posts (33.3% of cases).

Respondents indicated that in the past 90 days, they encountered misleading information available on the Internet in multimedia form, such as images, audio recordings, videos, or animations. Table 5.23 presents information on the frequency of such occurrences.

Population protection in hybrid warfare 333

TABLE 5.22 Distribution of frequency of fake news occurrences among respondents in the form of texts, emails, or websites

Frequency	Number of Indications	Percentage Value
Not at all	12	35.3
1–3 times	9	26.5
4–6 times	2	5.9
7–10 times	2	5.9
More than 10 times	9	26.5

Source: Own study

TABLE 5.23 Distribution of frequency of fake news occurrences among respondents in multimedia form

Frequency	Number of Indications	Percentage Value
Not at all	11	35.5
1–3 times	9	29
4–6 times	4	12.9
7–10 times	1	3.2
More than 10 times	6	19.4

Source: Own study

The results indicate that a significant majority of respondents (64.5%) were exposed to misleading information disseminated via the Internet in multimedia form. According to the respondents, the misleading information pertained to manipulation (57.9% of cases), half-truths (57.9% of cases), false events (42.1% of cases), the spread of fake news (52.6% of cases), deepfake (5.3%), phishing attempts (5.3%), the presentation of sponsored posts (31.3% of cases), and propaganda (5.3%).

According to respondents, the misleading multimedia information available on the Internet was mostly created using AI. Table 5.24 presents respondents' opinions indicating the involvement of AI in the creation of misleading multimedia content.

The results presented in Table 5.24 indicate a dominant belief among respondents regarding the involvement of AI in creating misleading multimedia content targeting the civilian population during a hybrid warfare. Respondents indicated that the misleading content pertained to the following thematic areas:

- current domestic politics (64% of cases),
- current foreign policy (60% of cases),

TABLE 5.24 Assessment of AI involvement in creating misleading multimedia content

Assessment	Number of Indications	Percentage Value
All	2	8.3
Majority	8	33.3
At least half	5	20.8
Minority	5	20.8
Artificial intelligence was rarely used	0	0
Not at all, everything was most likely created by humans	4	16.7

Source: Own study

- socio-economic situation (56% of cases),
- cultural issues (20% of cases),
- local armed conflicts (32% of cases),
- international armed conflicts (28% of cases),
- policies of international organizations (20% of cases),
- current domestic politics of another country (24% of cases),
- current foreign policy of another country (20% of cases),
- socio-economic situation of another country (20% of cases),
- cultural issues in another country (8% of cases),
- local armed conflict involving another country (4% of cases),
- international armed conflict involving another country (12% of cases),
- policies of an international organization in which another country participates (12% of cases),
- significant national event/situation (12% of cases),
- significant international event/situation (12% of cases).

According to respondents, misleading information contributed to decisions related to conducting kinetic attacks (4.2% of cases), carrying out cyberattacks (20.8% of cases), local political decisions (8.3% of cases), and international political decisions (16.7% of cases). In the opinion of the respondents, as a result of actions taken based on misleading information, the consequences for the civilian population could include:

- experiencing hunger (37.5% of cases),
- experiencing thirst (25% of cases),
- sustaining injuries (56.3% of cases),
- illnesses (50% of cases),
- experiencing excessively high temperatures (6.3% of cases).

Half of the respondents believe that misleading information did not contribute to any further actions. Respondents indicated that, to their knowledge, the following types of cyberattacks were observed in their country within a year from the date of the survey:

- (D)DoS attack (Distributed Denial of Service) on the websites of important institutions (9 mentions),
- (D)DoS attack (Distributed Denial of Service) on critical infrastructure: hospitals, telecommunication systems, banks, logistics, electricity production, etc. (seven mentions),
- Attack paralyzing critical infrastructure (ten mentions),
- Surveillance, wiretapping, espionage, theft of important information (seven mentions),
- I am not aware of any major cyberattacks (seven mentions).

Cyberattacks, according to respondents, contributed to kinetic attacks (21.4% of cases), other cyberattacks (14.3% of cases), influenced local political decisions (7.1% of cases), and influenced international political decisions (21.4% of cases). In 35.7% of cases, respondents believe that cyberattacks did not have any indirect consequences.

Similarly to the misleading information spread on the Internet, respondents were asked if they believed that as a result of a cyberattack, the civilian population might have been exposed to:

- Hunger (33.3% of cases),
- Thirst (11.1% of cases),
- Injury (77.8% of cases),
- Disease (33.3% of cases),
- Exposure to excessive heat (22.2% of cases),
- Exposure to extreme cold (22.2% of cases).

In addition, respondents indicated that they feared other consequences resulting from a cyber attack:

- loss of life (57.7% of cases),
- financial loss (26.9% of cases),
- exposure to stress (42.3% of cases),
- feeling fear (34.6% of cases),
- exposure to anger (11.5% of cases),
- disruption of services (7.7% of cases),
- loss of job (11.5% of cases),
- loss of contacts (11.5% of cases),
- loss of confidence (11.5% of cases),
- financial penalties (7.7% of cases).

336 Civil Protection and Domestic Security in Hybrid Warfare

None of the respondents indicated a fear of reputational damage.

Respondents used a five-point scale when assessing the preparedness of their country in various aspects of state system organisation to detect, respond to and counter computer security incidents. A score of 1 indicated a complete lack of preparedness, while a score of 5 indicated the ability to implement best practices in the area of cyber security. Respondents were also given the opportunity to indicate a situation in which the assessed component is not implemented in their country. Table 5.25 presents the obtained results.

Respondents were also asked how they shaded the current preparedness of their country in various aspects of the organisation of the state system to detect, respond to and counter information threats. A rating of 1 indicated a complete lack of preparedness, while a rating of 5 indicated the ability to implement best practices in the area of cyber security.

TABLE 5.25   Assessment of the readiness of state institutions to counter computer security incidents

Institution	Capacity Assessment						
	1	2	3	4	5	Not Applicable	Average
Central state body	7	9	3	2	2	1	3.5
Regional state bodies	7	6	5	1	2	–	3.2
Local authorities – local level	12	4	7	–	1	1	3.1
Local self-government – regional level	7	8	4	–	1	1	2.7
Police services	8	5	4	1	3	–	3.3
Rescue services	6	7	3	1	6	–	4.2
Special services	6	6	3	1	4	–	3.4
Specialist services and units in the field of cyber security	2	8	5	2	4	–	4.1
Critical infrastructure	6	7	7	–	1	–	3.1
State civil institutions	5	7	7	1	1	–	3.3
Education and knowledge exchange system	9	8	2	2	1	1	2.9
Armed forces	1	7	8	3	2	1	4.1
Private companies and institutions	6	7	3	2	1	–	2.8
Population	8	6	5	1	1	–	2.9

Source: Own study

Population protection in hybrid warfare

TABLE 5.26 Assessment of the organisation of the state system for detecting, responding to and countering information threats

Institution	Capacity Assessment						Average
	1	2	3	4	5	Not applicable	
International organisations in which my country participates	4	5	5	2	3	–	3.5
International organisations in which my country does not participate but with which it cooperates	3	6	4	1	3	–	3.1
Central government	3	7	5	1	2	–	3.1
Regional authorities	3	5	5	2	2	–	3.1
Local authorities – local level	4	4	6	1	2	–	2.9
Local self-government – regional level	3	6	5	1	2	1	2.9
Police services	3	5	5	1	4	–	3.5
Rescue services	3	3	3	2	4	2	3.1
Special services	2	4	4	2	4	–	3.3
Specialised cyber security services and units	3	4	5	1	5	–	3.7
Critical infrastructure	2	4	5	3	3	–	3.5
State civil institutions	2	6	4	2	2	–	2.9
Education and knowledge exchange system	4	4	3	3	3	–	3.2
Armed forces	2	4	3	2	6	–	3.8
Private companies and institutions	4	4	4	2	3	–	3.1
Population	5	2	3	4	3	–	3.3

Source: Own study

Respondents were also given the opportunity to indicate a situation in which the assessed component is not implemented in their country. Table 5.26 presents the obtained results.

In addition to assessing the preparedness of state institutions to respond to cyber threats, respondents were asked to rate the country's preparedness to detect, respond to and counter hybrid threats. A rating of 1 indicated a complete lack of preparedness, while a rating of 5 indicated the ability to implement best practices in the area of protection against hybrid threats. Respondents were also given the opportunity to indicate a situation in which the assessed component is not implemented in their country. Table 5.27 presents the results obtained.

Respondents also commented on their own preparedness to detect, respond to and counter computer security incidents, information manipulation. A score of 1 indicated a complete lack of preparedness and a score of 5 indicated the ability to implement cyber security best practices. Table 5.28 presents the obtained results.

Respondents indicated that their knowledge of cyber hazard and cybersecurity practices stemmed from:

TABLE 5.27   Assessment of the organisation of the state system for detecting, responding to and countering hybrid threats

Institution	Capacity Assessment					Not Applicable	Average
	1	2	3	4	5		
International organisations in which my country participates	1	6	7	1	2	–	3.2
International organisations in which my country does not participate but with which it cooperates	2	6	5	1	4	–	3.5
Central government	2	4	7	1	4	–	3.7
Regional authorities	1	7	4	2	4	–	3.7
Local authorities – local level	2	6	4	2	3	–	3.3
Local self-government – regional level	1	7	5	1	3	–	3.3
Police services	1	3	7	2	4	–	3.7
Rescue services	–	3	7	2	6	–	4.3
Special services	1	3	6	2	6	–	4.2
Specialised cyber security services and units	–	4	8	–	6	–	4.1
Critical infrastructure	1	3	7	3	4	–	4.0
State civil institutions	–	5	7	1	4	–	3.7
Education and knowledge exchange system	2	5	5	2	4	–	3.7
Armed forces	–	3	6	1	6	2	3.9
Private companies and institutions	2	4	4	3	3	1	3.3
Population	3	3	4	3	3	1	3.2

Source: Own study

Population protection in hybrid warfare   339

TABLE 5.28   Assessment of own preparedness to detect and respond to computer security incidents, information manipulation and countering them

Institution	Capacity Assessment					
	1	**2**	**3**	**4**	**5**	**Average**
I encrypt drives on all computers	12	2	1	1	–	1.5
I regularly update computers, phones and other devices	5	2	3	2	5	3.4
I do not use ICT devices with outdated software	7	1	4	1	4	3.0
I use strong passwords (at least 12 characters, upper case, lower case, numbers, symbols, no keywords in them	4	2	6	2	4	3.6
I use different passwords for different websites	4	4	5	2	2	3.0
I do not share passwords with others	5	1	4	4	6	4.3
I use password managers	9	1	2	1	2	2.1
Where possible, I use multi-component authentication, including physical keys.	7	1	4	–	4	2.7
I use the best available security features on my devices, such as mobile device biometrics	5	2	2	2	6	3.5
I use disk encryption on my computers	9	2	2	1	1	1.9
I use up-to-date antivirus protection on my devices and computers	2	3	4	2	4	3.2
I use a split account model with different permissions, I do not work every day on an account with full administrator rights	5	4	2	1	4	2.9
I always analyse emails, instant messaging, etc. websites for expectations of such a message and the compatibility of the context and the recipient	4	3	4	3	4	3.6
I regularly back up my devices	5	6	3	2	1	2.6
I only use my own external drives, I always scan other people's drives when connected for danger	7	5	1	3	–	2.1
I regularly follow information on websites	7	2	2	1	4	2.7
Studying and learning about cyber threats and information hazards.	7	4	3	1	1	2.2
I always check information from several sources	2	4	3	3	6	4.1
I know where I can report attempted phishing attacks	9	2	3	1	2	2.4

Source: Own study

- professional knowledge (2 indications),
- friends (14 indications),
- private study (1 indication),
- mandatory in-service training (1 indication),
- local/national portals (2 indications),
- foreign portals (1 indication),
- podcasts (1 indication),
- classic video forms, e.g. YouTube, Vimeo (6 indications),
- short films – Tik Tok, YouTube Shorts, Instagram Reels (3 indications),
- blogs (7 indications),
- official documents and safety standards (3 indications),
- prepared by public authorities and subordinate institutions in the county cyber security (1 indication).

The majority of respondents indicate that they have no experience of a simulated phishing/disinformation/social engineering attack. The lack of such experience is indicated by 87% of respondents. Respondents also indicate a lack of formal knowledge of the existence of a formal cyber security framework at their country level (73.9% of respondents). At the same time, respondents have knowledge of the existence of a reporting system for threats, both security incidents and information threats. In 20.8% of cases they are able to use this system, while in 54.2% they declare knowledge of the system and lack of ability to use it. Respondents would like communication between civilians and public services in an emergency to take place via the following:

- SMS messages (14 indications),
- special application for smartphones (13 indications), and
- standard communicators for smartphones (6 indications),
- smart local systems, e.g. large screens, digital noticeboards, audible announcements (12 indications)
- television (15 indications)
- online communication (7 indications)
- social media (13 indications).

When assessing methods to counter information and social engineering attacks, respondents indicate that:

- Cyberattack simulations are a good and necessary form of exercise and, as such, should be organized as frequently as possible, with as many companies/institutions as possible implementing them. They are considered a more effective method than training and awareness campaigns (7 indications).

Population protection in hybrid warfare 341

- Cyberattack simulations are a good and necessary form of exercise, but they should be avoided if organized only occasionally. Regular training and information campaigns about real attacks are much more important, as these simulations are limited in scope (3 indications).
- Caution should be exercised regarding the frequency and form of cyberattack simulations, as they may foster inappropriate attitudes among people, such as treating every message with distrust or ignoring real threats (4 indications).
- Simulated attacks should not be used to induce additional stress. Appropriate, regular, and mandatory training sessions are sufficient (5 indications).
- An approach should be adopted that assumes someone will inevitably click on the wrong link or page, but training and informational campaigns should not be abandoned (4 indications).
- The approach that assumes someone will inevitably click on the wrong link or page is a reason why conducting training and awareness campaigns is ineffective (1 indication).

The respondents provided their opinions on which solutions should be implemented to create an effective cybersecurity and information protection system, particularly to counteract threats arising from new technologies such as artificial intelligence. A rating of 1 indicated an ineffective solution, while a rating of 5 indicated an optimal and effective solution among the various approaches and methods currently used worldwide. The results obtained are presented in Table 5.29.

TABLE 5.29   Assessment of self-preparedness for detecting, responding to, and counteracting computer security incidents and information manipulation

| Institution | Capacity Assessment | | | | | |
	1	2	3	4	5	Average
Elements of pre-school, primary and secondary education	2	1	3	1	10	4.5
Elements of academic and vocational education	–	3	3	1	8	3.9
Mandatory training and use of safety mechanisms (practice) in the organisational environment	2	2	2	1	10	4.4
International legal standards laying down detailed requirements	1	3	2	2	7	3.7

(*Continued*)

342 Civil Protection and Domestic Security in Hybrid Warfare

TABLE 5.29 (*Continued*)   Assessment of self-preparedness for detecting, responding to, and counteracting computer security incidents and information manipulation

Institution	Capacity Assessment					
	1	2	3	4	5	Average
National legislation imposing specific requirements	–	3	2	1	8	3.7
Regional and local authority regulations imposing specific requirements	1	3	2	1	8	3.8
Standards and frameworks developed by formal organisations (international, national, local government)	1	1	3	1	8	3.7
Standards and frameworks developed by industry organisations	1	2	2	1	8	3.7
Standards, frameworks, guidelines developed by organisations dedicated to cyber security tasks	2	1	1	1	10	4.1
Thematic portals, blogs, websites, audio and video material	3	–	1	2	9	3.9

Source: Own study

Respondents identified technologies that could potentially be sources of new threats in the future, with negative consequences for the civilian population:

- Decision-making algorithms in ML/AI (1 indication),
- Predictive algorithms in ML/AI (1 indication),
- Generative artificial intelligence, LLM (1 indication),
- Internet of Things (IoT) (2 indications),
- Wearable devices and IT solutions that are passively engaging to people (6 indications),
- Human-machine interface, where people can interact with computers, etc. (5 indications),
- Smart solutions for personalized medicine (6 indications),
- Autonomous cars and other vehicles (e.g., drones) (2 indications),
- Autonomous agents and communication systems (5 indications),
- Electromobility (6 indications).
- Decentralized banking (1 indication),
- Decentralized energy systems (power grids) (1 indication),
- Instant communication (4 indications),
- VR/AR (2 indications),
- Holography (2 indications),
- Quantum communication (1 indication),
- Data analysis from multiple connected sources (1 indication).

An interesting observation is that respondents do not perceive smart urban systems as a source of new threats to the civilian population.

In response to new threats, respondents identified the new technologies they hope will effectively counter hybrid threats in the future:

- Decision-making algorithms in ML/AI (6 indications),
- Predictive algorithms in ML/AI (4 indications),
- Generative artificial intelligence, LLM (2 indications),
- Internet of Things (IoT) (2 indications),
- Wearable devices and IT solutions that are passively engaging to people (1 indication),
- Human-machine interface, where people can interact with computers, etc. (5 indications),
- Smart solutions for personalized medicine (3 indications),
- Autonomous cars and other vehicles (e.g., drones) (7 indications),
- Autonomous agents and communication systems (3 indications),
- Electromobility (1 indication),
- Decentralized energy systems (power grids) (1 indication),
- Smart urban systems (3 indications),
- Instant communication (5 indications),
- Holography (3 indications),
- Data analysis from multiple connected sources (7 indications).

Respondents do not see potential in technologies such as decentralized banking, VR/AR, and quantum communication for effectively countering hybrid threats. Respondents assessed the potential of national entities to develop solutions that would enable the use of new technologies to protect against hybrid warfare. A rating of 1 indicated a lack of potential both currently and in the future, while a rating of 5 indicated high activity in developing solutions both currently and in the future. The results are presented in Table 5.30.

In the context of other technologies that may help in hybrid warfare or prevent them, respondents believe that:

- Predictive algorithms can help model situational and crisis conditions, allowing better planning of preventive actions and forecasting (75% of respondents),
- Modern telecommunications networks have a sufficient level of resilience that can be relied upon in conflict situations (43.5% of respondents),
- It is necessary for the state to have various communication channels, with protection of availability adequately planned for different categories of modern conflicts and crisis situations (73.9% of respondents),

TABLE 5.30 Assessment of the potential of national actors to develop solutions to use new technologies to protect against hybrid warfare

	Capacity Assessment					
Institution	1	2	3	4	5	Average
Civilian research institutes	4	2	4	2	3	2.9
Military research institutes	2	3	4	2	4	3.2
Civilian universities	2	2	4	1	3	2.5
Military universities	1	2	3	2	4	2.8
Military	2	–	6	1	5	3.3
State security and defence enterprises	1	2	5	1	4	2.9
Companies operating outside the security and defence sector	1	2	6	–	2	2.2
Public institutions	2	1	5	1	2	2.2
Educational institutions	2	2	4	1	3	2.5
Start-ups	–	2	3	1	2	1.8
International organisations in which my country is active	3	1	3	1	3	2.2
International research projects	–	3	3	2	4	2.9
Central government and public institutions	1	3	4	2	2	2.5
Local government and its institutions	2	2	5	–	1	1.7

Source: Own study

- Institutions and private individuals will privately ensure the availability of various communication channels, with protection of availability adequately planned for different categories of modern conflicts and crises (52.2% of respondents),
- The strategic action of the state should be to support decentralization in various systems by increasing resilience to threats (82.6% of respondents),
- Solutions based on data analysis and social media monitoring can be useful in planning and preventing the effects of hybrid warfare (77.3% of respondents),
- The widespread use of solutions based on data analysis and social media monitoring by the state, due to privacy and anonymity concerns, is not an appropriate way to counter hybrid warfare (77.3% of respondents),
- Possibility of combining security and privacy (78.3% of respondents),

- Smart urban systems can be useful in crisis situations, for example, they can help in more efficient management of evacuations or provide greater resilience to threats (95.5% of respondents),
- The development of artificial intelligence should be regulated due to the risks that may be associated with it (76.2% of respondents),
- Technological development will occur in an uncontrolled manner, and restrictions and best practices will develop one way or another (50% of respondents),
- School education provides adequate educational elements to distinguish disinformation from true information (63.6% of respondents),
- Local public administration has effective methods for reaching the population with crisis management information (59.1% of respondents).

Furthermore, respondents believe that as regards developing capabilities for offensive actions in cyberspace (information operations, cyberattacks):

- The state should develop offensive capabilities in the field of information operations (81.8% of respondents),
- The state should develop offensive capabilities in the field of cyberattacks (81.8% of respondents),
- The state has the right to carry out offensive actions in cyberspace (information operations, cyberattacks) in response to similar actions taken against my country (85.7% of respondents),
- The state has the right to use classical offensive actions (kinetic attacks, sabotage, traditional offensive intelligence operations, etc.) in response to cyber actions taken against my country (81% of respondents),
- No regulations are needed regarding the use of offensive actions in cyberspace (47.6% of respondents),
- In the future, international regulations on the use of offensive operations and cyberattacks, similar to treaties on various types of weapons, will be established, leading to the de-escalation of such actions (86.4% of respondents),
- Offensive actions in cyberspace (information operations, cyberattacks) should be used only in the most critical situations and only at the highest level of escalation (77.3% of respondents),
- States have the right to keep information about existing vulnerabilities in telecommunications systems secret in order to use them for actions against other states (59.1% of respondents),

TABLE 5.31 Quantitative summary of identified protection mechanisms

Code Tree	Number of Codes	Percentage share
Education	1,859	94.37
Humanitarian aid	31	1.57
Shelters	29	1.47
Ensuring energy security	15	0.76
Cybersecurity	9	0.46
Medical assistance	8	0.41
Psychological support	4	0.20
Civilian protection	3	0.15
Protection of critical infrastructure	3	0.15
Shelter areas	3	0.15
Building resilience	2	0.10
Emergency management	2	0.10
Warning systems	1	0.05
Border security	1	0.05

Source: Own study

- The development of new technologies should be subject to international control by independent bodies, which could block or prohibit the development of technologies with potentially high risks to societies (81.8% of respondents).

In parallel with the survey study, an additional analysis of media reports was conducted, searching for codes indicating protective actions taken towards the civilian population. The results are presented in Table 5.31.

The analysis of the data collected in Table 5.31 indicates that the dominant protective mechanism is education (94%), suggesting that it is perceived as a key element in building awareness and skills among civilians necessary to cope with military and non-military threats. Other protective mechanisms have significantly lower scores, which may indicate their narrower application or insufficient coverage in media reports.

Table A5.1 presents data illustrating the connections between the identified protective mechanisms and the identified military and non-military threats.

In Table A5.1 summarizing the quantitative analysis of identified protective mechanisms, education emerges as the most represented protective mechanism. Analysing the connections between protective mechanisms and military and non-military threats, it was observed that education is strongly associated with military threats, such as conventional actions (e.g., the use of missiles, artillery, bombs), as well as with non-military threats, such as propaganda. This indicates that education is widely used as a means of preparing the population to cope with various threats. However, it may also suggest that the preparation of the population is incomplete in the context of hybrid warfare threats.

Other protective mechanisms identified in media reports are significantly less represented. The concept of "civil protection" was identified in only 0.15% of cases and is mainly associated with shelling and riots. This could suggest that a range of threats arising from hybrid warfare is not being adequately addressed in the area of civil protection. Civilian warning systems were identified at a level of 0.05%, representing a marginal share.

In the correlation table, connections are only shown with the code "missiles". Cybersecurity was identified at a level of 0.46% and shows obvious connections with cyberattacks and propaganda. Another identified mechanism is energy security, which reached a level of 0.76%. In the correlation table, energy security is associated with threats such as occupation, import bans, and areas such as murders, rapes, and kidnappings. However, understanding these correlations requires further research. Shelters were identified at a level of 1.47% and are mainly associated with military actions (shelling, bombs, bombardment, air raids, rockets, artillery) and propaganda. On the other hand, places of refuge, which show marginal presence in media reports, are linked with bombs, private military companies (PMCs), and propaganda. This result may suggest an influence on the physical security of the civilian population through the use of PMCs, for example, by spreading disinformation about shelters or the need to seek refuge in them. Humanitarian aid was the second most prominent identified protective mechanism and shows connections with both conventional and unconventional military actions (e.g., missiles, artillery, infantry, siege, bombs, shelling, diversionary activities) as well as non-military activities (e.g., election interference, corruption, protests, crime, disinformation, famine). The contexts in which humanitarian aid was discussed in the media highlight its importance but also suggest the need for further research into its connections with non-military activities. Additionally, medical assistance was identified, which has only one connection with conventional military activities. Border security was identified as a marginal protective mechanism, discussed in the context of terrorist attacks, terrorism, and destabilizing activities.

The analysis of the media reports indicates that there are mechanisms in place for the protection of the civilian population in the hybrid war in Ukraine. However, there are also certain gaps that may suggest either the marginalization of these areas in the media or that existing solutions are insufficient to achieve full protection of the civilian population. Assuming that this is the result of a lack of comprehensive solutions, it seems that there is a need for a coordinated and balanced approach to civilian protection. This approach should account for the diversity of threats and implement appropriate protective mechanisms accordingly.

APPLICATION OF THE SIX WAYS TO DIE MODEL IN THE ANALYSIS OF THE DIRECT AND INDIRECT EFFECTS OF HYBRID WARFARE ON THE CIVILIAN POPULATION

An analysis of the survey results and media reports shows that many hybrid warfare actions are aimed at direct or indirect effects on the civilian population. The direct effects include injuries, lack of access to food, water, medical care, and exposure to low temperatures, which can lead to death or permanent health damage. The results obtained point to the "Six Ways to Die" model. The "Six Ways to Die" model is a tool that allows for identifying areas impacting the health and life of the civilian population and defining the network of dependencies on critical infrastructure necessary for the proper functioning of the state in these areas. The model assumes that the primary task of the state is to eliminate factors that could lead to death in six key areas (Bennett, Gupta, 2010):

- hunger,
- thirst,
- trauma,
- illness,
- too high a temperature,
- too low a temperature.

The elimination of threat sources should be addressed in relation to three levels of needs: the individual, groups of citizens, and the state as an organization. For each level of need, the provision of conditions for survival can be described through the processes used to achieve them (Figure 5.2).

An example of a process ensuring access to food, which may be disrupted as a result of threats generated by hybrid warfare, is illustrated in Figure 5.3.

Considering the situation depicted in Figure 5.3, we observe that a customer wishing to purchase food needs a resource in the form of payment means, namely a payment card. The use of a payment card to pay for purchases requires the store offering the goods to have a resource in the form of a payment terminal. The payment terminal, in order to charge the customer's account, must have access to a service provided by a payment processor, which must be certified by one of the payment system operators (e.g., Visa, MasterCard). Additionally, the payment processor must be authorized by the Central Bank of the country in which it is registered.

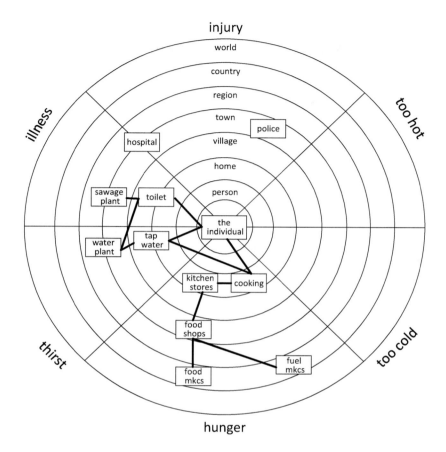

FIGURE 5.2 Illustration of the six ways to die model with the processes for personal protection

Source: Mohorčich (2022)

To complete the transaction, the payment system operator must be able to establish a connection and exchange data with the transaction system of the customer's bank as well as the bank servicing the store.

A cyberattack, such as a DDoS attack that blocks the ability to connect with the payment system operator, can result in the loss of the ability to purchase food. Prolonged unavailability of this service could lead to hunger in the area affected by the threat.

An example of cutting off access to services that fulfil basic needs can be seen in the situation described in a Polish Press Agency (PAP) article. The article outlines the conditions faced by the residents of Mariupol, occupied by the Armed Forces of the Russian Federation. The prior shelling

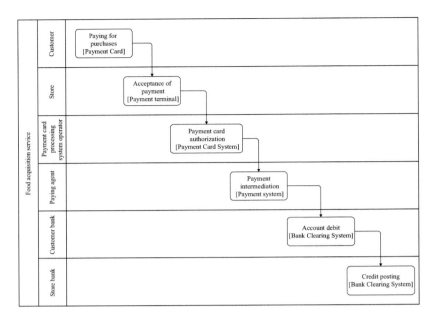

FIGURE 5.3 Example of the process for food acquisition service implementation

Source: Own study based on Kisilowski et al. (2021)

of civilian infrastructure, combined with persecution, forced relocations, and the activities of collaborators, led to a severe reduction in access to drinking water, food, and basic hygiene products for the civilian population. This dire situation forced people to resort to eating pigeon meat. Oleksandr Lazarenko, the director of one of Mariupol's clinics, points out that consuming pigeon meat poses an additional threat to the lives of civilians, exposing them to diseases. Pigeons are carriers of many viral, bacterial, and fungal infections, making their meat potentially contaminated. Eating it can lead to illnesses such as histoplasmosis, encephalitis, ornithosis, toxoplasmosis, and other dangerous diseases, which are particularly hazardous for children and the elderly. Without proper treatment, some of these diseases can be fatal (Polish Press Agency [PAP], 2022).

The referenced article illustrates how the effects of one or a group of threats (bombardment, persecution, collaboration) can escalate, creating conditions conducive to the emergence of additional threats (risk of infectious diseases). In this case, the destruction of civilian infrastructure led to restricted access to food, resulting in hunger. This situation then forced the civilian population to rely on available food sources, thereby increasing the risk of infectious diseases. If illness occurs, the ability to receive medical assistance is limited due to the lack of access to healthcare, which can lead to death from disease or injuries sustained.

The Cybersecurity and Infrastructure Security Agency (CISA) employs the "Six Ways to Die" methodology at the central level of U.S. public administration. CISA defines critical state functions, and then, by creating a table of these critical functions, sequentially defines the processes that support their implementation. Critical state functions are understood as those functions of the government and private sector that are so vital to the United States that their disruption, damage, or destruction would have a harmful impact on public safety, national economic security, national public health, or any combination of these areas (Moteff et al., 2003, pp.107-56)). The critical functions have been divided into four groups (Table 5.32).

The concept presented in relation to the central level of public administration aligns with the approach outlined in the "Six Ways to Die" methodology. By identifying critical functions and determining the goals to be achieved, one can proceed to identify services, their constituent processes, and designate their operators. Defining the processes that deliver key services paves the way for identifying the resources that ensure the resilience of those services. In this context, resilience is understood as a characteristic of a system, process, or resource that influences the reduction of risk levels associated with the threat in question. Resilience is achieved when it is possible to maintain or restore functioning to a predefined level within an acceptable time frame after an incident occurs. Resilience is attained through the cumulative effect of technical, organizational, educational, and other measures that protect the system, process, or resource from threats (Itich-Drabarek et al., 2023, pp. 247–407).

The results of a survey conducted on a group of 40 individuals affected by the consequences of hybrid warfare in Ukraine confirmed that the effects of military actions are perceived by the civilian population as a threat to life and health through exposure to hunger, thirst, injuries, diseases, excessively high temperatures, and excessively low temperatures (Table 5.33). Table also includes data indicating the duration of experiencing the life- and health-threatening negative effects of hybrid warfare.

The results of the survey confirm the necessity of taking actions to ensure the continuity of services that protect the civilian population from the effects of hybrid warfare listed in Table 5.33. Protective measures for the resources necessary to deliver key services can be determined using the methodology discussed in the chapter "Management of Critical Infrastructure Safety in the Context of Hybrid Warfare Threats". However, it is not feasible to guarantee uninterrupted access

TABLE 5.32 National critical function set

Connect	Distribute	Manage	Supply
• Operate core network	• Distribute electricity	• Conduct elections	• Exploration and extraction of fuels
• Provide cable access network services	• Maintain supply chains	• Develop and maintain public works and services	• Fuel refining and processing fuels
• Provide internet based content, information, and communication services	• Transmit electricity	• Educate and train	• Generate electricity
• Provide internet routing, access, and connection services	• Transport cargo and passengers by air	• Enforce law	• Manufacture equipment
• Provide positioning, navigation, and timing services	• Transport cargo and passengers by rail	• Maintain access to medical records	• Produce and provide agricultural products and services
• Provide radio broadcast access network services	• Transport cargo and passengers by road	• Manage hazardous materials	• Produce and provide human and animal food products and services
• Provide satellite access network services	• Transport cargo and passengers by vessel	• Manage wastewater	• Produce chemicals
• Provide wireless access network services	• Transport materials by pipeline	• Operate government	• Provide metals and materials
• Provide wireline access network services	• Transport passengers by mass transit	• Perform cyber incident management capabilities	• Provide housing
		• Prepare for and manage emergencies	• Provide information technology products and services
		• Preserve constitutional rights	• Provide materiel and operational support to defence
		• Protect sensitive information	• Research and development
		• Provide and maintain infrastructure	• Supply water
		• Provide capital markets and investment activities	
		• Provide consumer and commercial banking services	
		• Provide funding and liquidity services	
		• Provide identity management and associated trust support services	
		• Provide insurance services	
		• Provide medical care	
		• Provide payment, clearing, and settlement services	
		• Provide public safety	
		• Provide wholesale funding	
		• Store fuel and maintain reserves	
		• Support community health	

Source: CISA

Population protection in hybrid warfare

TABLE 5.33 Negative effects of hybrid warfare threatening life or health

	Perception of Phenomenon (%)	Duration of Perception			
		Up to 24 h (%)	Up to 48 h (%)	Up to 72 h (%)	Over 72 h (%)
Hunger	25	50	22.2	5.6	22.2
Thirst	18.8	66.7	22.2	–	11.1
Injuries	9.4	27.3	–	9.1	63.6
Illnesses	34.4	68.8	18.8	6.3	6.3
Excessive high temperatures	18.8	33.3	33.3	–	33.3
Excessively low temperatures	9.4	14.3	14.3	14.3	57.1

Source: Own study

to key services under hybrid warfare conditions. Achieving such a level of availability is also not possible in peacetime conditions.

The survey results (Table 5.33) suggest that civilians should be prepared to mitigate the effects of hybrid warfare, such as hunger, thirst, injuries, diseases, excessively high and low temperatures, on their own for up to 72 hours. This conclusion points to two essential requirements for the civilian safety model under hybrid warfare conditions:

- Systemic actions should protect the civilian population from the loss of continuity in key services that prevent hunger, thirst, injuries, diseases, and exposure to excessively high or low temperatures beyond 72 hours.
- Individual actions by the civilian population should be organized in a way that ensures protection from hunger, thirst, injuries, diseases, and exposure to excessively high or low temperatures for up to 72 hours.

Proper planning and implementation of both systemic and individual actions are contingent upon access to reliable information. This observation is confirmed by available reports and media coverage of the war in Ukraine and the Israeli-Palestinian conflict.

The lack of access to information hinders the ability to carry out specific actions, and consequently, it obstructs the execution of the entire process. The result of blocking a process that delivers essential services or products to the civilian population may expose them to conditions leading to permanent health damage or death due to prolonged exposure.

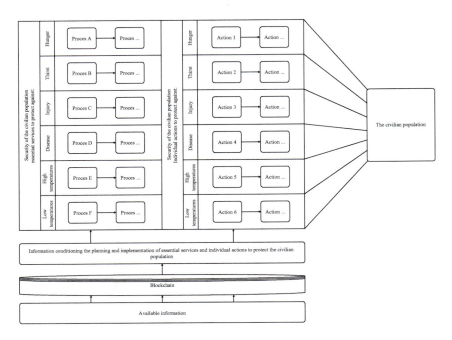

FIGURE 5.4   Civilian security model

Source: Own study

A more dangerous issue related to information access is the lack of data integrity. Unauthorized modification of data, even if it is publicly available, can lead to the improper execution of established processes for providing essential goods and services. In such a scenario, the process is carried out, but its outcomes are harmful to the civilian population. An example of the consequences of data integrity breaches could be the alteration of Crisis Management Plans, which define evacuation sites. In this case, the modification of public data could result in directing civilians to a location exposed to threats, such as shelling, instead of guiding them to a safe zone.

In this context, Figure 5.4 presents a modification of the Six Ways to Die model, incorporating the dimension of access to reliable information.

BLOCKCHAIN TECHNOLOGY IN CIVILIAN PROTECTION

In the context of the confessions and analyses presented so far in the protection of civilians in a hybrid war situation, it becomes extremely important to look for technological solutions for communication and data exchange, which in their assumptions will offer features relevant to this type of conflict. Two main characteristics for such a system should be identified as:

- Offer the ability to protect information by eliminating potential single points of failure, while increasing resilience when parts of the system may be decommissioned, attacked or inaccessible;
- The possibility of deeper authentication and ensuring the reliability of the information placed in the communication system, together with full transparency and verifiability of operations in the system.

For the above, the target system for the exchange of information and communication must above all offer technical solutions in the field:

- decentralisation and dispersal,
- providing security mechanisms for data at rest, in motion and during processing,
- replication, reliability and data integrity,
- full performance verification with deep user authentication.

A technological solution that can collectively offer a communication system is blockchain. Consideration of this type of solution dates back to 1991 and an article (Haber, Stornetta, 1991, pp. 99–111), but it was not more widely studied and implemented in practice until a paper (Nakamoto, 2008) in which a Bitcoin digital currency based on a public blockchain system was proposed and whose practical implementation was presented in 2009.

Blockchain technology is a system of distributed records that enables the creation of secure and transparent digital records. Blockchain works by establishing a decentralised network of nodes that participate in the verification and validation of transactions, ensuring their consistency and immutability (Puthal et al., 2018, pp. 6–14). Over the last 15 years, a number of technological solutions have emerged that implement the original assumptions of a cryptographically strong, distributed, transparent and at the same time anonymous blockchain, with publications or practical solutions from 2015 to 2024 indicating a particular interest in this technology. In addition to applications related to digital currencies (such as Bitcoin), use cases are being sought where blockchain can either solve existing limitations or offer unique and desirable solutions. Among the uses of this approach, any system that requires the non-repudiation of an operation performed, the protection of the integrity of a record entry or the full verifiability of the data and operations exchanged is indicated. Thus, blockchain is being tested for tasks such as notarial contracts (e.g.

the distribution of company shares to shareholders), digital business contracts or settlements in decentralised electricity production systems. It can also be used as a distributed registry with a high level of integrity protection to store sensitive data, such as medical data.

The above issues indicating the various features of a blockchain system can find invaluable application in the case of the protection of societies where the impact of hybrid conflicts often takes place in the digital sphere – cyberspace, information space, social networking, digital information exchange, etc. The impact of actors in hybrid conflicts on civilians in the digital world boils down to using the methods offered by the digital sphere to produce primarily negative phenomena in the psychological and mental spheres of people through, among other things, intensive propaganda campaigns and sowing false information (fake news) targeting the lowering of trust, undermining authorities and the systems in which they operate.

How can blockchain respond to problems in the fight against disinformation? An example of an area of research where blockchain is being used as an integrity and non-repudiation control mechanism is the search for solutions to combat disinformation and falsely generated multimedia material, including the use of AI (deepfake) on the Internet. Using the solution architecture presented in the paper (Qureshi et al., 2021, pp. 1786–1793) as an example, the traditional approach using watermarking solutions to detect the violation of authenticity, originality and authorship of multimedia materials is enhanced by using a blockchain to store metadata related to watermarked videos posted online (such as content identifier, content type, watermark embedding encoding or speech and video features). The transparency and immutability of the blockchain is then used to retrieve information that can be used in the process of detecting deepfake material.

A similar idea of using blockchain in detecting and combating disinformation spread through fake news was proposed in Wang et al. (2023). The article draws attention to the significant risks of the modern media space, in which any information can be distributed almost freely, modifying existing information without the possibility of claiming actual, physical authorship of that information. This feature is permanently exploited by various actors conducting influence campaigns in ongoing hybrid conflicts in the information space. The proposal (Wang et al., 2023) is for media publications to go into blockchain-based data storage systems, which will allow full lifecycle management of media information with full verifiability of operations on this information.

What features of blockchain technology enhance network communication and the security of data exchange? Blockchain, which offers built-in mechanisms for preserving the resilience or integrity, as well as the non-repudiation of the actions performed in an information system, seems an adequate technological candidate to help preserve the trust of users in situations of uncertainty. In addition, cyber attacks are also one of the main tools in this type of conflict, both those aimed at reducing the availability and stability of systems (denial of service attacks) and attacks aimed at stealing or modifying information, often aimed at stealing money. Blockchain in the context of the indicated cyber threats is characterised by a high level of data security due to its cryptography and decentralised architecture, which eliminates single points of failure (Zubaydi et al., 2023; Moosavi, Taherdoost, 2023, pp. 58–72). In addition, systems using blockchain for data storage are more resilient to typical cyber attacks than traditional databases (Benjamin, 2021; Xu, 2016).

An important concept for the application of a blockchain-based system is presented in an article (Biswas, Muthukkumarasamy, 2016, pp. 1392–1393) for securing communication between distributed IT systems using smart city systems as an example. Within this concept, blockchain complements the system architecture in terms of:

- Layers of data storage – offering a distributed ledger mechanism (i.e. what is at the heart of blockchain),
- Protocol layers – using well-known blockchain protocols such as Ethereum, NXT or Telehash alongside classic data communication protocols for wide area networks (WAN) and local area networks (LAN).

In this way, a distributed system of multiple nodes in an indicated smart city, while performing various operational functions for such a city and, above all, for the population increasingly living in this type of system, receives an important enhancement of system cyber security through the previously indicated features of blockchain technology: strong cryptography, decentralisation, resilience or transparency. The article (Zubaydi et al., 2023) provides a summary of the various concepts for securing distributed networks using the example of Internet of Things networks precisely by means of blockchain.

A generalisation of the considerations for which blockchain technology is one solution is communication systems in general with high resilience and confidentiality. Between the trends of centralising data processing and decentralising computing (e.g. the Internet of Things), another paradigm referred to as fog computing is developing (Chiang, Zhang, 2016, pp. 854–864). The use of fog computing as a mechanism for network and data security is indicated by a study (Kott et al., 2016). The proposed system assumes that a system characterised by greater uncertainty from an external attacker's point of view will provide greater resilience to attacks. Its direct implementation is to split the data into multiple fragments and disperse them to multiple nodes, e.g. to end-user devices or servers. The premise is that if the system is partially compromised and chunks of data are captured, they are useless to the attacker. At the same time, the remaining, unattacked parts of the system are supposed to continue to be useful to the system's users by performing the task of communication and data exchange. The final technological solutions require the right trade-off between accessibility and confidentiality depending on the tasks and operational circumstances. Blockchain technology may be one implementation of this concept. It is also worth citing a study in which the concept of a cyber-aggregate is used for proposing a distributed information hiding system for a network of Internet of Things device nodes (Bieniasz, Szczypiorski, 2018). The concept involves a layered architecture of the system in terms of: application layer, file system, device memory sectors and physical memory management. Each of these layers contains, in addition to the core task execution component, a complementary layer-specific information hiding component. As a whole, the system offers a distributed communication protocol via steganographic channels combining network steganography and data storage steganography in the network nodes. Within the scope of the article (Bieniasz et al., 2022), a working prototype of the system realising the concept from the article (Bieniasz, Szczypiorski, 2018, pp. 24–28) was implemented to be subsequently tested for security and performance. Operational parameters were evaluated according to the challenges defined by Kott et al. (2016), in particular in terms of the distribution of data fragments, the complexity of network management, the speed of data transfer, the disk occupancy of the end device and the use of its computing power. Security The developed system provides first and foremost the nature of a logical connection between distributed parts of the data chain The system could only be properly compromised if an attacker took over the secret generation function module that addresses the data fragments placed in the system. Without it, the captured parts, e.g. by compromising one or more devices, would be useless.

In summary, blockchain technology and, more broadly, technologies offering a distributed architecture with strong data security mechanisms represent an important area of development in the context of protecting cyberspace and, above all, its users in the face of growing disinformation threats and cyber attacks in the face of hybrid conflicts targeting specific societies. Thus, the search for secure information technologies has an increasingly important role, having long since gone beyond merely protecting individual network and computer users. The NATO Science and Technology Organisation, in its 2020 report on Breakthrough Technology Concepts for 2020–2040, identified blockchain technology as one of them in the areas of secure communication and secure data storage, thus important and groundbreaking solutions are to be expected in this area, thus generally enhancing the resilience of civilians in the face of hybrid conflicts (NATO, 2020).

CONCLUSIONS OF CHAPTER

This chapter presents an analysis of civilian protection mechanisms and international humanitarian law concerning the protection of civilians in the context of hybrid warfare. Additionally, a study was conducted on civilians directly affected by the war in Ukraine, along with an analysis of media reports, to better understand the effectiveness and application of these mechanisms. As part of this analysis, the research hypothesis posed at the beginning of the chapter was positively verified. The materialization of threats resulting from hybrid warfare leads to complex consequences for the civilian population, necessitating the implementation of multifaceted systemic and individual actions to effectively mitigate these effects.

The "Six Ways to Die" model identifies six primary pathways through which hybrid warfare can lead to fatal consequences: hunger, thirst, injuries, diseases and extreme temperature conditions (both excessively high and low temperatures). Analysing the study results within these six categories allows for the assessment of the threats posed by hybrid warfare and their interconnections.

In the context of hybrid warfare, hunger represents one of the most serious threats to the civilian population, caused by both military and non-military actions as well as extreme weather conditions. The effects of hunger include both physical consequences, such as malnutrition and food-related diseases, and psychological impacts, such as stress and the weakening of social bonds. Among particularly vulnerable groups, hunger posed a significant threat, especially for children and the elderly. Most respondents in this section reported experiencing hunger for up to 24 hours, with slightly fewer indicating that the duration ranged from 48 to more than 72 hours. Efforts to minimize the impact of hunger were undertaken at both systemic and individual levels. In the first case, respondents assessed these efforts as either ineffective or only partially effective. In the case of individual actions, the majority of people rated them as partially effective. Thirst, another critical threat, is directly linked to the lack of access to drinking water, which can result from military actions and attacks on water infrastructure. Respondents indicated that attacks on water supply systems, along with direct military and non-military actions, were the primary causes of experiencing thirst. The consequences of this include serious health risks, such as dehydration and an increased risk of infectious diseases, which can lead to death in the absence of appropriate remedial actions, a concern also highlighted by the respondents. Among particularly vulnerable groups, the effects of thirst were especially significant for children. Similar to the experience of hunger, most respondents in this section reported experiencing thirst for up to 24 hours, with slightly fewer indicating that this period lasted from 48 to more than 72 hours. As with hunger, systemic and individual actions were taken to address thirst, but according to the respondents, these efforts were mostly ineffective or only partially effective.

Physical injuries, directly resulting from warfare activities such as ground operations and airstrikes, represent the third threat pathway in the "Six Ways to Die" model. The study results show that injuries such as gunshot wounds, fractures, and other bodily harm, as well as forced migration, were primarily the result of direct armed conflicts and the consequences of these actions. Additionally, respondents indicated that extreme weather events also contributed to injuries. Non-military actions were another significant cause. The consequences of injuries included both physical effects and non-physical impacts, such as trauma in children. The impact of injuries on other vulnerable groups was at a lower, but still significant, level. Respondents were convinced that systemic actions taken to address injuries were ineffective or only partially effective. Individual actions were rated better in this category. The duration of injuries typically exceeded 72 hours. Diseases constitute the fourth threat pathway identified in the "Six Ways to Die" model.

The study results indicate that the causes of illnesses were directly linked to armed conflicts and extreme weather events. Non-military actions were also a significant contributing factor. When identifying the consequences of threats that led to illness, respondents pointed to the worsening of pre-existing conditions and limited access to first aid as key physical consequences. To a lesser extent, they noted an increased risk of infectious diseases, injuries, and skin conditions caused by exposure to high temperatures and flames, as well as an elevated risk of infections in overcrowded temporary shelters and disabilities in children. In the area of non-physical consequences that led to illnesses, respondents mainly highlighted psychological, social, and financial impacts. The materialization of threats resulting in illness primarily affected vulnerable groups, particularly the elderly and individuals with disabilities. Similar to the case of injuries, the duration of illness often exceeded 72 hours. Both systemic and individual efforts to address these issues were largely assessed as ineffective or only partially effective.

Extreme temperatures, especially excessive heat, pose a significant threat to the health of the civilian population, particularly in the context of infrastructure damage caused by warfare. Respondents indicated that the primary causes of the consequences of excessive heat were both natural weather phenomena and military and non-military actions. The main consequences of excessive heat identified by the respondents included heat strokes, the intensification of local non-physical conflicts and financial difficulties. In the context of particularly vulnerable individuals, excessive heat primarily affected those who were ill and individuals with disabilities. Those experiencing excessive heat typically felt its effects within time frames of up to 24 hours, up to 48 hours, and beyond 72 hours. Respondents noted that both systemic and individual actions taken in response to events causing them to experience excessive heat were generally partially effective or somewhat effective.

Excessively low temperatures, like excessive heat, pose a significant threat to the health and lives of the civilian population. The study results indicate that military and non-military actions, along with extreme weather events, were the main causes of experiencing excessively low temperatures. These conditions led to severe health consequences, such as hypothermia, respiratory diseases, and death, as well as non-physical effects like anxiety and weakened social bonds. The impact of excessively low temperatures on particularly vulnerable individuals primarily affected children, but it was also significant for the elderly, individuals with disabilities, and pregnant women. The duration of these effects was most commonly assessed as lasting beyond 72 hours. In terms of systemic and individual actions, they were generally evaluated as rather ineffective or only partially effective.

All six areas demonstrated significant impacts that threatened the health and lives of the surveyed civilians, as well as those around them and particularly vulnerable individuals. In each of the identified areas, the need for specific resources to minimize the threats and their consequences was also highlighted.

In the conducted study, in addition to the areas discussed above, issues related to cyber threats were examined, which represent both a tool of attack and a specific area of concern. The study results indicate that the civilian population is exposed to various forms of threats arising from the use of information and communication technologies in hybrid warfare. It seems appropriate, therefore, to consider including cyberspace as an additional, cross-cutting area within the "Six Ways to Die" model, as it can influence all traditional categories of threats, such as hunger, thirst, injuries, diseases, and extreme temperature conditions.

A high percentage of respondents use IT systems daily, indicating a significant dependence on technology in both private and professional spheres. The related risks include widespread exposure to disinformation and informational manipulation, which can be used as tools in hybrid warfare. In the study, as many as 64.8% of respondents reported encountering misleading information, suggesting that cyberspace is being used to destabilize society through informational chaos, a finding also confirmed by media reports on the war in Ukraine. The study revealed that disinformation, in both text and multimedia forms, is a common phenomenon encountered by most respondents. They indicated that disinformation often involved manipulation, half-truths, and false events.

Particularly concerning is the use of artificial intelligence (AI) in creating these contents, highlighting the increasingly advanced technological aspects of hybrid warfare. The study's findings suggest that cyberattacks are materializing and can lead to real, physical threats to the civilian population.

Respondents observed that the effects of cyberattacks could include experiences of hunger, thirst, injuries, and illness. Moreover, cyberattacks can be linked to kinetic attacks and other forms of direct violence, underscoring their role as a catalyst in the escalation of hybrid warfare. The respondents' assessments of the readiness of state institutions to counter cyber and hybrid threats varied (from moderate to low), which, in the event of physical threat materialization, exacerbates the risks for the civilian population. Respondents identified many technologies that could become both sources of new threats and tools for countering these threats. Technologies such as artificial intelligence, the Internet of Things (IoT), autonomous systems, and smart urban solutions are seen as crucial both for the escalation of conflicts and for managing them. Respondents also expressed strong support for developing offensive capabilities in cyberspace and for regulating new technologies, reflecting their awareness of potential threats and the need to protect civilians in a rapidly evolving technological environment.

Experts interviewed emphasized the crucial role of cyberspace and informational activities in influencing the civilian population during hybrid wars. One of the primary threats identified by the experts are phishing attacks, which aim to gain access to sensitive information such as financial data or online banking credentials.[1] Furthermore, the experts highlighted that traditional methods of information interception and disinformation dissemination have been enhanced with modern technologies, significantly altering the nature of contemporary hybrid warfare. Artificial intelligence, particularly in the form of large language models (LLMs), enables the generation of content that can elicit strong emotional responses from recipients. These emotional responses can be used to mobilize previously passive social groups and lead to the stigmatization of other groups, thereby endangering the personal safety of civilians. For example, this can manifest as scapegoating, a phenomenon that often accompanies crises and social changes. In this process, certain individuals or social groups are stigmatized and perceived as a threat to social integrity, which leads to increased negative emotions towards them. This, in turn, can result in direct attacks on these individuals, threatening their health and lives.

Additionally, the evolving nature of espionage and information gathering, particularly in the era of social media, highlights how easily societal behaviours can be influenced. A prime example is the scandal involving Cambridge Analytica, a company that provided political consulting services, which demonstrated how easily voter preferences can be manipulated during the electoral process and the far-reaching consequences this can have. In this case, people were manipulated using publicly available information or data that individuals provided to the company, either knowingly or unknowingly. Based on this information, Cambridge Analytica created personal profiles, identifying ways to influence those individuals. This was most often done through targeted advertisements displayed on a popular social media platform, containing primarily false information designed to evoke specific emotional responses. Such emotionally charged reactions were intended to lead to specific and desired actions. The effectiveness of this strategy lies in bypassing the conscious decision-making process, overriding logical thinking, and redirecting actions toward those desired by Cambridge Analytica's clients. By inducing this state of heightened emotional arousal, which shuts down critical and logical thinking, it became much easier to manipulate people and their behaviours. Understanding the mechanisms of these manipulations and their potential consequences could significantly reduce vulnerability of the society to similar practices in the future.

The conclusions drawn from the analyses of hunger, thirst, injuries, diseases, and extreme temperatures primarily focus on physical threats that directly impact the health and lives of civilians, with their effects being easily identifiable and immediate. In contrast, threats related to cyberspace and technology are indirect in nature, yet they can lead to equally serious physical consequences, as well as destabilize society and create uncertainty, which can directly influence decision-making. The analysis of all sections in this chapter reveals that different forms of threats within a hybrid warfare are interrelated and mutually reinforcing. For instance, disruptions in access to food and water caused by military actions can exacerbate health problems, such as diseases or injuries. These threats can be further amplified by cyberattacks, which disrupt the functioning of critical infrastructure systems, such as power grids or telecommunications networks.

As regards protecting civilians during hybrid warfare, ensuring the effectiveness of protective actions (both at the systemic and individual levels) is a crucial element. The surveyed population, on average, rated systemic actions as rather ineffective. Individual actions were evaluated slightly better, but both require effort to achieve optimal protection for civilians. This highlights that, in addition to systemic preparedness, social and individual preparedness—building societal resilience—is also critically important (more on this topic in the chapter *The Role of Communities in Hybrid Warfare*). The analysis of research and expert assessments identified education as the dominant form of increasing public awareness about threats and ways to protect against them. However, the key to education is not rote learning but rather fostering critical thinking at the individual level. According to one expert, only on a solid foundation of critical thinking can resilience be effectively built.

In the context of identifying protective mechanisms in the analysis of media reports on the war in Ukraine, in addition to education, other elements of protective mechanisms identified include humanitarian aid, shelters, energy security, and cybersecurity. In the next stage, an attempt was made to analyse the connections between the identified protective mechanisms and the codes and keywords previously identified in military and non-military threats. The results and analysis are described in Table 5.32. The analysis revealed both strengths and weaknesses of the identified mechanisms in relation to the threats. Considering the overall results of the code correlations, both military and non-military actions have a varied impact on the analysed protective mechanisms, which expose existing gaps in the protection of civilians (as also indicated by the respondents).

The analysis conducted in this chapter confirms that the impacts of hybrid warfare on civilian populations are complex due to the interconnectedness of tactics across various domains, their cascading nature, and the predominance of non-military actions over military ones (both conventional and unconventional). The ratio of non-military actions to military actions is 3.69:1, meaning that for every military action, there are nearly four non-military actions. Additionally, the ratio of non-military actions to conventional military actions is 193.7:1, indicating that non-military actions are almost 194 times more frequent than conventional military actions (see Chapter 3). In this situation, systemic measures may be insufficient, as reported by respondents. It is worth considering, in this context, a more in-depth preparation of civilians to build mature resilience through critical thinking education. The analysis conducted showed that respondents indicated that in most cases, the mentioned effects were felt for over 72 hours, suggesting that systemic measures may not be effective, for example, due to shelling. Therefore, at least within this time frame, civilians should be independently prepared for protective tasks.

Considering the conclusions drawn from the analyses conducted so far, there is a need to evaluate the effectiveness of existing solutions for civilian protection in the context of hybrid warfare. Primarily, efforts should focus on establishing clear definitional frameworks for these two concepts, which still evoke controversy among researchers and practitioners. The lack of uniform definitions leads to a gap in the ability to build resilience in systems and societies, affecting the perceptions of both decision-makers and the societies as such. As a result, protective measures become less effective, as confirmed by reports from international humanitarian organizations, such as the *Protection of Civilians in Armed Conflict* report mentioned in this chapter. The need for systematic and individual enhancement of civilian protection in hybrid wars is also highlighted by experts, who, like the authors, believe that at this stage, there are only attempts to create effective systems. In addition to the systems mentioned in this chapter, additional indirect or regional solutions can also be identified, such as the Comprehensive Approach to Crisis Management (NATO, 2024a, 2024b), Resilience-Based Management (EU, 2018), Whole-of-Government Approach (Christensen, Lægreid,

2007), Human Security Approach (UN, 2024), Comprehensive Security Framework (National Security Strategy of Japan, 2022), Integrated Crisis Management Framework (Buhagiar, Anand, 2021, pp. 2–14) or National Resilience Framework developed by Great Britain (GOV.UK, 2022). In most countries, systems are a collection of more or less integrated approaches, ranging from military readiness to civil defence, infrastructure protection, and educational programs aimed at combating, for example, disinformation (EU vs Disinfo website). There are approaches that provide some protection against certain aspects of hybrid warfare, but there is no comprehensive system, and most approaches are imperfect, because actions are decentralized and fragmented, which means they do not comprehensively address hybrid threats.

Current mechanisms for civilian protection, although they make efforts to ensure safety in hybrid wars, are insufficient. On the other hand, full protection of civilians in such a complex environment seems impossible. Therefore, a potential solution may be a flexible, adaptive, and responsive system aimed at shifting from a reactive approach to a more proactive one (this necessity was also highlighted by experts) (Figure 5.5).

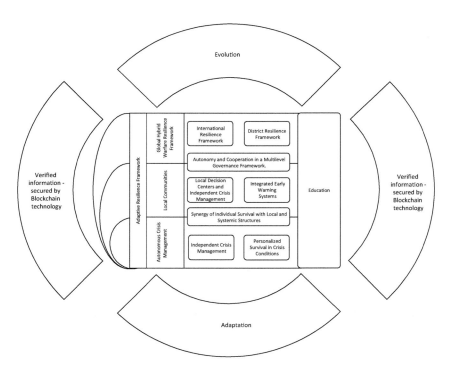

FIGURE 5.5   Comprehensive hybrid warfare resilience framework

Source: Own study

The framework for this system could be based on the critical impacts of hybrid wars on civilian populations. One such framework, applicable at international, regional, and individual levels, could be the "Six Ways to Die" model. This model should consider additional critical impacts resulting from actions across various domains of hybrid warfare, integrate regional specifics, adopt a proactive approach to public education, shift the individual paradigm, and allow for flexibility in adjusting protective priorities to changing conditions and local social contexts. Such an approach could significantly enhance the effectiveness of protective measures in the context of hybrid warfare.

NOTE

1 For the full responses of the experts, see Appendix 4.

REFERENCES

Benjamin, N., (2021), How Effective Is Blockchain in Cybersecurity? *ISACA Journal*, 4. Available at: https://www.isaca.org/resources/isaca-journal/issues/2021/volume-4/how-effective-is-blockchain-in-cybersecurity. Accessed: 10 July 2024.

Bennett, M., and Gupta, V., (2010), *Dealing in Security: Understanding Vital Services and How They Keep You Safe.* Available at: http://resiliencemaps.org/files/Dealing_in_Security.July2010.en.pdf Accessed: 16 July 2024.

Bieniasz, J., Bąk, P., and Szczypiorski, K., (2022), *StegFog: Distributed Steganography Applied to Cyber Resiliency in Multi Node Environments.* IEEE. https://doi.org/10.1109/ACCESS.2022.3199749. Accessed: 09 July 2024.

Bieniasz, J., and Szczypiorski, K., (2018), *Towards Empowering Cyber Attack Resiliency Using Steganography*, 2018 4th International Conference on Frontiers of Signal Processing (ICFSP), France, 2018, pp. 24–28. https://doi.org/10.1109/ICFSP.2018.8552068. Accessed: 09 July 2024.

Biswas, K., and Muthukkumarasamy, V., (2016), *Securing Smart Cities Using Blockchain Technology*, 2016 IEEE 18th International Conference on High Performance Computing and Communications; IEEE 14th International Conference on Smart City; IEEE 2nd International Conference on Data Science and Systems (HPCC/SmartCity/DSS), Sydney, NSW, Australia, https://doi.org/10.1109/HPCC-SmartCity-DSS.2016.0198. Accessed: 07 July 2024.

Buhagiar, K., and Anand, A., (2021), Synergistic Triad of Crisis Management: Leadership, Knowledge Management and Organizational

Learning.*International Journal of Organizational Analysis*, ahead-of-print. Emerald Publishing. 31(2) https://doi.org/10.1108/IJOA-03-2021-2672. Available at: https://www.researchgate.net/publication/354108480_Synergistic_triad_of_crisis_management_leadership_knowledge_management_and_organizational_learning#fullTextFileContent. Accessed: 16 July 2024.

Cabinet Office, 2022. The UK Government Resilience Framework. Available at: https://assets.publishing.service.gov.uk/media/63cff05 6e90e071ba7b41d54/UKG_Resilience_Framework_FINAL_v2.pdf. Accessed: 16 July 2024.

Chiang, M., and Zhang, T., (2016), Fog and IoT: An Overview of Research Opportunities. *IEEE Internet of Things Journal*, 3(6), pp. 854–864, Available at: https://ieeexplore.ieee.org/document/7498684. Accessed: 09 July 2024.

Christensen, T., and Lægreid, P., (2007), The Whole-of-Government Approach to Public Sector Reform. *Public Administration Review*, 67(6). JSTOR, pp. 1059–1066, Available at: https://www.jstor.org/stable/4624667. Accessed: 17 July 2024.

Cybersecurity and Infrastructure Security Agency (CISA) (n.d.) National Critical Functions Set. Available at: https://www.cisa.gov/. Accessed: 19 July 2024.

Diakonia International Humanitarian Law Centre, (2024), *Basic Principles of International Humanitarian Law.* Available at: https://www.diakonia.se/ihl/resources/international-humanitarian-law/basic-principles-ihl/. Accessed: 16 July 2024.

Act on Civil Protection and Civil Defense in Poland, (2024), Available at: https://isap.sejm.gov.pl/isap.nsf/download.xsp/WDU20240001907/T/D20241907L.pdf, Accessed: 10 December 2024.

Encyclopedia of Public Administration, *Internal Security.* Available at: http://encyklopediaap.uw.edu.pl/index.php/Bezpieczeństwo_wewnętrzne, Accessed: 15 June 2024.

EUR-Lex, (2024), EU Legislation Database: Civil Protection. Available at: https://eur-lex.europa.eu/content/help/eurlex-content/experimental-features.html. Accessed: 16 July 2024.

European Commission, (2020), *Communication from the Commission to the European Parliament, the Council, the European Economic and Social Committee and the Committee of the Regions – The EU Security Union Strategy.* Available at: https://eur-lex.europa.eu/legal-content/PL/TXT/?uri=CELEX:52020DC0605. Accessed: 15 June 2024.

European Council – Council of the European Union, (2024), *EU Civil Protection.* Available at: https://www.consilium.europa.eu/en/policies/civil-protection/. Accessed: 10 July 2024.

European Parliament and Council, (2013), *Decision No 1313/2013/EU of the European Parliament and of the Council of 17* December

2013 *on a Union Civil Protection Mechanism. OJ L 347, 20. 12.2013.* Available at: https://eur-lex.europa.eu/legal-content/EN/TXT/?uri=CELEX:32013D1313. Accessed: 16 July 2024.

European Parliament and Council, (2021), Regulation (EU) 2021/836 of the European Parliament and of the Council of 20 May 2021 Amending Decision No 1313/2013/EU on a Union Civil Protection Mechanism. OJ L 185, 26.5.2021. Available at: https://eur-lex.europa.eu/legal-content/EN/TXT/?uri=CELEX:32021R0836. Accessed: 16 July 2024.

European Resilience Management Guideline, (n.d.), *European Resilience Management Guideline. Smart Mature Resilience Project.* Available at: https://smr-project.eu/fileadmin/user_upload/Documents/Resources/Non-WP_publications/SMR-EMRG-handbook-WWW-compressed.pdf. Accessed: 23 July 2024.

Finance Strategists, (2023), Blockchain Transaction Verification, Meaning and How It Works. Available at: https://www.financestrategists.com. Accessed: 11 July 2024.

Global Protection Cluster, (2023), Protection of Civilians Policy, Global Protection Cluster. Available at: https://www.globalprotectioncluster.org/sites/default/files/2023-07/2023_protection_of_civilians_policy.pdf. Accessed 16 Aug. 2024.

Global Protection Cluster, (2024), Protection of Civilians, Global Protection Cluster (2024). Available at: https://www.globalprotectioncluster.org/themes/protection_civilians. Accessed 16 Aug. 2024.

gov.pl, (2024), *Międzynarodowe prawo humanitarne.* Available at: https://www.gov.pl/web/dyplomacja/miedzynarodowe-prawo-humanitarne. Accessed: 16 July 2024.

Government of Japan, (2022), National Security Strategy of Japan. Available at: https://www.cas.go.jp/jp/siryou/221216anzenhoshou/nss-e.pdf. Accessed: 16 July 2024.

Haber, S., and Stornetta, W.S., (1991), How to Time-Stamp a Digital Document. *Journal of Cryptology*, 3, 99–111. https://doi.org/10.1007/BF00196791. Accessed: 05 July 2024.

Hosanagar, K., (2021), How the Blockchain Will Impact the Financial Sector, Knowledge at Wharton. Available at: https://knowledge.wharton.upenn.edu. Accessed: 07 July 2024.

Integrated Food Security Phase Classification (IPC), (2024), Integrated Food Security Phase Classification, Available at: https://www.ipcinfo.org. Accessed: 14 July 2024.

International Code of Conduct Association, (2024), The International Code of Conduct for Private Security Service Providers (ICoC), Available at: https://icoca.ch/the-code/. Accessed: 27 November 2024.

International Committee of the Red Cross, Customary IHL Database. Available at: https://www.icrc.org/en/law-and-policy/customary-ihl. Accessed: 16 July 2024.

ISACA, (2021), *How Effective Is Blockchain in Cybersecurity. ISACA Journal*, 4, pp.5–16, Available at: https://www.isaca.org/resources/isaca-journal/issues/2021/volume-4/how-effective-is-blockchain-in-cybersecurity. Accessed: 07 July 2024.

Itich-Drabarek, I., Misiuk, A., Mitkow, Sz., and Bryczek-Wróbel, P., (2023), *Encyklopedia Bezpieczeństwa Narodowego*. Warsaw: *Dom Wydawniczy ELIPSI*.

Kashi Komijani, M., (2023), *Explaining the Dimensions of Hybrid War from the Perspective of International Humanitarian Law.* Presented at the 5th National Conference on Innovation and Research in Psychology, Law, and Cultural Management, *Qom University*, June 2023. Available at: https://www.researchgate.net/publication/371399433_Explaining_the_dimensions_of_hybrid_war_from_the_perspective_of_international_humanitarian_law. Accessed: 16 July 2024.

Kisilowski, M., Skomra, W., Smagowicz, J., Szwarc, K, and Wiśniewski, M. (2021), *Management of Critical Infrastructure Security and Continuity of Essential State Services, University of Technology*, Poland.

Kitler, W., (2023), Internal Security in the Aspect of Contemporary Challenges of Theory and Practice of the Problem. *Wiedza Obronna*, 282(1). https://doi.org/10.34752/2023-f282. Available at: https://wiedzaobronna.edu.pl. Accessed: 15 June 2024.

Kolb, A.G., Hrushko, M., Teteriatnyk, H., Chepik-Trehubenko, O., and Kotliar, O., (2021), Peculiarities of Realization of the International Mechanism for the Protection of the Rights of Victims of Armed Conflict in the East of Ukraine. *Cuestiones Políticas*, [online] 39(71). https://doi.org/10.46398/cuestpol.3971.17. Accessed: 15 July 2024.

Kott, A, Swami, A., and West, B., (2016), *The Fog of War in Cyberspace,* tech. rep., *US Army Research Laboratory*. Available at: https://www.researchgate.net/publication/309956945_The_Fog_of_War_in_Cyberspace Accessed: 09 July 2024.

Lonardo, L., (2021), *EU Law Against Hybrid Threats: A First Assessment.* In S. Hummelbrunner, L. Kirchmair, B. Pirker, A.-C. Prickartz, and I. Staudinger (eds.), *Shaping the Future of Europe – Second Part.* European Papers, Vol. 6, No. 2. https://doi.org/10.15166/2499-8249/514.Availableat:https://www.europeanpapers.eu/en/system/files/pdf_version/EP_eJ_2021_2_19_Articles_SS2_6_Luigi_Lonardo_00514.pdf. Accessed: 10 July 2024.

MacLachlan, K., (2022), *Protection of Civilians – A Constant Point of Reference in a Changing Security Environment.* Available at: https://www.nato.int/docu/review/pl/articles/2022/06/17/ochrona-ludnosci-cywilnej-staly-punkt-odniesienia-w-zmieniajacym-sie-srodowisku-bezpieczenstwa/index.html. Accessed: 16 June 2024.

Marcinko,M.,Stefańska,M.,andKolaj,M.,(eds.),(2019),*Międzynarodowe Prawo Humanitarne*. Polski Czerwony Krzyż. Available at: https://

pck.pl/wp-content/uploads/2020/10/mph_odpowiadamy_na_twoje_pytania.pdf. Accessed: 16 July 2024.

Marcinko, M., (2020), *Jakie są podstawowe zasady międzynarodowego prawa humanitarnego?* Available at: https://pck.pl/wp-content/uploads/2020/10/mph_odpowiadamy_na_twoje_pytania.pdf. Accessed: 15 May 2024.

Mohorčich, J., (2022), People Die in Six Ways and Each is Politics: Infrastructure and the Possible. *Contemporary Political Theory*, 21(2). Available at: https://doi.org/10.1057/s41296-021-00518-5. Accessed: 16 July 2024.

Moosavi, N., and Taherdoost, H., (2023), Blockchain Technology Application in Security: A Systematic Review. *Blockchains*, 1(2), pp. 58–72. https://doi.org/10.3390/blockchains1020005. Accessed: 04 July 2024.

Moteff, J., Copeland, C., and Fischer, J. (2023), Critical Infrastructures: What Makes an Infrastructure Critical? Report for Congress, Resources, Science, and Industry Division. USA Patriot Act, Section 1016. Available at: https://irp.fas.org/crs/RL31556.pdf, Accessed: 24 July 2024.

Nakamoto, S., (2008), Bitcoin: A Peer-to-Peer Electronic Cash System. Available at: https://bitcoin.org/bitcoin.pdf.

NATO, (2016), *NATO Policy for the Protection of Civilians*. Endorsed by the Heads of State and Government at the North Atlantic Council meeting in Warsaw, 8–9 July 2016. Press Release (2016) 135. Available at: https://www.nato.int/cps/en/natohq/official_texts_133945.htm. Accessed: 16 July 2024.

NATO, (2019), *NATO Joint Warfare Centre Hosts Seminar on Protection of Civilians. Seminar Held at Joint Warfare Centre*, Stavanger, Norway, 2–4 September 2019. Available at: https://www.jwc.nato.int/articles/nato-joint-warfare-centre-hosts-seminar-protection-civilians. Accessed: 16 July 2024.

NATO, (2020), Science & Technology Trends 2020–2040. Available at: https://www.nato.int/nato_static_fl2014/assets/pdf/2020/4/pdf/190422-ST_Tech_Trends_Report_2020-2040.pdf. Accessed: 09 July 2024.

NATO, (2022), *Human Security: Approach and Guiding Principles.* Available at: https://www.nato.int/cps/en/natohq/official_texts_2085 15.htm. Accessed: 15 June 2024.

NATO, (2024a), A "Comprehensive Approach" to Crises. [online] NATO. Available at: https://www.nato.int/cps/en/natohq/topics_51633.htm?selectedLocale=en. Accessed: 23 July 2024.

NATO, (2024b), *Resilience, Civil Preparedness and Article 3*. Available at: https://www.nato.int/cps/en/natohq/topics_132722.htm. Accessed: 15 June 2024.

NATO Allied Command Operations, (2021), *The Protection of Civilians Allied Command Operations Handbook*. Available at: https://shape.nato.int/news-archive/2021/the-protection-of-civilians-allied-command-operations-handbook. Accessed: 10 July 2024.

Polish Press Agency (PAP), (2022), *Mieszkańcy Mariupola z głodu jedzą gołębie, brakuje wody pitnej*. Available at: https://www.pap.pl/aktualnosci/news%2C1269876%2Cmieszkancy-mariupola-z-glodu-jedza-golebie-brakuje-wody-pitnej.html. Accessed: 19 July 2024.

Puthal, D., Malik, N., Mohanty, S.P., Kougianos, E., and Das, G., (2018), Everything You Wanted to Know about the Blockchain: Its Promise, Components, Processes, and Problems. *IEEE Consumer Electronics Magazine*, 7(4). https://doi.org/10.1109/MCE.2018.2816299. Accessed: 06 July 2024.

Qureshi, A., Megías, D., and Kuribayashi, M., (2021), *Detecting Deepfake Videos Using Digital Watermarking*, 2021 Asia-Pacific Signal and Information Processing Association Annual Summit and Conference (APSIPA ASC), Tokyo, Japan. Available at: https://www.researchgate.net/publication/358729656_Detecting_Deepfake_Videos_using_Digital_Watermarking, Accessed: 05 July 2024.

Sari, A., (2019), *Legal Resilience in an Era of Grey Zone Conflicts and Hybrid Threats*. Exeter Centre for International Law Working Paper, 2019/1. *University of Exeter - School of Law*. Available at: https://papers.ssrn.com/sol3/papers.cfm?abstract_id=3315682. Accessed: 17 July 2024.

Schweizerische Eidgenossenschaft, (2021), *International Code of Conduct for Private Security Service Providers*. As amended 10 December 2021. Available at: https://icoca.ch/wp-content/uploads/2024/08/INTERNATIONAL-CODE-OF-CONDUCT_Amended_2024.pdf. Accessed: 20 July 2024.

Sharma, S., Ibrahim, S., Ahmad, I., Qureshi, S., and Ishfaq, M., (2022), Blockchain Technology: Benefits, Challenges, Applications, and Integration of Blockchain Technology with Cloud Computing. *Future Internet*, 14(11), Available at: https://www.mdpi.com/1999-5903/14/11/341. Accessed: 04 July 2024.

Singh, S.K., and Kumar, S., (2021), Blockchain Technology: Introduction, Integration and Security Issues with IoT. https://arxiv.org/abs/2101.10921. Accessed: 07July 2024.

Smart Mature Resilience, (2018), European Resilience Management Guideline. Available at: https://smr-project.eu/fileadmin/user_upload/Documents/Resources/Non-WP_publications/SMR-EMRG-handbook-WWW-compressed.pdf. Accessed: 27 July 2024.

Switzerland and International Committee of the Red Cross (ICRC), (2008), The Montreux Document on Private Military and Security Companies. Available at: https://www.eda.admin.ch/eda/en/home/foreign-policy/international-law/international-humanitarian-law/private-military-security-companies/montreux-document.html. Accessed: 19 July 2024.

The Wall Street Magazine, (2023), How Are Transactions Verified in Blockchain: The Ultimate Guide to Trust. Available at: https://www.thewallstreetmagazine.com. Accessed: 05 July 2024.

Treaty on the Functioning of the European Union (TFEU), (2024), Consolidated Version, as Amended by the Amsterdam Treaty (1997), the Treaty of Nice (2001), the Treaty of Lisbon (2007) and EU Council Decision Amending Article 136 (2011). Available at: https://www.jus.uio.no/english/services/library/treaties/09/9-01/tfeu_cons.html#history. Accessed: 16 July 2024.

United Nations, (2024), Human Security Unit. Available at: https://www.un.org/humansecurity/. Accessed: 16 July 2024.

United Nations Department of Peace Operations, (2020), *The Protection of Civilians in United Nations Peacekeeping Handbook*. Available at: https://peacekeeping.un.org/sites/default/files/dpo_poc_handbook_final_as_printed.pdf. Accessed: 16 July 2024.

United Nations Department of Peace Operations, (2023), *The Protection of Civilians in United Nations Peacekeeping*. Ref. 2023.05. Available at: https://globalprotectioncluster.org/sites/default/files/2023-07/2023_protection_of_civilians_policy.pdf. Accessed: 10 July 2024.

United Nations Security Council, (2024), Protection of Civilians in Armed Conflict - Report of the Secretary-General (S/2024/385. Available at: https://reliefweb.int/report/world/protection-civilians-armed-conflict-report-secretary-general-s2024385-enarfrrueszh. Accessed: 20 July 2024.

Wang, X., Xie, H., Ji, S., Liu, L., and Huang, D., (2023), Blockchain-Based Fake News Traceability and Verification Mechanism. Heliyon, 9(7), e17084, Available at: https://pubmed.ncbi.nlm.nih.gov/37449155/. Accessed: 27 July 2024.

Widłak, T., (2012), Martens Clause against the Notion of 'Humanity' in International Law. *International Humanitarian Law*, III. pp. 173–187, Available at: https://www.academia.edu/4615813/Klauzula_Martensa_na_tle_pojęcia_ludzkość_w_prawie_międzynarodo-wym_Martens_Clause_Against_the_Notion_of_Humanity_in_International_Law. Accessed: 16 July 2024.

Witlin, L., (2008), Mirror-Imaging and Its Dangers. *SAIS Review of International Affairs*, 28(1), pp. 89–90. Johns Hopkins University Press. Available at: https://www.researchgate.net/publication/236805126_Of_Note_Mirror-Imaging_and_Its_Dangers. Accessed: 16 July 2024.

Xu, J.J., (2016), Are Blockchains Immune to All Malicious Attacks? *Financial Innovation*, 2(25). https://doi.org/10.1186/s40854-016-0046-5. Accessed: 07 July 2024.

Zubaydi, H.D., Varga, P., and Molnár, S., (2023), Leveraging Blockchain Technology for Ensuring Security and Privacy Aspects in Internet of Things: A Systematic Literature Review. *Sensors*, 23(2). https://doi.org/10.3390/s23020788. Accessed: 07 July 2024.

CHAPTER 6

Utilizing new technologies for population protection in hybrid warfare

CHALLENGES FOR TECHNOLOGY DEVELOPMENT FROM THE POINT OF VIEW OF HYBRID CONFLICT AND THE PROTECTION OF THE POPULATION IN THE FACE OF IT

Hybrid warfare and its intensity in its impact on societies today is greatly enhanced by the development of technology and the ubiquity of the information space. Strategies and solutions to prevent, counter, anticipate and defend against this type of threat must be developed on the basis of new, coherent mental models regarding new technologies, in particular their dual role in the life of societies. On the one hand, they are often the solution to important human problems and, on the other hand, one should also be aware that they can be the catalyst for hybrid threats with new means, methods, tactics and strategies. Thus, negative actors in hybrid warfare can often increase the reach of their actions by representing new options for influencing societies.

Globalisation and international cooperation has increased the speed of developing new technologies and making them widely available to large audiences. The creation of new technologies is seen as an important aspect of building the advantage of states and societies, while they can open up new fields of negative impact. This chapter will look at which technological areas, in particular, have the greatest potential for growth. It is worth pointing out that some of these may not necessarily be the latest conceptually, but are only now possible in practice as the next step of development in a given technological branch.

The dark side of this development, unfortunately, is that new technological developments may increasingly become the new 'battle space' in hybrid conflicts. In this context, many international actors see

DOI: 10.4324/9781003503859-7

373

technology as a new domain of influence and hybrid warfare, extending the previous spaces of this confrontation, in particular the traditionally kinetic and intelligence spaces. In some cases, the area of technology may even become the core area of a hybrid operation. This is most often the case when the adaptation and development of a given technology takes place without proper, pre-sequential threat modelling. This is a common problem when technologies are primarily geared towards quick sales and profits (achieving *time-to-market* as quickly as possible), with naïve disregard for aspects of security, reliability, trustworthiness, impact on the environment or human impact. In addition, an important aspect is that technologies, especially communications, are further open at the user layer, where the primary tool of influence in hybrid conflicts is simply 'weaponised' information. "Armed" information becomes a means of deception in hybrid threats, as well as hybrid war, and is used by state and non-state actors to achieve a specific goal. New concepts such as narrative warfare and cognitive warfare are also emerging. Information can be used by both state and non-state actors to create targeted narratives, build false impressions, opinions and raise the temperature of political disputes. Ultimately, such operations lead to destabilisation, unrest and long-term negative effects on entire societies and the organisation of cooperation between societies.

This chapter will identify three dimensions related to new technologies and their ability to protect and defend societies in hybrid conflicts using selected examples:

- Conceptual, organisational and formal-normative developments to guide technology security and the development of technology for security in the face of increasing intensity of hybrid conflicts. Attention will be directed to examples of approaches from good practice to regulation. This section will first contract the Zero Trust architecture for natively resilient ICT networks and general trends related to the security of information technology production, so that it is the development of security and resilience issues that are already present at the design stage of new technologies. Here, the assumptions of the NIS2 directive within the European Union as well as the new cyber-strategy of the US government in this area will be indicated. It will also be shown the organisational development related to responding to threats in the technology area in a vertical (horizontal, teams) and horizontal (cooperation, knowledge sharing, consortia, etc.) horizon. A final example will be the reference when concepts and regulations for security try to keep up with technological progress. Efforts to regulate AI security in the European Union through the AI Act will be pointed out, which may contribute to reducing, for example, AI-induced disinformation. A final example will be the EU's directive for cyber resilience – the Cyber Resilience Act (CRA), which defines the requirements for different technologies to enhance common cyber resilience.

- The development of technologies offering specific features and functionalities relevant to protection in the face of hybrid conflicts, e.g. secure communication systems and secure ICT networks or cloud computing. Relevant examples of the implementation of various technological concepts that have already been able to be positively verified in the practice of hybrid conflicts will be pointed out, including in the face of Russia's aggression in Ukraine in 2022.
- Development of technologies to combat vulnerabilities in other technologies. This section will discuss the strands of development of systems for cyber security and technologies to combat disinformation, fake multimedia material or fraud attempts (e.g. phishing), as well as the broad development of cyber security systems in the area of threat detection and response. A key aspect from a development perspective will be the identification of efforts to automate and autonomise cyber security operational processes.

CONCEPTUAL, ORGANISATIONAL AND FORMAL-NORMATIVE DEVELOPMENT IN THE AREA OF NEW TECHNOLOGIES FOR RESILIENCE IN THE FACE OF HYBRID CONFLICTS

In 2022. The Defence Information Systems Agency (DISA), in collaboration with the National Security Agency (NSA), together carrying out various technological support tasks in the areas of information and communications technology (ICT) and communications or, explicitly, electronic intelligence for the main actors in the US homeland and external security system, presented the second, current version of the Zero Trust Reference Architecture model (Department of Defense, 2022) for use by the US Department of Defence. The significance of such documents is usually that, in the years to come, various US agencies, including the military, will adapt to the requirements introduced by such studies. It will further extend beyond borders, particularly into the NATO area, where we can expect to see an increasingly rapid adaptation of the concept by other countries as part of their own cyber security strategies and by the international cyber security ecosystem, including by hardware and software solution providers, in company operations, consulting or research in the area of cyber security. The document introduces important assumptions for a universal understanding of technological, architectural and process issues, encompassing the digital ecosystem, networks, services, but also human behaviour in the long-term building of a secure cyberspace and cyber resilience.

What is the Zero Trust concept? To quote the introduction to the document, referring to Special Publication 800–207 (Rose et al., 2020) of the US Agency for Standards and Technology (NIST):

> Zero Trust is the term for an evolving set of cybersecurity paradigms that move defenses from static, network-based perimeters to focus on users, assets, and resources. Zero Trust assumes there is no implicit trust granted to assets or user accounts based solely on their physical or network location (i.e., local area networks versus the Internet) or based on asset ownership (enterprise or personally owned).

Overall, the Zero Trust approach is intended to provide a strategy, a framework for operating and thinking about the overall security of critical assets and processes against cyber threats by modifying existing assumptions for secure ICT and specialised network architectures, such as Industrial Systems Networks (Operational Technology, OT) or critical networks. The first change is to move away from the assumption of distinguishing zones in systems and networks with attribution of a feature and level of 'trust'. This paradigm has existed in ICT since the dawn of digital systems, e.g. realising a security model based on 'hierarchical privilege rings' in processors and operating systems (Schroeder, Saltzer, 1972; Karger, Herbert, 1984, p. 2). For classical data communication networks, this approach is implemented by means of *the* perimeter *model* and perimeter-based security. This approach is presented ideologically in Figure 6.1.

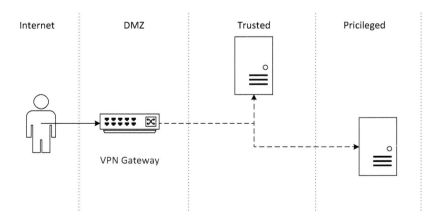

FIGURE 6.1 Perimeter-based security model

Source: Own study

Although this approach has seemed natural and adequate for many years, cyber-attackers have adapted their tactics and techniques to this model, focusing in the initial phases of an attack on gaining footholds in higher-trust zones, as well as acquiring access data in various ways, particularly to accounts with the highest privileges. This means that systems of this type, on the one hand, which are more resistant from the outside, become vulnerable to internal threats, and this is how an attacker who has broken through the security that is around the assets can be considered. This feature has also been pointed out in earlier studies on the Zero Trust model, including what is considered to be an important formulation of the concept itself in a 2010 report by John Kindervag and colleagues (Kindervag, 2010). Zero Trust means introducing a permanent move away from assigning a trust feature at the boundary of a system or network. Instead, there is to be continuous verification of operations performed and access control with multi-level permissions, with the assumption that each user is to have only the permissions needed to perform a given action and nothing more. Secondly, the Zero Trust reference document points to the challenges of having to develop and apply a holistic set of cyber security solutions and processes, in every layer and technological dimension of today's digital systems. Without this, it will not be possible to effectively combat the most sophisticated cyber threats.

The model directly defines the seven Fundamental Principles:

- Assumption that there are no default or explicit zones with an assigned 'trust' level in the networks.
- Identity-based authentication and authorisation are strictly enforced for all connections and access to infrastructure, data and services.
- Machine-to-machine (M2M) authentication and authorisation are strictly enforced for communication between servers and applications.
- Risk profiles, generated in near real time from monitoring and assessing user and device behaviour, are used to authorise users and devices to resources.
- All sensitive data is encrypted both during transmission and storage.
- All incidents are to be continuously monitored, collected, stored and analysed to assess safety compliance.
- The management and distribution of security policies are centralised.

For this, the model defines seven pillars on which the Zero Trust architecture is to be built together. Each pillar, in relation to the selected system context, indicates a set of mechanisms and cyber security operations, including directly designating specific types of technological solutions to meet the objectives of the pillar:

- The User Dimension: securing, restricting and enforcing personal and non-personal access to Data, Applications, Resources and Services includes the use of identity controls such as multi-factor authentication (MFA) and privileged access management (PAM) for privileged functions. Organisations need the ability to continuously authenticate, authorise and monitor activity patterns to manage user access and privileges while protecting and securing all interactions.
- Device dimension: real-time continuous authentication, inspection, assessment and patching of device vulnerabilities in the enterprise are critical functions. Solutions such as Mobile Device Managers, Comply to Connect programmes or Trusted Platform Modules (TPMs) provide data that can be useful for assessing device trust, determining authorisation and restricting access. Other assessments should be carried out for each access request (e.g. investigating device vulnerability status, software version, protection status, enabling encryption and proper configuration, etc.) The ability to identify, authenticate, inventory, authorise, isolate, secure, remediate and control all devices is essential to the Zero Trust approach.
- Network Dimension: Segmenting (both logically and physically), isolating and controlling the network/environment (local and external) with granular access and policy restrictions. As networks become more and more extensive with macrosegmentation, microsegmentation provides greater protection and control over Data, Applications, Resources and Services. Controlling privileged access, managing internal and external data flows and preventing attackers from being able to take over portions of the network is key.
- The Applications dimension: Applications include tasks in local systems or services, as well as applications or services running in a cloud environment. ZT requirements span the entire application stack, from the application layer to the hypervisor. Securing and properly managing the application layer, as well as compute containers and virtual machines, is critical to ZT deployment. Application delivery methods, such as proxies, enable additional security covering decision points and enforcement of ZT requirements. Developed source code and shared libraries are verified using DevSecOps development practices to secure applications from the very beginning of development.

- Data dimension: understanding the Data, Applications, Resources and Services within an organisation is critical to the successful implementation of a ZT architecture. Organisations need to categorise their Data, Applications, Resources and Services in terms of application criticality and use this information to develop a comprehensive data management strategy as part of an overall ZT approach. This can be achieved by capturing consistent, valid data, categorising data, developing schemas and encrypting data at rest and in transit. Solutions such as DRM, DLP, software-defined environments and granular data labelling support the protection of critical systems.
- Visibility and Analytics dimension: contextual details provide a better understanding of performance, behaviour and activity in other ZT pillars. This visibility improves anomaly detection and provides the ability to dynamically make security policy changes and access decisions in real time. In addition, other monitoring systems, such as sensor data in addition to telemetry, will be used to help complete the picture of what is happening to the environment and help trigger alerts used to respond. Networks will capture and control traffic, going beyond network telemetry and delving into the packets themselves to accurately detect network traffic and observe current threats and target defences more intelligently.
- Automation and Orchestration Dimension: manual security processes need to be automated in order to take action quickly and at scale based on security policies across the organisation. SOAR-type systems improve security and reduce response times. Security orchestration integrates security information and event management (SIEM) and other automated security tools and helps to manage different security systems. Automated security response requires defined processes and consistent enforcement of security policies across all environments to ensure proactive command and control.

One of the key areas for improving the security of technology and increasing reliance on it is to identify a clear purpose for thinking about its security right from its inception. The intensification of the focus on this aspect of technology, i.e. 'security by design', has been influenced by various events, mainly cyber attacks and geopolitical friction, which together have a significant context in hybrid conflicts and human impact. In the Zero Trust model referred to, the assumptions for the security of technology since its inception have been in the pillar of the Applications dimension. Alongside this, the focus of various regulations on this aspect of cyber security is apparent. It can be surmised that this is the aftermath of the various high-profile cyber-attacks of 2015–2022, in which deficiencies in securing the production and delivery of applications were spectacularly exposed, revealing the major impact of these deficiencies on large organisations, including government, local government or the military. This is to the advantage of the attackers in the sense that, in terms of the assumptions of the implementation of hybrid conflicts, attacks of this type realise the raising of public distrust in their own states. Examples of larger attacks and the use of cyberspace for this purpose:

- Ukraine power plant attack (December 2015) – Ukraine was the victim of one of the world's first documented cyber attacks that led to large-scale disruption of energy infrastructure. The attack is attributed to the Sandworm group, possibly linked to Russian military intelligence. It resulted in the disruption of three regional power plants, disrupting the power supply to more than 230,000 households. The attack used malware to gain access to SCADA (Supervisory Control and Data Acquisition) systems that manage industrial control networks at power plants, among others. This software, combined with social engineering techniques, enabled the attackers to remotely take control of the systems and physically disable the transmission lines. Moreover, in doing so, they blocked operators from restoring power by sabotaging the operation of the back-up software, delaying the response to the situation. This type of attack on Ukraine's energy infrastructure has significant implications for the entire international community. This is the first time that a cyber-attack has led to physical power outages of this scale, highlighting the potential risks to critical systems around the world. The event also highlighted the growing role of cyberspace as a new battlefield, where attacks on infrastructure can be just as destructive as traditional military action, which is particularly exploited in hybrid conflicts.
- SolarWinds attack (December 2020) – this attack was disclosed in December 2020, but was probably ongoing from mid-2019. It is currently considered to be one of the most complex and dangerous cyber attacks in recent years. A group linked to Russian intelligence is believed to have been behind the attack, which has been circumstantially confirmed by a US security agency investigation. There are also traces of a Chinese connection to this attack. The attack involved infecting an update package for SolarWinds' Orion software, which is used to manage IT infrastructure in thousands of companies and organisations around the world. By inserting malicious code into legitimate update channels for this software, they were able to gain access to systems for a number of organisations. The list of targets

included the US government and federal agencies, technology companies and private companies (including FireEye, a cyber security technology provider, and Microsoft). As a result, they were able to steal sensitive data and monitor user activity for months before being detected. In the end, the attack probably affected 18,000 SolarWinds customers, although not all of them realised the attack in full. Nevertheless, the attack affected the US Department of the Treasury and the US Department of Commerce, among others, affecting national security concerns. This means that the attackers, in addition to the strategic objective of acquiring information through digital espionage, affected public perceptions of US preparedness and resilience to such attacks, which can be considered a type of hybrid conflict operation. Ultimately, the scale, complexity and longevity of this attack changed perceptions of cyber security, highlighting weaknesses in global technology supply chains and the need to strengthen protection measures in the digital realm. Another important lesson is that private companies themselves do not necessarily care about the security of the technologies they create and stronger regulation in this area is needed.

- Log4Shell vulnerability disclosure in the log4j library (December 2021) – The vulnerability in the log4j library was one of the most serious threats to many IT systems worldwide. The library is widely used in applications written in Java (a popular language for developing many systems) to log system events. The vulnerability, named Log4Shell, allowed remote code execution (RCE), which enabled attackers to take control of an application without having privileges. The scale of the threat proved to be very large due to the widespread use of this library in web applications, cloud servers and systems, and even network infrastructure or popular virtual machine management systems. Within hours of the vulnerability being made public, many organisations – from small to large – could see automated attempts to exploit the vulnerability because, as mentioned, this could be done remotely. Behind the mere attempt to exploit the vulnerability, attempts to carry out various types of cyber-attacks were observed, from ransomware to data theft and taking over computing resources to mine cryptocurrencies. In response to the discovery of the vulnerability, companies had to immediately implement response plans and workarounds, and the library update itself was only delivered after several hours. In many cases, too, despite the availability of the update, it was not possible to carry out the process immediately. The Log4Sehll vulnerability highlighted another dimension of the technology's dependency, this time on open source components, which are often not controlled, secured or verified in any way. In addition, a significant problem that was identified during this incident was that many system owners were not aware at all that such a vulnerability could affect them. This means there is often a lack of control over what the software being produced actually consists of. There is also speculation that knowledge of the vulnerability and how it could be exploited was in Russia's wider offensive plan in cyberspace for use during the attack on Ukraine in February 2022, but the plan was burned by the public disclosure of the vulnerability itself and efforts around the world to remove or mitigate it.

- Using cyber attacks in a full-scale military invasion in February 2022 in Ukraine – Russia's 2022 invasion of Ukraine demonstrated how cyber attacks have become a key element of new conflicts, accompanying traditional warfare. Russia's previous actions in Ukraine since the first invasion in 2014 can be seen as tests of possibility, which in February 2022 took on a dimension of hitherto unknown intensity in the operation and use of cyberspace as a new field of influence in conflicts. From the very beginning of this campaign, Ukraine was the target of coordinated cyber-attacks aimed at destabilising key infrastructure, government and military systems. One of the most significant attacks targeted Ukrainian communication systems, banks, as well as energy grids. Groups with links to the Russian government and military, such as Sandworm or APT28 (Fancy Bear), were responsible for most of these attacks. In one of the most advanced incidents, the WhisperGate malware was used to destroy data and prevent systems from being restored. Another attack, targeting Viasat, paralysed satellite communications, affecting the operation of the Ukrainian army and civilian infrastructure. These actions were designed to undermine morale, hamper communications and disorganise Ukraine's defence operations. The war in Ukraine has shown how crucial a role cyber attacks can play in modern conflicts, affecting every aspect of a state's functioning, from administration to the economy and critical infrastructure, thereby impacting society. The lesson for all is that enhancing the resilience of states must accelerate exponentially in the face of the technological revolution on the one hand, and the rapid rise of hybrid conflicts on the other.
- Ransomware attacks – Between 2018 and 2023, ransomware attacks have become one of the most serious threats in cyberspace, affecting both businesses and government institutions around the world. Ransomware is malicious software that

encrypts a victim's data and demands a ransom in exchange for decrypting it. During this period, the number of such attacks has increased dramatically and attackers have begun to use increasingly sophisticated techniques, which has significantly increased the scale and cost of incidents. Ransomware attacks were no longer limited to data theft and blocking. A 'double extortion' model was introduced, where, in addition to encrypting data, hackers threatened to expose it if the ransom was not paid. Such actions were designed to increase pressure on victims and increase the chances of receiving payment. Well-known groups such as Ryuk, REvil, DarkSide and Conti have carried out massive attacks on sectors such as healthcare, education, energy and public administration. It is also often speculated that the indicated ransomware groups are inspired or even supported by various state actors who are keen to sow panic and lower confidence as part of the intensification of hybrid conflicts. An interesting example is the attack on the Colonial Pipeline in 2021, which caused gas supply disruptions on the US East Coast. Another high-profile incident was the attack on healthcare systems during the COVID-19 pandemic, which caused major disruption to the hospital operations of many hospitals. The response to these actions was the formation of a number of groups cooperating and coordinating targeting actions. It also demonstrated the importance of teams of cyber-security and IT engineers, the judiciary, security services (Police, Counterintelligence) or national incident response teams joining together in joint action.

To date, the way cyber security and cyber resilience frameworks have been provided in organisations has mainly been based on the voluntary application of the dissemination of good practices and the use of corresponding technology. Sanctioned rules for the application of cyber security appeared mainly in the area of creation or operation in regulated areas. The spectacular cyber attacks have shown that the approaches indicated need to change a lot more, and that more and more cyber security rules simply need to be enforced by way of requirements for the operation of all – from the level of private companies, to local governments, institutions, government or the military. With cyber attacks only going to get more and more complex and intense, the evolution of legislation and regulation in the world's major economic areas is apparent.

The evolution in efforts to legally order cyber security can be traced back to the European Union. In 2016, the first NIS Directive is adopted, This directive imposed a number of obligations on Member States, including the establishment of specific types of institutions for cyber security and the introduction of cooperation mechanisms.

In addition, the directive defined certain obligations for ensuring NIS, in particular in relation to the groups of key and important actors defined by the directive. On top of this, there was a requirement to report centrally on the state of cyber security and to take corrective action in the long term. A review of the implementation of this directive (Wrzosek, 2020) noted that:

- The directive introduced a minimum set of requirements, and each Member State could adopt different ways of implementation, including in terms of cyber security requirements or how to enforce them. Thus, a disharmony in cyber resilience was created in the context of the European Union as a whole
- The directive did not cover a number of actors that are equally important from the point of view of the development of cyber threats to be within the scope of such requirements.

Other shortcomings or inadequacies were also identified, which led to the development and adoption of an update to the directive referred to as NIS 2, which came into force in 2023. The NIS 2 directive gives even greater importance to cyber security management systems in traditionally understood security, including civil protection and national security. In addition to the existing indication of national and sectoral computer security incident response teams, the European Cyber Crisis Management Network (EU-CyCLONe) has been formally established, which will support the coordination of large-scale cyber security incident management at Union level. In addition, there has been an increased focus on the use of measures and tools for the ongoing assessment of risks in cyberspace and the cooperation of actors to share knowledge about them. Against the backdrop of the described examples of cyber threats in recent years, the NIS 2 Directive introduces requirements for all actors to manage their technology supply chain. For technology manufacturers, this means new, formally established requirements in the process of creating, delivering and maintaining technology, including those related to responding to and mitigating emerging vulnerabilities. In addition, it formally entrenches the process of security certification of digital products, on the basis of which member states may introduce new types of requirements for technology providers for specific tasks, and the lack of certification or loss of certification may mean for technology buyers the directive will mean that greater vigilance must be exercised when acquiring technology, and technology providers are expected to prove at the delivery stage that they will deliver secure technology. It will also become important to control, monitor and evaluate other actors over time to determine whether they can actually be an adequate and trusted technology supplier, in order to exclude those posing a higher risk. Overall, it is intended to be a collaborative strengthening of resilience, for which the ideological source is an understanding of the fundamental principle of 'secure by design'. A key aspect for the directive is the introduction of a catalogue of penalties (NIS2 Directive, 2024) for non-compliance by covered entities, with the aim that this will force them to actually increase their level of cyber resilience.

In parallel, in the US, despite a longer history in the systemic management of cyber security in the context of the country's cyber resilience, new strategies for action were needed. In March 2023, the US government unveiled a new strategy for cyber security (National Cybersecurity Strategy, 2023) for the entire country. One of the main goals of the strategy is to understand the need to increase the resilience of critical infrastructure and the country as a whole even more deeply. This includes measures to raise security standards in sectors such as energy, finance, transport and telecommunications. The government intends to invest in upgrading outdated systems and introduce new regulations that force private companies to manage risks more effectively. As part of this, investment needs have been identified for the development of modern technologies, such as artificial intelligence and machine learning, which can help identify threats and automate cyber security operations. Critical infrastructure is also to be subjected to regular audits and penetration testing to detect vulnerabilities and weaknesses more quickly.

One of the key elements of the strategy is the formulation of a new role for the central US government in the area of cyber security. In previous approaches, which relied heavily on the private sector, the new strategy will see the government take a more proactive role in providing security. The government administration has recognised that private actors often do not have the resources or motivation to effectively protect critical infrastructure, such as energy or telecommunications networks. Consequently, the strategy emphasised closer public-private cross-sector cooperation and the establishment of new regulations to raise security standards. In addition, a new approach to accountability for insufficient cyber security efforts was proposed. Technology companies and IT service providers are to be obliged to take more responsibility for the security of the products and services they introduce. The strategy also points to the need to develop more rigorous standards for software design, so that security is integral to the entire product development process – from conception to deployment and operation. The strategy also includes guidelines on the responsibility for implementing security and the need to inform customers of potential vulnerabilities and threats. One of the explicitly stated tools to achieve the goal will be for each software developer to provide a full list of dependencies (components, libraries) with the software, the so-called Software Bill of Materials.

The strategy also strongly hints at coordination and cooperation activities. The government is to work more deeply with allies and partners to jointly counter the threats coming from cyberspace. Among other things, the need for decisive action in the fight against cybercrime and increased resources in this area was pointed out. Ransomware attacks, which in recent years have targeted key sectors of the US economy such as healthcare, energy or transport, were identified as one of the main threats, with the attackers aiming to cause confusion and sow panic, which fits in with hybrid conflicts. The strategy explicitly points to other countries that the US sometimes targets – Russia, China, Iran and North Korea. The US plans to strengthen its defensive and even retaliatory cyber-attack capabilities. The strategy also calls for close cooperation with allies, such as NATO countries, to coordinate cyber operations.

The US government's actions are quickly being translated into practical action, the implementation of requirements or implementing regulations. One action is the introduction of requirements for transitioning fully to post-quantum cryptography by 2035, with the understanding that institutions are to prepare for this today. Another important factor in the success of the strategy is having adequate staff resources to carry out cyber security tasks. The director of the US National Security Agency (NSA), in an interview in September 2024 (Cybersecurity is National Security, 2024), explicitly identifies cyber security as a domain joined together with others representing national security interests. On top of this, in early September 2024, the US presidential administration announced (Coker, 2024) that dealing with cyber-security is being elevated to a public service and that choosing cyber-security as a career path has been described as 'choosing to serve the country'. This indicates how cyber security, including the protection of information space and users of information systems, is becoming a common security concern of societies. This is an important indicator for the international community as a whole, including NATO countries, as many times US-initiated cyber-security initiatives have become international standards of conduct. Nevertheless, important initiatives linking national security with cyber security, as well as grassroots social initiatives along the lines of civil defence were already emerging in Poland in 2019 in the form of the Polish Civic Cyber Defence, among others. At the NATO level, a key initiative is the annual Locked Shields cyber defence exercise, in which the cyber security services of the military, civilian services and private citizen cybersecurity experts jointly exercise protection against various threats to critical infrastructure (e.g. power plants, logistics systems or drinking water supply).

A major challenge to any effort trying to place technology within security is its accelerating development. In the last three years we have seen this challenge to artificial intelligence and machine learning.

On the one hand, we have high hopes for this technology as a new milestone in industrial development (an event on the scale of the steam engine, electricity and the invention of the internet). On the other hand, as pointed out earlier, negative uses or risks of AI were quickly found, such as using it to automatically create social media disinformation nets through bots or to generate fake multimedia material, and overall to raise the threat level in hybrid conflicts (Mazzucchi, 2022). Therefore, the question of regulating requirements that would impose security, ethics or self-control mechanisms on the creators of these technologies immediately arises. An example of an attempt in this regard is the EU AI Act, passed in 2024. The AI Act is a first-of-its-kind global piece of legislation that creates a legal framework to regulate the development and implementation of AI systems. On the one hand, the act aims to protect people from the dangers of inappropriate use of technology, while on the other hand, it seeks to encourage innovation and the development of artificial intelligence in Europe.

In 2024, the European Union adopted the Cyber Resilience Act (CRA), a directive aimed at increasing the resilience of digital products and services brought to the European market. The CRA is a response to the growing threats in cyberspace and the increasing frequency of attacks that affect public institutions, businesses and individual consumers alike. The directive is a key element of the EU's strategy to strengthen digital security. The main objective of the CRA is to raise cyber security standards for digital products and services, including devices and software. The directive applies to a wide range of solutions, from simple IoT (Internet of Things) devices to complex operating systems and industrial software. The key idea is to make minimum cybersecurity standards mandatory at the design and market implementation stages of products.

The directive requires manufacturers and suppliers to keep their products cyber-proof throughout the lifecycle of the devices, meaning that security updates and patches must be available for a certain period of time after the product is launched. Manufacturers and suppliers must not neglect their products once they have been sold – they must ensure that they remain secure and protected from new threats. This introduces greater accountability throughout the product lifecycle. This approach aims to ensure that digital products are more resilient to attacks and offer a higher level of security for users. In addition, manufacturers must provide adequate data protection measures or access control mechanisms. On top of this, they must also provide detailed technical documentation to enable recipients to verify compliance with the requirements of the directive. Digital products and services are to be subject to a conformity assessment before they are placed on the EU market. This assessment is to verify that they meet the cybersecurity requirements of the directive. Depending on the level of risk associated with the product in question, the assessment can range from the manufacturer's internal compliance procedures to an external audit by independent certification bodies. In the event of non-compliance with the CRA, manufacturers may be subject to sanctions, including financial penalties that can amount to several per cent of the company's annual turnover, in order to discourage manufacturers from neglecting cyber security issues.

The CRA Directive is an important step in building the resilient and secure digital infrastructure needed to continue to grow the economy based on new technologies and in the face of threats such as hybrid conflicts. It introduces high security standards, but also requires cooperation between businesses, governments and authorities to ensure effective protection against cyber threats. Consumers are expected to gain greater confidence that the products they use meet high security standards, which can increase confidence in new technologies. In turn, manufacturers, despite the challenges of compliance, can gain a competitive advantage by providing more secure and resilient products.

DEVELOPMENT OF TECHNOLOGY FUNCTIONALLY OFFERING RESILIENCE AND SECURITY IN THE FACE OF HYBRID CONFLICT

In the context of faiths that place hybrid conflicts ahead of efforts to protect civilians, it becomes important to build technological solutions that, by design, offer embedded mechanisms relevant to this type of conflict that offer absolute credibility, availability, confidentiality, integrity and accountability. Therefore, those technologies that offer one or more capabilities such as:

- The absence or minimisation of single points of failure, which in the face of an emergency increases resilience when some parts of the system may be decommissioned, attacked or inaccessible;
- Deep authentication and ensuring the reliability of the information placed in the communication system, together with full transparency and verifiability of operations in the system;
- Architecturally supporting greater resilience through, among other things, adequate decentralisation and dispersion, while ensuring replicability of data or communication channels;
- Provided data security mechanisms at rest, in motion and during processing, including using quantum and post quantum cryptography solutions;
- Ensure redundancy in operation so that if part of the system fails, the others can take over unnoticed in service delivery, communication and data processing roles;

- Increasing autonomy in action that ultimately leads to self-organisation, self-defence and self-repair of digital systems in the face of hybrid threats;
- Meeting the assumptions of the Zero Trust model described in the previous section.

This subsection will discuss various examples of technologies that are being developed for the indicated characteristics and thus indicate their usefulness in protecting societies and in enhancing the cyber resilience of states in the face of hybrid conflicts.

Mission Critical LTE (MC-LTE) technology targets mission-critical communication systems, particularly for emergency services, the military and critical infrastructure management organisations. MC-LTE is based on Long-Term Evolution (LTE) networks, widely used in mobile communications, but is specifically tailored to meet extremely stringent requirements for reliability, low latency and data security. These networks must operate even under the most extreme conditions, such as natural disasters, overcrowded commercial networks or hostile operations. The systems are also designed to be resilient and fully functional even in the event of partial infrastructure failure. This enables MC-LTE to support operations where people's health and lives, as well as public safety, depend on the quality of communications. One of the main applications of MC-LTE is to support communications for emergency services such as the police, fire brigade, ambulance service or anti-terrorist units. In such situations, the rapid exchange of information with integrity is crucial. MC-LTE provides real-time data transmission for rapid decision-making and coordination, for example, video from the scene of an incident can be transmitted to command centres to assess the situation and better manage resources. MC-LTE can also be key in sectors managing critical infrastructure such as power grids, water supply, public transport or aviation. For railway systems, MC-LTE can be used to communicate between trains and traffic management centres, ensuring safe and efficient control. In energy, the technology allows remote monitoring and control of power grids, which is particularly important in emergency situations such as breakdowns or cyber attacks. MC-LTE supports large-scale operations and also provides high resilience to disruptions and cyberattack attempts. MC-LTE natively employs encryption and advanced authentication mechanisms to protect against unauthorised access and data interception attempts. In addition, MC-LTE is more resilient to interference and DDoS (Distributed Denial of Service) attacks that could cripple classic LTE networks.

The capabilities of mobile networks in terms of their resilience to emergencies are being considered and developed in future technology releases (IEEE Public Safety Technology Initiative, 2024).

One of the key advantages of 5G networks currently being deployed for mission-critical communications is its ability to support reliable low-latency communication (URLLC). With latency as low as one millisecond and robust reliability mechanisms, 5G can facilitate real-time data exchange and seamless coordination. This capability is crucial in scenarios where split-second decisions can make a difference, such as coordinating rescue efforts or remotely controlling unmanned vehicles (UAVs) or robots. Effective communication and connectivity are critical to emergency response operations as they enable rapid information exchange, resource coordination and timely decision-making. The 5G network is designed with redundancy mechanisms, including multiple levels of backup systems and on-the-fly failover capabilities. This redundant architecture ensures that even if some network components fail, alternative paths and resources can be automatically used to maintain connectivity and minimise service disruption. Furthermore, 5G networks offer advanced techniques to increase network availability, such as self-repair features. In the event of a localised outage or equipment failure, 5G networks can dynamically reconfigure themselves, rerouting traffic and adjusting resource allocation to maintain service continuity. This self-repair feature is particularly valuable in emergency situations where traditional maintenance and repair operations may be hindered or delayed.

Another mechanism specific to 5G networks is the ability to dynamically create separate network slices (network slicing). This mechanism allows a single physical 5G network to be logically divided into multiple virtual networks, each tailored to the specific requirements of different use cases or applications. By dividing the network into such slices, dedicated chunks can be allocated for different purposes, such as a dedicated slice for emergency services with guaranteed bandwidth, very low latency and highest priority. This ensures that critical emergency communications are not disrupted by congestion or interference from traffic on another network. Splitting the network provides the means to prioritise bandwidth for different needs ensuring the necessary resources to deliver the service.

The next evolution of mobile networks, 6G networks are expected to offer further solutions related to improving resilience, reliability and usability in crisis situations such as hybrid conflicts. Research and projects are already underway to define the assumptions of next-generation 6G networks, including for mission-critical communications applications. Some of the key improvements envisaged for 6G include increased data rates, improved spectral efficiency in radio communications, enhanced security and support for integrating different types of networks, including satellites or unmanned aerial vehicle (UAV) networks. One area of development within 6G networks is the increase in peak data rates through the use of higher frequency bands, such as terahertz (THz) spectrum, and advanced antenna technologies such as intelligent reflective surfaces (IRS) and holographic beamforming. In addition, 6G networks are expected to make greater use of artificial intelligence (AI) and machine learning (ML) within a common management system to enable more efficient resource allocation, predictive analytics and self-optimisation capabilities. It should be emphasised that the indicated aspects of enhancing network security in the face of various threats are realised and will be developed in the years to come.

Nevertheless, ahead of the advent of 6G network solutions, it is worth noting the accelerated adaptation of the use of satellite-based networking in recent years. Communications using satellites have been around for many years, but before that the development of their use was gradual. The main uses that have emerged are satellite television, voice communication in special conditions or, finally, the delivery of Internet networks to geographically inaccessible places. The largest project in this area is the Starlink satellite network currently under development by SpaceX. The idea at SpaceX was initiated as early as 2004, but the actual implementation of the project began in 2015–2016, with the aim of launching the first satellites of the future constellation into low earth orbit (LEO) in 2019 with the possibility of providing Internet access and network connectivity in general to every corner of the world. By 2024, the Starlink network already includes more than 5,000 satellites. On top of this, since 2022 SpaceX has been developing a parallel dedicated Starshield network for use exclusively for the US government. On the one hand, the commercial use of this type of network has increased, allowing the Internet to reach places in the world where cellular or fibre-optic networks still have not reached. On the other hand, satellite networks have quickly revealed their special role as a solution for crisis situations or even armed conflicts, including hybrid ones. With the launch of the Starlink network for Ukraine after the outbreak of Russia's armed aggression in February 2022, it was possible to maintain strategic connectivity to the world or internal connectivity for critical infrastructure, among other needs (Antoniuk, 2022).

In parallel, the development of ICT networks includes increasing the resilience of the Internet itself and the wide area networks traditionally used for all communications between people. The classic Internet network was and is a major development of the 1960s and 1970s, but the design and organisation of the network was not designed for the challenges that have arisen particularly in the last ten years, including hybrid conflicts. One of the key weaknesses of this network is the limitations of the key protocol for establishing communication between independent networks building the Internet, the Border Gateway Protocol (BGP). As indicated in (Perrig et al., 2017), these limitations include:

- Risks of failure and interruption of communication due to the lack of separation between the control layer and the data layer. By attacking the BGP routing function, the network can be led to malfunction. It should be pointed out here that high-profile attacks of this type have occurred at the inter-state level, such as the 2010 attack in which a Chinese telecom operator took over as much as 15% of all global Internet traffic for 16 minutes (Demchak, Shavitt, 2018).
- Lack of separation and isolation in the event of failure – failure of a single BGP node can result in communication failure across the entire network.
- Low scalability – related to the fact that changes to the BGP protocol must be propagated throughout the network, resulting in an increase in load as the number of nodes increases.
- Single path – BGP in the end relies on the selection of a single path from source to destination. There is no mechanism for balancing traffic or choosing an alternative in the face of failure.

Add to this the widespread shortcomings of natively designed authentication and authorisation mechanisms. Solutions have been added over the years more along the lines of trying to patch the problem. Solutions such as RPKI, BGPsec and DNSSEC have been proposed, but their adoption has been slow and inadequate in the face of challenges to more resilient wide area networks. To counter this, there is a need for the development of network architectures for wide area networks, including the Internet, that will offer embedded solutions that offset the indicated limitations of traditional Internet networks, thus following a 'secure by design' approach. One of the more important proposals is the SCION network architecture, developed since 2009. A summary of the assumptions of this architecture can be found in (Perrig et al., 2017), as well as in a comprehensive monograph (Chuat et al., 2022). The SCION network directly addresses each of the problems and, in particular, takes into account different types of network threats – from BGP path acquisition to DDoS attacks. On the back of the research project, the company Anapaya Networks (Anapaya, 2024) was founded to commercialise the SCION architecture. One of its major achievements is the implementation of a secure network for the financial industry in Switzerland. A recent publication by the creators of SCION (Wyss et al., 2024) discussed at a NATO conference on conflicts in cyberspace pointed to the potential for the traditional Internet and its providers to evolve towards a secure network such as that offered by the SCION architecture by also combining several other mechanisms that together will offer different levels of protection for network traffic: encryption, control, filtering, authentication and prioritisation.

The basis for the operation of the indicated ICT networks with security-enhancing solutions is the Software Defined Networking (SDN) paradigm. SDN technology is also indicated as the basis for implementing any of the assumptions defined in the Zero Trust model. SDN introduces the assumption that the existing three-layer model of data and communications networks – control plane, data plane and management plane – should be separated into dedicated network components (devices, software), instead of integrating parts of these layers in almost every network device. An important assumption for the operation of SDN is an approach in which the network initially does not allow data to be transmitted and connections to be established, making the essence of the operation consistent with the Zero Trust approach. This is due to the essence of the underlying SDN network protocol, Openflow (McKeown et al., 2008, pp. 69–74). It is only by defining connections or introducing dynamic authentication mechanisms that data transfer can be achieved. The separation of the control and data transmission layer also allows more elaborate decision logics to be achieved, going beyond the capabilities of the previously classically used firewalls. In addition, the SDN-based network development model allows new functionalities to be added by extending the management and control software, when the software and hardware in the data transmission layer do not need to be modified. This allows SDN networks to be ready to change and evolve in a more dynamic way than in classic ICT networks. New mechanisms can thus be developed, including new security mechanisms in response to emerging threats. The SDN approach can be seen today in many ICT technologies as a basis for building any new solutions.

Another important strand of technological development in the area of networks and IT resources is the use of public clouds (cloud computing). As early as the 1960s, the idea emerged that data processing and computing would one day become the same public utility as electricity or water (Garfinkel, 2011). The development of approaches to the commonality of computing services developed in parallel with the capabilities of computers, servers and ICT networks. A watershed moment for cloud computing came in 2006 when Amazon launched Amazon Web Services (AWS), offering an on-demand Elastic Compute Cloud (EC2) service. AWS allowed users to rent computing power and store data on external servers, enabling them to avoid upfront costly IT infrastructure investments, shifting costs towards operational costs. This 'on-demand' model was the beginning of the rapid growth of cloud computing. The next big providers, Microsoft and Google, presented their first cloud solutions as early as 2008. The development of cloud computing and, above all, the technologies fundamental to the realisation of this area have had a major impact on the overall development of IT and ICT in the last 20 years. On the one hand, cloud computing has initially made use of existing developments to offer a new model for data processing, while on the other hand, its development has given rise to new ideas and technologies that are being adapted in the other direction to classic ICT environments, which translates into jointly intertwined technological developments. One of the primary areas of impact of the development of cloud computing is the influence on the use of software-defined technologies everywhere, where this was not possible or limited until now.

The development of cloud computing is based on three basic service models that offer different levels of management and control for users:

- IaaS (Infrastructure as a Service) – The most basic model in which a cloud provider provides infrastructure such as servers, networks and storage. Users are responsible for managing the operating system, applications and data. Examples include AWS, Microsoft Azure and Google Cloud.
- PaaS (Platform as a Service) – In the PaaS model, the cloud provider offers a platform on which users can develop, test and deploy applications. Users do not have to manage the infrastructure, allowing them to focus on the code and logic of the application. Examples include Google App Engine or Microsoft Azure App Service.
- SaaS (Software as a Service) – In the SaaS model, users are given access to off-the-shelf applications running in the cloud, without having to manage the infrastructure, platform or code. Examples include Gmail, Microsoft 365 or Salesforce.

Further intermediate models or even the possibility of moving cloud technologies back to on-premises environments in the face of requirements for data security or generally regulated practical applications are also emerging.

In addition to technologies aimed at solving the problem of computing in different ways, the development of cloud computing has also offered important conceptual advances in enhancing the cyber security and cyber resilience of ICT infrastructures. An example of this is the BeyondCorp model (Ward, Beyer, 2014, pp. 6–11) proposed by Google and implemented in Google Cloud, which is considered one of the first practical realisations of the Zero Trust idea of an enhanced authentication system based on an extensive role and permission model. In the BeyondCorp system, access is constantly verified and monitored regardless of the user's location (Figure 6.2). Thus, there is no need to define internal or external zones, and access is granted after verification of the device from which the employee is making the connection, as well as through credentials.

As shown in Figure 6.2, the BeyondCorp architecture consists of several important components. *The Access Proxy* provides access to all internal applications and to which you must connect to gain this access. You must have a *Managed Device* of your choice in order to connect.

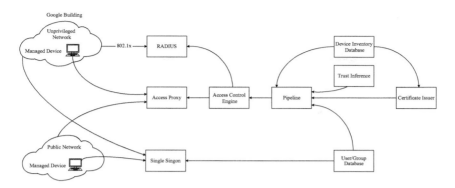

FIGURE 6.2   BeyondCorp architecture
Source: Own study based on Ward, Beyer (2014)

Essential to the entire component is the *Access Control Engine*, which performs the authorisation process on the basis of information received from the other components, e.g. information about correct user authentication, user or device group membership or user location. The *Single Sign-on* Portal allows central verification of the authentication components presented by the user. *Device Inventory Database* and *User/Group Database* are databases with user and computer accounts. The Trust Inference component is responsible for assigning a dynamic level of trust to a user session, and *the Certificate Issuer* allows device certificates to be managed. All data is passed to the Access Control Engine component so that it can make the right security decisions. Analysing this approach, it is apparent that there is a real move away from the classic perimeter model and a reliance on trust models for access allocation. The development of this vision has also been undertaken in the area of traditional ICT networks, referring to the approach proposed by Google as the Software Defined Perimeter (SDP) model. SDP[1] is based on the premise that access to network resources should be controlled based on the identity of the user rather than the location from which the network traffic originates (perimeter). Traditional solutions, such as firewalls or virtual private networks (VPNs), are based on the assumption that the user inside the protected network is secure and that threats only come from outside. This model becomes inadequate in cloud and hybrid environments, where network boundaries are blurred and users and resources are in different locations. SDP creates dynamic security boundaries that are invisible to unauthorised users, thereby minimising the attack surface. In practice, this means that users who have not been verified cannot even see the available resources. A diagram of how SDP works is shown in Figure 6.3. Three key components are defined within SDP:

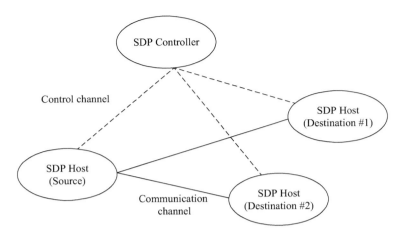

FIGURE 6.3 Architecture of the SDP solution

Source: Own study based on Zscaler (2024)

- SDP Controller (SDP Controller) – the main management centre that is responsible for verifying a user's identity and authorising their access to resources.
- Client – a user or device that requests access to a resource. The consumer first authenticates against the SDP controller.
- Provider (Gateway/Resource) – a resource that is protected within the SDP. Access is only granted if the controller confirms the identity and rights of the consumer.

One of the important features of using cloud computing is that the data in it has high mobility and rapid portability. Data is not stored locally and can be accessed from almost anywhere in the world. One of the in-built mechanisms of cloud computing in particular is the ability to replicate data quickly, including taking advantage of geographical dispersion. Such a solution is crucial and important when, in the face of hybrid conflicts, it may sometimes be necessary to suddenly move data to another location before an aggressor can access it. An example of implementation in a crisis situation was shown by Russia's attack on Ukraine in 2022. This use of the cloud was pointed out by Microsoft (Defending Ukraine, 2022) in its June 2022 report on defending Ukraine in cyberspace. Among its five main conclusions, the report pointed out that defence in the face of new conflicts now requires most countries to have the ability to rapidly move operations and data across borders to other countries. Russia targeted, among others, Ukraine's government data centre in an early missile attack, and other servers 'on the ground' were similarly vulnerable to attack by conventional weapons. Russia also targeted local computer networks with its devastating wiper malware attacks. However, the Ukrainian government successfully maintained its civilian and military operations, acting quickly to move its digital infrastructure to the public cloud in various data centres across Europe. The success of Ukraine's cyber resilience efforts is also indicated by a study (Kott et al., 2024, pp. 82–89), which summarises the factors relevant to cyber resilience and how they can be realised as part of its defence by Russia in 2022. The study identifies the factors cited throughout the chapter:

- Willingness to quickly change systems and replace each other. Replacing the use of satellite communications offered by Viasat with solutions from SpaceX was cited as an example.
- The ability to receive some attacks in parts of the network while maintaining the availability of others. This is possible in highly decentralised and distributed networks. Ukraine has taken advantage of its dispersion across multiple telecom operators, which has proven to be a natural resilience of ICT networks in Ukraine (resillience-by-design).
- Readiness for rapid reconfiguration and transfer of resources. In this respect, successes have been achieved through the aforementioned use of cloud computing in safe countries in the West, and this has allowed the continuity of state operations to be maintained in the face of an incipient conflict.
- The paradigm of continuously creating, maintaining and updating resources for data exchange to ensure security against attacks. An example is the aforementioned public cloud backups, so that Ukraine's critical data could be securely managed in the face of conflict. In the area of secure communications, the establishment of a direct, highly secure communication line between the Ukrainian military and the US European Command is particularly noteworthy. This line was specifically designed to be resistant to detection and interference by hostile forces.

DEVELOPMENT OF TECHNOLOGIES TO DEFEND OTHER TECHNOLOGICAL AREAS AGAINST ATTACKS IN THE FACE OF HYBRID CONFLICTS

Another dimension of considering technology in the context of hybrid conflicts is the use of technological solutions to combat threats. As indicated earlier, a very important, and negative, use of technology in hybrid conflicts is the widespread spread of disinformation and false multimedia material to make specific impacts on societies and populations.

In a report discussing the use of the cyber domain in Russia's aggression against Ukraine in 2022, it was pointed out that the cyber influence operation was well prepared using the long experience of the intelligence services in this type of operation, transferring it to cyberspace. One of the false narratives launched on 24 February 2024 was the introduction by some ten different websites of a narrative about US-funded biological laboratories. This story was further replicated by a further more than 300 Russian-controlled sites. Another example of the use of this approach was the narrative that Ukraine was using a hospital in Mariupol as a troop grouping site, for which the hospital was evacuated. Two days later, Russia bombed this hospital and Russia's representative at the United Nations described this as 'fake news'. In general, such various narratives favouring the aims of the aggressor have appeared and continue to appear. It is also important to note that the action of such actors is not limited to the targeted country directly, but also to other countries e.g. allies. In addition, other themes are taken into account, such as the Covid-19 pandemic-related influence operation targeting New Zealand or Canadian society.

The relevance and increasing intensity of the use of disinformation or generally deceiving Internet users in various ways (phishing) is obvious. To date, one of the main efforts is education and awareness raising, but these efforts are difficult to scale and respond to any and all emerging threats. Thus, the cybersecurity and technology research community has been looking for years for various solutions to combat disinformation or deceptive multimedia material in general in a more automated and scaled way. Ideally, such threats should be extinguished at the point where they occur before they reach a wider audience.

One of the basic scenarios for combating sites or messages used in practice is the effort of various companies and communities to monitor emerging threats on an ongoing basis. Projects are emerging that aggregate information about emerging phishing attack attempts, e.g. for websites that are recognised as phishing sites, there is the OpenPhish portal (OpenPhish, 2024). Various organisations have web scanners that attempt to detect such sites using built-in algorithms and make them public to others. Such sources of knowledge of emerging phishing sites are used by web browser providers, where they can keep the list of dangerous sites up to date. A user, should he or she attempt to access such a site, will be informed that the site is unsafe or even prevented from accessing it. In addition, information about phishing sites is reported to domain registrars, who can block or even disable such domains. The same is true for social networks, where it is possible to report perceived attempts at misinformation or misleading multimedia material. What are the problems and challenges with the current approach?

Utilizing new technologies for population protection

- These actions are not proactive but reactive, take time and do not happen immediately. This means that before access to misleading material is blocked or removed, certain groups of people may become aware of it. Attempts at rectification may not be as effective as the information sown through such an operation.
- The means and monitoring of this type of phishing are limited – to specific types, such as websites, and scanning the Internet takes a long time. Many communication channels are not covered by any design or solution, leaving attackers with plenty of opportunities to reach their targets.
- Algorithms for detecting complex and advanced phishing still need to be developed and various studies are being conducted in this area. Detecting disinformation can be considered a challenge still. Research is also underway in relation to building technological solutions that allow for immediate responses to detected threats, or even building new ways of doing things that make it impossible or very limited to share this type of material.
- There is no common approach and no possibility to block or remove detected material that is considered false and dangerous. Designated domains with websites, on the one hand, are easy to block; on the other hand, removing all messages on social networks that spread false information seems to be a major challenge today.

The publication (Parikh, Atrey, 2018, pp. 436–441) defines seven types of false information:

- visual: This type of fake news uses graphic elements such as videos or images.
- messages for specific types of users: they are targeted by fake accounts and their target audience may belong to a specific age group, gender or culture.
- Post-based fake news: these mainly appear on social media platforms. Posts can be messages on Facebook or X, using visual material.
- Network-based fake news: a form of fake news spread by a network of Facebook friends, LinkedIn associates or members of an organisation.
- Knowledge-based fake news: presents a scientific or reasonable explanation of an unresolved issue. Such stories are designed to spread false information.
- Fake news based on style: this type of fake news focuses on the way the content is presented to the audience; most fake news comes from sources that are not journalists, so the writing style may vary.

- Position-based fake news: focuses on how statements are made in an article. The themes of position-based stories tend to be vague, with little information and lots of statements (false arguments).

As technological solutions that can allow the detection of phishing, disinformation or fake news, it is possible to identify essentially three groups of solutions with different scopes of application in relation to the types of fake material:

- Digital watermarking
  - Use: Multimedia materials (image, video, sound) and other objects in which a watermark can be embedded.
- Analytical methods that use a variety of algorithmic methods, including artificial intelligence and machine learning to detect a threat in a given data type or different data types. Including
  - Application: Analysis of any material: multimedia, text, web pages, etc.
- Post fact-checking with the community involves the community analysing suspicious material and providing public feedback on detected threats. This is how the aforementioned OpenPhish works, for example, and previously various media portals invested in 'fact-checking' services.
  - Use: all fake material, targeting news and web portals.

Over the past few years, various methods have been proposed to analyse the material and detect among them false material in the form of disinformation or false information, including phishing:

- Zhao proposes the concept of using a method that does not depend on artefact identification, but relies on a tagging mechanism to prevent Deepfake multimedia images. The labelling is to use a neural network in an encoder-decoder structure to embed watermarks in facial features. The injected label will link to features that identify the face in the image, so it will be sensitive to translational face substitutions (i.e. Deepfake) and resistant to conventional image modifications (e.g. resizing and compression). In the compound, it will be possible to identify whether watermarked images have been forged by Deepfake methods based on the existence of a label. Experimental results show that the method can achieve an average detection accuracy of more than 80%, confirming the effectiveness of the proposed method in implementing Deepfake detection (Zhao et al., 2023, pp. 4591–4600).

- The study (Caramancion, 2023, pp. 0042–0046) presents the concept of using a large language model to detect fake news. The researcher presented the capabilities of the ChatGPT model for the task of assessing presented material as either false or true. Using a selected dataset as an example, the model demonstrated 100% performance in distinguishing between true and false news.
- The publication (Alquran, Banitaan, 2022, pp. 155–160) proposes the use of data mining methods in the social network space to detect fake messages. The researchers focused on selecting the best features of text messages to enhance the performance of selected machine learning models.
- As the authors point out (Chai et al., 2022, pp. 790–803), web-based phishing attacks are evolving and remain a major threat in the area of social engineering attacks. To date, phishing detection methods of this type have mainly focused on URLs, neglecting the other two important modalities of a Web page: textual information and the visual layer. Moreover, the interpretability of these methods based on deep machine learning is limited, which reduces the reliability of the model and prevents relevant and useful information from being obtained. The indicated paper formulates a potential solution to the problems presented by using a multimodal hierarchical attention model that jointly learns deep fraud cues from the three main modalities to detect phishing more effectively. The proposed method not only learned improved deep cues to better detect phishing, but also provided a hierarchical interpretation system from which phishing threat information could be developed.
- Researchers in (Matsumoto et al., 2021, pp. 19–20) use graph transform-based neural networks to analyse communication grids to detect those that propagate false information. Effectiveness has been demonstrated on, among others, a dataset cross-referenced to the Twitter platform (now X).
- (Afchar et al., 2018, pp. 1–7) presents a proposed algorithm for detecting manipulated faces in video footage (deepfakes) using Deepfake and Face2Face methods. The paper is based on deep machine learning. Two networks of this type, both with a small number of layers, were used to focus on the mesoscopic properties of the images. They were evaluated on both an existing dataset and a dataset created from online videos. The tests showed a detection rate of more than 98% for Deepfake and 95% for Face2Face.

In the context of the development of technologies to defend other technological areas against attacks in the face of hybrid conflicts, the overall development of cyber security systems is relevant. The previous subsection focused primarily functionally on the mechanisms for securing, preventing and architecture supporting cyber resilience (Prevent). Within this subsection, an important area of cyber security development will be identified in the area of detection (Detect) and remediation of systems (Correct) when security and prevention mechanisms are breached.

Classic solutions, whether developed as off-the-shelf commercial products, as open-source projects or undergoing a continuous search for new mechanisms in the field of computer security incident detection and response, include:

- IDS/IPS systems: intrusion detection systems (IDS) and intrusion prevention systems (IPS) are tools used to monitor network traffic or system activity to detect suspicious activity that may indicate an attempted security breach.
  - IDSs act as passive systems – they do not take preventive action, but only detect and record potential incidents, which they report to administrators.
  - Intrusion prevention systems (IPSs), unlike IDSs, not only detect threats, but also actively take preventive action to block suspicious traffic or stop malicious activity. IPSs must operate in an 'inline' mode, meaning that they are placed directly in the path of network traffic or the execution path of subsequent process steps, so that they can intervene in harmful activity immediately.
    There are two types of IDS/IPS systems:
  - Network (NIDS/NIPS) – monitors network traffic in real time. It scans data packets transmitted over the network and compares them with a database of known threat signatures. If it detects suspicious traffic, it generates an alert and, in IPS mode, can block the traffic.
  - Host (HIDS/HIPS)) -monitors activity on individual hosts (servers, computers) by analysing system logs, processes and other indicators of device-level activity. When a threat is detected, it can trigger an alert (IDS mode) or lead to various actions to block or stop activity (IPS mode).
- Endpoint Detection and Response (EDR) systems – is the evolution of HIDS systems in conjunction with the development of classic anti-virus systems. EDR allows activity to be tracked at different ends, threats to be detected and incidents to be responded to automatically or manually. Thanks to its ability to monitor processes in real time, EDR can detect various threats such as malware, ransomware or advanced fileless malware activities.

- Security Information and Event Management (SIEM) systems are tools that collect, analyse and correlate data from various sources to identify anomalies and potential threats. SIEM combines data from systems such as IDS, IPS, firewalls, servers, applications and end devices to provide a comprehensive view of an organisation's security situation. The key functions of SIEM are:
  - Data collection and correlation – SIEM collects logs and events from different systems and correlates them, identifying potential threats.
  - Real-time monitoring – SIEM systems enable real-time monitoring of security events, allowing for rapid detection of incidents.
  - Reporting and analysis – SIEM offers analytical tools to help report incidents, identify causes and create remediation strategies.

    The main challenges of SIEM systems are the permanently growing volumes of logs to be analysed, the need to maintain and develop in such a way that the system is ready and responsive to threat signals.
- Orchestration, automation and response (SOAR) systems are tools that integrate the various security systems available on the network into a single execution tool, automating and coordinating incident response activities. SOAR allows tasks such as data analysis, incident classification and the initiation of appropriate corrective actions to be performed automatically.

A further anticipated evolution in the context of the growing challenges of cyber resilience, including in the face of increasing hybrid threats, relates primarily to the widespread automation and autonomisation of operations. This ties in with the central finding that in cyber security operations, it is most difficult to scale the teams of personnel working on things of detection and response to threats. On the other hand, the vision of the future battlefield in various conflicts is of autonomous systems fighting each other, controlled by autonomous agents, as the study points out (Kott, 2018, pp. 55–70). This means that a very important area of cyber defence development is solutions for automation, autonomisation, system-to-system cooperation, etc. with a gradual reduction in the need for human intervention, leaving them only with the most difficult tasks that are not solvable by automatons at the time.

Within the framework of the aforementioned publication (Kott, 2018), as well as a second one defining a reference architecture for defence agents (Théron et al., 2020, pp. 1–21), assumptions for the existence of autonomous defence agents are indicated. These agents are to

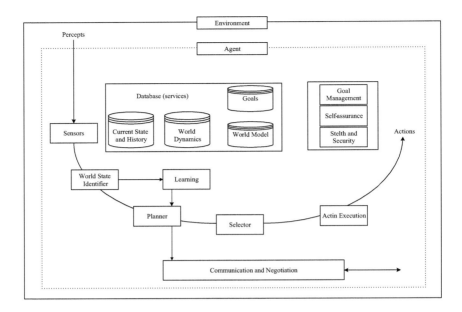

FIGURE 6.4   Architecture for an autonomous defence agent

Source: Own study based on Kott (2018) and Théron et al. (2020)

be transparently deployed to different systems jointly networked, while being a decentralised network to work together for common cyber resilience, especially in the face of conflicts of different nature, including hybrid. An illustrative drawing of the operating architecture of such an agent is shown in Figure 6.4.

Five key functionalities have been defined for each agent:

- Detecting and identifying the state of the environment. This functionality enables the agent to extract data from the environment in which it operates, as well as from itself, in order to understand the current state of the environment. This world state detection and identification functionality relies on components to continuously create an 'environment model', determine the 'current state', maintain a 'state history', 'sensors' and 'current state identification'. Descriptions of the current state of the environment are captured by the sensing function in the agent, while identification of the current state of the environment is based on (1) processed descriptions of the current state of the environment and (2) learned patterns of the environment. Once a suspicious current ambient state pattern is identified (e.g. a cyber attack), the 'ambient state identification' function proceeds to trigger the 'action planning and selection' function.

- Action planning and selection by the agent. The action planning and selection function allows an agent to propose one or more actions and then send them to a selector. The selector decides on an action or set of actions to perform in order to respond to a detected suspicious environmental state pattern. The function attempts to select response actions appropriate to this detected suspicious pattern. The action selection function seeks a solution based on the proposed response plans in the context of the goals set for the agent and in the face of the defined constraints and requirements of the execution environment. The proposed response plan is analysed by the action selector in light of the agent's current objectives, as well as any constraints and execution requirements. The proposed response plan is then reduced by those elements that do not fit the situation and supplemented with pre-, preparatory, preventive or post-implementation actions. The action selector thus creates an executable response plan, which is then forwarded to the action implementer.
- Cooperation and negotiation of activities by the agent. The cooperation and negotiation of activities by the agent function is used to:
  - exchanging information with other agents or the central Command & Control node. An example of a situation where this function is used is when an agent cannot achieve satisfactory results on its own and
  - negotiating with other agents the details of consolidated conclusions or results based on the environment.

    Collaboration and negotiation are based in this system on a continuous flow of data in all directions and on the basis of data acquired in-house by each agent (i.e. knowledge generated through the learning and improvement function).
- Agent action execution. The action execution function defines the actions to be taken by the agent, based on the adopted response plan in the previous steps, as well as the monitoring of the execution and its effects. It must also provide the means to scale the plan's assumptions or even dynamically modify the plan if necessary. Given the technical configuration of the environment, the execution function executes each planned action in the planned sequence. The monitoring function collects feedback on the execution of the plan in order to monitor the execution status of each scheduled action. Any status other than "done" is to trigger corrective execution actions. If warning signals are identified by either of the previous two functions, the

execution adjustment function will adjust the execution of the actions according to the circumstances or modify the response plan.

- Agent learning and knowledge improvement. The premise is that each agent, based on the experience gained, uses it to improve its performance over time. This mechanism analyses the agent's 'reward' function (the distance between goals and action results) and their impact on the agent's knowledge. The results are fed back to the action improvement function. The improvement function combines the results (propositions) from the learning function with the current items delivered to the agent.

The indicated architecture should be considered as a concept proposal for autonomous agents, adopted as a reference model for NATO as a whole. The reference model primarily organises the language of description and also summarises the various considerations in the field of autonomous defence agents into an overall model. Current implementations of these concepts may vary, and it is certainly possible to identify significant needs for proposing specific technologies that could realise more and more assumptions for these systems. The evolution of the aforementioned cyber security systems such as IDS/IPS, EDR, SIEM and SOAR holistically in the ICT network architecture can realise some of the functionalities related primarily to the observation of the environment and the execution of actions (e.g. network reconfiguration in the face of a threat). With regard to the remaining of the main functionalities and, above all, greater autonomy in the whole process from detection to response to threats, we are at the research and development stage with trials of the first commercial solutions for this purpose.

An example of a development in the area of cyber threat data exchange functions between systems is the spread of the Structured Threat Information eXpression (STIX) format. This is a standardised language created in 2012 by MITRE and OASIS. It is used to specify, capture, characterise and communicate standardised cyber threat information (Barnum, 2014). A publication (Okada et al., 2021, pp. 109–114) presents the possibility of using STIX-formatted cyber threat knowledge in a software-driven network (SDN) to have the system dynamically reconfigure the network to block communication with malicious hosts. This approach allows for a more coordinated incident response based on actual cyber threat information, enabling organisations to be more precise in committing resources to incident response. The automation of incident response systems using shared threat information may prove essential to increase situational awareness and reduce response times compared to human action.

Based on the successes of solutions such as the STIX format for exchanging about cyber threats, aspirations and efforts to introduce standardised knowledge exchange languages in the different layers of cyber defence systems are evident. Computer security incident response plans are undergoing a similar evolution. From the beginning, they were mainly defined in the form of high-level documents (incident management policies and procedures) that were primarily usable by humans. The need for the idea of fleshing out such documents into more detailed procedure manuals was quickly recognised. This is how detailed playbooks began to be developed, i.e. procedures that define how to respond to specific types of security incidents. They define technical instructions and procedures that help to effectively respond to detected threats, such as denial of service attacks, ransomware attacks or data leaks. For organisations, the creation of playbooks means the establishment of an organisational memory and standardisation in the operation of different security teams. Finally, playbooks have become the basis for a further stage of evolution related to their representability in cyber security systems and towards ever greater automation and autonomisation. They became the basis for the creation of SOAR-type systems, which programmatically represent the playbooks previously developed in document form. On top of this, a SOAR system having integrations with various computer systems can perform actions in the target systems within the next steps of a procedure, replacing human actions.

Again, SOAR system technologies are being developed as stand-alone solutions from different manufacturers with often features unique only to that manufacturer, ultimately reducing the key interoperability for cyber resilience. Faced with this challenge, two important projects are being developed:

- CACAO project (OASIS, 2024) Playbooks – i.e. introducing standardisation in the area of structured definition of incident response plans (playbooks), extending the capability of the STIX format
- Project OpenC2 (OpenC2, 2024a, 2024b) – i.e. the introduction of a standardised command and control protocol for cyber-security systems and information systems in general, for consistent issuing of commands in the face of detected threats in networks or on end devices.

The CACAO project is tasked with standardising the definition and use of two important terms often used by organisations for cybersecurity: actions and playbooks. An action represents any security activity or operation (referred to as a security action or simply an activity) that an organisation may undertake to detect, investigate, prevent, mitigate or remediate a specific cyber security breach that has occurred or may occur. A playbook is a workflow for security orchestration that contains a set of steps (security actions) to be performed based on a logical process and can be performed ad-hoc, periodically or triggered by an automated or manual event or observation. The playbook provides guidance on how to deal with a specific security event, incident, problem, attack or breach. In addition, the CACAO project (OASIS, 2024) has defined a structured playbook format standard. The JSON file, which is widely used in code-driven infrastructures, is used for the machine description of playbooks. This allows cybersecurity developers to conveniently create solutions that consume and use playbooks in this format for use in systems. CACAO has also supported the creation of a SOAR reference implementation, SOARCA (COSSAS, 2024), which natively supports playbooks in the CACAO Playbooks v2.0 format. The SOARCA project is open and accessible to all, as part of the COSSAS community working on open implementations of cyber security solutions (COSSAS, 2024).

The OpenC2 project has proposed a language definition in the form of a Command & Control (C&C) protocol for network security and ICT systems. OpenC2 is defined broadly and flexibly enough to provide a low entry threshold for manufacturers in implementing its capabilities in their cyber security products. Current ways of building cyber-security architectures, as mentioned earlier in this section, are based on integrations that are costly to develop and maintain and rely heavily on proprietary solutions from each vendor, with the accuracy of using a standardised approach based on REST APIs and the HTTP protocol. The approach offered by OpenC2 goes deeper to ensure interoperability between tools, vendors, technologies and programming languages. OpenC2 simply encodes the 'actions' part of the process for responding to security incidents. It is based on the nouns and verbs required to encode human intentions and decisions and machine-readable instructions, enabling automated courses of action.

The input to the system is the OpenC2 Language Specification (OpenC2 Language Specification), a definition for the implementation of cyber security functions by individual practical systems (OpenC2 Actuator Profiles) and instructions for adapting OpenC2 operations to specific environments, e.g. the selection of appropriate transport protocols or message encoding (OpenC2 Transfer Specifications). In OpenC2, the components of a Control Command are Actions (what is to be done), Targets (what is the object of the action), optional Trigger definitions (what is to trigger the execution of the command) and Control Command arguments that affect how the command is executed. An Action in combination with an Objective is sufficient to describe a complete Command.

Finally, work on the missing 'link' in the autonomisation of agents has also accelerated in recent years, i.e. in terms of creating the ability to understand situations in the environment without human intervention in such a way that such a decision-making centre can perform a complete process as defined in (Théron et al., 2020). In terms of research, the use of approaches combining algorithm development in the areas of artificial intelligence (AI), machine learning (ML), large language models (LLM) and reinforcement learning (RL) is evident.

- In Babar et al. (2024, pp. 168–169), the authors focus on developing an environment for teaching autonomous agents in a Reinforcement Learning (RL) approach. The environment simulated the conditions of a fully functional ICT environment using one of the available datasets. The developed environment allows for the learning and testing of a defensive agent, while implementing the simulation of offensive agents.
- In Nguyen and Reddi (2023, pp. 3779–3795), various approaches in the application of reinforcement learning using deep neural networks to cyber security problems are summarised. Particularly noteworthy are the referenced studies and concepts related to the application of RL solutions in detecting threats in networks or, more specifically, for detecting malware on hosts.
- A publication (Wiebe et al., 2023) presented the possibility of using RL in a multi-agent approach to learn network defence tactics over time. The authors' proposal also indicates a pioneering approach in combining multi-agent learning with reinforcement learning for application in a cyber defence task. The paper presents an implementation of a defence agent learning and preparation environment, analyses different cooperative approaches in agent learning, and demonstrates how a defence agent adapts its tactics in the presence of offensive agents.
- A study (Hammar, Stadler, 2021, pp. 509–517) proposes to investigate finding the optimal defensive strategy in calculating the occurrence of an incident based on finding the optimal stop point. This way of formulating the problem, based on the theory of dynamic programming, makes it possible to determine this threshold based on, among other things, observations of the environment. Taking into account the fact that, in the test model, the defender only has access to a limited amount of knowledge from measurements of the environment and cannot directly observe the attacker, it was proposed to model the stopping problem using a partially observed Markov decision process. (POMDP). We obtain the optimal policy for the network defender by simulating a series of episodes for the POMDP process in which an intrusion takes place and in which the defender continuously updates its policy based on the results of the previous episodes.

We use a reference learning algorithm with reinforcement to update the policy. This approach allowed us to find an effective defence policy despite the uncertainty of the attacker's behaviour and despite the large state space of the model.

- Loevenich et al. (2024, pp. 1–10) proposes to extend the design of an autonomous agent for network defence to monitor and execute defensive actions in a preset network segment. The authors use advances in artificial intelligence development to define a hybrid architecture that combines deep reinforcement learning (DRL), large language models (LLM) and rule-based models. The motivation stems from the fact that modern network segments in cloud computing use software-defined network (SDN) controllers, which enables the deployment of such agents and other cyber security tools. The proposed agent uses the DRL model and the chatbot uses the LLM model as a conversational interface with human operators. The proposed agent has been tested for two offensive strategies in a simulated environment along with the use of various cyber defence services on the network (monitoring, analysing, decoying, removing the attacker and restoring systems). A chat interface was developed using a RAG approach using cyber security knowledge graphs. The final results indicate that the developed agent can enhance the defence capabilities of critical ICT networks.

The main efforts of commercial companies in the area of autonomisation of cyber operations are seen in products such as:

- Microsoft Copilot for Security (Microsoft, 2024) – a platform that integrates on the one hand the ecosystem of security tools from Microsoft with AI technologies, in particular generative artificial intelligence. Through extensive integration, it is possible to create a loop between observations, response planning and deployment of actions to mitigate threats in real time. Here, generative AI provides a bridge that first supports humans working with the platform, e.g. by recommending actions to be taken, and ultimately can be a significant replacement for humans in this type of operation.
- Google Security Operations platform – as part of its ecosystem of cyber security tools and service support through Mandiant, Google has integrated the use of artificial intelligence into the operational area of cyber security in its solutions (Corde, 2024). Google declares that their cyber-security ecosystem continuously fed with threat intelligence and using artificial intelligence will detect more, respond faster and relieve the operational burden on humans.

Complementing in the area of technology development for civil protection in the face of hybrid conflicts is the widespread dissemination of knowledge and information about threats, as pointed out in Microsoft's report on the example of aggression in Ukraine in 2022 (Defending Ukraine, 2022). In cyber security, the discipline of implementing threat intelligence and knowledge dissemination processes is Cyber Threat Intelligence. The history of the origin of CTI is linked to the occurrence of the term *intelligence* in the name, a reference to traditional intelligence analysis. At this point, one can refer to the US Central Intelligence Agency (CIA) studies on what intelligence is, (Warner, 2002) among others, but the term itself can have many understandings in different countries. A good approach suggested in Sajdak (2024) is that intelligence analysis should be related to data and information. The example cited in the Sajdak (2024) chapter on CTI in the area of cyber security can be shown as follows:

- Data: e.g. IP address
- Information: the above IP address was assigned to the control server of the selected malware
- Analysis: The aim of the attackers using the above malware was to destabilise several logistics companies, key to the food supply chain within the European Union.

CTI has been more widely disseminated by top cyber security companies such as Mandiant, CrowdStrike and Microsoft. A 2013 report by Mandiant (Mandiant, 2013) summarizing around 7 years of incident response on the first Advanced Persistent Threat type group code-named APT1, attributed to the Chinese government, is recognised as a milestone in the development of CTI reporting provided by private cybersecurity entities. From then until now, various activities around CTI have proliferated, from public threat reporting through commercial solutions and platforms available for a fee, to the development of the discipline in various security teams or government services.

On the technology side, CTI is supported by, among other things, the STIX project mentioned earlier, which provides cyber threat knowledge in a structured form that is ready for use in end-to-end cyber security systems. This reduces the time from the emergence of information to securing end-to-end networks, as this type of structured form of threat information delivery allows it to be directly translated into network configuration, security rules in NIDS/EDR/SIEM systems or action plans in SOAR systems. However, as the main challenge of CTI is becoming the amount of data available to be processed in such a way that it becomes useful for use in cyber-security operations and systems, significant research efforts on application technologies for CTI and its increasing dissemination have been observed in recent years:

- Clairoux-Trepanier tested the use of large language models (LLMs) in the task of analysing posts from cybercrime forums for the extraction of CTI-relevant information. The model had to analyse each post and suggest ten key parameters relevant to the task of establishing defence mechanisms. A success rate of 98% was achieved, but areas for further development or, in general, methods for the use of LLM in CTI were also identified (Clairoux-Trepanier et al., 2024).
- Huang and Xiao proposed the use of large language models to construct knowledge graphs from CTI data. The aim of the approach is to potentially uncover unknown and invisible at first glance relationships between different CTI objects, and thus find better threat models corresponding to the reality in cyberspace. One of the example applications presented in the publication was to segment attack tactics and techniques in such a way as to show the full range with regard to the exploitation of single vulnerabilities. Using a knowledge graph, it was possible to uncover five times more behaviours leading to attacks against the identified vulnerabilities than when analysing individual reports (Huang, Xiao, 2024).
- The MITRE-sponsored TRAM (Threat Report ATT&CK Mapper) project (Centre for Threat-Informed Defense, 2024) allows the automation of the mapping of cyber threat reports (CTI) to tactics and techniques from the MITRE ATT&CK catalogue (MITRE, 2024). Threat intelligence providers, threat intelligence platforms and analysts can use TRAM to more easily and consistently integrate ATT&CK into their cyber security systems. It can identify up to 50 common ATT&CK techniques in text documents. It also supports model enhancement by annotating additional data and rebuilding the model.

SUMMARY

Cyber resilience is becoming a key feature of any information technology for states and societies to use in order to be ready in the face of an intensification of threats against people – from typical cybercrime to the use of cyberspace as a new battlefield within conflicts and hybrid threats. Empirical confirmation for this requirement came with Russia's aggression against Ukraine in 2022, where cyberspace, in conjunction with other areas of military conflict, was an important area of attempted impact. However, it is noteworthy that with foresight in this area, Ukraine, together with the help of allies, was able to prepare adequately for this intensity of the situation. In (Kott et al., 2024) it is described how it was cyber resilience in the broadest sense, rather than cyber security per

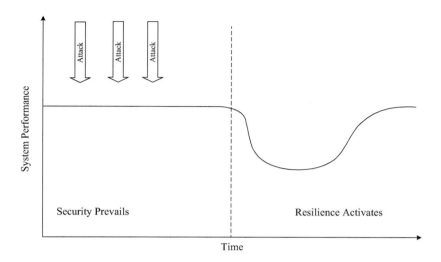

FIGURE 6.5   Cyber security with cyber resilience

Source: Kott et al. (2024)

se, that contributed to Ukraine's defence in cyberspace. The publication identifies that cyber-security is important, but is mainly responsible for taking and deflecting the onslaught phase of cyber-attacks. Far more important is the long-term systemic capability to restore full operations, which is just referred to as cyber resilience. Figure 6.5 of the origin (Kott et al., 2024) defines precisely this relationship of cyber security and cyber resilience.

Over the space of this chapter, three dimensions of building long-term cyber resilience are discussed – the organisational-conceptual-legal dimension, the dimension of technologies fundamental to cyber resilience and the dimension of technologies to protect information systems from threats. A number of examples for each dimension are presented:

- Various documents (NIS2, US Cyber-strategy, AI Act, CRA), concepts (Zero Trust) and organisational efforts for cyber-resilience.
- Fundamental technologies for secure communications and networks: mechanisms within 4G/5G/6G networks, the development of more secure wide area network architectures, the development of the SDN paradigm, and cloud computing.
- Technologies for even more secure information systems. Here, two threads were pointed out:
  - combating attacks on users of information systems, who are mainly influenced by social engineering (disinformation, fake news or phishing)

- the development of network detection and response architectures towards automation and autonomous processes with a vision of "self-defending" and "self-repairing" networks of the future.

Pointing to these dimensions was meant to show how much we are already doing as societies and our institutions (science, business, politics), and how much there is still important and relevant fields to cover or develop. One can have a sense of the enormous opportunities in contributing to this area, but on the other hand, reality is only becoming more and more complex that one can only be rightly concerned about whether one will ever be able to keep up in this perpetual race between threats in cyberspace and how to deal with them. Certainly, one can be optimistic that, using the example of the actions taken in the hybrid conflict in Ukraine, the technologies available, the coordination and the organisation of efforts have actually made it possible to demonstrate in practice that cyber resilience is already possible. Going forward, it is important that these technologies become more and more accessible, and that awareness of threats is a driver for action in increasing the resilience of our societies, rather than a stunner in active measures.

BIBLIOGRAPHY

Afchar, D., Nozick, V., Yamagishi, J., and Echizen, I., (2018), *MesoNet: A Compact Facial Video Forgery Detection Network*. 2018 IEEE International Workshop on Information Forensics and Security (WIFS), Hong Kong, China. https://doi.org/10.1109/WIFS.2018. 8630761. Accessed: 6 July 2024.

Alquran, H., and Banitaan, S., (2022), *Fake News Detection in Social Networks Using Data Mining Techniques*. 2022 IEEE World AI IoT Congress (AIIoT), Seattle, WA, USA, https://doi.org/10.1109/AIIoT54504.2022.9817287. Accessed: 18 July 2024.

Anapaya, (2024), Anapaya Networks: Secure, Reliable, and Transparent Internet Connectivity. Available at: https://www.anapaya.net. Accessed:19 July 2024.

Antoniuk, D., (2022), How Elon Musk's Starlink Satellite Internet Keeps Ukraine Online. Available at: https://kyivindependent.com/how-elon-musks-starlink-satellite-internet-keeps-ukraine-online/. Accessed: 14 July 2024.

Babar, A., Li, L., Taylor, A., and Zulkernine, M., (2024), *Towards Autonomous Network Defense: Reinforcement Learning Environment for a Defense Agent*. 2024 IEEE Canadian Conference on Electrical and Computer Engineering (CCECE), Kingston, ON, Canada.https://doi.org/10.1109/CCECE59415.2024.10667139. Accessed: 19 July 2024.

Barnum, S., (2014), Standardizing Cyber Threat Intelligence Information with the Structured Threat Information eXpression (STIX™), Version 1.1, Revision 1, 20 February. Available at: https://stixproject. github.io/about/STIX_Whitepaper_v1.1.pdf. Accessed: 9 July 2024.

Caramancion, K.M., (2023), *Harnessing the Power of ChatGPT to Decimate Mis/Disinformation: Using ChatGPT for Fake News Detection.* 2023 IEEE World AI IoT Congress (AIIoT), Seattle, WA, USA. https://doi.org/10.1109/AIIoT58121.2023.10174450. Accessed: 17 July 2024.

Chai, Y., Zhou, Y., Li, W., and Jiang, Y., (2022), An Explainable Multi-Modal Hierarchical Attention Model for Developing Phishing Threat Intelligence. *IEEE Transactions on Dependable and Secure Computing*, 19(2). https://doi.org/10.1109/TDSC.2021.3119323. https://scion.org/wp-content/uploads/2024/07/SCION_thecompletebook-2022.pdf. Accessed: 8 July 2024.

Chuat, L., Legner, M., Basin, D.A., Hausheer, D., Hitz, S., Müller, P., and Perrig, A., (2022), *The Complete Guide to SCION – From Design Principles to Formal Verification, Information Security and Cryptography*. Cham: Springer. Accessed: 9 July 2024.

Clairoux-Trépanier, V., Beauchamp, I.-M., Ruellan, E., Paquet-Clouston, M., Paquette, S.-O., and Clay, E., (2024), The Use of Large Language Models (LLM) for Cyber Threat Intelligence (CTI) in Cybercrime Forums. https://doi.org/10.48550/arXiv.2408.03354. Accessed: 18 July 2024.

Coker, H., (2024), Service for America: Cyber Is Serving Your Country. Available at: https://bidenwhitehouse.archives.gov/oncd/preparing-our-country-for-a-cyber-future/service-for-america/ Accessed: 12 July 2024.

Corde, C., (2024), Introducing Google Security Operations: Intel-Driven, AI-Powered SecOps at RSA. Available at: https://cloud.google.com/blog/products/identity-security/introducing-google-security-operations-intel-driven-ai-powered-secops-at-rsa. Accessed: 13 July 2024.

COSSAS, (2024a), Open Source Security Automation Software (COSSAS). Available at: https://cossas-project.org. Accessed: 8 July 2024.

COSSAS, (2024b), SOARCA. Available at: https://github.com/COSSAS/SOARCA. Accessed: 14 July 2024.

Cybersecurity is National Security, (2024), Podcast, 5 September. Available at: https://www.nsa.gov/Podcast/View/Article/3876300/cyber-security-is-national-security/. Accessed: 4 July 2024.

Demchak, C.C., and Shavitt, Y., (2018), China's Maxim – Leave No Access Point Unexploited: The Hidden Story of China Telecom's BGP Hijacking. *Military Cyber Affairs*, 3(1). https://digitalcommons. usf.edu/cgi/viewcontent.cgi?article=1050&context=mca. Accessed: 10 July 2024.

Department of Defense (DOD) Zero Trust Reference Architecture, (2022), Ver. 2.0, Joint Defense Information Systems Agency (DISA) and National Security Agency (NSA). Available at: https://dodcio.defense.gov/Portals/0/Documents/Library/(U)ZT_RA_v2.0(U)_Sep22.pdf. Accessed: 15 July 2024.

Garfinkel, S., (2011), The Cloud Imperative. Available at: https://www.technologyreview.com/2011/10/03/190237/the-cloud-imperative/. Accessed: 11 July 2024.

Hammar, K., and Stadler, R., (2021), *Learning Intrusion Prevention Policies through Optimal Stopping*. 2021 17th International Conference on Network and Service Management (CNSM), Izmir, Turkey. https://doi.org/10.23919/CNSM52442.2021.9615542. Accessed: 6 July 2024. Available at: https://www.multicians.org/protection.html. Accessed: 2 July 2024.

Huang, L., and Xiao, X., (2024, October), *CTIKG: LLM-Powered Knowledge Graph Construction from Cyber Threat Intelligence*. Proceedings of the First Conference on Language Modeling (COLM 2024), Philadelphia, PA, USA. Accessed: 9 July 2024.

IEEE Public Safety Technology Initiative, (2024), How Does 5G Enhance Mission-Critical Communication? Available at: https://publicsafety.ieee.org/topics/how-does-5g-enhance-mission-critical-communication. Accessed: 1 July 2024.

Karger, P.A., and Herbert, A.J., (1984), *An Augmented Capability Architecture to Support Lattice Security and Traceability of Access*. 1984 IEEE Symposium on Security and Privacy, Oakland, CA, USA, pp. 2–2. https://doi.org/10.1109/SP.1984.10001. Accessed: 19 July 2024.

Kindervag, J., (2010), No More Chewy Centers: Introducing the Zero Trust Model of Information Security. Updated on 17 September 2010. Available at: https://media.paloaltonetworks.com/documents/Forrester-No-More-Chewy-Centers.pdf. https://www.jstor.org/stable/26554997. Accessed: 6 July 2024.

Kott, A., (2018), Intelligent Autonomous Agents Are Key to Cyber Defense of the Future Army Networks. *The Cyber Defense Review*, 3(3), JSTOR. Accessed: 13 July 2024.

Kott, A., et al. (2024), Russian Cyber Onslaught Was Blunted by Ukrainian Cyber Resilience, Not Merely Security. *Computer*, 57(08). Available at: https://www.computer.org/csdl/magazine/co/2024/08/10633827/1ZlBeQxYT1S. Accessed: 10 July 2024.

Loevenich, J.F., Adler, E., Mercier, R., Velazquez, A., and Lopes, R.R.F., (2024), Design of an Autonomous Cyber Defence Agent using Hybrid AI models. *2024 International Conference on Military Communication and Information Systems (ICMCIS)*, Koblenz, Germany. https://doi.org/10.1109/ICMCIS61231.2024.10540988. Accessed: 3 July 2024.

Mandiant (2013). APT1: Exposing One of China's Cyber Espionage Units. Available at: https://www.mandiant.com/sites/default/files/2021-09/mandiant-apt1-report.pdf.Accessed: 19 July 2024

Matsumoto, H., Yoshida, S., and Muneyasu, M., (2021), *Propagation-Based Fake News Detection Using Graph Neural Networks with Transformer*. 2021 IEEE 10th Global Conference on Consumer Electronics (GCCE), Kyoto, Japan. https://doi.org/10.1109/GCCE53005.2021.9621803. Accessed: 5 July 2024.

Mazzucchi, N., (2022), AI-Based Technologies in Hybrid Conflict: The Future of Influence Operations. *Hybrid CoE Paper*, 14. Available at: https://www.hybridcoe.fi/publications/hybrid-coe-paper-14-ai-based-technologies-in-hybrid-conflict-the-future-of-influence-operations/. Accessed: 13 July 2024.

McKeown, N., Anderson, T., Balakrishnan, H., Parulkar, G., Peterson, L., Rexford, J., Shenker, S., and Turner, J., (2008), OpenFlow: Enabling Innovation in Campus Networks. *SIGCOMM ComputerCommunication Review*, 38(2). Available at: https://doi.org/10.1145/1355734.1355746. Accessed: 7 July 2024.

Microsoft, (2022), Defending Ukraine: Early Lessons from the Cyber War. Available at: https://blogs.microsoft.com/on-the-issues/2022/06/22/defending-ukraine-early-lessons-from-the-cyber-war/. Accessed: 4 July 2024.

Microsoft, (2024), Microsoft Copilot for Security. Available at: https://www.microsoft.com/en-us/security/business/ai-machine-learning/microsoft-copilot-security. Accessed: 10 July 2024.

MITRE, (2024), ATT&CK Matrix for Enterprise. Available at: https://attack.mitre.org. Accessed: 2 July 2024.

National Cybersecurity Strategy, (2023), National Cybersecurity Strategy, March 2023. Available at: https://bidenwhitehouse.archives.gov/oncd/national-cybersecurity-strategy/. Accessed:8 July 2024.

Nguyen, T.T., and Reddi, V.J., (2023), Deep Reinforcement Learning for Cyber Security. *IEEE Transactions on Neural Networks and Learning Systems*, 34(8). https://doi.org/10.1109/TNNLS.2021.3121870. Accessed:17 July 2024.

NIS2 Directive, (2024), NIS2 Fines. Available at: https://nis2directive.eu/nis2-fines/. Accessed: 5 July 2024.

OASIS, (2024), Security Playbooks Version 2.0. Available at: https://docs.oasis-open.org/cacao/security-playbooks/v2.0/security-playbooks-v2.0.html. Accessed: 12 July 2024.

Okada, S., Fujiwara, Y., Fujimoto, M., Matsuda, W., and Mitsunaga, T., (2021), *Efficient Incident Response System on Shared Cyber Threat Information Using SDN and STIX*. 2021 IEEE International Conference on Computing (ICOCO). https://doi.org/10.1109/ICOCO53166.2021.9673536. Accessed: 2 July 2024.

OpenC2, (2024a), Open Command and Control (OpenC2). Available at: https://openc2.org. Accessed: 15 July 2024.

OpenC2, (2024b), Open Command and Control (OpenC2). Available at: https://openc2.org. Accessed: 11 July 2024.

OpenPhish, (2024), OpenPhish: Phishing Threat Intelligence. Available at: https://www.openphish.com. Accessed: 12 July 2024.

Parikh, S.B., and Atrey, P.K., (2018), *Media-Rich Fake News Detection: A Survey*. 2018 IEEE Conference on Multimedia Information Processing and Retrieval (MIPR). IEEE. https://ieeexplore.ieee.org/document/8397049. Accessed: 3 July 2024.

Perrig, A., Szalachowski, P., Reischuk, R.M., and Chuat, L., (2017), *SCION: A Secure Internet Architecture*. Cham: Springer. Accessed: 17 July 2024.

Rose, S., Borchert, O., Mitchell, S., and Connelly, S., (2020), *Zero Trust Architecture, SP* 800-207. NIST. https://doi.org/10.6028/NIST.SP.800-207. Accessed: 11 July 2024.

Sajdak, M. (ed.), (2024), *Introduction to IT Security*, Vol. 1. Krakow: Securitum. https://wdbit1.sekurak.pl. Accessed: 4 July 2024.

Schroeder, M.D., and Saltzer, J.H., (1972, March), A Hardware Architecture for Implementing Protection Rings. *Communications of the ACM*, 15(3), pp. 157-170. Accessed: 7 July 2024.

Théron, P., Kott, A., Drašar, M., Rzadca, K., LeBlanc, B., Pihelgas, M., Mancini, L., and de Gaspari, F., (2020), Reference Architecture of an Autonomous Agent for Cyber Defence of Complex Military Systems. In *Adaptive Autonomous Secure Cyber Systems*. Cham: Springer. https://link.springer.com/chapter/10.1007/978-3-030-33432-1_1. Accessed: 11 July 2024.

Ward, R., and Beyer, B., (2014), BeyondCorp: A New Approach to Enter-prise Security. 39(6). https://www.usenix.org/system/files/login/articles/login_dec14_02_ward.pdf. https://www.usenix.org/publications/login/dec14/ward. Accessed: 16 July 2024.

Warner, M., (2002). Wanted: A Definition of Intelligence. *Studies in Intelligence*, 46(3). Available at: https://www.cia.gov/resources/csi/static/Wanted-Definition-of-Intel.pdf. Accessed: 7 July 2024.

Wiebe, J., Al Mallah, R., and Li, L., (2023), *Learning Cyber Defence Tactics from Scratch with Multi-Agent Reinforcement Learning*. 2nd International Workshop on Adaptive Cyber Defense. https://arxiv.org/abs/2310.05939. Accessed: 5 July 2024.

Wrzosek, M., (2020). The NIS Directive and NIS 2: What Does It Mean and why Is It Important? Available at: https://cyberpolicy.nask.pl/przeglad-dyrektyw-nis-co-oznacza-i-dlaczego-jest-istotny/. Accessed: 3 July 2024.

Wyss, M., Meier, R., Roma, L., Krahenbuhl, C., Perring, A., and Lenders, V., (2024), *On Building Secure Wide-Area Networks over Public Internet Service Providers*. CyCon 2024: Over the Horizon, 16th

International Conference on Cyber Conflict, NATO CCDCOE. https://ccdcoe.org/uploads/2024/05/CyCon_2024_Wyss_Meier_Roma_Krahenbuhl_Perrig_Lenders-1.pdf. Accessed: 18 July 2024.

Zhao, Y., Liu, B., Ding, M., Liu, B., Zhu, T., and Yu, X., (2023), *Proactive Deepfake Defence via Identity Watermarking.* 2023 IEEE/CVF Winter Conference on Applications of Computer Vision (WACV), Waikoloa, HI, USA, https://doi.org/10.1109/WACV56 688.2023.00458.Accessed:1 July 2024.

Zscaler, (2024), What Is Software-Defined Perimeter? Available at: https://www.zscaler.com/resources/security-terms-glossary/what-is-software-defined-perimeter. Accessed: 15 July 2024.

CHAPTER 7

The role of communities in hybrid warfare

COMMUNITY IN AN ENVIRONMENT OF HYBRID WARFARE

Wars and conflicts such as the Russia-Georgia war (2008), Russia's annexation of Crimea (2014), the war in Ukraine (2022) or the most recent war in the Middle East (2023) have attracted the attention of the international community as well as researchers and practitioners, not only because of the effects of military operations, but also because of the large-scale unconventional and non-military actions undertaken in them. The reasons for the increasing use of hybrid strategies are complex and subject- and region-specific, but one of the main reasons is the low cost of hybrid operations compared to classical military operations. The effects of hybrid action also appear more effective from the tactical side, which is due, among other things, to the lack of preparation for the spectrum of this type of action. Above and beyond this, hybrid warfare in Ukraine, for example, has never been formally declared, which creates legal problems and, as a result, these actions are often conducted in the so-called grey zone (i.e. between a state of peace and war). In addition, global interdependence on technology and information, has reinforced hybrid actions and consequently threats have become difficult to combat (Hoffman, 2007). The nature of hybrid warfare is its vagueness and deniability, but it is important to emphasise that these attributes are dependent on the phase of hybrid strategy implementation. As a reminder, previous chapters have proposed an understanding of the field as a hybrid strategy with two phases of implementation. The first is a hybrid conflict in which large-scale and formal military actions of regular militaries are not implemented, while the second phase is a hybrid war which is not only a continuation of the first phase, but also a significant reinforcement of it using military actions of state actors who also implement unconventional and non-military actions. All these activities

420   DOI: 10.4324/9781003503859-8

generate hybrid threats increasingly targeting societies and communities. The consequences of this have been extensively described in previous chapters. This chapter will describe the roles of communities in this type of warfare. The role of communities in hybrid warfare is multifaceted, encompassing both the vulnerabilities that can be exploited by adversaries and the resilience that can be cultivated to counter such threats. Understanding hybrid warfare allows resilience to be enhanced in all its dimensions.

The aim of the chapter will be to explore the role of communities in a hybrid war environment, with a particular focus on their contribution to building resilience. The choice of communities has been informed by the belief that if communities are unable to build a resilience strategy, solidarity within society and within the state structure weakens, common purpose disappears and fragmentation inevitably follows, meaning that the will to survive, no matter how strong, alone is insufficient compared to the threat. However, we should caution against treating resilience as a 'miracle cure' which, as (Bilban, 2016, pp. 1–10) notes, has recently become a 'fashionable' recommendation among scientists (McLennan, 2024).

Although the chapter deals with communities, for the sake of logic, a distinction will be made between the definitions of society and community, which was considered necessary because the response to hybrid threats will be different at the level of society and at the level of community. The essence of this difference is, in the author's opinion, important because there is a stronger element of community in a community (personal relationships, shared values and often territoriality), which have a far different meaning than less personal relationships, shared interests, where territoriality is only one of many conditioning factors.

According to dictionary definitions, society means all people in mutual relations resulting from living conditions, division of labour and participation in cultural life; also: all citizens of a given district, city, etc.; while a community is people living in a certain area or belonging to a certain professional or social group (Słownik Języka Polskiego PWN, 2024). According to Ferdinand Tönnies' classic sociological definition, personal and direct ties (e.g. family, religion, place of residence) are important in a community as mentioned above. In contrast, society is characterised by ties that are less personal and direct and by rational values (Tönnies, 1957, pp. 33–65). Hybrid strategies target both societies and communities, but taking into account the complex nature of the ties between these actors. Andersson, for example, argues that the creation of divisions is more easily achieved at the level of societies than communities, due to the rational nature of the former's ties to the latter (Andersson, 2021, pp. 363–375).

Arsalan Bilal, on the other hand, argues that given the perspective of the aggressor, the nature of deeper community ties can be paradoxically exploited, for example, for community and social polarisation (Bilal, 2021).

Another fairly universal distinction between society and communities is the position these actors occupy at the levels of state organisation: local, regional and national. However, as this topic is not the purpose of this publication, it will not be considered further.

THE ROLE OF COMMUNITIES IN PROVIDING INFORMATION – MOBILISATION AND SUPPORT NETWORKS

UN information (UN OCHA, 2003) has shown that communities that have been forced to migrate as a result of conflict develop a much better system for collecting and sharing information than what humanitarian organisations had to offer. This observation was developed further in their research by, among others, Leaning and Meier (2008), who highlighted that in wartime settings, communities were many times unable to rely on high-tech solutions, and therefore community methods and tools were unconventional. The examples they gave referred to communities and living conditions where access to today's civilian technological solutions was difficult. With increasing digitalisation and the development of personal mobile devices, we have witnessed over the past two decades the use of high-tech solutions that allowed some communities to defend themselves against oppression and violence. We saw this during the Green Movement protests in Iran in 2009, when the authorities of the Islamic Republic of Iran were forced to switch off GSM antennas and block the internet, or during the Arab Spring of 2011, when numerous countries in the Middle East and North Africa had to follow Iran's lead, with greater or lesser success. The war in Syria that began in 2011 was probably the first instance of armed conflict that coincided with the transition from Web 1.0 to Web 2.0 (i.e. from one generated by the owners of digital content to one generated by the users of that content). It was also arguably the first conflict to be reported in real time precisely from users equipped with smartphones (Janjeva et al., 2022).

Over time, smartphones have become a common tool for citizen journalism and the defence of civil liberties. Today, the vast majority of intelligence material comes from unclassified sources, which also explains the attitude of separating the virtual domains of countries such as China, Iran or Russia from the infrastructure of Western countries. State apparatuses have also begun to exploit the fact that every smartphone is a source of potentially valuable information, as we see not only from the apps created for information gathering, but also from their use for espionage purposes. An example of this is the use of the GPS location function in smartphones, which enabled the Ukrainian authorities to estimate the day before the invasion how many people were in the capital and how many had left it the following day: within ten hours of the start of the invasion (a fifth of the population had left Kyiv, allowing for better planning of evacuation and humanitarian assistance) (Janjeva et al., 2022). Thus, the community is able to provide key real-time intelligence also unwittingly. At the same time, however, communities still have to expect to lose some services for their own safety and have to rely on other means of information, such as when Google switched off traffic data in Ukraine during the 2022 invasion (Janjeva et al., 2022).

Not only the devices, but also the data technology itself and its potentially hostile applications have gained the attention of researchers and the international community, as best demonstrated by the controversy surrounding Huawei's 5G technology. The radio wave spectrum used in 5G technology, and we are already standing at the threshold of 6G development, allows for almost uninterrupted transmission of large data packets and 'total connectivity'. The potential for further development of mobile device technology allows communities to be used as a link in the state's early warning system also in the real-time dimension. This is because smartphones can work with the right applications as a short-wave network, which does not need telecommunications antennas other than those that smartphones already have built in. This means that even in conditions where an aggressor has removed some of the critical infrastructure for telecommunications, communities could still be able to inform the authorities of threats. This has been proven, for example, by research on community action using smartphones during the war in Syria (Janjeva et al., 2022), which began in 2011, and the subsequent Russian invasion of Ukraine in 2022 (Zarembo et al., 2024).

Communities as information providers are also, in the author's view, crucial because of their polycentric nature, which enables polycentric defence; moreover, because of the lack of a single decision-making centre, polycentrism forces flexibility due to limited resources, competition, especially in limiting the abuse of power, and experimentation, e.g. in the face of insufficient resources provided by a central decision-making centre (Alshamy et al., 2023). Examples in the information sphere include the LiveUAMap portal or Demagog.

Zarembo et al. (2024), in their study, noted that the respondents they surveyed could be divided into three groups, depending on the purpose of the smartphone use: to escape, to resist and for mundane purposes. However, according to numerous sources, even casual, smartphone use can, in some circumstances, result in an incident being recorded, so in the author's view this is not a group that should be devalued. Communities can also play a key role in crowdfunding, surveillance of the infosphere and physical environment and documenting war crimes (Zarembo et al., 2024). In addition to documenting war crimes, information extracted from mobile devices also allows for the extraction of other data, such as geocoding of locations (Bilous et al., 2024). However, Russia's occupation of Crimea in 2014 had already shown that community mobilisation and solidarity networking went beyond conventional frameworks: in response to the invasion of the 'green men', communities of modellers, various enthusiasts and computer scientists and technicians formed Aerorozvidka. Initially the group was informal, but over time they registered as an entity, from which another offshoot was created in late 2021/early 2022: the Centre for Innovation and Development of Defence Technologies. This community provides the Ukrainian services and military with reconnaissance assets based on unmanned aerial vehicles (BALs) (Kandrik, Pala, 2024).

Communities were also a key element of state resilience during the Russian invasion also in terms of mobilisation for armed defence. For example, the authorities in Kyiv decided to form volunteer battalions and territorial defence troops already during the first invasion in 2014 (Horyń, Tomasik, 2022). The aspect of territoriality is, as we know from Ferdinand Tönnies' theory, one of the key community bonding factors, and, according to the author, it also influences the effectiveness of the defence measures implemented by, among others, territorial defence troops.

COMMUNITIES IN HYBRID WARFARE

Hybrid warfare challenges communities to survive and adapt to changing conditions. Communities pushed to the brink are forced to measure themselves against both the physical and non-physical effects of hybrid activities, which are highly networked and often cascading (as discussed in previous chapters of this book). As assessed by Kaim et al. (2024), wars often reveal multiple vulnerabilities that affect many aspects of life, from family relationships to the risk of physical harm or even loss of life. In certain situations, people may have to sacrifice their lives for a greater cause or to protect their loved ones.

The Protection of Civilians in Armed Conflict report estimates that in 2023, in 25 major armed conflicts, including hybrid wars, some 150 million civilians were affected by hostilities (killed, wounded, displaced, victims of sexual violence, victims of landmines and unexploded ordnance, missing persons, etc.) (United Nations Security Council, 2024). Furthermore, according to the report Global Trends: Forced Displacement in 2023, the number of people displaced by conflict and war has reached 117.3 million (UNHCR, 2023). These statistics show that civilians, including local communities, suffer both short-term and long-term consequences of wars. For example Chad, Briggs (2020, pp. 45–57) note that assessments carried out during the reconstruction of post-conflict regions revealed that some attacks aimed not only at immediate destruction, but also at traumatising communities over the long term, preventing them from returning to normal functioning. Attackers often exploited gaps in community defences, striking at key community resources, which could include the destruction of agricultural land by installing landmines, the devastation of health and environmental infrastructure, and other actions designed to undermine the ability to rebuild. Such tactics, have often been observed in civil wars and have been linked to ethnic cleansing. Similar methods are used in hybrid warfare, where the main objective is to weaken a society's resilience, making it more vulnerable to new threats. For example, disinformation in a military setting can have the effect of exposing civilians to violence, disrupting access to key resources such as health care and causing severe physical and psychological suffering, further destabilising societies (Katz, 2021).

In contrast, a World Bank (WB) report shows that around 2 billion people worldwide, half of them extremely poor, live in countries affected by conflict and violence. By 2030, as many as two-thirds of the extreme poor may live in such areas. The number of civil wars has tripled since 2007, and modern conflicts are characterised by increasing complexity, including an increase in the number of armed groups. Today's wars last longer and the economic losses from violence amount to $14.3 trillion, or about 12.6% of global GDP. Conflicts affect not only the poorest countries, but also middle-income countries, where victims outnumber those in low-income countries. Moreover, interpersonal and criminal and gender-based violence poses a serious threat to development and social well-being. Approximately half a million people a year die as a result of violence, with gender-based violence and violence against children being particularly severe, especially in conflict-affected areas. Currently, as (WB) highlights, the world is facing the largest forced displacement crisis in history, with more than 100 million displaced people, more than half of whom are internally displaced. Women and children account for 70% of all forcibly displaced people. Climate change is exacerbating these problems, causing further displacement and loss of livelihoods. In such conditions, violence, as during the COVID-19 pandemic, further exacerbates the crises, particularly affecting women.

The role of communities in hybrid warfare is more complex than in more traditional conflicts and wars where it is mainly related to direct survival, military or humanitarian support. In hybrid warfare, these groups must additionally deal with, for example, information manipulation, cyber attacks, Psyops operations or cognitive strategies. Above all,

all these activities are today supported by AI, which, in the assessment (Ilyas, 2023, pp. 1–22), influences each of the instruments of hybrid warfare: military, political, economic, civilian and information. The effectiveness of the implementation of protective and defensive actions by these groups is determined by resilience. This concept has been described quite extensively in the literature however, as assessed by some authors (e.g. Shannon Houck, 2022), it tends to target peacetime threats rather than war and even more so hybrid war. There is still a lack of consensus on the very definition of this issue as well as a clear framework delineating the necessary areas of resilience in hybrid war-time threats. Instead, there should be agreement that resilience building cannot be shifted to communities, but must be closely integrated into systemic solutions. The experience of war in Ukraine and the Middle East shows that adequately prepared civilians can support defence, but also make a significant contribution to protection (physical and digital), pre-medical or humanitarian efforts. Shannon Houck, in the context of resilience during an invasion, points out that even the use of bricolage (the ability to improvise and solve problems creatively) requires preparation. For example, as Houck argues, *one Ukrainian woman reportedly threw a jar of cucumbers from her balcony to destroy a drone*; another example is one brewery that began producing 'Molotov cocktails' with a label 'expressing the attitude of the civilian population towards the aggressor' (Houck, 2022). However, it is important to consider whether this form of resilience exposes communities to escalating aggression.

CONCEPTUALISING RESILIENCE IN THE CONTEXT OF HYBRID WARFARE

The sheer volume of research on resilience, combined with its interdisciplinary nature, means that the concept has been defined in many ways. As Cretney (2014, pp. 627–640) cited after Clark (2024, pp. 720–740) points out, it is a word with multiple meanings. An important constant, however, is the idea of an adaptive response to disruption. Resilience can be broadly understood as a dynamic process involving positive adaptation in the context of significant adversity. War is a powerful adversity in this regard; it is one of the major stressors that individuals (and the wider systems to which their lives are linked, including families, communities and ecosystems) can experience (Clark, 2024). So, not surprisingly, there is a wealth of research on resilience in conflict and post-conflict settings. These variously explore the ways in which resilience is measured, people's coping mechanisms and adaptive responses, cultural and contextual factors shaping the expression and sources of resilience in conflict-affected environments (Clark, 2024).

While some scholars have emphasised that incorporating a resilience lens into conflict analyses can offer new insights into individuals' experiences of war, others have raised concerns that resilience-focused research leads to highly generalised conclusions about war-affected populations and neglects intersectional identities. According to Keelan and Brown, for example, the results of a limited study of Palestinian children and young men in Gaza have been uncritically applied to homogenise Palestinian resilience in general, reinforcing the problematic Western belief that Palestinians are a homogenous group (Keelan, Brown, 2022, pp. 459–471, cit. Clark, 2024, p. 723).

Resilience has been described as a notoriously slippery concept and, according to Simon and Randalls, its ultimate generality makes it applicable to almost anything (Clark, 2024).

Alexandros Lordos and Daniel Hyslop assess that the existing toolkit for conflict prevention and mitigation, developed after two world wars and based on diplomacy, trade and international norms, is becoming less and less effective in the face of new forms of asymmetric and hybrid conflicts (Lordos, Hyslop, 2021, pp. 417–452). Consequently, the need to build different forms of resilience (e.g. national, social, community, individual or hybrid) is increasingly discussed. Simpson et al. assess that cultivating resilience capacities can provide the foundation for transformative social change that can bring together diverse social, civic and institutional stakeholders (Simpson et al., 2016, pp. 1–40). In contrast, *the UN Joint Guidelines on Assistance for Building Resilient Societies* emphasise that, from a development perspective, investments in resilience help reduce economic and human losses in crises, while protecting development achievements and reducing human suffering (United Nations, 2020). Lordos and Hyslop, point to a wide range of approaches to resilience that take into account different concepts of conflict stages (such as resilience before, during and after conflict), system levels (individual, household, community, institution or state), resilience resources (e.g. personal characteristics, social capital, material resources, institutional practices) and assessment methods (participatory, quantitative, qualitative, case study) (Lordos, Hyslop, 2021). The International Organisation for Migration in Ukraine sees resilience as proactively, wisely and sustainably dealing each day with new realities, which contributes to strengthening communities (International Organization for Migration [IOM], 2024).

There are two main streams in the literature that reflect methodological approaches. The first focuses on resilience as the ability to prevent violence by maintaining cooperative strategies in the face of increasing social stressors. This strand includes research that looks at how communities can counteract pressures that could lead to conflict. The second strand of research focuses on resilience, understood as the ability of individuals, communities and institutions to cope with the consequences of violence that has already occurred, without compromising mental health, social functioning or key institutional capacities. Methodological approaches in resilience research vary according to the research perspective. Socio-ecological approaches analyse the dynamics of multi-stakeholders from a systems theory perspective, involving them in the research process, which allows for a holistic understanding of resilience mechanisms. In contrast, psychological and anthropological approaches focus on individuals' responses to conflict-related stressors, using empirical methods to study resilience at the individual and societal levels. The two approaches are complementary, creating a composite picture of conflict resilience that considers both systemic and individual aspects of survival and adaptation under threat (Lordos, Hyslop, 2021).

In addition to the dominant strand of literature that focuses on psychosocial aspects of resilience, there are also studies dedicated to specific sources of resilience, such as access to material resources, information, technical knowledge and adaptive organisational strategies (Clark, 2022, pp. 22–25). This type of research pays particular attention to the analysis of household and institutional resilience in conflict-affected regions.

However, the diverse nature of academic research on resilience in the context of war seems less consistent than the development of frameworks for practitioners (Lordos, Hyslop, 2021), which provide structured guidelines, mainly based on systems theory (for example, the United Nations Joint Guidelines for Building Resilient Societies (United Nations, 2020), Hybrid Resilience Framework EU (Giannopoulos et al., 2020), Sendai Framework for Disaster Risk Reduction (2015–2030), Framework for Disaster Resilience UNDRR (United Nations Office for Disaster Risk Reduction [UNDRR], 2015), Framework for Assessing Resilience (CEPAD,; Lordos, Hyslop, 2021) see a gap in these solutions in the absence of specific guidelines for assessing the risk landscape for specific subpopulations in the context of conflict. In response to this problem, they propose 7 Principles and Guidelines for an Integrated Science of Conflict Resilience (Lordos, Hyslop, 2021):

- Principle 1: Integrate a System-Wide Perspective With Agent-Focused Research
- Principle 2: Contribute Toward a Cumulative Science of Conflict Resilience around an Agreed Taxonomy of Resilience Capacities
- Principle 3: Become Versatile in the Use of Appropriate Qualitative and Quantitative Methodologies
- Principle 4: Develop distinct Research Protocols and Approaches for the Assessment of Individual, Household, Community, Institutional, and National Resilience

- Principle 5: Leverage Analytic Methods That Are Suitable for Detection of Cross-Systemic Linkages
- Principle 6: Engage with Stakeholders Across Multiple Systems and Levels, to Maximize Resilience-Enhancing Insight, Planning, and Action
- Principle 7: Adjust Resilience Assessment Priorities as the Conflict and Peace System Evolves over Time, and as Local Understanding of Resilience Processes Matures.

Mitchell and Harris (2012, pp. 1–6), cited by Buheji and Mushimiyiman, divide resilience into four phases: the exposure phase, the vulnerability phase, the adaptation phase and the recovery phase. Exposure is the phase in which individuals or communities are exposed to shocks, while vulnerability encompasses the vulnerabilities and consequences that occur during this time. In the adaptation phase, individuals or communities begin to cope with the situation by accepting change and shocks, while in the recovery phase they work to gradually adjust to the new normal. The strength of resilience depends on the level of resilience in each of these phases and the ability to successfully move to the next stages of recovery (Buheji, Mushimiyimana, 2024, pp. 120–136).

In addition to the concepts discussed above, resilience is defined, for example, as the capacity of individuals, households, communities, cities, institutions, systems and societies to prevent, resist, absorb, adapt, respond and recover positively and effectively in the face of a wide range of threats, while maintaining acceptable levels of functioning and without compromising long-term prospects for sustainable development, peace and security, human rights and well-being for all (United Nations, 2020). The Interpeace Frameworks for the Assessment of Resilience, on the other hand, indicate that resilience refers to a variety of endogenous characteristics, capacities, resources and responses that potentially enable individuals, communities, institutions and societies to peacefully cope with the impact of past conflicts and violence, as well as to prevent new and emerging patterns of conflict and violence (Simpson et al., 2016). In another study (Lordos, Hyslop, 2019) analysing and integrating different concepts of resilience, they define it as the ability of agents at different levels (i.e. individuals, households, communities, institutions, nations) in a complex social system to respond appropriately to stressors and shocks, in an effective and timely manner, without compromising long-term prospects for sustainable development, inclusive growth, reducing chronic vulnerability, preventing new conflicts, maintaining peace and security, promoting human rights, and ensuring access to livelihoods and well-being for all. Resilience can manifest in a variety of agent responses in complex systems, depending on the temporal relationship to the stressor (e.g. prevention before the stressor;

resistance during the stressor; recovery after the stressor) and the level of innovation in the response (i.e. whether it is absorptive, adaptive or transformative).

Examples of conceptual frameworks of resilience show that it is not a universally accepted area. For example, according to Pamela Aall and Chester A. Crocker, despite the wide range of definitions of resilience, a key element is the ability to cope with stress without breaking down (Aall, Crocker, 2019). In their assessment, it is worth looking at three different interpretations of resilience. The first approach, derived from engineering, emphasises the physical properties that enable individuals or communities to return to their original state despite significant pressure (the squeezing effect of a rubber ball) (Aall, Crocker, 2019). An example of this is where social infrastructure in Ukraine, is being rebuilt with the aim of restoring pre-conflict functions and despite the destruction caused by the war. This approach emphasises the ability to return to the status quo, maintaining the sustainability of institutions, social relations and economic patterns. The second approach to resilience emphasises the adaptive qualities of individuals and systems. Although structures may change, entities, while adapting to new circumstances, retain part of their original identity (Aall, Crocker, 2019). An example of this is the Gaza Strip, where, despite ongoing conflict and changes in the social environment, communities adapt to new conditions, retaining certain traditions and cultural identities while changing their survival strategies. The third approach to resilience refers to a more radical change that leads to a complete shift in structure and modes of operation compared to the original state (Aall, Crocker, 2019). As an example, Ukraine, faced with a hybrid war, has transformed its social and economic models to better meet new challenges, moving from traditional structures to modern, integrated systems based on innovation and international cooperation (Aall, Crocker, 2019).

Yulia Kurnyshova points out that in the literature, resilience is often seen as a process of social adaptation in the face of complex shocks and implies adaptation, partnership and self-reliance on the part of individuals and communities, as well as shifting responsibility to those communities by promoting reflexive self-governance, awareness strategies, risk management and adaptation (Kurnyshova, 2022). In this context, resilience requires individuals and communities to take care of their own well-being and security, rather than relying on government safeguards (Humbert, Joseph, 2019, pp. 216–223). However, it is worth noting that this understanding of resilience is met with criticism. As Kurnyshova points out, the example of Ukraine demonstrates that resilience has a deeply political dimension and seeks to empower individuals as active participants in their own vulnerability reduction, enabling them to make the right decisions and avoid maladaptations in their newly created environment. In this way, everyday practices of resilience create actors, among whom civil society organisations, grassroots groups and networks play a key role. Resilience is not the result of a one-off action, but rather the result of long-term, ongoing efforts and investments that adapt to changing conditions. In the context of war, the traditional understanding of resilience has focused on the ability to resist armed attacks. This encompasses not only the readiness of armed forces to carry out their tasks, but also the ability of society to resist and recover from attacks, thus minimising civilian casualties and providing continuous support to the needs of the armed forces. This ensures that military resources are not overcommitted to resolving civilian crises (Christie, Berzina, 2022, pp. 2–4). Shannon Houck, in her research on resilience preparedness processes, emphasises that resilience is a key factor in enabling societies to effectively resist threats. Her analysis leads to the conclusion that a lack of will to defend sovereignty significantly undermines a society's ability to resist. Although there is growing interest in the topic of resilience, Houck points out an important gap in the approach to societal preparedness. Contemporary strategies mainly focus on building civilian resilience in the face of natural disasters, natural catastrophes and emergency response, which is undoubtedly important, but insufficient in the context of hybrid warfare threats. It is necessary to develop cognitive readiness, determination and motivation to fight. The resilience-building process, according to Houck, should include preparing individuals and entire communities for the psychological challenges of an invasion: before the invasion arrives (where anticipation and uncertainty dominate), during the invasion itself (when coping, acceptance of the situation and community unity become crucial), and after the invasion ends (where psychological changes resulting from the experience occur). As an example of the successful implementation of this approach, Houck points to Ukraine, which, after 2014, adopted a society-wide strategy to strengthen both the government and the civil sector, with a particular focus on psychological resilience. This has enabled Ukraine, according to Houck, to remain determined, confident of victory, innovative and united in the face of conflict. According to the author, other nations can learn from this example by adapting similar strategies to strengthen their own resilience to potential threats (Houck, 2022).

TYPOLOGIES OF RESILIENCE

A review of research on resilience indicates that three types of resilience can be distinguished: individual, social (community) and national (societal) (Kimhi et al., 2023).

National resilience is an important aspect of the survival and stability of societies in the face of a variety of threats, both external and internal. The concept encompasses a wide range of activities and mechanisms that enable a society to cope with crises, as well as to adapt to new conditions once they occur. In the academic literature, national resilience is often defined as the ability of a society to maintain functionality and integrity in the face of significant threats. As assessed by Goodwin et al. (2023), research on national resilience points to four key components that play a critical role in its maintenance: patriotism, optimism, social integration and trust in public and political institutions. These factors are critical in the context of high-intensity conflicts, where a society needs to mobilise its resources not only militarily, but also socially and psychologically. For example, Israeli society during the Al-Aqsa intifada was able to maintain a high level of resilience due to a strong sense of national identity, supported by social integration and trust in institutions. Analogous mechanisms could be observed in the Ukrainian context following the annexation of Crimea in 2014 and the Russian invasion in 2022, where social mobilisation, at both formal and informal levels, played a key role in maintaining social stability (Goodwin et al., 2023). In their study of Ukraine's national resilience (Goodwin et al., 2023), they found that a strong sense of national identity and belonging were key factors in maintaining the resilience of Ukrainian society in the face of war with Russia. Despite difficult conditions, such as the 2022 invasion, Ukrainians showed high levels of optimism and national pride, which contributed to strengthening resilience at the societal level. Strong social relations and mutual trust among citizens and between citizens and institutions played a key role in maintaining national resilience. The model shows that a society with high levels of trust and cohesion is better able to cope with crisis situations. Above this, despite the loss of income for many members of society, no reduction in national resilience has been observed. Economic losses are accepted as part of a larger struggle for independence and survival, suggesting that a strong national identity can neutralise the negative impact of financial problems. Ukrainian speakers showed higher levels of national resilience compared to those who spoke Russian showing that a strong linguistic identity has a direct impact on feelings of belonging and resilience during war. Social resilience as assessed by Koubová and Kimhi (2024) (formerly national resilience) refers to a society's perceived ability to successfully cope with adversity and to quickly return to its pre-threat state once the threat is removed. It includes four factors: trust in the country's leaders, trust in state institutions, social unity and willingness to contribute to the welfare of the country, i.e. patriotism.

Social resilience as noted by Christie and Berzina (2022) has different practical meanings in different expert communities. From a national security and defence perspective, there is a strong overlap with civilian preparedness, with the difference that social resilience emphasises the wider range and diversity of actors who should work together to ensure a certain level of resilience. Social resilience in this context can be understood as the ability of a nation to draw on all elements of society to resist, recover, learn and adapt in the face of major shocks, including armed attacks, to minimise harm to the population and to support the continuity of essential public services, including security and national defence. Elements of society include individuals, civil society organisations, private enterprises and public institutions. In addition to technical factors, societal resilience also depends on intangible factors, such as the degree of social bonds and social trust between individuals and between individuals and civil society, the private sector and the public sector, enabling a combination of top-down and bottom-up responses.

Saja, distinguish four groups of social resilience (Saja et al., 2021, pp. 790–804, Kupenko et al., 2023, pp. 154–168):

- as the capacity of individuals – people, social units, social systems – to cope with, resist and/or recover from disasters,
- as the capacity of social mechanisms to cope with a disaster, including mechanisms for decision-making and resource utilization,
- as the capacity and reliability of public structures, resources and processes to anticipate, cope with and recover from disasters,
- as the capacity to cope with disasters, adapt or transform when the previous capacity has already been exceeded.

Defining community resilience first requires an understanding of community itself, which can include place, individual and collective identity, social being and collective action. It can also mean, a group of people with different characteristics, united by social ties and acting together in specific geographical locations or contexts (Kimhi et al., 2023a, 2023b, 2023c; Olcese et al., 2023).

A community resilience perspective is understood as the ability to anticipate risk, mitigate impact and rapidly recover by surviving, adapting, evolving and growing in the face of turbulent change. Resilient communities are not only prepared to prevent or minimise loss or damage to life, property and the environment, but also have the capacity to quickly return citizens to work, reopen businesses and restore other essential services needed for full and timely recovery (Olcese et al., 2023). Similarly, they believe (Kimhi et al., 2023a, 2023b, 2023c), arguing that community resilience refers to their ability to cope with challenges, recover from traumatic events and return to normal functioning. Taking into account factors such as social trust (mutual support between members), local leadership (the ability of leaders to manage in a crisis) and the ability to organise and respond to a crisis (preparedness for disasters, such as missile attacks, emergencies), they found that communities with higher levels of community resilience are more resilient to war-related stressors and their members recover more quickly from traumatic events (Yanakiev et al., 2023).

As assessed by Olcese et al. (2023), community resilience refers to the ability of a group of people to adapt and respond effectively to crises and disasters, enabling them to return to pre-disruption functioning. Community resilience is described in the literature from different perspectives. Norris et al. (2008, pp. 127–50, cited in Olcese et al., 2024) define it as the process that links the adaptive capacity of social networks to a positive trajectory of action after a disruption. Other authors point out that community resilience is the ability to adapt to the resources and losses resulting from natural disasters (Cox, Perry, 2011, pp. 395–411 cited in Olcese et al., 2024) or recognise the crucial readiness of communities to take responsibility for their own development, particularly in the context of coping with disruption-induced change (Matarrita-Cascante et al., 2017, pp. 105–123 cited in Olcese et al., 2024). In practice, community resilience encompasses the community's actions related to coping with crisis situations or stressful events, which includes helping to reduce their impact and activating transformative capacities. Every community has the capacity to develop resilience; however, communities need to be able to live with change through adaptation as well as transformation. Above and beyond this, developing resilience can enhance a community's ability to thrive in dynamic environments characterised by unpredictability and novelty. This construct should be understood as the capacity of community members to engage in coordinated action projects in their context, despite events and structures that may cause constraints to such projects. The emphasis is therefore on the community planning and design phase that follows a critical event, and the prevention of a possible subsequent event. In fact, community resilience is not only related to the aftermath of a traumatic event, but also to the preparation of the community for the event itself (community preparedness), which occurs through the strengthening of protective factors that may contain the harm associated with the event. The literature lists several factors as components of community resilience, and among them are local knowledge, community skills and training on risk communication, collective efficacy and empowerment, and community competence. Another key factor for community resilience is the physical and mental health services that can be offered after a disaster. The literature also highlights the importance of governance and leadership in disaster management economic investments such as access and presence of resources, employment and policy decisions to reduce the socio-economic impact of disasters. The importance of preparedness for response planning and sustainable recovery and the active involvement of stakeholders in disaster response planning is highlighted. Another factor is the network of relationships and communities, which includes social support and community cohesion. Finally, the importance of information and communication includes infrastructure, real-time information, meaning sharing and other elements of dealing with emergencies. The above aspects can play a role in alleviating the stress of a traumatic event and help facilitate coping (Olcese et al., 2023). Eshel and Kimhi (2015, pp. 109–117) argue that resilience should be analysed simultaneously in terms of its adaptive and pathogenic components. In another study (Eshel, Kimhi, 2015, pp. 109–117), it was hypothesised that, respectively, a community's successful adaptation, positive functioning or competence would not be sufficient to guarantee its resilience, without simultaneously considering its level of vulnerability. The study conducted assessed this vulnerability by means of a sense of threat after adversity. The results confirm that Community Social Vulnerability Resilience (COM-SVR) is indeed a measure of resilience. Elements that promote resilience, such as individual and national resilience, well-being and Sense of Coherence (SOC), positively predicted COM-SVR, while community size inversely predicted this measure of community resilience. The key role of vulnerabilities, which form part of the balance of predictors, was revealed in pathway models run separately for the strength and vulnerability components of COM-SVR. The results clearly indicate that examining Community Resilience (CR) in terms of strength, without simultaneously considering its vulnerability, can lead to a loss of information that may be crucial to understanding the whole picture of the multidimensional nature of community responses to adversity and trauma. Positive as well as negative cognitive appraisals determine the assessment of and responses to stressful situations. A high SOC represents a positive cognitive appraisal that reduces the traumatic impact of stressful experiences and reinforces people's beliefs about their ability to cope successfully with adversity. In this role, SOC is a mediator of the relationship between COM-SVR and its predictors. The present results indicate that this is indeed the case for the associations of subjective resilience at the individual level and national level, well-being and community size with subjective resilience at the community level (Eshel, Kimhi, 2015, pp. 109–117). The data show that individual, community and national resilience tend to correlate with each other in times of war, such that resilient individuals are also inclined to attribute higher levels of resilience to both their close community and their country (Eshel, Kimhi, 2015, pp. 109–117).

COMMUNITY RESILIENCE AND
ROLES IN HYBRID WARFARE

A case study in the Ukraine war

There is a growing trend of discussion of Ukraine's resilience in academic and open studies. As Clark (2024, pp. 720–740) notes, reference to it is repeated in media articles and reports on the war (Wilson, 2022). There are also several studies on this topic (Goodwin et al., 2023; Kimhi et al., 2023a, 2023b, 2023c; Kurapov et al., 2023, pp. 167–74; Giordano et al., 2024).

Oleg Romanchuk, director of the Ukrainian Institute of Cognitive Behavioural Therapy and the Institute of Mental Health at the Ukrainian Catholic University, emphasises that in a situation of war, resilience is not only a coping mechanism for dealing with trauma and stress, but also the basis of a collective effort leading to victory. Both individual (community) and national resilience is based on the strength of social bonds, a commonality of values and a sense of belonging to a larger whole, of which shared goals and historical heritage are an integral part. Key elements of this resilience are trust, cooperation and mutual support at the family, community and national level. The ability to regulate emotions and adapt to new challenges is also an important factor, making it possible to function even in the most difficult circumstances. Resilience here is not just an innate trait, but an ability that can be developed and strengthened by taking deliberate action, both at the individual and collective level. In his view, the war, despite its hardships and pain, became for many Ukrainians a time for the birth of new psychological strength and national unity (Romanchuk, 2023). Local communities in Ukraine were a key factor in sustaining resilience and supporting state structures under difficult wartime conditions. According to the Ukrainian Center for Independent Political Research (UCIPR), local communities were involved in preparing for harsh winter conditions by purchasing generators and seeking alternative heating methods in the face of the energy crisis. This was particularly evident in the Kharkiv region, where power cuts were paralysing businesses. Local communities were also taking steps to assess war damage and reconstruct damaged buildings. Remote sensing technologies were used to collect data on damaged property, which was entered into the State Register of Damaged and Destroyed Property. This enabled damage to be assessed and compensation to be sought. IDPs in various regions of Ukraine organised themselves to secure housing and employment assistance. Civil society organisations and international donors actively participated in this process, working with local authorities. Communities continued to provide financial and moral support to the Armed Forces of Ukraine, despite a decline in donations due to the deteriorating economic situation. The public continued to be involved in helping the army, albeit with fewer and fewer resources. Families of soldiers, especially prisoners of war, regularly organised demonstrations, reminding the authorities and the public of the need to work for the release of prisoners. Communities engaged in debates on the renaming of villages and streets, leading to tensions, but at the same time strengthening civic engagement and improving public consultation, particularly in the Nikolaev region. In some regions, such as the Nikolaev region, communities supported the reconstruction of local democratic mechanisms, including transparent public decision-making, even though the wartime law restricted some local government decisions. Local communities and businesses were involved in the construction of defence fortifications, although they faced difficulties such as insufficient insurance mechanisms, low wages and supply problems. Above this, they supported the authorities' efforts to bring those suspected of collaborating with the aggressor to justice, demonstrating the high level of public support for anti-collaboration measures. Various international organisations continued their activities in Ukraine, providing support targeted at specific institutions, community groups and foundations. Despite economic difficulties, communities continued to support humanitarian projects, organising aid for IDPs and other groups in need (Ukrainian Center for Independent Political Research, 2024).

The International Organisation for Migration (IOM) in Ukraine reports that at the beginning of the war, people did not sleep or eat for days, hiding in basements. They had to endure long and difficult journeys to reach safe places and were completely exhausted physically and emotionally. When the evacuation trains arrived in Lviv, psychologists noticed fear, anxiety, anger and apathy in the evacuees. These emotions and psychological reactions became common in places such as overcrowded train stations and humanitarian centres. The war separated many families, both physically and emotionally. Many have experienced feelings of loneliness, caused by a lack of understanding within the family or a divergence of views. Children draw tanks, guns, grenades and their knowledge of the war comes from television or their families. Some children have witnessed the horrors of war and this has affected their emotions and development. Many Ukrainians have experienced displacement for the second time in the last eight years. Those who have gone through previous displacement often become leaders and encourage others to take action. Once basic needs are met, people develop unique resilience strategies to cope with new realities and rebuild their lives. An example of this is a 13-year-old girl who, through a mobile game in which houses can be designed, found a way to process her emotions after her home was destroyed. Psychological interventions based on art and games help children who have difficulty expressing their feelings in words. Communities that welcome displaced people strengthen them by providing new opportunities, which helps build resilience. People who have experienced war have begun to develop new ways of coping, often leading to a strengthening of their resilience (IOM Ukraine, 2024).

The *Resisting Russia* report analyses the role of civilians and local communities in Ukrainian resistance to the Russian invasion, with a particular focus on the first four months of the 2022 war. As the study states, civilian action is an integral part of Ukraine's defence efforts and contributes to maintaining the country's political sovereignty and territorial integrity. Civilian actions in the first four months of the war involve both physical, psychological and digital spaces. For example, the 'IT Army of Ukraine' group brought together volunteers from Ukraine and abroad to conduct cyber attacks on Russian infrastructure, government websites and social media. Civilians used OSINT methods to monitor Russian troop movements by analysing satellite data, social media and other open sources. City residents blocked the movement of Russian military columns by standing on the roads and protesting. Civilians addressed Russian soldiers directly, appealing for them to stop fighting, and informed the families of Russian soldiers about their plight via social media. Ukrainians abroad organised protests, fund-raisers and information campaigns to raise international awareness and put pressure on host governments. The public opposed attempts to organise illegal referendums in the occupied territories.

Volunteers organised the evacuation of civilians from areas under combat or occupied by the Russians. NGOs and community groups delivered food, medicine and other essential supplies to those most in need. Above and beyond this, evidence of Russian crimes against civilians was collected and made public to increase international pressure on Russia. Civilians used social media and traditional media to maintain public morale, sharing stories of heroism and solidarity. In addition, there was widespread use of national symbols, anthems, poetry and art as a means of strengthening national unity, and the creation of memes, songs and other cultural content to uplift and unite society in the face of aggression. The authors of the report highlight that the war in Ukraine demonstrates that through cyber warfare, the use of open sources of information and other forms of unconventional resistance, societies and communities, can play a significant role in hybrid warfare (see Kepe, Demus, 2023 in broader terms).

In turn, the report *Unbroken: How Communities Adapted To War* indicates that Ukrainian local communities adapted to the realities of full-scale war by focusing on reconstruction, strategic planning and citizen involvement in decision-making processes. According to the authors of the report, there are key factors that have contributed to the resilience of local communities:

The team – united and dedicated management teams at various levels have been key to keeping the community functioning. Leaders and managers in sectors such as education, health and social care demonstrated professionalism and dedication.

Stability – the continuation of proven management practices has allowed communities to maintain basic services and invest in development despite budget difficulties caused by the war.

Initiative – the emergence of numerous volunteer initiatives and the willingness of local people to sacrifice their own resources to help others have been crucial in supporting IDPs and the Armed Forces of Ukraine.

Development – communities have continued to plan strategically and invest in their development, which has maintained prospects for long-term growth and recovery.

Solidarity – cooperation between residents and local authorities in pursuit of a common goal has made it possible to respond quickly to challenges and to coordinate activities effectively.

Communication – effective communication between authorities and residents and within management teams was essential for building trust and responding quickly to community needs.

International assistance – support from international partners and NGOs has provided the necessary resources for the reconstruction and development of conflict-affected communities.

Other factors include confidence in the Armed Forces of Ukraine, hope for victory and the experience of residents who survived the occupation contributed to psychological and social resilience (see wider Centre UA, 2024).

Kurnyshova and Makarychev (2022) in the context of Ukraine's resilience introduce the concept of hybrid resilience, which means that resilience is not a uniform, monolithic phenomenon, but encompasses different levels and spheres of social and political life. This approach assumes that resilience develops at both national and local levels, and that its formation depends on the cooperation of various actors: state, local and grassroots. The authors emphasise that Ukraine's resilience is based on cooperation between state structures and civil society. Resilience at the societal level is understood as society's response to challenges, such as the war, which triggered an anti-imperial moment that united society in resistance against Russia. Ukraine has strengthened its sense of national identity and has clearly moved away from cultural and historical ties with Russia. On the institutional level, it strengthened public institutions, including the military sector, thanks to earlier decentralisation reforms. Reforms of public institutions played a key role, enhancing their ability to deal with threats. Strong institutions, especially government and the military, allow not only for effective defence against aggression, but also for the promotion of social resilience. The local level also refers to decentralisation reform, which has been a key element in building resilience at this level. This gave local communities autonomy and enabled them to respond more effectively to a war crisis by organising humanitarian aid, securing infrastructure and supporting the military. This points to the ability of local communities to self-organise, which was an important element of Ukrainian resistance. Local authorities, thanks to the reform, were able to respond to the war and continue their activities despite the difficult conditions. A final dimension of resilience relates to the information warfare that Ukraine is waging against Russian propaganda and disinformation. The growth of the media space, as well as an effective information policy, has been key to maintaining national unity and high morale. The Ukrainian media took steps to ensure a unified message, focusing on mobilising the public and supporting the government. Access to Russian disinformation channels was also restricted.

At the same time, Kurnyshova, Makarychev, criticise theories of resilience suggesting that it should develop independently of the state. In the case of Ukraine, they argue, such an approach is too radical, as the state has played a key role in building resilience through reform and security provision. Institutional reforms, particularly those relating to the military and decentralisation, have been fundamental to an effective response to the war. In the context of war, the state-society opposition does not apply here, as the two are mutually supportive (Kurnyshova, Makarychev, 2022, pp. 88–110).

Clark, analysing the discourse on resilience in the context of the war in Ukraine, draws attention to the multidimensional role played by the concept at both national and international levels. Drawing on Ish-Shalom's theory of the 'concept at work', she points out that resilience is selectively used in a way that favours Western political objectives, leading to the marginalisation of countries in the Global South, which are also affected by the conflict but are often overlooked in this discourse. In contrast to traditional framings linking resilience to neoliberal practices that promote individual responsibility and marketisation, Clark suggests that in the case of Ukraine, resilience has a much broader political function. It is presented not as something yet to be developed, but as an already existing and fundamental characteristic of the Ukrainian people. However, as he goes on to note, there is a risk, a risk of homogenising the human experience through a discourse of resilience. In the realities of conflict, where survival often becomes a necessity rather than a choice, attributing resilience to individuals as an innate or expected trait can lead to the dehumanisation of individual stories and limit the possibility of expressing vulnerability. President Zelenski, in his rhetoric, often refers to narratives of resilience, which, Clark argues, can paradoxically limit the space for a more nuanced understanding of how different individuals experience war and cope with its consequences. The study of resilience in Ukraine also needs to take into account the fact that the war, now in its third year, is leading to fatigue, which may reduce enthusiasm for continued military support from Western states. In turn, changing geopolitical priorities, the escalation of new conflicts and wars and the upcoming US presidential election may further test the sustainability of international support. Clark predicts that, as the geopolitical landscape changes, the concept of resilience may gain traction at the domestic level in Ukraine itself, while losing its centrality in the international rhetoric surrounding the war (see wider Clark, 2024, pp. 720–740).

The study (Kimhi et al., 2022, pp. 1005–1023) analysed levels of community and societal resilience as well as positive and negative indicators of coping among the population of Ukraine and five neighbouring countries-Poland, Estonia, the Czech Republic, Lithuania and Slovakia-in the context of war (psychological variables included hope, morale, well-being, feelings of threat, stress symptoms and perceived threats). The key findings are that respondents from Ukraine reported the highest levels of both social and community resilience and hope compared to the other countries surveyed. Paradoxically, they simultaneously reported the highest levels of stress symptoms and perceived threat, the lowest levels of wellbeing and relatively low morale. In all six countries, hope emerged as the strongest and most consistent predictor of both community and social resilience. Perceived threats were also significant predictors of resilience in all countries. Differences were observed between countries in the levels of psychological variables, reflecting their unique geopolitical, historical and socio-cultural backgrounds. For example, Estonia reported the lowest sense of threat and perceived threat, which may be due to NATO membership serving as a deterrent mechanism against existential threats. As assessed by (Kimhi et al., 2023) in the context of Ukraine, high resilience and hope may coexist with high levels of stress and perceived threat.

A case study in the Israel-Gaza war

As in the case of the war in Ukraine, in the context of the war between the State of Israel and Hamas that began on 7 October 2023, the discourse on the resilience of Israeli and Gaza societies and communities is expanding in academic and open literature. Previous studies of Israeli resilience during periods of conflict, such as the rocket attacks in 2011 and in the aftermath of Operation Protective Edge and also during the ongoing tensions in Gaza (2022), characterised Israeli communities as exhibiting particularly high levels of resilience. In their study (Kaim et al., 2024), they identified four key relevant variables that are consistently associated with community resilience: community resilience, level of hope, government support (specifically being a supporter of the government as opposed to being against it) and religiosity (specifically being ultra-Orthodox as opposed to being secular). Kaim et al. (2024), noted that in the early days of the Israel-Gaza conflict, Israel's resilience was very high, but in an identical study a month later there was a significant drop in resilience levels. This means that the initial effect of the so-called 'Rally 'Round the Flag' (as in Ukraine) see also (Berlinschi et al., 2022, pp. 283–301) and is short-lived. Notwithstanding, community and societal resilience are highly correlated, demonstrating that they are entities integrated in social cohesion, which has been positively and consistently linked to social resilience, highlighting its role as a key psychological resource in coping with crises. Extending this thought, community resilience indicated a dynamic interaction between individuals and their communities, reflecting not only the community's ability to meet the needs of its members, but also the extent to which individuals draw strength from their social ties. This means that a resilient community is not just an aggregator of resilient individuals. Individual resilience does not necessarily scale up to the level of a community or society, a community's resilience – encompassing its social networks, shared resources and collective efficacy – can instead spread to affect social resilience. Therefore, if many social units within a society demonstrate resilience, this collective resilience can serve as the basis for the overall resilience of the society. This relationship is evident when communities facing crises effectively mobilise resources, provide mutual support and maintain their functional integrity, which in turn contributes to the stability and resilience of society as a whole. In this way, community resilience works synergistically to strengthen and amplify the resilience of society as a whole. Thus, co-modernity plays an important role in building resilience in Israel. Above and beyond this, hope as a psychological resource supports individuals and communities to remain positive and motivated in the face of difficulties (a result similar to the study of resilience and from conflict zones in Ukraine and Poland (Kimhi et al., 2023a, 2023b, 2023c). The other variables – government support – showed that being a supporter of the government, compared to an opponent, had a significant effect on the level of social resilience. In contrast, a negative association with social resilience was observed among ultra-Orthodox individuals compared to secular individuals. However, it is important to note that religious groups in Israel have different levels of resilience. The predictor 'religious' often refers to orthodox individuals, but not to the stricter practices of the ultra-orthodox community. A religious group may operate with cultural and social mechanisms that are more positive for resilience. These may include, for example, strong community support networks, a collective sense of identity and shared values that provide psychological comfort and practical help in crisis situations. Ultra-Orthodox Jews, despite having high social capital in their community, are known in Israel for their insularity, with a lifestyle that is strongly religiously focused, often with limited engagement with the secular world. As a result, they may have limited access to national resources, information and support systems that are crucial for resilience in the current war. Above and beyond this, the argument may be the dissonance between the recommendations of religious leaders and the crisis management strategies of the authorities. These elements may contribute to the fact that the ultra-Orthodox community shows lower levels of social resilience compared to their religious, traditional and secular counterparts. Conversely, in the case of social resilience levels within the secular group, these may be influenced by factors such as potentially weaker social ties or a lack of unifying narratives, which can often be provided by a degree of religious belief. As highlighted by Kaim et al. (2024), it is important to recognise that these differences in the same social context suggest that other mediating factors play a role beyond religiosity itself for social resilience. The role of religious beliefs needs to be interpreted alongside factors such as community structure, socioeconomic status, access to resources and the relationship between levels of religiosity and government institutions.

Erlan argue that the intensity of the 7 October 2023 attack, combined with the failure of Israeli intelligence and military operations, as well as the forced evacuation of citizens from northern and southern areas of the country, has significantly undermined the resilience of Israeli society to date. In their analysis of Israel's national resilience, based on the results of a nine-week survey conducted by the Institute for National Security Studies (INSS) since the start of the conflict (Erlan et al., 2023), they argue that a large majority of Israeli Jewish society (82%) recognise that the sense of solidarity has increased since the start of the war. Also, an overwhelming majority (96%) expresses support for the goals of the war that have been announced by the political authorities. Confidence in the Israeli Defense Forces (IDF) remains very high, with a large proportion of respondents believing that the IDF is capable of winning the Gaza conflict. Some 90% of respondents remain optimistic about the possibility of society returning to normalcy and development after the war. However, despite these positive indicators, the survey results also reveal the complexity of the situation. For example, only 25% of respondents trust the current government, around 33% report a high sense of security, and more than half of respondents state that their daily lives have been significantly disrupted by the war. Nearly half of the respondents also expressed concerns about Israel's future social situation after the end of hostilities. As assessed by Erlan et al. (2023), these differences in results may be interpreted as an expression of Israeli society's need to cope with the feelings of humiliation, pain and frustration that the events of 7 October triggered. These results may also reflect a widespread belief that Israel is engaged in an inevitable and just war, which was necessitated by an unexpected, brutal attack by Hamas. Consequently, there is a growing ethos of patriotism in the population that reinforces support for the IDF and the goals of the conflict. Unity and mobilisation are highlighted by the widespread mobilisation of reservists, unanimity in the media and the rebuilding of IDF operational capabilities. Kimhi et al. (2023a, 2023b, 2023c), in a comparative analysis of resilience levels and protective and vulnerability factors among the Ukrainian civilian population during the ongoing Russo-Ukrainian war with analogous data collected among the Israeli population during the 2021 armed conflict, noted differences in conflict specificities. The most important findings are that the Ukrainian sample had significantly higher levels of stress symptoms, feelings of threat and perceived threats compared to the Israeli sample. Despite these strong negative feelings, Ukrainian respondents reported significantly higher levels of hope and social resilience compared to their Israeli counterparts, and slightly higher individual and community resilience. Ukrainian respondents' protective factors (levels of hope, well-being and morale) were better predictors of the three types of resilience (individual, community and social) than the vulnerability factors (feelings of threat, stress symptoms and level of threat). The best predictors of the three types of resilience were hope and wellbeing. In light of these results, the war in Ukraine is perceived as an imminent threat to sovereignty, which may have an impact on increasing feelings of national unity and social resilience. In contrast, the conflict in Israel was not perceived as a threat to the existence of the state, which may explain the lower levels of social resilience in this population. It appears, therefore, that a war that threatens a country's independence and sovereignty may, under certain conditions, increase the social resilience and hope of the population at risk, despite a lower sense of well-being and higher levels of stress, feelings of threat and perceived threats. Hope plays a key role in shaping resilience, even in the face of high levels of stress and perceived threat. High levels of hope can help individuals and communities to remain positive and motivated. In a situation of conflict that threatens the existence of the state, psychological factors have a greater impact on levels of resilience than traditional demographic variables. A widespread sense of threat may offset differences based on age, gender or socio-economic status. Adini et al. (2022) similarly Kimhi et al. (2023a, 2023b, 2023c), in a study of social resilience in

Ukraine and Gaza, find that the social resilience of the Ukrainian population is significantly higher than that of the Israeli population. Similarly, levels of hope were significantly higher in the Ukrainian sample compared to the Israeli sample. In contrast, the perceived wellbeing of the Israeli sample was significantly higher compared to the Ukrainian sample. The sense of threat was significantly higher in the Ukrainian sample compared to the Israeli sample. The implication is that societies at war may exhibit high levels of stress, sense of threat and perceived threats, while at the same time exhibiting high levels of hope for a better future and social resilience (Project Engage, 2024).

In addition to Ukraine and Israel, a region particularly affected by hybrid warfare is the Gaza Strip, whose residents, as assessed by Al-Muhannadi, Buheji (2024a, 2024b), are at risk of losing their resilience, due to a loss of capacity to cope with a variety of escalating political, economic, social, financial, medical and environmental stressors and challenges occurring simultaneously. As assessed by the authors of this study, residents in Gaza were in a stage of gradual recovery despite the siege, but the conflict of 7 October 2023, affected their ability to be resilient beyond the phases of exposure[1] and vulnerability. Consequently, many residents in Gaza were stuck in the first two stages of resilience, i.e. they tolerated the exposure and vulnerability phases, but could not move into the adaptation and recovery phases. Al-Muhannadi, Buheji (2024 citing Callamard (2022) emphasise that Israel's actions towards Palestinians, in particular Gaza residents, constitute a form of apartheid. These policies, based on segregation and exclusion, were aimed at systematically undermining the resilience of the Palestinian community. In addition to military action, Israel has intensified its blockade of the Gaza Strip, restricting access to resources necessary for survival, including medical and humanitarian supplies, which has had a direct impact on the community's ability to cope with the crisis. Gaza's infrastructure – water supply, sanitation, medical and energy facilities – has also been targeted and deliberately destroyed, further exacerbating the food security and health crises. Restrictions on the movement of Gaza residents prevented access to specialised medical care, and agriculture, which could have been the basis for survival, was almost completely eliminated by the deliberate destruction of agricultural land.

In response to threats, the people of Gaza, in the assessment of the authors of this study, have shown exceptional resilience as a result of the values with which they identify. Al-Muhannadi, Buheji (2024), abstracted ten dominant values that build social resilience in war (2023):

- Deep family and community ties,
- Collective respect of the community,

- courage and perseverance,
- leadership and care,
- resourcefulness,
- High optimism and love of life despite difficulties,
- continued adaptability to extreme conditions,
- spiritual strength and acceptance,
- kindness, generosity and social cohesion,
- a unique, resilient identity and global solidarity.

The materialisation of these values is manifested in individual and community attitudes towards the impact of the conflict. Al-Muhannadi, Buheji (2024) recognise that one of the key manifestations of resilience observed among the people of Gaza was strong social cooperation and solidarity, regardless of the origin or social status of individuals. The community showed particular cohesion in the face of difficult conditions, where experiencing suffering and challenges together built a sense of communal responsibility. At moments of intense bombardment and in the aftermath, Gaza residents came together to support each other, sharing resources, offering shelter to those who had lost their homes, and organising themselves for clean-up and reconstruction work. Another important aspect was the extraordinary mental resilience shown by residents, despite the immense stress and trauma. They drew strength from their family ties, their social belonging and in many cases, their deep faith. Community leaders, teachers and the elderly played key roles in providing emotional support, sustaining morale and offering hope and a sense of purpose during these difficult times. Medical staff at Al-Shifa Hospital, for example, continued to care for the wounded during the conflict, despite the critical lack of resources and the immediate threat to their lives. Many families had emergency supplies such as food, water and basic medical kits and lighting. Civil defence, despite some equipment shortages and dependence on unstable energy sources, tried to respond to emergencies. However, the evacuation of the population was poorly organised and the available shelters were often inadequate, contributing to high casualty rates. While the resistance of the population also manifested itself in the decision to remain on their land, increased awareness of the use of local shelters should be considered to minimise the loss of life. In response to the intense bombardment by Israeli forces, which used carpet bombing to increase civilian casualties, Gaza residents quickly adapted to the new, unprecedented situation. Families acted quickly, moving to safer locations, often taking advantage of the hospitality of friends and relatives. Their ability to adapt, as well as their persistence in finding innovative solutions, enabled them to continue their daily routines, even under extreme conditions.

MODELS OF RESILIENCE

In the context of the role of communities in hybrid warfare and resilience, it is worth mentioning models to support these processes. There are both direct and indirect, formal and less formal studies that focus on community resilience in hybrid war. For example: NATO Resilience Guidelines, Joint Communication on Increasing Resilience and Bolstering Capabilities to Address Hybrid Threats, European Union Security Union Strategy, European Programme for Critical Infrastructure Protection, Hybrid Threats and Resilience Framework. Researchers from RAND's Global Strategic Partnership (GSP), developed a conceptual framework that identified three distinct phases of societal resilience: Prepare, Respond and Recover:

- The Preparedness phase consists of all activities undertaken prior to a crisis or incident to ensure that awareness and assessment of potential threats, hazards and vulnerabilities has occurred and that the necessary resources and relationships are in place to enable an effective response. It includes the subtasks Anticipate, Build **and** Educate.
- The response phase includes all activities that take place after a crisis has occurred to effectively mitigate the immediate effects of the crisis. Key priorities may include obtaining and maintaining accurate situational awareness, communicating between stakeholders and committing the necessary resources. This phase includes three subtasks: Understand, Inform and Mobilise.
- The recovery phase follows the passage or mitigation of the initial crisis. It consists of both short-term tasks to ensure that civilians have been removed from immediate danger and resources have been restored to their previous locations, and longer-term activities to return the community to its pre-crisis state and ensure that response personnel and equipment are restored to readiness. The sub-tasks included in this phase are Reset, Regenerate and Innovate.

The above phases are not sequential, but can be integrated and coexist. An element of a phase is the dependency of the preceding phase while feeding and preempting the following phase. As the authors note, crises can be networked and cascaded, meaning that actors may have to act in several tasks simultaneously. Social resilience here is a cyclical process.

In addition to organisational models of resilience, there are also scientific proposals like Agile Resilience developed by Buheji and Mushimiyiman (2024). The model emphasises self-sustainability and internal strengthening of the Gaza community by investing in local resources and skills so that the community can better prepare for future challenges.

Key elements (frameworks) of the model include: Flexibility, i.e. the ability to adapt quickly to changing conditions and modify strategies when needed. Responsiveness, i.e. the ability to respond quickly to new challenges and take advantage of emerging opportunities, and innovation, understood as encouraging creative thinking and continuous improvement of solutions. Components of the model are: food security: promoting urban agriculture, home gardens and sustainable cultivation practices to increase local food production. investment in water treatment technologies such as portable purification stations; renewable energy sources: developing solar and wind energy projects to reduce dependence on external energy supplies. installation of solar panels on residential and public buildings; healthcare: strengthening the healthcare system through the establishment of mobile clinics and community health programmes, based on efficient and resilient models; education and skills development: ensuring continuity of education through e-learning and vocational training programmes that will increase employment opportunities and develop the local labour market; psychological and community support: developing psychological support programmes, promoting social solidarity and initiatives that support the mental health and well-being of residents (Al-Muhannadi, Buheji, 2024; Kupenko et al., 2023, pp. 154–168).

Buheji, 2024, pp. 22–33) have also developed a model in what they call 'resilience fatigue'. which refers to the exhaustion of the ability of individuals and communities to adapt in the face of ongoing stress and trauma. The authors propose a framework of 'collective pain' and 'collective happiness' that aims to offset the negative effects of trauma by enhancing positive social experiences. A key element is the understanding that while pain and trauma are inevitable in the context of conflict, positive aspects of social life can be strengthened through conscious action, ultimately increasing the overall resilience of the community.

The key components of the model are collective pain (the shared experience of suffering, trauma and loss by the community and collective happiness the shared experience of joy, hope and a sense of community that can counteract the negative effects of trauma).

The authors also propose a model of intervention that aims to: identify and measure collective pain, enhance collective happiness, develop community leaders, a multidisciplinary approach (see ext. [Buheji, 2024]).

CONCLUSIONS

Hybrid warfare is undoubtedly a complex and multidimensional threat, making it one of the most serious challenges to national and international security. The hallmark of this type of warfare is the combination of military and non-military actions which, as demonstrated in previous chapters, are deeply networked and can lead to cascading effects. In such a context, the role of local communities takes on particular importance, becoming a key element in building resilience to hybrid threats. The analysis of conflicts such as the war in Ukraine or the Israeli-Palestinian conflict proves that local communities are not just passive recipients of the effects of hybrid actions, but active participants in countering these threats. These communities perform a range of functions: from relief, rescue and humanitarian operations, providing key intelligence, to social mobilisation and creating networks of support and solidarity. Using both traditional communication methods and modern technologies – such as smartphones, social media and OSINT tools – communities are able to respond effectively to the dynamically changing conditions of conflict. A key lesson from the case studies is the importance of community resilience, understood as the ability to adapt, survive and recover in the face of threats. This resilience is based on several factors. Strong social and family ties. Communities based on trust, support and solidarity are more resilient to destabilising actions. In crisis situations, these communities show the ability to mobilise quickly and help each other.

Trust in institutions and leadership. A high level of trust in local and central government, as well as in public institutions, strengthens social cohesion and facilitates coordination in crisis situations. Hope and optimism. A positive attitude and the belief that difficulties can be overcome are important for maintaining community morale. Research has shown that high levels of hope correlate with higher levels of both individual and community resilience. Adaptability and innovation. Communities that are able to adapt quickly to new conditions, use available resources creatively and innovate are more resilient to disruption from hybrid activities. Cultivating shared values and identities. A strong national or cultural identity unifies a community and increases its ability to resist attempts at destabilisation and polarisation.

In practice, local communities can play a key role in monitoring and detecting threats, e.g. by observing the local environment and using technological tools, communities can quickly identify potential threats and inform the relevant services; countering disinformation, e.g. through education and awareness-raising on methods of information manipulation; logistical and humanitarian support, e.g. in emergency situations local communities are often the first source of help for those affected, organising material and psychological support. Building psychological resilience e.g. by experiencing difficulties together and supporting each other emotionally.

However, it should be taken into account that actions taken by communities, especially in the context of resilience, should take into account regional and cultural differences. So far, despite existing solutions to promote resilience, there is no universally accepted framework for community resilience in hybrid war. Despite the important role of local communities, their importance is often underestimated in defence strategies and security policies. Most existing models focus on the state level or society as a whole, overlooking the unique needs and potential of local communities. There is therefore a need to redefine resilience-building approaches that take full account of the role of these communities.

NOTE

1 Mitchell, Harris (2012, pp. 1–6) divide resilience into four phases: (1) the exposure phase, (2) the vulnerability phase, (3) the adaptation phase and (4) the recovery phase. Exposure is the phase in which individuals or communities are exposed to shocks, while vulnerability is the weaknesses and consequences that emerge during a period of shock. In the adaptation phase, the individual or community begins to cope with the situation and accept the changes and shocks, while in the recovery phase these actors, being individuals or communities, work to gradually or systematically better adapt to the new normal. Therefore, it can be seen that the strength of resilience depends on the level of resilience for each post-shock phase and the ability to recover from the phase to the next phase.

REFERENCES

Aall, P., and Crocker, C.A., (2019), Building Resilience and Social Cohesion in Conflict. *Global Policy Journal*, 10(4), Available at: https://www.globalpolicyjournal.com/articles/conflict-and-security/building-resilience-and-social-cohesion-conflict. Accessed: 4 Sept. 2024.

Adini B., Stolero N., and Peleg K., (2022), Societal Resilience in Countries During Human-Made Conflicts. ENGAGE Project, Available at: https://www.project-engage.eu/societal-resilience-in-countries-during-human-made-conflicts/. Accessed: 30 August 2024.

Al-Muhannadi, K., and Buheji, M., (2024), Value-Based Resilience – Stories from Gaza (during War 2023). Research Gate. Available at: https://www.researchgate.net/publication/377245015. Accessed: 25 Sept. 2024.

Alshamy, Y., Coyne, C.J., Goodman, N.P., and Wood, G., (2024), Polycentric Defense, Ukraine Style: Explaining Ukrainian Resilience against Invasion. *Journal of Public Finance and Public Choice*, 39(1). Available at: https://doi.org/10.1332/251569121X16795569226712. Accessed: 31 Aug. 2024.

Andersson, D.E., (2021), Spontaneous Order and the Hayekian Challenge to Interdisciplinary Social Scientists. *Atlantic Economic Journal*, 49(4). Available at: https://doi.org/10.1007/s11293-022-09735-8. Accessed: 9 Sept. 2024.

Berlinschi R., Farvaque E., Fidrmuc, J., Harms P., Steiner N., Mihailov A., Neugart M., and Stanek P., (2022), Rallying Around the EU Flag: Russia's Invasion of Ukraine and Attitudes Toward European Integration. *SSRN Electronic Journal*. 10.2139/ssrn.4189233, Available at: https://www.researchgate.net/publication/362764002_Rallying_Around_the_EU_Flag_Russia's_Invasion_of_Ukraine_and_Attitudes_Toward_European_Integration. Accessed: 30 August 2024.

Bilal, A., (2021), Hybrid Warfare – New Threats, Complexity, and 'Trust' as the Antidote. *NATO Review*. Available at: https://www.nato.int/docu/review/articles/2021/11/30/hybrid-warfare-new-threats-complexity-and-trust-as-the-antidote/index.html. Accessed: 14 Sept. 2024.

Bilban, C., (2016), Resilience: Silver Bullet in Challenging Hybrid Warfare? [online]. Available at: https://www.researchgate.net/publication/325285480. Accessed: 29 Aug. 2024. https://doi.org/10.13140/RG.2.2.25155.91684.

Bilous, V., Bodnenko, D., Khokhlov, O., Lokaziuk, O., and Stadnik, I., (2024), Open Source Intelligence for War Crime Documentation. Workshop Cybersecurity Providing in Information and Telecommunication Systems (CPITS 2024), 3654. ISSN 1613-0073.

Briggs, C. M., (2020), Climate change and hybrid warfare strategies. *Journal of Strategic Security*, 13(4), 45–57. Available at: https://digitalcommons.usf.edu/jss/vol13/iss4/4. Accessed: 05 August 2024.

Buheji, M., (2024), Avoiding Resilience Fatigue-Navigating 'Collective Pain' and 'Collective Happiness' in Gaza (War of 2023/2024). *International Journal of Psychological and Behavioral Sciences*, 14(1). Available at: https://www.researchgate.net/publication/377780889. Accessed: 6 Sept. 2024.

Callamard A., (2022), Israel's Apartheid against Palestinians: Cruel System of Domination and Crime Against Humanity. Amnesty International. Available at: https://www.amnesty.org/en/latest/news/2022/02/israels-apartheid-against-palestinians-a-cruel-system-of-domination-and-a-crime-against-humanity/. Accessed: 30 August 2024.

Cascante M., Trejos D., Qin B., Joo H., and Debner Sigrid D., (2017), Conceptualizing Community Resilience: Revisiting Conceptual Distinctions. *Community Development*. 48, Available at: https://www.researchgate.net/publication/309399068_Conceptualizing_community_resilience_Revisiting_conceptual_distinctions. Accessed: 27 August 2024.

Centre UA, (2024), Communities of War. Available at: https://centreua.org/wp-content/uploads/2024/03/Communities_of_war_web.pdf. Accessed: 14 Sept. 2024.

Christie, E.H., and Berzina, K., (2022), NATO and Societal Resilience: All Hands on Deck in an Age of War. *Policy Brief.* Available at: https://www.gmfus.org/news/nato-and-societal-resilience-all-hands-deck-age-war. Accessed: 2 Sept. 2024.

Clark, J. N., (2022), Thinking About Resilience as a Social-Ecological Concept. In: *Resilience, Conflict-Related Sexual Violence and Transitional Justice.* 1st Edition. Routledge, Available at: https://www.taylorfrancis.com/chapters/oa-mono/10.4324/9781003323532-2/thinking-resilience-social-ecological-concept-janine-natalya-clark?context=ubx&refId=c843c612-3695-4591-a5c7-37b3f7ad75fb. Accessed: 11 August 2024.

Cox R., and Perry, K. M., (2011). Like a Fish Out of Water: Reconsidering Disaster Recovery and the Role of Place and Social Capital in Community Disaster Resilience. *American Journal of Community Psychology.* 48, Available at: https://www.researchgate.net/publication/49803975_Like_a_Fish_Out_of_Water_Reconsidering_Disaster_Recovery_and_the_Role_of_Place_and_Social_Capital_in_Community_Disaster_Resilience. Accessed: 24 August 2024.

Cretney, R., (2014), Resilience for Whom? Emerging Critical Geographies of Socio-Ecological Resilience. *Geography Compass, 8*(9), Available at: https://compass.onlinelibrary.wiley.com/doi/10.1111/gec3.12154. Accessed: 15 August 2024.

Eshel, Y., Kimhi, S., (2015), Community Resilience of Civilians at War: A New Perspective. *Community Mental Health Journal* 52. Available at: https://link.springer.com/article/10.1007/s10597-015-9948-3#citeas. Accessed: 27 August 2024.

Giannopoulos, G., Smith, H., and Theocharidou, M., (2020), *The Landscape of Hybrid Threats: A Conceptual Model.* Luxembourg: Publications Office of the European Union. Available at: https://op.europa.eu/en/publication-detail/-/publication/b534e5b3-7268-11eb-9ac9-01aa75ed71a1, Accessed: 19 August 2024.

Giordano F., Lipscomb S., Jefferies F., Kwon, Kyong A., and Giammarchi M., (2024), Resilience Processes Among Ukrainian Youth Preparing to Build Resilience with Peers During the Ukraine-Russia War. *Frontiers in Psychology*, 15, Available at: https://www.frontiersin.org/journals/psychology/articles/10.3389/fpsyg.2024.1331886/full. Accessed: 27 August 2024.

Hoffman, F. G. (2007). *Conflict in the 21st Century: The Rise of Hybrid Wars.* Arlington, VA: Potomac Institute for Policy Studies, Available at: https://www.potomacinstitute.org/images/stories/publications/potomac_hybridwar_0108.pdf. Accessed: 3 Sept. 2024.

Horyń, W., and Tomasik, R., (2022), Territorial Defense Forces in Hybrid Warfare in the Light of Experience of the Conflict in Ukraine. *Scientific Journal of the Military University of Land Forces*, 54(1). https://doi.org/10.5604/01.3001.0015.8028.

Houck, S., (2022), Psychological Capabilities for Resilience. *War on the Rocks*. Available at: https://warontherocks.com/2022/12/psychological-capabilities-for-resilience/. Accessed: 5 Sept. 2024.

Humbert, C. and Joseph, J., (2019), Introduction: The Politics of Resilience: Problematising Current Approaches, *Resilience*, 7(3), Available at: https://www.tandfonline.com/doi/full/10.1080/216932 93.2019.1613738#d1e93. Accessed: 23 August 2024.

Ilyas, M. D., (2023)., The Impact of Artificial Intelligence on Hybrid Warfare: Case of Russia-Ukraine War. *Journal of Liaoning Technical University,* 17(11). Available at: https://www.researchgate.net/publication/375164694_The_Impact_of_Artificial_Intelligence_on_hybrid_warfare_Case_of_Russia-Ukraine_war. Accessed: 11 August 2024.

International Organization for Migration (IOM), (2024), Building Resilience Helps People Carry on during Wartime. Available at: https://ukraine.iom.int/stories/building-resilience-helps-people-carry-during-wartime. Accessed: 11 Sept. 2024.

Janjeva, A., Harris, A., and Byrne, J., (2022), The Future of Open-Source Intelligence for UK National Security. RUSI Occasional Papers, June.

Kaim, A., Siman Tov, M., Kimhi, S., Marciano, H., Eshel, Y., and Adini, B., (2024), A Longitudinal Study of Societal Resilience and Its Predictors during the Israel-Gaza War. *Applied Psychology: Health and Well-Being*, 16 (3), First published: 21 March 2024. Available at: https://iaap-journals.onlinelibrary.wiley.com/doi/full/10.1111/aphw.12539. Accessed: 18 Sept. 2024. https://doi.org/10.1111/aphw.12539.

Kandrik, M., and Pala, T., (2024), *Unconventional Forms of Civil Participation in Defence: Preliminary Observations from the Russo-Ukrainian War.* Central European Digital Media Observatory, Available at: https://www.researchgate.net/publication/381408034_Unconventional_Forms_of_Civil_Participation_in_Defence_Preliminary_observations_from_Russo-_Ukrainian_War. Accessed: 3 Sept. 2024.

Katz, E., (2021), Liar's war: Protecting civilians from disinformation during armed conflict. *International Review of the Red Cross.* 102, 1–24. Available at: https://www.researchgate.net/publication/355298190_Liar's_war_Protecting_civilians_from_disinformation_during_armed_conflict. Accessed: 3 Sept. 2024.

Kepe, M., and Demus, A., (2023), Resisting Russia: Insights into Ukraine's Civilian-Based Actions during the First Four Months of the War in 2022. Available at: https://www.rand.org/pubs/research_reports/RRA2034-1.html. Accessed: 13 Sept. 2024.

Kimhi, S., Baran, M., Baran, T., Kaniasty, K., Marciano, H., Eshel, Y., and Adini, B., (2023a), Prediction of Societal and Community Resilience among Ukrainian and Polish Populations during the Russian War against Ukraine. *International Journal of Disaster Risk Reduction*, 93, 103792. Available at: https://doi.org/10.1016/j.ijdrr.2023.103792. Accessed: 6 Sept. 2024.

Kimhi, S., Eshel, Y., Marciano, H., and Adini, B., (2023b), Impact of the War in Ukraine on Resilience, Protective, and Vulnerability Factors. *Frontiers in Public Health.* Available at: https://www.frontiersin.org/journals/public-health/articles/10.3389/fpubh.2023.1053940/full. Accessed: 20 Sept. 2024.

Kimhi, S., Kaim, A., Bankauskaite, D., Baran, M., Baran, T., Eshel, Y., Dumbadze, S., Gabashvili, M., Kaniasty, K., and Koubova, A., (2023c), A Full-Scale Russian Invasion of Ukraine in 2022: Resilience and Coping within and beyond Ukraine. *Applied Psychology: Health and Well-Being.* First published: 09 July 2023. Available at: https://iaap-journals.onlinelibrary.wiley.com/doi/full/10.1111/aphw.12466. Accessed: 16 Sept. 2024. https://doi.org/10.1111/aphw.12466.

Koubová, A., and Kimhi, S., (2024), Prediction of Individual, Community and Societal Resilience in the Czech Republic compared to Slovakia during the War in Ukraine. *BMC Public Health*, 24-583, Available at: https://www.researchgate.net/publication/378437597_Prediction_of_individual_community_and_societal_resilience_in_the_Czech_Republic_compared_to_Slovakia_during_the_war_in_Ukraine. Accessed: 24 August 2024.

Kupenko, O., Kostenko, A., Kalchenko, L., Pehota, O., and Kubatko, O., (2023), Resilience and Vulnerability of a Person in a Community in the Context of Military Events. *Problems and Perspectives in Management*, 21(1). Available at: https://doi.org/10.21511/ppm.21(1).2023.14. Accessed: 12 Sept. 2024.

Kurapov, A., Kalaitzaki, A., Keller, V., Danyliuk, I., and Kowatsch, T., (2023), The Mental Health Impact of the Ongoing Russian-Ukrainian War 6 Months after the Russian Invasion of Ukraine. *Front Psychiatry*, 27(14), 1134780, Available at: https://pubmed.ncbi.nlm.nih.gov/37575573/. Accessed: 27 August 2024.

Kurnyshova Y., (2022), Hybrid Resilience in Insecure Times: Russia's War and Ukrainian Society. *CIDOB*, Available at: https://www.cidob.org/en/publication/hybrid-resilience-insecure-times-russias-war-and-ukrainian-society. Accessed: 30 August 2024.

Kurnyshova, Y., (2023), Ukraine at War: Resilience and Normative Agency. *Central European Journal of International and Security Studies*, 17(2), 80–110. Available at: https://www.cejiss.org/ukraine-at-war-resilience-and-normative-agency. Accessed: 15 Sept. 2024. https://doi.org/10.51870/UXXZ5757.

Kurnyshova, Y., and Makarychev, A., (2022), Hybrid Resilience in Insecure Times: Russia's War and Ukrainian Society. *CIDOB Report*, Available at: https://www.cidob.org/en/publications/hybrid-resilience-insecure-times-russias-war-and-ukrainian-society. Accessed: 27 August 2024.

Lordos, A., and Daniel H., (2021), The Assessment of Multisystemic Resilience in Conflict-Affected Populations. In Michael Ungar (ed.), *Multisystemic Resilience: Adaptation and Transformation in*

Contexts of Change. New York: Oxford Academic. Available at: https://academic.oup.com/book/41117/chapter/350425087. Accessed: 17 August 2024.

McLennan, M., (2024), The Global Risk Report 2024. *World Economic Forum.* Available at: https://www.weforum.org/publications/global-risks-report-2024/. Accessed: 4 Sept. 2024.

Mitchell, T., and Harris, K., (2012), *Resilience: A Risk Management Approach* (ODI Background Note, pp. 1–6). London: Overseas Development Institute. Available at: https://cdn.odi.org/media/documents/7552.pdf. Accessed: 21 August 2024.

Norris F., Stevens S., Pfefferbaum B., Wyche K. and Pfefferbaum R., (2008), Community Resilience as a Metaphor, Theory, Set of Capacities, and Strategy for Disaster Readiness. American Journal of Community Psychology. 41, Available at: https://www.researchgate.net/publication/5691020_Community_Resilience_as_a_Metaphor_Theory_Set_of_Capacities_and_Strategy_for_Disaster_Readiness. Accessed: 26 August 2024.

Olcese, M., Cardinali, P., Madera, F., Camilleri, A., and Migliorini, L., (2024), Migration and Community Resilience: A Scoping Review. *International Journal of Intercultural Relations.* 98, Available at: https://www.researchgate.net/publication/376888740_Migration_and_community_resilience_A_scoping_review. Accessed: 26 August 2024.

Project Engage, (2024), Societal Resilience in Countries during Human-Made Conflicts. Available at: https://www.project-engage.eu/societal-resilience-in-countries-during-human-made-conflicts/. Accessed: 22 Sept. 2024.

PWN, (2024), Społeczeństwo. *Słownik Języka Polskiego PWN.* Available at: https://sjp.pwn.pl/szukaj/społeczeństwo.html. Accessed: 05 August 2024.

Robin Goodwin, Yaira Hamama-Raz, Elazar Leshem, Menachem Ben-Ezra, (2023), National Resilience in Ukraine Following the 2022 Russian Invasion, *International Journal of Disaster Risk Reduction*, 85. Available at: https://www.sciencedirect.com/science/article/pii/S2212420922007063. Accessed: 23 August 2024.

Romanchuk, O., (2023), Psychological Resilience in a Time of War: Individual and National Dimension. Ukrainian Institute of Cognitive-Behavioural Therapy. Available at: https://i-cbt.org.ua/psychological-resilience-in-a-time-of-war/. Accessed: 9 Sept. 2024.

Saja, A. A. M., Teo, M., Goonetilleke, A., and Ziyath, A. M., (2021), A Critical Review of Social Resilience Properties and Pathways in Disaster Management. *International Journal of Disaster Risk Science*, 12, Available at: https://www.researchgate.net/publication/356077593_A_Critical_Review_of_Social_Resilience_Properties_and_Pathways_in_Disaster_Management. Accessed: 24 August 2024.

Simpson, G., Makoond, A., Vinck, P., and Pham, P. N., (2016)., *Assessing Resilience for Peace: A Guidance Note*. Geneva, Switzerland: Interpeace. Available at: https://www.peacebuildingdata.org/_files/ugd/70de91_7dd55ea5c457495ea3f0ec2c6283b3fd.pdf, Accessed: 17 August 2024.

Tönnies, F., (1957), *Community and Society* (C. P. Loomis, Trans.). East Lansing: Michigan State University Press.

Ukrainian Center for Independent Political Research, (2024), Publications: Analytical Reports. Available at: http://www.ucipr.org.ua/en/publications/analytical-reports. Accessed: 10 Sept. 2024.

UNHCR, (2023), Global Trends: Forced Displacement in 2023. Available at: https://www.unhcr.org/global-trends-report-2023. Accessed: 5 Sept. 2024.

United Nations Office for Disaster Risk Reduction (UNDRR), (2015), Sendai Framework for Disaster Risk Reduction 2015–2030. Available at: https://unsdg.un.org/sites/default/files/2021-09/UN-Resilience-Guidance-Final-Sept.pdf. Accessed: 4 Sept. 2024.

United Nations Security Council, (2024), Protection of Civilians in Armed Conflict – Report of the Secretary-General (S/2024/385) [EN/AR/FR/RU/ES/ZH]. [online] Available at: https://reliefweb.int/report/world/protection-civilians-armed-conflict-report-secretary-general-s2024385-enarfrrueszh. Accessed: 4 Sept. 2024.

United Nations Sustainable Development Group, (2020), *UN Common Guidance on Helping Build Resilient Societies*. Available at: https://unsdg.un.org/sites/default/files/2021-09/UN-Resilience-Guidance-Final-Sept.pdf. Accessed: 19 August 2024.

Wilson, A., (2022), Resilient Ukraine. RUSI Commentary. Available at: https://rusi.org/explore-our-research/publications/commentary/resilient-ukraine. Accessed: 7 Sept. 2024.

Zarembo, K., Knodt, M., and Kachel, J., (2024), Smartphone Resilience: ICT in Ukrainian Civic Response to the Russian Full-Scale Invasion. *Media, War & Conflict*, 0(0). Available at: https://doi.org/10.1177/17506352241236449. Accessed: 2 Sept. 2024.

Conclusion

War, on the one hand, is a well-known phenomenon and on the other is an ever-evolving one. It is nowadays defined in many ways, including hybrid warfare. However, no matter how we conceptually define the phenomenon, every war will be one of the most difficult and acute human experiences. Above all, each one will cause unimaginable suffering to millions of people.

The hybrid warfare addressed in this book is still a vague concept in both the research and practice space. Nevertheless, it specifically affects civilians at all levels of collectivity within the state structure. The nature of the hybrid strategies conducted is often subtle, increasing the difficulty (especially at the civilian level) of responding appropriately to threats. Recommendations or recommendations issued are difficult for societies to implement (mainly due to the intensity of hybrid threat vectors).

This book attempts to analyse this phenomenon, focusing on understanding it in the context of civilian protection and the effectiveness of systems aimed at providing security. This study, like any, has its limitations, in the form of the limited availability of up-to-date empirical data and the difficulty in clearly defining the hybridity environment. However, despite these challenges, this book seeks to highlight key trends and propose a framework of analysis that can provide a foundation for future research and implementation of effective civil protection strategies.

Chapter 1 attempts to characterize the phenomenon of hybrid warfare, highlighting its complexity and the multidimensional challenges it poses to contemporary societies and security systems. Analysing the complex mechanisms underlying this type of warfare, the activities, categories, and roles of the various actors involved in the implementation of hybrid strategies are identified. It has been shown how these elements coexist to create networks of hybrid effects, which in turn amplify the overall impact of hybrid threats. Based on the literature review, a clear separation between the concepts of hybrid conflict and hybrid war has been proposed and eleven main characteristics of hybrid war have been identified that can form a framework for further research. As a result of the analyses carried out, it was also proposed that hybrid warfare should be understood as a phase of hybrid strategy involving networked military (conventional and unconventional) and non-military actions carried out by state and non-state actors in order to achieve strategic advantage, often by inducing destabilizing cascading effects. Above, the

DOI: 10.4324/9781003503859-9

roles of actors in this type of war have been identified and defined. While non-state actors (e.g. terrorist groups, private military companies) play an important role in hybrid actions, the analysis shows that the role of state actors is dominant. Non-military actions are a key element of hybrid strategies. This is confirmed by the Gerasimov Doctrine, suggesting that non-military actions can be four times as important as military actions in achieving strategic objectives. Analysis has shown that the ratio of non-military to military actions is 3.69:1, and as high as 193.7:1 for conventional actions.

Although the chapter is not exhaustive, it is an important introduction to further research and analysis and thus points to the need for continued exploration of hybrid warfare strategies and methodologies. It is necessary in order to develop more robust defence and protection mechanisms for civilians.

One of the most important elements in ensuring the security of civilians is critical infrastructure (CI). Chapter 2 presents the relationship between critical services (UK) and CI facilities on the basis of process management theory as applied in management and quality sciences. The chapter analyses the international formal and legal considerations related to the designation and management of UK and CI security. The results of the analysis of international approaches to UK and CI security management served as research material identifying the necessary stages of the Methodology for Security Management of Key Services (MESSM) as an integral element of ensuring the security of the population during a hybrid conflict. The chapter discusses the stages of the MESSM methodology, defining how to set up the analysis team, establish safety thresholds for the functionality of UK components, identify the resources required to provide UK, generate Adverse Event Scenarios (AES), estimate risk, formulate and solve decision problems, and implement protective measures. A complementary element of the MESSM methodology is the identification of facilities that can replace lost UK components as a result of threat materialization. In summary, the chapter presents a comprehensive approach to the security management of critical services in the context of hybrid conflicts. An examination of the threats arising from the ongoing hybrid war in Ukraine indicates the need for a change in the approach to identifying and managing the security of CI. The selection of critical facilities should be linked to key services and the resources required to maintain their business continuity. CI security management should be based on a situational model of these infrastructures, which takes into account: the functionalities performed, interpreted as components of the key services; the threats to which the resources are vulnerable; the safeguards applied in response to identified threats; and the interdependencies between resources resulting from the organization of processes. This model integrates functionalities with resources exposed to

Conclusion

threats, the materialization of which may lead to damage or destruction of the resource, negatively affecting the availability of the functionality. Threats indicate the need for safeguards to ensure the correct operation of resources and access to functionality. The information gathered in the situational model of the resource provides a basis for further action:

- Risk assessment: on the basis of the estimated risk, the availability of the functionality is predicted in the event of a specific hazard. If the predicted value of the functionality does not reach the established safety threshold, a decision problem is formulated taking into account the hazards that are the source of the given risk.
- Creation of AES: the data from the situation model allows the development of a dependency network to identify AES. The determination of these scenarios is based on the probability of a hazard occurring and the vulnerability of the resource to that hazard. For each scenario, the value of the risk associated with the hazards contained in it can be determined. If the risk does not allow a safety threshold to be reached, a decision problem is formulated for the hazards present in the scenario. Determining the probability of a hazard occurring subject to the materialization of another hazard uses Bayes' theorem. A detailed example of the mechanism for creating AES for crisis management can be found in the literature.
- Decision problem formulation: the solution to the decision problem is to determine a set of safeguards for each identified threat to achieve the safety threshold. This method is a modification of the Analysis Interconnected Decision Areas (AIDA) approach. The resulting set of safeguards from the problem solution serves as a recommendation to the resource operator for action in response to the risks associated with the resource's vulnerabilities.

In addition, the use of a situational model of CI makes it possible to identify resources that can replace those that have lost the ability to perform their functions (elements of the critical service). Using the assumptions of analogy theory and the assessment criteria derived from the characteristics of the resources mapped in the model, it is possible to quickly identify similar resources and integrate them into the delivery of the key service, either temporarily or permanently.

Chapter 3 touches on the complexity and dynamics of hybrid warfare and the impact on civilian populations and internal security. The analysis confirmed that the threats in hybrid warfare create a web of flexible linkages between military and non-military actions that interact with each other in ways that lead to cascading effects. Nineteen distinct domains of hybrid action were confirmed in the study, of which the information, political, air, maritime, intelligence, and land domains stand out in particular. These domains are not isolated, but interpenetrate each other and adapt seamlessly to the operational environment and the strategic objectives of the aggressor. It is also important to point out the evolution of the cognitive domain and artificial intelligence. This combination is a critical area of interest due to its potential to manipulate perception and influence social behaviour on a large scale. Above this, the findings indicate that conventional military threats continue to dominate, but non-military threats play an important role in initiating or reinforcing these threats. The media focus on visible military activities can obscure public perception of the subtleties of non-military threats (e.g. disinformation, propaganda), which can directly lead to measurable consequences in security and societal resilience at all levels. Additionally, in the context of hybrid threats given the involvement of state as well as non-state actors, this relationship creates a feedback loop of action and response. This relationship contributes to the complexity of a system in which threats are difficult to identify and can escalate rapidly, affecting civilians in multidimensional ways. Traditional security measures that rely on centralized, institutional responses may not be sufficient to respond in all phases of civilian protection. In the face of all this, it is worth considering the decentralization of responsibility and the empowerment of smaller communities and individuals. By promoting awareness and adaptive response capacity at the micro level, societies can better navigate hybrid threats.

The next chapter discussed mechanisms for the protection of civilians and international humanitarian law on the protection of civilians in the context of hybrid war. In addition, a fact-intensive survey of civilians directly affected by the war in Ukraine was conducted, together with an analysis of media reports, to better understand the effectiveness and application of these mechanisms. The analyses showed that the materialization of hybrid threats leads to direct and indirect consequences for civilians. Attempts to date to mitigate hybrid activities and the resulting threats in both the conflict and hybrid war phases still do not provide effective protection mechanisms, as the statistics of casualties and victims in the war in Ukraine and the Middle East can attest. Systemic interventions in the war in Ukraine proved less effective than the individual actions of the surveyed population, who experienced health and life-threatening effects such as hunger, thirst, illness, injury, excessive heat, and excessive cold. Based on the six Ways to die model, the survey methodology should be supplemented with an element of information that, through materialization, can influence the decisions of the civilian population. To this end, the implementation of the Blockchain concept for the protection of information in the relationship between security actors and the public was proposed. Above and beyond this, the analyses showed that the civilian population should be prepared to self-manage their own security for at least 72 hours. It is worth mentioning here that many security mechanisms only teach schematic threat perceptions (e.g. do not click on a suspicious link), but hybrid threats elude schematics. Therefore, the preparation of civilians in terms of their ability to build a response to hybrid threats and to interact in the civil protection system should be extended to a triadic, mature, and critical analysis of network threats. Civilians, especially in a hybrid war situation, should ask themselves questions such as whether the information they receive is reliable, whether and how I can verify it, whether acting on it will be safe for me and my family, or whether it is disinformation designed to make me make unfavourable decisions. This is just an example showing that in modern hybrid warfare, which is evolving very dynamically, much more attention needs to be paid to protective mechanisms than has been the case so far.

Modern hybrid warfare uses advanced technologies and the information space to impact societies. In response to these threats, it is necessary to develop new technological models that take into account the dual role of technologies: as tools for protection and as potential catalysts for hybrid threats. Globalization and international cooperation are fostering the development and sharing of new technologies, which creates both opportunities and risks. On the one hand, technologies such as cloud computing, 5G networks, and secure communication systems can provide protection for CI. On the other hand, these same technologies can be used as tools in information warfare and cyberattacks, destabilizing societies. In the context of hybrid wars, as confirmed by analyses in a study of media reports, communication and information technologies play a key role in expanding the battlefield. Examples such as narrative warfare and cognitive warfare show how "weaponized" information becomes a tool to influence societies. In order to effectively protect civilians from these threats, it is important to develop technologies that not only enhance security, but are also capable of detecting and neutralizing threats such as disinformation or cyberattacks.

The final chapter discusses the role of communities in hybrid warfare. The role of civilians should, as already mentioned, be expanded to include competences that will allow them to effectively respond and interact with defence and security systems. It should be emphasized that the war in Ukraine and the Middle East has shown that these communities are becoming a key element in both shaping the course of the conflict and minimizing its consequences. Analyses of academic studies and open sources point to the importance of community resilience as those who interact with societal and national resilience. Resilience, like hybrid warfare, is a concept for which there is no consensus on its definition, but there are attempts to explore community resilience factors, which may include: strong social and family ties; trust in institutions and leadership; hope and optimism, adaptability and innovation; cultivation of shared values and identities. However, it is important to mention that both factors and models of resilience should take into account the regionalization and nature of a given society. Undoubtedly, local communities, despite being underestimated in the literature, can play a particularly important role in the security system in hybrid war.

The main conclusions presented above clearly demonstrate the complexity, multidimensionality, and non-obviousness of hybrid warfare. This implies the need for a new holistic, but at the same time space-saving development of strategies that will allow the civilian population to anticipate and respond to hybrid threats.

Appendix 1: Characteristics of the research methods used

Given the definitional ambiguity of the issue of hybrid warfare, the authors decided to empirically test three hypotheses:

- H1: Hybrid warfare is a phase of a broader, flexible, and integrated hybrid strategy. In its first phase, this strategy takes the form of a hybrid conflict, which in feedback may use elements (features) of hybrid warfare.
- H2: Hybrid warfare is characterized by the integrated and flexible use of both military (conventional and unconventional) and non-military means by state and non-state actors to achieve strategic advantage and leads to the creation of a complex networked hybrid system in which the actions of one element trigger a reaction in other areas (cascade effect).
- H3: The materialization of hybrid warfare threats leads to a variety of specific consequences for the civilian population, which requires the application of multifaceted systemic and individual measures to effectively minimize these impacts.

The above hypotheses require methodological choices to be made, including decisions on issues such as which sources should be considered and what is the list of characteristics to be investigated under each hypothesis.

Secondary source analysis was used in the study. The analysis of the available literature on the subject allowed for a survey of the state of knowledge on hybrid warfare and the establishment of a theoretical framework. The theoretical framework adopted from the literature analysis was compared with the results of the empirical research. Empirical research was conducted on secondary sources in the form of media reports describing the war in Ukraine.

The analysis of secondary sources made it possible to adopt a period of analysis that was adequate for the characteristics of modern hybrid warfare. Furthermore, the collection of primary data through observation would have been impossible in terms of time, workload, and researcher safety.

A systematic literature review was used to examine the literature on the subject and a content analysis method was used to analyse media reports.

The analysis of secondary sources was complemented by surveys of civilians affected by the hybrid war between Ukraine and the Russian Federation.

SYSTEMATIC LITERATURE REVIEW

A systematic literature review was chosen as a research method to identify leading issues raised in the scholarly discussion on hybrid warfare and hybrid conflict. The systematic review was chosen because it involves strict procedures for searching and selecting articles for review, and therefore provides a tool that allows for repeated study results for given parameters (Snyder, 2019).

The exploration of the existing literature on hybrid warfare and hybrid conflict was based on the identification of available studies, which in turn was facilitated by a defined set of keywords. The selection of relevant articles for bibliometric research focused on the construction of a query covering various terms, synonyms, and abbreviations related to hybrid war and hybrid conflict.

A literature search was conducted in two scientific databases: Web of Science Core Collection (WoSCC) and Scopus. These databases were chosen because they are the most commonly used when conducting literature searches and are leading databases with significant scientific impact (Visser et al., 2021). After analysing the initial search results, it was decided to use Scopus as the database that contains a wider range of papers.

The choice of keywords was based on a scoping study framework (Arksey, O'Malley, 2005). A scoping study aims to map literature related to a topic or research area to support the identification of key concepts, research gaps, or evidence to inform practice, policy-making, and research. Search strings were modified to cover a wide range of studies describing hybrid warfare. This was achieved by iteratively modifying the search string to include new keywords or add new constraints.

Based on the above keyword considerations, a search query was formulated for titles, keywords, and abstracts, with a time limit. Studies published after 2014 were sought. The choice of the time restriction is driven by the desire to map features of contemporary hybrid warfare and hybrid conflict correlated with the case of the war in Ukraine under analysis. No other exclusion criteria were applied, so documents of all types

Appendix 1: Characteristics of the research methods used 465

could be considered. The query was entered into the Scopus databases on 30 April 2024, where:

- A1.1 – Hybrid warfare enquiry,
- A1.2 – Hybrid conflict enquiry,

"proxy wars" OR "gray wars" OR "Unlimited war" OR "Reflexive control" OR "Reflexive control" OR "New generation war" OR "Aggression below the threshold of conflict" OR "Non-linear warfare" OR "Complex war" OR "Political warfare" OR "Cyber warfare" OR "Information warfare" OR "Hybrid operations" OR "Asymmetric warfare" OR "Guerrilla warfare" OR "Ambiguous warfare" OR "Irregular warfare" OR "Ambiguous warfare" OR "Fourth-generation war" OR "Fifth-generation war" AND PUBYEAR > 2013 AND PUBYEAR < 2024

$$(A1.1)$$

"Hybrid conflict" OR "Irregular conflict" OR "Asymmetric conflict" OR "Conflict in the gray zone" OR "Low-intensity conflict" OR "Subconventional conflict" OR "Subversive actions" OR "Non-standard actions" OR "Conflict below the threshold of war" OR "Mixed actions" OR "Multidimensional conflict" AND PUBYEAR > 2013 AND PUBYEAR < 2024

$$(A1.2)$$

The choice of keywords and the design of the query are very important, as the results may change if a different query is used. This selection was made in accordance with the aim of the article, i.e. the broad identification of works on hybrid warfare and hybrid conflict. The query (A1.1) returned 18,458 papers while the query (A1.2) returned 4,648 papers.

We conducted an analysis to identify co-occurrence networks for keywords using the VOSviewer approach and tool. Co-occurrence analysis aims to analyse features of information. It is applicable to keywords, authors, study classifications, and other record fields in books, chapters, articles, reports, and other literature (Morris, 2000). There are three basic types of co-occurrence analysis: (i) co-occurrence of authors (co-operation analysis), (ii) co-occurrence of authors and keywords (coupling analysis), (iii) co-occurrence of keywords (co-word analysis) (Lou, Qiu, 2014).

The study decided to use keyword co-occurrence analysis. This analysis yielded the results most relevant to the content of the article. It concerns the analysis of keywords indicated by authors in their papers and indexed by bibliometric databases. Indexing is done by analysing the words used in the abstracts of the papers. This method of quantitative analysis makes it possible to discover the structure of the research area in the collection of papers under consideration and its potential relevance to the discipline. The co-occurrence of keywords creates a map in which the size of the nodes corresponds to the frequency of the keyword, while the lines show the relationships between the corresponding keywords (Fox, 2018). The identified network of relationships divides the analysed output into thematic clusters. This makes it possible to identify the leading themes addressed in the research and to identify knowledge gaps.

The bibliometric data obtained from the queries were made available in the data set of the study (Wisniewski et al., 2024).

CONTENT ANALYSIS

Media reports were taken from the two portals, PAP (Polish Press Agency) and Defence24.

The choice to analyse media reports as a research method in the context of hybrid warfare was dictated by the specificity of this type of conflict, in which military actions (conventional and unconventional) are closely linked to non-military actions including mainly information and propaganda operations. In these types of wars, information plays a key role, influencing the perceptions of the public, decision-makers, and actors involved in the conflict. Media messages can shape public opinion and influence decision-making, which, if based on erroneous or manipulated information, can lead to serious consequences such as escalation of the conflict, misjudgement of threats, or inappropriate political or military action. Above and beyond this, civilians may make decisions influenced by media messages that directly affect their security. Inappropriate actions resulting from disinformation or propaganda, such as wrong decisions to evacuate, choosing a place of refuge, or trusting false threat information, can put their health or lives at risk. Therefore, analysis of media reports is crucial to understanding the dynamics of the conflict itself.

PAP is one of the main sources of information in Poland. As the national news agency, PAP delivers news to the media, public and private institutions, as well as to individual audiences. PAP has an extensive network of correspondents both at home and abroad, which enables it to provide information from various sources and regions, ensuring a wide range of news. Its long history of activity has allowed it to develop working methods that guarantee the reliability of information. Information is verified and confirmed before it is published. Indirectly, PAP's reliability is confirmed by frequent quotations of PAP reports by other participants in the information market in Poland.

The Defence24 portal is recognized as a reliable source of information in the area of security, defence, and military affairs, both in Poland and internationally. Defence24 focuses on defence, national security,

Appendix 1: Characteristics of the research methods used

military technology, and geopolitics. The portal employs defence and security experts, including analysts, ex-military and industry specialists. The portal is respected by defence and security professionals.

The choice of two news portals was dictated by two aspects. Firstly, the authors used two sources of information to verify the results of the content analysis. Secondly, the synthesis of information from PAP (general news portal) and Defence24 (specialist portal) provides a broad information spectrum.

Media reports were extracted from both portals using the data scraping method. Data scraping is a method of automatically collecting data from various online sources, such as websites, social networks, or forums, online. It involves the use of computer programmes, called scrapers, which analyse the structure of a website to identify data of interest and then extract the data in a structured way, such as in a tabular format (Babaritskii, 2024).

In research, data scraping is used in the analysis of large data sets, especially in fields such as sociology, economics, marketing, or market analysis. This method allows for the rapid acquisition of information about user behaviour, market trends, or social opinions, making it a valuable tool in empirical research.

The task of article retrieval was performed automatically using the Python language and libraries supporting the automatic retrieval of data from the indicated textual web sources, including LangChain (LongChain) and BeautifulSoup (BeautifulSoup).

Subsequently, all downloaded reports for each portal separately were merged and stored in a single file. The files thus combined were subject to content analysis. Media reports were collected from the date of Russia's full-scale aggression against Ukraine (24 February 2022) until 30 April 2024.

Articles on the portals were searched using an internal search engine. Whether an article was analysed was determined by the article's thematic assignment to the Ukraine war thread. The final sample selected included 1,769 articles from PAP and 4,187 articles from Defence24.

It was decided to use a mixed-methods approach using text mining and keyword occurrence statistics in a set of secondary sources. As a first step, a quantitative content analysis was adopted (Coe, Scacco, 2017). Keywords for each hypothesis were identified based on the results of the literature analysis and the authors' experience. A dictionary of keywords divided into thematic categories was used to code the content of the collected media reports. All keywords were used in the content language of the articles. Lemmatization was implemented automatically according to the algorithms of the IT tool used to ensure that all possible instances of keywords were recognized. In a further step, the encoding of the texts with the accepted keywords was carried out. The coding was programmed in such a way that the programme would code the sentence in which the keyword occurred, as well as one sentence before and one sentence after. This produced a three-sentence fragment of text encoded with a specific code. Analyses were carried out using MAXQDA text mining and quantitative text analysis software. The frequency of keywords in the total number of words in the document was calculated. It was checked whether the frequency of one keyword was correlated with the frequency of another keyword. Statistics indicating cross-coding were calculated. If a piece of text coded with code A had a part in common with a piece of text coded with code B, the programme considered such a piece of text as a common part of both codes. In this way, the authors established the fact of co-occurrence of thematic issues.

A set of content analysis data was made available in the data set of the study (Wisniewski et al., 2024).

SURVEYS

We conducted a survey among people affected by the hybrid war in Ukraine. Due to the specificity and difficulty in accessing respondents, the survey was conducted among two groups of respondents:

- Civilians in Ukraine – the survey in this group included residents of Ukraine who directly experienced the effects of the war.
- People residing in refugee centres in Poland – the second research group consisted of people who had also experienced the effects of war, but had left the conflict zone and were currently residing in refugee centres in Poland.

Despite efforts and physical outreach to refugee centres in Poland and to locations in Ukraine where the survey could be conducted, the final survey sample was 40 people. These limitations were due to several factors. Firstly, the complex political and social situation in the conflict-affected regions made direct contact with potential respondents difficult. Secondly, living conditions in refugee centres and the stress of forced migration affected the limited availability of people willing to participate in the survey. Despite measures taken, such as a personal visit to the centres and a detailed explanation of the questionnaire, the number of respondents remained limited. In spite of this, the data collected provides important insights into the experiences and needs of those affected by the hybrid war. The results of this study should be seen as preliminary and exploratory, which can form the basis for further, more extensive research.

Appendix 1: Characteristics of the research methods used

The study was conducted by means of a questionnaire survey using the CAWI (Computer-Assisted Web Interviewing) technique (Manfreda et al., 2006). A questionnaire containing closed and open-ended questions was made in the Google Forms tool.

The main objective of the study was to identify and analyse civilians' experiences of hybrid warfare. The data collected was intended to optimize strategies to protect civilians from the complex challenges arising from hybrid conflicts. The questionnaire contained 144 questions divided into three sections:

1. The first section collects data on the characteristics of the respondent while maintaining their anonymity. The questions in this section related to personal characteristics such as age, gender, education, or membership of a high-risk group.
2. The second section collects data on experienced hazards and methods of responding to them. The hazards have been divided into six areas that can lead to death or permanent damage to health. The division of hazards was done in analogy with the Six Ways to Die method. Within this section, the authors asked respondents about:
   a. experiencing a threat to life or permanent damage to health,
   b. reasons for feeling at risk of death or permanent damage to health,
   c. organized threat response methods (actions by state or local authorities),
   d. individual methods of responding to threats,
   e. assessing the effectiveness of organized and individual hazard response methods.
3. The third section focuses on the impact of digital threats on population security in hybrid warfare.

The survey was conducted between 01.03.2024 and 14.04.2024. A questionnaire in Ukrainian and English was used. The results obtained were published on the Zendoo platform (Wisniewski et al., 2024). The Zendoo platform is dedicated to supporting open science and increasing the visibility and accessibility of EU-funded research results. The platform is managed by CERN on behalf of the European Commission. The mission of the repository is to support the implementation of the EU's open science policy by providing a trusted and comprehensive space for researchers to share the results of their research, such as data, software, reports, presentations, posters, and more (Zendoo).

BIBLIOGRAPHY

Arksey, H., and O'Malley, L., (2005), Scoping Studies: Towards a Methodological Framework. *International Journal of Social Research Methodology*, 8, 19–32. https://doi.org/10.1080/1364557032000119616.

Babaritskii, P., (2024), Solving the Problem of Market Failure Associated with Data Scraping: The Behavior Regulatory Pattern. *Journal of Legal Affairs and Dispute Resolution in Engineering and Construction*, 16, 03724002. https://doi.org/10.1061/JLADAH.LADR-1111.

BeautifulSoup, Available at: https://www.crummy.com/software/Beautiful-Soup/. Accessed: 9 Sept. 2024.

Coe, K., and Scacco, J.M., (2017), Content Analysis, Quantitative. In J. Matthes, C.S. Davis, and R.F. Potter (eds.), *The International Encyclopedia of Communication Research Methods*. Wiley, pp. 1–11. https://doi.org/10.1002/9781118901731.iecrm0045.

Fox, A., (2018). Keywords Co-Occurrence Analysis of Research on Sustainable Enterprise and Sustainable Organisation. *Journal of Corporate Social Responsibility Leadership*, 5, 47–66.

LongChain, Applications That Can Reason. Powered by LangChain [WWW Document]. Available at: https://www.langchain.com. Accessed: 13 Sept. 2024.

Lou, W., and Qiu, J., (2014), Semantic Information Retrieval Research Based on Co-Occurrence Analysis. *Online Information Review*, 38, 4–23. https://doi.org/10.1108/OIR-11-2012-0203.

Manfreda, K.L., Batagelj, Z., and Vehovar, V., (2006), Design of Web Survey Questionnaires: Three Basic Experiments. *Journal of Computer-Mediated Communication*, 7, 0–0. https://doi.org/10.1111/j.1083-6101.2002.tb00149.x.

Morris, T.A., (2000), Structural Relationships within Medical Informatics. *Proceedings of the AMIA Symposium*, 590–594.

Snyder, H., (2019), Literature Review as a Research Methodology: An Overview and Guidelines. *Journal of Business Research*, 104, 333–339. https://doi.org/10.1016/j.jbusres.2019.07.039.

Visser, M., Van Eck, N.J., and Waltman, L., (2021), Large-Scale Comparison of Bibliographic Data Sources: Scopus, Web of Science, Dimensions, Crossref, and Microsoft Academic. *Quantitative Science Studies*, 2, 20–41. https://doi.org/10.1162/qss_a_00112.

Wisniewski, M., Bieniasz, J., and Wróblewski, W., (2024), UK 2024 Survey on Civil Protection and Domestic Security in Contemporary Hybrid Warfare. https://doi.org/10.5281/ZENODO.13767999.

Appendix 2: Results of analysis of media reports characterizing the war in Ukraine

The appendix contains the results of an analysis of media reports characterizing the war in Ukraine. Media reports were taken from two portals, PAP (Polish Press Agency) and Defence24. Two aspects dictated the choice of two news portals. First, the authors use two sources of information to verify the content analysis results. Secondly, synthesizing information from PAP (general news portal) and Defence24 (specialized portal) provides a broad information spectrum.

A description of the applied research method of media reports is included in Appendix 1.

Appendix 2 contains the detailed results of the research in the area:

- A1.1
- A2.1
- A2.2
- A2.3
- A2.4
- A2.5
- A4.1
- A4.2
- A4.3
- A4.4
- A4.5
- A5.1

TABLE A1.1 Summary of the percentage linkage of codes indicating hybrid warfare features with other codes

Code Tree		Ambiguity	Flexibility	Complexity	Integration of Means	Destabilizing Actions	Asymmetry	New Technologies	Subliminality
Code Frequency		1	40	9	1	113	12	5	7
Conventional operations > Manoeuvres	983		2.50%			2.65%	8.33%		
Conventional operations > Armed conflict	36					0.88%			
Other > Tactics	331		2.50%				8.33%		14.29%
Other > Tools	278				100%	6.19%	8.33%		42.86%
Prevention	23					1.77%			
Response	382		7.50%	11.11%		3.54%			14.29%
Preparation	1,262		2.50%		100%	7.08%	25.00%		14.29%
Counteracting	90					1.77%			
Irregular operations, hybrid actions, and below the war threshold > Destabilization	112					99.12%			
Irregular operations, hybrid actions, and below the war threshold > Restoration	433					2.65%			
Actors in conventional operations > Regular armed forces	816		7.50%	11.11%		0.88%	8.33%		

(*Continued*)

Appendix 2: Results of analysis of media reports

TABLE A1.1 (*Continued*) Summary of the percentage linkage of codes indicating hybrid warfare features with other codes

Code Tree		Ambiguity	Flexibility	Complexity	Integration of Means	Destabilizing Actions	Asymmetry	New Technologies	Subliminality
Code Frequency		1	40	9	1	113	12	5	7
Actors in conventional operations > Army	7,887		27.50%	22.22%		23.89%	50%	40%	71.43%
Actors in irregular, hybrid, and below-threshold operations > Private military companies	40		10%			1.77%	8.33%		
Actors in irregular, hybrid, and below-threshold operations > Terrorist groups	554					7.96%			
Actors in irregular, hybrid, and below-threshold operations > Cybercriminal groups	64					0.88%			
Non-military measures > Cyberattacks	47						8.33%		14.29%
Non-military measures > Intimidation	71					1.77%			

(*Continued*)

474 Appendix 2: Results of analysis of media reports

TABLE A1.1 (*Continued*)   Summary of the percentage linkage of codes indicating hybrid warfare features with other codes

Code Tree	Ambiguity	Flexibility	Complexity	Integration of Means	Destabilizing Actions	Asymmetry	New Technologies	Subliminality
Code Frequency	1	40	9	1	113	12	5	7
Non-military measures > Political measures	8				0.88%			
Non-military measures > Offensive actions in cyberspace	18							14.29%
Non-military measures > Propaganda	956	2.50%			6.19%	16.67%		14.29%
Non-military measures > Disinformation	177		11.11%		5.31%			
Non-military unconventional actions > Sabotage actions	118	5.00%				8.33%		28.57%
Non-military unconventional actions > Diversionary actions	230	5.00%			4.42%	8.33%		28.57%
Domains > Information	3,516	7.50%		100%	14.16%	8.33%		
Domains > Diplomatic	789				5.31%	8.33%		
Domains > Political	3,069	100%	2.50%	22.22%		30.09%	8.33%	20%	42.86%
Domains > Intelligence	1,781		7.50%			3.54%			14.29%

(*Continued*)

Appendix 2: Results of analysis of media reports

TABLE A1.1 (*Continued*) Summary of the percentage linkage of codes indicating hybrid warfare features with other codes

Code Tree		Ambiguity	Flexibility	Complexity	Integration of Means	Destabilizing Actions	Asymmetry	New Technologies	Subliminality
Code Frequency		**1**	**40**	**9**	**1**	**113**	**12**	**5**	**7**
Domains > Legal	1,718		10%			3.54%			
Domains > Social	340		2.50%			9.73%	16.67%		14.29%
Domains > Cultural	212								14.29%
Domains > Military	950		12.50%	11.11%		11.50%	16.67%		28.57%
Domains > Economic	783		2.50%			10.62%	8.33%		
Domains > Cyberspace	38			11.11%					
Domains > Maritime	2,004			11.11%		6.19%			28.57%
Domains > Land	1,427		2.50%			6.19%	8.33%		28.57%
Domains > Air	2,473		17.50%	33.33%		3.54%			

Source: Own work

TABLE A2.1 Summary of the percentage linkage of codes indicating military activities (conventional and unconventional) with other codes

Code Tree		Unconventional Military Action					Conventional Military Action		
		Intelligence Activities	Guerrilla Warfare	Special Operations	Sabotage Activities	Diversionary Activities	Maritime Operations	Air Operations	Land Operations
Code size		7	2	3	118	230	2	1	4
Conventional operations > Manoeuvres	983				2.54%	3.48%			25.00%
Conventional action > Armed conflict	36				0.85%	0.43%			
Conventional measures > Psychological factor	2				0.85%	0.43%			
Others > Synergistic effect	28					0.43%			
Other > Social media	34					0.43%			
Other > Tactics	331					2.61%			
Other > Tools	278				5.08%	2.61%			
Other > Techniques	142				0.85%	0.87%			
Crisis management > Response	382				0.85%	3.04%			25.00%
Crisis management > Preparation	1,262				11.02%	9.57%			
Crisis management > Prevention	90				0.85%				
Irregular, hybrid, and below the threshold of conflict actions > Destabilization	112					2.17%			

(*Continued*)

Appendix 2: Results of analysis of media reports 477

TABLE A2.1 (*Continued*) Summary of the percentage linkage of codes indicating military
activities (conventional and unconventional) with other codes

Code Tree		Unconventional Military Action					Conventional Military Action		
		Intelligence Activities	Guerrilla Warfare	Special Operations	Sabotage Activities	Diversionary Activities	Maritime Operations	Air Operations	Land Operations
Code size		7	2	3	118	230	2	1	4
Irregular, hybrid, and below the threshold of conflict actions > Reconstruction	433				0.85%	2.17%			
Irregular, hybrid, and below conflict threshold actions > Psychological factor	2				0.85%	0.43%			
Features of hybrid warfare > Flexibility	40				1.69%	0.87%			
Features of hybrid warfare > Destabilizing actions	113					2.17%			
Features of hybrid warfare > Asymmetry	12				0.85%	0.43%			
Features of hybrid warfare > Below the threshold of war	7				1.69%	0.87%			
Actors in conventional action > Regular armed forces	816				4.24%	2.61%			
Actors in conventional action > Special forces	33					1.30%			

(*Continued*)

478 Appendix 2: Results of analysis of media reports

TABLE A2.1 (*Continued*) Summary of the percentage linkage of codes indicating military activities (conventional and unconventional) with other codes

Code Tree		Unconventional Military Action					Conventional Military Action		
		Intelligence Activities	Guerrilla Warfare	Special Operations	Sabotage Activities	Diversionary Activities	Maritime Operations	Air Operations	Land Operations
Code size		7	2	3	118	230	2	1	4
Actors in conventional action > Army	7,887	42.86%		33.33%	29.66%	30.87%			50%
Actors in irregular, hybrid, and below pro actions > Private military companies	40	14.29%			4.24%	3.04%			
Actors in irregular, hybrid, and below pro actions > Guerrilla groups	83			33.33%	4.24%	1.30%			
Actors in irregular, hybrid, and below pro actions > Terrorist groups	554	14.29%			8.47%	6.09%			
Actors in irregular, hybrid, and below pro actions > Cybercrime groups	64					0.43%			
Non-military operations > Cyberattacks	47				0.85%	0.43%			
Non-military action > Intimidation	71				0.85%	0.87%			
Non-military activities > Terrorist activity	10					0.43%			

(*Continued*)

Appendix 2: Results of analysis of media reports

TABLE A2.1 (*Continued*)   Summary of the percentage linkage of codes indicating military activities (conventional and unconventional) with other codes

Code Tree	Code size	Unconventional Military Action					Conventional Military Action		
		Intelligence Activities	Guerrilla Warfare	Special Operations	Sabotage Activities	Diversionary Activities	Maritime Operations	Air Operations	Land Operations
Code size		7	2	3	118	230	2	1	4
Non-military operations > Psychological operations	6	14.29%			0.85%	0.43%			
Non-military action > Propaganda	956				14.41%	5.65%			
Non-military operations > Disinformation	177	14.29%			2.54%	2.17%			
Domains > Informational	3,516	42.86%	50%	33.33%	22.03%	16.96%			
Domains > Diplomatic	789				0.85%	2.17%			
Domains > Political	3,069	14.29%			10.17%	5.65%	50%		
Domains > Intelligence	1,781	100%	50%	33.33%	19.49%	14.78%			25.00%
Domains > Legal	1,718				6.78%	2.17%			
Domains > Social	340				0.85%	2.61%			
Domains > Military	950		50%		5.08%	4.35%			
Domains > Economic	783				1.69%				
Domains > Cyberspace	38					0.43%			
Domains > Water	2,004				4.24%	13.91%	100%		
Domains > Land	1,427				3.39%	3.04%	50%		100%
Domains > Air	2,473	14.29%		33.33%	5.93%	4.35%	50%	100%	

Source: Own work

480   Appendix 2: Results of analysis of media reports

TABLE A2.2 Summary of the percentage linkage of codes indicating conventional hybrid warfare with other codes

Code Tree		Manoeuvres	Military Operations	Demonstrations of Force	Defensive Action	Territorial Defence
Code size		983	11	1	11	17
		Conventional measures				
Others > Synergistic effect	28	0.10%				
Other > Social media	34					
Other > Public opinion	26	0.10%				
Other > State of war	7					
Other > Tactics	331	2.34%			9.09%	
Other > Tools	278	1.22%				
Other > Techniques	142	0.41%				
Crisis management > Prevention	23					
Crisis management > Response	382	1.53%				5.88%
Crisis management > Preparation	1,262	5.70%				11.76%
Crisis Management > Prevention	90	0.20%				
Irregular, hybrid, and below the threshold of conflict > Asymmetric operations	1	0.10%				
Irregular, hybrid, and below the threshold of conflict actions > Destabilization	112	0.31%				
Irregular, hybrid, and below the threshold of conflict > Hybrid conflict	1	0.10%				
Irregular, hybrid, and below the threshold of conflict actions > Reconstruction	433	0.51%			9.09%	
Irregular, hybrid, and below the threshold of conflict actions > Political factor	1					

Armed Conflict	Urban Areas	Conventional Warfare	The Political Factor	The Economic Factor	The Psychological Factor	Maritime Operations	Air Operations	Land Operations
36	1	3	1	5	2	2	1	4
						Conventional military action		
2.78%					50%			
2.78%								
2.78%								25.00%
13.89%								
2.78%								
			100%					

(*Continued*)

Appendix 2: Results of analysis of media reports

TABLE A2.2 (*Continued*) Summary of the percentage linkage of codes indicating conventional hybrid warfare with other codes

Code Tree		Manoeuvres	Military Operations	Demonstrations of Force	Defensive Action	Territorial Defence
Code size		983	11	1	11	17
		Conventional measures				
Irregular, hybrid, and below the threshold of conflict actions > Economic factor	5					
Irregular, hybrid, and below conflict threshold actions > Psychological factor	2					
Features of hybrid warfare > Flexibility	40	0.10%				
Features of hybrid warfare > Destabilizing actions	113	0.31%				
Features of hybrid warfare > Asymmetry	12	0.10%				
Actors in conventional action > Regular armed forces	816	3.97%			9.09%	5.88%
Actors in conventional action > Special forces	33	0.10%				
Actors in conventional action > Army	7,887	29.70%	9.09%	100%	63.64%	29.41%
Actors in irregular, hybrid, and below pro actions > Private military companies	40	0.31%				
Actors in irregular, hybrid, and below pro actions > Guerrilla groups	83		9.09%			
Actors in irregular, hybrid, and below pro actions > Terrorist groups	554	1.53%	18.18%			
Cybersecurity > Data confidentiality	2	0.10%				

Appendix 2: Results of analysis of media reports

Armed Conflict	Urban Areas	Conventional Warfare	The Political Factor	The Economic Factor	The Psychological Factor	Maritime Operations	Air Operations	Land Operations
36	1	3	1	5	2	2	1	4

Conventional military action

				100%				
					100%			
2.78%								
5.56%								
13.89%			100%	40%	100%			50.00%
2.78%		33.33%						

(*Continued*)

484 Appendix 2: Results of analysis of media reports

TABLE A2.2 (*Continued*) Summary of the percentage linkage of codes indicating conventional hybrid warfare with other codes

Code Tree		Manoeuvres	Military Operations	Demonstrations of Force	Defensive Action	Territorial Defence
Code size		983	11	1	11	17
		Conventional measures				
Cybersecurity > OT systems	45	0.20%				23.53%
Non-military operations > Cyberattacks	47	0.10%				
Non-military action > Intimidation	71	0.20%				
Non-military activities > Terrorist activity	10	0.10%				
Non-military action > Diplomatic action	12	0.10%				
Non-military action > Propaganda	956	3.56%				
Non-military operations > Disinformation	177	0.20%				5.88%
Unconventional military operations > Sabotage operations	118	0.31%				
Unconventional military operations > Diversion operations	230	0.81%				
Domains > Informational	3,516	10.27%	18.18%		9.09%	11.76%
Domains > Diplomatic	789	0.92%				
Domains > Political	3,069	5.70%	36.36%	100%	9.09%	5.88%
Domains > Intelligence	1,781	5.80%			18.18%	5.88%
Domains > Legal	1,718	3.87%	18.18%			11.76%
Domains > Social	340	0.41%				
Domains > Cultural	212	0.41%				
Domains > Military	950	3.56%				
Domains > Economic	783	1.32%				
Domains > Cognitive	10	0.10%				
Domains > Space	59	0.10%				
Domains > Water	2,004	12.72%				
Domains > Land	1,427	10.17%			9.09%	11.76%
Domains > Air	2,473	24.52%			9.09%	

Source: Own work

Armed Conflict	Urban Areas	Conventional Warfare	The Political Factor	The Economic Factor	The Psychological Factor	Maritime Operations	Air Operations	Land Operations
36	1	3	1	5	2	2	1	4

Conventional military action

Armed Conflict	Urban Areas	Conventional Warfare	The Political Factor	The Economic Factor	The Psychological Factor	Maritime Operations	Air Operations	Land Operations
2.78%					50%			
2.78%					50%			
2.78%					50%			25.00%
11.11%					50%			
		33.33%						
13.89%			100%	20%		50%		
5.56%		33.33%						25.00%
5.56%		33.33%		20%				
2.78%								
8.33%								
2.78%				100%				
						100%		
					50%	50%		100%
8.33%				20%		50%	100%	

TABLE A2.3 Summary of the percentage linkage of codes indicating unconventional military activities of hybrid warfare with other codes

Code Tree	Code size	Electronic Warfare	Asymmetric Operations	Proxy War	Attacks on Civilians	Hybrid Operations	Destabilization	Hybrid Warfare	Hybrid Conflict
Code size		2	1	1	8	1	112	2	1
		Irregular, Hybrid, and Below the Threshold of Conflict Activities							
Conventional operations > Manoeuvres	983		100%				2.68%		100%
Conventional actions > Defensive actions	11								
Conventional actions > Territorial defence	17								
Conventional actions > Armed conflict	36						0.89%		
Conventional action > Political factor	1								
Conventional measures > Economic factor	5								
Conventional measures > Psychological factor	2								
Other > Cascade effect	2								
Others > Synergistic effect	28								
Other > Social media	34								
Other > Public opinion	26								
Other > Tactics	331								
Other > Tools	278					100%	6.25%		
Other > Techniques	142								
Crisis management > Prevention	23						1.79%		
Crisis management > Response	382						3.57%	50%	
Crisis management > Preparation	1,262						7.14%	100%	
Crisis management > Prevention	90						0.89%		
Features of hybrid warfare > Flexibility	40								
Features of hybrid warfare > Destabilizing actions	113						100%		
Features of hybrid warfare > Asymmetry	12								

Appendix 2: Results of analysis of media reports

Reconstruction	Cascade Effect	Attack on Civilians	The Political Factor	The Economic Factor	The Psychological Factor	Intelligence Activities	Guerrilla Warfare	Special Operations	Sabotage Activities	Diversionary Activities
433	2	1	1	5	2	7	2	3	118	230
						Unconventional				
1.15%									2.54%	3.48%
0.23%										
									0.85%	0.43%
			100%							
				100%						
					100%				0.85%	0.43%
	100%									0.43%
										0.43%
0.23%										
1.15%										2.61%
1.85%					50%				5.08%	2.61%
0.69%									0.85%	0.87%
0.92%									0.85%	3.04%
4.62%									11.02%	9.57%
0.69%									0.85%	
									1.69%	0.87%
0.69%										2.17%
									0.85%	0.43%

(*Continued*)

488 Appendix 2: Results of analysis of media reports

TABLE A2.3 (*Continued*)   Summary of the percentage linkage of codes indicating unconventional military activities of hybrid warfare with other codes

Code Tree		Electronic Warfare	Asymmetric Operations	Proxy War	Attacks on Civilians	Hybrid Operations	Destabilization	Hybrid Warfare	Hybrid Conflict
Code size		2	1	1	8	1	112	2	1
		Irregular, Hybrid, and Below the Threshold of Conflict Activities							
Features of hybrid warfare > Below the threshold of war	7								
Actors in conventional action > Regular armed forces	816			100%			0.89%		
Actors in conventional action > Special forces	33								
Actors in conventional action > Army	7,887		100%		12.50%		24.11%		100%
Actors in irregular, hybrid, and below pro actions > Private military companies	40						1.79%		
Actors in irregular, hybrid, and below pro actions > Guerrilla groups	83								
Actors in irregular, hybrid, and below pro actions > Terrorist groups	554						8.04%		
Actors in irregular, hybrid, and below pro actions > Cybercrime groups	64						0.89%		
Actors in irregular, hybrid, and below pro actions > Separatist forces	7								
Cybersecurity > Cyber defence	1								
Non-military operations > Cyberattacks	47								
Non-military action > Intimidation	71						1.79%		
Non-military activities > Terrorist activity	10								

Appendix 2: Results of analysis of media reports 489

Reconstruction	Cascade Effect	Attack on Civilians	The Political Factor	The Economic Factor	The Psychological Factor	Intelligence Activities	Guerrilla Warfare	Special Operations	Sabotage Activities	Diversionary Activities
433	2	1	1	5	2	7	2	3	118	230
						Unconventional				
									1.69%	0.87%
1.85%									4.24%	2.61%
										1.30%
17.09%		100%	40%	100%		42.86%		33.33%	29.66%	30.87%
0.69%						14.29%			4.24%	3.04%
								33.33%	4.24%	1.30%
0.69%						14.29%			8.47%	6.09%
0.23%										0.43%
0.23%										
0.23%										
0.23%									0.85%	0.43%
									0.85%	0.87%
										0.43%

(*Continued*)

TABLE A2.3 (*Continued*)   Summary of the percentage linkage of codes indicating unconventional military activities of hybrid warfare with other codes

Code Tree		Electronic Warfare	Asymmetric Operations	Proxy War	Attacks on Civilians	Hybrid Operations	Destabilization	Hybrid Warfare	Hybrid Conflict
Code size		2	1	1	8	1	112	2	1
		Irregular, Hybrid, and Below the Threshold of Conflict Activities							
Non-military action > Political action	8		100%				0.89%		100%
Non-military operations > Psychological operations	6								
Non-military action > Propaganda	956						6.25%		
Non-military operations > Disinformation	177					100%	5.36%		
Domains > Informational	3,516						14.29%		
Domains > Diplomatic	789						5.36%		
Domains > Political	3,069		100%			100%	30.36%		100%
Domains > Intelligence	1,781				12.50%		3.57%		
Domains > Legal	1,718						3.57%	100%	
Domains > Social	340						9.82%		
Domains > Cultural	212								
Domains > Military	950						11.61%		
Domains > Economic	783			100%	12.50%		9.82%	50%	
Domains > Cyberspace	38								
Domains > Water	2,004						5.36%		
Domains > Land	1,427						6.25%		
Domains > Air	2,473	50%		100%			3.57%		

Source: Own work

Reconstruction	Cascade Effect	Attack on Civilians	The Political Factor	The Economic Factor	The Psychological Factor	Intelligence Activities	Guerrilla Warfare	Special Operations	Sabotage Activities	Diversionary Activities
433	2	1	1	5	2	7	2	3	118	230
						Unconventional				
						14.29%			0.85%	0.43%
2.77%					50%				14.41%	5.65%
0.46%						14.29%			2.54%	2.17%
5.77%					50%	42.86%	50%	33.33%	22.03%	16.96%
3.23%									0.85%	2.17%
17.09%			100%	20%		14.29%			10.17%	5.65%
6.00%						100%	50%	33.33%	19.49%	14.78%
6.93%				20%					6.78%	2.17%
3.00%									0.85%	2.61%
1.39%										
4.85%							50%		5.08%	4.35%
9.70%			100%						1.69%	
										0.43%
5.31%									4.24%	13.91%
2.77%	50%				50%				3.39%	3.04%
3.70%	50%			20%		14.29%		33.33%	5.93%	4.35%

TABLE A2.4 Percentage breakdown of non-military action codes with other codes

Code Tree		Cyberattacks	Intimidation	Food Security	Humanitarian Crises	Terrorist Activity	Political Pressure
Code frequency		47	71	19	12	10	1
Conventional operations > Manoeuvres	983	2.13%	2.82%			100%	
Conventional operations > Territorial defence	17						
Conventional operations > Armed conflict	36						
Conventional operations > Psychological factor	2						
Other > Social media	34						
Other > Public opinion	26						
Other > Tactics	331	6.38%					
Other > Tools	278	6.38%	7.04%				
Other > Techniques	142						
Emergency management > Prevention	23						
Emergency management > Response	382	4.26%	1.41%			10%	
Emergency management > Preparations	1,262	6.38%	2.82%			10%	
Emergency management > Counteracting	90		1.41%				
Irregular, hybrid, and below conflict threshold operations > Asymmetric actions	1						

International Isolation	Operations of Special Forces	Economic Measures	Internal Conflict Generation	Political Measures	Diplomatic Measures	Psychological Operations	Offensive Measures in Cyberspace	Propaganda	Information Warfare	Disinformation
1	1	1	1	8	12	6	18	956	15	177
					8.33%			3.66%		1.13%
										0.56%
								0.10%		
								0.10%		
								0.10%		1.13%
								0.21%		
								0.84%	6.67%	1.69%
	100%							3.14%	6.67%	6.21%
								0.52%		1.69%
								0.31%		0.56%
								1.36%		
	100%				8.33%	5.56%		5.02%	6.67%	3.95%
								0.52%		1.13%
				12.50%						

(*Continued*)

494 Appendix 2: Results of analysis of media reports

TABLE A2.4 (*Continued*) Percentage breakdown of non-military action codes with other codes

Code Tree	Cyberattacks	Intimidation	Food Security	Humanitarian Crises	Terrorist Activity	Political Pressure
Code frequency	47	71	19	12	10	1
Irregular, hybrid, and below conflict threshold operations > Hybrid operations	1					
Irregular, hybrid, and below conflict threshold operations > Destabilization	112	2.82%				
Irregular, hybrid, and below conflict threshold operations > Hybrid conflict	1					
Irregular, hybrid, and below conflict threshold operations > Restoration	433	2.13%				
Irregular, hybrid, and below conflict threshold operations > Psychological factor	2					
Features of hybrid warfare > Flexibility	40					
Features of hybrid warfare > Impacting political decisions	11					
Features of hybrid warfare > Complexity	9					
Features of hybrid warfare > Destabilizing actions	113	2.82%				
Features of hybrid warfare > Asymmetry	12	2.13%				
Features of hybrid warfare > Below war threshold	7	2.13%				

International Isolation	Operations of Special Forces	Economic Measures	Internal Conflict Generation	Political Measures	Diplomatic Measures	Psychological Operations	Offensive Measures in Cyberspace	Propaganda	Information Warfare	Disinformation
1	1	1	1	8	12	6	18	956	15	177
										0.56%
				12.50%				0.73%		3.39%
				12.50%						
								1.26%		1.13%
								0.10%		
								0.10%		
								0.10%		0.56%
										0.56%
				12.50%				0.73%		3.39%
								0.21%		
							5.56%	0.10%		

(*Continued*)

TABLE A2.4 (*Continued*) Percentage breakdown of non-military action codes with other codes

Code Tree		Cyberattacks	Intimidation	Food Security	Humanitarian Crises	Terrorist Activity	Political Pressure
Code frequency		47	71	19	12	10	1
Actors in conventional operations > Regular armed forces	816			5.26%			
Actors in conven-tional operations > Army	7,887	21.28%	12.68%	26.32%	33.33%	30%	
Actors in irregular, hybrid, and below-threshold operations > Little green men	11						
Actors in irregular, hybrid, and below-threshold operations > Private military companies	40	2.13%	1.41%			10%	
Actors in irregular, hybrid, and below-threshold operations > Guerrilla groups	83						
Actors in irregular, hybrid, and below-threshold operations > Terrorist groups	554		1.41%	10.53%		100%	
Actors in irregular, hybrid, and below-threshold operations > Cybercriminal groups	64	17.02%					
Cybersecurity > IT systems	9	2.13%					
Military unconven-tional operations > Intelligence actions	7						
Military unconven-tional operations > Sabotage actions	118	2.13%	1.41%				

Appendix 2: Results of analysis of media reports

International Isolation	Operations of Special Forces	Economic Measures	Internal Conflict Generation	Political Measures	Diplomatic Measures	Psychological Operations	Offensive Measures in Cyberspace	Propaganda	Information Warfare	Disinformation
1	1	1	1	8	12	6	18	956	15	177
								1.67%		0.56%
				33.33%	33.33%	38.89%	24.58%		6.67%	21.47%
								0.21%		
								3.35%		2.82%
								0.31%		
								2.72%	6.67%	1.69%
							16.67%	0.52%		1.69%
							5.56%			
					16.67%					0.56%
					16.67%			1.78%		1.69%

(*Continued*)

TABLE A2.4 (*Continued*) Percentage breakdown of non-military action codes with other codes

Code Tree		Cyberattacks	Intimidation	Food Security	Humanitarian Crises	Terrorist Activity	Political Pressure
Code frequency		47	71	19	12	10	1
Military unconventional operations > Diversion actions	230	2.13%	2.82%			10%	
Domains > Information	3,516	19.15%	11.27%		16.67%	30%	
Domains > Diplomatic	789	6.38%	5.63%	15.79%	16.67%		100%
Domains > Political	3,069	10.64%	14.08%	10.53%		20%	100%
Domains > Intelligence	1,781	14.89%	5.63%	5.26%		10%	
Domains > Legal	1,718	8.51%	2.82%				
Domains > Social	340	2.13%	1.41%	5.26%			
Domains > Cultural	212	2.13%					
Domains > Military	950	6.38%	4.23%	5.26%	8.33%		100%
Domains > Economic	783	4.26%	1.41%	5.26%	8.33%		
Domains > Cognitive	4						
Domains > Cognitive sphere	10						
Domains > Cybersecurity	8	6.38%					
Domains > Cyberspace	38	6.38%					
Domains> Space	59						
Domains > Maritime	2,004	4.26%	4.23%	10.53%	16.67%	10%	
Domains > Land	1,427		5.63%	15.79%	8.33%		
Domains > Air	2,473	4.26%	2.82%		8.33%		

Source: Own work

Appendix 2: Results of analysis of media reports

International Isolation	Operations of Special Forces	Economic Measures	Internal Conflict Generation	Political Measures	Diplomatic Measures	Psychological Operations	Offensive Measures in Cyberspace	Propaganda	Information Warfare	Disinformation
1	1	1	1	8	12	6	18	956	15	177
						16.67%		1.36%		2.82%
				12.50%	16.67%	33.33%	22.22%	19.77%	100%	36.72%
				37.50%	100%		5.56%	2.09%	13.33%	5.08%
100%		100%		100%	16.67%	16.67%	16.67%	15.59%	40%	23.16%
		100%			8.33%	16.67%	16.67%	5.65%	6.67%	9.04%
				12.50%	8.33%		11.11%	4.81%	6.67%	6.78%
				12.50%				3.66%	6.67%	3.39%
							5.56%	0.84%		1.13%
	100%			12.50%		16.67%	5.56%	4.18%	13.33%	7.34%
	100%	100%						3.35%	13.33%	1.13%
								0.21%		0.56%
								0.21%		1.13%
						16.67%		0.10%		
							5.56%	0.42%		3.39%
								0.10%		0.56%
			100%	12.50%	8.33%		5.56%	4.39%	6.67%	4.52%
				25.00%				2.82%		1.69%
				12.50%			11.11%	4.18%		2.82%

TABLE A2.5 Summary of the percentage linkage of codes indicating hybrid conflict actors with other codes

Code Tree		Regular Armed forces	Special Forces	International Organizations	Army
Code frequency		816	33	14	7.887
Conventional operations > Manoeuvres	983	4.78%	3.03%		3.70%
Conventional operations > Military operations	11				0.01%
Conventional operations > Demonstrations of power	1				0.03%
Conventional operations > Defence operations	11	0.12%			0.09%
Conventional operations > Territorial defence	17	0.12%			0.06%
Conventional operations > Armed conflict	36	0.25%			0.06%
Conventional operations > Conventional warfare	3				
Conventional operations > Political factor	1				0.01%
Conventional operations > Economic factor	5				0.03%
Conventional operations > Psychological factor	2				0.03%
Other > Synergy effect	28	0.25%			0.14%
Other > Social media	34				0.05%
Other > Public opinion	26				0.04%
Other > Tactics	331	1.59%	6.06%		1.24%
Other > Tools	278	1.23%			0.89%
Other > Techniques	142	0.37%			0.42%
Prevention	23				0.06%
Response	382	1.84%	6.06%	7.14%	1.26%
Preparation	1,262	5.64%	3.03%	21.43%	4.55%
Counteracting	90	0.12%			0.18%

Little Green Men	Irregular Forces	Separatist Forces	Private Military Companies	Guerrilla Groups	Terrorist Groups	Cybercrime Groups
11	**1**	**7**	**40**	**83**	**554**	**64**
			7.50%		2.71%	
				1.20%	0.36%	
					0.18%	
					0.18%	
			2.50%		0.18%	
			2.50%	2.41%		1.56%
9.09%			10%		1.08%	
			7.50%		0.36%	4.69%
					0.54%	
					0.18%	
			7.50%	1.20%	1.44%	3.13%
		28.57%	45.00%	4.82%	3.97%	1.56%
			2.50%		0.54%	

(*Continued*)

502 Appendix 2: Results of analysis of media reports

TABLE A2.5 (*Continued*) Summary of the percentage linkage of codes indicating hybrid conflict actors with other codes

Code Tree	Regular Armed forces	Special Forces	International Organizations	Army
Code frequency	816	33	14	7.887
Irregular, hybrid, and below conflict threshold operations > Asymmetric operations	1			0.01%
Irregular, hybrid, and below conflict threshold operations > Proxy war	1	0.12%		
Irregular, hybrid, and below conflict threshold operations > Attacks on civilians	8			0.01%
Irregular, hybrid, and below conflict threshold operations > Destabilization	112	0.12%		0.34%
Irregular, hybrid, and below conflict threshold operations > Hybrid warfare	1			0.01%
Irregular, hybrid, and below conflict threshold operations	433	0.98%	14.29%	0.94%
Irregular, hybrid, and below conflict threshold operations > Political factor	1			0.01%
Irregular, hybrid, and below conflict threshold operations > Economic factor	5			0.03%
Irregular, hybrid, and below conflict threshold operations > Psychological factor	2			0.03%
Features of hybrid warfare > Flexibility	40	0.37%		0.14%
Features of hybrid warfare > Impacting political decisions	11			0.01%
Features of hybrid warfare > Complexity	9	0.12%		0.03%
Features of hybrid warfare > Destabilizing actions	113	0.12%		0.34%

Appendix 2: Results of analysis of media reports

Little Green Men	Irregular Forces	Separatist Forces	Private Military Companies	Guerrilla Groups	Terrorist Groups	Cybercrime Groups
11	1	7	40	83	554	64
			5.00%		1.62%	1.56%
		14.29%	7.50%		0.54%	1.56%
			1			
			5.00%		1.62%	1.56%

(*Continued*)

504 Appendix 2: Results of analysis of media reports

TABLE A2.5 (*Continued*)   Summary of the percentage linkage of codes indicating hybrid conflict actors with other codes

Code Tree		Regular Armed forces	Special Forces	International Organizations	Army
Code frequency		816	33	14	7.887
Features of hybrid warfare > Asymmetry	12	0.12%			0.08%
Features of hybrid warfare > New technologies	5				0.03%
Features of hybrid warfare > Below war threshold	7				0.06%
Features of hybrid warfare > Impact on society	1				0.01%
Cybersecurity > Artificial intelligence	17	0.12%			0.11%
Cybersecurity > IT systems	9				0.08%
Cybersecurity > OT systems	45	0.25%			0.10%
Non-military measures > Cyberattacks	47		3.03%		0.13%
Non-military measures > Intimidation	71				0.11%
Non-military measures > Food security	19	0.12%			0.06%
Non-military measures > Humanitarian crises	12				0.05%
Non-military measures > Terrorist activity	10				0.04%
Non-military measures > Diplomatic actions	12				0.05%
Non-military measures > Psychological operations	6				0.03%
Non-military measures > Offensive operations in cyberspace	18				0.09%
Non-military measures > Propaganda	956	1.96%			2.98%
Non-military measures > Information war	15				0.01%

Little Green Men	Irregular Forces	Separatist Forces	Private Military Companies	Guerrilla Groups	Terrorist Groups	Cybercrime Groups
11	1	7	40	83	554	64
			2.50%			
						1.56%
			2.50%			
			2.50%			12.50%
			2.50%		0.18%	
					0.36%	
			2.50%		1.81%	
						4.69%
18.18%			80%	3.61%	4.69%	7.81%
					0.18%	

(*Continued*)

TABLE A2.5 (*Continued*)   Summary of the percentage linkage of codes indicating hybrid conflict actors with other codes

Code Tree		Regular Armed forces	Special Forces	International Organizations	Army
Code frequency		816	33	14	7.887
Non-military measures > Disinformation	177	0.12%			0.48%
Military unconventional operations > Intelligence actions	7				0.04%
Military unconventional operations > Special operations	3				0.01%
Military unconventional operations > Sabotage actions	118	0.61%			0.44%
Military unconventional operations > Diversion actions	230	0.74%	9.09%		0.90%
Military unconventional operations > Land operations	4				0.03%
Domains > Information	3,516	12.50%	3.03%	14.29%	9.40%
Domains > Diplomatic	789	1.10%	6.06%		1.99%
Domains > Political	3,069	7.11%	6.06%	14.29%	7.59%
Domains > Intelligence	1,781	6.00%	9.09%		7.32%
Domains > Legal	1,718	4.29%	3.03%		4.84%
Domains > Public administration	6				0.01%
Domains > Social	340	0.98%			0.85%
Domains > Cultural	212	0.37%	3.03%	7.14%	0.48%
Domains > Military	950	4.04%	6.06%		3.36%
Domains > Economic	783	1.96%			1.80%
Domains > Critical infrastructure	16				0.04%
Domains > Cognitive	10	0.25%			0.06%
Domains > Cybersecurity	8				0.03%
Domains > Cyberspace	38				0.09%
Domains> Space	59	0.12%			0.15%
Domains > Maritime	2,004	6.00%	3.03%	21.43%	5.97%
Domains > Land	1,427	5.76%	3.03%	7.14%	8.15%
Domains > Air	2,473	10.54%	15.15%	7.14%	8.33%

Source: Own work

Little Green Men	Irregular Forces	Separatist Forces	Private Military Companies	Guerrilla Groups	Terrorist Groups	Cybercrime Groups
11	1	7	40	83	554	64
			12.50%		0.54%	4.69%
			2.50%		0.18%	
				1.20%		
			12.50%	6.02%	1.81%	
			17.50%	3.61%	2.53%	1.56%
			100%	13.25%	15.16%	23.44%
		28.57%	12.50%		1.62%	
9.09%	14.29%	75.00%		9.64%	10.11%	9.38%
9.09%	14.29%	100%		12.05%	6.86%	14.06%
27.27%	14.29%	80%		3.61%	5.05%	1.56%
					0.18%	
			7.50%	1.20%	0.90%	3.13%
			5.00%		0.36%	
			30%	2.41%	3.61%	3.13%
			10%		1.26%	
						1.56%
				1.20%	0.36%	6.25%
					0.36%	3.13%
			12.50%	4.82%	3.43%	6.25%
9.09%			30%	6.02%	3.25%	1.56%
9.09%			10%	6.02%	6.32%	

TABLE A4.1 Summary of the percentage linkage of codes indicating hybrid warfare domains with other codes

Code Tree		Informational	Diplomatic	Political	Intelligence	Legal	Public Administration	Social	Cultural
Code Size		3,516	789	3,069	1,781	1,718	6	340	212
Conventional operations > Manoeuvres	983	2.87%	1.14%	1.82%	3.20%	2.21%		1.18%	1.89%
Conventional operations > Military operations	11	0.06%		0.13%		0.12%			
Conventional actions > Demonstrations of force	1			0.03%					
Conventional actions > Defensive actions	11	0.03%		0.03%	0.11%				
Conventional operations > Territorial defence	17	0.06%		0.03%	0.06%	0.12%			
Conventional action > Armed conflict	36	0.11%		0.16%	0.11%	0.12%		0.29%	
Conventional actions > Conventional warfare	3		0.13%		0.06%	0.06%			
Conventional action > Political factor	1			0.03%					
Conventional measures > Economic factor	5			0.03%		0.06%			
Conventional measures > Psychological factor	2	0.03%							
Other > Cascade effect	2								

Military	Economical	Critical Infrastructure	Cognitive	Cognitive	Cybersecurity	Cyberspace	Cosmic	Marine	Land	Air
950	783	16	4	10	8	38	59	2,004	1,427	2,473
3.68%	1.66%			10%			1.69%	6.24%	7.01%	9.75%
									0.07%	0.04%
									0.14%	
0.32%	0.13%									0.12%
	0.64%									0.04%
									0.07%	
									0.07%	0.04%

(*Continued*)

Appendix 2: Results of analysis of media reports

TABLE A4.1 (*Continued*) Summary of the percentage linkage of codes indicating hybrid warfare domains with other codes

Code Tree		Informational	Diplomatic	Political	Intelligence	Legal	Public Administration	Social	Cultural
Code Size		3,516	789	3,069	1,781	1,718	6	340	212
Others > Synergistic effect	28	0.09%		0.26%	0.17%			0.29%	
Other > Social media	34	0.28%	0.13%	0.13%	0.11%	0.12%		0.29%	
Other > Public opinion	26	0.06%		0.29%	0.06%	0.06%		0.29%	
Other > State of war	7	0.03%	0.13%		0.06%	0.17%			
Other > Tactics	331	0.97%	0.38%	0.78%	0.39%	0.17%		0.88%	0.47%
Other > Tools	278	1.31%	1.52%	2.12%	0.67%	0.47%		3.24%	0.47%
Other > Techniques	142	0.20%		0.16%	0.17%	0.17%		0.29%	0.94%
Crisis management > Prevention	23	0.06%	0.13%	0.07%		0.06%			
Crisis management > Response	382	1.14%	1.52%	1.63%	1.18%	1.92%		0.59%	0.94%
Crisis management > Preparation	1,262	3.27%	4.06%	4.11%	4.44%	2.79%	33.33%	7.35%	3.30%
Crisis management > Prevention	90	0.09%	0.63%	0.23%	0.22%	0.76%		1.18%	
Irregular, hybrid, and below the threshold of conflict > Asymmetric operations	1			0.03%					
Irregular, hybrid, and below the threshold of conflict operations > Proxy warfare	1								
Irregular, hybrid, and below the threshold of conflict activities > Attacks on civilians	8				0.06%				

Appendix 2: Results of analysis of media reports

Military	Economical	Critical Infrastructure	Cognitive	Cognitive	Cybersecurity	Cyberspace	Cosmic	Marine	Land	Air
950	783	16	4	10	8	38	59	2,004	1,427	2,473
	0.13%					2.63%	1.69%	0.10%		0.08%
	0.13%							0.15%	0.14%	0.08%
	0.26%									
									0.14%	
1.68%	0.77%					2.63%		0.90%	2.17%	2.02%
2.63%	3.32%					15.79%	5.08%	0.35%	0.91%	0.61%
0.21%	0.77%			10%			3.39%	0.70%	0.98%	0.73%
0.21%								0.10%	0.07%	0.08%
2.32%	1.40%					2.63%	5.08%	1.45%	2.52%	1.78%
4.32%	3.70%	6.25%	25.00%	20%	12.50%	2.63%	6.78%	4.24%	4.41%	4.12%
0.74%	0.51%							0.25%	0.28%	0.20%
	0.13%									0.04%
	0.13%									

(*Continued*)

512   Appendix 2: Results of analysis of media reports

TABLE A4.1 (*Continued*)   Summary of the percentage linkage of codes indicating hybrid warfare domains with other codes

Code Tree		Informational	Diplomatic	Political	Intelligence	Legal	Public Administration	Social	Cultural
Code Size		3,516	789	3,069	1,781	1,718	6	340	212
Irregular, hybrid, and below the threshold of conflict operations > Hybrid operations	1			0.03%					
Irregular, hybrid, and below the threshold of conflict actions > Destabilization	112	0.46%	0.76%	1.11%	0.22%	0.23%		3.24%	
Irregular action, hybrid, and below the threshold of conflict > Hybrid warfare	2					0.12%			
Irregular, hybrid, and below the threshold of conflict > Hybrid conflict	1			0.03%					
Irregular, hybrid, and below the threshold of conflict actions > Reconstruction	433	0.71%	1.77%	2.41%	1.46%	1.75%		3.82%	2.83%
Irregular actions, hybrid, and below conflict threshold > Cascade effect	2								
Irregular, hybrid, and below the threshold of conflict actions > Political factor	1			0.03%					
Irregular, hybrid, and below the threshold of conflict actions > Economic factor	5			0.03%		0.06%			

Military	Economical	Critical Infrastructure	Cognitive	Cognitive	Cybersecurity	Cyberspace	Cosmic	Marine	Land	Air
950	783	16	4	10	8	38	59	2,004	1,427	2,473
1.37%	1.40%							0.30%	0.49%	0.16%
	0.13%									
2.21%	5.36%						3.39%	1.15%	0.84%	0.65%
									0.07%	0.04%
	0.64%									0.04%

(*Continued*)

TABLE A4.1 (*Continued*) Summary of the percentage linkage of codes indicating hybrid warfare domains with other codes

Code Tree		Informational	Diplomatic	Political	Intelligence	Legal	Public Administration	Social	Cultural
Code Size		3,516	789	3,069	1,781	1,718	6	340	212
Irregular, hybrid, and below conflict threshold actions > Psychological factor	2	0.03%							
Features of hybrid warfare > Ambiguity	1			0.03%					
Features of hybrid warfare > Flexibility	40	0.09%		0.03%	0.17%	0.23%		0.29%	
Features of hybrid warfare > Influencing political decisions	11			0.36%	0.06%				0.47%
Features of hybrid warfare > Complexity	9			0.07%					
Features of hybrid warfare > Spectrum of tools	1	0.03%							
Features of hybrid warfare > Grey area	2			0.03%					
Features of hybrid warfare > Destabilizing actions	113	0.46%	0.76%	1.11%	0.22%	0.23%		3.24%	
Features of hybrid warfare > Asymmetry	12	0.03%	0.13%	0.03%				0.59%	
Features of hybrid warfare > New technologies	5			0.03%					
Features of hybrid warfare > Below the threshold of war	7			0.10%	0.06%			0.29%	0.47%
Features of hybrid warfare > Impact on society	1	0.03%							

Military	Economical	Critical Infrastructure	Cognitive	Cognitive	Cybersecurity	Cyberspace	Cosmic	Marine	Land	Air
950	783	16	4	10	8	38	59	2,004	1,427	2,473
									0.07%	
0.53%	0.13%								0.07%	0.28%
	0.26%							0.05%	0.07%	0.08%
0.11%						2.63%		0.05%		0.12%
1.37%	1.53%							0.35%	0.49%	0.16%
0.21%	0.13%								0.07%	
0.21%								0.10%	0.14%	

(*Continued*)

TABLE A4.1 (*Continued*) Summary of the percentage linkage of codes indicating hybrid warfare domains with other codes

Code Tree		Informational	Diplomatic	Political	Intelligence	Legal	Public Administration	Social	Cultural
Code Size		3,516	789	3,069	1,781	1,718	6	340	212
Actors in conventional action > Regular armed forces	816	2.90%	1.14%	1.89%	2.75%	2.04%		2.35%	1.42%
Actors in conventional action > Special forces	33	0.03%	0.25%	0.07%	0.17%	0.06%			0.47%
Actors in conventional activities > International organizations	14	0.06%		0.07%					0.47%
Actors in conventional action > Army	7,887	21.08%	19.90%	19.52%	32.40%	22.24%	16.67%	19.71%	17.92%
Actors in irregular, hybrid, and below pro actions > Green people	11			0.03%	0.06%	0.17%			
Actors in irregular, hybrid, and below pro actions > Private military companies	40	1.99%	0.63%	0.98%	3.03%	1.86%		0.88%	0.94%
Actors in irregular, hybrid, and below pro actions > Guerrilla groups	83	0.31%		0.26%	0.56%	0.17%		0.29%	
Actors in irregular, hybrid, and below pro actions > Terrorist groups	554	2.39%	1.14%	1.82%	2.13%	1.63%	16.67%	1.47%	0.94%
Actors in irregular, hybrid, and below pro actions > Cybercrime groups	64	0.43%		0.20%	0.51%	0.06%		0.59%	
Actors in irregular, hybrid, and below pro actions > Separatist forces	7		0.25%	0.03%	0.06%	0.06%			
Cybersecurity > Artificial intelligence	17	0.11%		0.10%		0.23%			

Appendix 2: Results of analysis of media reports

Military	Economical	Critical Infrastructure	Cognitive	Cognitive	Cybersecurity	Cyberspace	Cosmic	Marine	Land	Air
950	783	16	4	10	8	38	59	2,004	1,427	2,473
3.47%	2.04%			20%			1.69%	2.45%	3.29%	3.48%
0.21%								0.05%	0.07%	0.20%
								0.15%	0.07%	0.04%
27.89%	18.14%	18.75%		50%	25.00%	18.42%	20.34%	23.50%	45.06%	26.57%
									0.07%	0.04%
1.26%	0.51%							0.25%	0.84%	0.16%
0.21%						2.63%		0.20%	0.35%	0.20%
2.11%	0.89%					5.26%	3.39%	0.95%	1.26%	1.42%
0.21%					12.50%	10.53%	3.39%	0.20%	0.07%	
										0.04%

(*Continued*)

518 Appendix 2: Results of analysis of media reports

TABLE A4.1 (*Continued*) Summary of the percentage linkage of codes indicating hybrid warfare domains with other codes

Code Tree		Informational	Diplomatic	Political	Intelligence	Legal	Public Administration	Social	Cultural
Code Size		3,516	789	3,069	1,781	1,718	6	340	212
Cybersecurity > Cyber defence	1			0.03%					
Cybersecurity > Data confidentiality	2	0.06%			0.06%				
Cybersecurity > IT systems	9	0.03%	0.13%		0.06%	0.12%			
Cybersecurity > OT systems	45	0.17%		0.07%		0.17%		0.29%	
Non-military operations > Cyberattacks	47	0.26%	0.38%	0.16%	0.39%	0.23%		0.29%	0.47%
Non-military action > Intimidation	71	0.23%	0.51%	0.33%	0.22%	0.12%		0.29%	
Non-military action > Food security	19		0.38%	0.07%	0.06%			0.29%	
Non-military operations > Humanitarian crises	12	0.06%	0.25%						
Non-military activities > Terrorist activity	10	0.09%		0.07%	0.06%				
Non-military action > Political pressure	1		0.13%	0.03%					
Non-military action > International isolation	1			0.03%					
Non-military actions > Special forces actions	1								
Non-military action > Energy action	0								
Non-military action > Economic action	1			0.03%	0.06%				
Non-military action > Provoking internal conflict	1								
Non-military action > Political action	8	0.03%	0.38%	0.26%		0.06%		0.29%	
Non-military action > Diplomatic action	12	0.06%	1.52%	0.07%	0.06%	0.06%			

Appendix 2: Results of analysis of media reports

Military	Economical	Critical Infrastructure	Cognitive	Cognitive	Cybersecurity	Cyberspace	Cosmic	Marine	Land	Air
950	783	16	4	10	8	38	59	2,004	1,427	2,473
								0.05%		
										0.04%
						2.63%		0.05%		
									0.14%	
0.32%	0.26%	6.25%			37.50%	7.89%		0.10%		0.08%
0.32%	0.13%							0.15%	0.28%	0.08%
0.11%	0.13%							0.10%	0.21%	
0.11%	0.13%							0.10%	0.07%	0.04%
								0.05%		
0.11%										
0.11%	0.13%									
	0.13%									
								0.05%		
0.11%								0.05%	0.14%	0.04%
								0.05%		

(*Continued*)

TABLE A4.1 (*Continued*) Summary of the percentage linkage of codes indicating hybrid warfare domains with other codes

Code Tree		Informational	Diplomatic	Political	Intelligence	Legal	Public Administration	Social	Cultural
Code Size		3,516	789	3,069	1,781	1,718	6	340	212
Non-military operations>Psychological operations	6	0.06%		0.03%	0.06%				
Non-military actions > Offensive actions in cyberspace	18	0.11%	0.13%	0.10%	0.17%	0.12%			0.47%
Non-military action > Propaganda	956	5.38%	2.53%	4.86%	3.03%	2.68%		10.29%	3.77%
Non-military operations > Information warfare	15	0.43%	0.25%	0.20%	0.06%	0.06%		0.29%	
Non-military operations > Disinformation	177	1.85%	1.14%	1.34%	0.90%	0.70%		1.76%	0.94%
Unconventional military operations > Intelligence operations	7	0.09%		0.03%	0.39%				
Unconventional military action > Guerrilla warfare	2	0.03%			0.06%				
Unconventional military operations > Special operations	3	0.03%			0.06%				
Unconventional military operations > Sabotage operations	118	0.74%	0.13%	0.39%	1.29%	0.47%		0.29%	
Unconventional military operations > Diversion operations	230	1.11%	0.63%	0.42%	1.91%	0.29%		1.76%	
Conventional military operations > Maritime operations	2			0.03%					
Conventional military operations > Air operations	1								
Conventional military opera-tions > Land operations	4				0.06%				

Source: Own work

Appendix 2: Results of analysis of media reports

Military	Economical	Critical Infrastructure	Cognitive	Cognitive	Cybersecurity	Cyberspace	Cosmic	Marine	Land	Air
950	783	16	4	10	8	38	59	2,004	1,427	2,473
0.11%										
0.11%					37.50%	2.63%		0.05%		0.08%
4.21%	4.09%		50%	20%	12.50%	10.53%	1.69%	2.10%	1.89%	1.62%
0.21%	0.26%							0.05%		
1.37%	0.26%		25.00%	20%		15.79%	1.69%	0.40%	0.21%	0.20%
										0.04%
0.11%										
										0.04%
0.63%	0.26%							0.25%	0.28%	0.28%
1.05%						2.63%		1.60%	0.49%	0.40%
								0.10%	0.07%	0.04%
										0.04%
									0.28%	

TABLE A4.2 Overview of the interconnectedness of hybrid warfare domains

Code Tree		Information	Diplomatic	Political	Intelligence	Legal	Public Administration	Social	Cultural
Code Size		3,516	789	3,069	1,781	1,718	6	340	212
Domains > Informational	3,516		8.37%	7.40%	18.36%	6.29%	16.67%	9.12%	9.91%
Domains > Diplomatic	789	1.88%		5.28%	3.26%	4.31%		1.76%	3.30%
Domains > Political	3,069	6.46%	20.53%		10.22%	10.94%	16.67%	37.35%	21.23%
Domains > Intelligence	1,781	9.30%	7.35%	5.93%		4.89%		3.24%	2.83%
Domains > Legal	1,718	3.07%	9.38%	6.13%	4.72%			10%	8.02%
Domains > Public administration	6	0.03%		0.03%					
Domains > Social	340	0.88%	0.76%	4.14%	0.62%	1.98%			5.66%
Domains > Cultural	212	0.60%	0.89%	1.47%	0.34%	0.99%		3.53%	
Domains > Military	950	2.59%	4.82%	7.04%	4.10%	3.32%		6.76%	4.72%
Domains > Economic	783	1.42%	4.69%	6.26%	2.30%	2.97%		11.18%	6.60%
Domains > Critical infrastructure	16	0.03%			0.06%				
Domains > Cognitive	4	0.09%		0.03%				0.29%	
Domains > Cognitive	10	0.14%		0.07%	0.17%			0.59%	
Domains > Cybersecurity	8			0.03%					
Domains > Cyberspace	38	0.48%	0.13%	0.16%	0.17%	0.06%		0.59%	
Domains > Space	59	0.14%	0.25%	0.10%	0.11%	0.06%			
Domains > Maritime	2,004	4.72%	4.82%	3.39%	5.90%	5.70%		1.18%	0.94%
Domains > Land	1,427	2.45%	2.53%	2.80%	3.14%	4.95%		2.06%	2.36%
Domains > Air	2,473	7.20%	3.42%	2.93%	5.67%	4.25%		1.18%	2.83%

Source: Own work

Appendix 2: Results of analysis of media reports 523

Military	Economical	Critical Infrastructure	Cognitive	Cognitive	Cybersecurity	Cyberspace	Cosmic	Water	Land	Air
950	783	16	4	10	8	38	59	2,004	1,427	2,473
9.58%	6.39%	6.25%	75.00%	50%		44.74%	8.47%	8.28%	6.03%	10.23%
4.00%	4.73%					2.63%	3.39%	1.90%	1.40%	1.09%
22.74%	24.52%		25.00%	20%	12.50%	13.16%	5.08%	5.19%	6.03%	3.64%
7.68%	5.24%	6.25%		30%		7.89%	3.39%	5.24%	3.92%	4.08%
6.00%	6.51%					2.63%	1.69%	4.89%	5.96%	2.95%
2.42%	4.85%		25.00%	20%		5.26%		0.20%	0.49%	0.16%
1.05%	1.79%							0.10%	0.35%	0.24%
	6.26%		25.00%	10%		7.89%	1.69%	2.89%	2.59%	2.18%
5.16%							1.69%	2.64%	1.47%	0.81%
								0.20%		0.12%
0.11%				20%		2.63%				
0.11%			50%			2.63%			0.14%	
							1.69%	0.10%		
0.32%			25.00%	10%			6.78%	0.20%	0.35%	0.12%
0.11%	0.13%				12.50%	10.53%		0.60%	0.56%	0.53%
6.11%	6.77%	25.00%			25.00%	10.53%	20.34%		14.44%	11.40%
3.89%	2.68%			20%		13.16%	13.56%	10.28%		11.28%
5.68%	2.55%	18.75%				7.89%	22.03%	14.07%	19.55%	

TABLE A4.3 Overview of linkages between conventional and non-military threats

Code Tree		Slavery	Occupation	Chemical Weapons	Unmanned Systems	Weapons of Mass Destruction	Nuclear Attack	Chemical Attack	Manoeuvres	Fire Support	Landmine	Ambushes	Patrols	Special Forces
Number of codes		511	518	14	710	10	10	3	983	9	39	84	231	50
Influencing elections	258	0.98%	1.74%		0.42%		10%		0.81%				0.3%	
Homicides	100	0.59%	0.39%						0.20%					
Mutilations	24		0.19%								2.56%			
Collaboration	27		1.16%						0.10%			2.38%		
Fake news	26				0.28%				0.10%					
Espionage	34	0.20%	0.19%		0.14%				0.10%					2.00%
False accusations	3													
Nepotism	7								0.10%					
Corruption	139	0.39%			0.14%				0.20%					
Attacks on civilians	8													
Internal voltages	2												0.43%	
Intimidation	71	0.20%							0.20%				0.43%	
Psychological operation	2													
Political changes	5													
Social tensions	1				0.14%									
Riots	141	0.20%	1.93%										1.30%	
Protests	258	0.98%	1.74%		0.42%		10%		0.81%				0.43%	
Poverty	8	0.20%												
Price increases	35													
Export ban	21													
Import ban	26								0.10%					
Surveillance	12		0.19%											
Fraud	14	0.20%												
Extortion	2		0.19%											
Extremism	9								0.10%					2.00%
Spreading disinformation	3													
Polarization	16	0.20%											0.43%	
Drinking water supply interruptions	4													

Appendix 2: Results of analysis of media reports

Scouting	Bullets	Artillery	Drones	Tanks	Infantry	Siege	Bombing	Cluster Bomb	Bombshells	Raid	Rockets	Fire	Kinetic
106	3,107	2,930	692	2,521	993	58	501	26	1,320	197	3,969	1,828	45
0.94%	0.23%	0.10%	0.43%	0.16%			0.60%		0.38%		0.18%	0.55%	
	0.03%	0.17%		0.04%			0.20%	3.85%	0.53%		0.10%	0.38%	2.22%
0.94%					0.20%	1.72%							
0.94%				0.04%					0.23%		0.05%	0.11%	
	0.03%	0.03%	0.29%								0.05%	0.16%	
			0.14%						0.08%	0.51%	0.08%	0.05%	
									0.15%				
		0.03%	0.14%	0.16%							0.08%	0.11%	
				0.04%									
	0.13%	0.10%		0.08%					0.30%		0.13%	0.27%	
											0.03%		
				0.04%									
			0.14%										
	0.26%	0.17%		0.20%	0.10%		0.40%		0.30%	1.02%	0.18%	0.38%	
0.94%	0.23%	0.10%	0.43%	0.16%			0.60%		0.38%		0.18%	0.55%	
	0.03%										0.03%		
	0.03%				0.10%							0.11%	
				0.04%							0.05%	0.05%	
	0.03%	0.03%		0.04%					0.08%		0.03%		
		0.03%					0.20%		0.08%		0.03%	0.05%	
										0.51%			
						1.72%							
	0.06%				0.10%						0.03%		
		0.07%		0.08%									
												0.05%	

(*Continued*)

TABLE A4.3 (*Continued*) Overview of linkages between conventional and non-military threats

Code Tree		Slavery	Occupation	Chemical Weapons	Unmanned Systems	Weapons of Mass Destruction	Nuclear Attack	Chemical Attack	Manoeuvres	Fire Support	Landmine	Ambushes	Patrols	Special Forces
Number of codes		511	518	14	710	10	10	3	983	9	39	84	231	50
Power cuts	6													
Persecution	20		0.19%											
Beatings	35	0.20%	0.58%											
Crime	22		0.19%											
Disinformation	177	0.59%	0.19%	7.14%	0.28%				0.20%			2.56%		
Theft	38	0.20%	0.39%		0.14%									
Temperatures too low	28				0.14%				0.20%					
Disease	44	0.39%	0.19%									2.56%	0.43%	
Injuries	54	0.20%	0.77%											
Desire	32		0.39%											
Hunger	130	0.59%	0.77%		0.28%							2.56%	0.43%	
Intimidation	71	0.20%							0.20%				0.43%	
Manipulation	34	0.20%	0.19%											
Humanitarian crisis	13		0.19%											
Rape	196	0.78%	1.74%		0.28%			33.33%	0.61%	11.11%		1.19%	1.30%	2.00%
Abduction	35	1.17%	1.16%											2.00%
Kidnapping	74	0.59%	1.35%				10%		0.31%				0.43%	
Terrorist attacks	147		0.97%		0.14%				0.31%				0.43%	
Terrorism	139		0.97%						0.20%				0.43%	
Destabilizing actions	113	0.39%	0.39%						0.31%				0.43%	
Propaganda	956	4.70%	5.98%		1.83%		10%		3.56%		5.13%	2.38%		
Diplomatic action	12								0.10%					
Psychological warfare	1													
Psyop	12								0.10%					
Psychological operations	6	0.20%	0.19%											
Activities in cyberspace	5													2.00%
Cyberattack	43								0.10%					2.00%
Information warfare	15													

Source: Own work

Appendix 2: Results of analysis of media reports

Scouting	Bullets	Artillery	Drones	Tanks	Infantry	Siege	Bombing	Cluster Bomb	Bombshells	Raid	Rockets	Fire	Kinetic
106	3,107	2,930	692	2,521	993	58	501	26	1,320	197	3,969	1,828	45
											0.03%	0.11%	
	0.03%										0.03%		
	0.03%	0.07%		0.04%	0.10%	1.72%	0.20%		0.15%				2.22%
							0.20%		0.15%		0.03%		
	0.16%	0.24%	0.29%	0.36%	0.10%	1.72%	0.20%		0.61%	0.51%	0.25%	0.44%	2.22%
	0.03%		0.14%	0.08%							0.15%	0.05%	
	0.03%	0.07%	0.14%	0.08%	0.10%				0.15%		0.03%	0.05%	
		0.07%										0.05%	
	0.10%	0.07%		0.04%			0.20%		0.15%		0.05%	0.16%	
	0.06%										0.03%	0.05%	
	0.39%	0.48%	0.29%	0.04%	0.20%		1.00%		0.45%		0.05%	0.38%	
	0.13%	0.10%		0.08%					0.30%		0.13%	0.27%	
				0.04%							0.03%		
							0.40%		0.15%		0.05%		
	0.39%	0.31%	0.29%	0.20%	0.30%		1.00%	3.85%	0.98%		0.25%	0.44%	
0.94%	0.03%	0.03%		0.08%	0.20%		0.20%		0.08%		0.08%	0.22%	
		0.03%		0.08%			0.20%		0.08%		0.03%	0.05%	
2.83%	0.19%	0.07%	0.14%	0.12%	0.20%		0.60%		0.30%	0.51%	0.23%	0.66%	2.22%
2.83%	0.13%	0.03%		0.12%	0.20%		0.60%		0.23%	0.51%	0.13%	0.55%	2.22%
0.94%		0.03%		0.12%	0.20%	1.72%			0.15%		0.15%	0.22%	
2.83%	1.54%	1.33%	1.88%	1.47%	0.91%	5.17%	1.80%		2.42%	4.06%	1.84%	1.31%	6.67%
									0.08%		0.03%		
	0.03%			0.08%	0.20%							0.05%	4.44%
		0.07%		0.08%							0.03%	0.05%	
		0.03%					0.20%		0.15%		0.05%		

TABLE A4.4 Overview of linkages between unconventional military and non-military threats

Code Tree		Torture	Proxy
Number of codes		162	9
Influencing elections	258	1.23%	
Homicides	100	10.49%	
Mutilations	24	1.23%	
Collaboration	27		
Fake news	26		
Espionage	34		
Corruption	139		
Intimidation	71	0.62%	
Riots	141		
Protests	258	1.23%	
Economic sanctions	2		
Polarization	16		
Persecution	20	0.62%	
Beatings	35		
Crime	22		
Disinformation	177	0.62%	
Theft	38		
Temperatures too low	28		
Disease	44		11.11%
Hunger	130		
Intimidation	71	0.62%	
Manipulation	34		11.11%
Rape	196	13.58%	
Abduction	35	0.62%	
Hijacking	74	4.32%	
Terrorist attacks	147	1.85%	
Terrorism	139	1.85%	
Destabilizing actions	113		
Propaganda	956	1.85%	
Psyop	12		11.11%
Psychological operations	6		
Cyberattack	43		

Source: Own work

Appendix 2: Results of analysis of media reports

Private Military Companies	Intelligence Activities	Sabotage Activities	Diversionary Activities
405	7	118	230
0.74%		0.85%	0.43%
0.99%	14.29%	1.69%	0.43%
0.99%			
		1.69%	1.30%
0.25%		0.85%	0.43%
0.49%	14.29%	1.69%	1.30%
			0.43%
0.25%		0.85%	0.87%
1.23%		0.85%	0.87%
0.74%		0.85%	0.43%
0.25%			
			0.87%
0.25%			
0.25%			
1.23%	14.29%	2.54%	2.17%
0.25%			
0.25%			
0.25%			
0.49%			0.43%
0.25%		0.85%	0.87%
		0.85%	
0.74%			
		0.85%	0.43%
0.49%		2.54%	2.17%
0.25%		2.54%	1.74%
0.49%			2.17%
7.90%		14.41%	5.65%
	14.29%	0.85%	0.43%
0.25%		0.85%	0.43%

530 Appendix 2: Results of analysis of media reports

TABLE A4.5 Summary of the connections between the characteristics of hybrid warfare and military and non-military threats

Code Tree		Destabilization	Synergy	Integration of Measures	Subliminality
Number of codes		19	28	1	7
Conventional measures > Slavery	511	5.26%			
Conventional operations > Occupation	518	5.26%			
Conventional operations > Unmanned systems	710		3.57%		
Conventional operations > Manoeuvres	983	5.26%	3.57%		
Conventional operations > Patrols	231				
Conventional actions > Missiles	3,107		3.57%		
Conventional operations > Artillery	2,930		28.57%		
Conventional operations > Drones	692		3.57%		
Conventional actions > Tanks	2,521		21.43%		
Conventional operations > Infantry	993		7.14%		
Conventional actions > Raid	197		3.57%		
Conventional actions > Rockets	3,969			100%	14.29%

Appendix 2: Results of analysis of media reports

Application of New Technologies	Asymmetry	Multidimensionality	Complexity	Ambiguity	Flexibility
5	12	1	9	11	40
					7.50%
	8.33%				2.50%
	8.33%				
2			11.11%	9.09%	17.50%
					15.00%
					5.00%
			22.22%	18.18%	10%
	8.33%				2.50%
					10%

(*Continued*)

Appendix 2: Results of analysis of media reports

TABLE A4.5 (*Continued*) Summary of the connections between the characteristics of hybrid warfare and military and non-military threats

Code Tree		Destabilization	Synergy	Integration of Measures	Subliminality
Conventional actions > Shelling	1,828				
Conventional > Kinetic actions	45		7.14%		
Conventional > Non-kinetic	12		7.14%		
Unconventional measures > Proxy	9				
Unconventional activities > Private military companies	405		3.57%		
Unconventional operations > Sabotage operations	118				28.57%
Unconventional operations > Diversionary operations	230	15.79%	3.57%		28.57%
Non-military action > Influencing elections	258	10.53%			
Non-military activities > Espionage	34	5.26%			
Non-military action > Corruption	139	5.26%	3.57%		
Non-military action > Riots	141	5.26%			
Non-military action > Protests	258	10.53%			

Application of New Technologies	Asymmetry	Multidimensionality	Complexity	Ambiguity	Flexibility
					2.50%
			11.11%		
	8.33%				10%
	8.33%				5.00%
	8.33%				5.00%
				9.09%	
				9.09%	

(*Continued*)

534 Appendix 2: Results of analysis of media reports

TABLE A4.5 (*Continued*) Summary of the connections between the characteristics of hybrid warfare and military and non-military threats

Code Tree	Destabilization	Synergy	Integration of Measures	Subliminality
Non-military action > Economic inequality	1			
Non-military action > Polarization	16	5.26%		
Non-military action > Radicalization	10			
Non-military action > Crime	22			
Non-military operations > Disinformation	177	10.53%		
Non-military action > Famine	130	5.26%		
Non-military operations > Terrorist attacks	147	5.26%		14.29%
Non-military operations > Terrorism	139	5.26%		14.29%
Non-military actions > Destabilizing actions	113	100%		
Non-military action > Propaganda	956	10.53%		14.29%
Non-military action > Cyberattack	43			14.29%

Source: Own work

Application of New Technologies	Asymmetry	Multidimensionality	Complexity	Ambiguity	Flexibility
	8.33%				
	16.67%				
	8.33%				
			11.11%		
			11.11%	9.09%	
20%	8.33%		11.11%	18.18%	
20%	8.33%		11.11%	18.18%	
	16.67%			9.09%	2.50%

TABLE A5.1   Summary of the connections between protective mechanisms and military and non-military threats

Code Three	Civilian Population	Warning Systems	Education	Cybersecurity
Number of codes	3	1	1,859	9
Conventional measures > Aerial strikes	9		0.05%	
Conventional measures > Captivity	511		1.45%	
Conventional measures > Occupation	518		0.65%	
Conventional measures > Unmanned systems	710		1.78%	
Conventional measures > Torpedo attacks	1		0.05%	
Conventional measures > Manoeuvres	983		3.23%	
Conventional measures > Fire support	9		0.05%	
Conventional measures > Land mining	39		0.11%	
Conventional measures > Traps	84		0.27%	
Conventional measures > Patrols	231		0.65%	
Conventional measures > Offensive operations	21		0.05%	
Conventional measures > Fights in the city	6		0.05%	

Border Security	Ensuring Energy Safety	Shelters	Shelter Locations	Medical Assistance	Humanitarian Aid
1	15	29	3	8	31

6.67%

3.23%

(*Continued*)

TABLE A5.1 (*Continued*)   Summary of the connections between protective mechanisms and military and non-military threats

Code Three	Civilian Population	Warning Systems	Education	Cybersecurity
Number of codes	3	1	1,859	9
Conventional measures > Special forces	50		0.43%	
Conventional measures > Medical evacuation	4		0.05%	
Conventional measures > Reconnaissance	106		0.27%	
Conventional measures > Missiles	3,107	100%	7.32%	
Conventional measures > Artillery	2,930		11.14%	
Conventional measures > Drones	692		1.67%	
Conventional measures > Tanks	2,521		12.86%	
Conventional measures > Infantry	993		5.43%	
Conventional measures > Siege	58		0.16%	
Conventional measures > Bombing	501		1.24%	
Conventional measures > Cluster bomb	26		0.11%	
Conventional measures > Bombs	1,320		2.37%	

Appendix 2: Results of analysis of media reports

Border Security	Ensuring Energy Safety	Shelters	Shelter Locations	Medical Assistance	Humanitarian Aid
1	15	29	3	8	31
				12.50%	3.23%
		3.45%			3.23%
					3.23%
					3.23%
		17.24%			
		24.14%	33.33%		3.23%

(*Continued*)

TABLE A5.1 (*Continued*) Summary of the connections between protective mechanisms and military and non-military threats

Code Three		Civilian Population	Warning Systems	Education	Cybersecurity
Number of codes		3	1	1,859	9
Conventional measures > Air raid	197			0.27%	
Conventional measures > Rockets	3,969			11.83%	
Conventional measures > Gunfire	1,828	33,33%		3.50%	
Conventional measures > Kinetic	45			0.05%	
Conventional measures > Non-kinetic	12			0.05%	
Unconventional measures > Tortures	162			0.11%	
Unconventional measures > Private military companies	405			1.83%	
Unconventional measures > Intelligence activities	7			0.05%	
Unconventional measures > Sabotage actions	118			0.32%	
Unconventional measures > Diversionary activities	230			0.91%	
Unconventional measures > Irregular actions	4			0.05%	

Appendix 2: Results of analysis of media reports

Border Security	Ensuring Energy Safety	Shelters	Shelter Locations	Medical Assistance	Humanitarian Aid
1	15	29	3	8	31
		6.90%			
		17.24%			
		6.90%			3.23%
			33.33%		
					3.23%

(*Continued*)

TABLE A5.1 (*Continued*) Summary of the connections between protective mechanisms and military and non-military threats

Code Three	Civilian Population	Warning Systems	Education	Cybersecurity
Number of codes	3	1	1,859	9
Non-military actions > Influencing elections	258		0.54%	
Non-military actions > Killings	100		0.11%	
Non-military actions > Fake news	26		0.05%	
Non-military actions > Nepotism	7		0.05%	
Non-military actions > Corruption	139		0.22%	
Non-military actions > Intimidation	71		0.16%	
Non-military actions > Social discontent	3		0.05%	
Non-military actions > Riots	141	33.33%	0.22%	
Non-military actions > Protests	258		0.54%	
Non-military actions > Poverty	8		0.05%	
Non-military actions > Export ban	21		0.05%	
Non-military actions > Import ban	26			

Appendix 2: Results of analysis of media reports

Border Security	Ensuring Energy Safety	Shelters	Shelter Locations	Medical Assistance	Humanitarian Aid
1	15	29	3	8	31
					3.23%

6.67%

6.45%

3.23%

6.67%

(*Continued*)

544 Appendix 2: Results of analysis of media reports

TABLE A5.1 (*Continued*)   Summary of the connections between protective mechanisms and military and non-military threats

Code Three	Civilian Population	Warning Systems	Education	Cybersecurity
Number of codes	3	1	1,859	9
Non-military actions > Economic sanctions	2		0.05%	
Non-military actions > Polarization	16		0.05%	
Non-military actions > Radicalization	10		0.05%	
Non-military actions > Persecutions	20		0.11%	
Non-military actions > Beatings	35		0.16%	
Non-military actions > Crimes	22		0.05%	
Non-military actions > Disinformation	177		0.27%	
Non-military actions > Theft	38		0.16%	
Non-military actions > Excessively low temperatures	28		0.16%	
Non-military actions > Illness	44		0.11%	
Non-military actions > Injuries	54		0.27%	
Non-military actions > Hunger	130		0.27%	

Border Security	Ensuring Energy Safety	Shelters	Shelter Locations	Medical Assistance	Humanitarian Aid
1	15	29	3	8	31

6.45%

3.23%

3.23%

(*Continued*)

546 Appendix 2: Results of analysis of media reports

TABLE A5.1 (*Continued*) Summary of the connections between protective mechanisms and military and non-military threats

Code Three	Civilian Population	Warning Systems	Education	Cybersecurity
Number of codes	3	1	1,859	9
Non-military actions > Intimidation	71		0.16%	
Non-military actions > Rape	196		0.75%	
Non-military actions > Abduction	35		0.05%	
Non-military actions > Kidnapping	74			
Non-military actions > Terrorist attacks	147		0.27%	
Non-military actions > Terrorism	139		0.27%	
Non-military actions > Destabilizing actions	113		0.11%	
Non-military actions > Propaganda	956		1.94%	11.11%
Non-military actions > Psyop	12		0.05%	
Non-military actions > Cyberattack	43		0.16%	33.33%
Non-military actions > Information warfare	15		0.05%	

Source: Own work

Border Security	Ensuring Energy Safety	Shelters	Shelter Locations	Medical Assistance	Humanitarian Aid
1	15	29	3	8	31
	6.67%				
	6.67%				
100%					
100%					
100%					
		3.45%	33.33%		

Appendix 3: Glossary

Aggression Below the Threshold of Conflict – This refers to military actions whose scope and scale are intentionally limited and maintained by the aggressor at a level that is below a threshold that can be relatively clearly identified as regular, open war. The objective of this sub-threshold aggression is to achieve established goals while simultaneously creating difficulties in reaching a decision-making consensus in international security organizations. This concept highlights active measures used to exert influence without triggering full-scale conflict (Koziej, 2015).

Ambiguous Warfare is characterized as hostile actions aimed at obscuring the situation or undermining the decision-making process of the opponent. The main objective is to confuse or surprise the adversary. These actions fall below the threshold of war and make the use of military force unlikely (Iskandarov, Gawliczek, 2023, pp. 96–107).

Ambiguous warfare applies in situations in which a state or non-state belligerent actor deploys troops and proxies in a deceptive and confusing manner with the intent of achieving political and military effects while obscuring the belligerent's direct participation (Connell, Evans, 2015, p. 1).

Asymmetric Warfare is understood in the literature as a confrontation between parties with significantly different levels of military power, where non-standard weapons and tactics are often used to neutralize the opponent's advantage and exploit its weaknesses. Irregular conflict, on the other hand, is characterized by actions aimed at disrupting or subverting power by forces operating outside conventional military structures (Encykolpedia Bezpieczeństwa Narodowego, 2024).

Compound Warfare is the simultaneous use of a regular or main force and an irregular or guerrilla force against an enemy. In other words, the compound warfare operator increases his military leverage by applying both conventional and unconventional force at the same time (Huber, 2004, p. 1). Compound warfare is a combination of conventional and irregular warfare, including elements of both used to reach the common goal (Huovinen, 2011).

Appendix 3: Glossary

Cyber Warfare involves the actions by a nation-state or international organization to attack and attempt to damage another nation's computers or information networks through, for example, computer viruses or denial-of-service attacks (Definition Cyber Warfare, RAND, 2024).

Equivocal Warfare refers to actions in which the aggressor uses deceptive and misleading strategies to achieve political and military objectives, masking its immediate role. Complex conflict, on the other hand, as described by Thomas M. Huber, is the simultaneous use of regular and irregular forces against an opponent, which increases military superiority through the use of both conventional and irregular methods of warfare. All of these types of war are reflected in the concept of hybrid warfare, which combines a variety of methods and tactics to gain strategic advantage (Popov, 2019).

Forward Defence (FD) defines hybrid warfare as a component of a broad range of state actions, involving diplomatic, informational, military, and economic means (DIME) across various phases of competition, from cooperation to competition, including actions in the "grey zone" up to deterrence and armed conflict. The grey zone, in FD's assessment, is defined as the area of defensive and offensive actions between cooperation and armed conflict, serving as a key element in understanding hybrid warfare (Atlantic Council (2024), Scowcroft Center for Strategy and Security).

Grey Zone Warfare – Grey wars, or conflicts in the grey zone, refer to wars in which groups or entities seek to achieve their objectives while minimizing the extent and scale of actual combat. These conflicts often involve a blend of conventional and unconventional tactics, including political manipulation, economic pressure, and cyber operations, allowing actors to operate below the threshold of open warfare (Wasiuta et al., 2018).

The grey zone is an intermediate space separating competition conducted according to conventional guidelines governing interstate political relations from direct and continuous armed confrontation. Conflicts in the grey zone focus on discrepancies perceived as significant, at least from the aggressor's perspective. The strategies employed are multidimensional and synchronized (hybrid), with their implementation being gradual, typically aimed at achieving long-term objectives (Jordan, 2020, pp. 1–24).

Guerrilla Warfare is typically an integral part of that longer, protracted struggle. However, guerrilla warfare in and of itself is merely a method which may be pursued by insurgents or state actors as a part of more traditional warfare. Many insurgencies rely not only on guerrilla tactics but also on clandestine, small-scale, armed operations, or terrorism, and indeed may be too weak to engage in guerrilla warfare at all until late in their development. And the contemporary, largely urban insurgencies in Iraq and Afghanistan often rely on a set of battlefield tactics foreign to traditional guerrilla warfare.

Aspects of tactics and territory also distinguish insurgency from civil war. One of insurgency's defining characteristics is the insurgent's unwillingness to engage in a direct military conflict with his opponent. Thus, while insurgencies seek to control territory, their control remains fluid. Civil war, however, is characterized by two subnational parties, each in control of a specific portion of territory, engaging in conventional conflict. As Galula says, "Civil War soon resembles an ordinary international war except that the opponents are fellow citizens." As insurgencies gain strength and firmer control over territory, their conflict may transform into a civil war – but this is by no means necessarily so (Elsevier, 2024).

Hybrid Actions can be a combination of selected forms of symmetric and asymmetric warfare, where the acting forces conduct conventional military operations while simultaneously making determined attempts to gain control over the local population in the area of combat operations by ensuring security and stability (Russel, 2002, pp. 120–122; McCuen, 2008, p. 108).

Information Warfare is an operation conducted in order to gain an information advantage over the opponent. It consists in controlling one's own information space, protecting access to one's own information, while acquiring and using the opponent's information, destroying their information systems and disrupting the information flow. Information warfare is not a new phenomenon, yet it contains innovative elements as the effect of technological development, which results in information being disseminated faster and on a larger scale (deepportal.hq.nato.int, 2024).

Irregular Warfare – The Pentagon defines irregular warfare as a campaign to secure or coerce the attitudes of states or other groups through indirect, non-assignable, or asymmetric actions. In practice this means actions that fall below the level of traditional armed conflict between nation-states. It is an approach to war that emphasizes the importance of local partnerships and gaining legitimacy and influence among local populations rather than occupying or controlling territory (Noyes, Egel, 2023; Summary of the Irregular Warfare Annex to the National Defense Strategy, 2020).

Multinational Capability Development Campaign (MCDC) – The MCDC definition emphasizes that hybrid warfare employs the synchronized use of multiple instruments of power, tailored to the specific weaknesses of the opponent. These actions encompass the full spectrum of social functions and aim to achieve synergistic effects. Such a strategy has far-reaching impacts on societies, national governments, and international institutions, necessitating integrated responses and adaptations to changing conditions (MCDC, 2019).

New Generation Warfare (Russian Origin) – This term refers to technologically advanced military operations that integrate modern information technologies with the use of diverse, highly precise weapon systems and robotic control systems. Key changes in the "rules of war" include the increasing role of non-military options in achieving political and strategic objectives, as well as the blurring of distinctions between strategic, operational, and tactical actions, and between offense and defence. The use of remote engagement in combat operations and attacking enemy targets on their territory directly from a distance become a primary tactic (Chekinov, Bogdanov, 2013).

Non-Linear Warfare – The concept of "non-linear" describes that the conflict does not have clear front lines or district friendly/enemy areas. Non-linear warfare relies on the subversion and division of the enemy's social and political structure allowing the aggressor to do their will by any means, not just brute force. The idea of NLW comes from the approach that it has no bounds and sometimes functions with limited planning, thus allowing a state to exploit an opportunity. Non-linear warfare employs many measures that would not seem like warfare although the goal, as in all war, is to force the enemy to do your will. In NLW, instead of tanks doing all the work, propaganda, political and social agitators, and cyberattacks do most of the forcing. This does not mean kinetic action or hard tactics remain unutilized (Schnaufer, 2017, pp. 17–31).

Political Warfare is the logical application of Clausewitz's doctrine in times of peace. In broadest definition, political warfare is the employment of all the means at a nation's command, short of war, to achieve its national objectives. Such operations range from such overt actions as political alliances, economic measures, and white propaganda to such covert operations as clandestine support of friendly foreign elements, black psychological warfare, and even encouragement of underground resistance in hostile states (Theohary, Weiss, 2023).

Proxy War is a military conflict in which one or more third parties directly or indirectly support one or more state or non-state combatants in an effort to influence the conflict's outcome and thereby to advance their own strategic interests or to undermine those of their opponents. Third parties in a proxy war do not participate in the actual fighting to any significant extent, if at all. Proxy wars enable major powers to avoid direct confrontation with each other as they compete for influence and resources. Direct means of support by third parties consist of military aid and training, economic assistance, and sometimes limited military operations with surrogate forces. Indirect means of support have included blockades, sanctions, trade embargoes, and other strategies designed to thwart a rival's ambitions (Baugh, 2024).

Proxy Warfare – Proxy wars are a phenomenon richly represented in the history of armed conflicts. Their character and specificity are defined not by the method of conducting military operations, but by the instrumentalization of the conflict (war) for the purposes of states that are not actively involved. This instrumentalization can take various forms. In every case, however, the scale and nature of this instrumentalization are determined by the interests and political goals of the "third party" (Bryjka, 2021).

Rand Corporation – Andrew Radin at the Rand Corporation notes that hybrid warfare is described as a set of covert or denied actions, supported by conventional or nuclear armed forces, aimed at influencing the domestic politics of target states. He emphasizes that hybrid warfare significantly impacts the internal politics of these countries, highlighting the role of the population in resisting or responding to Russian actions (Radin, 2017).

Reflexive Control (Russian Origin) – Reflexive control can be understood in two ways. In the first sense, it refers to the art of manipulating individuals and human communities, while in the second, it is seen as a specific method of social control. Broadly speaking, reflexive control can be defined as informational influence on the awareness and will of subjects. These subjects can include individuals as well as human communities such as families, groups, nations, societies, and civilizations. This concept helps to understand not only the behaviour of an adversary but also their ability to perceive themselves and other entities, including those attempting to gain control over their actions. Other models, such as behavioural or psychoanalytic ones, can provide insights into the rival's dynamics (Kublik, 2019, pp. 23–32).

Royal United Services Institute (RUSI) – In the context of this definition, the Royal United Services Institute (RUSI) adds that hybrid warfare is a strategy that integrates conventional, irregular, cyber, and subversive actions, blurring the formal distinction between war and peace. This perspective emphasizes the adaptability and multidimensionality of hybrid warfare, aiming to utilize the full spectrum of available means to achieve strategic advantage, often through actions that are covert or difficult to attribute clearly (Meath Baker, 2017).

Unlimited War (Chinese Origin) – The term "unlimited war" generally refers to a type of conflict in which there are no clear limitations or boundaries on the objectives' scope or duration of the war. In an unlimited war, both sides may be willing to use any means necessary to achieve their goals, which can result in high levels of destruction, casualties, and suffering. This concept emphasizes total commitment and the potential for conflicts to escalate beyond traditional constraints, affecting not only military targets but also civilian populations and infrastructure (Weisiger, 2013).

REFERENCES

Atlantic Council (2024) Forward Defense. Available at: https://www. atlanticcouncil.org/programs/scowcroft-center-for-strategy-and-security/forward-defense/ (Accessed: 17 March 2025).

Baugh, L.S., (2024), Proxy war, Encyclopedia Britannica, 5 September. Available at: https://www.britannica.com/topic/proxy-war. Accessed: 23 June 2024.

Bryjka, F., (2021), Wojny Zastępcze. Warsaw: Polski Instytut Spraw Międzynarodowych. Available at: https://www.researchgate.net/publication/349956085_WOJNY_ZASTEPCZE. Accessed: 16 June 2024.

Chekinov, S. G., and Bogdanov, S. A., (2013), The Nature and Content of a New Generation War. Military Thought (4). Available at:

https://www.semanticscholar.org/paper/The-Nature-and-Content-of-a-New-Generation-War-Chekinov-Bogdanov/c8874593b1860de12 fa40dadcae8e96861de8ebd, Accessed: 16 May 2024.

Elsevier (2024), Guerrilla warfare – definition, ScienceDirect. Available at: https://www.sciencedirect.com/topics/social-sciences/guerrilla-warfare#definition, Accessed: 17 March 2025.

Encyclopedia Bezpieczeństwa Narodowego, Itrich-Drabrek J., Misuk A., Mitkov Sz., and Bryczek-Wróblel P., (red.), (2024), Elipsa, Warszawa, Available at: https://encyklopedia.revite.pl. Accessed: 11 May 2024.

Huber, Thomas M., (2004), Compound Warfare: A Conceptual Framework. Stockton, CA: University of the Pacific.

Huovinen, P. (2011) Hybrid Warfare – Just a Twist of Compound Warfare? Views on warfare from the United States Armed Forces perspective. National Defence University, Department of Military

History, Senior Staff Officer Course 63, Finnish Army. Available at: https://www.doria.fi/bitstream/handle/10024/74215/E4081_HuovinenKPO_EUK63.pdf Accessed: 17 March 2025).

Iskandarov, K., and Gawliczek, P., (2023), Hybrid Warfare as a New Type of War. The Evolution of Its Conceptual Construct. In The Russian Federation and International Security. Difin Publishing House. Available at: https://www.researchgate.net/publication/373118996_HYBRID_WARFARE_AS_A_NEW_TYPE_OF_WAR_THE_EVOLUTION_OF_ITS_CONCEPTUAL_CONSTRUCT#fullTextFileContent(PDF). Accessed: 27 June 2024.

Jordan, J., (2020), International Competition Below the Threshold of War: Toward a Theory of Gray Zone Conflict, Journal of Strategic Security, vol. 14, no. 1, 2020, JSTOR, Available at: https://www.jstor.org/stable/26999974?seq=1 Accessed 17 Mar. 2025

Koziej, S. (2015), Sub-threshold aggression, Available at: https://koziej.pl/wp-content/uploads/2015/11/Agresja-podprogowa.pdf, Accessed 16 April 2024

Kublik, E., (2019), Strategic Meaning of Reflexive Control Methods in the CO. Kultura Bezpieczeństwa, No. 33. DOI: 10.5604/01.3001.0013.1944. Accessed: 19 June 2024.

MCDC Countering Hybrid Warfare Project, (2019), Countering Hybrid Warfare. Available at: https://assets.publishing.service.gov.uk/media/5c8141e2e5274a2a51ac0b34/concepts_mcdc_countering_hybrid_warfare.pdf. Accessed: 11 June 2024.

McCuen, J.J., (2008), Hybrid Wars. Military Review, no. 2. Accessed: 25 June 2024.

MCDC Countering Hybrid Warfare Project, (2019), Countering Hybrid Warfare. Available at: https://assets.publishing.service.gov.uk/media/5c8141e2e5274a2a51ac0b34/concepts_mcdc_countering_hybrid_warfare.pdf, Accessed: 11 June 2024.

Meath Baker, C., (2017), 'Hybrid Warfare in the Middle East: We Must Do Better', RUSI, 7 March. Available at: https://www.rusi.org/explore-our-research/publications/commentary/hybrid-warfare-middle-east-we-must-do-better. Accessed: 12 June 2024.

NATO (2020) Information Warfare, DEEP Portal, NATO. Available at: https://www.nato.int/nato_static_fl2014/assets/pdf/2020/5/pdf/2005-deepportal4-information-warfare.pdf Accessed: 17 March 2025.

Noyes, A., Egel, D. (2023) Winning the Irregular World War, RAND Corporation. Available at: https://www.rand.org/pubs/commentary/2023/11/winning-the-irregular-world-war.html, Accessed: 17 March 2025.

Popov, V., (2019), Robust Civil-Military Relations—One of the Most Powerful Tools to Counteract Russian Hybrid Warfare: The Case of Ukraine. March. Available at: https://apps.dtic.mil/sti/pdfs/AD1073658.pdf (PDF). Accessed: 24 May 2024.

Radin, A., (2017), Hybrid Warfare in the Baltics: Threats and Potential Responses. RAND Corporation. Available at: https://www.rand.org/t/RR1577. Accessed: 13 June 2024.

RAND Corporation (2024) Cyber warfare. Available at: https://www.rand.org/topics/cyber-warfare.html (Accessed: 17 March 2025).

Russel J., Asymmetric Warfare, [w:] P. David (red.), The Big Issue: Command and Combat in the Information Age, SCSI, Shrivenham 2002, Available at: http://www.dodccrp.org/files/Potts_Big_Issue.pdf. Accessed: 17 March 2025.

Schnaufer, Tad A. II., (2017), Redefining Hybrid Warfare: Russia's Non-linear War against the West." Journal of Strategic Security 10, no. 1, Available at: https://digitalcommons.usf.edu/jss/vol10/iss1/3/, Accessed: 17 March 2025.

Theohary, C.A. and Weiss, M.A. (2023), What Is "Political Warfare"', Congressional Research Service Report IF11127. Available at: https://www.congress.gov/crs-product/IF11127, Accessed: 17 March 2025.

U.S. Department of Defense (2020) Irregular Warfare Annex to the National Defense Strategy – Summary. Available at: https://media.defense.gov/2020/Oct/02/2002510472/-1/-1/0/Irregular-Warfare-Annex-to-the-National-Defense-Strategy-Summary.PDF, Accessed: 17 March 2025.

Wasiuta, O., Klepka, R., Kopeć, R. (2018), Niemilitarne metody prowadzenia wojny hybrydowej. Vademecum bezpieczeństwa. Wydawnictwo Libron, Kraków.

Weisiger, A., (2013), Logics of War: Explanations for Limited and Unlimited Conflicts. Ithaca and London: Cornell University Press. Available at: https://library.oapen.org/bitstream/handle/20.500.12657/30789/642713.pdf?sequence=1&isAllowed=y. Accessed: 18 June 2024.

Appendix 4: Interview questionnaire

RESPONSES PROVIDED BY EXPERT 1

Dear Sir,

In our pursuit of a better understanding and the development of strategies for counteracting and protecting the civilian population from the consequences of hybrid conflicts, I respectfully request your expert answers to questions aimed at delving into the nature of hybrid conflicts, identifying the main threats to the civilian population, and discussing potential protection strategies. These questions relate to both the theoretical characterization and definition of hybrid conflicts, as well as the practical aspects of protection against their effects. Our goal is to gain an insightful perspective on hybrid conflict issues from an expert viewpoint, which will enhance our understanding of the challenges and possible directions for action.

Below, I present a set of questions whose answers will assist us in developing a comprehensive picture of the situation and potential solutions:

I. Characterization of hybrid conflicts
1. Could you elaborate on what exactly you understand by the term "hybrid conflicts/wars" and why are they so difficult to define unambiguously?

    These are conflicts fought by an array of different means – from military (invasion) to economic (using a key dependency such as gas or water to force political decisions detrimental to a state's interest – Moldova) to political (influence over election) to criminal (for example, strategic corruption – Russia in Ukraine), as well as cyber (attacks on infrastructure – Baltic states). They are often networked and incorporate a significant element of disinformation. To be clear, I do not consider them to be a new form of warfare – using a variety of means has always been a key element of state strategy.

The key difficulty I see in defining hybrid conflicts is the threshold beyond which they become wars – there is no defined threshold. Hybrid actions are also by design difficult to attribute with reasonable certainty, making it more difficult to ascertain who the adversary is.

2. **In your opinion, what are the main features of hybrid warfare, and how do they affect the security of the civilian population?**

   The key variable is uncertainty and a lack of clarity: sub-threshold activities create uncertainty as to whether we're in a state of peace or war, and whether war is just around the corner. This can be more destabilizing that an objectively worse, but clear situation, such as a declared war, as it might be easier to identify means of coping. This in turn can increase the perceptions of insecurity.

3. **What do you consider the main types of actions/tactics involved in hybrid conflicts? Could you identify these types and provide examples?**

   See response to Q1, I included it there.

4. **Please indicate, in your assessment, the actors in hybrid wars and describe their impact on the dynamics and effectiveness of hybrid conflicts.**

   Key actors include governments and government agencies and the armed forces which can either orchestrate or directly perform actions related to hybrid warfare. Their involvement is likely to increase effectiveness along the military and political realms while decreasing deniability. Alongside them, a variety of actors can be involved, from private companies to whole structures that are theoretically independent yet practically tied to governing structures – such as Gazprom or the Wagner Group. The latter might have a more freedom of manoeuvre but fewer means at their disposal, but their effectiveness depends on their goals: while they might not be able to take or hold territory the way a military unit would, they can sow chaos and create instability.

II. **Identification and analysis of threats to the civilian population**

   1. **In your opinion, what are the threats to the civilian population in the context of hybrid conflicts? Please rank the types of threats hierarchically.**

      a. *Mental health issues related to a lack of stability, certainty, and predictability*

558   Appendix 4: Interview questionnaire

   b. *Social and political consequences, including stunted national economic development and an ineffective political system*
   c. *Fraying of social ties and cohesiveness*
   d. *Health and well-being issues related to limited provision of healthcare that goes with limited national economic development*
   e. *Threats of physical harm*

2. **Could you indicate what you believe are the current effects of hybrid threats?**

   All of the above are occurring in different areas (a and c in Ukraine, b and c in Moldova, d in Moldova, e in Ukraine).

3. **What do you think are the critical consequences of threats to the civilian population in hybrid wars?**

   I think the answer to the above includes both threats and consequences. The overall consequence is a deterioration of the living environment and the overall feeling of security and stability, which then translates into worse social, economic, and political outcomes, such as increased polarization. It can also result in the deterioration of the international security environment.

4. **Which of the following effects do you consider critical for the civilian population in hybrid warfare:**

   a. *hunger*
   b. *thirst*
   c. *injuries*
   d. *Illnesses*
   e. *exposure to extreme heat*
   f. *exposure to extreme cold*
   g. *all of the above*

   All of the above, but these are primarily true at the more militarized end of hybrid warfare and less likely to happen (though not impossible, especially if attacks on infrastructure are included) if sub-threshold, non-military means are being used.

5. **How do you think attacks on critical infrastructure affect the daily lives of the civilian population?**

   This question would be much better answered through a literature review than expert opinions – there's a lot of evidence out there about these impacts. Briefly, it decreases civilians' access to key services, including provision of electricity, heat, and healthcare, which brings about both short- and long-term negative effects (worse health outcomes, more limited educational opportunities for children, and mental health consequences). In the medium to long term, it can decrease trust in government and fray social cohesion.

6. **Can and how do informational actions in hybrid warfare, in your opinion, destabilize the personal security of civilians or affect it?**

    Disinformation, especially at the local/tactical level, can have a direct negative impact on protection outcomes, especially if it distorts information about available services, safe evacuation routes, and military movements and behaviour vis-à-vis civilians. For a detailed analysis, please see https:// civiliansinconflict.org/wp-content/uploads/2023/11/CIVIC_ Disinformation_Report.pdf

7. **In your opinion, how do cyber actions – aimed directly at information infrastructure and at the civilian population – impact societies and everyday life today?**

    In some cases, they can increase insecurity and societal divisions as well as preferences for international alliances (disinformation in African states, for example), but their impact varies very widely in different contexts.

III. **Protection of the population in hybrid conflicts**

1. **Do you believe there is a protection system for the population in hybrid wars?**

    There are attempts at systems, such as NATO's Comprehensive Approach. In most states, the "systems" are a jigsaw puzzle of different approaches, from military preparedness to civil defence to infrastructure protection and educational programmes aimed at combatting disinformation. However, beyond the Comprehensive Approach, I am not aware of approaches being explicitly labelled as protection systems against hybrid wars.

2. **Do you believe any system currently provides effective protection for the civilian population?**

    No, there are approaches that provide some protection from some aspects of hybrid warfare, but there is no "system" and most approaches are imperfect.

3. **Do you believe there is a protection system for information infrastructure in hybrid wars?**

    Again, I am not aware of a "system." There are different approaches applied by a variety of institutions, including support for independent journalism, education (especially in assessing the validity of information and teaching critical approaches), or specific initiatives aimed at analysing and de-bunking disinformation (EU vs Disinfo website). They are, however, decentralized/fragmented and don'tnecessarily address the entirety of hybrid threats/disinformation.

4. **Do you believe any protection system for information infrastructure currently offers effective protection, including considering the impact on the civilian population?**

   No. A degree of protection can be offered, but it's unlikely to be fully effective.

5. **In your opinion, what factors need to be met for the effectiveness of a system in protecting the civilian population in hybrid wars?**

   I don't think it's possible to entirely protect any population against hybrid war, mostly because it's impossible to predict what means will be used and against whom. However, any remotely effective approach will need to be adaptable and responsive, as hybrid approaches can evolve quickly.

6. **What do you believe are the critical areas that ensure the safety of civilians in hybrid wars?**

   Protection of infrastructure and countering disinformation. These will enable other approaches.

7. **In which areas, in your opinion, should civilians be prepared in the context of hybrid warfare?**

   If you mean geographical areas, then anywhere there is a contest for influence or resources. Africa and Eastern Europe are particularly exposed, but so are Western nations, especially to hybrid means short of open warfare.

Thank you for sharing your expert knowledge and insights. Your contribution is invaluable to our study on hybrid conflicts and will significantly contribute to our efforts to understand the challenges and develop effective strategies for protecting the civilian population.

With respect
Wojciech Wróblewski PhD
Internal Security Institute
Fire University
wwroblewski@apoz.edu.pl
Michał Wiśniewski PhD Eng.
Faculty of Management
Warsaw University of Technology
michal.wsiniewski@pw.edu.pl
Jędrzej Bieniasz PhD
Assistant Professor @ Cybersecurity Division, Institute of Telecommunications, FEIT (WEiTI), WUT, Poland
Head @ Cybersecurity Center, WUT, Poland
Warsaw University of Technology
jedrzej.bieniasz@pw.edu.pl

RESPONSES PROVIDED BY EXPERT 2

Dear Sir,

In our pursuit of a better understanding and the development of strategies for counteracting and protecting the civilian population from the consequences of hybrid conflicts, I respectfully request your expert answers to questions aimed at delving into the nature of hybrid conflicts, identifying the main threats to the civilian population, and discussing potential protection strategies. These questions relate to both the theoretical characterization and definition of hybrid conflicts, as well as the practical aspects of protection against their effects. Our goal is to gain an insightful perspective on hybrid conflict issues from an expert viewpoint, which will enhance our understanding of the challenges and possible directions for action.

Below, I present a set of questions whose answers will assist us in developing a comprehensive picture of the situation and potential solutions:

I. Characterization of hybrid conflicts

1. **Could you elaborate on what exactly you understand by the term "hybrid conflicts/wars" and why are they so difficult to define unambiguously?**

    Hybrid conflict is a form of conduct that can be placed somewhere on the spectrum between war and peace. It is an action of a nature outside the patterns of traditional military action.

    Hybrid conflict is used by states, quasi-state organizations, legitimate international organizations, terrorist or criminal organizations, or interest groups (with a common political, social, or moral interest occurring online or physically) to create internal or external policy (in other states or regions of the world).

    The above actors can lead to social or political destabilization, involving the incitement of social unrest and conflicts aimed at changing the attitudes of social groups towards specific issues. Such changes in perceptions of reality may be stirred up in order to create or reinforce social unrest that can affect the political scene and may even lead to regime change or subversion.

560 Appendix 4: Interview questionnaire

In the simplest terms, the aim of hybrid warfare is to gather information that can be used to achieve predetermined goals. Such an abstract approach, however, causes a problem in bringing the subject matter into depth for those who are interested in it. Thus, the difficulty in defining hybrid wars precisely is partly due to their nature and the fact that it is a phenomenon that is very difficult to grasp unambiguously. In addition, the ever-changing geopolitical situation together with very rapidly modernizing tools (due to technological developments) do not make this task any easier.

2. **In your opinion, what are the main features of hybrid warfare, and how do they affect the security of the civilian population?**

Hybrid warfare is characterized by the willingness of an external actor to effect change without the use of directly military tactics and excluding the direct involvement of military resources. One aspect of hybrid warfare is the multiplicity and dispersion of actors actively engaged in it. This causes a problem in the way in which unwanted actions by external actors can be countered. In a way, hybrid warfare is an extension of tactics native to proxy wars (fought through intermediaries), where parties not directly involved in the conflict support one of the parties militarily, financially, or with their knowledge.

Often the results of hybrid warfare are felt more in the geopolitical space, e.g. due to a change in relations between states (political aspect). Nevertheless, part of the effort is aimed at destabilizing the social situation (social aspect), as in the case of directly or indirectly influencing election results. In addition, there is also the possibility of indirectly influencing the financial situation of the civilian population (financial aspect), e.g. by influencing stock market prices or disrupting stock market activities, which may have further repercussions on unemployment rates, investment opportunities, or raising capital on international markets.

3. **What do you consider the main types of actions/tactics involved in hybrid conflicts? Could you identify these types and provide examples?**

The most important activities are carried out to create disruption – more generally in the (1) social, (2) political, (3) financial, (4) military, (5) critical infrastructure, and more specifically in the (6) health system, (7) justice system, (8) banking system, (9) transport and logistics in the broad sense, and (10) IT infrastructure. This is not a closed catalogue. Depending on the purpose of a particular action, the utility of specific elements of the state or society may be most appropriate to achieve a given objective. For example, the efficient use of religious views may foster changes in legislation that may lead to protests and social unrest.

As has already been mentioned, some of the activities may be aimed at creating social unrest; increasing social divisions and undermining trust in particular social groups; or influencing the results of an election or referendum. In addition, it can also be subsidizing organizations or entities that can influence the above activities, or hacking and using data for the above purposes (through controlled leaks of personal data and information in general, or blackmailing decision-makers). It can also be all activities aimed at reducing military capabilities (e.g. by undermining confidence in decision-makers of states wishing to purchase military systems or equipment).

4. **Please indicate, in your assessment, the actors in hybrid wars and describe their impact on the dynamics and effectiveness of hybrid conflicts.**

   As was mentioned at the beginning, some of the main actors actively involved in hybrid warfare are (1) states. Having statehood has a lot of advantages, one of which is having resources and people who can use these resources creatively. Using their military, secret services, and other resources, states can influence the economic, social, and political situation of other states (not necessarily neighbouring states).

   Other actors may be (2) quasi-state organizations (or parastatals) fighting either for territory or for their international recognition as having full independence and self-determination. Further potential actors are (3) legitimate international organizations, (4) terrorist organizations, or (5) criminal organizations, which may act independently raising funds for their activities or may be supported by other actors. Another example is (6) interest groups, which may be formalized or not necessarily (e.g. ad hoc in nature). They may also direct their activity online or in a stationary form. Such groups may have a common political, social, or moral interest to influence internal or external policy-making in their countries of normal activity or in other regions of the world.

564   Appendix 4: Interview questionnaire

II. Identification and analysis of threats to the civilian population

1. **In your opinion, what are the threats to the civilian population in the context of hybrid conflicts? Please rank the types of threats hierarchically.**

   There are quite a number of potential risks associated with the occurrence of hybrid wars and their potential wide-ranging consequences for civilian populations. This is due, among other things, to the multi-faceted and intricate nature of modern social systems and the way they operate. The more developed economies of the world rely on complex systems and technologically advanced elements that are inextricably linked. Dysfunction in one of these inter-dependent elements causes disruption, obstruction, or inefficiency in other systems. Thus, for example, a disruption or collapse of the banking system can cause an inability to check or use one's own funds (either by withdrawing them directly or using non-cash settlements) or a disruption in communication between banks (e.g. in the SWIFT system) can affect problems with incoming and outgoing transfers. Similarly, disconnection from IT systems can have far-reaching consequences for the functioning of citizens. If there is a collapse in electricity or gas transmission systems as a result of external actors, citizens will feel it immediately. The situation is similar with disruptions to, for example, rail transport. The same could be true if there is a disruption in the availability of systems facilitating the location of objects such as GPS or Galileo, which would affect the ability to travel without problems.

   All of the above situations cause difficulties and a kind of inconvenience in everyday life. However, it is difficult to prioritize the magnitude of these risks.

2. **Could you indicate what you believe are the current effects of hybrid threats?**

   The answer in para. 1.

3. **What do you think are the critical consequences of threats to the civilian population in hybrid wars?**

   The consequences resulting from hybrid warfare for the civilian population are complex. They range from physical to livelihood and psychological. It should be noted that there are short-term consequences such as famine as well as long-term consequences such as livelihood instability. Nevertheless, the hybrid nature of war leaves this catalogue open.

Appendix 4: Interview questionnaire 565

4. **Which of the following effects do you consider critical for the civilian population in hybrid warfare:**
    a. *hunger*
    b. *thirst*
    c. *injuries*
    d. *Illnesses*
    e. *exposure to extreme heat*
    f. *exposure to extreme cold*
    g. *all of the above*

    All the above-mentioned effects. Although they apply more to the military stage they can also occur below the threshold of war.

5. **How do you think attacks on critical infrastructure affect the daily lives of the civilian population?**

    At an institutional level, an attack on the health service results in an inability to use its services. It does not require much imagination to realize how important a part of modern existence the health service is. Conversely, attacks on cultural institutions can cause public confusion and a loss of trust in those institutions that have not taken sufficient measures to protect their resources. At times, these types of events can serve as perfect surrogate topics acting as a distraction from other social or political problems.

    Another example concerns undersea cables. Potentially, gaining access to undersea fibre-optic cables can cause direct and indirect risks to citizens. Other critical infrastructure (its location, role, and access) may be at risk if the transmitted information is accessed. Disruption of such fibre-optic cables may threaten total or partial inability to transmit and receive information. In addition, depending on the role such cables play (civilian or military), the lives and health of citizens may be at risk if their integrity is compromised and information (e.g. location and geolocation data of critical or military infrastructure) is obtained.

6. **Can and how do informational actions in hybrid warfare, in your opinion, destabilize the personal security of civilians or affect it?**

    The personal security of civilians may be at risk in the case of electronic warfare aimed at disrupting the transmission of information or its acquisition. The same is true with regard to propaganda activity targeting a particular section of society. Various actors may wish to take advantage of some already existing social divisions in this regard and seek only to amplify them. This can be done using a process known in English as scapegoating. This is a phenomenon that accompanies crises and major social change. In this process, a person, individuals, or specific social groups are identified as a threat to social integrity. A process of stigmatization occurs in this respect and these persons or groups are identified as socially undesirable or threatening. Due to the strong amplification of negative emotions directed at these very people, their safety is at risk, as they may become the target of direct attacks that threaten their health and life.

7. **In your opinion, how do cyber actions – aimed directly at information infrastructure and directly at the civilian population – impact societies and everyday life today?**

Given the fast-changing reality and the rapid development of tools used for cybercrime, it is extremely difficult to predict the direction of these threats.

One of the most obvious influences on the civilian population in the current situation is phishing emails designed to access and steal sensitive information (e.g. financial, including access to online banking). In this regard, there is a need to inform the population in the public space about the threats that are occurring and how to protect themselves against them. This is necessary due to the increasing level of sophistication with which civilians are attempting to deceive themselves. This is a direct result of the continuous improvement in software and the resulting cyber threats. These threats are not going to disappear and it is therefore necessary to raise awareness among citizens so that they are best prepared and know how to react in the face of these threats and who to inform if they do occur.

III. **Protection of the population in hybrid conflicts**

1. **Do you believe there is a protection system for the population in hybrid wars?**

At the current stage of technology development and accessibility, the number and frequency of hybrid threats have increased. From a geopolitical point of view, due to, among other things, the effects of globalization, the possibilities of influencing almost every region of the world have expanded and the need for global actors to be active influencing as many places in this geopolitical architecture as possible has increased. This in turn increases the quantity and quality of attacks and the vulnerability of civilian populations. It seems that the best way to strengthen the protection of civilians and critical infrastructures (especially

Appendix 4: Interview questionnaire

those managed by civilians) at present is to communicate these threats and offer knowledge on how to counter these dangers by not succumbing to manipulation techniques (for example, social engineering).

2. **Do you believe any system currently provides effective protection for the civilian population?**

   I believe that there is no effective system in place to protect civilians in hybrid warfare.

3. **Do you believe there is a protection system for information infrastructure in hybrid wars?**

   As mentioned earlier, it seems that there is no way to completely eliminate threats in order to protect critical infrastructure (including IT). It has been said, and is still very much the case, that the weakest element in any system is always man and his susceptibility to manipulation (especially in the field of social engineering). Education is, in this respect, one of the most important elements in countering attacks on IT infrastructure.

4. **Do you believe any protection system for information infrastructure currently offers effective protection, including considering the impact on the civilian population?**

   Does not exist

5. **In your opinion, what factors need to be met for the effectiveness of a system in protecting the civilian population in hybrid wars?**

   As the level of militarization increases (which accelerated after Russia's invasion of Ukraine in 2022), it can be assumed that the military involvement of states in hybrid activities also increases. This is due, among other things, to the need to counter efforts by other actors and armies of the world using hybrid actions. Such preventive, intelligence, and counter-intelligence conduct has the potential to mitigate to some extent the actions of other actors. However, it is difficult to determine to what extent they can have the impact of significantly eliminating them. A change from a reactive to a proactive approach (including training and public information on these threats), and more flexibility to adapt priorities to the prevailing situation as regards the protection of critical infrastructure (including IT assets), is also required.

6. **What do you believe are the critical areas that ensure the safety of civilians in hybrid wars?**

   First and foremost, protecting the credibility and integrity of information, critical infrastructure and education and building resilience at micro levels.

7. **In which areas, in your opinion, should civilians be prepared in the context of hybrid warfare?**

Emphasis should be placed on education on cybersecurity and psychological and information resilience. It must be emphasized that traditional forms of information interception and the spread of disinformation have recently been enhanced by modern methods that can be used for these purposes. The advent of artificial intelligence (AI) that we have seen since November 2022, in particular LLMs (large language models) and in the form of advanced algorithms, has taken hybrid conflicts to the next level. These models are able to (re)produce information in a way that can affect individuals by eliciting an emotional response. This emotional response can lead to actions desired by the party trying to elicit it. This can occur by stirring up the activity of hitherto passive social groups who may wish to bring about the stigmatization of other social groups.

Given this, the paramount role of education in countering this type of manipulation must once again be emphasized. It seems that critical thinking is the only solid foundation on which to build resistance to any attempts at manipulation, especially in view of the increasing availability and accuracy of algorithms, e.g. those responsible for the production of so-called deep fakes (i.e. the manipulation of an image – both photo and video format – to make it appear real).

Furthermore, spying and information gathering in the age of social media is changing in nature. This is illustrated by scandals such as the one involving Cambridge Analytica (which was supposed to provide political consulting services) showing how easily the will of voters can be influenced during the electoral process and how far-reaching the consequences can be. In this case, people were manipulated using publicly available information, or what people gave to the company (knowingly or not). From this information, Cambridge Analytica built a personal profile, indicating ways in which this person could be influenced. This was most often through dedicated adverts displayed on a popular social networking site containing primarily false information designed to arouse the expected emotions. The emotional arousal created in this way was intended to be directed towards a specific and desired action. The effectiveness of this strategy lies in disabling conscious decision-making, bypassing the process of logical thinking and redirecting

Appendix 4: Interview questionnaire

actions to those that were desired by Cambridge Analytica's clients. By achieving this kind of state of high emotional arousal disabling critical and logical thinking, people and their behaviour could be manipulated much more easily. Hence, explaining what these manipulative processes consisted of could potentially reduce vulnerability to such practices in the future.

Thank you for sharing your expert knowledge and insights. Your contribution is invaluable to our study on hybrid conflicts and will significantly contribute to our efforts to understand the challenges and develop effective strategies for protecting the civilian population.

With respect
Wojciech Wróblewski PhD
Internal Security Institute
Fire University
wwroblewski@apoz.edu.pl
Michał Wiśniewski PhD Eng.
Faculty of Management
Warsaw University of Technology
michal.wsiniewski@pw.edu.pl
Jędrzej Bieniasz PhD
Assistant Professor @ Cybersecurity Division, Institute of Telecommunications, FEIT (WEiTI), WUT, Poland
Head @ Cybersecurity Center, WUT, Poland
Warsaw University of Technology
jedrzej.bieniasz@pw.edu.pl

Index

Note: **Bold** page numbers refer to tables; *italic* page numbers refer to figures and page numbers followed by "n" denote endnotes.

Aall, P. 430
Abdyraeva, C. 251
academic perspective 26–28, **29–30**, 31
ACO *see* Allied Command Operations (ACO)
action planning 405
action selection function 405
active PMCs 101
actors, hybrid warfare 143–144; connections 149, *149*; non-state actors 1, 9, 11, 33, 43, 73, 86, 87, 144–151, 229, 230, 234, 235, 250, 252, 255, 257, 273, 282, 292, 301, 374, 457, 458, 460, 463; state actors 144–150, 383, 420, 458; types 144–149
adaptation phase 429, 450n1
Adini, B. 444
adverse event scenarios (AES) 185, 187, 190–192, *191*, 196–198, 206, **208**, 209, 210, 214, 224, 458, 459; decision problem 216, **217**, *217*, 218, **218**; generation 224
AEI *see* American Enterprise Institute (AEI)
affiliated forces 146
agent action execution 405–406
agent intelligence 97
agglomerative methods 65
Agile Resilience 447
AI *see* artificial intelligence (AI)

AIDA method *see* Analysis of Interconnected Decision Areas (AIDA) method
Allied Command Operations (ACO) 295
Amazon Web Services (AWS) 393, 394
Ambiguous Command Structure 23
American Enterprise Institute (AEI) 9
Analysis of Interconnected Decision Areas (AIDA) method 224, 459
analytics dimension 379
Andersson, D.E. 421
AnonGhost 116, 237
anthropological approaches 428
applications dimension 378, 379
Armed Forces of Ukraine 8, 437, 439
artificial intelligence (AI) 2, 16, 21, 123, 234, 281, 333, **334**, 341, 345, 361, 362, 374, 385–387, 391, 400, 409, 410, 426, 460
Art of Achieving Political Goals Without Use of Force: War by Non-military Means (Stoilova) 106
al-Assad, B. 44, 102
asymmetric warfare 1, 48, 244
Atlantic Council hybrid conflict 11, *12*
ATM 218, 219, 223, 225n7
automation dimension 379
autonomous defence agent 404, *404*, 406

571

Autonomous Republic of Crimea 23
auxiliary forces 146
AWS *see* Amazon Web Services (AWS)
Azzuni, A. 132, 133

Babar, A. 409
Bachmann, S.-D. 7
balanced warfare 56, 57
Balcerowicz, B. 10, 11
Bartosz, A.A. 56
battlefield management systems
(BMS) 90
BCP *see* business continuity planning
(BCP)
Behrendt, P. 38
Bergaust, J.C. 12, 21
Bernal, A. 122
Berzina, K. 433
BeyondCorp model 394, *395*
BGP *see* Border Gateway Protocol
(BGP)
Bilal, A. 43, 60, 86, 422
Bilms, K. 41, 42; *The Science of
Military Strategy* 40
black intelligence 97
black propaganda 111, 251
Blackwater USA model 101
blockchain technology 354–358
Bloomberg's assessment 129
blue cluster 16, 17, 19
Bluszcz, J. 126
BMS *see* battlefield management
systems (BMS)
Bogdanov, S. 48
Border Gateway Protocol (BGP) 391,
392
"bouncing back" 124
bow-tie method 280
Brayer, C. 132, 133
Briggs, C.M. 7, 122–124, 425
Brooks, D. 100
Brown, R. 231
Buheji, M. 429, 445–448
Burt, T. 114, 115
business continuity planning (BCP)
182, 218, 219
business entity 96, 169, 218; essential
services 218–223

CACAO project 407, 408
Cambridge Analytica 362, 363
Carlucci, P. 68
Case-Based Reasoning (CBR) 219
Castro, N. de 100
CCP *see* Chinese Communist Party
(CCP)
Central Intelligence Agency (CIA) 411
Central Military Commission (CMC)
36, 41
Centre for Innovation and
Development of Defence
Technologies 424
Centre for Strategic and International
Studies (CSIS) 7
ChatGPT 401
Check Point Software Technologies
Ltd. 116
Chekinov, S. 48
China: media warfare strategy 37,
39; military, hybrid warfare
35–43
Chinese Communist Party (CCP) 3,
36, 37, 39–41, 63; hybrid
warfare 35, 42, **42–43**
Chivvis, C.S. 58–59, 242, 246
Christie, E.H. 433
CI *see* critical infrastructure (CI)
CIA *see* Central Intelligence Agency
(CIA)
CIMIC *see* civil-military cooperation
(CIMIC)
civilian intelligence operations 97
civilian population 2, 6, 24, 57, 72,
112, 132, 136, 280, 282,
359–362, 364, 366, 426,
444, 459–463; assessment
314, **314**, 315, **315**, 317, 318,
318, **319**, 320–322, **321**,
322, 324, **325**, 326, **326**,
328, 328–331, **329**, **331**,
332, 333–335, 342, 343,
346, 347; conflicts and wars
293–309; direct or indirect
effects 348–354
civil-military cooperation (CIMIC)
92, 99
civil protection approach 2, 3

civil protection system 2, 291–293, 347, 384, 411, 457, 461; blockchain technology 354–358; cyberspace 292, 301, 332–348, 356, 358, 361–363; mechanisms 293–309; six ways to die model 348–354, *354*; threat perception *see* threat perception
civil society organisations 431, 433, 436
Clairoux-Trepanier 412
Clark, J.N. 426, 436, 440–441
Clark, M. 50–51
Clausewitz, C. von 1, 6, 10, 11, 22
cloud computing 4, 375, 393, 394, 396, 397, 410, 413, 461
Cloudflare report 116
CMC *see* Central Military Commission (CMC)
coding method 74
cognitive domain 231, 232, 253, 254, 281, 460
cognitive operations 2, 23, 121–125, 150, 251, 252, 301, 309
cognitive strategies 425
Cold War 49–51, 59, 100, 102, 103, 109, 119, 122
colour revolutions 44, *56*, *58*
Command & Control (C&C) 405, 408
Communist Party of China (CPC) 7, 36, 62
communities, hybrid warfare 424–426
Community Resilience (CR) 433–447, 449, 450, 461, 462
Community Social Vulnerability Resilience (COM-SVR) 435
competency matrix 186, 187, **188**
Computer-Assisted Web Interviewing (CAWI) technique 469
computer security 167, 175, 336, **336**, 338, **339**, 341, 384, 402, 407
conceptual developments, hybrid conflicts 374–388
conduct of warfare 45, 239

Conference on Security and Cooperation in Europe (CSCE) 49
Conflict in the 21st Century: The Rise of Hybrid Wars (Hoffman) 26
conflict phase 6, 20–22, 24, 74, 87, 91, 100, 106, 136, 256
contemporary strategies 235, 431
content analysis method 464, 466–468
continuous scale 275, **276**
Control Command 408
Conventional Armed Forces in Europe (CFE) 50
conventional military action 48, 87, 89–91, 94–96, 98, 104, 105, 114, 121, 141, 150, 247, 249, 364
conventional military threat 262–263, **264**, 266, 281, 460; quantitative summary 257, **258–259**
conversion propaganda 111
co-occurrence map, hybrid warfare 13, *14*
cooperative strategies 427
Corera, G. 49
COSSAS 408
counter-propaganda 111
COVID-19 pandemic 122, 175, 178, 181, 225n7, 383, 398, 425
CrashOverride 134
Cretney, R. 426
Crimea 43, 54, 99, 102, 109, 115, 144, 146, 301, 420, 424, 432
crisis management 135, 173, **183–184**, 224, 293, 345, 354, 443, 459
Critical Entity Resilience Directive (CER) directive 178, **178**, 179, 181–183, 185
critical infrastructure (CI) 3, 16, 20, 35, 51, 63, 114, 115, 141, 142, 203, **204**, **205**, 223–225, 232–234, 236, 238, 246, 270, 301, 304, 305, 308, 312, 316, 319, 323, 329, 335, 348, 363,

382, 385, 386, 389, 391, 423, 458–459, 461; adverse event scenarios (AES) 206, **208**, 208–210; attributes 193, **194–195**; Critical Entity Resilience Directive (CER) directive 178, **178**, 179, 181–183, 185; decision problem 211, *212*, 213, **213**, 214, **214**; evolution of security management 168–185; interdependence threats 206, **207**; links 203, *205*; MESSM application 201–218; MESSM methodology 186–201; security management 166–168; Situation Model 193, **194–195**, 194–197, 199, 215, 223–225; threats impacts 206, **206**
Critical Infrastructure Protection 16, 17, 20, 35, 51, 63, **178**
Crocker, C.A. 430
CSIS *see* Centre for Strategic and International Studies (CSIS)
customary law 297, 298, 300
cyber attacks 116, 234, 236, 248, 257, 267, 335, 357, 358, 379, 380, 382, 383, 389, 404, 425, 438
cyber operations 6, 23, 27, 35, 36, 63, 115–117, 120, 124, 144, 234–236, 239, 386, 410
cyber resilience 375, 376, 383–385, 389, 394, 397, 402–404, 407, 412–414, *413*
Cyber Resilience Act (CRA) 375, 387, 388
cybersecurity 4, 16, 17, 20, 25, 116, 118, 139, 167, 169, 315, 322, 325, 338, 341, 347, 351, 364, 376, 386, 387, 398, 407, 408, 411
Cybersecurity and Infrastructure Security Agency (CISA) 169, 351, **352**

cyberspace 47, 54, 63, 94, 114, 117, 123, 125, 137, 139, 143, 230, 234–237, 292, 301, 332–348, 356, 358, 361–363, 376, 380, 382, 384, 386, 387, 392, 396, 398, 412–414
Cyber Threat Intelligence (CTI) 411, 412
cyber warfare 106, 116, 118, 122, 301, 303, 438

Danyk, Y. 7, 122–124
Al Dardari, A. 129
data dimension 379
data mining methods 401
data scraping method 467
DDoS attacks *see* distributed denial of service (DDoS) attacks
deceptive warfare 51
decision-making task (ZP) 192, **192**, 198, **201**, 218–219, 221
decision problem: adverse event scenarios (AES) 216, **217**, *217*, 218, **218**; critical infrastructure (CI) 211, *212*, 213, **213**, 214, **214**; formulation 224, 459
Deepfake methods 400–401
deep reinforcement learning (DRL) 410
Defence Information Systems Agency (DISA) 375
Defence24 portal 466, 467
defensive propaganda 111
dendrogram 65
destabilization activities 86, 95, 96, 104–106, 110, 114, 132, 136, 139, 141, 144, 149, 150
device dimension 378
dictionary 11, 12, 95, 421, 467
digital colonization 123
digital security actions 315
Diplomatic, Informational, Military, Economic (DIME) 11, 75n1
direct actions 98, 99, 319
DISA *see* Defence Information Systems Agency (DISA)

discrete scale 275, **275**
disinformation 2, 4, 6, 8, 9, 12, 17, 20, 22, 23, 33, 35, 37, 43, 45, 48, 54, 64, 71, 75n2, 86, 89, 91, 93–96, 98, 103, 105–110, 112, 114–116, 118, 120–124, 133, 134, 136, 137, 139–141, 143, 147, 149, 150, 166, 231, 234, 236–238, 245, 249, 251, 252, 257, 262, 263, 267, 268, 271, 281, 283, 284, 301–303, 312, 316, 319, 323, 327, 345, 347, 356, 358, 361, 362, 365, 375, 387, 397–400, 425, 440, 449, 460, 461, 466
DiSiNFO vs EU report 109
distributed denial of service (DDoS) attacks 108, 116, 236, 237, 335, 349, 389, 392
diversionary actions 88, *89*, 93, 94, 104, 139, 147
divisive methods 65
domains: codes 231, *232*; comparion with hybrid threats and 239, **240–241**; hybrid warfare 230–255
domestic security *see* hybrid warfare
dominant protective mechanism 346, **346**
Donetsk People's Republic (DPR) 308–309
Donnelly, J. 230
DRL *see* deep reinforcement learning (DRL)
Dudin, M.N. 125
Dugin, A. 51, 52
Dupuy, A.C. 133

Economic and Energy Aspects of Hybrid Threats to National Security (Mitrović) 126
economic intelligence 96
economic security actions 315, 318, 322, 325

Economic war to energy war: Ukraine war reflects new dimensions of warfare (Jain) 243
education sector 128
Elastic Compute Cloud (EC2) 393
electronic intelligence 97, 375
Encyclopaedia of National Security 10, 92
Endpoint Detection and Response (EDR) 402, 406, 411
energy security 132–134, 347, 364
Erlan 443, 444
ES *see* essential services (ES)
Eshel, Y. 435
Essential Security against Evolving Threats (ESET) 118, 120
essential services (ES) 141, 223–225, 308, 312, 353, 433; business entity 218–223; components 219, *220*; evolution of security management 168–185; MESSM methodology 186–201; security management 166–168
EU *see* European Union (EU)
European Commission 12, 33, 107, 129, 173, 178, 230, 234, 255, 291, 469
European Cyber Crisis Management Network (EU-CyCLONe) 384
European Programme of Critical Infrastructure Protection (EPCIP) 172–175, 179
European Union (EU) 107, 109, 112, 113, 126, 128, 130, 131, 134–136, 291, 294, 295; AI Act 387; Civil Protection Mechanism 297; directives 179, **179–181**; hybrid warfare 32–35, **34**
European Union Agency for Cybersecurity (ENISA) Threat Landscape Report 2022 108

Europe's Preparedness to Respond to Space Hybrid Operations (Robinson) 238
EU vs DiSiNFO report 109
expert interviews, hybrid warfare 63–64
exposure phase 429, 450n1
EY 173

Face2Face methods 401
Fahmi, I. 24
fake news occurrences 332, **333**, 399–401
Farkas, J. 114
Farley, J. 230
Fave, D. 118
5G networks 390
food acquisition service, payment system 348–349, *350*
food blockades 130–132, 137
food security actions 315, 318, 322, 325
formal-normative developments, hybrid conflicts 374–388
Fourth Hague Convention (1907) 299
Fox, A.C. *255*
Freier, N. *58*
Fridman, O. 44
Fuller, J.F.C. 94

Galeotti, M. 132
Gawliczek, P. 242; *Hybrid Warfare as a New Type of War. The Evolution of Its Conceptual Construct* 27
Gaza Strip 95, 109, 116, 129, 132, 134–136, 430, 445
Gazprom 148
GDP 127–129, 241, 425
Geneva Conventions (1949) 297, 298, 300
genset 223
Gerasimov, V. 1, 45–49; concept 47, *47*; doctrine 45, 150, 458
Giannopoulos, G. 234, 242, 245, 248
gibridnaya voyna 44, 51
Gibson, K.H. 33

Giesea, J. 98; *Hybrid Intelligence as a Response to Hybrid Warfare* 97
Giles, K. 112, 113
Glenn, R.W. *58*
Global Conflict Tracker 5
Global Energy Security Index 133
Global Protection Cluster (GPC) 296, 297
Golden Triangle 97
Goncalves, C.P. 234, 235
Goodwin, R. 432
Google Security Operations platform 410
Goransson, M.B. *58*
GPS 239, 270, 423
Gray, C.S. 151
Great Limitroph 54
Great March of Return 109
Green Movement 422
grey intelligence 97
grey propaganda 111
grey zone 11, 75n2, 420; warfare 11, 75n2, 228, 244, 420
grouping methods 65
group propaganda 111
GSM 422
guerrilla warfare 23, 53, 87, 92–93, 100, 104, 147
Guidelines for an Integrated Science of Conflict Resilience 428–429

Hague Conventions: of 1899 297, 298; of 1907 297, 298
Hague Law 297, 298
Hamas terrorist tactics 24, 25, 109, 110, 116, 117
Harris, K. 429, 450n1
healthcare sector 128
health-related actions 314, 318, 321, 325, 328
Helsinki Final Act 49
Hensoldt Analytics 251
hierarchical clustering methods 65
Hoffman, F.G. 1, 7, 9, 26, 27, 44, 48, 49, *58*; *Conflict in the 21st*

Century: The Rise of Hybrid Wars 26; *The Landscape of Hybrid Threats* 150
hospital operator 201–203, 206, 209, 215, 217
host intrusion detection systems (HIDS) 402
host intrusion prevention systems (HIPS) 402
Houck, S. 426, 431
housing security actions 315, 322, 325
How China's Cognitive Warfare Works: A Frontline Perspective of Taiwan's Anti-Disinformation Wars (Hung and Hung) 122
Huang, L. 412
Huawei's 5G technology 423
human-induced military threats 312, 316, 319, 323
human-induced non-military threats 312, 316, 319–320, 323
Human Rights Watch (HRW) 132
Hung, T.-C.: *How China's Cognitive Warfare Works: A Frontline Perspective of Taiwan's Anti-Disinformation Wars* 122
Hung, T.-W.: *How China's Cognitive Warfare Works: A Frontline Perspective of Taiwan's Anti-Disinformation Wars* 122
Huntington, S. 92
Huskaj, G. 114
hybrid actions 3, 21, 22, 25, 35, 64, 134, 138, 145, 247, 248, 250, 420, 449, 458, 460
HybridCoE 11
Hybrid Conflict, Hybrid Warfare, and Resilience (Preziosa and Meulman) 9
hybrid conflicts 1, 3–6, 33, 47, 55, 64, 73–75, 373–375; advantage 60; comparison with hybrid warfare 7–26;

issue 13, *14*, 17, **18–19**; phase 87, 91, 100, 106, 108, 118, 122, 133, 139, 148, 150; resilience *see* resilience; technological attacks 397–412
hybrid intelligence 97, 98
Hybrid Intelligence as a Response to Hybrid Warfare (Giesea) 97
hybrid interference theory 21
hybrid strategies 5, 6, 13, 17, 20–22, 22, 35, 40, 58–60, 63, 73, 74, 87, 104, 106, 108, 110, 133, 135, 137, 139, 148, 150, 229, 234, 237, 242, 243, 250, 257, 420, 421, 457, 458, 463
hybrid threats 1–4, 9, 11–13, 20, 27, 33, 103, 126, 133, 144, 145, 167, 231, 234, 238, 239, 241, 242, 246–248, 252, 282, 291, 292, 337–338, **338**, 343, 362, 365, 373, 374, 389, 403, 412, 421, 449, 457, 460–462; comparion with domains and 239, **240–241**; identification and characterisation 255–271; methodical approach 271–281; security impacts 228–230
hybrid warfare 1–4, 457–459, 461, 462; academic perspective 26–28, **29–30**, 31; actors *see* actors; characteristics 5–7; Chinese Communist Party 35, 42, **42–43**; Chinese military 35–43; civilian protection *see* civilian protection strategies; communities 424–426; community resilience 436–447; comparison with hybrid conflict 7–26; concepts 27, 28, 64–72; content analysis method

466–468; conventional military action 87, 89–91, 94–96, 98, 104, 105, 121; critical infrastructure *see* critical infrastructure (CI); domains 230–255; environment 420–422; essential services *see* essential services (ES); expert interviews 63–64; features 65, **66–67**; Gerasimov's concept 47, *47*; hybrid threats *see* hybrid threats; intensity 59; issue 13, 14, *14*, **15**; military actions 87–89, *88*; military force 59; mobilisation and networks 422–424; negative effects 353, **353**; non-military actions 106–118; operations 32–35, **34**, 86–87; overview 68, **69**; population-based orientation 59–63; psychological warfare 118–143; resilience *see* resilience; resilience framework 365, *365*; Russian perspective 43–59, 61, **61–62**; secondary source analysis 463, 464, 467; section 469; survey 468–469; systematic literature review 464–466; technologies 343, **344**; test three hypotheses 463; theoretical model strategy 22, *22*; think tanks' definition 31, **31–32**; unconventional military operations 92–106, *105*

Hybrid Warfare as a New Type of War. The Evolution of Its Conceptual Construct (Iskandarov and Gawliczek) 27

Hyslop, D. 427

ICT *see* information and communications technology (ICT)

IDPs 436, 437, 439

IHL *see* international humanitarian law (IHL)

Ilnitsky, A.M. 55

Improvised Explosive Devices (IEDs) 304

individual propaganda 111

information and communications technology (ICT) 171–173, 182, 234, 235, 374–376, 391, 393–395, 397, 406, 408–410

information security actions 315

information warfare 16, 17, 23, 36, 44, 50–51, 106–108, 110, 112–113, 119, 121–122, 135–137, 139, 228, 234, 283, 303, 440, 461

Infrastructure as a Service (IaaS) 394

Institute for National Security Studies (INSS) 443

intelligence activities 87, 89, 96–98, 104, 105, 139, 147, 250, 267

intense information warfare 23, 135

interdomain interconnections 254, 254–255

Intermediate-Range Nuclear Forces (INF) Treaty 50

internal intelligence 96

International Committee of the Red Cross (ICRC) 298, 307

International Criminal Court 302

International Criminal Tribunal for the Former Yugoslavia 10, 300

international humanitarian law (IHL) 102, 116, 132, 262, 293, 297–303, 305, 308, 309, 359, 460

International Labour Organization (ILO) 129

International Lunar Research Station (ILRS) 39

International Organisation for Migration (IOM) 427, 437, 438

International Team for the Study of Security Verona (ITSS) 118
Internet of Things (IoT) 20, 357, 358, 362, 387
Interpeace Frameworks for the Assessment of Resilience 429
intrusion detection systems (IDS) 402, 403, 406
intrusion prevention systems (IPS) 402, 403, 406
irregular warfare 1, 7, 27, 228, 255
Ish-Shalom's theory of the 'concept at work' 440
Iskandarov, K. 242; *Hybrid Warfare as a New Type of War. The Evolution of Its Conceptual Construct* 27
Islamic Republic of Iran 422
ISO 31000:2018 184, 277–279
Israel-Gaza war, case study 441–446
Israeli Defense Forces (IDF) 443, 444
Israeli-Palestinian conflict 7, 24, 113, 304, 353, 449
Israeli Red Alert 237
Isserson, G. 49
IT systems 270, 332, 357, 361, 381

Jain, S.: *Economic war to energy war: Ukraine war reflects new dimensions of warfare* 243
Jarecka, U. 112, 114
Jensen, B. 7
Johnson, H. 112
joint operations 235
Joint Psychological Operations Doctrine 119
JSON file 408

Kaim, A. 424, 442, 443
Kakhovka dam 131, 305, 306
Kartapolov, A.V.: *Military Review* 48
Kashi Komijani, M. 300, 301
Keelan 427
Khamzatov, M. 58
Kim, A. 56–57
Kimhi, S. 432, 435, 444

Kindervag, J. 377
Kiselyova, V.A. 51
Kitler, W. 291, 292
Kolb, A.G. 308, 309
Kołodziejczyk, A. 112
Komleva, N. 54, 55
Korhonen, I. 128
Koubová, A. 432
Kremlin's Troll Army 113
Kurnyshova, Y. 430, 439, 440
Kylo project 9

The Landscape of Hybrid Threats (Hoffman) 150
large language models (LLM) 362, 401, 409, 410, 412
Law on the Protection of the Population and Civil Defence 293
Leaning 422
legal security actions 315, 322
legal warfare 36, 39, 40, 42, 249
lemmatization 467
Liflander, C.-M. 236
limitrophic wars 54, 55
"little green men" 23, 43, 54, 147
LLM *see* large language models (LLM)
local communities 1, 2, 4, 425, 436–438, 440, 449, 450, 462; resilience 439
Loevenich, J.F. 410
Log4Shell vulnerability 381–382
Long-Term Evolution (LTE) 389
Lordos, A. 427
Lowenthal, M.M. 249
Luhansk People's Republic (LPR) 308

machine learning (ML) 16, 20, 234, 385, 386, 391, 400, 401, 409
MacLachlan, K. 293, 303
Magda, E. 27
Makarychev, A. 439, 440
Manko, O. 23–24, 93
Mao Zedong 36
Martens Clause 299, 300

Martens, F. 299
mass propaganda 111
Mattis, P. 38, 48
Maxar Technologies 239
MAXQDA 468
media messages 244, 466
media warfare strategy 37, 39
Meier 422
mental warfare 55
MESSM *see* Methodology of
    Essential Services Security
    Management (MESSM)
Messner, Y. 51–53
methodological approaches, resilience
    research 427–428
Methodology of Essential Services
    Security Management
    (MESSM) 458; adverse
    event scenarios 191, **191**;
    application 201–218;
    characteristics 187, **189**;
    decision-making problem
    192, **192**; framework 191,
    191, 193; methodology
    186–201; risk estimation
    procedure 187, **190**;
    safeguards implementation
    192, **192**
Meulman, F.H.: *Hybrid Conflict,*
    Hybrid Warfare, and
    Resilience 9
Microsoft Copilot for Security 410
Middle East 3, 5, 7, 24, 40, 59, 74,
    150, 236, 243, 308, 420,
    422, 426, 460, 461
Mikhieiev, Y. 23, 24, 93
military: intelligence 96, 120, 139,
    380; manoeuvres 38, 90, *91*,
    135, 141, 148, 150; support
    98, 99, 441; threat code 266,
    268, **269**
military actions 1, 3, 12, 22, 26,
    28, 42, 47, 48, 63, 87–89,
    88, 93, 141, 144, 244, 247,
    257, 299, 364, 380, 445,
    457–459, 466
Military Concept for the Protection
    of Civilians 295

military force 6, 7, 9–11, 24, 25, 33,
    41, 59, 63, 102, 126, 146,
    149, 150, 230, 244, 308;
    hybrid warfare 59
Military Review (Kartapolov) 48
military service providers (MSPs) 100
Mimran, T. 236, 237
Mission Critical LTE (MC-LTE)
    technology 389
Mitchell, T. 429, 450n1
Mitkov, M. 239
MITRE 406
MITRE-sponsored TRAM 412
Mitrović, M. 132; *Economic and*
    Energy Aspects of Hybrid
    Threats to National Security
    126
mixed-methods approach 467
mobility security actions 315, 318,
    322, 325
Model of Essential Service (MES)
    196–198, **197**
Montreux Document Forum 305
Al-Muhannadi, K. 445, 446
MUK 198, **198**
Mumford, A. 68
Mushimiyiman 429, 447

national critical function 169, **170**,
    351, **352**
national resilience 432, 435, 436,
    443, 461
national security 7, 11, 16, 37, 87, 96,
    97, 114, 123, 126, 133, 134,
    145, 233, 243, 249, 292,
    381, 384, 386, 433, 466
National Security Agency (NSA) 117,
    375, 386
National Security Strategy of Russia
    114
natural threats 312, 316, 319, 323,
    326, 327, 329
naval operations 90
Neklessa, A. 58
Nemeth, W.J. 26
Netanyahu, B. 116, 237
network-centric warfare 44, 51, 52
network dimension 378

network intrusion detection systems
(NIDS) 402, 411
network intrusion prevention systems
(NIPS) 402
network warfare theory 51–52
Neumayer, C. 114
Neumeyer, M. 7
"new generation warfare" (Russian)
44, 48, 50, 121
Nguyen, T.T. 409
Niejelov, W.M. 44
NIS Directive 173–175, **176–177**, 178,
179, 383, 384
non-lethal service providers 100
non-military actions 1, 3, 33, 44–48,
50, 63, 70, 71, 73, 98, 125,
130, 132, 136, 137, 143,
149, 150, 229, 235, 257,
262, 281, 359–361, 364,
420, 448, 457–459, 466;
codes frequency 137, *137*;
hybrid warfare 106–118;
layered graph 138, *138*;
network diagram 141,
142; propaganda and
disinformation 139,
140–141
non-military threats 263, **264, 265**;
code 268, **269**; quantitative
summary 257, **259–261**
non-state actors 1, 9, 11, 33, 43, 73,
86, 87, 144–151, 229, 230,
234, 235, 250, 252, 255,
257, 273, 282, 292, 301,
374, 457, 458, 460, 463
non-state-sponsored operations 235
non-verbal propaganda 111
Non-War Military Activities
(NWMA) 40–42
North Atlantic Treaty Organization
(NATO) 11, 12, 32–35, **34**,
43, 57, 59, 63, 107, 112,
113, 119, 125, 133–136,
228, 229, 236, 238, 245,
247, 292, 293, 295, 297,
364; Science and Technology
Organisation 358
NotPetya attack 115

OASIS 406–408
offensive propaganda 111
oil refinery 201–203, 206, 209–211,
214, 215
Olcese, M. 434
Olech, A. 113
'on-demand' model 393
OpenC2 project 407, 408
open-source intelligence (OSINT) 97,
438, 449
operational intelligence 96
operational PSYOPs 118–119
orchestration, automation and
response (SOAR) systems
403, 406–408, 411
orchestration dimension 379
organisational developments, hybrid
conflicts 374–388
organisation assessment 336–338,
337–338
Other Active Measures (OAA) 11, 75n2

Panarin, I. 51
partially observed Markov decision
process (POMDP) 409
passive PMCs 101
People's Liberation Army (PLA) 36,
38, 40–42
People's Republic of China (PRC)
35–41
perimeter-based security model 376,
376, 395
personal protection, six ways to die
model 348, *349*
Peskov, D. 7
phishing attacks 117, 362, 375,
398–401
physical security actions 314, 318,
321, 325
Pifer, S. 100
Platform as a Service (PaaS) 394
PMCs *see* private military companies
(PMCs)
PN-EN ISO 31000:2018 184
Polish Institute of International
Affairs (PISM) 95
Polish Press Agency (PAP) 167, 349,
350, 466, 467

political intelligence 96
POMDP *see* partially observed Markov decision process (POMDP)
Popov, V. 58
population-based orientation 59–63
power sharing equipment 221, **222**
Prague Security Studies Institute (PSSI) 238–239
preparation phase 22, 91, 148
preparedness assessment 338, **339**
preparedness phase 447
Preziosa, P.: *Hybrid Conflict, Hybrid Warfare, and Resilience* 9
Prigozhin, Y.V. 103
private military companies (PMCs) 10, 48, 60, 87, 89, 98, 100–105, 138, 145–148, 150, 249, 250, 266, 267, 305, 347
private security companies (PSCs) 100
process management theory 169, 458
Procter, C. 135
Project OpenC2 407, 408
Prońko, J. 272
propaganda campaigns 91, 107, 109–114, 118–122, 136, 137, 139, **140–141**, 141, 147–151
Protection Analytical Framework (PAF) 296, *296*
Protection of Civilians in Armed Conflict report 295, 302, 303, 364, 424
proxy forces 60, 146
proxy warfare 72
psychological operations (PSYOPs) 35, 38, 46, 48, 53, 55, 59, 89, 91, 92, 98, 105, 106, 118–121, 139, 150, 267, 428
psychological security actions 315, 321, 325
psychological warfare 36, 38, 39, 44, 48, 63, 94, 95, 118–143
PSYOPs *see* psychological operations (PSYOPs)
public opinion warfare 36, 37

Putin, V. 51, 101, 108
Python language 467

quasi-state organizations 148

Rally 'Round the Flag' 442
Randalls 427
RAND Corporation 107, 118, 124, 248
RAND Europe 173
ransomware attacks 382–383, 386, 407
Rauta, V. 146
recovery phase 429, 445, 447, 450n1
Red Alert app 116, 237
red cluster 16, 17, 19, 20
Reddi, V.J. 409
reflexive control (Russian) 44, 125, 138
Reilly, J. 230
Reinforcement Learning (RL) 409
research method 13, 68, 90, 231; characteristics 463–469
resilience 9, 34, 124, 126, 151, 171–173, 175, 181, 185, 186, 195, 213, 225n4, 242, 249, 256, 274, 293, 302, 310, 343, 345, 351–358, 363, 364, *365*, 374, 426–435; approach 430; Community Resilience 433–447, 449, 450; cyber resilience 375–376, 383–385, 389, 394, 397, 402–404, 407, 412–414, *413*; fatigue 448; local communities 439; methodological approaches 427–428; models 302–303, 447–448; national resilience 432, 435, 436, 443; social resilience 124, 151, 432–433, 439–445, 447; strategies 437; types 431–435
Resisting Russia report 438
respondents 167, 314–338, **333**, 340–346, 359–362, 364, 423, 441, 443, 444, 468,

469; age structure 310, 310; materialization 313, 313; perceptions 311, **311**, 312, **312**
response phase 447
risk assessment 126, 276, **277**, 278, 279, 459; methodologies 172, **183–184**, 183–185
risk estimation 185, 187, **190**, 274
risk management theory 271–281
risk strategy assignment 279, *280*
risk value estimation 224
Robbins, S.P. 10
Robinson, J.: *Europe's Preparedness to Respond to Space Hybrid Operations* 238
Romanchuk, O. 436
Russia: cyberattack 115, 133; financial markets 23; perspective 43–59, 61, **61–62**, 235; propaganda 109, 112, 113, 440
Russia-Georgia war 420
Russian Federation 6, 7, 23, 35, 43, 45, 46, 48, 50, 59, 60, 62, 113, 120, 121, 125, 151, 235, 304, 349, 464
Russian Hybrid Warfare report 60
Russian Wagner Group (PMC Wagner) 102, 103

sabotage actions 87–89, *89*, 92, 94–96, 104, 105, 132, 139, 141, 147, 148
sabotage and reconnaissance groups (SRG) 8
Sajdak, M. 411
Samdesk 73
Sanchez, L. 27
Sanders, P. 143
Sari, A. 301–303
scapegoating 271, 362
Schmidt, J. 24
The Science of Military Strategy (Bilms) 40, 41
SCION network 392
SCOPUS database 13, 182, 464, 465
scrapers, computer programmes 467

Seashell Blizzard group 115
secondary source analysis 463, 464, 467
Second Hague Convention 299
Security Information and Event Management (SIEM) 379, 403, 406, 411
security management 3, 166–168, 193, 218, 223, 384, 458; evolution of 168–185
security policy 31, 293, 302, 377, 379, 450
self-confessed anomie 283n1
self-preparedness assessment 341, **341–342**
Sellevag, S.R. 12, 21
Sense of Coherence (SOC) 435
Sheikh, A. 133
Sherr, J. 49, *50*
Siman-Tov, D. 122
Simon 427
Simpson, G. 427
Singh, A. 38–39
6G networks 390, 391
"six ways to die model" 311, 348–354, 359–361, 366, 460; civilian protection strategies 348–354, *354*; methodology 169; personal protection 348, *349*
Smith, H. 234
social cohesion 256, 270, 315, 322, 325, 331, 442, 446, 449
social resilience 124, 151, 432, 433, 439–445, 447
social security actions 315, 322, 325
society-wide strategy 431
socio-ecological approaches 428
Software as a Service (SaaS) 394
Software Defined Networking (SDN) 393, 406, 410, 413
Software Defined Perimeter (SDP) model 395, 396, *396*
solar panels 223, 448
SolarWinds attack 115, 380–381
Source, Time, Audience, Subject, Mission (STASM) 110, 114
South Caucasus region 54, 242–243

SpaceX's Starlink system 239
special military operation 6, 36, 87,
89, 94, 98–100, 102, 104,
105, 146, 312, 316, 319,
323, 327, 329
special missions 98
special reconnaissance 98, 99
Spice domain 238
state actors 144–150, 383, 420, 458
State of Israel 24, 441
state-sponsored operations 235
Stensones, N.A. 7–8
Stoilova, V.: *The Art of Achieving
Political Goals Without
Use of Force: War by
Non-military Means* 106
strategic PSYOPs 118–119
Structured Threat Information
eXpression (STIX) format
406, 407, 411
Sun Zu 5–6
surrogate forces 146
survival strategies 430
Svechin, A. 49
Sykulski, L. 53
systems theory 428

tactical PSYOPs 118–119
technical intelligence 96
Terrados, J.J. 48
terrorism 6, 17, 19, 26, 35, 51, 53, 73,
95, 119, 127, 145, 166, 171,
255, 262, 267, 291–293, 347
Theocharidou, M. 234
theory of war 1
Thiele, R. 239
think tanks 31, **31–32**, 52, 117
threat perception 36, 257, 281, 298,
303, 305, 311, 312, **312**,
461; actions 318; civilian
population *see* civilian
population; groups 312;
high temperatures 326–329,
327–329; hybrid threats
291–296; illness 323–326,
324–326; injuries 319–322,
320–322; life-threatening

311, **311**; low temperatures
329–332, **330–332**;
respondents *see* respondents;
thirst perception 316–319,
317–319
Three Warfares (3W) policy 35–40
threshold of conflict 6, 10, 12, 21, 41,
63, 64, 229, 247, 256
Tönnies, F. 421, 424
Torreados, J.J. 33
transform-based neural networks 401
treaty law 297, 298
Trotsky, L. 56
Tsymbursky, V. 54

UCIPR *see* Ukrainian Center for
Independent Political
Research (UCIPR)
Ukraine power plant attack 380
Ukraine war 236, 243, 249, 420,
423, 426, 427, 430–432,
442, 444, 445, 449, 463,
464, 467, 468; case study
436–441; global food
supplies 131
Ukrainian Center for Independent
Political Research (UCIPR)
436, 437
Ukrainian Institute of Cognitive
Behavioural Therapy 436
ultra-Orthodox 442, 443
UMCP 171
*Unbroken: How Communities
Adapted To War* report 438
unconventional military operations
87, 92–106, *105*
unconventional military threats
256, 257, 263, **265**, 266;
quantitative summary 257,
259, 262
UNDP *see* United Nations
Development Programme
(UNDP)
UNDPO *see* United Nations
Department of Peace
Operations (UNDPO)
UNICEF report 136

Index

unifying propaganda 111
Union Civil Protection Mechanism 294
Union Mechanism for Civil Protection 171
United Kingdom (UK) 101, 117, 121, 134, 166, 182, 219, 458
United Nations Department of Peace Operations (UNDPO) 295, 296
United Nations Development Programme (UNDP) 129
United Nations (UN) Policy on the Protection of Civilians in Peacekeeping Operations 295–297
United States (US), 34, **34**, 38–40, 51, 59, 101, 103, 104, 117, 119–121, 134, 168, 169, 182, 238, 351, 374, 375, 381, 382, 385, 386, 391, 441
the UN Joint Guidelines on Assistance for Building Resilient Societies 427
unlimited war (Chinese) 36
unmanned aerial vehicle (UAV) 97, 100, 173, 390, 424
unrestricted warfare methods 35
UN Security Council Secretary-General 302, 303
UPS 223
USA Patriot Act 168
U.S. Department of Defence 32–34, **34**, 56
user dimension 378
US National Security Agency (NSA) 117, 375, 386

Valente, M. 126
Vdovytskyi, Y. 60
verbal propaganda 111

Verrocchio, M. 118
visibility dimension 379
Vladimirov, A. 58
Vorobyova, I.N. 51
VOSviewer program 13, 20, 465
Voyenno-Promyshlennyy Kurier 45
vulnerability phase 429, 445, 450n1

Wagner Group 102, 103, 146, 148, 268
Walecki, O.W. 44
war propaganda 111, 112
Weapons of Mass Destruction (WMD) 262, 263, 266
web-based phishing attacks 401
Weitz, R. 44
white intelligence 97
white propaganda 111
Wigell, M. 21
wiper malware 114, 116, 236, 237, 397
World Bank (WB) 129, 130, 425
World Health Organization (WHO) 116

X-axis correlation 263, 267, 268, 282n1
Xiao, X. 412

Yakymiak, S. 60
Y-axis correlation 263, 266, 267, 282n1
yellow cluster 16, 17, 19

Zarembo, K. 423
Zelensky, V. 108, 120, 441
Zendoo platform 469
Zero Trust 374, 376–379, 389, 393, 394, 413
Zero Trust Reference Architecture model 375
Zhao, Y. 400